ILLINOIS
REAL ESTATE
LICENSE LAW AND PRINCIPLES

A simplified explanation of the essential
knowledge every licensee needs to know to
pass the state real estate license exam.

DAVID A. MCGOWAN & DR. STEPHANIE KROL

LEMNISCATE-INFINITY

Illinois Real Estate License Law and Principles: A Simplified Explanation of the Essential Knowledge Every Licensee Needs to Know to Pass the State Real Estate License Exam
Published by Lemniscate-Infinity Press
Wheaton, IL

Disclaimer:

The content in this book is not intended to serve as legal advice, financial advice, tax advice, real estate advice, or any other form of professional advice. The authors of this book are not attorneys, tax advisors, financial advisors, or professionals in other related fields, and as such, nothing within this book should be interpreted as legal advice, tax advice, financial advice, or any other type of professional advice. The information provided is for general knowledge and educational purposes only. Readers seeking professional guidance in any specific area are encouraged to consult with qualified experts in those respective fields. The authors and publishers of this book disclaim any responsibility for how readers may apply or interpret the information contained herein.

Readers are advised to verify the status of licensee law with the state of Illinois, as our digital and/or printed publication may not always reflect the most current provisions. License law is subject to frequent modifications and updates, and these changes can occur at any time. We strongly encourage all readers to conduct their due diligence in ensuring the accuracy and up-to-date nature of licensee law and its relevant provisions. The authors and publishers of this book do not assume responsibility for any discrepancies between the book's content and the current state of licensee law.

QUANTITY PURCHASES: Schools, companies, professional groups, clubs, and other organizations may qualify for special terms when ordering quantities of this title. For information, email: school@inlandreschool.com

Publisher's Cataloging-in-Publication data

Names: McGowan, David A., author. | Krol, Stephanie, author.
Title: Illinois real estate license law and principles : a simplified explanation of the essential knowledge every licensee needs to know to pass the state real estate license exam / David A. McGowan & Dr. Stephanie Krol.
Description: Wheaton, IL: Leminscate-Infinity Press, 2023.
Identifiers: ISBN: 979-8-9867781-0-5, Subjects: LCSH Real estate agents—Licenses—Illinois. | Real estate agents—Illinois—Examinations, questions, etc. | BISAC STUDY AIDS / Professional | STUDY AIDS / Study Guides | BUSINESS & ECONOMICS / Real Estate / General, Classification: LCC HD278 .M34 2023 | DDC 333.33076—dc23

Cover and interior design by Victoria Wolf, Wolf Design and Marketing, Editor Jennifer Bisbing, copyright owned by David A. McGowan & Dr. Stephanie Krol.

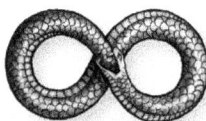

LEMNISCATE-INFINITY
PRESS

To all our new, current, and future students,

As two educators deeply committed to the belief that genuine learning is a collaborative journey, we have always sought a more student-centered approach to instruction and content. This book stands as our answer to a profound question: How can we put the student first, making the process of learning and absorbing content not only effective but also meaningful?

In the realm of real estate, a field we both admire and love, this dedication carries even greater significance. It's a tribute to those of you excited to embark on this educational adventure, and to those who have already dedicated themselves to the world of real estate. Your pursuit of knowledge and your commitment to the profession inspire us every day.

This book is a testament to our shared passion for education, for real estate, and for the endless potential of every student. We offer it with the hope that it will empower you, our students, to reach new heights and redefine the way you learn and grow.

With gratitude and excitement,

David McGowan & Dr. Stephanie Krol, Real Estate Visionaries: School Owners, Traditional & Online Educators, Decades-Long Brokers of Excellence

CONTENTS

INTRODUCTION

DEAR READER,

Welcome to Illinois Real Estate License Law and Principles!

The goal of this book is to prepare you for a successful, fulfilling, and profitable career in real estate in Illinois.

Your success starts with one precious thing: knowledge.

Ready?

Let's begin.

ABOUT THE BOOK

Illinois Real Estate License Law and Principles is a simple and easy-to-follow explanation of the essential elements every pre-license student needs to know to pass the Illinois state and national real estate license exam. Seasoned real estate practitioners who are recognized and trained educators carefully wrote and edited the book to maximize student learning and retention. Its student-focused style is straightforward, step by step, and written in a way that is easy to understand.

This book is for individuals who:

- Are pre-license students

- Are considering starting a real estate career

- Want to reignite his or her former real estate career

In these pages, you will learn about the Illinois Real Estate Act of 2000. It is the premise of the law that allows you to act as a licensee in representing the interest of buyers, sellers, landlords, and tenants. This book will refer to its laws and statutes as necessary in order for you to have a firm grasp and working knowledge of how the real estate business works in Illinois. Along with covering Illinois state laws, this book also includes the necessary and applicable national laws as well.

As a reader, you will also discover and learn:

- Recommendations

- Guidelines

- Helpful insights

- Real-world tips

The majority of quoted material in this book comes from the Illinois Real Estate Act of 2000. All sources are referenced. Each one has been carefully vetted. If you ever want to do further reading, search for the source online.

A note about real estate forms: The real estate industry uses a wide variety of forms. Forms can vary from brokerage to brokerage. In light of that, only certain sample forms are included in this textbook. These are strictly for educational purposes and not intended for business. For real estate forms, always refer to your designating managing broker.

FROM THE AUTHORS

Dear Reader,

This book was carefully crafted with the express purpose of showing you the intriguing and ever-evolving world of real estate in the United States. It is strategically written to maximize your learning so you can pass both the national and Illinois state-specific real estate license exams. After passing the exams and contracting with a brokerage, you will start your new career as a real estate broker. What is exciting about this is that you get to create your own identity. This includes the opportunity to decide:

- The specialization you want to pursue

- Your work hours

- Your income goals

It also includes the opportunity to develop your professional network in a live classroom, online, or both. You do this through the experiences you gain interacting with the instructor and other students. It's possible that one or more will be a cooperating broker in future transactions.

One of our greatest joys is watching our students succeed and be recognized for their own achievements in the industry.

Real estate is full of challenges. Remember that Inland Real Estate School is always here to support you in your endeavors.

David McGowan and Dr. Stephanie Krol

ABOUT THE AUTHORS

David McGowan

David is currently the founder, president, and CEO of Professional Studies Institute, Inc., DBA Inland Real Estate School. In addition, he is a managing broker for Inland Commercial Brokerage and has served in this capacity since 2001.

With over forty-five years of experience as a real estate practitioner and more than forty years as a real estate educator, David has taught well over 20,000 students. Under his leadership, Inland Real Estate School's average pass rate for Illinois real estate exams is higher than the state average.

David is past president of the Northern Illinois Commercial Association of REALTORS® and former regional director of the Real Estate Educators Association. He has also been the Director of Education for the Chicago Association of REALTORS®. David is a member and a former director of the Association of Illinois Real Estate Educators.

Stephanie Krol

Dr. Stephanie is the vice president, co-owner, and COO of Inland Real Estate School. She has a proven reputation of excellence and professionalism among clients and peers alike. In higher education management, she is recognized as a multi-award-winning educator, speaker, and dean. In real estate, she has been investing and brokering for over twenty-five years.

She believes variety in work is the *spice* of life. Along with being the co-owner of Inland Real Estate School, she is also:

- A full-time certified publishing consultant
- Author of What the Pet Food Industry Is NOT Telling You

- An imprint owner and publishing services boutique owner for specialized self-publishing services

- A functional medicine practitioner and certified health and well-being coach for people and pets

- A certified raw dog nutrition specialist and pet health advocate

Today, Dr. Stephanie feels fortunate that she gets to live her values and pursue her purpose. She is an evolved entrepreneur following her passions, doing things her way, and building strong relationships along the way. Her multidimensional approach includes luxury residential, estates, equine facilities, residential, and commercial spaces. She has developed an expansive network of business owners, property owners, and civic leaders in Chicago, western suburban Illinois, and western Michigan. In the realm of publishing, she is growing her network nationally and internationally.

ABOUT INLAND REAL ESTATE SCHOOL

Few schools have earned a reputation for supporting their students beyond the completion of their pre-licensing course as Inland Real Estate School has and does. We have developed a solid reputation for supporting our students long after they've completed their education. We provide consulting services focused on helping you develop your professional reputation and identity, so you can enhance your real estate career.

What can you expect from engaging with Inland Real Estate School?

- We offer one-on-one tutoring. If a student needs additional assistance, we are available to make that happen.

- We implement the best reading materials available in the industry. They are designed to help you understand the concepts and enhance your understanding in preparation for the state exam.

- Whether you are an Inland Real Estate School student or coming to us from another school, we provide real customer service. It is backed by the guidance you need to get through the program as well as the state exam.

What makes Inland different?

- Our staff has over sixty years of combined experience in providing education and training to the Illinois real estate market.

- Inland is not only supported by specialists with formal educational degrees, but also brokers with practical real life experience.

- Our instructors respond to our students' questions and inquiries in a timely manner and are available via phone and email.

- Our updated flexible course options provide our students with the flexibility of selecting a program that meets their schedule and time availability.

- Our programs are available in different mediums to meet the needs of our students.

- Our faculty has over forty years of experience in residential and commercial real estate as a broker and managing broker.

- Having a school run and owned by two proven successful educators with actual market experience makes all the difference in your learning and passing the state exam. Our results and referrals prove it.

Be sure to visit our website and follow us on social media. See the resource section at the end of the book for more details.

Disclaimer: Nothing in this book is intended to be legal advice, financial advice, tax advice, real estate advice, or any other type of professional advice. Always seek your own professional expert guidance. This book makes no financial guarantees or promises. A real estate career depends on your effort, your commitment, additional education beyond your license, and a large variety of other factors.

CHAPTER 1:

WELCOME TO THE WORLD OF REAL ESTATE AS A BUSINESS

LEARNING GOALS:

By the end of this lesson, you will:

- Recognize the benefits of a career in real estate
- See how vast the real estate industry reaches
- Know the top twenty-four foundational real estate terms
- Understand what real property is
- Learn the five types of real property and be able to give examples of each
- Discover the people and businesses that make the real estate industry work

YOU AND YOUR REAL ESTATE CAREER

There's no doubt that you are seriously considering a career as a real estate broker. There are *countless* perks to this exciting career choice. Here are five compelling reasons that make this career and industry fascinating and engaging.

1. You are your own boss. People want freedom. They want the ability to decide things for themselves and live their lives in a way that they choose to live them. If you've ever dealt with bosses who are incompetent, unethical, or just plain miserable to work for, you can say goodbye to that with this career choice. Being a broker creates freedom from bad bosses and unfulfilling work environments. You also get to say goodbye to punching clocks and tedious commuting. As your own boss, you get to say how your career evolves.

2. You can make great money. Although money may not be your primary focus, money touches everything in our lives. Maybe you're disappointed right now because you're struggling to make ends meet. Perhaps you simply don't have the financial margin that you want. Maybe you know you were made for more. It could just be that you're convinced that if you had the right opportunity, you could excel. You can earn significant returns from real estate. A handful of great clients every month can open up the financial margin—or even financial freedom—that you want. Whether it's a larger home for your family, a European vacation, supporting your favorite charity, or saving for retirement, being a broker opens the door to growing your bank account. There are few careers that can do that.

3. You can make time for family and friends. Like we said, it's all about people! As with any career, responsibility is required. What's so intriguing about being a broker is that you set and change your schedule as you need to do so. You have the power to manage your time in a way that works best for you. This means you can easily attend your children's or grandchildren's extracurricular events. It means you have time to go to family reunions, create date nights, and/or attend other special events. Likewise, it opens up the door for pursuing hobbies you enjoy. Your career is not causing you to miss out on life. As long as you are cognizant of your time management, being a broker can be a relationship-friendly career choice.

4. You get to experience a wonderful array of variety. Doing the same thing every single day can get *boring* fast. Having the same conversations with the same people about the same things for years on end is not a bad thing. However, many people are not wired for the nonstop monotony that is oftentimes associated with desk jobs. If you know that you're not meant to go to a job year after year and sit at the same desk for decades, being a broker could be the ideal career for you. You will never have two days exactly the same. You always have the opportunity to meet new people and see new places. People say variety is the spice of life. If that's true, being a broker is a *super spicy* career choice.

5. **You help people fulfill their dreams.** Being a broker is not only about making your dreams come true. It's also about turning *dreams into reality* for your clients. Imagine standing in front of a beautiful house. Standing with you is a family consisting of both parents and two young children. Their smiles are beaming as you hand over the keys to their dream home. This is the place where they will celebrate birthdays, have parties, watch their children grow up, and make all sorts of new and wonderful memories together. You're not simply selling a house; you're opening the door to their future. The homes in which people live contain countless moments, memories, and conversations that are significant to people. Whether it's helping someone buy or sell, few things can be more fulfilling and satisfying than helping someone achieve their dreams.

REAL ESTATE AS A BUSINESS

Real estate, as a business, is sprawling, multifaceted, and fascinating. This industry is constantly evolving. It is impacted by a wide variety of factors, some of which can be controlled and many of which we have no real control over. What does the new cafe that you love have in common with your friend's boutique store? What does your salon have in common with the latest chain store that just had a grand opening? Each of them has one characteristic in common. Each results from a real estate transaction. We're constantly surrounded by the reality of real estate as a business. Financially, real estate is an overwhelmingly vast business. It involves everything from the simplest of transactions to more advanced, sophisticated transactions. Whether it's for $100,000 or multi-billion dollars, these transactions happen every single day. Accordingly, a sprawling industry, such as real estate, requires a wide array of people, job titles, and skill sets in order to keep the business moving forward.

There are two bodies of law that regulate the real estate industry:

1. The Illinois Real Estate License Act of 2000 (RELA)

    -   RELA is commonly referred to as "The Act." It is considered a sunset provision. This means that because of its nature, it must be reenacted by legislative action every ten years. The Illinois Department of Financial and Professional Regulation (IDFPR) oversees the implementation of The Act.

    -   ILCS stands for the Illinois Compiled Statutes.

2. The Rules And Regulations

    -   The Rules And Regulations come from the body of law known as the Illinois Administrative Code.

Although you need to be aware of both bodies of law since each one will impact your real estate performance, the state exam will focus only on The Act. A detailed discussion of The Act will be presented in Chapter 30.

RELA and the Rules And Regulations provide the most current, accurate, and applicable definitions for real estate professionals doing business. Definitions are the starting point for clear communication. If people define a term differently, then they will have communication problems. Knowing real estate terms, terminology, and definitions, as well as being able to communicate them easily to buyers and sellers, is an essential skill that you must develop. Below are the top twenty-four most commonly used terms in the real estate industry, followed by their definitions.

TOP TWENTY-FOUR REAL ESTATE TERMS (IN ALPHABETICAL ORDER)

1. Adjustable-Rate Mortgage

An adjustable-rate mortgage is one of the top five most popular types of mortgage loans. Sometimes called ARMs, these loans are also lesser known as variable-rate mortgages or tracker mortgages. On this type of loan, the interest rate periodically adjusts based on an index that shows the lender's cost of borrowing on the credit markets. Although commonly based on one-year intervals, the interest rate can change every twelve months. There are some hybrid ARMs that may allow for interest adjustment in as short as six-month intervals. These hybrids can also provide for a combination of a fixed interest rate for a named period of time, and a conversion to an annual adjustment. (Example: The 5/25 means that for the first five years of the loan's interest, the APR is fixed. However, starting in the sixth year, the interest rate converts to an annual adjustable rate.) The ARM loan will always provide a profit due to the lender, commonly known as the margin. The combination of the lender's base rate (index), plus the lender's profit (margin), defines the new interest rate the consumer will be charged for the next period of time. As you know, the lender is a for-profit institution. They need to be conscientious of making a profit not only on the day they grant you the loan but also ten to thirty years into the future. Therefore, the interest rates they charge today are intended to provide a profit now and ten-plus years from now too. Because of this expectation, the fixed-rate loan provides the lender with that security. What if you grant the lender consent to alter the interest rates every twelve months? If you do, they only have to look toward the next twelve months with regard to their profitability. By granting the lender the right to alter the rate every twelve months based upon the then-current cost of funds (the index), they can charge a lower interest rate recognizing that if they need to increase it within twelve months, they can do so. During the loan term, by nature, the interest rate will fluctuate up and down (increase and decrease).

2. Agent

The terms agent, broker, managing broker, property manager, and leasing agent get thrown around frequently and many people believe each term has the same definition. This is inaccurate. These terms are not interchangeable.

The most common definition in most industries is that an agent is an industry professional who has either an implied or expressed authorization to act for and/or represent another party. Typically, the context is business specifically defined.

Thus, a real estate agent is someone who represents sellers, buyers, landlords, and tenants of real estate, or real property. He/she serves as the transaction facilitator in real estate and works under the supervision of a sponsoring broker. Ultimately, an agent's responsibility and goal is to bring the sellers and buyers, landlord, and tenant together. This creates the transaction, which provides the agent a commission, which is an agreed percentage of the property's sale price.

3. Appraisal

An appraisal is a professional opinion or estimate of the value of real estate by a licensed appraiser as of a given date. An appraisal's hallmark characteristic is that it is completely unbiased.

4. Broker

In Illinois, a broker, under the supervision of a sponsoring broker, is someone who represents sellers, buyers, landlords, and tenants of real estate or real property. The sellers and buyers could be individuals, companies, or firms. This action is done for a commission. The broker generally represents the client under the guidance and supervision of a sponsoring broker. This allows the broker to represent clients throughout the state of Illinois. Under the authority and direct supervision granted by the sponsoring broker, the broker exercises the fiduciary duties designed to protect the best interests of the client.

5. Brokerage

The term brokerage has two definitions.

- The first definition is that a brokerage is a real estate company that has the primary responsibility to act as a middleman, bringing consumers together in order to facilitate a transaction. It represents buyers, sellers, landlords, and/or tenants, who are pursuing real estate possibilities. The brokerage acts as a broker, utilizing the services of a designated managing broker and broker to facilitate the creation and completion of real estate transactions. You can view it as the connecting point between brokers and consumers. The properties bought and sold may be industrial, residential, commercial, or agricultural. License categories in Illinois feature residential leasing agents, brokers, and managing brokers. (You'll learn more about them later.)

- The second definition of brokerage is the act or function of representing buyers, sellers, landlords and tenants.

6. Buyer's Agent

A buyer's agent is the agent for the buyer. Buyer agents help buyers find a new home and/or property. They assist in the search process and help the buyers with creating offers. The goal is to obtain the best deal possible for the buyer/tenant, and ultimately assist in helping a buyer purchase the desired property. A buyer's agent can function in residential or commercial property, or both.

7. Closing Costs

Closing costs are the fees (expenses) that are paid at the closing of a real estate transaction. These expenses are in addition to and on top of the price of the property. Both the buyer and the seller will incur closing costs in order to complete the transaction.

The closing can be the most exciting time in the real estate transaction process for the buyer and the seller. It is when the money and documents are transferred so that the transfer of ownership can go to the buyer. An effective closing is present when both parties fulfill their contractual agreements.

8. Contingencies

A contingency is a type of clause in a contract. In a typical contract, there will always be specific components that need to be met in order to complete the transaction. These are referred to as contingencies. Contingencies are one or more conditions that must be met prior to the delivery of the deed. In other words, the contingency defines one or more conditions and/or actions that must be fulfilled in order for the transaction to be finalized.

9. Designated Agent

The Act states that a "designated agent means a sponsored licensee named by a sponsoring broker as the exclusive legal agent of a client" (225 ILCS 454/1-10). In the year 2000, the state of Illinois coined the term "designated agent." It literally gave the managing broker the right to delegate the agency responsibilities to individual agents. The duties that the agent would take responsibility for consist of "COLD AC" which stands for Care, Obedience, Loyalty, Disclosure, Accountability, and Confidentiality.

10. Designated Managing Broker

The designated managing broker is appointed by the sponsoring broker to take responsibility for the day-to-day operation of the brokerage as well as take responsibility for overseeing the activities of the licensees. Should the licensee violate license law, the designated managing broker may also be held responsible for failure to properly supervise the actions of the licensee.

11. Fixed-Rate Mortgage

Fixed rate refers to a loan that is a fully amortized mortgage loan. The note's interest rate is fixed and thus stays the same through the term of the loan. As a result, the payment amounts and the duration of the loan are fixed. The borrower benefits from having a payment that stays consistent, which makes it easier to budget because the **cost** is fixed.

12. Home Inspection

The Home Inspector License Act of Illinois defines this term:

> "Home inspection" means the examination and evaluation of the exterior and interior components of residential real property, which includes the inspection of any two or more of the following components of residential real property in connection with or to facilitate the sale, lease, or other conveyance of, or the proposed sale, lease or other conveyance of, residential real property:
>
> 1. Heating, ventilation, and air conditioning system
>
> 2. Plumbing system
>
> 3. Electrical system
>
> 4. Structural composition
>
> 5. Foundation
>
> 6. Roof
>
> 7. Masonry structure or
>
> 8. Any other residential real property component as established by rule.

In other words, a home inspection examines and reports on a series of details about the condition of a residential real estate property. These are most commonly used when a house is on the market to be sold. These inspections are done by licensed home inspectors.

In contrast, in the commercial realm, multiple inspections take place. Typically, a structural engineer and/or environmental specialist is tasked with the inspections.

13. Land

Land is defined as that which nature has created. It includes everything below the surface to the center of the Earth, the surface and all decorative vegetation on the surface, and everything above to infinity.

14. Licensee

Real estate licensee means an individual who holds an active license as a real estate broker, designated managing broker, or residential leasing agent.

15. Listing

Listing is a generic term that refers to a property in which a designated sponsoring broker using a designated agent has been engaged by the seller to market the property in pursuit of a ready, willing, and able buyer or tenant.

16. Listing Agent

A listing agent is also known as and called a seller's agent. He/she is a licensee under the authority of a sponsoring broker and has a legal, written contract with the owner who wants to sell/lease the home or property. The agent legally represents the owner. His or her goal is to price and market the property and ultimately sell/lease it in order to receive a commission. The listing agent works exclusively with the home seller/landlord, keeping their best interest constantly in mind. The goal is to guide the seller/landlord step by step through every aspect of the process, from marketing the property to closing. Furthermore, a listing agent will assist in preparing the property to sell/lease. In the residential sector, the listing agent will list the home in the MLS, show the home to buyers/tenants (whether one on one or open houses), and negotiate with the homebuyer.

17. Market

Real estate market is another term for real estate business. The business cannot exist without the market, and the market cannot exist without the business. The real estate market is the profession of buying, selling, or renting real estate, and real property. This includes housing, land, and buildings. The market does not exist on its own inside its own bubble. It is impacted by several variables and forces, including but not limited to the economy, supply and demand, interest rates, demographics, along with government policies and subsidies.

18. Offers and Contracts

As a verb, an offer means to make something available for sale.

As a noun, an offer is a proposal that is conditional in nature. It is made by either a buyer or a seller. It is a formal request to purchase real estate. The goal is to sell or buy real estate property. If a written offer is accepted, it becomes a legally binding contract.

Thus, a real estate contract is a legally enforceable written agreement between two or more parties. A verbal agreement may be legal, with limited exceptions, and is not enforceable in a court of law. The purpose of the contract is to facilitate real estate being purchased, sold, exchanged, or some other type of conveyance. Conveyance is the legal act or process of transferring or conveying ownership or interest in real estate from one owner to another.

19. Preapproval Letter

In mortgage lending, preapproval is the determination by a lender establishing what a borrower is qualified for. The preapproval letter is the written evaluation that outlines the range of what the buyers are approved for budget-wise, after verifying the buyer's employment, credit score, and cash availability. In other words, it's a preliminary financial evaluation of a potential borrower. The purpose is to give the borrower a financial landscape and overview, which includes an estimated interest rate, along with the maximum principal amount.

A prequalification letter is a preliminary determination of what a buyer can afford that does not incorporate confirmation of credit, employment, or income. It is purely an estimate based upon information verbally given by the buyer to the loan officer. It does not have as much impact on defining the buyer's financial capability as a preapproval letter may have.

20. Realtor/REALTOR®

A REALTOR® is a member of the National Association of REALTORS® (NAR). It's possible that a REALTOR® can be a broker, agent, or appraiser. Additionally, even real estate sales professionals, along with other real estate professionals, can be REALTORS®. Each one must pay dues, meet a certain set of standards (adhere to a detailed code of conduct), and be an expert in his or her field.

Note: REALTOR® is a federally registered trademark and has a design standard. "The preferred form of the term is REALTOR®—in all caps, and using the registered trademark symbol. If using the symbol isn't possible, then the next best form is in all caps: REALTOR." NAR

21. Real Estate

While you may think it is unnecessary that we're defining real estate, its definition holds the utmost importance. Real estate is property that comprises the land, along with all human-made additions to the land. Also included in real estate are:

- Any natural resources: minerals, water, vegetation

- Immovable property related to natural resources

- Human-made improvements intended to remain with the property

- Real estate often gets confused with personal property. The key distinction is that personal property is not permanently attached to the land. Personal property can be a massive list. It includes items like furniture, crops, tools, vehicles, boats, and so on.

22. Real Property

Real property is defined as the land, human-made improvements, and rights of ownership, which consists of five elements:

- Possession

- Quiet enjoyment

- Disposition

- Exclusion

- Control

One simple way to remember is by this acronym: "Passing Quizzes Drives Effective Classes."

23. Sponsoring Broker

The Act defines sponsoring broker as:

> "The broker who certifies to the Department his, her, or its sponsorship of a licensed managing broker, broker, or a residential leasing agent." (225 ILCS 454/1-10)

Let's simplify the definition of sponsoring broker. The sponsoring broker is an entity (whether human or a legal entity such as a corporation) that authorizes the licensee to conduct real estate activities. It is imperative for the licensee to realize that all business opportunities belong to the sponsoring broker as well as future commissioned earnings. The licensee works on behalf of, in the name of, and under the authority of the sponsoring broker.

In Illinois, each and every licensee is associated with a sponsoring broker either as an employee or independent contractor. State regulation requires the licensee to enter into a written relationship agreement with the sponsoring broker that dictates the relationship either as an employee or independent contractor.

A licensee participates in offering brokerage services on behalf of the sponsoring broker. The law also outlines clear expectations of sponsoring brokers. Each sponsoring broker through a designated managing broker is responsible for guiding licensees through their first years as an agent, as well as being available to assist licensees throughout their affiliation with the sponsoring broker.

24. Title Insurance

Title insurance is a form of indemnity insurance. (Indemnity is security or protection against a loss or other financial burden.) Title insurance provides protection to both the mortgagee (lender) and the purchasers (mortgagors). It safeguards against potential losses arising from disputes over property ownership and title defects that may not be revealed in a public record search. Purchasers are protected from unlisted claimants, such as forged documents, errors in legal descriptions, and other errors. The purpose of title insurance is not to fix title defects, but rather to provide financial coverage for title defects. If required, the title company is obligated to legally defend its policyholder against any claims concerning land ownership. Generally, it is paid for with a one-time premium at closing by the seller.

Illinois recognizes two different types:

1. Owner's coverage (mortgagee)

2. Lender's protection (mortgagor)

You finished learning the top twenty-four real estate definitions. Congratulations!

Recommended Activity

One of the best ways to know if you actually know a definition is to explain it to someone else. If you have a family member or friend near you, have them verbally quiz you on the terms. This repetition will ground the definitions in your mind while giving you the opportunity to practice how you articulate each definition.

The reason knowing definitions is important in the real world is that the moment a potential client catches a licensee not using a term correctly, or explaining something in hard-to-understand terms, it is an instant turnoff and creates mistrust.

Being articulate and speaking with certainty using real estate lingo showcases your expertise and builds trust. And trust builds profitable and fulfilling careers.

REAL PROPERTY AND EXAMPLES

What is real property? Real property is legally defined as the land, plus improvements and the rights of ownership. This includes elements created by nature as well as permanent human-made improvements to the land, such as fences, structures, driveways, and so forth.

We can classify real property by its general type. There are five categories. They consist of:

1. Residential

2. Commercial

3. Industrial

4. Agricultural

5. Special purpose

A real estate professional can specialize in one or more of the above categories. Let's look at definitions and distinctions of each category.

Residential

Residential property refers to property that is used or intended to be used for the purpose of providing residential living facilities. Residential property includes:

- Single family homes

- 2-4 unit buildings

- Townhomes

- Condominiums

- Coach homes

- Manor homes

- Quads

- Mobile homes

- And similar types of dwellings

Residential property can be located in rural, urban, or suburban areas.

Commercial

The term commercial has two definitions. In the generic sense, it includes agricultural, industrial, and special purpose. In the specific sense, it is defined as business property and includes three different types of properties:

1. **Multifamily**

   These are housing structures with five or more living units. These structures are generally considered to be commercial and may require a higher down payment and possibly a higher interest rate because of the added risk to the lender.

2. **Office**

   An office can be a room, set of rooms, or a building that is used and designated as a location for commercial or professional work.

3. **Retail**

   Retail is selling goods or items to the public who will use them for business or personal purposes. This is different from wholesale, which is selling to a retailer. Types of retail stores can include, but are not limited to, supermarkets, specialty stores, department stores, convenience stores, warehouse stores, discount stores, and superstores. Examples include Target, IKEA, Kohl's, Costco, Kroger, Rite Aid, Home Depot, and so on.

Industrial

Industrial real estate includes buildings where product is manufactured or stored, such as warehouses, repositories, factories, depots, buildings that deal in logistics, and even land that is located within industrial districts within a city or state.

Agricultural

Agricultural real estate property includes farmland, forestry, orchards, and ranches.

Special Purpose

The fifth and final category of real property is called special purpose. This category includes:

- Cemeteries
- Churches
- Government-held lands
- Public use
- Schools
- Surgical hospitals

Government-held lands means the same as government-owned lands. It is land or other assets that are legally owned by the government. This property can be titled at any level (federal, state, or local level). Public access is at the government's discretion.

Public use means public property. It's specifically dedicated to and for public use. It's a subset of state property. Examples include public streets, freeways, courthouses, public school buildings, state universities, information centers, libraries, some parks, and so forth.

Each of the five categories of real property has two underlying market divisions. You might view them as branches on a tree. These branches or divisions are:

1. Rental
2. Sales

To summarize, the five types of real property are:

1. Residential
2. Commercial
3. Industrial
4. Agricultural
5. Special purpose

THE PEOPLE AND BUSINESSES THAT MAKE THE REAL ESTATE INDUSTRY WORK

Business is all about people. It's about building relationships and supporting each other, all in an effort to achieve a worthwhile goal and build fulfilling careers. The business of real estate is no different.

The real estate industry, like you learned earlier, is multifaceted. It is one of the largest and most varied industries in the US. It is a truly interdependent industry that relies on a wide variety of professionals in order to make all the systems and transactions work. As you know, interdependent means two or more people or things that are dependent on one other. The real estate business is not as simple as brokerages or real estate office branches. Although when you think of real estate, you may think of a brokerage first, the industry is exceptionally broad and includes other elements. The real estate industry includes property management, development, subdivision, home inspection, and more.

There are a variety of specialties that are separate, yet an essential part of the real estate industry. These separate specializations consist of:

1. Appraisal

2. Auctions

3. Consulting

4. Financing

5. Home inspection

6. Property management

7. Subdivision and development

8. Training and education

You've already learned about appraisals. Let's look at details related to these other businesses that serve to support the real estate industry.

Auctions

If you've used eBay, you already know what an auction is. In real estate, an auction is a sales event. Just like with eBay, each hopeful buyer places his or her competitive bid with the desire to win the item being auctioned. The auction may be open (public) or closed.

Consulting

Consulting is the act of providing advice or guidance. This advice and guidance come from an expert, trained professional, and/or a type of specialist. Advice is given without conflict of interest. The consultant is neutral, has no hidden agenda, and shows no biases.

Financing

The real estate finance industry focuses on providing funding for both commercial and residential real estate. This is the funding that allows the real estate transaction to take place. The majority are financed as mortgage loans, where a loan originator does his or her part in order to facilitate the transaction.

Home Inspection

The real estate industry has a variety of inspectors. Each one plays a specific role in giving potential buyers a clear and accurate assessment of a specific aspect of the home and/or property, or a broad overview. A home inspection is an examination focusing on the home's condition. It is noninvasive, visual, and limited. Nothing is taken apart. After the inspector prepares the written report, he/she delivers it to the client or clients. Having this knowledge is an asset to the clients. It allows them to make decisions based on evidence. The written report is not a guarantee of the future condition of the house. In your mind, never combine a home inspector with a real estate appraiser. Those jobs are separate and distinct. While usually not required, a home inspection can reduce a buyer's risk by identifying potential structural problems in the early stages of buying a home. In many cases, the buyer may be granted a short period following the acceptance of the offer by the seller to conduct their home inspection. Generally, it is the buyer's responsibility to engage a provider and pay for a home inspection.

In the state of Illinois, home inspectors are required to be licensed by the State. Also, in Illinois, home inspection is a regulated industry. The American Society of Home Inspectors (ASHI), which is one of several home inspector training organizations, says that "Illinois law creates the Illinois Home Inspector License Act and establishes a Home Inspector Advisory Board within the Division of Real Estate (DRE) for the Illinois Department of Financial and Professional Regulation (IDFPR) the regulatory agency that oversees home inspectors." A home inspection is the most common and widely used type of inspection. You can read the full Home Inspector License Act here: http://www.ilga.gov/legislation/ilcs/ilcs5.asp?ActID=1359&ChapterID=24

Besides the home inspector, other types of inspections that are done by specialists include:

- Roof

- Plumbing

- Septic

- Heating, ventilation, and air conditioning (HVAC)

- Thermal imaging

- Tree health

What does a home inspector not inspect? What is not usually included?

- Asbestos

- Lead paint

- Pest and rodent control

- Radon gas (a naturally occurring radioactive gas)

- Swimming pools, spas, and hot tubs

- Toxic mold

When searching for a home inspector, agents can recommend that clients look for one who has an affiliation with groups, such as:

- The American Society of Home Inspectors

- The International Society of Certified Home Inspectors

- The National Institute of Building Inspectors

Each of the above associations is well respected. Each website has a search feature, so agents or clients can quickly locate a member in his or her area.

Property Management

This industry focuses on the oversight, maintenance, marketing, and management of one or more properties on behalf of the owner/s. These properties can be commercial, residential, agricultural, and industrial real estate. Much of the time, they fall in the category of investment properties. Examples include apartments, retail shops, shopping centers, and detached houses.

Subdivision and Development

These terms are often used together. A subdivision is the division or splitting of a lot, tract, or parcel of land into two or more lots, sites, plots, or other divisions of land for the purpose of sale, or the purpose of building development (whether immediate or future). In other words, you divide a single property into two or more smaller pieces. A development is also known as a real estate development or property development. It is the human-made improvement and construction on the land in order to generate value. It is a business process that includes a variety of activities. These activities include, but are not limited to:

- Renovation

- Re-lease of existing buildings

- Raw land purchases

- The sale of developed land or parcels

Real estate developers are the professionals who coordinate development activities. They oversee the process from idea to reality. Real estate development is not the same as construction, although there can be overlap.

Training and Education

Real estate training and education are found in a variety of places, including but not limited to:

1. Educational institutions like universities and colleges

2. Trade organizations

3. Private schools

4. Companies

The training can take place in person or virtually, depending on the nature of the educational opportunities. Group work may or may not be required.

Each state sets its own minimum standards and requirements for licensing education for those seeking a real estate license. Continuing education (CE) requirements are also determined and set by the licensee's home state. The goal of CE classes and training is to keep the licensee up to date with the best practices.

Licensing and CE do not take the place of or preclude the designating managing broker from taking the responsibility for providing skill set training designed to help licensees grow their real estate careers. Having a real estate license does not necessarily ensure success in the industry. There is an entirely separate body of knowledge that must be mastered in order to be able to successfully represent the best interest of buyers and sellers.

You're now at the end of chapter one. It's time for your chapter quiz. Without referring back to the text, see how well you can answer these questions. The answer key is in the back of the book. Good luck!

CHAPTER 1 QUIZ

1. There are a number of different loan programs available to the purchaser of a residential home. Which type of mortgage loan program can the purchaser of a townhouse acquire that periodically adjusts the interest rates based on an index that reflects the cost to the lender for lending the money?

    a. Adjustable rate
    b. Fixed rate
    c. 30-year fixed
    d. Graduated payment loan

2. Sam and Martha are interested in purchasing an investment building. They have a friend, Mark Dillon, who recently acquired his real estate license. If Mark agrees to work with Sam and Martha, the role Mark is going to play is:

    a. The agent of the loan officer, who will provide the necessary funds to purchase the property
    b. The attorney, who will provide Sam and Martha with the necessary legal advice regarding the purchase of the property
    c. The real estate agent charged with the responsibility of representing the best interest of Sam and Martha
    d. Simply a friend providing advice on what they need to do

3. A real estate agent is someone who has acquired a broker's license and is generally charged with the responsibility to represent the best interest of which party:

    a. Seller of real estate
    b. Buyer of real estate
    c. Landlord
    d. Whoever has hired (engaged) the broker

4. Karen, having recently graduated from college, is interested in purchasing a condo rather than moving back in with her parents. In order for her to secure a loan, the lender wishes to verify the current value of the property. Which of the following terms is a professional judgment of the property's value on a specific date?

    a. Home inspection report
    b. Appraisal
    c. Estimate
    d. Home value report

5. A real estate licensee is someone who represents sellers and/or buyers of real estate or real property. The sellers and buyers could be:

    a. Individuals
    b. Companies
    c. Firms
    d. All of the above

6. Andrew wants to start his own business. As he has an interest in real estate, he thought it might be best to start a real estate brokerage office. If Andrew has the funding necessary to start the business, what other credentials will be required in order to make the business operational? Who has the credentials and can legally exercise the option of starting their own brokerage and employing other real estate agents?

    a. Any real estate agent who has successfully passed the state broker exam
    b. Only a broker
    c. Only a designated managing broker
    d. An attorney working under court-ordered supervision

7. What term is frequently used to represent the action within the real estate industry that reflects the representation of buyers, sellers, landlords, and/or tenants in the pursuit of real estate possibilities?

    a. Brokerage
    b. Buyer's agency
    c. Property management agreement
    d. Licensee

8. Quinton is looking to buy a new home for his family. In order to better understand the markets and available housing, which professional would most likely be the choice to give Quinton some insight and direction into the marketplace?

    a. Seller's agent
    b. Buyer's agent
    c. Leasing agent
    d. Property manager

9. Closing costs are the expenses that are in addition to and on top of the price of the property. They are payable by:

    a. The buyer only

    b. Both the buyer and seller are responsible for paying their respective closing costs

    c. Seller only

    d. Either party, depending upon the written agreement by and between the seller's and buyer's attorney

10. The sales contract is the binding agreement between buyer and seller that will ultimately fulfill the desire to deliver the deed. The contract lays out terms and conditions that the buyer and seller agree to regarding the transaction. Provisions within this contract that establishes certain obligations of either party are generally considered to be:

    a. Closing costs

    b. Contingencies

    c. Preapproval letter

    d. Power of attorney

11. Which of the following individuals has been granted written authority to execute legal documentation on behalf of the owner who wants to sell/lease the home or property?

    a. Listing agent

    b. Seller's agent

    c. Attorney-in-fact

    d. Buyer's agent

12. When a buyer makes an application for a mortgage, the lender will confirm the buyer's credentials, which might include verifying employment and the financial capability to repay the debt. An essential element of judging the buyer's financial capability is looking at their history of satisfying the debt to other creditors. Which of the four documents used in processing the mortgage loan would give the lender an understanding of the buyer's responsibility for the repayment of debt?

    a. Credit report

    b. Preapproval letter

    c. Pre-authorization letter

    d. Satisfaction of mortgage

13. There are different professional associations that licensees may elect to participate in. When a licensee secures their license, which of the following professional associations does the licensee automatically belong to?

    a. The local board of REALTORS®
    b. National Association of REALTORS®
    c. Association of Real Estate Professionals
    d. There is no professional association the licensee automatically belongs to after securing their real estate license.

14. Special-purpose properties are generally highly specialized with regard to their use, resulting in a limited supply. Many times, this requires a specialized means of appraisal in order to establish a market value. Which of the following is NOT included in the category of special purpose real property?

    a. Places of worship
    b. Colleges
    c. Construction sites
    d. Cemeteries

15. There are five categories of real property. Which of the following would not fall in the realm of real property?

    a. Special purpose
    b. Apartment buildings consisting of five or more units
    c. Rental properties
    d. Motor homes

16. Licensees are required to complete continuing education to further enhance their knowledge of real estate law so they can better protect the interest of their clients. The requirements for continuing education must be met before the licensee can renew their licenses. Said requirements are established by:

    a. The designated managing broker
    b. The Federal Government
    c. The state licensing agency
    d. The local board in REALTORS® in conjunction with the National Association of REALTORS®

17. Development activities include all of these, except which one?

    a. Renovation
    b. Repurpose of existing buildings
    c. Home inspections
    d. Raw land purchases

18. Real estate skill set training and practical education can be provided through:

    a. State-approved educational venues
    b. The sponsoring broker to ensure the licensee can successfully protect the interests of the consumer
    c. Professional vocational schools licensed under the state's department of education
    d. Such education is not required so long as the licensee uses simple common sense on how to protect the financial interests of their client

19. Who or what sets the minimum standards and requirements for those who seek to obtain a real estate license?

    a. Sponsoring broker
    b. Board of REALTORS®
    c. Federal Government
    d. State regulatory agency responsible for the oversight of professional industries

20. In order for the buyer to fully understand the physical condition of the property, there will generally be a home inspection by a licensed home inspector. Who has the responsibility of paying for the services of this home inspector?

    a. Buyer
    b. Seller
    c. Brokerage
    d. Agent or broker

CHAPTER 2:

REAL ESTATE INDUSTRY DYNAMICS

LEARNING GOALS:

By the end of this lesson, you will:

- Have an overview of real estate economics
- Recognize the impact of supply and demand
- Understand what the Federal Reserve does and how it applies to the real estate industry

REAL ESTATE ECONOMICS

Economics is the branch of social science that focuses on the production, consumption, and transfer of wealth, as well as the distribution and consumption of goods and services.

Real estate economics applies these techniques to the real estate market. It researches, studies, and uncovers answers to countless questions, including ones like these:

- To what extent is it possible to predict supply and demand?

- To what extent is it possible to predict pricing patterns?

Real estate economics can be narrowed down to a smaller focus. Most studies focus on residential real estate markets. However, other markets such as commercial, industrial, and agricultural can be studied as well. As you read earlier, the real estate market is another word for real estate business. The business cannot exist without the market, and the market cannot exist without the business. The real estate market is the profession of buying, selling, or renting real estate and real property. This includes housing, land, and buildings. The market does not exist on its own; it is not contained inside its own bubble. It is impacted by several variables and forces, including but not limited to the economy, supply and demand, interest rates, demographics, along with government policies and subsidies.

Let's start with supply and demand.

SUPPLY AND DEMAND

Supply and demand is the basic concept of our economic system. Like any market, there are always ups and downs. As such, if the interest rates increase beyond what the consumer is comfortable paying, that could cause demand to decrease. This decrease results in an abundance of real estate available with few buyers to take action. Here we have low demand with high inventory. As with any retailer, this will bring about reductions in price to attract what few buyers currently exist in the marketplace to make a purchase. Supply and demand has been called both an economic model and also a theoretic model. Here, of course, we're applying it specifically to the study of real estate. Like any asset in the world, real estate is subject to the forces of supply and demand. The focus of supply and demand in the real estate market is price determination. It works to explain and describe the ever-evolving interaction between home sellers and buyers. In a competitive market, house prices can fluctuate until they settle at a point where the quantity demanded (at the current asking price) will equal the quantity that is supplied (also at the current asking price). This generates an economic equilibrium between the selling prices and the available **properties**. It's the ebb and flow between how willing people are to buy and sell and the asking and selling prices of the real estate. With housing, when housing demand is high and supply is low, house prices usually increase. This is known as a "seller's market" because the market favors sellers at that point in time. When the housing supply is high, it is common for homeowners to decrease their asking prices because there is less demand in the market. This is known as a "buyer's market." There are a number of components that impact supply and demand for real estate.

There are four primary factors that affect the concept of supply:

1. **Labor force**: This concept deals with the availability of skilled construction professionals. Frequently, when a market takes a downward turn, developers tend to reduce the number of units being constructed. This causes the developers to lay off skilled construction craftspeople rather than keeping them on the payroll. These craftspeople also may have families they need to support, resulting in many of them pursuing alternative forms of employment. This reduces the number of skilled workers to construct additional housing when the economy returns. The loss of skilled craftspeople results in a shortage of available housing when the demand begins to increase.

2. **Construction costs**: Whenever construction costs go up, this impacts supply. Many of the components used in the construction of real estate are made from various elements. Imagine if your local Home Depot ran out of wood. This would create a demand for it. Those who need lumber would drive for hours in order to get it and/or order it online. Consequently, lumber prices would most likely increase. This financial burden is passed on to the home builder, who most likely will increase his or her rates to cover the added cost. Meaning, costs are passed down ultimately to the end user, usually buyers and renters/tenants. These increased prices can cause the entire market to slow down even further. Another example is when using PVC pipe to bring fresh water to the building, the cost of that pipe could have a direct impact on the value of the real estate. PVC is a form of plastic that is a derivative of oil. If the cost of a barrel of crude oil goes up, the cost of producing the PVC pipe will also likely increase. If the cost to produce the pipe increases, the manufacturer likely will pass that increased cost onto the developer, who then passes it on to the consumer. This ultimately impacts the value of the real estate. If the cost of construction increases substantially, it may cause a negative reaction by the consumer, thereby reducing interest in new construction.

3. **Government controls**: The government has been charged with the responsibility to protect your health, welfare, and safety. The key factor is the word safety. You deserve a safe environment, which means a safe structure to raise your family in. When it comes to the real estate market, the biggest influence the government has is the establishment of regulations that define the number of housing units that can exist within a given geographical space. For example, the city has determined the most probable lot size is

25' x 125'. This lot size, common in many older communities, amounts to 3,250 square feet. Consider a typical professional football playing surface, which is typically one acre in size, or 43,560 square feet. Based on the city lot described above, we could get 13.9 homes (lots) into one acre of land. If the municipality sets a housing standard of one home per acre, it is clear to see that the government intervention involving the size of the lots will have a direct impact on the quantity and availability of housing.

- Permits: With new home construction, the housing supply is affected by permits. Permits are the necessary legal approval required in order for construction or expansion to take place. If granted, this permission is given in the form of a permit, which could be a building permit or construction permit. At times, the government creates "red tape." As you probably know, this is an idiom. It points out requirements or steps that seem to be excessive, redundant, or rigid. This red tape can mean that getting new homes on the market takes a longer time. When this happens, there are fewer houses on the market. As such, this causes house prices to increase. It should also be noted that if the municipality issues an abundance of building permits, this may create an environment where developers are putting up more homes than the economy can bear.

- **Financial policies**: With government policies in the context of real estate, usually the topic focuses on the Federal Reserve (also known as the Federal Reserve System or the Fed). It is the US's central banking system. Overseen by a board, it regulates and supervises the practices of lending and banking institutions. You can instantly and easily see how decisions made there can impact the real estate industry. Their changes are most commonly in response to laws that have been enacted by the US government's legislature. Its ultimate goal is to generate and produce banking system stability. The Federal Reserve defines what it does as: "Supervising and regulating banks and other important financial institutions to ensure the safety and soundness of the nation's banking and financial system and to protect the credit rights of consumers. Maintaining the stability of the financial system and containing systemic risk that may arise in financial markets." The source of funds to purchase real estate, generally, comes from financial institutions. They justify lending the money by charging interest as their profit. The amount of interest can severely impact housing affordability. For example, the difference in a monthly payment of a $400,000 mortgage with an interest of 3% compared to an 8% loan can be as much as $1,248.64 per month. The impact on the required income is going to reduce the number of qualified buyers substantially. This could result in an increase in required annual income by over $50,000.

WHAT ADDITIONAL FACTORS IMPACT THE SUPPLY OF REAL ESTATE?

They include but are not limited to:

- **Active listings:** These play an essential role in the supply of real estate. Greater supply is created by a higher number of active listings. This gives homebuyers and investors more options from which to choose.

- **Employment:** Employment is unique because there is a case for it to impact both supply and demand. Most commonly, employment is listed as a factor under demand. However, the availability of employment can also have a direct impact on the supply of real estate. Employment centers often rely on the central financial district (CFD) to fund business operations and expansion. Both of these factors can be a catalyst for the increased need for housing. This can cause a surge in construction and the supply of housing units. Central financial districts are generally considered to form a hub within a metropolitan area. In many communities, the compensation that a person may be entitled to usually has a direct connection to that financial core that the community has been built around, a central financial district. If there is a source of income in a given community, it often acts as an incentive that attracts consumers. Suburbs are oftentimes defined by their relationship to a localized financial district.

- **Immigration:** Immigration is also a smaller factor. When more immigrants move into a specific city, it can generate higher demand for real estate.

WHAT INFLUENCES DEMAND?

Demand can be influenced, impacted, and/or changed by several factors, just like supply. The top factors are the following in alphabetical order:

- **Demographics:** This is the statistical study of human populations. Demographic analyses can include a wide array of data including but not limited to education, ethnicity, nationality, religion, spending habits, age ranges, number of children, income, and so on. A demographic study can be a city, state, country, or worldwide. It can study whole societies, specific groups, or subsets of groups.

- **Economy:** Probably the most obvious of them all, when there is a "good economy," it is almost always marked by more movement. People buy more homes. Young people will move out of their parents' home and begin renting on their own, or possibly purchase. A good economy usually means more movement of cash, people, and assets. A bad economy usually means just the opposite.

- **Income:** When someone is considering making a financial decision, such as renting or buying, it always comes down to his or her income. What can they afford? What is the percentage of the mortgage or rent payment to their monthly income? Is that correlation reasonable and healthy, or not? Are they growing their wealth, or looking at a chasm of debt?

- **Interest rates:** In general terms, when interest rates are low, the demand for real estate increases. When interest rates are high, the demand for real estate usually decreases. The significance of low interest rates and what makes it appealing is that it means the cost of borrowing is less than it has been. This gives many homebuyers the opportunity to purchase larger homes. Thus, they can invest more money into their home. For example:

  - A $350,000 home with 10% down results in a mortgage amount of $315,000.

  - With an interest rate of 3% per year, the monthly principal and interest payment amounts to $1,328. This would require an annual income of $57,000.

  - If the interest rate would increase to 4.5% annually, this would increase the monthly payment to $1,596. This increase would require an annual income of $68,402.

  - This would result in a required increase in salary by 20%. If the economy is only averaging a 3% per year increase in salaries, this would dramatically impact a potential buyer's desire to buy a home or would force the buyer to reduce the targeted purchase price.

  - To be able to afford a home on a $57,000 per year salary at 4.5%, the consumer would have to drop their target purchase price to just above $260,000 as compared to the $350,000 noted above.

- **Population:** Population growth or decline can be impacted by how well a geographical area attracts or repels people. It's common knowledge that every person needs a place to live. As the population grows, so does its need for housing. In 2019, the US population was 328.2 million. It's still growing! However, this growth does not mean the population in all states and cities is growing at the same rate. Within this topic is also the dynamic of how certain states or cities grow more (or grow faster) than others. For example, let's say that City A has a booming job market. This is attracting new people to live there. Its population is increasing. However, the other side of the coin is that those people are exiting City B because its job market keeps deteriorating. Thus, City A's population is growing while City B's population is diminishing. Simultaneously, demand in one city increases while demand in another city decreases. This is a fascinating dynamic that's constantly happening in the US.

At this point, you can see how there is a dynamic dance or synergy between these two forces. Now that you've learned about real estate economics, it's time for a chapter quiz.

CHAPTER 2 QUIZ

1. Which social science focuses on the production, consumption, and transfer of wealth, and the distribution and consumption of goods and services?

    a. Sociology
    b. Economics
    c. Business
    d. Micro-business

2. Real estate economics applies to which of the following?

    a. Residential
    b. Commercial
    c. Industrial
    d. All of the above
    e. None of the above

3. Real estate business is an industry consisting of multiple facets. Which of the following would not constitute a facet of the real estate industry as it exists within the market?

    a. Buyer representation
    b. Seller representation
    c. Lender representation
    d. Landlord representation

4. The real estate market is able to exist and yet there is a question as to whether or not it can exist and thrive within its own individual bubble. Which of the statements below would best reflect the real estate industry's existence within its own unique bubble?

    a. The real estate industry is impacted by a number of variables as well as forces that help to define its parameters. Therefore, the real estate industry is of a nature that it cannot exist within its own unique bubble but is directly impacted by influences from other realms including buyer sentiments and industry standards.
    b. Due to restraints established by society, the real estate industry is limited to the simple act of representing the best interest of a seller in a real estate transaction.
    c. Unlike other industries, the demand for real estate does not have an impact on the availability and pricing of such.
    d. The government does not have any influence over the real estate industry, and as such, is not a factor in defining the parameters and conditions under which business activities can be performed.

5. Which term reflects the amount or quantity of a commodity, product, or service available and the desire of buyers for it?

    a. Supply
    b. Demand
    c. Supply and demand
    d. None of the above

6. Supply and demand focus on which of the following?

    a. Price determination
    b. The interaction between homebuyers and sellers
    c. Both of the above
    d. None of the above

7. In a competitive market, house prices can fluctuate until they settle at a point where the quantity demanded (at the current asking price) will equal the quantity that is supplied (also at the current asking price). What does this generate?

    a. Greater supply and demand
    b. Less supply and demand
    c. Interest rate increases
    d. An economic equilibrium

8. A city in California has a vibrant job market and is attracting new people who want to settle down there. However, the supply of houses is low. Since the demand is high, how does that affect prices?

    a. House prices usually stay the same.
    b. House prices usually decrease.
    c. House prices usually increase.
    d. None of the above

9. Construction companies and project managers are finding it difficult to find and hire the specialists and skilled laborers that they need in order to complete housing projects. What has been created?

    a. A reduction in the available supply of new housing designed to meet the demands of the consumers
    b. A general increase in the demand for real estate because of the creative nature that unskilled specialists can bring to the marketplace
    c. An environment that discourages potential specialists from entering the construction industry due to government interference in construction standards
    d. The lack of skilled craftspeople in constructing homes does not have any influence on the availability or supply of new housing.

10. When construction costs increase, what almost always happens?

    a. The market stays the same
    b. The market slows down
    c. The market speeds up
    d. None of the above

11. The Federal Reserve regulates and supervises the practices of which financial institutions?

    a. Lending institutions
    b. Banking institutions
    c. Both of the above
    d. None of the above

12. What is the ultimate goal of the Federal Reserve?

    a. Banking system stability
    b. Government accountability
    c. Credit bureau accountability
    d. To control government cash flow

13. For new home construction or expansions, what is the necessary legal approval required in order to complete those projects?

    a. A listing contract executed by a real estate licensee approved by the local municipality to represent the developer in pursuit of a potential buyer.
    b. Building permit
    c. An executed sales contract establishing that there is an interested buyer to assume the ownership of the property upon completion of the project.
    d. None of the above

14. Demographics can best be defined as a reflection of which of the following:

   a. The natural need of society to establish a place to live. The extent of the population defines the need for real estate and also governs the nature of the demographics.

   b. A reflection of the general concept that the desire to purchase real estate has nothing to do with financial capability but simply the need to provide a financial platform to grow personal wealth.

   c. The study of the human population including various levels of education, national origin, various age ranges, spending habits, and the potential study of society and subsets.

   d. A reflection of the direction the money market is taking and how we define the availability of funds in the pursuit of real estate investments.

15. Population growth generally has the same growth rate in all major US cities.

   a. This is a true statement as society has evolved into a consistency regarding the general growth of the population.

   b. This is true, as the government has established the maximum population density that can be defined and achieved in a given marketplace.

   c. This is false because the general population within the US has not changed for over 100 years.

   d. This is false as there are a number of factors that impact population growth, such as employment opportunities and housing availability.

16. Which of the following can influence people to move to a new city?

   a. Good economy in the city
   b. Healthy job market in the city
   c. Low interest rates
   d. All of the above

17. A bad economy usually means less movement of:

   a. Money
   b. People
   c. Assets
   d. All of the above
   e. None of the above

18. In general terms, when interest rates are low, the demand for real estate will:

    a. Increase as housing becomes more affordable

    b. Decrease as the economy is shaky and as such consumers tend to be cautious in purchasing real estate, which many consider to be an unstable investment opportunity.

    c. Hold steady as people oftentimes consider the future as being defined by what happens in the economic climate. If interest rates go down, that is a potential sign of a pending recession or depression.

    d. Hold steady because lenders are now more cautious about loaning money and create more restrictions that limit a buyer's ability to qualify for the debt.

19. When a purchaser is interested in acquiring a new home, and they find themselves in a position where they have to borrow money from a lender, the lender is concerned with the buyer's ability to meet the monthly debt. Which of the following factors does a lender specifically look at to judge a buyer's eligibility?

    a. The number of foreclosures that had been reported in a specific neighborhood.

    b. The number of siblings that a buyer has that may be used as cosigners or backup resources.

    c. The buyer's gross income and the commitments the buyer has incurred regarding repayment of other debt.

    d. The financial strength of the municipality where the property in question is located and as to whether or not the governmental services provided are adequate to meet the needs of any purchaser of the property.

20. Demand for housing has been impacted by a number of different facets. Which of the following would not be considered a factor that could influence the demand for real estate?

    a. Interest rates

    b. Demographics

    c. Population

    d. Accessibility to the stock market

CHAPTER 3:

REAL ESTATE PRACTITIONERS AND PROFESSIONAL ORGANIZATIONS

LEARNING GOALS:

By the end of this lesson, you will:

- Recognize the variety of specialists who support the real estate industry
- Discover a variety of professional real estate organizations

REAL ESTATE INDUSTRY PROFESSIONALS

The real estate business is inseparable from people. While some people or schools may only be obsessed with statistics, information, facts, and profit, there is a much bigger picture to see. Our stance at Inland is that our business is 100% about people.

There is a wide variety of people that is required to make the real estate industry keep running and thriving. As mentioned earlier, this industry is exceptionally interdependent. For example:

- Homebuyers are dependent on brokers to guide them and ultimately help them buy or sell their houses.

- Brokers are dependent on sponsoring brokers to guide them, be an example, and give them advice when they need to know something.

- Home inspectors are dependent on homebuyers to hire them, so they can continue to support themselves and their families.

- The list keeps going and going.

Here is a list of professionals that most residential and commercial brokers interact with on some type of recurring basis:

- Brokerage owners

- Brokers

- Commercial property managers

- Designated managing brokers

- Escrow officers

- Foreclosure specialists

- Investors

- Lease administrators

- Leasing agents

- Leasing consultants

- Leasing managers

- Loan officers

- Loan underwriters

- Managing brokers

- Mortgage brokers

- Mortgage loan originators

- Office managers

- Property developers

- Property inspectors

- Real estate appraisers

- Real estate associates

- Real estate attorneys/lawyers

- Real estate clerks

- Real estate consultants/analysts

- Real estate managers

- Residential property managers

- Title examiners

Beyond that, brokers will interact with people outside of the industry too. These could include the neighbors who live beside the houses that are for sale, cleaning company employees, yard maintenance employees, locksmiths, roofing companies, plumbers, electricians, and so on. All of this builds evidence to the irrefutable fact that you, as a future real estate professional, must develop and cultivate incredible people skills. Hands down, it is one of the most essential skills if you truly want to build a career that is sustainable, fulfilling, and profitable.

PROFESSIONAL REAL ESTATE ORGANIZATIONS

Let's begin with the definition of an organization. Specifically, we are talking about trade organizations. These organizations generate and foster cooperative relationships amongst members and practitioners. At times, these may be referred to as a business association, a sector association, an industry trade group, or an industry body. The point is that the trade organization operates in a specific industry.

Once again, the topic here centers all around people. In this context, it specifically applies to those who operate within and/or with the real estate industry. The landscape of professional real estate organizations is broad and has grown in its scope and diversity over the last few years. Below, we will highlight a variety of trade organizations in chronological order.

The National Association of REALTORS® (NAR)

Date founded: 1908

NAR is the largest trade organization in the real estate industry. In fact, it's the largest trade organization of all the industries within the US. It boasts over 1.6 million members. These members include NAR's affiliated societies, institutes, and councils, which are engaged in every aspect of the real estate industry, both residential and commercial. NAR is an advocate for ownership rights and works with the real estate industry to facilitate instruction to make real estate practitioners better, as well as working to improve property ownership for the consumer.

National Association of Real Estate Brokers (NAREB)

Date founded: 1947

As their website states, NAREB is "the nation's oldest and most historic black real estate trade association." Their African-American members are called Realtists. One of their main focuses is equal housing opportunities for all. They also seek to "partner with other real estate trade groups, civil rights organizations, fair and equal housing advocates, and financial services institutions to make sustainable homeownership for African Americans and other minorities realizable."

The National Association of Hispanic Real Estate Professionals® (NAHREP)

Date founded: 1999

NAHREP is another vibrant association in the world of real estate. On their website, they share this: "We are The Voice for Hispanic Real Estate® and proud champions of homeownership for the Hispanic community. Homeownership is the symbol of the American Dream, the cornerstone of wealth creation and a stabilizing force for working families. Our role as trusted advisors and passionate advocates is to help more Hispanic families achieve the American Dream in a sustainable way that empowers them for generations to come."

Asian American Real Estate Association of America (AREAA)

Date founded: 2003

AREAA is "a national nonprofit trade organization dedicated to improving the lives of the Asian American and Pacific Islander (AAPI) community through homeownership" (AREAA website). Its mission statement highlights their purpose: "AREAA is dedicated to promoting sustainable homeownership opportunities in Asian American communities by creating a powerful national voice for housing and real estate professionals that serve this dynamic market."

The National Association of Gay and Lesbian Real Estate Professionals (NAGLREP)

Date founded: 2007

The NAGLREP website states it is a "mission driven organization that is part business and part advocacy." Their mission is to "advocate on behalf of the rights of the lesbian, gay, bisexual, and transgender (LGBT) community as it relates to housing and discrimination laws."

There are more professional organizations as well below, listed in alphabetical order:

- American Guild of Appraisers (AGA)
- American Real Estate Society (ARES)
- Association of Commercial Real Estate Professionals (ACRP)
- Association of Independent Mortgage Experts (AIME)
- Commercial Real Estate Development Association (NAIOP)
- International Association of Real Estate Professionals (IARP)
- International Council of Shopping Centers (ICSC)
- National Association of Appraisers (NAA)
- National Association of Broker Price Opinion Professionals (NABPOP)
- National Association of Expert Advisors (NAEA)
- National Association of Mortgage Brokers (NAMB)
- National Association of Real Estate Advisors (NAREA)
- National Association of Residential Property Managers (NARPM)
- National Association of Transaction Coordinators (NATC)

There are also commercial real estate organizations. Here is an overview:

- Building Owners and Managers Association International (BOMA)

- Certified Commercial Investment Institute (CCIM)

- Commercial Real Estate Women (CREW)

- Institute of Real Estate Management (IREM)

- International Council of Shopping Centers (ICSC)

- National Multifamily Housing Council (NMHC)

- Society of Industrial and Office REALTORS® (SIOR)

- The Appraisal Institute

- Urban Land Institute (ULI)

All in all, this is in no way an exhaustive or comprehensive list of real estate trade organizations. This is a high-level overview. Each organization has its own respective policies, requirements, structures, and codes of conduct. For more information on each of the organizations, you can visit their websites. This chapter's reading contained a wide array of acronyms. Review those prior to taking the chapter quiz.

CHAPTER 3 QUIZ

1. When someone wants to become a real estate agent, he/she is usually drawn to this career because of a desire for:

    a. Being his or her own boss
    b. Income possibilities
    c. Flexible schedule
    d. All of the above

2. A career in real estate includes:

    a. Working with a wide variety of people
    b. Variety
    c. Needing outstanding people skills
    d. All of the above

3. Real estate brokers interact with:

    a. Only buyers and sellers
    b. Sponsoring brokers
    c. Property inspectors
    d. All of the above

4. AREAA focuses on which of the following?

    a. African Americans
    b. Asian Americans
    c. LGBT Americans
    d. Hispanic

5. What is the biggest trade organization in the US?

    a. NAR
    b. NAREB
    c. NAHREP
    d. AREAA

6. NAREB, NAHREP, AREAA, and NAGLREP have which characteristics in common?

    a. Seeking to end discrimination
    b. Focuses exclusively on commercial real estate
    c. All of the above
    d. None of the above

7. NAREB focuses on which of the following?

    a. African Americans

    b. Asian Americans

    c. LGBT Americans

    d. Hispanic

    e. None of the above

8. Does NAR target a specific demographic?

    a. Yes, African Americans

    b. Yes, Asian Americans

    c. Yes, the LGBT community

    d. Yes, Hispanic

    e. No

9. NAGLREP focuses on which of the following?

    a. African Americans

    b. Asian Americans

    c. LGBT Americans

    d. Hispanic

10. Which of the following is not a commercial real estate organization?

    a. Institute of Real Estate Management (IREM)

    b. National Multifamily Housing Council (NMHC)

    c. The Appraisal Institute

    d. National Association of Multilingual Attorneys (NAMA)

CHAPTER 4:

REAL PROPERTY DISTINCTIONS AND DETAILS

LEARNING GOALS:

By the end of this lesson, you will:

- Know the detailed definition of land
- Have a deeper understanding of real property
- Know the differences between real property and personal property
- Understand the differences between fixtures and trade fixtures
- Know how crops, plants, and trees are classified
- Understand how law affects real estate

DISTINCTIONS ARE EVERYTHING in life and business. A distinction is a type of difference or contrast between similar people or things. Any professional, especially a master in one's field, has a very high level of distinctions. People who are new to a field usually know fewer distinctions than those with more time invested. As you read this book, you will learn not only definitions, but you'll also learn a variety of insightful distinctions. This is not simply to fill your head with knowledge. The purpose is to equip you for what awaits you in the realm of real estate as a business.

LAND, REAL ESTATE, AND REAL PROPERTY DEFINITIONS

Consumers often confuse these three terms. As a real estate licensee, you need to know the correct definition of each term as each pertains to the law.

1. **Land**

   - Land is unique, immobile, and indestructible. You can view land as something created by God, Mother Nature, or evolution. It is pure, unaltered by human beings.

   - It includes the surface of the earth and everything above, technically to infinity. It also includes everything below the surface to the center of the earth. Although we can't actively use all of that as a result of physical limitations and/or governmental restrictions, the theory of the law is that those elements belong to the property owner.

   - In other words, land includes the following:

     - The earth's surface and underlying soil.

     - Objects attached naturally to the surface of the earth. Examples include plants, trees, etc.

     - Substances and minerals in the subsurface.

     - The air above the earth, continuing up into space.

2. **Real estate**

   - Real estate refers to the combination of the land plus any human-made improvement that has been attached to the land with the expectation to remain.

     - In this context, the term improvement means a permanent, human-made addition to land. The term improvement is subjective. Real property improvements do more than repair or replace. These improvements are permanent. Each one adds value to the property.

- The ownership of real estate may encompass additional governmental restrictions with regard to how you can use the land and the type of structure and/or placement of the structure on the site.

- Improvement examples include but are not limited to structures, driveways, concrete slabs, and pipes embedded into the soil (such as the water pipe). It can also be any utility source that is added to the land.

3. **Real property**

- Real property combines the land, the improvements, and the bundle of rights. The bundle of rights when added to real estate provides the property owner with the greatest level of ownership. The bundle of rights consists of five elements:

  - **Possession** is the right to occupy all or part of the property

  - **Control** is the right to control the use of the property within limits established by government or deed restrictions

  - **Exclusion** is the right to control who may have access to your property

  - **Quiet enjoyment** is the right to enjoy the property without interference of third parties

  - **Disposition** is the right, at the owner's discretion, to dispose of the property by sale, lease, gift or will

As a real estate licensee, you need to take the responsibility to assist others in either buying and/or selling real estate. Thus, it is imperative that you understand the correct definition and interpretation of land, real estate, and real property.

PERSONAL PROPERTY

Personal property covers all other forms of properties that one may possess, such as automobiles, livestock, money, and furniture. These are items the consumer has the right to take with them from location to location. Specifically, the law indicates that personal property is any item that has not been attached to the building or the land with the intent to leave it behind upon transfer. Personal property always attaches to the person, not to the land.

An **appurtenance** is defined as real property. It is associated with the property, while not directly being a part of the real property. An appurtenance is generally immovable and always relates to the land. An example of an appurtenance might be parking spaces. Other examples include in-ground swimming pools, fences, water rights, easements, and sheds. When a property is sold, an appurtenance usually transfers to the new owner/s. Note: An easement allows an individual or an organization (who does not own the land) to use the land of a property owner for a specific purpose. It is a non-possessory right to use and/or enter into someone else's real property, although he/she does not actually own the property. You will learn more about easements and their impact on the property owners and the people who use them in a later chapter.

Personal property is also referred to as **personalty** or *chattel*, originally a French word. The words *chattel* and cattle originated from the Medieval Latin word *capitale*. It relates to the Latin word for "head."

Sometimes, clear-cut definitions exist in the world of real estate. Occasionally they can be tricky to discover and/or interpret because sometimes it will come down to the law. Words that we may use in everyday life often have an entirely different meaning in various aspects of law. As you continue through this book, we will explain how the different interpretations can impact the application of a specific term or phrase.

This brings us to three interesting aspects of what is and what is not real property:

1. Fixtures and trade fixtures

2. Plants

3. Manufactured homes

FIXTURES AND TRADE FIXTURES

In Illinois, a **fixture** is an item that was once personal property but has since been attached to the real property with the expectation or intent to make it a portion of the real property. A fixture is attached or fastened to a building or the land with the expectation that it will not be removed. Examples of non-fixtures (i.e., personal property) include: freestanding washers and dryers, dining room tables, couches, televisions, beds, potted plants, grilling equipment, rugs, and so forth.

A **trade fixture** is personal property that belongs to the business entity or business owner that owns and operates the business currently existing within the property. The business operation usually includes equipment and/or objects that are generally considered to be a permanent part of the improvement and would ordinarily stay with the property. However, the item in question is used for business purposes and thus, is a trade fixture. Under the law, when a trade fixture is removed, there is an expectation that any damage that the item created to the physical structure will be replaced or repaired in order to return the space to its original condition. Trade fixtures may be removed (taken out, extracted) prior to the expiration of the lease or the close of the sale if the business owner was also the owner of the building being sold. An example of this might be the hardwood lanes used in a bowling alley. If the business is relocating, the lanes, which are an integral part of business operations, can be taken to the new site. The party removing the lanes would just need to ensure that the concrete foundation that stabilized the lanes would be returned to the original condition when the business first acquired the space. Commercial trade fixtures can include restaurant booths, barstools, hair salon wash basins, gym equipment, gasoline station pumps, neon signs, storage tanks, and the like.

However, at times there are disagreements between buyers and sellers, and they go to court over fixtures. How do you legally know if something is a fixture or not? In many real estate circles, an easy-to-remember acronym to help you answer that question is M.A.R.I.A. (The original source is unknown.) M.A.R.I.A. is a simple way to recall a framework for figuring out whether something is a fixture or not.

M.A.R.I.A. stands for:

M: Method of attachment: Is the item in question permanently fastened to the ceiling, wall, or floor? Have screws, cement, or something similar been used to fasten it?

A: Adaptability: Is the item an essential aspect of the house? If so, it may not be removed or taken out. One example is smoke detectors. Can they be removed? Of course. However, smoke detectors are considered to be a part of the house. It's a fixture.

R: Relationship of the parties: The relationship between the parties can dictate the outcome, as to whether or not an item is a fixture. When the dispute is between tenant and landlord, if the tenant is the party who installed the item in question and can remove it prior to the expiration of the lease and repair all damage caused by the installation, the tenant's rights will prevail.

When the dispute is between a buyer and seller regarding an item the seller had previously installed, if the item is an essential component to the enjoyment of the property, then a court would likely award the item in question to the buyer.

I: Intention: What was the intention of the party when the item in question was added or installed? When an owner installs something, he/she has in mind that it will either be permanent or temporary. If the intention is for an item to be permanent, it's a fixture. For example, if the owner installed a new heating system and ceiling fan when she originally moved in, those are considered fixtures. Here's another example. Let's say the party installed a flatscreen TV using an adjustable wall mount: the TV is considered to be personal property, but the adjustable mount is a fixture.

A: Agreement: What does the agreement or contract among the parties state? Legal documents usually feature a clause. Drafted by a lawyer, these lines or sections in the contract outline which items are included and excluded in the sale of the property.

In advance, you should know that when these cases go to court, the rulings have not been consistent within the State of Illinois. Although we do have definitions that are defined by the state, at times, unique or unusual circumstances or heated verbal disagreements occur. When a case goes to court, it all comes down to the judge's ruling.

There are two terms that you need to know concerning fixtures. They can include any addition or subtraction of personal property attached to real property.

1. Annexation: This is the conversion of personal property to real property.

2. Severance: This is the conversion of real property back to personal property.

Annexation is the act of transforming personal property into real property. For example, if a landowner buys wood and paint (both of which are personal property) and constructs a fence in the backyard, those items of personal property have now been converted to real property. When the house is sold, the fence stays.

Severance is not used in financial terms here. As you know, to sever means to cut off, break off, and separate two things. Severance occurs when real property is converted back to personal property. For example, a homeowner installed a wood picket fence fifteen years ago. A recent windstorm knocked down a good portion of the fence and the owner now elects to install a privacy fence in place of the wood picket fence. The elements that created the wood picket fence when they are taken out now become personal property, a function of exercising severance, that is, converting real property back into a personal property state.

As you can see, annexation and severance are opposites. They are two sides of the same coin.

VEGETATION

There are two categories of vegetation:

1. Vegetation for aesthetic purposes

2. Vegetation with the expectation of harvesting for profit.

Knowing the difference comes from answering this question: Was the vegetation planted and cultivated with the goal of generating a profit? If the answer is no, the vegetation is considered part of the real estate. If the answer is yes, the vegetation is considered personal property, but only for the current growing season. The seller does not have future rights to the land following the current growing season.

This brings us to a new term: **Emblements**. These are items of vegetation that are planted with the intent to harvest for a profit. They are considered personal property. In the context of common law, an emblement is an annual crop produced with the intent to sell for profit. It is a legal possession of the tenant/owner. There's an implied right for its harvest. Thus, an emblement is considered property of the tenant/owner. To simplify the transfer of land used in the production of emblements, the common targeted date for closing is March 1st. At this point, the land is probably between plantings and therefore is sitting dormant. This timing allows the conveyance of the land to take place without confusion as to who owns the growing emblement.

MANUFACTURED, MOBILE, AND MODULAR HOMES

What is the difference between real property and personal property when it comes to manufactured and mobile homes versus modular homes? The truth is that the differences are not always easy to detect, note, or distinguish. Generally speaking, manufactured housing, also known as mobile homes, is considered personal property. This is the case even though its transportability could be limited to a single trip to a mobile home park or land development where the utilities are hooked up, and the residents begin living inside the manufactured home. However, manufactured housing can possibly be viewed as, considered, or deemed to be real property if it becomes attached to the land permanently.

The Act says:

> "Manufactured home" and "mobile home" mean a "manufactured home", as defined in subdivision (53) of Section 9-102 of the Uniform Commercial Code. "Mobile home" means a factory-assembled, completely integrated structure, constructed on or before June 30, 1976, designed for permanent habitation, with a permanent chassis, and so constructed as to permit its transport, on wheels temporarily or permanently attached to its frame, that is a movable or portable unit that is constructed to be towed on its own chassis (comprised of frame and wheels) from the place of its construction to the location, or subsequent locations, at which it is connected to utilities for year-round occupancy for use as a permanent habitation, and designed to be used as a dwelling with or without a permanent foundation and situated so as to permit its occupancy as a dwelling place for one or more persons. The terms "manufactured home" and "mobile home" shall include units otherwise meeting their respective definitions containing parts that may be folded, collapsed, or telescoped when being towed and that may be expected to provide additional cubic capacity, and that are designed to be joined into one integral unit capable of being separated again into the components for repeated towing. The terms "manufactured home" and "mobile home" exclude campers and recreational vehicles." (430 ILCS 117/10)

The Act further defines a manufactured home as a:

factory-assembled, completely integrated structure designed for permanent habitation, with a permanent chassis, and so constructed as to permit its transport, on wheels temporarily or permanently attached to its frame, and is a movable or portable unit that is (i) eight body feet or more in width, (ii) 40 body feet or more in length, and (iii) 320 or more square feet, constructed to be towed on its own chassis (comprised of frame and wheels) from the place of its construction to the location, or subsequent locations, at which it is installed and set up according to the manufacturer's instructions and connected to utilities for year-round occupancy for use as a permanent habitation, and designed and situated so as to permit its occupancy as a dwelling place for one or more persons." (210 ILCS 115/2.1)

The Act continues and states:

- "The term 'mobile home' shall not include modular homes and their support systems. The words 'mobile home' and 'manufactured home' are synonymous for the purposes of this Act" (210 ILCS 115/2.1).

- "'Modular home' means factory built housing regulated by the Illinois Department of Public Health that consists of a building assembly or system of building sub-assemblies, designed for habitation as a dwelling for one or more persons, including the necessary electrical, plumbing, heating, ventilating, and other service systems, which is of closed or open construction and which is made or assembled by a manufacturer, on or off the building site, for installation, or assembly and installation, on the building site with a permanent foundation." (815 ILCS 362/5)

Here are more highlights from The Act related to this topic:

- Mobile homes and manufactured homes in mobile home parks must be assessed and taxed as chattel (personal property).

- Mobile homes and manufactured homes outside of mobile home parks must be assessed and taxed as real property.

- All mobile type homes constructed after June 15, 1976, are manufactured homes" (Illinois Compiled Statutes (35 ILCS 517/5). In other words, factory-built housing made before 1976 is termed as a "mobile home."

Every topic in this chapter is connected via one common ingredient; the law.

SOURCES OF LAW

Building on your knowledge from prior chapters, when it comes to real estate law in the State of Illinois, all roads lead to this primary source: The Real Estate License Act of 2000 (i.e., RELA or The Act). As you have seen by now, it is impossible to separate real estate from law. The two are uniquely bound. What does this mean for real estate professionals? Everything! It signifies that each licensee must keep up with applicable and relevant laws in the State of Illinois, along with federal laws. Where do the laws originate?

In the US, there are five primary origins and sources of law that affect real estate:

1. Federal

    ▪ United States Constitution

    ▪ Regulatory agencies

    ▪ Laws passed by Congress

2. State

    ▪ Constitutions

    ▪ State statutes

3. Local ordinances

    ▪ These are provisions of law created by governmental agencies below the state level, such as counties, townships, cities, villages, towns, and so on.

4. Common law

    ▪ This is law that has been primarily borrowed from England, France, or Spain. It is derived from custom and judicial precedent, as opposed to being derived from statutes.

5. Case law

    ▪ This is the law that has been established by court decisions as a result of lawsuits.

    ▪ Real estate professionals must have an updated working knowledge of several aspects of their careers. These include, but are not limited to, the following:

    ▪ License law

    ▪ Legal documents such as contracts, listing agreements, agent-broker agreements, office to purchase forms, etc.

    ▪ General property law

- General contract law

- The law of agency, which outlines and defines the legally binding relationship between a real estate professional and his or her clients.

In general, your sponsoring broker will have a wealth of knowledge in these areas. Ultimately, always refer to what the State of Illinois dictates. The purpose of RELA and laws in general is to protect the public. Real estate practitioners are required by law to be licensed in every state in the US. Licensing is a type of insurance that helps protect consumers from real estate crimes, dishonesty, and incompetence.

Now, it's time for your chapter quiz.

CHAPTER 4 QUIZ

1. The definition of land includes:

    a. Houses

    b. Garages

    c. Swimming pools

    d. All of the above

    e. None of the above

2. The definition of land also includes:

    a. Soil

    b. Plants

    c. Minerals in the subsurface

    d. All of the above

3. Real estate and land are the same thing.

    a. True

    b. False

4. Real estate includes:

    a. Only land

    b. Human-made structures and land

    c. Only human-made structures

    d. Soil and water

5. An improvement is each of the following except:

    a. A development on the land

    b. A series of potted plants on the front porch

    c. Something permanently attached to the land

    d. An addition to the land

6. Fences, houses, other buildings, landscaping, and driveways are classified as which of the following?

    a. Real property

    b. Personal property

    c. Appurtenances

    d. Emblements

    e. Chattel

7. An appurtenance is generally immovable.

    a. True

    b. False

8. Which answer below most accurately describes personal property?

    a. Something attached or affixed to the land

    b. Movable

    c. Tangible

    d. Movable and tangible

9. Another word for personal property is which word below?

    a. Chattel

    b. Emblement

    c. Appurtenance

    d. Capitale

10. A Ming vase, having been given to the property owner as a wedding gift, is commonly referred to as which of the following?

    a. Emblement

    b. Personal property

    c. Real property

    d. Fee simple defeasible estate

11. Which of the following is an item that is attached to a building that is used in the operation of a business?

    a. Trade fixture

    b. Chattel

    c. Emblement

    d. Appurtenance

12. The acronym M.A.R.I.A. is a simple way to recall a framework for figuring out whether something is a fixture or not. What does the acronym M.A.R.I.A. stand for?

    a. Method, add-on, real, intention, agreement

    b. Method, appurtenance, relationship, instance, agreement

    c. Method, adaptability, relationship, intention, agreement

    d. Movable, add-on, relationship, intention, agreement

13. Two categories emerge when it comes to crops, plants, and trees. It centers around one question. What is that question?

    a. Who purchased the crops, plants, and/or trees?
    b. Is annual cultivation required?
    c. Is the land government owned?
    d. Is the land special purpose?

14. Which answer below is not correct when considering how the Illinois General Assembly defines the term manufactured home?

    a. Factory-assembled
    b. Permanent chassis
    c. Clear intention
    d. Movable

15. Mobile homes and manufactured homes found in mobile home parks must be assessed and taxed as chattel.

    a. True
    b. False

16. Which statement is false concerning the Real Estate License Act of 2000?

    a. It was amended in 2020.
    b. It's commonly called The Act.
    c. It does not apply to all real estate professionals.
    d. It is overseen by the IDFPR.

17. Which type of law has been established by court decisions as a result of lawsuits?

    a. Common law
    b. Local ordinances
    c. License law
    d. Case law

18. What is the primary purpose of RELA and laws in general?

    a. To protect the public
    b. To generate funding
    c. To oversee real estate taxes
    d. To extend its own reach

19. Which answer is best? Licensing protects consumers from _____.

    a. Real estate professionals lying or cheating
    b. Real estate professionals being incompetent
    c. All of the above
    d. None of the above

20. Which word fills in the blank accurately? "Mobile homes and manufactured homes outside of mobile home parks must be assessed and taxed as _____."

    a. Land
    b. Personal property
    c. Real property
    d. Real estate

CHAPTER 5:

ALL ABOUT HOMEOWNERSHIP

LEARNING GOALS:

By the end of this lesson, you will:

- Understand homeownership and how the real estate tax cycle works
- Learn tax benefits for homeowners
- Learn about 1031 exchanges
- Uncover the implications of housing affordability
- Know the top ten most common housing types
- Understand home insurance and federal flood insurance

THE INS AND OUTS OF HOMEOWNERSHIP

Homeownership has been a cornerstone of the American dream for decades. Ownership is intriguing and captivating on a number of different levels for people. On a tangible level, owning a home gives people a place to call their own. Since they own it, they call the shots and can enjoy life on their own terms. They can be creative, paint, build new rooms or spaces, and more. It possibly gives them the opportunity to have something they've always wanted, such as a home office, home theater, or garden. Purchasing a home also creates new future options that would not be possible otherwise. These new options could include planning to sell the house in the future and make a profit. Another option is the financial muscle allowing the homeowner to leverage his or her home equity to pay for or finance other large expenses.

For many Americans, owning a home is an essential part of the American dream that conveys a number of economic benefits, such as the ability to accumulate wealth and access credit by building home equity, reduce housing costs through the mortgage interest deduction, and gain long-term savings over the cost of renting. (HUD)

There are also numerous intangible benefits. These include having a place to belong, a sense of safety, feeling proud of oneself, a feeling of being settled, and peace of mind. It could also be a vision being fulfilled, such as a larger home for a growing family, or a quiet cabin during retirement. Homeownership can also be a method of elevating one's status. People can buy houses in unique areas or in expensive cities. They may purchase their home near country clubs, national parks, or landmarks. Homeownership is many times uniquely tied to the buyer's needs, wants, and dreams. The website Statista reports that between five million and six million homes have sold every year between 2012 and 2021 in the US. That's a lot of real estate! The only exception to sales is the year 2020. That year, homes sold in the US totaled 4.8 million.

Homeownership, at times, is called owner-occupancy. As you know, homeownership is a form of housing tenure where an individual not only owns the property consisting of the land and improvements but also lives in the property. These dwellings can encompass various styles, such as a single-family home, an apartment, a condominium, or even a housing cooperative. Although this is a short list, it is wise to remember that there are multiple housing configurations available to consumers.

THE REAL ESTATE TAX CYCLE

Just like having a baby, homeownership comes with tax benefits. However, before you learn about those. It's important to have an overview of what goes into the real estate tax cycle. In the background of real estate taxes, there are several factors in play. The County of Knox, State of Illinois, shares an excellent overview of the real estate tax cycle. It shows each position, and each position's main responsibilities. It is as follows:

Assessor:

- Establishes values

- Approves exemptions

- Updates name and address information

- Works splits and combinations

- Forwards this information to the county clerk

County clerk:

- Establishes the rates

- Monitors the TIF and enterprise abatements

- Calculates the tax dollar amounts

- Forwards this information to the treasurer

Treasurer:

- Prints and mails tax bills

- Collects tax dollars

- Distributes tax dollars to taxing bodies

- Conducts delinquent tax sale

To the IRS, the terms "real estate tax" and "property tax" are the same thing. Usually, the IRS uses the term "real estate tax." In contrast, most people call it "property tax." (Note that "property tax" is not the same as "personal property tax.") Property (real estate) tax is charged on property that is immovable. Immovable property consists of the human-made structures and land. Examples: house, building, and/or land. Homeowners either pay property tax directly to their respective local tax assessor's office, or pay indirectly via their monthly mortgage payments. As a licensee, you must understand if taxes will be prorated and how. Note that in some states, the tax cycle for the various taxing entities may actually begin in different months.

In Illinois, property taxes are paid one year in arrears. For example, the taxes being paid in the current year are actually taxes due for the prior year. We do not pay the current year's property taxes until the following year.

Because of this, every seller must give their buyer/s a real estate tax credit for the number of days that the seller owes on the property in that specific calendar year.

Example: Samantha is purchasing Alexander's home, and they have scheduled a closing for August 22 of this year. The taxes for the prior year have amounted to $14,022 and have already been paid. Since the taxes for the current year will not be paid until next year, what is the amount of proration that Alexander would owe Samantha for the current year's property taxes? In order to complete this problem, you must remember:

- Use a statutory month and statutory year unless otherwise indicated.

- Read the question carefully, as there may be information contained within the question that has no relevance to the question.

- Remember, the date of closing is a day of expense to the seller.

$14,022 ÷ 360 (Number of days within a statutory year) = $38.95

The closing is scheduled for August 22.

Determine how many full months the seller has owned the property in the current year.

January through July amounts to 7 full months.

7 full months × 30 days per statutory month = 210 days

In the month of the close, the seller is responsible for 22 days

210 days + 22 days = 232 days

232 days × $38.95 = $9,036.40

There will be a $9,036.40 credit to the buyer and a $9,036.40 debit to the seller.

TAX BENEFITS FOR HOMEOWNERS

Tax credits and deductions can potentially benefit homeowners! Each one lowers how much you would have had to pay in taxes. They each do this in their own unique way.

What is a **tax credit**? "A tax credit is a dollar-for-dollar reduction in the amount of income tax you would otherwise owe" (Energy.gov). Furthermore, the IRS defines a tax credit as: "Tax credit deducted from the amount of tax you owe. There are two types of tax credits: 1) A nonrefundable credit you are entitled to up to the amount of tax you owe. 2) A refundable tax credit is a refund you are entitled to even if it's more than what you owe."

What is a **tax deduction**? The IRS goes on to define a tax deduction as a "Deduction subtracted from your income *before* you calculate the amount of tax you owe." This deduction decreases your tax liability (or that of your company) by decreasing the taxable income. Usually, these are expenses you, as a taxpayer, have incurred in a calendar year.

Tax benefits of homeownership are extensive. Here is a short summary in alphabetical order: accidental loss, capital gains exclusion (profits from home sale), home office expenses, imputed rent, mortgage insurance premiums, mortgage loan interest deduction, moving costs, points and other closing costs, real estate taxes, second homes/vacation homes and solar energy. Next, let's go through each one so you can learn more details.

1. **Accidental loss:** Usually, accidental loss (also known as accidental damage) is defined as loss of value, and/or damages. The key is the word accidental. The source or cause of the loss or damage must be accidental, as in unforeseen or unintended. It cannot be something that was done on purpose, which would make it a deliberate act. To be clear, these acts or events cause harm or damage. However, in their essence, they are accidental. To file a claim, both the event and the accompanying injury must be classified as an accident.

2. **Capital gains exclusion:** This is one of the most popular real estate terms and economic concepts. It means the profits from the sale of an owner-occupied house. The key is that the value of the asset has increased over the holding period.

   - Primary residence

     - A tax-free capital gain is available.

     - The owner must have occupied the property as a primary dwelling for two consecutive of the last five years.

     - A single name of the deed will result in a $250,000 tax-free capital gain.

     - A married couple with both of their names on the deed will receive a $500,000 tax-free capital gain.

   - Investment real estate

     - There is no tax-free capital gain on investment properties. However, there is a separate taxing structure created by the Federal Government when it comes to investment real estate. Rather than being based on the investor's income, it is a flat percentage of the capital gain. Although it may be beneficial for you to be aware of the schedule, it is not at this time considered a testable component. When looking at your capital gain exposure, it is wise to speak directly with your accountant.

- If you want to defer your obligation to pay a capital gains tax until some point in the future, you need to exercise a 1031 exchange. You'll learn more about this topic below.

3. **Home office expenses:** Both office space and office expenses are usually deductible on your taxes when you own or run a business from home or are self-employed. Renters also benefit from this. You must meet the requirements laid out by the IRS, which communicate that the space used is used exclusively and regularly. Here's what the IRS website currently conveys about this topic: "You can deduct expenses for a separate freestanding structure, such as a studio, garage, or barn, if you use it exclusively and regularly for your business. The structure does not have to be your principal place of business or the only place where you meet patients, clients, or customers. These expenses may include mortgage interest, insurance, utilities, repairs, and depreciation. Regardless of the method chosen, there are two basic requirements for your home to qualify as a deduction: 1) Regular and exclusive use. 2) Principal place of your business." As always, it's important to check back regularly with your accountant. Changes do happen. You want to stay up to date.

4. **Imputed rent:** This is the financial benefit that a rental household gains when compared with a similar rental household. This is not very common.

5. **Mortgage insurance premium (MIP):** A mortgage insurance premium, also known as a MIP, is paid by a homeowner who takes out one or more loans that are funded by the Federal Housing Administration (FHA). Currently, the Further Consolidated Appropriations Act of 2020 allows tax deductions for mortgage insurance premiums. MIPs are a means by which FHA-approved lenders guard themselves against borrowers who are labeled as high risk. As you know, it's more probable that a high-risk borrower will default on a loan as opposed to mid/low-risk borrowers. Finally, any mortgage insured by FHA mandates that the borrower carry MIP for the full life of the loan.

6. **Mortgage loan interest deduction:** First, let's define the financial term interest. Interest is the profit the lender earns from having granted you the loan. In this context, we're talking about interest specifically on a mortgage loan. This deduction gives taxpayers who are homeowners the opportunity to lower their taxable income by the amount of total interest paid on their loan. Their loan is secured and backed by their principal house (residence). Sometimes, it is backed by a second house.

7. **Moving costs:** Many people think moving costs are still deductible. Here is what the IRS says about this topic. Under the new tax law, moving deductions are no longer currently permitted. Moving for work does not qualify you either. The only people who currently qualify and can deduct moving expenses are active duty military members and their families. This change came into play when the Tax Cuts and Jobs Act of 2017 was enacted.

8. **Points and other closing costs**: About points, the IRS states: "Points are prepaid interest and may be deductible as home mortgage interest, if you itemize deductions on Schedule A (Form 1040), Itemized Deductions. If you can deduct all of the interest on your mortgage, you may be able to deduct all of the points paid on the mortgage." Whether or not closing costs are tax deductible depends. The possibility of having these as deductions requires homeowners to do their research. A variety of factors go into this math puzzle. It may be best for the homeowner to work with a financial advisor and/or tax strategist. By doing so, they receive a global view and understanding and ultimately make the best decision for themselves. When you think of a tax strategy, you want to focus on its optimization, given your current circumstances and context as a homeowner. Prepayment penalties are tax deductible. You will learn more about points in the chapter about financing.

9. **Real estate taxes**: Also called real property taxes, the IRS states: "Deductible real estate taxes are generally any state or local taxes on real property levied for the public welfare. The charge must be uniform against all real property in the jurisdiction at a like rate." This benefit is specifically designed to boost and inspire homeownership.

10. **Second homes and vacation homes:** Yes, there are tax deduction possibilities for second homes and vacation homes as well. These deductions make owning a second residence more attainable. Second homeownership costs can possibly be greatly lowered. How? Through the homeowner taking advantage of tax deductions on any or all of the following: property taxes, mortgage interest, and rental expenses. There are different guidelines for owning a rental property as opposed to a second residence. The best recommendation is to always speak directly with your accountant.

11. **Solar energy:** The investment tax credit (ITC), which is frequently referred to as the federal solar tax credit, mandates how solar energy deductions work, who qualifies, and the percentages. This applies both to residential and commercial. Property owners are able to deduct a specific percentage off their federal taxes.

For details on solar deductions for property owners, refer to:

- The U.S. Department of Energy's downloadable PDF called "Homeowner's Guide to the Federal Tax Credit for Solar Photovoltaics."

- Your accountant

For details on solar deductions for companies and business owners, refer to:

- The U.S. Department of Energy's downloadable PDF called "Guide to the Federal Investment Tax Credit for Commercial Solar Photovoltaics."

- Your accountant

WHAT IS A 1031 EXCHANGE?

Speaking of tax benefits, it's important to define and talk about 1031 exchanges. Capital gains taxation can be deferred only on investment real estate using a 1031 exchange. Undertaking an exchange is a common strategy for tax deferment. It is also called a "Starker exchange" or a "like-kind exchange." The property must meet the IRS's definition in order to qualify. Section 1031 of the US Internal Revenue Code allows a taxpayer to defer recognition of capital gains and related federal income tax liability, on the exchange of certain types of property. In short, by implementing a 1031 exchange, property owners can defer taxation of capital gains. The IRS states:

> "Like-kind property: Properties are of like-kind if they're of the same nature or character, even if they differ in grade or quality. Real properties generally are of like-kind, regardless of whether they're improved or unimproved. For example, an apartment building would generally be like-kind to another apartment building. However, real property in the United States is not like-kind to real property outside the United States.

> Like-kind exchange (when you exchange real property used for business or held as an investment solely for other business or investment property that is the same type or "like-kind") have long been permitted under the Internal Revenue Code. Generally, if you make a like-kind exchange, you are not required to recognize a gain or loss under Internal Revenue Code Section 1031. If, as part of the exchange, you also receive other (not like-kind) property or money, you must recognize a gain to the extent of the other property and money received. You can't recognize a loss.

> Under the Tax Cuts and Jobs Act, Section 1031 now applies only to exchanges of real property and not to exchanges of personal or intangible property. An exchange of real property held primarily for sale still does not qualify as a like-kind exchange.

A transition rule in the new law provides that Section 1031 applies to a qualifying exchange of personal or intangible property if the taxpayer disposed of the exchanged property on or before December 31, 2017, or received replacement property on or before that date.

Thus, effective January 1, 2018, exchanges of machinery, equipment, vehicles, artwork, collectibles, patents and other intellectual property and intangible business assets generally do not qualify for non-recognition of gain or loss as like-kind exchanges. However, certain exchanges of mutual ditch, reservoir or irrigation stock are still eligible for non-recognition of gain or loss as like-kind exchanges.

Reporting a like-kind exchange: Form 8824 is used to report a like-kind exchange. Form 8824 Instructions provide information on general rules and how to complete the form.

Who qualifies for the Section 1031 exchange? Owners of investment and business property may qualify for a Section 1031 deferral. Individuals, C corporations, S corporations, partnerships (general or limited), limited liability companies, trusts and any other taxpaying entity may set up an exchange of business or investment properties for business or investment properties under Section 1031." (IRS)

Can property that increased in value greatly since its purchase be exchanged for other property? The answer most likely is yes. The owner of the property only incurs tax liability on a sale if and when the property or additional capital is received. Capital gains are only created once the property is sold. Once it is sold, the capital gain will be taxed. In order to defer paying capital gains tax, the property that is exchanged is required to be real estate of greater or equal value. Keep in mind that the tax is only being deferred. It is not being forgiven or eliminated.

This type of tax-deferment strategy is exceptionally complicated. The government imposes and enforces very strict guidelines which must be followed. It is in the best interest of each owner to work with a tax specialist who is highly qualified and has experience with Section 1031.

THE ESSENTIAL CHARACTERISTIC OF HOUSING: AFFORDABILITY

If homeownership is the dream, how does one get there? Where do you begin? The way the dream of homeownership becomes a reality comes down to the affordability of housing. When you were a teenager, you were probably like most other teens. You were excited about learning how to drive and having a new freedom in your life. In every movie, the sixteen-year-old always wants to get his or her license. What else do they want? A car! To teenagers, car ownership is infinitely exciting. However, at the end of the day, it all comes down to one thing: Money. Can he/she (or his or her family) actually afford a car? Likewise, with buying a house, it also comes down to money (financing). Housing affordability focuses on being able to own and operate a house. There is a wide variety of how much spending and earning power individuals and couples have. These dynamics affect what they can afford and ultimately affect where they live. There are several factors to explore and questions to answer before one buys a house. These questions include but are not limited to the following financial and nonfinancial questions:

Financial questions:

1. What's my housing budget?

2. What's my credit score?

3. How much money should I save for my down payment?

4. How much are closing costs?

5. What is a guesstimate of moving expenses?

6. Once I move in, what additional variable and fixed expenses will I have?

7. What are similar homes selling for in or near this neighborhood?

Nonfinancial questions:

1. Why do I want to buy a house?

2. How long do I anticipate living in my new house?

3. What are the neighborhood, schools, and/or social life like?

4. Does the location suffer from floods, tornadoes, or other natural disasters?

5. Does the house have any issues?

6. How old are the roof and appliances?

7. What's included and isn't included when I buy?

8. What is the seller's reason for selling?

9. How long has the house been on the market?

A few things tend to happen when someone owns a home. It shows that they are there for the long haul. After moving into their new place, they're more likely to establish roots in the community and be involved in any number of ways. Where they live is where they will shop and conduct other business transactions. Also, some research says that crime is lower in communities where homes are purchased, rather than in rental communities.

As you know, purchasing a house can be challenging financially. It depends on a variety of factors including income, location, and more. The government takes steps toward making homeownership more attainable for the broader population. There are a variety of different government subsidies. These include but are not limited to first-time homebuyer grants and programs, the Good Neighbor Next Door program, and FHA loans. Each subsidy is structured and designed as a way to lower the costs of purchasing a house. There are also numerous informational resources online to help people who want to purchase a home. As you probably already know, the biggest deduction is the federal income tax deduction for mortgage interest. To be able to implement this deduction, a family must generate enough income. This justifies being able to itemize their deductions on their tax returns, instead of taking the standard deduction. Seek guidance from your tax accountant about this if you want to learn more.

HOUSING STYLES AND TYPES

Housing seemingly comes in a number of styles, especially when you look around internationally and throughout history. Common home styles nowadays in the US vary from state to state and region to region.

Housing Styles

These styles include, but are not limited to, the following: Double pen (double cell), hall and parlor, central passage (central hallway), shotgun house, side-hall (side-passage), bungalow, cottage, ranch style or rambler, high house, gamble front, split-level house, courtyard, Cape Cod, farmhouse, French country, colonial, craftsman, contemporary, and so on.

Housing Types

Not only have styles evolved, but also housing structures have evolved in the US over the decades as well. Currently, there is a wide variety of housing types. These include but are not limited to the following alphabetized list:

1. **Adult communities:** These are commonly called active adult communities, retirement homes, or retirement communities. In this context, "active" simply means independent. To be clear, these are not nursing homes or assisted living homes. The purpose of these real estate developments is to facilitate a lifestyle for older adults that is comfortable, independent, and enjoyable. Many of these communities offer a wide range of activities, services, and amenities.

2. **Apartment complexes**: These structures have two or more apartments. An apartment is a self-contained unit of housing. This means it usually has its own front door, bathroom, and kitchen. An apartment only occupies a section or part of a specific building. There may be one or more buildings in an apartment complex. Apartment complexes may have two occupants or 200+ occupants. It depends on the size of the complex. They can be one, two, three, or more stories high, thus either low-rise or high-rise. Low-rise are a few stories high, but usually below 115 feet in height. A high-rise is any tall building.

3. **Condominiums:** Otherwise known as condos, these are single-family residences contained in a multifamily building. Condominiums fall under the umbrella of residential properties. One of the main appeals of owning a condo is property ownership without having the responsibility of external maintenance, updates, and care. All outside maintenance, along with management, is overseen and completed by some type of governing association, and/or by a team of outside contract workers. Many condominium facilities have features and amenities such as but not limited to elevators, pools, hot tubs, basketball and/or tennis courts, gyms, and so forth. The ownership of these amenities, structures, and grounds is shared among all unit owners. Which types of buildings can be legally structured as condominiums? High-rise buildings, low-rise buildings, and even detached structures such as single-family homes. Individual unit owners are responsible for the property taxes on their condos.

4. **Converted Use:** "Property whose use has been changed to a use other than what its improvements were originally constructed for is identified as 'converted-use' property. This occurs primarily because of the basic principles of change and anticipation, wherein changing economic conditions and a revision of the property owner's anticipated future benefits estimate have influenced the change in use. These properties sell at market value for the new use, which is commonly different from, if the property retained its original use. As a result, a significant degree of interior and exterior remodeling is often needed to convert these properties into their new retail, office or some other type of new use" (Arizona Department of Revenue).

Said another way, the property was originally residential, commercial, industrial, agricultural, or special purpose. However, it was converted to a different property type to fulfill a different purpose. Examples: An office building was converted into an apartment building. An old church was converted into a house. An old industrial building was converted into loft condominiums.

5. **Cooperative:** Cooperatives, also known as co-ops, are owned by a corporation and managed by its residents. Co-ops share similarities with condos in that many have

facilities and features that are shared among the owners. Also in common is that co-op unit residents pay their portion of the maintenance and care expenses of the building. This payment is part of a monthly assessment (fee). The largest difference between condos versus co-ops is ownership. Co-ops, in contrast to condos, are not owned by the tenants residing there. Rather than ownership, they buy shares of stock of the corporation, which does in fact own the co-op building/s. The tenant is a shareholder of the corporation, which is the owner.

Instead of having a deed, each shareholder purchases shares in the corporation. For all intents and purposes, this entitles and allows them to live in a unit of the co-op as well as access and use common areas and amenities. Although it can depend on the co-op, in order to have a larger unit, more shares must be purchased. Smaller units usually require fewer shares.

What about maintenance? Usually, the daily operations of a co-op are overseen by a governing board. The board members consist of residents, who were elected by their fellow residents.

Each potential shareholder must apply to live at the co-op. The co-op application is very similar to other housing applications in that it includes personal history and financial information. Each application submitted is reviewed and ultimately accepted or rejected, by the board. This means that even if a potential shareholder is able to finance his or her purchase, he/she may be denied due to other factors (whether financial or of another nature).

A few more facts about cooperatives include:

- Buyers do not actually purchase a specific unit within a building/complex. They lease the unit.

- Shareholders do not have a property deed or title. The corporation grants proprietary leases to the shareholders which grants them the right to occupy their respective units.

- Property taxes are the responsibility of the corporation. Although the occupants contribute to the payment of the property taxes, their contribution is not tax-deductible.

6. **Mixed-use Developments (MUDs):** At times, these are referred to as high-rise developments. These structures combine residential and nonresidential buildings together. They functionally integrate two or more of the following aspects: institutional,

commercial, residential, cultural, and industrial. Think of them as multipurpose and multiuse. A MUD can be one or more buildings, or even an entire neighborhood. What might be included? Any number of things! For example, a MUD may include cafes, restaurants, retail shops, filling stations, parks, retail stores, multifamily housing, and more. To learn more, read about how Toronto has implemented MUDs. In the US, in the early 1990s, Portland was already implementing MUDs in an effort to decrease traffic flow. Specifically, this Oregon city implemented a "light rail system" (known as MAX). It helps encourage and facilitate the mixing of different spaces (housing, work, and commercial) into one harmonious zone.

7. **Manufactured Housing:** Manufactured housing is commonly known as "mobile homes" in the US. These types of dwellings are a type of prefabricated housing. They are assembled in factories and then transported to their respective sites. Each one is taken to a parcel of land, where it is installed or assembled. Manufactured housing has a variety of other commonly used names, including: mobile home, trailer, trailer home, house trailer, static caravan, residential caravan, or simply caravan. Manufactured housing not only includes mobile homes but also includes panelized and precut.

   The phrase mobile home generally is said in reference to prefabricated housing that was constructed prior to 1976. When the National Manufactured Housing Construction and Safety Standards Act of 1976 was created, the term mobile home was phrased out. Why? Because that is the year they became federally regulated. However, in everyday use, the term mobile home has embedded itself into the English language and is very common to this day.

8. **Modular Homes:** These are also called prefabricated homes. These homes are typically constructed in modules within a factory and transported to a site. There, they're assembled like a jigsaw puzzle and permanently attached to a foundation. This transforms the once-vacant land into a parcel of real estate. In contrast to other options for home buyers, modular homes are usually much more budget-friendly. Because of this, they are growing in popularity in the US. It is important to recognize that various states have their own definitions and interpretations of modular homes.

9. **Planned Unit Development:** These developments, also referred to as PUDs, are a type of regulatory process and autonomous building development. It is a designed grouping that contains housing, recreation areas and/or buildings, business/retail centers, along with industrial zones. A PUD exists within one subdivision (like a neighborhood), or within one complete and contained specific development (like a town or city).

10. **Timeshares:** Sometimes referred to as "vacation ownership," a timeshare is a type of vacation real estate featuring shared rights. Timeshares have numerous purchasers who are entitled to a specific period of time each year that allows them the ability to enjoy the property. The most common time frames are one to two weeks. This model is used with a wide variety of properties, from condos and units to campgrounds and high-end vacation resorts.

As of the date of this book's publication, statistically, the states with the most timeshares are generally considered to be destination states and may include Arizona, California, Colorado, Florida, Hawaii, Nevada, and South Carolina.

As you can see, the variety and richness of both the styles of houses and types of housing are driven by several components, including but not limited to human creativity, necessity, flow, and functionality.

THE REALITY OF HOMEOWNER INSURANCE

Homeowner's insurance is also known as home insurance. This type of insurance primarily covers and protects a homeowner's private residence. It covers losses and damages. These include the house itself (inside and outside), along with the contents and assets (personal property) inside of the house itself. Common disasters, but not all, are covered most of the time. Accidents and theft are almost always included. Most lenders require that homeowners have a home insurance policy. Plus, the policy must have certain requirements (coverage levels). There are different coverage types included, selected, and/or required. With each of those is a coverage limit, which is either a percentage or a range of dollar amounts.

A mortgage payment is usually a homeowner's largest monthly expense. Thus, it stands to reason that homeowners must implement smart insurance policies in order to protect what is commonly referred to as their biggest investment. The lender protects itself by requiring the homebuyer to acquire homeowner insurance. This ensures the property owner will be able to fund any repairs or reconstruction in the event of a disaster. Frequently, the lender will put the buyer on a budget plan, whereby 1/12 of the annual insurance premium is added to the monthly mortgage payment. When the annual bill is due, the lender can make the payment to the insurance carrier in a timely manner.

NATIONAL FLOOD INSURANCE ACT OF 1968

If you have ever experienced a severe flood, you know what a horrible experience it can be. You and your community are in trouble. People are frantically trying to secure their valuables and quickly move their vehicles to higher or safer ground. The circumstances that a severe flood causes can be dangerous, scary, and emotionally difficult.

The National Flood Insurance Act of 1968 is a piece of United States legislation. Because of it, the National Flood Insurance Program (NFIP) was created. NFIP is run by the Federal Emergency Management Agency (FEMA). The purpose of NFIP is to actively help renters and homeowners rebuild their dwellings and businesses following a flood. Insurance companies who offer home insurance do not always offer flood insurance, so the government subsidizes the NFIP. NFIP makes flood insurance available to homeowners who: 1) live in participating communities and/or 2) live within the boundaries of NFIP-designated floodplains. This gives homeowners the opportunity to purchase flood insurance through a private company. However, it's the government, not the private company, which sets the rates.

> "The National Flood Insurance Program (NFIP) is the primary source of flood insurance coverage for residential properties in the United States. The NFIP has two main policy goals: (1) to provide access to primary flood insurance, thereby allowing for the transfer of some of the financial risk of property owners to the Federal Government; and (2) to mitigate and reduce the nation's comprehensive flood risk through the development and implementation of floodplain management standards." (Congressional Research Service)

Review those prior to taking the chapter quiz.

CHAPTER 5 QUIZ

1. Homeownership can possibly provide:

    a. Peace of mind
    b. Stability
    c. New options
    d. All of the above
    e. None of the above

2. In the real estate tax cycle, what does the County Clerk do?

    a. Establishes home values
    b. Approves exemptions
    c. Prints and mails tax bills
    d. All of the above
    e. None of the above

3. To the IRS, the terms "real estate tax" and "property tax" are the exact same thing.

    a. True
    b. False

4. In Illinois, taxes are paid in arrears.

    a. True
    b. False

5. Which phrase helps describe a tax credit?

    a. Incurred expenses in a calendar year
    b. Decreasing the taxable income
    c. Dollar-for-dollar reduction
    d. It is not recognized in Illinois.

6. If a loss or damage occurs in a 1902 Victorian home that was unforeseen or unintended, what is the specific tax benefit called?

    a. Claim loss
    b. Accidental loss
    c. Appurtenances
    d. Home insurance loss

7. Sarah just sold her home. Her profits from the sale of a house were $75,000. Which word defines what this money is called?

    a. Capital Gains
    b. Mortgage loan interest deduction
    c. Points and closing costs
    d. Deferment

8. Can people who rent a home or apartment benefit from home office expenses if they own or run a business from their residence or if they are self-employed?

    a. Yes
    b. No

9. Any mortgage financed by the FHA requires the borrower to have which of the following?

    a. High credit score
    b. Life insurance policy naming the FHA as the beneficiary
    c. Mortgage insurance
    d. All of the above

10. An active duty military member and her family are moving across the country. According to the Tax Cuts and Jobs Act of 2017, can she deduct moving costs on her taxes?

    a. Yes
    b. No

11. Which of the following is a simple definition for points?

    a. Standard deduction
    b. Itemized deductions
    c. Prepaid interest
    d. None of the above

12. Which of the following describes a 1031 exchange?

    a. Capital gains taxation
    b. Federal solar tax credit
    c. Sales tax issued at closing
    d. Strategy for tax deferment

13. Can property that increased in value greatly since its purchase be exchanged for other property?

    a. Yes
    b. No

14. One of the main appeals of condo ownership is property ownership without having the responsibility of which of the following?

    a. Lawn maintenance and repairs

    b. Real estate taxes

    c. Property taxes

    d. None of the above

15. Which of the following is an example of a converted-use property?

    a. A small factory is now a retail center

    b. An old barn is now a single-family home

    c. A cafe is transformed into a barbershop

    d. All of the above

16. In a co-op, unit residents pay their portion of the maintenance and care expenses of the building.

    a. True

    b. False

    c. It depends on the co-op

    d. Co-ops are prohibited from charging maintenance fees by law

17. Who oversees the National Flood Insurance Program?

    a. The state government in which the homeowner resides

    b. Federal Emergency Management Agency

    c. The Environmental Protection Agency

    d. National Domestic Preparedness Office

18. Which type of housing has numerous purchasers who own a specific amount of time within a given time frame?

    a. Condos

    b. Co-ops

    c. MUDs

    d. Timeshares

19. Which type of housing is a designed grouping that contains housing, recreation areas and/or buildings, business/retail centers, along with industrial zones that exist within one subdivision?

    a. A MUD
    b. Converted-use
    c. Manufactured housing
    d. A PUD

20. Which of the following are prefabricated homes?

    a. Modular homes
    b. Manufactured housing
    c. Mobile homes
    d. All of the above

CHAPTER 6:

LAW OF AGENCY I

LEARNING GOALS:

By the end of this lesson, you will:

- Understand the law of agency and related terms
- Know the minimum services provision in The Act
- Clearly understand a fiduciary's role and responsibilities
- Know what puffing and fraud mean
- Understand designated agency

REAL ESTATE AGENCY, or simply agency, is a special relationship between a licensee and the client, whether that be a buyer, seller, landlord, or tenant. This relationship requires the agent to take responsibility and extend to the client the fiduciary duties.

Within a seller agency, the agent represents the property seller in a real estate transaction. Within a buyer agency, the agent represents the buyer.

LAW OF AGENCY: RELATED TERMS

First, let's begin with definitions directly from The Act (225 ILCS 454/1-10).

- "The Act" means the Real Estate License Act of 2000.

- "Agency" means a relationship in which a broker or licensee, whether directly or through an affiliated licensee, represents a consumer by the consumer's consent, whether expressed or implied, in a real property transaction.

Note: This is also known as "agency relationship." Agency relationships are commonplace in a wide variety of professions. An agent in commercial law (sometimes called a manager in non-real estate professions) is someone who has the authority and permission to act on behalf of a client (known as the principal) and can make a legal relationship with a third or different party. (In real estate, the principal can be the buyer or the seller.)

- "Applicant" means any person, as defined in this Section, who applies to the Department for a valid license as a managing broker, broker, or residential leasing agent.

- "Board" means the Real Estate Administration and Disciplinary Board of the Department as created by Section 25-10 of this Act.

- "Broker" means an individual, entity, corporation, foreign or domestic partnership, limited liability company, registered limited liability partnership, or other business entity other than a residential leasing agent who, whether in person or through any media or technology, for another and for compensation, or with the intention or expectation of receiving compensation, either directly or indirectly:

  1. Sells, exchanges, purchases, rents, or leases real estate.

  2. Offers to sell, exchange, purchase, rent, or lease real estate.

  3. Negotiates, offers, attempts, or agrees to negotiate the sale, exchange, purchase, rental, or leasing of real estate.

  4. Lists, offers, attempts, or agrees to list real estate for sale, rent, lease, or exchange.

5. Whether for another or themselves, engages in a pattern of business of buying, selling, offering to buy or sell, marketing for sale, exchanging, or otherwise dealing in contracts, including assignable contracts for the purchase or sale of, or options on real estate or improvements thereon. For purposes of this definition, an individual or entity will be found to have engaged in a pattern of business if the individual or entity by itself or with any combination of other individuals or entities, whether as partners or common owners in another entity, has engaged in one or more of these practices on two or more occasions in any twelve-month period.

6. Supervises the collection, offer, attempt, or agreement to collect rent for the use of real estate.

7. Advertises or represents himself or herself as being engaged in the business of buying, selling, exchanging, renting, or leasing real estate.

8. Assists or directs in procuring or referring of leads or prospects, intended to result in the sale, exchange, lease, or rental of real estate.

9. Assists or directs in the negotiation of any transaction intended to result in the sale, exchange, lease, or rental of real estate.

10. Opens real estate to the public for marketing purposes.

11. Sells, rents, leases, or offers for sale or lease real estate at auction.

- "Brokerage agreement" means a written or oral agreement between a sponsoring broker and a consumer for licensed activities to be provided to a consumer in return for compensation or the right to receive compensation from another. Brokerage agreements may constitute either a bilateral or a unilateral agreement between the broker and the broker's client, depending upon the content of the brokerage agreement. All exclusive brokerage agreements shall be in writing.

- "Client" means a person who is being represented by a licensee.

- "Compensation" means the valuable consideration given by one person or entity to another person or entity in exchange for the performance of some activity or service. Compensation shall include the transfer of valuable consideration, including without limitation, the following:

  1. commissions

  2. referral fees

  3. bonuses

4. prizes

5. merchandise

6. finder fees

7. performance of services

8. coupons or gift certificates

9. discounts

10. rebates

11. a chance to win a raffle, drawing, lottery, or similar game of chance not prohibited by any other law or statute

12. retainer fee

13. salary

- "Confidential information" means information obtained by a licensee from a client during the term of a brokerage agreement that (i) was made confidential by the written request or written instruction of the client, (ii) deals with the negotiating position of the client, or (iii) is information the disclosure of which could materially harm the negotiating position of the client, unless at any time:

  - the client permits the disclosure of information given by that client by word or conduct;

  - the disclosure is required by law; or

  - the information becomes public from a source other than the licensee.

  - "Confidential information" shall not be considered to include material information about the physical condition of the property.

- "Consumer" means a person or entity seeking or receiving licensed activities.

- "Customer" means a consumer who is not being represented by the licensee.

- "Exclusive brokerage agreement" means a written brokerage agreement that provides that the sponsoring broker has the sole right, through one or more sponsored licensees, to act as the exclusive agent or representative of the client and that meets the requirements of Section 15-75 of this Act.

- "License" means the privilege conferred by the Department to a person who has fulfilled all requirements prerequisite to any type of licensure under this Act.

- "Licensed activities" means those activities listed in the definition of "broker" under this Section.

- "Licensee" means any person, as defined in this Section, who holds a valid unexpired license as a managing broker, broker, or residential leasing agent.

Although terms and definitions are not the most interesting topics to read, it's imperative that real estate professionals understand and can articulate each term accurately.

Note: Client and customer cannot and should never be used interchangeably. They are neither the same term nor do they have the same implications. Here is the distinction between a client and a customer.

1. **Customer:** A party to whom you owe the duties of fairness and honesty. The concept of "specific question with specific answer" applies. Examples: How many bedrooms are there? How many bathrooms are there? What's the size of the backyard? Those questions result in a specific answer. However, if a *customer* asks how good the school system is, a licensee cannot answer that. Why? It is an opinion to which a customer is not entitled to.

2. **Client:** A party with whom you owe only the duties of fairness and honesty. Nothing more and nothing less.

Agency relationships in Illinois must follow the law, as dictated by Article 15 of The Act. It clearly lays out the responsibilities, duties, and rights of all involved parties. Whenever a lawsuit is considered, The Act is the source from which the lawyers work. The Act was written to protect all the people who are legally involved in real estate transactions, including but not limited to homebuyers and sellers, renters, tenants, brokers, property managers, and so on.

Real estate transactions are not ultimately about real estate. They're about people. The transactions are about the dreams and goals that people have, whether their dreams lay in the residential or commercial realm.

As such, there are laws in place to protect consumers. Let's start with the bare minimum and build from there.

MINIMUM SERVICES IN ILLINOIS

In Section 15-75: Exclusive Brokerage Agreements of The Act, there is a portion of law that is commonly called the "minimum services provision." It was enacted to ensure the consumer is protected and receives what is generally considered to be the absolute minimum services owed to the client by the broker. Below, you'll read three sections quoted from this part of The Act, followed by Inland's rationale to help you understand it better.

The provision of The Act starts with the following statement:

All exclusive brokerage agreements must be in writing and specify that the sponsoring broker, through one or more sponsored licensees, must provide, at a minimum, the following services:

1. Accept delivery of and present to the client offers and counteroffers to buy, sell, or lease the client's property or the property the client seeks to purchase or lease."

   Note: You see, the designated broker has a fiduciary obligation to protect and care for the absolute best interests of the client. Should it be a buyer client, the licensee needs to participate in assisting the buyer in understanding the market conditions and how to develop the offer.

2. Assist the client in developing, communicating, negotiating, and presenting offers, counteroffers, and notices that relate to the offers and counteroffers until a lease or purchase agreement is signed and all contingencies are satisfied or waived."

   Note: Just as the licensee has an obligation to protect the interest of the buyer, as the seller's designated agent, the broker has an obligation to ensure the seller understands the nature, structure and contents of the offer. In addition, the seller's designated must also remain involved with the transaction right up to the actual closing.

3. Answer the client's questions relating to the offers, counteroffers, notices, and contingencies.

   Note: As you will read below, the licensee has an obligation to care about the best interest of his or her client above all else. This provision requires the licensee to answer the client's specific questions with specific answers.

Said another way, the first obligation under minimum service provision is to accept delivery of all offers from your client. This could also include assisting them in developing the offer. If the client doesn't have first-hand experience in the market, you will need to educate them with an up-to-date comparative market analysis (CMA). (You will read more about CMAs later.) As you can see, while the first obligation requires you to accept the offer for the client, the second obligation not only requires you to help develop the offer in preparation for submission but also requires you to deliver the offer in a timely manner. The third obligation under minimum services is to answer all of their questions. Take responsibility to walk your client through this process. It could make a difference in whether they get the property or not. The law dictates that our responsibility is to protect the public. This also includes the responsibility to answer your client's questions regarding the transaction to ensure that they are able to make an informed decision regarding how they should proceed. Keep in mind that when answering client questions, know your limitations. If the question involves a topic that is financial or legal in nature, or involves the building's structural integrity, refer your client to the appropriate professional so he or she can receive accurate and complete information.

FIDUCIARY DEFINITION AND RESPONSIBILITIES

As you've learned, agency is a special legal and strict relationship between the client and licensee, wherein the licensee is responsible for undertaking specific duties commonly known as fiduciary. Usually, a fiduciary carefully oversees and manages money or other assets for their clients and/or customers.

Known by the nickname "COLD AC," the fiduciary duties as defined by The Act include:

- Care

- Obedience

- Loyalty

- Disclosure

- Accountability/Accounting

- Confidentiality

Let's explore the details of each fiduciary duty, following the COLD AC acronym:

Care: Although it should go without saying, you must care about your client, the transaction, other people involved, and the project as a whole. Care for the interest of the client above all others. It is not to be taken lightly. Furthermore, no client wants to feel like he/she is merely a product on an assembly line in a factory. How would you want to be treated? What would you expect if the roles were reversed? Questions like that are great to ask because they compel you to explore the way in which you can show and express care in different ways during the life of the agency relationship.

Obedience: Obey the legal instruction of the client. Think of this as the context being the signed legal contract. It is not blind obedience to anything he/she wants. Furthermore, unethical requests or one that breaks the law are obviously not to be followed. Being obedient should never cross lines into any territory that's unlawful and/or unethical. When faced with an illegal or unethical instruction, the law basically wants you to educate your client as to why it is illegal or unethical. If they are unwilling to accept the explanation, disassociate.

Loyalty: Loyalty means being faithful. Always remember who you are responsible for. Your goal is not to make everyone happy, as that's rarely possible. You have fiduciary duties to the principal and only the principal. Loyalty is paramount. The best interests of the principal supersede all other people's interests, including your own. Your goal is to advance the principal's goals. It's not about you or your commission, career advancement, and so on. All conflicts of interest must be avoided at all costs.

This brings up the topic of being a dual agent. Dual agency occurs when you have a single real estate licensee that is representing both the buyer and seller simultaneously. In the state of Illinois, it is permissible to be in a dual agent relationship only if you have the expressed written permission from all parties, which would be the buyer and the seller. In our state, you need to show three pieces of evidence for the consent of dual agency; one signed by the seller, one signed by the buyer, and the sales contract signed by both. If you are in a dual agency relationship, the focal point is literally on what you're *not* allowed to do. When you are the agent of a client, you have six fiduciary duties, which is what you're currently learning about. In the realm of those duties, it is the broker's responsibility to provide the client with direction when it comes to value. For the seller, give the seller a market evaluation that provides them direction with the costs and what the sales price will likely be. With the buyer, if he/she is the client, give the buyer an analysis of the market so he/she knows what the house should be offered up for on the market. If you find yourself in a dual agency situation, you're *not* allowed to help the buyer or seller when it comes to the value. Any recommendation that you give to one side could very easily be harmful to the other. As a dual agent, you can do everything that you need to do except provide guidance on value.

Disclosure: You must disclose any relevant facts and material information that could influence or impact the principal's decision to own, buy, or sell. This includes disclosure of any personal interest that you, as a licensee, may have or intend to have in the property. Nothing is to be hidden, misconstrued, or withheld.

This brings us to a number of important terms: material facts, physical defects, latent defects, and patent defects.

1. **Material facts**

   - In a real estate transaction, a material fact is a fact that any reasonable person would recognize as pertinent to the decision-making process of the principal. It can affect whether or not the principal chooses to continue with the potential transaction or not. (As you recall, a principal can be a buyer or seller.)

   - Hiding, suppressing, or manipulating this fact would most likely result in the principal making a different decision. It could possibly result in legal action.

   - In short, a material fact is any factor that may impact a party's ability to buy, own, or sell a property.

LAW OF AGENCY I | 87

2. **Physical defects**

- A physical defect is any material imperfection in the property. It is a type of flaw, incompleteness, deficiency, or inadequacy.

- There are two forms of physical defects that the seller must disclose:

  a. Latent defects

    - Latent defects are defined as those defects in the property that the seller is aware of but are neither visible nor recognizable to the buyer. It's possible that the buyer has a lack of knowledge concerning what defects may look like or perhaps the defect is out of view. In a residential transaction, the buyers do not typically crawl into the attic or the crawlspace and may not be aware of defects in those areas of the home.

  b. Patent defects

    - Patent defects are defects found in the property that are both known to the seller and visible and recognizable to the buyer. Examples include but are not limited to a crack in the foundation and water leaks visible on the kitchen ceiling. The caveat the broker should recognize is that while a defect may be visible, a buyer may not recognize it as a defect.

What must be disclosed? Here is The Act's answer:

"All latent material adverse facts pertaining to the physical condition of the property that are actually known by the licensee and that could not be discovered by a reasonably diligent inspection of the property by the customer." (225 ILCS 454/15-25a)

The Act talks about the duties of licensees representing clients. It states:

"A licensee must disclose to the client material facts concerning the transaction of which the licensee has actual knowledge, unless that information is confidential information. Material facts do not include the following when located on or related to real estate that is not the subject of the transaction: (i) physical conditions that do not have a substantial adverse effect on the value of the real estate, (ii) fact situations, or (iii) occurrences and acts at the property." (225 ILCS 454/15-15)

In 225 ILCS 454/15-25a, The Act talks about what a licensee can do for clients when acting as a dual agent. It states licensees must:

"Disclose all latent material defects in the property that are known to the licensee."

When a dual agent is unaware of or unable to identify a defect, and the seller does not reveal it, the licensee is not liable to the buyer for failure to disclose.

Licensees are required by law to disclose information about physical defects and material facts to all parties, not only the principal. During the client relationship, as various physical defects and material facts come to light, the seller must be made aware of them. Furthermore, the licensee must disclose them to the consumers. Disclosure forms are used. Most of the time, they are filled out and signed by the seller. This can happen either during the signing or prior to the seller signing the listing agreement. When a defect comes to light after the disclosure has been prepared, the seller is required to revise the disclosure with the updated information.

Nowadays, in accordance with the obligation of full disclosure, the seller is required to disclose known defects. Because of the need to be transparent, the seller now has an obligation to provide the residential or commercial buyer with advance notice of known defects in the property. The law does not differentiate between residential and commercial properties regardless of size when it comes to the obligation of disclosure.

In a residential transaction, required disclosures include:

1. **Residential real property disclosure:** This communicates to the buyer all known latent and patent defects.

2. **Radon disclosure:** This is intended to communicate to the buy any known issues regarding the existence of radon.

3. **Lead paint disclosure:** This is required if the structure was built prior to 1978 where a young child or pregnant individual may reside.

You have probably already seen or read about the **Residential Real Property Disclosure Report**. The disclosure itself is straightforward. This important document places the responsibility for full disclosure directly on the seller. This responsibility is not on the shoulders of the licensee. The disclosure is for any seller who has a 1-4 unit residential property. Its purpose is to make known any and all material defects (whether visible or not) of which the seller/s are aware. The disclosure was originally designed to ensure that the seller of residential real estate conveys knowledge of any latent and patent defects to the buyer, prior to the buyer tendering an offer.

RESIDENTIAL REAL PROPERTY DISCLOSURE REPORT

(765 ILCS 77/5)

Section 5. Definitions. As used in this Act, unless the context otherwise requires, the following terms have the meaning given in this Section: "Residential real property" means real property improved with not less than one nor more than 4 residential dwelling units; units in residential cooperatives; or, condominium units, including the limited common elements allocated to the exclusive use thereof that form an integral part of the condominium unit. The term includes a manufactured home as defined in subdivision (53) of Section 9-102 of the Uniform Commercial Code that is real property as defined in the Conveyance and Encumbrance of Manufactured Homes as Real Property and Severance Act. "Seller" means every person or entity who:

(1) is a beneficiary of an Illinois land trust; or

(2) has an interest, legal or equitable, in residential property as:

   (i) an owner;

   (ii) a beneficiary of a trust;

   (iii) a beneficiary pursuant to testate 5 disposition, intestate succession, or a transfer on 6 death instrument; or

   (iv) a contract purchaser or lessee of a ground lease

"Seller" does not include a party to a transfer that is exempt under Section 15. "Prospective buyer" means any person or entity negotiating or offering to become an owner or lessee of a ground lease of residential real property by means of a transfer for value to which this Act applies. "Contract" means a written agreement by the seller and prospective buyer that would, subject to the satisfaction of any negotiated contingencies, require the prospective buyer to accept a transfer of the residential real property. (Source: P.A. 98-749, eff. 7-16-14; 99-78, eff. 7-20-15.)

Section 15. Seller exemptions. A seller in any of the following transfers is exempt from this Act, regardless of whether a disclosure report is delivered:

1. Transfers pursuant to court order, including, but not limited to, transfers ordered by a probate court in administration of an estate, transfers between spouses resulting from a judgment of dissolution of marriage or legal separation, transfers pursuant to an order of possession, transfers by a trustee in bankruptcy,

transfers by eminent domain, and transfers resulting from a decree for specific performance.

2. Transfers from a mortgagor to a mortgagee by deed in lieu of foreclosure or consent judgment, transfer by judicial deed issued pursuant to a foreclosure sale to the successful bidder or the assignee of a certificate of sale, transfer by a collateral assignment of a beneficial interest of a land trust, or a transfer by a mortgagee or a successor in interest to the mortgagee's secured position or a beneficiary under a deed in trust who has acquired the real property by deed in lieu of foreclosure, consent judgment or judicial deed issued pursuant to a foreclosure sale.

3. Transfers by a fiduciary in the course of the administration of a decedent's estate, guardianship, conservatorship, or trust. As used in this paragraph, "trust" includes an Illinois land trust.

4. Transfers from one co-owner to one or more other co-owners.

5. Transfers from a decedent pursuant to testate disposition, intestate succession, or a transfer on death instrument.

6. Transfers made to a spouse, or to a person or persons in the lineal line of consanguinity of one or more of the sellers.

7. Transfers from an entity that has taken title to residential real property from a seller for the purpose of assisting in the relocation of the seller, so long as the entity makes available to all prospective buyers a copy of the disclosure report furnished to the entity by the seller.

8. Transfers to or from any governmental entity.

9. Transfers of newly constructed residential real property that has never been occupied. This does not include rehabilitation of an existing home. (Source: P.A. 88-111.)

(765 ILCS 77/20)

Section 20. Disclosure report requirements. A seller of residential real property shall complete all items in the disclosure report described in Section 35. The seller shall deliver to the prospective buyer the written disclosure report required by this Act before the signing of a contract. (Source: P.A. 88-111.)

(765 ILCS 77/30)

Section 30. Disclosure report supplement. If, prior to closing, any seller becomes aware of an error, inaccuracy, or omission in any prior disclosure report or supplement document after delivery of that disclosure report or supplement to a prospective buyer, that seller shall supplement the prior disclosure report or supplement with a written supplemental disclosure, delivered by any method set forth in Section 50. (Source: P.A. 90-383, eff. 1-1-98; 91-357, eff. 7-29-99.)

(765 ILCS 77/35) Section 35. Disclosure report form.

The disclosures required of a seller by this Act shall be made in the following form:

RESIDENTIAL REAL PROPERTY DISCLOSURE REPORT

NOTICE: THE PURPOSE OF THIS REPORT IS TO PROVIDE PROSPECTIVE BUYERS WITH INFORMATION ABOUT MATERIAL DEFECTS IN THE RESIDENTIAL REAL PROPERTY BEFORE THE SIGNING OF A CONTRACT. THIS REPORT DOES NOT LIMIT THE PARTIES' RIGHT TO CONTRACT FOR THE SALE OF RESIDENTIAL REAL PROPERTY IN "AS IS" CONDITION. UNDER COMMON LAW, SELLERS WHO DISCLOSE MATERIAL DEFECTS MAY BE UNDER A CONTINUING OBLIGATION TO ADVISE THE PROSPECTIVE BUYERS ABOUT THE CONDITION OF THE RESIDENTIAL REAL PROPERTY EVEN AFTER THE REPORT IS DELIVERED TO THE PROSPECTIVE BUYER. COMPLETION OF THIS REPORT BY THE SELLER CREATES LEGAL OBLIGATIONS ON THE SELLER; THEREFORE THE SELLER MAY WISH TO CONSULT AN ATTORNEY PRIOR TO COMPLETION OF THIS REPORT.

Property Address: _____

City, State and Zip Code:_____

Seller's Name: _____

This Report is a disclosure of certain conditions of the residential real property listed above in compliance with the Residential Real Property Disclosure Act. This information is provided as of this _____ day of _____, 20_____. The disclosures herein shall not be deemed warranties of any kind by the seller or any person representing any party in this transaction.

In this form, "aware" means to have actual notice or actual knowledge without any specific investigation or inquiry. In this form, "material defect" means a condition that would have a substantial adverse effect on the value of the residential real property or that would significantly impair the health or safety of future occupants of the residential real property unless the seller reasonably believes that the condition has been corrected.

The seller discloses the following information with the knowledge that even though the statements herein are not deemed to be warranties, prospective buyers may choose to rely on this information in deciding whether or not and on what terms to purchase the residential real property. The seller represents that to the best of his or her actual knowledge, the following statements have been accurately noted as "yes" (correct), "no" (incorrect), or "not applicable" to the property being sold. If the seller indicates that the response to any

statement, except number 1, is yes or not applicable, the seller shall provide an explanation in the additional information area of this form.

	YES	NO	N/A	
1.				Seller has occupied the property within the last 12 months. (If "no," please identify capacity or explain relationship to property.)
2.				I currently have flood hazard insurance on the property.
3.				I am aware of flooding or recurring leakage problems in the crawl space and/or basement.
4.				I am aware that the property is located in a flood plain.
5.				I am aware of material defects in the basement or foundation (including cracks and bulges).
6.				I am aware of leaks or material defects in the roof, ceilings, or chimney.
7.				I am aware of material defects in the walls, windows, doors, or floors.
8.				I am aware of material defects in the electrical system.
9.				I am aware of material defects in the plumbing system (includes such things as water heater, sump pump, water treatment system, sprinkler system, and swimming pool).
10.				I am aware of material defects in the well or well equipment.
11.				I am aware of unsafe conditions in the drinking water.

12.				I am aware of material defects in the heating, air conditioning, or ventilating systems.
13.				I am aware of material defects in the fireplace or woodburning stove.
14.				I am aware of material defects in the septic, sanitary sewer, or other disposal systems.
15.				I am aware of unsafe concentrations of radon on the premises.
16.				I am aware of unsafe concentrations of or unsafe conditions relating to asbestos on the premises.
17.				I am aware of unsafe concentrations of or unsafe conditions relating to lead paint, lead water pipes, lead plumbing pipes or lead in the soil on the premises.
18.				I am aware of mine subsidence, underground pits, settlement, sliding, upheaval, or other earth stability defects on the premises.
19.				I am aware of current infestations of termites or other wood boring insects.
20.				I am aware of a structural defect caused by previous infestations of termites or other wood boring insects.
21.				I am aware of underground fuel storage tanks on the property.
22.				I am aware of boundary or lot line disputes.
23.				I have received notice of violation of local, state, or federal laws or regulations relating to this property, which violation has not been corrected.
24.				I am aware that this property has been used for the manufacture of methamphetamine as defined in Section 10 of the Methamphetamine Control and Community Protection Act.

Note: These disclosures are not intended to cover the common elements of a condominium, but only the actual residential real property including limited common elements allocated to the exclusive use thereof that form an integral part of the condominium unit.

Note: These disclosures are intended to reflect the current condition of the premises and do not include previous problems, if any, that the seller reasonably believes have been corrected.

If any of the above are marked "not applicable" or "yes," please explain here or use additional pages, if necessary:

_____

_____

_____

Check here if additional pages used: _____

Seller certifies that seller has prepared this report and certifies that the information provided is based on the actual notice or actual knowledge of the seller without any specific investigation or inquiry on the part of the seller. The seller hereby authorizes any person representing any principal in this transaction to provide a copy of this report, and to disclose any information in the report, to any person in connection with any actual or anticipated sale of the property.

THE SELLER ACKNOWLEDGES THAT THE SELLER IS REQUIRED TO PROVIDE THIS DISCLOSURE REPORT TO THE PROSPECTIVE BUYER BEFORE THE SIGNING OF THE CONTRACT AND HAS A CONTINUING OBLIGATION, PURSUANT TO SECTION 30 OF THE RESIDENTIAL REAL PROPERTY DISCLOSURE ACT, TO SUPPLEMENT THIS DISCLOSURE PRIOR TO CLOSING.

Seller: _____ Date: _____

Seller: _____ Date: _____

THE PROSPECTIVE BUYER IS AWARE THAT THE PARTIES MAY CHOOSE TO NEGOTIATE AN AGREEMENT FOR THE SALE OF THE PROPERTY SUBJECT TO ANY OR ALL MATERIAL DEFECTS DISCLOSED IN THIS REPORT ("AS IS"). THIS DISCLOSURE IS NOT A SUBSTITUTE FOR ANY INSPECTIONS OR WARRANTIES THAT THE PROSPECTIVE BUYER OR SELLER MAY WISH TO OBTAIN OR NEGOTIATE. THE FACT THAT THE SELLER IS NOT AWARE OF A PARTICULAR CONDITION OR PROBLEM IS NO GUARANTEE THAT IT DOES NOT EXIST. THE PROSPECTIVE BUYER IS AWARE THAT THE PROSPECTIVE BUYER MAY REQUEST AN INSPECTION OF THE PREMISES PERFORMED BY A QUALIFIED PROFESSIONAL.

Prospective Buyer: _____ Date: _____ Time: _____

Prospective Buyer: _____ Date: _____ Time: _____

(Source: P.A. 98-754, eff. 1-1-15.) ARTICLE 2: DISCLOSURES

ARTICLE 2: DISCLOSURES

(765 ILCS 77/40)

Section 40. Material defect.

(a) If a seller discloses a material defect in the Residential Real Property Disclosure Report, including a response to any statement that is answered "yes" except numbers 1 and 2, and, in violation of Section 20, it is delivered to the prospective buyer after all parties have signed a contract, the prospective buyer, within 5 business days after receipt of that report, may terminate the contract or other agreement with the return of all earnest money deposits or down payments paid by the prospective buyer in the transaction without any liability to or recourse by the seller.

(b) If a seller discloses a material defect in a supplement to this disclosure report, the prospective buyer shall not have a right to terminate unless: (i) the material defect results from an error, inaccuracy, or omission of which the seller had actual knowledge at the time the prior disclosure was completed and signed by the seller; (ii) the material defect is not repairable prior to closing; or (iii) the material defect is repairable prior to closing, but within 5 business days after the delivery of the supplemental disclosure, the seller declines, or otherwise fails to agree in writing, to repair the material defect.

(c) The right to terminate the contract, however, shall no longer exist after the conveyance of the residential real property. For purposes of this Act the termination shall be deemed to be made when written notice of termination is delivered to at least one of the sellers by any method set forth in Section 50, at the contact information provided by any seller or indicated in the contract or other agreement. Nothing in subsection (a) or (b) shall limit the remedies available under the contract or Section 55. (Source: P.A. 90-383, eff. 1-1-98.)

(765 ILCS 77/45)

Section 45. Other law. This Act is not intended to limit remedies or modify any obligation to disclose created by any other statute or that may exist in common law in order to avoid fraud, misrepresentation, or deceit in the transaction. (Source: P.A. 88-111.)

(765 ILCS 77/50)

Section 50. Delivery of disclosure report. Delivery of the Residential Real Property Disclosure Report provided by this Act shall be by:

(1) personal delivery or facsimile, email, or other electronic delivery to the prospective buyer at the contact information provided by the prospective buyer or indicated in the contract or other agreement;

(2) depositing the report with the United States Postal Service, postage prepaid, first class mail, addressed to the prospective buyer at the address provided by the prospective buyer or indicated on the contract or other agreement; or

(3) depositing the report with an alternative delivery service such as Federal Express or, UPS, delivery charges prepaid, addressed to the prospective buyer at the address provided by the prospective buyer or indicated on the contract or other agreement. For purposes of this Act, delivery to one prospective buyer is deemed delivery to all prospective buyers. Delivery to an authorized individual acting on behalf of a prospective buyer constitutes delivery to all prospective buyers. Delivery of the report is effective upon receipt by the prospective buyer. Receipt may be acknowledged on the report, acknowledged in an agreement for the conveyance of the residential real property, or shown in any other verifiable manner. (Source: P.A. 91-357, eff. 7-29-99.) (765 ILCS 77/55)

Section 55. Violations and damages. If the seller fails or refuses to provide the disclosure report prior to the conveyance of the residential real property, the prospective buyer shall have the right to terminate the contract. A seller who knowingly violates or fails to perform any duty prescribed by any provision of this Act or who discloses any information on the Residential Real Property Disclosure Report that the seller knows to be false shall be liable in the amount of actual damages and court costs, and the court may award reasonable attorney's fees incurred by the prevailing party. (Source: P.A. 90-383, eff. 1-1-98.)

Section 99. Effective date. This Act takes effect upon becoming law.

Statutes amended in order of appearance

765 ILCS 77/5

765 ILCS 77/15

765 ILCS 77/20

765 ILCS 77/30

765 ILCS 77/35

765 ILCS 77/40

765 ILCS 77/45

765 ILCS 77/50

765 ILCS 77/55

Accountability: Most of the time, the A in the acronym COLD AC stands for Accounting. We prefer to use the word Accountability because it references the direct responsibility a licensee has on behalf of his or her client. It is a more complete and accurate definition.

There are two types of accountability. They are:

1. Tangible

2. Financial

> **Tangible accountability** takes into consideration the broker's responsibility for the client's property. Consider when taking a listing, many times a seller will provide the broker with a key to gain access in order to show the property when the seller is not available. This also allows cooperating brokers access to the property without the need of having the listing broker join them. (A **cooperating broker** is the licensee that generally represents the interest of the buyer. Typically in a residential transaction, there will be two brokers. One represents the buyer. One represents the seller.) Because of this flexibility, the listing broker must assume responsibility for the tangible assets of the seller. Those tangible assets could be jewelry left in the jewelry box on top of the dresser, or a plaster of Paris figurine created by the seller's child as a birthday gift. Whether it be valuable financially or valuable emotionally, the broker must take responsibility should a loss or damage be incurred. Also, the property may be shown by cooperating brokers. If the property is not properly closed up (such as closing and locking the doors, turning off lights, securing the windows), the listing designated

agent may have some liability to the client. This does not indicate financial liability, but rather credible liability because the seller has literally entrusted the designated listing agent with the care of the property.

Financial accountability includes the proper maintenance and security of the clients' monies (escrow accounts). This includes the process of recording, categorizing, and summarizing financial transactions.

As a sponsored licensee, you are neither an accountant, nor are you required to maintain the escrow account. However, your sponsoring and designated managing brokers are responsible for clients' monies as they progress toward closing. In the chapters to come, you will learn what The Act states and requires for recordkeeping and escrow accounts.

All real estate transactions revolve around money and numbers. Accurate accounting is an absolute must. It's the final fiduciary duty. Agents in many states are required by law to keep accounting records. At any moment, he/she must be able to report the status of all funds received on behalf of the principal. The goal is to be an impeccable steward. Money, money trails, and documents must be safeguarded.

There are two illegal practices of which to take note:

1. **Commingling**: It is illegal to commingle (mix) clients' monies with the agent/licensee's personal funds or general business funds.

2. **Conversion**: Unauthorized use or withholding of money or property that rightfully belongs to another person is illegal. This is when a licensee uses escrow money as his or her own money.

Here are more details about commingling.

"Commingling Prohibited. Each sponsoring broker shall deposit only escrow money received in connection with any real estate transaction in an escrow account. The sponsoring broker shall not deposit personal funds in an escrow account, except the sponsoring broker may deposit from the sponsoring broker's own personal funds, and keep in any escrow account, an amount sufficient to avoid incurring service charges relating to the escrow account. The sum shall be specifically documented as being for service charges and the sponsoring broker shall have proof available that the amount of the sponsoring broker's own funds in the escrow account does not exceed the minimum amount required by the depository to maintain the account without incurring service charges. Transfer of funds as set forth in subsection (i)(4) shall not constitute commingling" Rules and Regulations

Confidentiality: Keep information in confidence. Never harm the negotiating position.

> Confidentiality is the fiduciary duty to which this concept is targeted. When it comes to your client, water cooler conversations within the office, which one might consider as innocent conversations, could very well be financially harmful to your client. Always ask yourself, "Would this information, if conveyed to another person, negatively impact my client's negotiating position?"
>
> As defined by The Act, "confidential information" means information obtained by a licensee from a client during the term of a brokerage agreement that …
>
> (i) was made confidential by the written request or written instruction of the client;
>
> (ii) deals with the negotiating position of the client; or
>
> (iii) is information the disclosure of which could materially harm the negotiating position of the client. (225 ILCS 454/1-10)

Confidential information must not be shared without the express written authorization given by the client. The law requires this disclosure. Note that confidential information does not include any material facts or information about the physical condition of the property or properties and its environment.

Although you now know a fiduciary's role and responsibilities, as well as the "COLD AC" acronym, there is also another fine line of which to be aware. Your principal weighs and measures every single word you say. In light of this, you should not make speculative or flippant statements. Doing so can create problems and reduce your effectiveness. When you are in a conversation with the principal, you must be clear with your words and ensure that he/she understands what you are saying. When you share a fact, you want the principal to clearly know that it's a fact. If you share an opinion, you want the principal to clearly know that it's an opinion. Sharing something speculative in nature requires you to clearly set forth to the client that it is indeed speculative and that he/she needs to make his or her own decision with regard to the topic at hand. When the lines get blurred and miscommunication takes place, this can open up a variety of difficult issues and obstacles.

PUFFING AND FRAUD

Other terms arise given the ongoing conversations of principals and licensees:

1. Puffing

2. Fraud

Puffing is the temptation or tendency for anyone in sales to exaggerate specific facts in order to make a sale. If you've watched late-night infomercials, you already know that many of them reek of puffing. It's generally viewed as an opinion and not a misrepresentation. Surprisingly or not, puffing is not against the law. However, if it crosses into fraud, it is illegal. This line is very fine and nuanced.

Fraud is a planned and *intentional* deception, misrepresentation, lie, or series of lies done in order to unfairly win or gain something. Fraud is a very broad term. Fraud tricks, deceives, and takes advantage of someone. It takes many forms, including but not limited to: mortgage scams, stolen tax refund fraud, affinity fraud, credit card fraud, mail fraud, healthcare fraud, identity fraud, voter fraud, Ponzi schemes, bank account fraud, and Internet fraud.

Under 815 ILCS 505/, the Consumer Fraud and Deceptive Business Practices Act, the Illinois General Assembly states:

> Section 2. Unfair methods of competition and unfair or deceptive acts or practices, including but not limited to the use or employment of any deception fraud, false pretense, false promise, misrepresentation or the concealment, suppression or omission of any material fact, with intent that others rely upon the concealment, suppression or omission of such material fact, or the use or employment of any practice described in Section 2 of the "Uniform Deceptive Trade Practices Act," approved August 5, 1965, in the conduct of any trade or commerce are hereby declared unlawful whether any person has in fact been misled, deceived or damaged thereby. In construing this section, consideration shall be given to the interpretations of the Federal Trade Commission (FTC) and the federal courts relating to Section 5 (a) of the Federal Trade Commission Act.

Agency law requires that licensees be conscious of the needs of their clients. One of the key factors that licensees need to be extremely concerned with would be the nature of misrepresentation. If the client is harmed as a result of misrepresentation and the department can define the misrepresentation as being negligent, the licensee will need to explain their actions to the disciplinary board. A few of the issues that the licensee needs to be conscientious of include:

- Providing the client with a false or inaccurate statement concerning a material fact

- Making a statement that the consumer/customer/client can justifiably believe is a statement of truth, but then subsequently learns that the broker's carelessness or negligence in making the statement causes harm to him or her

- Intentionally providing the client with information intended to induce or persuade the client into undertaking an illegal or contradictory action

- Failing to convey accurate information regarding the property that the client may have an interest in

Does it have to be their intention in order for a licensee to experience backlash or disciplinary action or legal action? The answer is no. As a licensee, it's your job to know what a material fact is and to convey them clearly. You can accidentally get in trouble for what you should have known in the first place. Your principal depends on you for accurate information. You must always provide just that.

Additionally, there are two other important and related factors concerning what we've covered: Megan's Law and stigmatized properties.

Megan's Law is named after Megan Kanka. Tragically, this seven-year-old was raped and murdered in 1994. Her assailant was her neighbor, Jesse Timmendequas. He was convicted of her murder. Due to the national attention this heart-wrenching case attracted, it led to the creation of Megan's Law. This law essentially created an online map of registered sex offenders. Law enforcement is required to disclose their locations to the public. "The Dru Sjodin National Sex Offender Public Website (NSOPW) is an unprecedented public safety resource that provides the public with access to sex offender data nationwide. NSOPW is a partnership between the U.S. Department of Justice and state, territorial and tribal governments, working together for the safety of adults and children" (NSOPW website). Meaning, anyone online can search by name and/or location. When a sex offender leaves jail or custody, he/she must keep law enforcement updated with job and residence changes. Federally, Megan's Law was put into place as a subsection of the Jacob Wetterling Crimes Against Children and Sexually Violent Offender Registration Act of 1994. This act only required sex offenders to register with local law enforcement. On a federal level, Megan's Law makes the sex offender registry public information. On a state level, Megan's Law might include both the sex offender registration and a community notification.

Does Illinois require listing agents to disclose if a registered sex offender lives near a listing? No, it does not. Buyer's agents, if and when asked, should give information to the clients about the NSOPW. Ultimately, in Illinois, it is the client's responsibility to learn whether or not a registered sex offender lives near the house that they are considering purchasing.

Stigmatized properties are the final caveat. When someone or something is stigmatized, it means that the person or object is viewed unfavorably, negatively judged, and/or viewed with disapproval. Commonly, anything stigmatized is viewed as bad or something to be ashamed of. While it's important to know what they are, stigmatized properties are not very common. These properties are ones that have a reputation. Generally speaking, the so-called reputation focuses on an event that took place on, in, or near the property. This type of property can easily and quite possibly be avoided and shunned by potential buyers and tenants due to one or more events that occurred inside or outside of the property. Examples of these events include but are not limited to:

- The occurrence of a criminal event such as murder, lynching, rape, and so on

- Someone died in the house by natural causes

- Someone died in the house by suicide

- Someone struggled with a horrible disease while living there

- A newborn was stolen from the house

- Another type of tragedy or horrible accident took place there

- The belief or sense that the house itself is haunted or cursed

- Anything similar that makes the house repel potential buyers

It is the history or the reputation that impacts a buyer's decision to purchase the property. Consider a property that has been occupied by a serial killer who uses their basement or crawl space as the primary site for their victims. This concept might make some people uneasy with regard to living on the property. Stigmatized properties can potentially bring up a whirlwind of emotions and negativity, as you can tell. The best advice for licensees is to seek out highly qualified legal advice if they ever consider taking on a stigmatized property as a listing. These types of properties are obviously not for the faint of heart because of the nature of conversations they can open up.

The Act (225 ILCS 454/15-20) states:

> Failure to disclose information not affecting physical condition. No cause of action shall arise against a licensee for the failure to disclose: (i) that an occupant of the property was afflicted with Human Immunodeficiency Virus (HIV) or any other medical condition; (ii) that the property was the site of an act or occurrence that had no effect on the physical condition of the property or its environment or the structures located thereon; (iii) fact situations on property that is not the subject of the transaction; or (iv) physical conditions located on property that is not the

subject of the transaction that do not have a substantial adverse effect on the value of the real estate that is the subject of the transaction.

DESIGNATED AGENCY AND AGENT INFORMATION

The realm of agency encompasses not only the representation of the seller but also includes representation of the buyer, landlord, and tenant.

Designated agency is currently legal in Illinois and several other states. It's a model of doing business that is very common, if not popular. It is depicted and covered in the written policies of the real estate companies that have elected this model.

A designated agent is someone who is authorized by the sponsoring broker to act as the exclusive agent for a specific principal. Approvals and authorizations come from the sponsoring broker.

Here are three related definitions from The Act, Section 15:

- "Designated agency" means a contractual relationship between a sponsoring broker and a client under Section 15-50 of this Act in which one or more licensees associated with or employed by the broker are designated as the agent of the client.

- "Designated managing broker" means a managing broker who has supervisory responsibilities for licensees in one or, in the case of a multi-office company, more than one office and who has been appointed as such by the sponsoring broker registered with the Department.

- Note: The designated managing broker is the only licensee within the company authorized to make decisions and supervise the actions of the sponsored licensees.

- "Designated agent" means a sponsored licensee named by a sponsoring broker as the exclusive legal agent of a client, as provided for in Section 15-50 of this Act.

- Note: In the year 2000, the state of Illinois coined the term "designated agent." It literally gave the managing broker the right to delegate the agency responsibilities to individual licensees. The duties that the agent would take responsibility for consist of "COLD AC." As you read earlier, these stand for: Care, Obedience, Loyalty, Disclosure, Accountability/Accounting, and Confidentiality. These six duties come into play with the fiduciary relationship under this concept of designated agency. Under the original common law of agency, the managing broker was always the designated agent of the seller, whether they have ever met that person or not. It really puts the managing broker and the seller in a precarious position. The fiduciary role always requires enormous responsibility and attention to detail.

What about the other agents who are not the designated agent? They may act as agents for the other party in the transaction if they choose. As you can see, this means that two licensees from the exact same real estate company have the ability to represent opposite parties in the sale of a property—and doing so without actually entering into dual agency. This business model allows licensees in the same office to represent both the buyers and the sellers in a real estate transaction. Within this model, it is the sponsoring agent who designates a different licensee, one to represent the buyer and the other to represent the seller.

As you know, licensed Illinois real estate agents are governed by the Illinois Real Estate License Act of 2000. Section 15-10 of The Act states:

> "Licensees shall be considered to be representing the consumer they are working with as a designated agent for the consumer unless there is a written agreement between the sponsoring broker and the consumer providing that there is a different relationship." (225 ILCS 454/15-10)

Unless given a written declaration of no agency, you are representing the best interests of the person you are working with as your client. As such, whether discussed or not, you owe that individual the fiduciary duties. Illinois is a state of presumption. It is presumed you are the agent of the party you are working with, even though nothing has been stated.

As noted above in 225 ILCS 454/15-10, the licensee is the designated agent of the individual *unless* an official form called "Notice Of No Agency" is executed. This form, signed by the consumer, declares the consumer's preference to be treated as a customer. Below is an example. It is not intended for business use. Always seek counsel from your designated managing broker and/or an attorney with regard to forms, contracts, and agreements.

It's now time for your chapter quiz.

CHAPTER 6 QUIZ

1. What is the term that describes a relationship in which a broker or licensee, whether directly or indirectly, represents a consumer by his/her consent in a real property transaction?

    a. Agency
    b. Brokerage
    c. Dual agency
    d. Broker agreement

2. What term's definition includes finder fees, discounts, and retainer fee?

    a. Referral
    b. Compensation
    c. Broker agreement
    d. None of the above

3. Which word below means a person who is not being represented by the licensee?

    a. Consumer
    b. Customer
    c. Candidate
    d. None of the above

4. The "minimum services provision" was enacted to:

    a. Ensure the consumer is protected
    b. Make sure licensees accept delivery of all offers from buyers
    c. Compel licensees to care for the absolute best interests of the client
    d. All of the above
    e. None of the above

5. "COLD AC" helps you remember your fiduciary duties as a licensee. What does that acronym stand for?

    a. Comprehensive, Obedience, Licensed, Disclosure, Accountability, Confidentiality
    b. Care, Observance, Loyalty, Disclosure, Accountability, Confidentiality
    c. Careful, Obedience, Law-abiding, Disclosure, Accounting, Confidence
    d. Care, Obedience, Loyalty, Disclosure, Accountability, Confidentiality

6. What occurs when you have a single real estate licensee that is representing both the buyer and seller simultaneously?

   a. Being a dual agent
   b. Being a fiduciary
   c. Being a sponsoring broker
   d. None of the above

7. Known material facts are to be disclosed to only the principal, not all parties.

   a. True
   b. False

8. Licensees are required by law to disclose information about physical defects and material facts.

   a. Depends on the circumstances
   b. True
   c. False

9. The Residential Real Property Disclosure Report is to be used with which of the following?

   a. Only a single residence
   b. A 1-4 unit residential property
   c. A 5-or-more unit residential property
   d. Apartment complexes
   e. None of the above

10. Which type of defects are defined as those defects in the property that the seller is aware of, but that are not visible to the buyer?

    a. Latent defects
    b. Patent defects
    c. Dormant defects
    d. Inspection defects

11. Accountability is not a fiduciary duty. It's the job of real estate bookkeepers or in-house support teams.

    a. True
    b. False

12. Mixing client money with your own funds is which of the following?

    a. Acceptable

    b. Conversion

    c. Fraud

    d. Commingling

13. As a licensee, you are able to share confidential information without the express written authorization given by the client if it's an advantageous decision given the circumstances.

    a. True

    b. False

14. You hear another licensee talking to a potential client. He says, "This is the most extraordinary property for this price you'll find within 50 miles of here. The neighborhood is amazing. The social life is phenomenal." What has he most likely just done?

    a. He is lying

    b. He is misrepresenting the listing

    c. He is puffing

    d. None of the above

15. What does the Dru Sjodin National Sex Offender Public Website (NSOPW) provide to the public?

    a. A list of sex offenses that have happened in the areas they search

    b. Where registered sex offenders live

    c. Where registered sex offenders currently work

    d. All of the above

16. Does Illinois require listing agents to disclose if a registered sex offender lives near a listing?

    a. No

    b. Yes

17. Which is an example of a stigmatized property?

    a. A house where a murder took place

    b. A property where lynching happened

    c. A home where someone committed suicide

    d. All of the above

    e. None of the above

18. According to The Act, which term is defined as "a sponsored licensee named by a sponsoring broker as the legal agent of a client"?

    a. Designated agent
    b. Dual agent
    c. Sponsoring broker
    d. Dual agency

19. Is it possible and legal for two licensees from the exact same real estate company to have the ability to represent opposite parties in the sale of a property?

    a. No
    b. Yes

20. You are representing the best interests of the person you are working with as your client unless you have which of the following written declarations?

    a. Nondisclosure agreement
    b. Designated broker
    c. Dual agency
    d. Notice of no agency

CHAPTER 7:

LAW OF AGENCY II

LEARNING GOALS:

By the end of this lesson, you will:

- See how agency is created and terminated
- Understand the differences between designated agent, special agent, and general agent
- Deepen your knowledge of agency types
- Learn about agency relationship disclosure

CREATION OF AGENCY

As you learned, The Act states that "agency means a relationship in which a broker or licensee, whether directly or through an affiliated licensee, represents a consumer by the consumer's consent" (225 ILCS 454/1-10). In a real estate transaction, this consent may be expressed or implied. Agency can be created in a formal or informal manner. Regardless of how they are formed, the law must be followed. This results in a fiduciary relationship being created. Agency is a privilege and responsibility that must be taken seriously.

In Illinois, an agency relationship may be created simply by working with someone. Let's say licensee Sarah meets a potential buyer (consumer). Most licensees, like Sarah, make an assumption that the consumer will be a client from the onset, even though there is nothing specifically stated or written between the parties.

The two ways in which agency is created are:

1. Express agency

2. Implied agency

Express agency is the most common method to create agency. Both the agent and the principal establish, lay out, and capture their roles, goals, and responsibilities in writing or orally. This agreement is where the principal authorizes the licensee to act as his or her agent. This is a formal and valid contract, whether it's a signed legal document or communicated verbally. Although a verbal contract is valid, it is unenforceable in court because it fails to comply with the Statute of Frauds (SOF). The SOF exists in US common law and requires that real estate contracts be in writing and signed by all parties to be enforceable in court. A contract is designed to protect both parties. Contracts and agreements (express or implied) are governed by US contract law. Express agency is *expressed* in writing or verbally, in contrast with *implied* agency.

Implied agency is exactly how it sounds. Imply means to strongly suggest or to infer. It is not direct. This type of agency is created or generated through the actions of two or more parties. Has a formal agreement or some sort of legal document been signed? No. Has either party directly verbalized the nature of the relationship (in that they are working together)? No. Without a written or verbalized agreement, the agent and principal nevertheless have created an agency relationship and are working together.

Whether it is express agency or implied agency, both are agency relationships unless there is specifically a declaration of "no agency."

What is no agency? In the state of Illinois, we actively work on what is known as a presumption of agency (implied agency). You are considered to be the agent of the party you are working with unless a written declaration exists (commonly known as Notice of No Agency).

When you engage a consumer and start talking with them, especially a buyer, and begin inquiring as to what they are looking for and how you can be of assistance, agency is created. The start of this conversation is also known as substantive contact. This occurs when a licensee solicits or receives information from a potential consumer. If you never address your role and allow the consumer to assume you are their agent, then your silence and actions establish you as the agent.

A no agency relationship means that there is neither a written agreement nor a fiduciary relationship in existence. When the licensee finds themselves in this position, the relationship with the individual needs to be based on customer status. When relating to an individual as a customer, the licensee is limited to treating the individual fairly and honestly. There are no other duties that are required. In fact, because of these limitations, the licensee must enter into a written declaration of no agency so that the individual is aware they shall refrain from:

- Seeking the agent's guidance, interpretation, opinion, or counsel. When treating an individual as a customer it must be clearly defined that the agent does not represent them nor assume any liability for their protection.

- Providing the licensee with confidential information. Just like being arrested, the accused individual must be granted Miranda rights, which basically stipulates that anything the individual may say can and will be used against them in a court of law. In this realm, any confidential information that the customer provides to the licensee can and should be used against them and contract negotiations. The statement of no agency must be given to the individual and retained in the office master file, should a question arise in the future as to whether or not the agent did overstep the limits and treat the individual as a client.

TERMINATION OF AGENCY

You now know how agency starts. How does it end? When is it terminated? This list is common law perceptions on termination of agency. At the present time, there are no specific policies in the state of Illinois that are in excess of what is stated below. In many states, agency will or can be terminated when one of the following circumstances occurs:

1. Death of the principal

2. Incapacity of the principal

3. Mutual agreement among all involved parties

4. The property suffered substantial destruction

5. Breach of contract by one of the parties (The guilty party could suffer liability and/

or damages.)

6. The principal goes bankrupt or applies for bankruptcy

7. If the lender files foreclosure proceedings

8. The agreement expires

9. The agreement is fulfilled and thus complete

Power of attorney (POA) is a type of legal authorization. It allows the recipient the legal authority to make decisions about another person's affairs. Those affairs usually center on the other person's medical care, property, and/or finances. Unless the power of attorney is written carefully, it could create an environment where a person may have restricted or unrestricted rights to take legal action on behalf of another. This could be a dangerous situation.

The "Illinois Power of Attorney Act" defines "incapacitated" as the following:

> "**Incapacitated**,' when used to describe a principal, means that the principal is under a legal disability as defined in Section 11a-2 of the Probate Act of 1975. A principal shall also be considered incapacitated if: (i) a physician licensed to practice medicine in all of its branches has examined the principal and has determined that the principal lacks decision-making capacity; (ii) that physician has made a written record of this determination and has signed the written record within 90 days after the examination; and (iii) the written record has been delivered to the agent. The agent may rely conclusively on the written record." (Section 755 ILCS 45)

TYPES OF AGENTS

All agents authorized by a principal do not have the same privileges and levels of authority. The principal may set an agent's limits of power inside of the agreement. There are five levels of authorized agents in Illinois you need to know about. They are:

1. Designated agent

2. Disclosed dual agent

3. Special agent

4. General agent

5. *Universal agent

As you recall, **designated agent** means a sponsored licensee named by a sponsoring broker as the legal agent of a client. He/she is someone who is authorized to act as the agent for a specific principal. This approval and authorization come from the sponsoring broker. Accordingly, he/she is the only licensee in the company with fiduciary responsibility toward the principal. Can other licensees in the same brokerage represent the other party in a real estate transaction? The answer is yes. This means two agents in the same brokerage can be working on the same transaction, each representing their own client.

A **disclosed dual agent** is a licensee who represents two clients simultaneously in a single transaction. In short, he or she is representing both the buyer and the seller in the same transaction.

A **special agent** is authorized to perform one task on behalf of the client. When acting as the agent of the seller, the licensee's role is to market the property. The sponsoring broker has the right to appoint the licensee as the designated agent as well. As a designated agent, the licensee will assume the responsibility for rendering the fiduciary duties to the client. To clarify, a special agent can also be a designated agent. For example, Margaret's firm has been hired by her client (the principal) as a listing agent. Margaret will assume responsibilities for marketing the property. This establishes her as a special agent. Her designated managing broker will also delegate the fiduciary duties upon Margaret to ensure the client's interests are met. When the home sells, the agency relationship ends.

A **general agent** is authorized to undertake multiple tasks in a specific area on behalf of the client. He or she does not have full power like a universal agent does. A principal can have one or more general agents working on his or her behalf. Example: Property managers can solicit tenants, negotiate the lease, address tenant issues, and work with contractors when making repairs to the property.

A **universal agent** is a licensee who acts on behalf of a principal and has the authority and full power to do whatever the client can do. This is by way of having power of attorney. This agent can buy and/or sell property, sign legal documents, and more. Commonly, he or she oversees matters of life and death. A principal can only have a single universal agent. Compared to the other types of agents, a universal agent is the most rare. *Note: Universal agent is a subject that is not traditionally used in real estate educational settings because this authorization is not common in the world of real estate.

TYPES OF AGENCY

Single agency: The focal point of this phrase is the word "single." Single agency is present when a single agent, broker, or firm represents the interests of either one seller or one buyer. The agent or firm is either the buyer's agent or the seller's agent. The buyer or seller may be a tenant or landlord. All of the agent or firm's legal responsibility and fiduciary duties are focused on a single principal. When it comes to real estate representation, single agency is the most popular representation. Can both a buyer and a seller be represented simultaneously in the same transaction by the same agent? The answer is no. Single agency restricts this. As you probably can guess, dual agency allows it.

Dual agency: The simplest way to describe dual agency is when the property owner/seller is allowing the real estate agent to also represent the potential buyer for his or her property. The same agent represents two principals in the same transaction simultaneously. Dual agency is currently allowed by Illinois law in real estate transactions. However, there must be "informed written consent" between all parties. The licensee must acquire three written evidences of consent to dual agency. These are:

1. Authorization established in the listing agreement signed by the seller

2. Authorization in a separate document signed by the buyer

3. Confirmation of consent to dual agency in the sales contract, which is signed by both the buyer and the seller

The unique characteristic of dual agency is that it calls for equal loyalty and professionalism from the agent to two different principals at the same time. He/she must honorably fulfill fiduciary responsibilities to one principal without ever compromising the interests or undermining the interests of the other principal. You can imagine that this can get interesting fast, especially when the parties' interests are not only separate, but many times are actually opposite. When acting as a dual agent, Illinois law specifically prohibits the licensee from discussing any aspect of pricing with either buyer or seller. The licensee can assist both clients with every aspect of the transaction, but *cannot* provide guidance on what the:

- Buyer should offer

- Seller should accept

What if an agent creates dual agency by implication or unintentionally? What if dual agency is not disclosed in that circumstance? Example: You are a licensee and have just met Steve. He is looking to purchase a home. You've established yourself as Steve's agent in order to protect his interests as you pursue a home. One of the options that has arisen happens to be your own personal listing. If you take Steve to look at this home and fail to disclose to him that you are the listing agent, this constitutes an undisclosed dual agency and may be the catalyst for your being brought before the disciplinary board. Not only could this result in a monetary fine of nearly $25,000, but it could also result in disciplinary action.

What happens if a client completely refuses dual agency representation? What can the agent do? The agent has the option of referring the client to another agent within in the office. This is likely the best outcome. In doing so, it is possible that this may produce a referral fee back to the referring agent. The other option is for the agent to withdraw. This restricts his/her representation in this transition to one client. He/she may do so without liability. This terminates the agency relationship to the party who refused dual agency.

To recap, single agency is an agreement where a buyer and seller are represented by two different agents who work in the same brokerage. Dual agency is an agreement where a single real estate agent represents both the buyer and seller in the same transaction simultaneously as their designated agent.

Buyer agency: In this type of agreement, the agent exclusively represents the buyer. The seller is not represented by the said agent directly or indirectly. Buyer agency can be implied (implication) or written (legal agreement). Under the Real Estate License Act of 2000 in the state of Illinois, buyer and seller agreements are referred to as brokerage agreements, commonly called representation agreements. Nowadays in Illinois, some licensees choose to specialize in only working with buyers or sellers, realizing they can make a choice as to who they represent.

Property management agency: In this type of agency, an agent or firm represents the property owner (landlord). The agent or firm's job is to oversee, maintain, market, lease, and manage a property on behalf of the owner. The management contract is a legal document that sets up and defines the relationship between the sponsoring broker and the owner of a rental property. Property owners employ property managers so they can avoid involvement in the daily property management responsibilities and tasks, as well as those tasks involved with having an office on-site. These tasks may include any variety of obligations but are not limited to: marketing, open houses, maintenance, tenant issues, paperwork, opening/closing the office, ordering repairs, coordinating schedules, etc. The property manager's responsibilities will depend on the terms of the agreement. Regardless, his or her role is to watch over the owner's investment, while working toward maximizing the owner's return and striving to meet the owner's objectives. Are property managers required to have a real estate license? In Illinois, the answer is yes. He/she must also provide their services under the direction and supervision of his or her sponsoring broker.

AGENCY RELATIONSHIP DISCLOSURE

As you know, in Illinois, agency disclosure is of the utmost importance to every consumer. It defines the working relationships between the agent and the consumer. Agency disclosure is required according to The Act.

Real estate licensees must disclose the parties that they respectively represent. This is not optional. It must never be taken casually. When a designated agency is present, before acting as a client's designated agent, he/she must disclose this fact to the client and it must be in writing. The written agreement must include the name/s of the sponsoring broker, designated agent, and client. What's the purpose of this disclosure requirement? First, it helps the client know in whom they are confiding and trusting. Second, it helps the client understand who exactly is acting in their best interest. Third, it is a reminder to the designated agent to maintain the duty of confidentiality and refrain from sharing any confidential information harmful to their client, even with members of their own office.

RESPONSIBILITIES TO THIRD PARTIES

The world of real estate transactions is not a bubble in which only agents and firms exist alongside buyers, sellers, tenants, and landlords. There is also a wide variety of third parties with whom you will interact frequently. A third party is a person or firm involved with the real estate transaction who is not the principal. The principal has a direct interest in the transaction, whereas a third party has an *indirect* interest in the transaction. The current law states that third parties are not owed fiduciary duties by agents, while principals are. Examples of third parties in real estate include escrow companies, lending institutions, home staging companies, property assessors, and so on.

Of course, you already know that the number one responsibility of an agent is always to the principal. Beyond that, the agent may have non-agency responsibilities to third parties who are involved. These may include, but are not limited to, the following:

- Adherence to state and federal real estate laws

- Ethical duties and obligations (from state regulators, professional real estate associations, and so forth)

- Adherence to the brokerage's code of conduct

It should go without saying that your preeminent goal should be responsibility. Be responsible for your words and actions everywhere you go and with whom everyone you speak. Not only do you represent yourself, but you also represent your brokerage and your clients. Plus, your career hinges on your reputation. In light of that, there's a strong argument that your entire career and financial future depend on your honesty and how you treat others.

Errors and Omissions Insurance

Errors and omissions insurance is commonly called E&O insurance or E&O coverage. It is a unique type of insurance commonly used by countless licensees. This type of professional liability insurance may exclude negligent acts other than errors and omissions, commonly called mistakes. It is often acquired by the sponsoring broker as an umbrella policy that the sponsored licensees can buy into. It protects the brokerage and its licensees against negligent actions and activities that are deemed inadequate, which may prompt an injured consumer to file a lawsuit. It also may cover unintentional misrepresentation and inaccurate professional advice. Often, it covers court costs along with any settlements up to the face value of the policy. In other words, E&O coverage provides protective coverage for any claim made against real estate sponsoring brokers and brokers, by reason of an error or omission, regarding his/her performance of professional services. Are all licensees' actions covered by E&O insurance? No. Do not expect that everything will be covered in your brokerage's umbrella policy. Never assume to know what's covered. Do your due diligence. For some licensee activities, an additional premium may be required. It's also possible that he/she will need a separate insurance policy to be issued. Illinois law does not require a sponsoring broker to have E&O insurance, although it is a good business practice to do so.

Sponsoring brokers and licensees must face the fact that claims are possible. Here are some commons scenarios when E&O coverage may protect them:

- Closing transaction delays as a result of the broker's mismanagement

- Discrimination, libel or slander

- Failure of the licensee to advise on a reasonable price

- Failure of the licensee to inspect property

- Listing a property that has an undisclosed structural flaw

- Failure to disclose a lien that is on a property

- Inadequate work

- Accusations of professional negligence

- Failure to provide reports and/or documentation

- Mishandling earnest money, security deposits or other monies

There are countless more scenarios than the ones written above. This is why E&O coverage is needed, necessary, and important. It may protect the licensee from claims that originate from customers, clients, consumers, tenants, and so on. Not only can licensees acquire E&O coverage, but it's also available to appraisers, property managers, and other real estate professionals so they can experience the benefits of its coverage.

E&O coverage does not cover every single type of claim. For example, if a licensee takes an action that is illegal or purposefully chooses to perform a malpractice or offense, E&O does not apply.

What are the most common types of liability claims? While there are no doubt statistics about this, it really comes down to the service or services that each specific licensee offers. Two licensees in the same brokerage may be at risk for drastically different liability issues because of the different nature of the services they each perform. Most licensees oversee a wide array of services which includes but is not limited to advertising, networking, conducting open houses, legal, insurance, and so on. Meeting a client's needs and fulfilling fiduciary duties while needing to fulfill other duties to third parties can be a delicate and sometimes complicated balancing act for each licensee. A licensee is expected to fulfill fiduciary duties while being accurate and truthful in their communications with clients and all other parties who are involved in any capacity.

Furthermore, claims can be made by anybody. This is what makes liability insurance so important. Getting slammed with legal fees without insurance can devastate a licensee's career, reputation, and financial viability. It can impact his/her family and their future financial goals.

Most brokerages offer an umbrella E&O policy. As a licensee, you may be required to participate in the premium cost. To understand the nature of the company policy and the coverage you may be eligible for, you should first check the company policies and procedures manual. After that, have a follow-up conversation with your designated managing broker.

Only services that are viewed in the eyes of the law as "professional services" are able to be insured and might be covered.

"Professional Service" means any personal service which requires as a condition precedent to the rendering thereof the obtaining of a license from a State agency or from the United States Patent Office or the Internal Revenue Service of the United States Treasury Department. (805 ILCS 10/ Professional Service Corporation Act).

Different insurance companies may define what is and is not covered under professional services differently. For example, at times, an insurance company will provide coverage for ancillary professional real estate services. Ancillary services are services that are *in addition to* your work as a licensee and brokerage. Ultimately, a licensee needs to do his/her due diligence and inquire of their designated managing broker as to what the brokerage offers in terms of E&O coverage.

This short chapter was filled with a variety of new terms, ideals, and distinctions. If you want to reread or review this chapter prior to taking your chapter quiz below, please take some time and do that now.

CHAPTER 7 QUIZ

1. The Act states that "a relationship in which a broker or licensee, whether directly or through an affiliated licensee, represents a consumer by the consumer's consent." What is this known as?

    a. Agency

    b. No agency

    c. Power of attorney

    d. Substantive contact

    e. None of the above

2. Which agency relationship is always a fiduciary relationship by nature?

    a. Single agency

    b. Dual agency

    c. Buyer agency

    d. All of the above

3. In which way or ways can agency be created?

    a. Expressed

    b. Implied

    c. Written

    d. Verbal

    e. All of the above

4. Illinois agents actively work on what is known as a presumption of agency, also known as implied agency.

    a. True

    b. False

5. Which word or words accurately fill in the blank? The licensing act is "You are considered to be the agent of the party you are working with, unless some other _____ exists."

    a. Verbal agreement

    b. Written declaration

    c. Substantive contact

    d. No agency

6. When you start a conversation with a consumer, especially a potential buyer, and begin inquiring as to what they are looking for and how you can be of assistance, which of the following best describes that scenario?

    a. Single agency
    b. No agency
    c. Substantive contact
    d. None of the above

7. A no agency relationship means that there is neither a written agreement nor a fiduciary relationship in existence.

    a. True
    b. False

8. In Illinois, agency may be terminated under which of the following circumstances?

    a. Death of the principal
    b. Incapacity of the principal
    c. Breach of contract
    d. All of the above

9. All agents authorized by a principal do have the same privileges and levels of authority.

    a. True
    b. False

10. According to The Act, which term below is defined as a "sponsored licensee named by a sponsoring broker as the legal agent of a client"?

    a. Designated agent
    b. Special agent
    c. General agent
    d. Universal agent

11. What is present when one agent, broker, or firm represents the interests of either one seller or one buyer?

    a. Property management agency
    b. Dual agency
    c. Single agency
    d. Buyer agency

12. With a first-year license, Sarah just asked a consumer to sign a dual agency representation. To her surprise, the consumer declined to do so. What can Sarah do?

    a. Create a single agency
    b. Withdraw with liability
    c. Withdraw with no liability
    d. Nothing

13. This is an agreement where a buyer and seller in the same transaction are represented by two different agents who work at the same brokerage.

    a. Buyer agency
    b. Property management agency
    c. Designated agency
    d. No agency

14. In Illinois, which is accurate concerning agency disclosure?

    a. It is exceptionally important.
    b. It defines the working relationships between the agent and the client.
    c. It is required according to The Act.
    d. All of the above

15. What's the purpose of the agency disclosure requirement?

    a. Assurance that all the other sponsored licensees that work in the same company do not obtain information that is confidential or private in nature
    b. To fulfill the law
    c. To stay in alignment with The Act
    d. All of the above

16. Are property managers required to have a real estate license in Illinois?

    a. No
    b. Yes
    c. Only if by direct request from the owner
    d. It depends on the county where the property is located

17. As the property manager, which action can he/she most likely not perform?

    a. Oversee the property
    b. Sell the property
    c. Market the property
    d. Lease the property
    e. None of the above

18. Buyer agency can be which of the following?

    a. Implied
    b. Express
    c. A and B
    d. Buyer agency is expressly prohibited by The Act.

19. Special agents are authorized to represent the principal in multiple business transactions.

    a. True
    b. False

20. Which of the following licensee designations would not be responsible for the fiduciary duties defined under agency law?

    a. A general agent acting as a designated agent
    b. Secret agent
    c. Special agent acting as a designated agent
    d. Designated agent

CHAPTER 8:

BROKERAGES, ILLINOIS LICENSES, AND OFFICE CULTURE

LEARNING GOALS:

By the end of this lesson, you will:

- Understand different types of brokerages
- Know the four levels of real estate licenses in Illinois
- Have a working knowledge of brokerage company culture and office dynamics
- Understand business planning and goal setting

TYPES OF BROKERAGES

As you learned earlier, a brokerage is a real estate company that represents buyers, sellers, landlords, and/or tenants in the pursuit of real estate possibilities. It is also the business or service of acting as a broker. You can view it as the connecting point between brokers and other parties. Its primary responsibility is to act as a middleman, bringing buyers and sellers together in order to facilitate a transaction. The properties bought and sold may be industrial, residential, commercial, agricultural, and special purpose.

Brokerage businesses may be legally structured as one of the following: Sole proprietorship (a company owned by one person), partnership, LLC (limited liability company), or corporation. Two main categories of brokerages are independent and franchises. Brokerage offices come in many varieties with different characteristics. It may be an independent office that is a "stand-alone" office that has no sister offices. An office may be part of a franchise that boasts multiple branches in one or more cities or states. Participation in a franchise commonly provides the licensee with regional or national exposure, credibility, marketing assets, and built-in systems. Transactions handled within a brokerage could be a wide variety of services, or it may only focus on offering one specific type of service or transaction.

FOUR LEVELS OF REAL ESTATE LICENSES

As you know, in order to purchase, exchange, or lease real property for other parties and receive compensation, a real estate license is always required by law.

Illinois has four levels of real estate licenses. They consist of:

1. Sponsoring broker

2. Designated managing broker

3. Broker

4. Residential leasing agent

Let's explore each license. Additionally, you will learn each one's scope of practice. Scope of practice describes the services that real estate professionals are deemed competent to perform and which actions they are permitted to take, all while staying in alignment and agreement with the terms of their professional license. Scope of practice encompasses processes, procedures, and actions that he/she is able to perform. All licensees must observe, respect, and honor the scope of practice.

1. Sponsoring broker

As you read earlier, in Illinois, each and every licensee is directly engaged by a sponsoring broker. This is a state law. A licensee must be sponsored by a sponsoring broker in order to acquire and maintain a real estate license in his or her state. The licensee will participate and offer brokerage services on behalf of the sponsoring broker.

Here are the two definitions of a sponsoring broker:

> "Sponsoring broker means the broker who certifies to the Department his, her, or its sponsorship of a licensed managing broker, broker, or a residential leasing agent." (225 ILCS 454/1-10)

> "Sponsoring broker means a person who operates a corporation, limited liability company, partnership, limited partnership, or limited liability partnership that is licensed by the Department, or an individual with a managing broker license who operates as a sole proprietor." (Section 1450.100 of the Rules And Regulations)

The sponsored licensees can be brokers, managing brokers, and/or leasing agents. The sponsoring broker can be an individual or a legal entity such as a corporation or LLC. More often than not, the sponsoring broker is a legal entity. It becomes the name of the entity under which all sponsored licensees conduct business.

The law also outlines clear expectations for sponsoring brokers. A sponsoring broker takes responsibility for supervising sponsored licensees through the designated manager broker. The sponsoring broker is required to provide assistance, support, and mentorship to all sponsored licensees in the realm of marketing, client relationships, and other business topics.

2. Designated managing broker

> "Designated managing broker means a managing broker who has supervisory responsibilities for licensees in one or, in the case of a multi-office company, more than one office and who has been appointed as such by the sponsoring broker registered with the Department." (225 ILCS 454/1-10)

Concerning designated managing brokers, The Act in 225 ILCS 454/10-55 states:

Designated managing broker responsibility and supervision.

A. A designated managing broker shall be responsible for the supervision of all licensees associated with a designated managing broker's office. A designated managing broker's responsibility includes implementation of company policies, the training of licensees and other employees on the company's policies as well as on relevant provisions of this Act, and providing assistance to all licensees in real estate transactions. The designated managing broker shall be responsible for, and shall supervise, all special accounts of the company.

B. A designated managing broker's responsibilities shall further include directly handling all earnest money, escrows, and contract negotiations for all transactions where the designated agent for the transaction has not completed his or her 45 hours of post-license education, as well as the approval of all advertisements involving a licensee who has not completed his or her 45 hours of post-license education. Licensees that have not completed their 45 hours of post-license education shall have no authority to bind the sponsoring broker.

A licensed designated managing broker has the supervisory responsibility for all of the licensees within their office. If the designated managing broker is supervising more than one office, then they would take on this role with all of their sponsored licensees. As the designated managing broker, they have the capability of performing all of the duties that their licensees undertake on behalf of the client. In addition, the designated managing broker must assume responsibility for oversight and direction of their sponsored licensees with regard to office policy and procedures.

Under Illinois law, an individual holding a managing broker's license is capable of fulfilling one of the three following activities:

1. Work as a broker under the supervision and direction of a designated managing broker.

2. Take responsibility to manage a real estate office on behalf of a designated managing broker and supervise all licensees associated with that office.

3. Start and own their own company.

C. Managing brokers are not required to be the owner/s. They may or may not be the owner. However, managing brokers are required by law to supervise each leasing agent and oversee the office. When it comes down to it, the managing broker is 100% responsible for the actions of the leasing agents. Leasing agents are employees. Managing brokers are the supervisors. All of this is within the context of the particular firms.

3. Broker

According to The Act, a "broker means an individual, entity, corporation, foreign or domestic partnership, limited liability company, registered limited liability partnership, or other business entity other than a residential leasing agent who, whether in person or through any media or technology, for another and for compensation, or with the intention or expectation of receiving compensation, either directly or indirectly:

1. Sells, exchanges, purchases, rents, or leases real estate.

2. Offers to sell, exchange, purchase, rent, or lease real estate.

3. Negotiates, offers, attempts, or agrees to negotiate the sale, exchange, purchase, rental, or leasing of real estate.

4. Lists, offers, attempts, or agrees to list real estate for sale, rent, lease, or exchange.

5. Whether for another or themselves, engages in a pattern of business of buying, selling, offering to buy or sell, marketing for sale, exchanging, or otherwise dealing in contracts, including assignable contracts for the purchase or sale of, or options on real estate or improvements thereon. For purposes of this definition, an individual or entity will be found to have engaged in a pattern of business if the individual or entity by itself or with any combination of other individuals or entities, whether as partners or common owners in another entity, has engaged in one or more of these practices on two or more occasions in any twelve-month period.

6. Supervises the collection, offer, attempt, or agreement to collect rent for the use of real estate.

7. Advertises or represents himself or herself as being engaged in the business of buying, selling, exchanging, renting, or leasing real estate.

8. Assists or directs in procuring or referring of leads or prospects, intended to result in the sale, exchange, lease, or rental of real estate.

9. Assists or directs in the negotiation of any transaction intended to result in the sale, exchange, lease, or rental of real estate.

10. Opens real estate to the public for marketing purposes.

11. Sells, rents, leases, or offers for sale or lease real estate at auction." (225 ILCS 454/1-10)

Brokers are licensed professionals who help people buy, sell, and/or rent real estate property. They serve as an intermediary between the parties they represent. They create, manage, and oversee the required legal paperwork in order to complete real estate transactions.

4. Residential leasing agent

In Illinois, leasing is considered a real estate activity. A residential leasing agent is a licensee who is employed by a sponsoring broker to engage in licensed activities limited to leasing *residential* real estate. Any leasing of *commercial* properties always requires a broker's or managing broker's license.

In simple terms, residential leasing agents work closely with the owners of the property in order to effectively market the property and achieve the property owner's objectives. These efforts attract new tenants/renters. Marketing may include any combination of offline and digital, including but not limited to: flyers, networking, offline and online advertisement, signs, social media, speaking engagements, community events, fairs, open houses, and/or any other type of promotion. Beyond that, they also give guidance, advice, and insights to renters in helping them find and lease properties.

Residential leasing agents are not self-employed. They may or may not be independent contractors. They always represent and act on behalf of the sponsoring broker/designated managing broker. Each residential leasing agent is expected to conduct brokerage services on behalf of the property owner/s. Similar to how employees in other industries are managed by supervisors/managers, leasing agents are directly supervised by the designated managing broker/s.

Although residential leasing agent responsibilities can vary, here are common responsibilities:

- Assist property owner in navigating the difficult and ever-changing nature of the property market

- Oversee all paperwork, including the signing of leases

- Serve as a landlord to the tenants

- Act on behalf of property owner

- Oversee marketing and advertising efforts in order to gain new tenants

- Show property/units to potential tenants and answer questions they have

BROKERAGE COMPANY CULTURE AND OFFICE DYNAMICS

Phrases like company culture, corporate culture, and organizational culture are mostly used interchangeably. Getting technical, company culture and corporate culture generally refer to a for-profit business. Organizational culture is commonly used for nonprofits. Still, in everyday language, the phrases mean the same thing. What's that? They mean the overall shared characteristics, qualities, and values of a business or organization. Some people use words like the company's vibe or energy. Licensees use the phrases to describe what it's like operating in the specific brokerage in which he/she works. Just as regions of the US vary from one another, likewise, company culture varies from brokerage to brokerage.

When starting out, it is helpful to learn about the company cultures of different brokerages.

Although the mechanics of how the brokerages work are the same, office cultures can differ drastically. Some brokerages may be more do-it-yourself and entrepreneurial, while other brokerages are highly supportive with training and mentorship. There's no right or wrong type of brokerage company culture. However, when you are starting your career, it is smart to seek out a brokerage that has a company culture that fits with how you're wired and that works well with your personality type.

Office dynamics center on how people in the brokerage communicate and function together. Just like anywhere else you have worked in the past, each brokerage has its own unique office dynamics. As you can imagine, licensee duties and obligations can be very fast paced. At times, the office may feel like a whirlwind of people coming and going, phone calls, text messages, emails, meetings, and paperwork. The real estate business is not for the faint of heart, as you can tell. In many ways, office dynamics always come down to people and projects. There's constant interaction between people and projects. All of those revolve around the most important skill in life—communication.

Each brokerage should have a handbook. Inside it, you will find all the company policies. Most of the time, there are also guidelines focused on office dynamics, behavior, and more.

The company policies in the handbook are to be known, understood, and followed by all agents. In 225 ILCS 454/10-40 of The Act, it states:

A. Company policy. Every brokerage company or entity, other than a sole proprietorship with no other sponsored licensees, shall adopt a company or office policy dealing with topics such as:

1. The agency policy of the entity

2. Fair housing, nondiscrimination, and harassment

3. Confidentiality of client information

4. Advertising

5. Training and supervision of sponsored licensees

6. Required disclosures and use of forms

7. Handling of risk management matters

8. Handling of earnest money and escrows

These topics are provided as an example and are not intended to be inclusive or exclusive of other topics. (225 ILCS 454/10-40)

One aspect of office dynamics that cannot be ignored is that of "water cooler talk." You have probably heard of the phrase before. It is defined as talking about confidential information about a client when you're with other brokers, in the office or involved in a business meeting. Although it is common to discuss non-work-related topics with coworkers, the focus here is on discussing matters that are confidential in nature. The license law was written with a primary intent to "protect the public." Within this law is the presumption that you will protect your clients' confidential information. Real estate licensees are social individuals and have been known to build close relationships with coworkers in the office. Inherent to that is the possibility that there may be what some people call "water cooler conversations." Frequently during these conversations, there may be idle chatter about what the licensees are doing, who they are working with, and so on. Remember, idle conversation can result in what may be considered innocent conversation, but in fact, these conversations can cause certain facts regarding your clients to come up and you never know if that friend, the other licensee, may actually have a buyer looking at our client's home. This means you just gave away information that could help the buyer, but harm the seller. That is why water cooler conversations and disclosing confidential information directly violates the licensee's duty of care and loyalty defined by the fiduciary duties.

BUSINESS PLANNING AND GOAL SETTING

Brokerages exist to facilitate real estate transactions. That is how they make money. Company policies and brokerage handbooks exist to help everyone involved know the rules to follow, know what to do in certain situations, and understand how to behave and conduct themselves. That brings us to the next topic, which is business planning. Now that all the ingredients are together in the same place, it's time to take action and *make* something happen. The foundation of business planning is having solid business skills.

It will come as no surprise to you that a wide variety of business skills are essential for a fulfilling and profitable career in real estate. Of all the industries in the US, there is a solid argument that real estate is one of the most demanding industries of all. Your skills encompass numbers, local knowledge, people skills, working with a variety of people with different backgrounds and personalities, staying up to date on trends, continuing education, managing your energy, and more.

One of the most essential business skills is setting goals. A goal is an idea of the future. It's the desired result that you want. It is an idea that you want to turn into reality. Goals are envisioned, planned, and lived out through action, all in order to achieve the desired result. Business professionals endeavor to reach goals within a finite time by setting deadlines. As you know, goals are essential for success. Depending on you, how you're wired, and where you work, you may have different goals than other agents. Also, goals will change and shift over time. Why don't people always achieve their goals? Any number of obstacles, whether external or internal, can deter or stop someone from reaching their goals. These goal killers include, but are not limited to, the following: vague goals, perfectionism, procrastination, not taking full responsibility, listening to anyone who discourages you, saying yes to too many projects, having a negative mindset, surrounding yourself with the wrong people, giving in to distractions (such as social media, TV, etc.), fear of success, fear of failure, not understanding the process of setting goals, lack of commitment, analysis paralysis, failure to plan, having too many goals, and so forth. Thus, one of your main goals is to be mindful of anything that can stop you from achieving your goals.

Here's a simple framework for goal creation and achievement:

1. Begin with the vision. What do you want to achieve? What do you want to see happen? Divide your vision into segments: Daily, weekly, monthly, quarterly, yearly, and five years from now.

2. Set a time limit. Do this for each goal. Since some goals are bigger than others, they may take anywhere from one hour to one year or longer to complete. However, having a deadline is essential.

3. Create an action plan for each goal. The action plan will consist of the steps to reach each goal. Small steps done consistently add up over time. The critical key to achieving your goals is to break them down into actionable, doable steps.

4. Track your actions daily. Without tracking, you are speculating or making assumptions. Track your leads. Track your calls. Track everything that is important. Some professionals call these key performance indicators (KPIs). They are what can make or break a business and a career.

5. Review your action plan weekly. Ask yourself clarifying questions like: Am I on track? If I'm not on track, what is getting in the way? How do I diminish or remove what's getting in the way, so I can focus on what's truly important?

6. Celebrate milestones and successes!

Ultimately, you want to pay special attention to how you are specifically wired. Do you perform best alone or on teams? Do you perform best with or without an accountability partner? How can you play to your strengths if you're an extrovert or an introvert? Customizing your approach to how you're personally wired will empower you to achieve your goals faster and more effectively.

Now it's time for your chapter quiz.

CHAPTER 8 QUIZ

1. How does a brokerage firm function?

    a. A middleman
    b. A connecting point
    c. A broker
    d. All of the above
    e. None of the above

2. A brokerage may only be legally structured as a partnership or an LLC.

    a. True
    b. False

3. Two main categories of brokerages are independent and franchises.

    a. True
    b. False

4. In order for a broker to qualify to become a managing broker, he/she must be a broker for a minimum of how many years?

    a. One
    b. Two
    c. Three
    d. Four
    e. Experience as a broker is not required.

5. How many levels of real estate licenses does Illinois currently have?

    a. Three
    b. Four
    c. Five
    d. Six

6. Which word means the services that real estate professionals are deemed competent to perform and which actions they are permitted to take, all while staying in alignment and agreement with the terms of their professional license?

    a. Company handbook
    b. Fiduciary
    c. Legal requirements
    d. Scope of practice

7. In Illinois, each and every licensee is directly engaged by which of the following?

    a. Sponsoring broker
    b. Brokerage owner
    c. Property owner
    d. Company president

8. Which of the following actions may be performed by a residential leasing agent?

    a. Assist property owner in navigating the difficult and ever-changing nature of the property market
    b. Oversee all paperwork, including the signing of leases
    c. Serve as a landlord to the tenants
    d. All of the above

9. According to The Act, whose responsibilities "include directly handling all earnest money, escrows, advertisement approvals, and contract negotiations for all transactions where the designated agent for the transaction has not completed his or her 45 hours of post-license education" by the license renewal date?

    a. Designated agent
    b. Sponsoring broker
    c. Designated managing broker
    d. Leasing agent

10. According to The Act, which term "means an individual, entity, corporation, foreign or domestic partnership, limited liability company, registered limited liability partnership, or other business entity other than a residential leasing agent who, whether in person or through any media or technology, for another and for compensation, or with the intention or expectation of receiving compensation, either directly or indirectly"?

    a. Broker
    b. Sponsoring broker
    c. Designated managing broker
    d. All of the above
    e. None of the above

11. Any leasing of commercial properties always requires a managing broker's or broker's license.

    a. True
    b. False

12. Licensed residential leasing agents may be employed or independent contractors depending on the policy of the sponsoring broker.

    a. True
    b. False

13. The phrases company culture, corporate culture, and organizational culture are mostly used interchangeably in every language.

    a. True
    b. False

14. Almost all brokerages have the same company culture.

    a. True
    b. False

15. In The Act, "every brokerage company or entity, other than a sole proprietorship with no other sponsored licensees, shall adopt a company or office policy dealing with" which topics?

    a. The agency policy of the entity
    b. Confidentiality of client information
    c. Required disclosures and use of forms
    d. All of the above
    e. None of the above

16. You're chatting with Mike in the break room one day in the brokerage. The conversation quickly turns to clients. He says, "The Johnson family on 15th Avenue are loaded! I had no idea. Their net worth is 1.4 million." What just happened?

    a. Mike broke his fiduciary duties by disclosing confidential information that could harm his client's negotiating position.
    b. Harmless water cooler talk
    c. Office gossip
    d. A and B

17. Disclosing confidential information directly violates which of the following?

    a. The licensee's duty of care and loyalty
    b. The licensee's fiduciary duties
    c. The brokerage's handbook
    d. All of the above

18. What is a simple and common starting point when creating a goal?

    a. Start with the vision
    b. Consider how much time it will take
    c. Consider how much money it will take
    d. None of the above

19. When setting goals, what is important to consider?

    a. How you are wired
    b. Whether you perform best alone or on a team
    c. Your strengths as an extrovert or an introvert
    d. All of the above
    e. None of the above

20. KPIs are also known in the context of business planning and goals as which of the following?

    a. Keeping People Involved
    b. Key Profit Indicators
    c. Key Performance Indicators
    d. Key Profit Initiative

CHAPTER 9:

SHOW ME
THE MONEY!
(COMPENSATION)

LEARNING GOALS:

By the end of this lesson, you will:

- Have a strong overview of compensation
- See how compensation works
- Know different responsibilities parties have
- Understand how compensation works on teams

EVEN IF YOU LOVE THE CAREER PATH you've chosen or the one you're moving toward, the ultimate goal of a business is to generate revenue. In this chapter, we'll talk about several important aspects of compensation. As referenced earlier, The Act states that "compensation is defined as the valuable consideration given by one person or entity to another person or entity in exchange for the performance of some activity or service" (225 ILCS 454/1-10). Examples of what is considered to be compensation as defined by The Act can be found in Chapter 8. In 225 ILCS 454/10-5 of The Act, compensation is covered in detail. Much of what follows will come directly from The Act.

EXCERPTS FROM THE ACT CONCERNING COMPENSATION

While acting in the capacity of a licensee, there are certain provisions the law looks at with regard to your brokerage activities.

A. Payment of compensation

1. No sponsored licensee shall pay compensation directly to a licensee sponsored by another sponsoring broker for the performance of licensed activities.

2. All compensation earned in a real estate transaction, whether a sale, lease, or property management, shall be paid directly to the sponsoring broker of the listing office. No licensee sponsored by a broker may pay compensation to any licensee other than his or her sponsoring broker for the performance of licensed activities unless the licensee paying the compensation is a principal to the transaction.

3. However, a non-sponsoring broker may pay compensation directly to a licensee sponsored by another or a person who is not sponsored by a broker if the payments are made pursuant to terms of an employment agreement that was previously in place between a licensee and the non-sponsoring broker, and the payments are for licensed activity performed by that person while previously sponsored by the now non-sponsoring broker. (If you were previously sponsored by Company A, and you leave them to join another company before a pending sale closes, your prior sponsoring broker has the right to pay you the commission you are due directly. It does not have to be paid to the new sponsoring broker.)

4. No licensee sponsored by a broker shall accept compensation for the performance of activities under this Act except from the broker by whom the licensee is sponsored, except as provided in this Section.

5. One sponsoring broker may pay compensation directly to another sponsoring broker for the performance of licensed activities.

6. Notwithstanding any other provision of this Act, a sponsoring broker may pay compensation to a person currently licensed under the Auction License Act who is in compliance with and providing services under Section 5-32 of this Act.

B. Disclosure of compensation

1. A licensee must disclose to a client the sponsoring broker's compensation and policy with regard to cooperating with brokers who represent other parties in a transaction.

2. A licensee must disclose to a client all sources of compensation related to the transaction received by the licensee from a third party.

3. If a licensee refers a client to a third party in which the licensee has greater than a 1% ownership interest or from which the licensee receives or may receive dividends or other profit-sharing distributions, other than a publicly held or traded company, for the purpose of the client obtaining services related to the transaction, then the licensee shall disclose that fact to the client at the time of making the referral. (The intent of this provision is to ensure that the client is aware there might be additional compensation to the licensee because of the use of an affiliated entity.)

4. If in any one transaction a sponsoring broker receives compensation from both the buyer and seller or lessee and lessor of real estate, the sponsoring broker shall disclose in writing to a client the fact that the compensation is being paid by both buyer and seller or lessee and lessor. In addition, a licensee must secure written authorization to act in a dual agency capacity from each client prior to taking such action.

5. Nothing in The Act shall prohibit the cooperation with or a payment of compensation to an individual domiciled in any other state or country who is licensed as a broker (salesperson) in his or her state or country of domicile or to a resident of a country that does not require a person to be licensed to act as a broker if the person complies with the laws of the country in which that person resides and practices there as a broker.

C. No compensation to persons in violation of Act; compensation to unlicensed persons; consumer.

1. No compensation may be paid to any unlicensed person in exchange for the person performing licensed activities in violation of this Act.

2. No action or suit shall be instituted, nor recovery therein be had, in any court of this State by any person for compensation for any act done or service performed, the doing or performing of which is prohibited by this Act to other than licensed managing brokers, brokers, or residential leasing agents unless the person was duly licensed hereunder as a managing broker, broker, or residential leasing agent under this Act at the time that any such act was done or service performed that would give rise to a cause of action for compensation.

3. A licensee may offer compensation, including prizes, merchandise, services, rebates, discounts, or other consideration to an unlicensed person who is a party to a contract to buy or sell real estate or is a party to a contract for the lease of real estate, so long as the offer complies with the provisions of subdivision (35) of subsection (a) of Section 20-20 of this Act.

4. A licensee may offer cash, gifts, prizes, awards, coupons, merchandise, rebates or chances to win a game of chance, if not prohibited by any other law or statute, to a consumer as an inducement to that consumer to use the services of the licensee even if the licensee and consumer do not ultimately enter into a broker-client relationship so long as the offer complies with the provisions of subdivision (35) of subsection (a) of Section 20-20 of this Act.

5. A licensee shall not pay compensation to an unlicensed person who is not or will not become a party to a real estate transaction in exchange for a referral of real estate services.

6. Nothing in this Section shall be construed as waiving or abrogating the provisions of the Real Estate Settlement Procedures Act (RESPA), 88 Stat. 1724. (225 ILCS 454/10-5)

HOW DO INDEPENDENT CONTRACTOR AND EMPLOYEE AGREEMENTS WORK?

Independent contractors have been a frequently discussed topic in the news over the last few years. The Act states the following regarding employment or independent contractor agreements.

"Every sponsoring broker must have a written employment or independent contractor agreement with each licensee the broker sponsors. The agreement shall address the employment or independent contractor relationship terms, including without limitation supervision, duties, compensation, and termination process. Notwithstanding the fact that a sponsoring broker has an employment or independent contractor agreement with a licensee, a sponsoring broker may pay compensation directly to a business entity solely owned by that licensee that has been formed for the purpose of receiving compensation earned by the licensee. A business entity that receives compensation from a sponsoring broker as provided for in this subsection (e) shall not be required to be licensed under this Act and must either be owned solely by the licensee or by the licensee together with the licensee's spouse, but only if the spouse and licensee are both licensed and sponsored by the same sponsoring broker or the spouse is not also licensed." (225 ILCS 454/10-20)

In the same section, The Act continues with the following:

Sponsoring broker; employment agreement.

a. A licensee may perform activities as a licensee only for his or her sponsoring broker. A licensee must have only one sponsoring broker at any one time.

b. Every broker who employs licensees or has an independent contractor relationship with a licensee shall have a written employment or independent contractor agreement with each such licensee. The broker having this written employment or independent contractor agreement with the licensee must be that licensee's sponsoring broker.

c. Every sponsoring broker must have a written employment or independent contractor agreement with each licensee the broker sponsors. The agreement shall address the employment or independent contractor relationship terms, including without limitation supervision, duties, compensation, and termination process.

d. (Blank).

e. Notwithstanding the fact that a sponsoring broker has an employment or independent contractor agreement with a licensee, a sponsoring broker may pay compensation directly to a business entity solely owned by that licensee that has been formed for the purpose of receiving compensation earned by the licensee. A business entity that receives compensation from a sponsoring broker as provided for in this subsection (e) shall not be required to be licensed under this Act and must either be owned solely by the licensee or by the licensee together with the licensee's spouse, but only if the spouse and licensee are both licensed and sponsored by the same sponsoring broker or the spouse is not also licensed. (225 ILCS 454/10-20)

EMPLOYMENT AND INDEPENDENT CONTRACTOR AGREEMENT COMPENSATION

Compensation is always outlined in a written agreement. By law, there must be a written employment/independent contractor agreement between every sponsoring broker and the licensees that he/she engages. This includes licensed personal assistants and non-practicing licensees. Regardless of the position held or title given, there must be a relationship agreement between the licensee and the sponsoring broker. As with other agreements, this legal contract defines the working relationship and outlines important details, such as compensation, responsibilities, rights, supervision, and termination. It must also be dated and signed by each of the parties. The sponsored licensees must be given an executed copy of this agreement.

Personal Assistants

It has been proven that using a personal assistant can substantially increase a licensee's income. Hiring a personal assistant can free up a broker's time so he or she can focus on more revenue-producing activities. The broker is able to delegate administrative tasks that would normally take up a significant amount of their time. This new freedom creates a greater time margin that allows the broker to meet with potential clients and generate business opportunities.

What are the advantages and disadvantages of utilizing a licensed personal assistant as compared to an unlicensed personal assistant? Let's look.

Employing an unlicensed personal assistant holds many advantages and disadvantages. The list includes but is not limited to the following:

- Advantages
    - May draft advertising copy and promotional materials for the licensee to review and approve
    - Placement of marketing materials with local vendors
    - Receive phone messages
    - Assist at an open house by managing visitors until the licensee is available to show them the property.
    - Basic administrative work
    - Online research
- Disadvantages
    - Cannot legally interface with consumers

- Cannot schedule appointments for the broker

- Must be paid a salary

- Cannot share in commissions

- Are compensated directly by the broker they support

- Broker must deduct, and when necessary, match tax withholdings

Section 1450.740 outlines which advertising activities unlicensed real estate assistants of a licensee can perform:

- He/she may place advertising

- He/she may place signage in front of listed properties

- He/she may develop marketing resources to enhance the licensee's activities

Engaging a licensed personal assistant holds many advantages and disadvantages as well. The list includes but is not limited to the following:

- Advantages

- Can be compensated either by commission and/or salary

- Is legally qualified to interface with consumers

- Is qualified to physically show properties and conduct open houses on their own

- Negotiate the sale

- Administrative work including paperwork concerning contracts, agreements, and disclosures

- Receive phone messages and give consumers information and/or answers over the phone

- Disadvantages

- Frequently, he/she is an independent contractor

- Must be compensated by a sponsoring broker

- Are required to have a written contract with the sponsoring broker

- Can become your next competitor and know the ins and outs of your business

BROKERAGE AGREEMENT COMPENSATION

In 225 ILCS 454/1-10 of The Act, it states the following:

> "Brokerage agreement" means a written or oral agreement between a sponsoring broker and a consumer for licensed activities to be provided to a consumer in return for compensation or the right to receive compensation from another. Brokerage agreements may constitute either a bilateral or a unilateral agreement between the broker and the broker's client depending upon the content of the brokerage agreement. All exclusive brokerage agreements shall be in writing.

This section states that each and every exclusive brokerage agreement must:

1. Be in writing

2. Must specify the required minimum services to be given to the consumer

In an exclusive right to sell listing agreement, a single licensee is designated as the seller's sole representative. This specific licensee has the exclusive right to market the property of the seller. In this type of agreement, only one authorized sponsoring broker receives compensation. This takes place regardless of whether the licensee or the seller makes the sale.

In a net listing agreement, the property seller sets a minimum price for which he/she is willing to sell the specified property. This minimum price would also include any closing costs and mortgage amounts that need to be satisfied as part of the sale. The licensee has the ability to offer the property at a price higher than the net amount the seller agreed to. Whatever amount above that minimum selling price that the licensee manages to bring in, the difference becomes his/her commission. In other words, the licensee keeps all compensation that is above the sale price. A net listing is legal in Illinois, although it is illegal in several other states in the US. In Illinois, net listings are highly discouraged due to the fact that there is a high potential for fraud to take place. Although legal, we view net listing agreements as unethical.

The cooperative commission refers to the sharing of commissions between brokers when one represents the interests of the seller and the other represents the interest of the buyer. In the residential sector, it is more common for brokers to share a commission that ultimately is paid by the seller. This results in few written buyer representation agreements being exercised. In the commercial realm, there are limited cooperative relationships as compared to the residential realm. This creates a higher probability that the buyer is going to have to compensate their own broker. The net result is fewer opportunities for cooperative broker sharing of commissions. At times, you may hear the phrase "sales force compensation." Know that phrase is a synonym for cooperative commission.

COMMISSION STRUCTURES

The commission structures are negotiable between the client paying the commission and the sponsoring broker receiving the commission. Based upon the application of the antitrust provisions, there is no standard commission rate that the industry charges the client. Every situation is unique. This results in a unique cooperative relationship to establish the fee that the sponsoring broker will earn while representing the client.

In the residential industry, it is a common practice between cooperating members of the MLS to share commissions. However, a client must grant consent *before* a broker can offer to share commissions with other sponsored brokers.

Consider this. A real estate office has ten agents. If each licensee is currently working with seven A-quality buyers, the office represents a total of seventy buyers. However, the office belongs to the MLS and it has 30,000 licensees participating. If each of those agents also represents seven buyers, that results in 210,000 potential buyers having access to your client's property. Your job is to market the property in the pursuit of a qualified buyer. Would you rather rely on the seventy buyers your office represents or the 210,000 potential buyers the MLS represents?

In the commercial industry, there is not a structured MLS like the residential industry enjoys. The net result is the broker representing the buyer frequently needs to negotiate and confirm the sharing of commission in writing *before* scheduling a showing.

Even though there is a presumption of commission sharing, not only does the seller need to grant the consent, but the seller also deserves to know what the commission split is going to be.

Diagram 9.1 below provides a simple example of how the commissions are generally shared between the two cooperating brokers involved in the transaction. By no means should this diagram be considered a definitive answer with regard to the sharing of commissions. There are many cases when, as the agent of the buyer, you might actually have to negotiate your share of the commission that would be payable, should your buyer prove to be the successful purchaser of the property. Always remember that any commission rate needs to be approved by the sponsoring broker, through the designated managing broker.

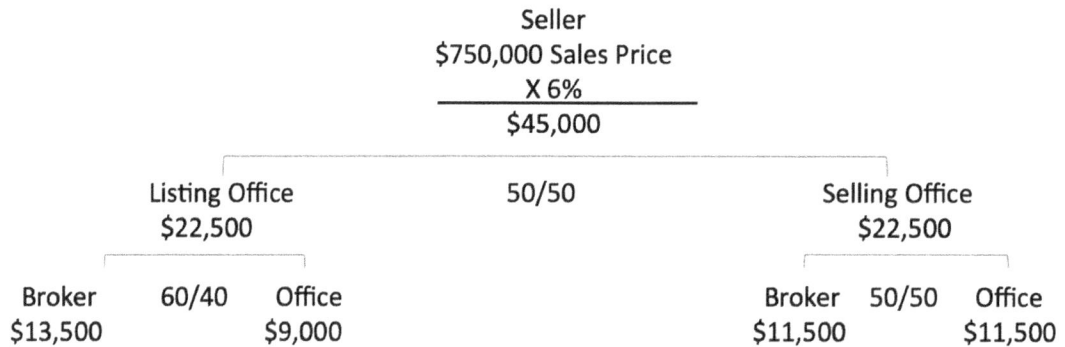

```
                            Seller
                      $750,000 Sales Price
                            X 6%
                     _____
                           $45,000

       Listing Office              50/50              Selling Office
         $22,500                                        $22,500

  Broker    60/40    Office                    Broker    50/50    Office
  $13,500            $9,000                    $11,500            $11,500
```

Diagram 9.1

The commissions earned by licensees vary from brokerage to brokerage. At the discretion of the designated managing broker, they are negotiable. Commissions are based on a property's selling price.

Examples of commission structures include the following in no particular order:

1. **A 100% commission split model**. In this model, the licensee pays all of his or her office and business expenses. This is done so he/she can keep 100% of the commissions from his or her sales. This does not necessarily mean the licensee can work on their own. They may still be required by law to be sponsored by a separate sponsoring broker.

2. **Production-based splits**. A certain percentage (split) is set initially. Let's say 40/60. The licensee gets 40% and the sponsoring broker gets 60%. This keeps happening until a specific production benchmark is achieved by the licensee. Let's say the benchmark is $30K. Once that is reached, then the percentage may go from 40/60 to 50/50. Once the next benchmark is reached—say $60K—then the percentage changes again. For example, it may go from 50/50 to 60/40. The licensee gets 60% and the sponsoring broker gets 40%. High producers can do exceptionally well and do so fairly quickly in this type of structure. This is not a standard commission split, but merely an example to illustrate the potential relationship you may have with your sponsoring broker. When you are interviewing for a brokerage office in the future, it's important that you inquire about the standard commission platform offered by the specific sponsoring broker.

3. **Cooperative transactions**: Let's define what this means, as it's not a term you hear on a regular basis. These transactions are commonplace in the real estate market. When

you assume the responsibility as the designated agent for a selling client, your duty is to market the property in a manner consistent with securing a buyer who is ready, willing, and able. In order to accomplish this, you need to use every marketing tool available, which would include the MLS. Imagine you currently are working with ten buyers yourself, and there are fifteen licensees in the office, each working with ten buyers. That provides you with 150 potential buyers. Compare that number to the over 210,000 buyers that may be represented by cooperating (co-op) brokers on the MLS. It only makes sense that you would seek cooperation from all of these co-op brokers to satisfy the needs of your seller client in finding a buyer who is ready, willing, and able.

4. **Franchise**: As noted above, a franchise affiliation provides additional exposure and resources which can increase both your sales volume and market recognition. As a result, the master franchisor (the entity that owns the franchise name), charges a certain percentage fee off the top. Money goes to them first before it's paid out to the sponsoring brokers and licensees.

5. **Salary**: Although not very common, some brokerages use a salary-based compensation plan. Usually, these brokerages employ a model called "fixed fee" and "fee for a service."

TEAMS AND COMPENSATION

Team members are usually compensated in one of four ways. From most common to least common, the compensation plan may consist of:

- Percentage-based
- Performance-based
- Flat rate
- Or some type of combination

The majority of licensees work for percentage-based compensation. When you walk into a brokerage office and encounter the administrative staff, it is likely that they are salaried, and working for an hourly rate. Performance-based means a licensee has agreed that his/her compensation is defined by his/her production.

Regardless of the agreement amongst the team members regarding commission splits, all compensation must flow through the sponsoring broker. The team can mutually define how the commission will be distributed. There are a variety of compensation plans for the team members to agree upon. Any and all compensation due to a team member must be paid through the sponsoring broker. Team members cannot compensate one another. Any agreement regarding the distribution of commission between the team members must be in writing and agreed to by the sponsoring broker. Distribution of said compensation would also be handled by the sponsoring broker, as "brokers may never pay brokers directly."

OTHER FACTS ABOUT COMPENSATION

Who can legally collect compensation in a real estate transaction in Illinois? The answer is only the sponsoring broker. After that, he/she can distribute the compensation to the licensee or licensees who were part of making the transaction possible.

In Section 1450.755, called recordkeeping, the Rules And Regulations state that "a sponsoring broker shall keep, or cause to be kept, escrow records, transaction records, and employment agreements and records reflecting the payment of compensation, as set forth in this Section. Records reflecting the payment of compensation for the performance of licensed activities shall be maintained for five years."

It's time for you to test your knowledge about compensation.

CHAPTER 9 QUIZ

1. The Act states that "No sponsored licensee shall pay compensation directly to a licensee sponsored by another sponsoring broker for the performance of licensed activities."

    a. True
    b. False

2. All compensation earned in a real estate transaction, whether a sale, lease, or property management, shall be paid directly to the sponsoring broker.

    a. True
    b. False
    c. More information is needed

3. Which of the following is true about this statement? "One sponsoring broker may pay compensation directly to another sponsoring broker for the performance of licensed activities."

    a. It is from The Act.
    b. It is a legal relationship.
    c. Brokers must be aware of this fact.
    d. All of the above.
    e. None of the above.

4. The Act states: "Notwithstanding any other provision of this Act, a leasing agent may pay compensation to a person currently licensed under the Auction License Act who is in compliance with and providing services under Section 5-32 of this Act."

    a. True
    b. False
    c. More information is needed

5. The Act states: "A licensee does not need to disclose to a client the sponsoring broker's compensation policy with regard to utilization of cooperating brokers."

    a. True
    b. False
    c. More information is needed

6. The Act states: "A licensee must disclose to a client all sources of compensation related to the transaction received by the licensee from a third party."

    a. True
    b. False
    c. More information is needed

7. The Act states: "Compensation may be paid to any unlicensed person in exchange for the person performing licensed activities in violation of this Act."

    a. Yes
    b. No

8. The Act states: "Every sponsoring broker must have an employment or independent contractor agreement with each licensee the broker sponsors."

    a. No.
    b. Yes, and it can be verbal.
    c. Yes, and it must be written.

9. Team members are always compensated the same way, regardless of his or her brokerage.

    a. True
    b. False
    c. More information is needed

10. Is it legal for team members in Illinois to compensate each other?

    a. Yes
    b. No

11. Compensation is always outlined in a written employment agreement. This is determined by each brokerage.

    a. True. The sponsoring broker determines the compensation plan.
    b. False. It's determined by the law.

12. Concerning compensation, it's common for a master franchisor to charge a certain percentage fee off the top to the licensees who work there.

    a. True
    b. False

13. A written employment agreement must be between the sponsoring broker and who else that works under her/him?

    a. Licensees

    b. Licensed personal assistants

    c. Non-practicing licensees

    d. All of the above

    e. None of the above

14. An employment agreement is a written agreement that is between a sponsoring broker and who else?

    a. Other brokers

    b. The brokerage owner

    c. Sponsored licensee

    d. None of the above

15. Daniel is a designated agent who is designated as his seller's sole agent. He has the exclusive right to market the property of the seller. Which type of listing agreement can define Daniel as the designated agent?

    a. Net listing agreement

    b. Exclusive agency listing agreement

    c. Exclusive right to sell listing agreement

    d. All of the above

16. In which ways can team members be compensated?

    a. Performance-based

    b. Percentage-based

    c. Flat rate

    d. A combination of A, B, and/or C

    e. All of the above

17. Concerning recordkeeping, how many years does a sponsoring broker need to keep escrow records, transaction records, employment agreements, and records showing compensation payments on file?

    a. 3 years

    b. 5 years

    c. 7 years

    d. 10 years

18. In the state of Illinois, who can legally collect a commission in a real estate transaction?

    a. Sponsoring broker
    b. Licensee
    c. Designated broker
    d. Only C and D

19. Janet is a new licensee who is a Type A personality. She starts at a popular brokerage on Monday. Her plan is to keep 100% of the commissions from her sales. Which compensation model will she opt for?

    a. Flat rate
    b. Production-based splits
    c. Salary
    d. None of the above

20. Because there are limited cooperative relationships in this sector, there is a higher probability that the buyer is going to have to compensate their own broker. Which realm is this?

    a. Residential
    b. Commercial
    c. Property management
    d. None of the above

CHAPTER 10:

PROTECTING THE PUBLIC

LEARNING GOALS:

By the end of this lesson, you will:

- Understand the purpose of antitrust laws
- Know the history of antitrust laws
- Understand common scams used by cybercriminals
- Learn smart practices to implement for your own cybersecurity

THE MOST VALUABLE ASSET in the real estate industry is not real estate. It is people. This is one reason why the real estate industry is a regulated industry. Protecting the public is why no individual can simply decide to sell real estate without having to go through the appropriate education, requirements, and training. To represent consumers in real estate transactions, a license is required. Continuing education, which is required for all licensees, is part of helping the licensees stay up to date with industry best practices and trends. Continuing education (CE) allows them to stay well-versed in applicable laws that dictate their scope of practice, responsibilities, and duties, as they strive to protect the best interests of consumers. In the real estate industry and other industries as well, the Federal Government, along with each state, stepped in to create strategic laws and measures to protect the public.

WHAT ARE ANTITRUST LAWS?

While most adults in the US have heard the term "antitrust laws" several times, it's very likely that not many people understand them. To start, let's begin with a clear definition and a historical overview.

In the mid-1880s, we were living in a country that was not fostering economic competition. As a result, citizens were dealing with monopolies where one person or one company controlled an entire industry. Here is a modern example. AT&T back in the 1960s and 1970s was the largest provider of phone service in the US. Literally, through each of its subsidiaries, AT&T controlled the phone system nationwide. Because of the Sherman Antitrust Act and what we lived through in the 1880s, the government has an obligation to ensure that every individual is able to secure services at a fair rate. This results in the government, when necessary, breaking up these large conglomerates that basically tell you as the consumer how you have to live. Antitrust enacted in 1890 is designed to give the consumer the ability to negotiate a fair price for services rendered without being told what they have to do. That is why we currently have discussions centered around the possibility of breaking up such entities as Amazon and Meta.

Antitrust laws are a collection of federal and state government laws. The purpose of the laws is to regulate the conduct and organization of business entities. This is commonly done in order to promote healthy competition. This competition, as you know, is a great benefit to consumers. Furthermore, antitrust laws are in place to keep the flow of trade moving forward. You can view it as a method of protecting against illegal activities that harm trade, such as monopolies, price-fixing, etc.

Keep in mind that antitrust laws were created and are designed to not only protect consumers but also to protect competition.

Free and open markets are the foundation of a vibrant economy. Aggressive competition among sellers in an open marketplace gives consumers—both individuals and businesses—the benefits of lower prices, higher quality products and services, more choices, and greater innovation. The FTC's competition mission is to enforce the rules of the competitive marketplace—the antitrust laws. These laws promote vigorous competition and protect consumers from anticompetitive mergers and business practices. The FTC's Bureau of Competition, working in tandem with the Bureau of Economics, enforces the antitrust laws for the benefit of consumers. (Federal Trade Commission)

Federal and state antitrust laws apply to the real estate industry. Violating an antitrust law is illegal.

A SUMMARIZED HISTORY OF ANTITRUST LAWS

Antitrust laws are not a modern development in the US. The Sherman Antitrust Act was the first of its kind. This federal statute came to fruition in 1890. It prohibits any activity that restricts interstate commerce and competition in the marketplace. It made trusts like cartels and monopolies illegal in an effort to stimulate fair economic competition. Violating the Sherman Antitrust Act results in harsh consequences. Individuals can face up to one million dollars in fines, along with potentially ten years in prison. Corporations can face up to one hundred million dollars in fines.

Historically speaking, what came into existence next that built upon the Sherman Antitrust Act was the Federal Trade Commission Act. This act, which was brought forth in September of 1914, created and established what is known as the Federal Trade Commission, commonly known as the FTC. This act outlaws dishonest, shady, and unethical methods of competition and practices that negatively affect commerce and trade.

In October of 1914, the Sherman Antitrust Act was amended by the Clayton Antitrust Act. The Clayton Antitrust Act came into the picture as part of the US's effort to keep trade flowing and support healthy and fair competition. This act's goal was to add further power and finesse to the nation's goal of protecting commerce and trade. It further defined different business practices which were deemed unethical, unfair, and immoral. These harmful practices include monopolies and price-fixing. This act outlaws mergers that are anticompetitive, along with discriminatory and cutthroat pricing.

The Sherman Antitrust Act, the Federal Trade Commission Act, and the Clayton Antitrust Act all continue to protect commerce and trade to this very day.

The Robinson-Patman Act was enacted in 1936. It's also known as the Anti-Price Discrimination Act and is an amendment to the 1914 Clayton Antitrust Act. This law forbids and outlaws anti-competitive business practices. Its primary focus is price discrimination.

ANTITRUST VIOLATIONS IN REAL ESTATE BROKERAGE

Antitrust violations exist in the real estate industry. These are the main categories:

1. Boycotting

2. Market division and customer allocation

3. Price-fixing

4. Tying agreements

Let's define each of these violations (illegal practices).

1. **Boycotting**: This is when two or more competitors or businesses choose to conspire against another, or they agree to withhold their business/patronage in order to reduce competition. This is sometimes called group boycotting. It is illegal and must be avoided. The FTC shares this definition:

   "Any company may, on its own, refuse to do business with another firm, but an agreement among competitors not to do business with targeted individuals or businesses may be an illegal boycott, especially if the group of competitors working together has market power. For instance, a group boycott may be used to implement an illegal price-fixing agreement. In this scenario, the competitors agree not to do business with others except on agreed-upon terms, typically with the result of raising prices. An independent decision not to offer services at prevailing prices does not raise antitrust concerns, but an agreement among competitors not to offer services at prevailing prices as a means of achieving an agreed-upon (and typically higher) price does raise antitrust concerns. Boycotts to prevent a firm from entering a market or to disadvantage an existing competitor are also illegal." FTC

   Here is another insightful explanation.

   "A group boycott occurs when two or more persons or entities conspire to restrict the ability of someone from competing. This is sometimes called a concerted refusal to deal, which unlike a standard refusal to deal, requires, not surprisingly, two or more people or entities. A group boycott can create per se antitrust liability. But the per se rule is applied to group boycotts like it is applied to tying claims, which means only sometimes. By contrast, horizontal price-fixing, market allocation, and bid-rigging claims are almost always per se antitrust violations." (Jarod Bona, Esq. The Antitrust Attorney Blog) Note: Per se is a Latin term that means by itself or in itself.

2. **Market division and customer allocation:** Although these are two different concepts, they overlap. Market division puts the focus on geography. Customer allocation puts the focus on people. Also known as dividing territories, market division is an illegal agreement by or between two or more companies or licensees to stay out of each other's territory. This action reduces competition within the agreed-upon areas. It is common for market division to include the division or splitting of geographical areas which naturally divides the customers. Both concepts are two of several anticompetitive practices outlawed under US antitrust laws.

The FTC conveys this information:

"Plain agreements among competitors to divide sales territories or assign customers are almost always illegal. Similarly, plain agreement among competing employers to not solicit or hire each other's employees are an unlawful allocation of employees in a labor market. These arrangements are essentially agreements not to compete: "I won't sell in your market if you don't sell in mine," or "I won't poach your employees if you don't poach mine." Individuals and companies that knowingly enter unlawful market-allocation agreements are routinely investigated by the FBI and other federal law enforcement agencies and can be criminally prosecuted. Potential penalties include lengthy terms of imprisonment (up to ten years) and large fines (up to $1 million for individuals, $100 million for companies, or twice the gain or loss from the offense). Where appropriate, the FTC may also bring a civil enforcement action." FTC

Here is a real estate industry example: (Note that the word "business" is interchangeable with "licensee"). Business A and Business B decide to not work in the same areas of the city. They divide the city in half. Business A takes the north part of the city. Business B takes the south part of the city. This type of scenario is called market division or client allocation, and it is illegal.

3. **Price-fixing:** The FTC defines this term as: "Price fixing is an agreement (written, verbal, or inferred from conduct) among competitors that raises, lowers, or stabilizes prices or competitive terms. Generally, the antitrust laws require that each company establish prices and other terms on its own, without agreeing with a competitor. When consumers make choices about what products and services to buy, they expect that the price has been determined freely on the basis of supply and demand, not by an agreement among competitors. When competitors agree to restrict competition, the result is often higher prices. Accordingly, price-fixing is a major concern of government antitrust enforcement."

As you can see, price-fixing disrupts the normal laws and rhythms of supply and demand. It gives the person/s and/or companies an edge over competitors, albeit an illegal edge. Price-fixing (artificially) imposes higher prices on customers. It can also lower incentives to innovate or take action on a specific transaction. Finally, it can raise barriers for consumers. The real estate process is particularly vulnerable to price-fixing because of several factors, including clients' being risk-adverse, multiple real estate professionals involved in the process, and high dollar amounts being attached to a single transaction.

A licensee must never agree with other licensees on commission rates. Each licensee has the responsibility to avoid talking about and/or colluding on any agreements regarding fees and/or compensation. It is illegal to set sale conditions, fees, and/or management rates. However, this is not applicable within an individual company where the sponsoring broker (through the designated managing broker), has the right to set standards regarding commission payments, which all sponsored licensees must agree with.

Collusion is a secret agreement or cooperation among licensees or brokerages that is intended to deceive consumers and/or is implemented for fraudulent purposes. It is illegal and can result in penalties by the courts.

4. **Tying agreements:** Also known as tie-in agreements, a tying agreement exists when a licensee offers an opportunity to a consumer, such as a lower commission rate, *if* the consumer buys their next property through that licensee. What makes this agreement illegal is when the licensee stipulates the reduction of the commission rate is contingent upon the consumer purchasing their new property from the licensee. By tying the benefit of the low commission rate to a secondary contract, the new property, the licensee is violating the consumer's right to utilize a competitor for the acquisition of their new property.

This type of agreement is like this statement: *I'm only going to do X if you do Y.* In other words, there is a condition set. In order to obtain what is desired, a consumer must undertake an additional obligation, even if it is not in his or her best interest. The benefit a consumer wants is tied to and contingent upon something else happening. Example: You can only purchase this land if you also purchase the land across the street from it.

At times, with these violations, disparagement comes into play. **Disparagement** is the act of making unflattering or negative statements about a person or thing. It shows that you have a negative opinion about the person or topic being spoken about. In other words, it is something said in person or written (physically or digitally) that is considered defamatory, degrading, demeaning, belittling, and/or slanderous. It is something potentially damaging to another person or business. In business terms, it comes across as the first business (who says or publishes something unflattering or negative) putting effort into harming a different business. Disparagement at times is connected to antitrust violations. It can also be a source of lawsuits.

Antitrust violations levy severe consequences. The FTC states:

> The penalties for violating the Sherman Act can be severe. Although most enforcement actions are civil, the Sherman Act is also a criminal law, and individuals and businesses that violate it may be prosecuted by the Department of Justice. Criminal prosecutions are typically limited to intentional and clear violations such as when competitors fix prices or rig bids. The Sherman Act imposes criminal penalties of up to $100 million for a corporation and $1 million for an individual, along with up to 10 years in prison. Under federal law, the maximum fine may be increased to twice the amount the conspirators gained from the illegal acts or twice the money lost by the victims of the crime, if either of those amounts is over $100 million. In addition to these federal statutes, most states have antitrust laws that are enforced by state attorneys general or private plaintiffs. Many of these statutes are based on the federal antitrust laws.

TELEPHONE CONSUMER PROTECTION ACT OF 1991 (DO NOT CALL REGISTRY)

As technology advances, people gain more and more wonderful benefits. The other side of the coin is that technology can create challenges (being addicted to a screen) and unwanted or unwelcome communications. The government has worked to protect the public from communications that are unwanted, unwelcome, or potentially harmful.

One of the first acts in this regard was the Telephone Consumer Protection Act of 1991.

Also known as TCPA, it was passed by the United States Congress in 1991 and signed into law as Public Law 102-243. This act restricts telemarketing (telephone solicitations) and the use of automated telephone equipment (i.e., robocalls). It protects consumers by limiting the use of automatic dialing systems, SMS text messages, artificial or prerecorded voice messages, and fax machines. Furthermore, it specifies numerous technical requirements for faxes, autodialers, and voice messaging and voicemail systems. In other words, it safeguards consumers from programs, software, and applications that are created and designed to send out mass solicitations.

A consumer who is solicited in this manner has the right to place a lawsuit against the person and/or firm that is breaking the law. If a licensee violates TCPA, whether it is the intention or not, he/she can be held liable for the violation. As you can tell, the TCPA's goal is to protect consumers from unwanted telephone solicitations.

TCPA's general provisions include the following. Unless the recipient (consumer) has given express consent beforehand, the TCPA and FCC rules under the TCPA generally include:

- Prohibiting solicitors from calling residences before 8 a.m., or after 9 p.m. (local time)

- Requiring that solicitors keep and maintain a company-specific "Do Not Call" list of consumers who requested to not be called. Note: This request must be honored for five years.

- Requiring that solicitors respect and honor the National Do Not Call Registry, in an effort to protect consumers

- Requiring that each solicitor provide his or her full name, the name of the person/ entity on whose behalf the call is being made, along with a phone number (or address) where that person or entity can be contacted

- No solicitations to residences that implement an artificial voice or a recording

- Prohibiting calls made using automated telephone equipment, an artificial or prerecorded voice to a cell phone, or any service for which the recipient is charged for the call

- Prohibiting autodialed calls (robocalls) that engage two or more lines of a multi-line business

- And even prohibiting unsolicited faxes (TCPA)

The laws are designed to protect consumers. The FTC has formally recognized the real estate industry as being a telemarketing industry. Therefore, all licensees are expected to honor and follow these laws.

The Do Not Call Act is a bill that modifies the penalties for violations of the Telephone Consumer Protection Act. Its goal as outlined on the US government site is to "deter obnoxious, nefarious, and outrageous telephone calls." It is designed to protect consumers from these types of calls and text messages.

What is the National Do Not Call Registry?

"The National Do Not Call Registry provides an easy and efficient way for consumers to tell companies they don't want to receive most telemarketing sales calls.

Robocalls that are sales calls are illegal whether a number is on the Registry or not, unless the caller has written permission from a consumer. Since its inception in 2003, the Registry has continued to grow. As of September 30, 2021, there were 244 million active registrations. Consumers can register multiple phone numbers on the Registry. Telemarketers and sellers must remove numbers added to the Registry from their call lists at least every 31 days. Organizations can access the Registry online. If a company violates the Do Not Call rules, consumers can report the call to the Federal Trade Commission (FTC) online or by calling the toll free number. Law enforcement officials review these complaints, as well as consumer registration and telemarketer access information, through the Consumer Sentinel Network, a secure online database maintained by the FTC." (FTC)

The Do Not Call Law establishes specific guidelines for when licensees are allowed and prohibited from contacting consumers. This topic centers around what is known as an established business relationship. 815 ILCS 402/1 defines an "established business relationship" as the following:

> "The existence of an oral or written transaction, agreement, contract, or other legal state of affairs involving a person or entity and an existing customer under which both parties have a course of conduct or established pattern of activity for commercial or mercantile purposes and for the benefit or profit of both parties. A pattern of activity does not necessarily mean multiple previous contacts. The established business relationship must exist between the existing customer and the person or entity directly, and does not extend to any related business entity or other business organization of the person or entity or related to the person or entity or the person or entity's agent including but not limited to a parent corporation, subsidiary partnership, company or other corporation or affiliate." (815 ILCS 402/1)

Licensees are allowed by the law to call consumers if and when they have an established business relationship, for up to 1.5 years (18 months) following the completion of the business activities.

How does an established business relationship work given the presence of the Do Not Call Registry? Here is an example. Sarah, a local real estate broker, drives past a home that she sold eleven months ago. She is surprised to see a for sale by owner sign in the front yard. Sarah would like to reach out and inquire if she could be of assistance, especially since she knows the owners. However, she knows that this couple is registered on the Do Not Call Registry. Does Sarah have the right to contact this couple? Yes. Sarah has the right to consistently contact the couple for up to 18 months following the completion of their last business activity.

When a consumer (lead) is on the registry and he/she makes inquiries and/or submits applications (in writing or online), a licensee is allowed to contact the consumer for up to three months after the inquiry or initial contact was made. Brokerage firms are required to have a separate "Do Not Call" policy in place. This applies whether or not the firm supports making cold calls. If a firm does not have a "Do Not Call" policy in place, it could be in violation for making any calls of a telemarketing nature. Fines may be levied when these violations occur, and fines may be given for every telemarketing call placed.

To stay in line with the Do Not Call Act and law, every brokerage firm needs to have these guidelines in place:

- Written how-to steps and procedures that follow the Do Not Call law.

- Oversee and enforce policy compliance.

- Train all employees and staff on the procedures.

- Make available phone numbers that the firm employees and staff are not permitted to call. (These will be specific to the said company).

- The company must maintain an internal Do Not Call Registry that lists names and numbers of consumers that the company has specifically been instructed not to call. The company must update this list every 31 days.

- If a call is made to a consumer that does not follow the law's guidelines, the company needs to be able to demonstrate and prove that the call was a mistake and not intentional.

THE JUNK FAX PREVENTION ACT OF 2005

If you have ever watched a movie from the '80s that shows an office, no doubt you saw a fax machine in the background. While fax machines are still common, they were heavily relied on in the '80s prior to the advancements of email being available for public use. With fax machines came the issue of unsolicited and unwelcome faxes. This went on for years, unchecked, with no real penalties for sending unsolicited faxes. For this reason, the Junk Fax Prevention Act of 2005 was signed into law. It allows the sending of unsolicited fax advertisements to persons and businesses with which the sender has an established business relationship. However, they must provide a method that allows the recipient to opt out of future fax notifications. Upon receipt of such declaration, the licensee must stop sending such advertisements. If there is no established business relationship between the sender and recipient, the sender should not send an unsolicited fax.

Concerning a fax advertising policy, the Federal Communications Commission (FCC) states:

"The Telephone Consumer Protection Act (TCPA), 47 U.S.C. § 227, restricts the use of the facsimile machine to deliver unsolicited advertisements. Specifically, the TCPA prohibits the use of "any telephone facsimile machine, computer, or other device to send an unsolicited advertisement to a telephone facsimile machine." The TCPA applies only to those facsimile messages that constitute "unsolicited advertisements." The statutory prohibition applies to such advertisements sent both to residential and business facsimile numbers.

In 2005, the Junk Fax Prevention Act amended the TCPA to permit the sending of unsolicited facsimile advertisements to individuals and businesses with which the sender has an established business relationship and to provide a process by which any sender must cease sending such advertisements upon the request of the recipient. On April 5, 2006, the Commission adopted rules to implement the Junk Fax Prevention Act.

Among other things, the Commission's rules in 47 CFR (Code of Federal Regulations) § 64.1200 require the sender of fax advertisements to obtain permission from the recipient before transmitting the fax. The fax sender must also provide notice and contact information on the fax that allows recipients to opt out of future fax transmissions from the sender and requires senders to honor opt-out requests within the shortest reasonable period of time, not to exceed 30 days. If there is an established business relationship between the recipient and the fax sender (as set forth in our rules), the recipient's permission is not required but the sender must have obtained the fax number in a permissible way, described in the FCC rules. These limitations do not apply to a fax that is not an advertisement, such as a fax that is solely transactional (e.g., confirming a purchase) or informational (e.g., an industry newsletter)." (FCC)

THE CAN-SPAM ACT OF 2003

If you remember when you signed up for your first email and started sending email communications for the very first time, no doubt a new reality came into being for you. You started receiving spam emails. These took several forms. They could feature everything from click-bait to emails that do seem professional and yet, are not welcome. Enter the CAN-SPAM Act of 2003.

The CAN-SPAM Act of 2003 (which is not associated with The Act) lays out standards that business professionals must comply with in terms of email marketing. Its goal is to control and ultimately diminish the number of deceptive and fraudulent commercial emails. The CAN-SPAM Act serves to protect email recipients, who have the right to say that they do not want unsolicited emails from you and/or your firm. This applies both to bulk emails and single "one-off" emails. It also applies whether you're using a CRM and sending one email to all contacts, or simply sending a quick email on the go from your smartphone to one recipient. The CAN-SPAM Act covers all emails sent that contain a commercial nature. This means that it includes new listing emails, newsletters, email sequences, updates, and the like. The FTC defines these emails as "any electronic mail message the primary purpose of which is the commercial advertisement or promotion of a commercial product or service."

This segment below comes directly from the FTC.

> The CAN-SPAM Act, a law that sets the rules for commercial email, establishes requirements for commercial messages, gives recipients the right to have you stop emailing them, and spells out tough penalties for violations. Despite its name, the CAN-SPAM Act doesn't apply only to bulk email. It covers all commercial messages, including email that promotes content on commercial websites. The law makes no exception for business-to-business email. That means all email—for example, a message to former customers announcing a new product line—must comply with the law. Each separate email in violation of the CAN-SPAM Act is subject to penalties of up to $43,280, so non-compliance can be costly. Following the law isn't complicated. Here's a rundown of CAN-SPAM's main requirements:

> 1. Don't use false or misleading header information. Your "From," "To," "Reply-To," and routing information—including the originating domain name and email address— must be accurate and identify the person or business who initiated the message.

> 2. Don't use deceptive subject lines. The subject line must accurately reflect the content of the message.

> 3. Identify the message as an ad. The law gives you a lot of leeway for how to do this, but you must disclose clearly and conspicuously that your message is an advertisement.

> 4. Tell recipients where you're located. Your message must include your valid physical postal address. This can be your current street address, a post office box you've registered with the U.S. Postal Service, or a private mailbox you've registered with a commercial mail receiving agency established under Postal Service regulations.

> 5. Tell recipients how to opt out of receiving future email from you. Your message must include a clear and conspicuous explanation of how the recipient can opt out of getting email from you in the future. Craft the notice in a way that's easy for an ordinary person to recognize, read, and understand. Creative use of type size, color, and location can improve clarity. Give a return email address or another easy Internet-based way to allow people to communicate their choice to you. You may create a menu to allow a recipient to opt out of certain types of messages, but you must include the

option to stop all commercial messages from you. Make sure your spam filter doesn't block these opt-out requests.

6. Honor opt-out requests promptly. Any opt-out mechanism you offer must be able to process opt-out requests for at least 30 days after you send your message. You must honor a recipient's opt-out request within 10 business days. You can't charge a fee, require the recipient to give you any personally identifying information beyond an email address, or make the recipient take any step other than sending a reply email or visiting a single page on an Internet website as a condition for honoring an opt-out request. Once people have told you they don't want to receive more messages from you, you can't sell or transfer their email addresses, even in the form of a mailing list. The only exception is that you may transfer the addresses to a company you've hired to help you comply with the CAN-SPAM Act.

7. Monitor what others are doing on your behalf. The law makes clear that even if you hire another company to handle your email marketing, you can't contract away your legal responsibility to comply with the law. Both the company whose product is promoted in the message and the company that actually sends the message may be held legally responsible. (FTC)

To avoid potential fines, you must be CAN-SPAM compliant.

Read the "Can-spam Act: A Compliance Guide for Business" found at this link to learn more: https://www.ftc.gov/business-guidance/resources/can-spam-act-compliance-guide-business

As you know, the FTC oversees enforcing laws held within the CAN-SPAM Act. It also has the power and the authority to levy fines against business owners, licensees, etc. Each violation can result in a fine that is up to $11,000. The FTC further states that it may add additional fines on commercial emailers for violating any one of the following illegal acts:

- The generation of email addresses using a technique known as a "dictionary attack." This type of attack randomly combines names, letters, and/or numbers into a wide variety of permutations.

- Harvesting. This is the process of obtaining ("harvesting") lists of email addresses using various methods. Many times, these email addresses come from sites or web services that have given notice that prohibits the transfer of email addresses for the purpose of sending email. For example, you cannot harvest someone's email from LinkedIn simply because he/she is a current first connection.

- Relaying emails via a computer or network without obtaining permission. One example is choosing to take advantage of open relays or open proxies without authorization.

- Implementing scripts or other automated methods in order to register for or obtain multiple email or user accounts to send commercial email. There are several shady and ill-advised Chrome extensions that run scripts. For example, using an extension or software to scrape email lists from LinkedIn is against LinkedIn's terms of service. If discovered, LinkedIn has the right to completely delete your profile. (FTC)

All email marketing must be in compliance with both the CAN-SPAM Act and the License Act. In addition, your firm may have special procedures or policies that you are requested to follow. In Illinois, the law states that sending an unsolicited advertising or fundraising email without obtaining the recipients' permission first may result in a fine. All electronic correspondence (which includes, but is not limited to, email, e-bulletin boards, and online discussion groups) must include the name of the licensee, the name of the company, and the company location. Your email and email marketing techniques are part of your reputation. Treat them with respect and integrity.

Furthermore, the Illinois General Assembly passed the Electronic Mail Act. It became effective on January 1, 2000. Concerning unsolicited or misleading electronic mail, The Act states:

(a) No individual or entity may initiate or cause to be initiated an unsolicited electronic mail advertisement if the electronic mail advertisement (i) uses a third party's Internet domain name without permission of the third party, or otherwise misrepresents any information in identifying the point of origin or the transmission path of an electronic mail advertisement or (ii) contains false or misleading information in the subject line.

(a-5) An initiator of an unsolicited electronic mail advertisement must establish a toll-free telephone number or valid sender-operated return electronic mail address that the recipient of the unsolicited electronic mail advertisement may call or electronically mail to notify the sender not to electronically mail any further unsolicited electronic mail advertisements.

(a-10) An initiator of an unsolicited electronic mail advertisement is prohibited from selling or transferring in any manner the electronic mail address of any person who has notified the initiator that the person does not want to receive any further unsolicited electronic mail advertisements.

(a-15) Each unsolicited electronic mail advertisement's subject line shall include "ADV:" as its first 4 characters. For any unsolicited electronic mail advertisement that contains information regarding the lease, sale, rental, gift offer, or other disposition of any realty, goods, services, or extension of credit, that may only be viewed, purchased, rented, leased, or held in possession by an individual 18 years of age and older, the subject line of each and every message shall include "ADV:ADLT" as the first 8 characters.

(b) This Section applies when the unsolicited electronic mail advertisement is delivered to an Illinois resident via an electronic mail service provider's service or equipment located in this State.

(c) Any person, other than an electronic mail service provider, who suffers actual damages as a result of a violation of this Section committed by any individual or entity may bring an action against such individual or entity. The injured person may recover attorney's fees and costs, and may elect, in lieu of recovery of actual damages, to recover the lesser of $10 for each and every unsolicited electronic mail advertisement transmitted in violation of this Section, or $25,000 per day. The injured person shall not have a cause of action against the electronic mail service provider that merely transmits the unsolicited electronic mail advertisement over its computer network.

(d) Any electronic mail service provider who suffers actual damages as a result of a violation of this Section committed by any individual or entity may bring an action against such individual or entity. The injured person may recover attorney's fees and costs, and may elect, in lieu of recovery of actual damages, to recover the lesser of $10 for each and every unsolicited electronic mail advertisement transmitted in violation of this Section, or $25,000 per day.

(e) The provisions of this Section shall not be construed to limit any person's right to pursue any additional civil remedy otherwise allowed by law.

(f) An electronic mail service provider may, upon its own initiative, block the receipt or transmission through its service of any unsolicited electronic mail advertisement that it reasonably believes is, or will be, sent in violation of this Section.

(g) No electronic mail service provider may be held liable for any action voluntarily taken in good faith to block the receipt or transmission through its service of any unsolicited electronic mail advertisement which it reasonably believes is, or will be, sent in violation of this Section.

Definitions, along with more details, can be found in 815 ILCS 511/1 of The Act.

OTHER SCAMS

The most prominent scam used by cybercriminals is called phishing. Phishing is when a cybercriminal or hacker pretends to be a legitimate business or other institution in order to steal confidential and/or sensitive information from the victim. It can also be a way to insert ransomware on the victim's laptop and/or network. There are several types of phishing attacks.

Phishing is usually deployed by emails, instant messages, and text messages. Most commonly, phishing is done through legitimate-looking and professionally designed emails. Email spoofing is the creation of email messages that use a forged or fake sender address. Many email protocols fail at having a reliable method for authentication. This makes it a fairly regular practice for spam and phishing emails to use spoofing. In this way, the criminal is able to mislead and trick the recipient into thinking that the source (origination) of the email is legitimate and trustworthy. Many phishing scams invite people to click on a link that leads to a fake website. Once there, the user is directed to enter personal information. These fake websites can look exceptionally convincing and realistic. In their Internet Crime Report 2021, the FBI Internet Crime Complaint Center reported that phishing scams were prominent in 2021. Their data states that there were 323,972 victims and that the reported losses totaled over $44,000,000. When compared to other computer crimes, phishing has twice as many incidents reported.

What does this mean for licensees? Each licensee must use extreme caution when sending anything confidential over email, text message, and social media. As you know, the real estate industry is fast paced. Therefore, it can be very easy to be caught up in the moment when you receive an email requesting information, and quickly work at sending the requested information back. However, you must always take a moment and pause. Confirm that you are sending the information to the actual recipient for whom it is intended. The smartest practice is to call the client or business and confirm the information. When calling, do not use the number that you received in the email. Find their number online via search or by what you have written down for them in your files, online documentation, or CRM.

Impact on Licensees

Licensees who decide to use any type of phone marketing and/or lead generation technology must use caution when using any type of autodialing or auto texting service. Here are three methods to stay in compliance with the TCPA:

- Confirm that the marketing software you use has written consent from the clients/leads/parties that you want to contact.

- Visit the Do Not Call Registry. It's found at telemarketing.donotcall.gov. This will help you avoid sending any type of automated communication to a consumer who is registered on the Do Not Call Registry.

- Does your brokerage have an internal Do Not Call List? If so, review the list and remove any additional leads and/or clients from your contact list.

SMART PRACTICES FOR YOUR OWN CYBERSECURITY

Safety is required because of threats like wire fraud, cybercrimes, phishing, and other scams and risks. Sometimes the problem is not that a licensee fell for a phishing scam and sent confidential information to a criminal. The problem is that the licensee did not have sufficient or adequate cybersecurity in place on his or her laptop and password-protected sites that he/she uses. Because of this lack of cybersecurity, once the licensee's computer or network is breached, it's possible that a criminal can access the confidential information of a licensee's current and previous clients. Such a breach can have staggering consequences. They can result in the licensee's or his or her clients dealing with financial loss and/or identity theft. Data breaches can and do happen. No company, organization, brokerage, or individual is immune. In fact, some of the largest data breaches in recent years include companies like Equifax, eBay, Yahoo, LinkedIn, Marriott International, and Adobe. A breach of eBay impacted 145 million people. When Yahoo was breached, it affected three billion people.

Wire fraud is a federal crime in the US. It involves electronically transmitting ("wiring") funds/money associated with fraud. Jurisdiction is claimed by the Federal Government if the illegal activities cross interstate or international borders. To protect yourself and your clients against wire fraud, do the following:

- Protect your email information.

- Never give out passwords. Avoid easy passwords like "password," "12345," and passwords related to common things people know or information people can easily find out, like your kid's birthday, your significant other's name, etc.

- Track every contact and every transaction. Have an electronic and/or paper trail of everything to maintain integrity.

- With the other party, verify all the information that is necessary, as well as what has been received and when.

- Keep account numbers safe.

- Install antivirus software on your computer, phone, and other devices.

- Do not share personal data that is not encrypted.

- Never open email attachments from anyone you do not know.

- Make sure wire instructions are clear and that the process is secure and encrypted.

- Call and verify a wire transfer with the party or agent before going through the steps online.

To protect yourself from cybercrime, here are guidelines:

- Use obnoxiously strong passwords. Use a combination of upper- and lower-case letters, along with a variety of numbers and symbols.

- Implement strong passwords for your laptops, work computers, tablets, smartphones, and for your home Wi-Fi network and office network.

- Always update any software when it is time. Software updates regularly include their own security advancements, which are designed to protect their users. Outdated software is more vulnerable to breaches.

- Implement social media security settings that will protect your accounts. If you use LinkedIn, Facebook, Twitter, and/or other social networks, review your security settings. Each social network will have different security options for you to review.

  - On LinkedIn, there are profiles and company pages. A profile is for an individual. A company page is for a business or nonprofit. A profile has different levels of security. Select how strong you want your security levels to be. A company page on LinkedIn is public and cannot be made private. As such, it has significantly fewer settings to review.

  - Similarly, Facebook has profiles and business pages. A profile is for an individual. A business page is for a business or nonprofit. Sometimes, a business page is called a Facebook page, or a "page" for short. Know that a profile is not a page, and a page is not a profile. People confuse those terms all the time.

    - Facebook profiles have the most detailed of all security settings with a wide variety of different options. You want to go through each security section slowly. Make sure you understand each part. Select the levels of security that you feel best about. What information are you comfortable with being public? What information do you only want approved friends to be able to see?

    - Unlike Facebook profiles, every Facebook page by default is public. They cannot be made private.

- Avoid using public Wi-Fi. Public Wi-Fi use is common in airports, hotels, coffee shops, and restaurants. It's also a hotbed for personal data being stolen. If you use public Wi-Fi a lot, it is recommended that you purchase a VPN (virtual private network). You can view a VPN as a secret tunnel that allows you to use the internet in a safe and private way. It's like your own private and secure network that you're using on a public network. It helps keep your information protected. VPNs mask your online identity and tasks, preventing other parties from viewing your online activities. Using a VPN on public Wi-Fi allows you to dramatically increase your online safety and security.

- Use two-factor authentication to protect your emails when you have the option to do so.

- Beware of any browser extensions that you use. Ensure that they are only requesting information that is necessary.

- Follow any guidelines outlined in your firm's office manual.

- Stay up to date with the current trends and software updates. Technology is constantly advancing and evolving. Likewise, how you protect yourself, your prospects and clients, and all related data will change (or at least must be updated) on a regular basis.

THE SOCIAL MEDIA LANDSCAPE

The social media landscape which has evolved dramatically over the years is a highly relevant and ever-evolving topic. Although the Internet had been around for years, the Internet truly emerged as a global commercial network in the '90s. The next digital revolution of sorts was spurred on by social media with the emergence of online social networks like Twitter, LinkedIn, Instagram, and Facebook.

A safety tip when it comes to Facebook is this: If a lead or client sends you a friend request on Facebook or any platform, call to confirm that it is him/her. Imagine if you accepted the friend request, and he/she started chatting with you. It could quickly turn into a phishing scam where the criminal is trying to obtain confidential information. When a friend request from a client is sent, simply call him/her directly to confirm that it is indeed him or her.

In recent years, we have also seen and experienced new social media platforms, such as TikTok and Snapchat. Keeping the public protected in light of ever-emerging and constantly evolving social networks is a challenge. It's safe to say that technology moves much faster than laws do. This makes it especially important to stay up to date with your brokerage's handbook concerning social media policies and practices.

As you have learned, there are initiatives and laws in place that licensees must know about and follow in order to protect themselves, their clients, and the public.

CHAPTER 10 QUIZ

1. Antitrust laws focus on which of the following?

    a. Stimulating healthy business competition
    b. Prohibiting business practices that restrain trade
    c. Protect consumers
    d. All of the above
    e. None of the above

2. According to the FTC, what is the foundation of a vibrant economy?

    a. Free and open markets
    b. Healthy competition
    c. A growing economy
    d. None of the above

3. Which piece of legislation outlaws trusts such as monopolies and cartels and was the first of its kind?

    a. The Federal Trade Commission Act
    b. The Sherman Antitrust Act
    c. The Clayton Antitrust Act
    d. None of the above

4. Which act outlaws mergers that are anticompetitive, along with discriminatory pricing and cutthroat pricing?

    a. The Federal Trade Commission Act
    b. The Sherman Antitrust Act
    c. The Clayton Antitrust Act
    d. None of the above

5. Tying or tie-in agreements exist when:

    a. Price-fixing takes place.
    b. A group boycott is happening.
    c. The consumer is required to undertake an additional activity in order to obtain the benefit of another.
    d. Two businesses divide a city by territory.

6. When competitors agree to restrict competition, the result is often an attempt to do which of the following?

    a. Raise prices
    b. Lower prices
    c. Create fewer options for buyers
    d. Boycott

7. Which antitrust violation disrupts the normal laws and rhythms of supply and demand?

    a. Price-fixing
    b. Boycotting
    c. Affiliated business
    d. Market division

8. A broker must never agree with other brokers on commission rates.

    a. True
    b. False
    c. More information is needed

9. What is a secret or illegal cooperation or conspiracy, especially in order to cheat or deceive others called?

    a. Boycotting
    b. Collusion
    c. Affiliated business
    d. Phishing

10. What is it called when two or more licensees or businesses choose to conspire against another, or they agree to withhold their business/patronage in order to reduce competition?

    a. Boycotting
    b. Collusion
    c. Affiliated business
    d. Phishing

11. You're watching a movie. A character says: "You can only purchase the property on 5th Street if you purchase the office building on 12th Avenue as well." Which word captures what just happened?

    a. Collusion
    b. Disparagement
    c. Tie-in agreement
    d. Extortion

12. Two brokerages decide to split the town. Brokerage A takes the east side and Brokerage B takes the west side. What is this antitrust violation known as?

    a. Boycotting
    b. Collusion
    c. Affiliated business
    d. Market division

13. If a licensee violates TCPA, whether it is intentional or not, he/she can be held liable for the violation.

    a. True
    b. False

14. The Do Not Call Law covers specific guidelines in terms of when it's allowed and not allowed for licensees to contact consumers.

    a. True
    b. False

15. When a consumer (lead) is on the registry and he/she makes inquiries and/or submits applications (in writing or online), a licensee is allowed to contact the consumer for up to _____ months after the inquiry or initial contact was made.

    a. Two
    b. Three
    c. Four
    d. Five

16. The Junk Fax Prevention Act of 2005 permits the sending of unsolicited fax advertisements to persons and businesses with which the sender has _____?

    a. An established business relationship
    b. A signed contract/agreement
    c. No relationship
    d. None of the above

17. The CAN-SPAM Act of 2003 applies to which of the following?

    a. The CRM of the licensee
    b. Sending one email to all contacts
    c. Sending an email to one recipient
    d. All of the above
    e. None of the above

18. What is the creation of email messages that use a forged or fake sender address known as?

    a. Email spoofing
    b. Fishing
    c. Clickbait
    d. None of the above

19. As a first-year licensee, you receive an email. At first, you think it's from your new client. Now, you're not sure. You don't remember if she has used this email before or not. What should you do?

    a. Email back and ask her if it's her new email
    b. Ignore it
    c. Call her to confirm
    d. None of the above

20. You're at a dinner with several licensees from other brokerages. A licensee you've never met says: "Brokerage A is the worst place to work! That's why I quit! They treat their clients like parts on a factory line. Their brokerage handbook is a joke." You notice other licensees are listening to him now. Which term below best describes what is happening?

    a. Disparagement
    b. Character assassination
    c. Gossip
    d. Venting

CHAPTER 11:

REAL PROPERTY OWNERSHIP INTEREST I

LEARNING GOALS:

By the end of this lesson, you will:

- Understand the meaning of ownership interest
- Know the four government powers
- Know how those government powers interact with real estate

OWNERSHIP INTEREST

When a young couple, James and Jasmine, purchases a house, they may believe that they simply own the house and property and that there's nothing more to the story. However, real estate is not always as simple as the difference between day and night. There are layers of distinctions. There are nuances. While it's accurate that the young couple has purchased the property, to be more specific, what has taken place is that they have now come into ownership of the property. This means that they have what is called "ownership interest" in the property. Ownership interest refers to the bundle of legal rights they now have as owners of the property. As you recall, real property combines the land, the improvements, and the bundle of rights. The bundle of rights when added to real estate provides the property owner with the greatest level of ownership. The bundle of rights consists of five elements:

1. Possession

2. Quiet enjoyment

3. Exclusion

4. Control

5. Disposition

Ownership interest is composed of a variety of rights, frequently referred to as the title. However, this term is problematic and inaccurate. The reason is that the title is a *concept* of ownership in real estate. There is no tangible title. This is similar to that which you hold on your car. The document that shows you have ownership in real estate is called the deed.

Each form of ownership outlines the interest and the potential limits of the ownership, and/or limits the rights concerning how the property is used. Ownership is ultimately a legal concept, and at times, it's complicated. It may be transferred, gained, and lost in a variety of ways and circumstances. When a property is acquired, it may come about from a direct purchase, an inheritance, being received as a gift, being found, and so on. Situations that can cause transfer or a loss of property include selling it, exchanging it, giving the property as a gift, legally losing the property (foreclosure, seizure, etc.), and so on.

Do James and Jasmine own the property and have rights? Absolutely. Can they do anything they please with the property? Not always. It depends on a variety of factors. Much of the time, the rights exist only up until the point of specific limitations. These boundaries are legal in nature. They can be created by either government limitations or private limitations from third-party entities. To push beyond the stated limits means the couple is taking actions outside of what they are legally able to do.

OWNERSHIP INTEREST AND THE LICENSEE

What does The Act say about licensee-owned property? There are several sections within the licensing act that establish what the law requires. Below are a few excerpts. The Advertising section (Section 10-30) of The Act conveys the following:

"A licensee shall disclose, in writing, to all parties in a transaction his or her status as a licensee and any and all interest the licensee has or may have in the real estate constituting the subject matter thereof, directly or indirectly, according to the following guidelines . . . A sponsored or inactive licensee selling or leasing property, owned solely by the sponsored or inactive licensee, without utilizing brokerage services of their sponsoring broker or any other licensee, may advertise "By Owner." For purposes of this Section, property is "solely owned" by a sponsored or inactive licensee if he or she (i) has a 100% ownership interest alone, (ii) has ownership as a joint tenant or tenant by the entirety, or (iii) holds a 100% beneficial interest in a land trust. Sponsored or inactive licensees selling or leasing "By Owner" shall comply with the following if advertising by owner: A sponsored or inactive licensee shall not use the sponsoring broker's name or the sponsoring broker's company name in connection with the sale, lease, or advertisement of the property nor utilize the sponsoring broker's or company's name in connection with the sale, lease, or advertising of the property in a manner likely to create confusion among the public as to whether or not the services of a real estate company are being utilized or whether or not a real estate company has an ownership interest in the property.

A sponsored licensee may not advertise under his or her own name. Advertising in any media shall be under the direct supervision of the sponsoring or designated managing broker and in the sponsoring broker's business name, which in the case of a franchise shall include the franchise affiliation as well as the name of the individual firm. This provision does not apply under the following circumstances: (1) When a licensee enters into a brokerage agreement relating to his or her own real estate, or real estate in which he or she has an ownership interest, with another licensed broker; or (2) When a licensee is selling or leasing his or her own real estate or buying or leasing real estate for himself or herself, after providing the appropriate written disclosure of his or her ownership interest as required in paragraph (2) of subsection (c) of this Section." (225 ILCS 454/10-30)

Here's a real-life scenario concerning showing licensee-owned property: When a licensee lists their own property for sale, whether it is the primary residence or an investment property, the law prohibits the licensee from undertaking a dual agency relationship as it would be impossible to effectively give the buyer the representation they deserve. If the licensee holds an open house on the property, the licensee *must* give the buyer a notice of no agency immediately upon engaging the buyer, reiterating the licensee is the agent of the seller. At the same time, the licensee *must* inform the buyer of his or her ownership interest.

GOVERNMENT POWERS

With ownership interest being a legal matter, the government weighs in. Not only does the Federal Government weigh in, but also state and local governments play a strong role. Whenever we talk about the government's impact on real estate, it's a smart move for you to quickly view them as a trifecta. There are federal, state, and local ordinances that have a direct impact on one's ownership and the ability to enjoy such.

There are four government powers. They are simple to remember because their acronym is "P.E.T.E." The government powers, in no particular order, are:

1. Police Power

2. Eminent Domain

3. Taxation

4. Escheat (or Escheatment)

Police Power

Police power is a constitutional law. It gives each state its own power and say in order to regulate behavior and enforce order within the state boundaries. The goal is to facilitate the physical safety of everyone in each state. It also seeks to improve morale, increase health and well-being, and improve its constituents' general welfare. In short, police power is the obligation of the state, county, or municipal governments to protect your health, welfare, and safety.

This brings us to the concept of **enabling acts**, which are provisions of law that grant each state and local jurisdictions the right to create laws that further enhance the objective of protecting public health, welfare, and safety. These laws relate specifically to certain issues within each state.

States are like people and have different personalities and obstacles for the most part. Enabling acts allows them to decide what is best for themselves and take appropriate action. Many states in the US passed their own state-level version of what is known as the Standard State Zoning Enabling Act. This allows municipalities to implement and enforce local zoning laws as a method to regulate land use. In addition to zoning, enabling acts give municipalities the power and right to establish and regulate building codes to meet the objective of protecting public safety.

The Tenth Amendment in the Bill of Rights states that the Federal Government only has powers that are delegated in the Constitution. If a power isn't listed in the Constitution, then it belongs to the states or to the people.

Eminent Domain

Eminent domain may seem like an odd or unique term. That's because it is. The term is Latin and means supreme lordship. The term was pulled from Dutch jurist Hugo Grotius' legal treatise entitled De Jure Belli et Pacis (On the Law of War and Peace), written in 1625. Here is a translated excerpt from his work:

> The property of subjects is under the eminent domain of the state, so that the state or he who acts for it may use and even alienate and destroy such property, not only in the case of extreme necessity, in which even private persons have a right over the property of others, but for ends of public utility, to which ends those who founded civil society must be supposed to have intended that private ends should give way. But it is to be added that when this is done the state is bound to make good the loss to those who lose their property.

Over 400 years after being written, the term and concept are very much alive and well today.

Eminent domain is the legal process in which the government has the right to take and seize private property when it is in the best interest of the public. Note that this is a *right*, not an obligation.

The majority of US states use the term eminent domain. In New York, it is commonly called appropriation. Louisiana calls it expropriation. Both terms mean the same.

What happens when a property owner objects to eminent domain? When this occurs, the government can employ a concept known as **condemnation** in order to seize the property. Essentially, the government is condemning the property. It has determined that the property is unsafe for the property owner to occupy. The government has the obligation to protect the property owner's safety by preventing further entry and use. It should be noted that eminent domain is the *right* of the government to take private property, while condemnation is the *process* frequently used to do so.

When eminent domain is employed, **just compensation** is required by state law. Just compensation is not necessarily fair compensation, although it does reflect what the government taking the property feels it is worth. The price offered may not reflect the price the owner feels they are entitled to. The law permits the property owner to challenge the government based on the amount of compensation being offered. Therefore, as the use of the property is for the public good, the government may exercise the right of condemnation.

Entities that have the power to initiate eminent domain in Illinois include but are not limited to the following: Illinois Department of Transportation, Forest Preserve District, Illinois municipalities, Illinois counties, Illinois townships, and Illinois State Tollway Authority.

The Act brings up a related concept called a **quick-take** in 735 ILCS 30, entitled Eminent Domain Act. This part of The Act outlines the quick-take procedure in detail. In a nutshell, a quick-take is an alternate type of condemnation in Illinois. This procedure allows an authority to acquire possession of a landowner's property before having to pay just compensation. The power to employ this type of condemnation is only given for particular types of projects. It will be no surprise to you that quick-takes are strictly regulated by the Illinois General Assembly.

The Eminent Domain Act says:

> "This Section applies only to proceedings under this Article that are authorized in this Article and in Article 25 of this Act. (b) In a proceeding subject to this Section, the plaintiff, at any time after the complaint has been filed and before judgment is entered in the proceeding, may file a written motion requesting that, immediately or at some specified later date, the plaintiff either: (i) be *vested with the fee simple title (or such lesser estate, interest, or easement, as may be required) to the real property, or a specified portion of that property, which is the subject of the proceeding, and be authorized to take possession of and use the property; or (ii) only be authorized to take possession of and to use the property, if possession and use, without the vesting of title, are sufficient to permit the plaintiff to proceed with the project until the final ascertainment of compensation. No land or interests in land now or hereafter owned, leased, controlled, or operated and used by, or necessary for the actual operation of, any common carrier engaged in interstate commerce, or any other public utility subject to the jurisdiction of the Illinois Commerce Commission, shall be taken or appropriated under this Section by the State of Illinois, the Illinois Toll Highway Authority, the sanitary district, the St. Louis Metropolitan Area Airport Authority, or the Board of Trustees of the University of Illinois without first securing the approval of the Illinois Commerce Commission.
>
> Except as otherwise provided in this Article, the motion for taking shall state: (1) an accurate description of the property to which the motion relates and the estate or interest sought to be acquired in that property; (2) the formally adopted schedule or plan of operation for the execution of the plaintiff's project; (3) the situation of the property to which the motion relates, with respect to the schedule or plan; (4) the necessity for taking the property in the manner requested in the motion and (5) if the property (except property described in Section 3 of the Sports Stadium Act or property described as Site B in Section 2 of the Metropolitan Pier and Exposition

Authority Act) to be taken is owned, leased, controlled, or operated and used by, or necessary for the actual operation of, any interstate common carrier or other public utility subject to the jurisdiction of the Illinois Commerce Commission, a statement to the effect that the approval of the proposed taking has been secured from the Commission, and attaching to the motion a certified copy of the order of the Illinois Commerce Commission granting approval. If the schedule or plan of operation is not set forth fully in the motion, a copy of the schedule or plan shall be attached to the motion.

Section 20-5-10. Preliminary finding of compensation. (a) The court shall fix a date, not less than five days after the filing of a motion under Section 20-5-5, for the hearing on that motion and shall require due notice to be given to each party to the proceeding whose interests would be affected by the taking requested, except that any party who has been or is being served by publication and who has not entered his or her appearance in the proceeding need not be given notice unless the court so requires, in its discretion and in the interests of justice. (b) At the hearing, if the court has not previously, in the same proceeding, determined that the plaintiff has authority to exercise the right of eminent domain, that the property sought to be taken is subject to the exercise of that right, and that the right of eminent domain is not being improperly exercised in the particular proceeding, then the court shall first hear and determine those matters. The court's order on those matters is appealable and an appeal may be taken from that order by either party within 30 days after the entry of the order, but not thereafter, unless the court, on good cause shown, extends the time for taking the appeal. However, no appeal shall stay the further proceedings prescribed in this Act unless the appeal is taken by the plaintiff or unless an order staying further proceedings is entered either by the trial court or by the court to which the appeal is taken. (c) If the foregoing matters are determined in favor of the plaintiff and further proceedings are not stayed, or if further proceedings are stayed and the appeal results in a determination in favor of the plaintiff, the court then shall hear the issues raised by the plaintiff's motion for taking. If the court finds that reasonable necessity exists for taking the property in the manner requested in the motion, then the court shall hear such evidence as it may consider necessary and proper for a preliminary finding of just compensation. In its discretion, the court may appoint three competent and disinterested appraisers as agents of the court to evaluate the property to which the motion relates and to report their conclusions to the court; and their fees shall be paid by the plaintiff. The court shall then make a preliminary finding of the amount constituting just compensation. (d) The court's preliminary finding of just compensation and any deposit made or security provided pursuant to that finding shall not be evidence in the further proceedings to ascertain finally the just compensation to be paid and shall not be disclosed in any manner to a jury impaneled in the proceedings. If appraisers have been appointed, as authorized under this Article, their report shall not be evidence in those further proceedings, but the appraisers may be called as witnesses by the parties to the proceedings.

Section 20-5-15. Deposit in court; possession. (a) If the plaintiff deposits with the county treasurer money in the amount preliminarily found by the court to be just compensation, the court shall enter an order of taking, vesting in the plaintiff the fee simple title (or such lesser estate, interest, or easement, as may be required) to the property, if such vesting has been requested and has been found necessary by the court, at a date the court considers proper, and fixing a date on which the plaintiff is authorized to take possession of and to use the property. (b) If, at the request of any interested party and upon his or her showing of undue hardship or other good cause, the plaintiff's authority to take possession of the property is postponed for more than ten days after the date of vesting of title or more than 15 days after the entry of the order of taking when the order does not vest title in the plaintiff, then that party shall pay to the plaintiff a reasonable rental for the property in an amount determined by the court. Injunctive relief or any other appropriate judicial process or procedure shall be available to place the plaintiff in possession of the property on and after the date fixed by the court for the taking of possession and to prevent any unauthorized interference with possession and the plaintiff's proper use of the property. The county treasurer shall refund to the plaintiff the amount deposited prior to October 1, 1973, that is in excess of the amount preliminarily found by the court to be just compensation. (c) When property is taken by a unit of local government for the purpose of constructing a body of water to be used by a local government-owned "public utility," as defined in Section 11-117-2 of the Illinois Municipal Code, and the unit of local government intends to sell or lease the property to a nongovernmental entity, the defendants holding title before the order that transferred title shall be allowed first opportunity to repurchase the property for a fair market value or first opportunity to lease the property for a fair market value.

Section 20-5-20. Withdrawal by persons having an interest. At any time after the plaintiff has taken possession of the property pursuant to the order of taking, if an appeal has not been and will not be taken from the court's order described in subsection (b) of Section 20-5-10 of this Act, or if such an appeal has been taken and has been determined in favor of the plaintiff, any party interested in the property may apply to the court for authority to withdraw, for his or her own use, his or her share (or any part thereof) of the amount preliminarily found by the court to be just compensation and deposited by the plaintiff, in accordance with the provisions of subsection (a) of Section 20-5-15 of this Act, as that share is determined by the court. The court shall then fix a date for a hearing on the application for authority to withdraw and shall require due notice of the application to be given to each party whose interests would be affected by the withdrawal. After the hearing, the court may authorize the withdrawal requested, or any part thereof as is proper, but upon the condition that the party making the withdrawal shall refund to the clerk of the court, upon the entry of a proper court order, any portion of the amount withdrawn that exceeds the amount finally ascertained in the proceeding to be just compensation (or damages, costs, expenses, or attorney fees) owing to that party.

Section 20-5-25. Persons contesting not to be prejudiced. Neither the plaintiff nor any party interested in the property, by taking any action authorized by Sections 20-5-5 through 20-5-20, inclusive, of this Act, or authorized under Article 25 of this Act, shall be prejudiced in any way in contesting, in later stages of the proceeding, the amount to be finally ascertained to be just compensation.

Section 20-5-30. Interest payments. The plaintiff shall pay, in addition to the just compensation finally adjudged in the proceeding, interest at the rate of 6% per annum upon: (1) Any excess of the just compensation finally adjudged, over the amount preliminarily found by the court to be just compensation in accordance with Section 20-5-10 of this Act, from the date on which the parties interested in the property surrendered possession of the property in accordance with the order of taking, to the date of payment of the excess by the plaintiff. (2) Any portion of the amount preliminarily found by the court to be just compensation and deposited by the plaintiff, to which any interested party is entitled, if the interested party applied for authority to withdraw that portion in accordance with Section 20-5-20 of this Act, and upon objection by the plaintiff (other than on grounds that an appeal under subsection (b) of Section 20-5-10 of this Act is pending or contemplated), authority to withdraw was denied; interest shall be paid to that party from the date of the plaintiff's deposit to the date of payment to that party. When interest is allowable as provided under item (1) of this Section, no further interest shall be allowed under the provisions of Section 2-1303 of the Code of Civil Procedure or any other law.

Section 20-5-35. Refund of excess deposit. If the amount withdrawn from deposit by any interested party under the provision of Section 20-5-20 of this Act exceeds the amount finally adjudged to be just compensation (or damages, costs, expenses, and attorney fees) due to that party, the court shall order that party to refund the excess to the clerk of the court and, if refund is not made within a reasonable time fixed by the court, shall enter judgment for the excess in favor of the plaintiff and against that party.

Section 20-5-40. Dismissal; abandonment. After the plaintiff has taken possession of the property pursuant to the order of taking, the plaintiff shall have no right to dismiss the complaint or to abandon the proceeding, as to all or any part of the property so taken, except upon the consent of all parties to the proceeding whose interests would be affected by the dismissal or abandonment.

Section 20-5-45. Payment of costs. If, on an appeal taken under the provisions of Section 20-5-10 of this Act, the plaintiff is determined not to have the authority to maintain the proceeding as to any property that is the subject of that appeal or if, with the consent of all parties to the proceeding whose interests are affected, the plaintiff dismisses the complaint or abandons the proceedings as to any property that is the subject of the appeal, the trial court then shall enter an order: (i) revesting the title to the property in the parties entitled thereto, if the order of taking vested title in the plaintiff; (ii) requiring the plaintiff to deliver possession of the property to the parties entitled to possession and (iii) making such provision as is just for the payment of damages arising out of the plaintiff's taking and use of the property and also for costs, expenses, and attorney fees, as provided in Section 10-5-70 of this Act. The court may order the clerk of the court to pay those sums to the parties entitled thereto out of the money deposited by the plaintiff in accordance with the provisions of subsection (a) of Section 20-5-15 of this Act.

Section 20-5-50. Construction of Article. The right to take possession and title prior to the final judgment, as prescribed in this Article and Article 25 of this Act shall be in addition to any other right, power, or authority otherwise conferred by law and shall not be construed as abrogating, limiting, or modifying any other right, power, or authority." (735 ILCS 30)

Vested: To vest means to grant, confer, or bestow property and/or property rights. When someone has a vested interest, it most commonly references his or her ability to rightfully and legally claim assets such as an estate, which has been conveyed or has been set aside for future use.

Historically, eminent domain was intended for the good of the people. Condemnation was to be done for a reason that, in essence, served what the government viewed as the greater good. In 2005, the definition of public use took a dramatic change due to a Connecticut court case called Kelo v. City of New London (545 U.S. 469). The case was resolved in the Supreme Court. The case centered upon employing eminent domain to transfer land from one private owner to another private owner. What was the outcome of this Supreme Court decision? The intent was to provide further economic development. In a final decision that was five against four, the Supreme Court held that a municipality has the right to use eminent domain as a means of community redevelopment, even if that requires transferring the seized property to private developers.

In what we may call a response to this Supreme Court decision, Illinois created the Equity in Eminent Domain Act in 2007. You can read all the details online by simply searching for Public Act 094-1055. This act is a very long read. Below is a summary. Let's start with the definitions from Section 1-1-5.

- "Acquisition of property," unless the context otherwise requires, includes the acquisition, damaging, or use of property or any right to or interest in property.

- "Blighted area," "blight," and "blighted" have the same meanings as under the applicable statute authorizing the condemning authority to exercise the power of eminent domain or, if those terms have no defined meaning under the applicable statute, then the same meanings as under Section 11-74.4-3 of the Illinois Municipal Code.

- "Condemning authority" means the State or any unit of local government, school district, or other entity authorized to exercise the power of eminent domain. (Public Act 094-1055)

The purpose of this public act in Illinois is to ensure that the government shows evidence and reasoning that an area is actually blighted before pressing forward with condemnation. To understand the nature of a blighted area, refer to the definition above.

Taxation

Taxation is a right of the government and a mandatory financial obligation of property owners, whether they are individuals or businesses. The purpose of the tax is to allow the government to generate revenue for public services. This includes everything from Medicare, the military, and well-maintained roads to our public parks and public libraries. Taxes occur at all levels of government (federal, state, and local) to varying extents. Property owners are subject to annual real estate property taxes. In addition, when owners sell a property for a profit, they are subjected to capital gains taxation.

Tax assessment, or assessment, is the job of determining the value of a property. This process is used to calculate a property tax. This is usually done by a government official called the assessor or tax assessor. His or her job is to determine the property value for the purpose of taxation.

For residential and commercial property owners in Illinois, the assessed value is 33.3% of market value, with the exception of Cook County. It has a floating schedule with residential housing being assessed as low as 10% of fair market value and as high as 25% for commercial property.

When a person or company fails to pay or chooses not to pay income taxes, a variety of consequences can erupt. Failure to pay only creates larger problems to handle. The IRS does work with people when they have a difficult time paying taxes. At times, people choose to start a payment plan with the IRS. When taxes are not paid and there's no payment plan set up, consequences may include any of the following: IRS notices will come in the mail. You will learn about the penalties and fees that at that point are unavoidable. You will be notified of the enforcement of tax debt collection and how that works. Ignoring notices usually means the IRS Automated Collection System, known as ACS, is triggered. The IRS uses ACS in an effort to collect unpaid taxes, also known as back taxes. ACS can issue a lien. A lien is a charge or claim against property that is made to enforce the payment of money. Another possible scenario is that ACS will levy the bank account and garnish wages in an effort to collect unpaid taxes. The interest starts accruing on the taxes owed. Those are the most common scenarios, although others do exist.

Escheat (Escheatment)

Escheatment is the procedure or process of a government taking ownership of unclaimed property, abandoned property, and estate assets. This most commonly happens when an individual's life comes to an end and has no known heirs and does not have a last will and testament. As you know, wills and testaments are legal documents. They express the deceased's final wishes and desires, concerning how his or her estate is to be distributed following his or her death. In the absence of an heir and a will, the government has the right to assume ownership. When it comes to granting escheat rights, each state in the US has its own regulations and rules. Sometimes these properties go to the state and at other times they go to the county where the property is located. In Illinois, real property escheats to the county where it's located and personal property escheats to the state. At times, you might hear the phrase "bona vacantia." This Latin phrase means "ownerless goods" or "vacant goods." Like escheatment, it's a legal term. It simply means a circumstance when a property is without a definite, clear, or known owner.

The Act covers all of this in 755 ILCS 20, which is known as the Escheats Act. The following comes directly from that section.

> Section 1. If any person dies owning any real or personal estate without any legacy, and leaving no known heirs or representatives capable of inheriting the same, or the legatees thereof are incapable of holding the same, and in all cases when there is no owner of real estate capable of holding the same, such real and personal estate shall escheat as provided in the Probate Act of 1975, as amended.

Section 2. In case the estate consists of personal property, letters of office shall be granted thereon, as in other cases, and the same shall be administered in conformity with the probate laws of this State. Should there be any balance left in the possession of the administrator after the payment of debts and costs of administration, the administrator shall report the same to the circuit court, with a statement of all the facts within his knowledge as to the heirship of the decedent, which facts shall constitute a part of his report, and be filed in the court; and the court shall enter an order directing the administrator to pay over the balance found in his possession to the county treasurer of the county, taking his receipt therefor, which receipt shall be filed with the county clerk and entered of record, and shall be a good and sufficient voucher to the administrator. The county clerk shall also charge the amount to the county treasurer as an escheat fund, specially designating from whose estate the same was derived.

Section 3. When the state's attorney of the county is informed or has reason to believe that any real estate within the county has escheated to the county by reason that any person owning the real estate has died without bequeathing the same, and leaving no heir capable of inheriting the same, or by reason of the incapacity of the legatee to hold the same, and such estate has not been sold according to law within five years after the death of the last owner, for the payments of the debts of the deceased, or if the state's attorney is informed, or has cause to believe that any such estate within the county has otherwise escheated to the county, it shall be the duty of the state's attorney to file a complaint in behalf of the county in the circuit court of the county, setting forth a description of the estate, the name of the last lawful owner thereof, the names of the parties in possession, and persons claiming such estate, if known, and the fact and circumstances in consequence of which such estate is claimed to have escheated, and alleging that by reason thereof the county has a right by law to such estate. The court shall enter an order against such persons, bodies politic or corporate, as alleged in the complaint, to hold, possess or claim such estate, requiring them to appear at the court on a designated return day, not less than 60 nor more than 90 days after the date thereof, and show cause why such estate should not be vested in the county. A certified copy of the order shall be served at least 10 days before the return day thereof. The court shall set forth in the order briefly the contents of the complaint, and require all persons interested in the estate to appear at the court on the return day so designated and show cause, if any, why the same should not be vested in the county; and the order shall be published for six weeks successively in some newspaper printed and published in the county, if any is there published; and if no newspaper is printed in the county, then the notice shall be published in some newspaper in the adjoining county thereto, the last insertion to be at least two weeks before the return day on which the parties are required to appear.

Section 4. All persons, bodies, politic, and corporate, named in such complaint as having possession rights or claimants of the estate, may appear and plead to such proceedings, and may deny the facts stated in the complaint, and the title of the county to the lands and tenements therein mentioned, at any time on or before the third day after the return day of the order, and any other person claiming an interest in such estate may appear and be made a defendant and plead to the complaint, by motion or by answer, within the time allowed for pleading; and if no person appears and pleads, or appearing, refuses to plead within the time, then judgment shall be entered vesting title in the county to the lands and tenements in such complaint claimed; but if any person appears and denies the title set up by the county, or denies any material facts in the complaint, an issue or issues shall be made up and tried as other issue of facts, and a survey may be ordered and entered as in other actions where the title or boundary of lands is drawn in question; and if, after the issues are tried, it appears from facts found or admitted that the county has good title to the lands and tenements in the complaint mentioned, or any part thereof, judgment shall be entered vesting title thereof in the county, and the county shall recover costs of the action against the defendant or defendants.

Section 5. When judgment is entered vesting title in the county to any land, tenements or hereditaments, such judgment shall contain a certain description of such estate, and shall be effectual for vesting the title in the county; and an order shall be entered directed to the sheriff of the county, commanding the sheriff to seize and take the lands, tenements and hereditaments so vested in the county into the sheriff's possession; and upon the return of such order of seizure, the state's attorney shall cause the record and process to be exemplified under the seal of the court, and cause the same to be recorded in the office of the recorder of the county; and such judgment shall preclude all parties and persons thereto, their heirs and assigns, so long as such judgment shall remain in force.

Section 6. Any party who has filed an appearance in the proceeding and the state's attorney, on behalf of the county, may appeal in the same manner as parties in other civil cases.

Section 7. The county treasurer shall keep just and true accounts of all moneys paid into the treasury, and if any person appears within ten years after the death of the intestate and claims any money paid into the treasury as his or hers, on legal representation such person may file a petition in the circuit court of such county, stating the nature of the claim and praying such money may be paid to the claimant. A copy of such petition shall be served upon the state's attorney of such county, who shall file an answer to the same, and the court shall thereupon examine the claim and the allegations and proofs, and if it finds that such person is entitled to any money paid into the county treasury, the court shall by order direct the county clerk to issue an order upon the county treasurer for the payment of the money, but without interest or costs. It is the duty of county boards to see that such amounts are paid in full without discount. A copy of the order of the court shall be a sufficient voucher for drawing such order. If any person appears and claims any lands vested in the county above stated, within five years after the judgment was entered, such person (other than such as were served with a copy of the order entered pursuant to Section 3 of this Act or filed an appearance in the proceeding, their heirs or assigns), may file a petition in the circuit court of the county in which the lands claimed lie, setting forth the nature of the claim and praying that the lands be relinquished to the petitioner. A copy of such petition shall be served on the state's attorney of the county, who shall file an answer. The court shall thereupon examine the claim and the allegations and proofs, and if it appears that such person is entitled to the lands claimed, the court shall enter an order accordingly, which shall be effectual for divesting the interest of the county in or to the lands, but no costs shall be adjudged against the county. All persons who fail to appear and file their petitions within the times limited, herein, shall be forever barred, saving, however, to minors and persons under legal disability the right to appear and file their petition as hereinabove set out, at any time within five years after their respective disabilities are removed. However, the county board of such county may cause such lands to be sold at any time after seizure, in which case the claimant shall be entitled to the proceeds of such sale in lieu of the lands, upon obtaining a judgment or order as hereinabove set out.

All persons beyond the limits of the United States, as to whom a right to petition under this Section is otherwise barred by this amendatory Act of 1961 or will be barred within one year after the effective date of this amendatory Act of 1961, may file a petition pursuant to this Section at any time within two years after such effective date. (755 ILCS 20)

Now, it's time for your chapter quiz.

CHAPTER 11 QUIZ

1. For a property owner, the bundle of rights and the title are the same thing.

    a. True
    b. False

2. Shannon and Mike just purchased their new home. After 10 years of living in an apartment, they are very excited. They both want to remodel. Specifically, they want to extend the backyard, build a room over the garage, and put up a metal fence around the property. Since they own the home, can they make those changes as they wish?

    a. Yes
    b. No
    c. Possibly. However, it depends on local zoning limitations.

3. Ownership is composed of a variety of rights, usually referred to as the _____.

    a. Brokerage agreement
    b. Deed
    c. Bundle of rights
    d. Title rights

4. When it comes to advertising, can a sponsored licensee legally advertise under his or her own name?

    a. Yes
    b. No
    c. More information is needed.

5. If a licensee has ownership interest in a property for sale, he/she must _____.

    a. Inform the potential buyers
    b. Sign a non-disclosure agreement
    c. Work through another licensee
    d. None of the above

6. What are the four government powers?

    a. Police protection, eminent dominance, transportation, and escheatment
    b. Police protection, eminent dominance, taxation, and escrow
    c. Police power, equity, taxation, and escrow
    d. Police power, eminent domain, taxation, and escheatment

7. The Escheats Act says the following. What goes in the blank? "The county treasurer shall keep just and true accounts of all moneys paid into the treasury, and if any person appears within _____ years after the death of the intestate and claims any money paid into the treasury as his or hers, on legal representation such person may file a petition in the circuit court of such county, stating the nature of the claim and praying such money may be paid to the claimant."

    a. 5

    b. 10

    c. 12

    d. 15

8. Sam recently passed away. He has no heirs and there is no will. His prize possession was his golden retriever named Dixie. In this circumstance, who takes responsibility for the ownership of Dixie?

    a. City

    b. County

    c. State

    d. Municipality

9. What is the procedure or process of a government taking ownership of unclaimed property, abandoned property, and estate assets?

    a. Unclaimed property initiative

    b. Government intervention

    c. Appropriation

    d. Escheatment

10. What can possibly happen if someone fails to pay his or her taxes?

    a. Penalties

    b. Fees

    c. Garnished wages

    d. Any of the above

    e. None of the above

11. In Illinois, real property escheats to the _____.

    a. State

    b. City

    c. County

    d. None of the above

12. What can the IRS use in an effort to collect unpaid taxes?

   a. Automated Collection System
   b. Automated Carryover System
   c. Back Taxes System
   d. Individual Tax Collection System

13. What is included in the mandatory financial charge that is imposed on taxpayers, whether they are individuals or businesses?

   a. Property taxes
   b. Income taxes
   c. Both A and B
   d. None of the above

14. Illinois created the Equity in Eminent Domain Act so that the government must show evidence and reasoning that an area is actually blighted before it can move forward with _____, thereby conveying ownership to a private developer.

   a. Taxation
   b. Condemnation
   c. Escheatment
   d. None of the above

15. Local governments can condemn both businesses and residences for private reasons or economic and financial reasons.

   a. True
   b. False
   c. Depends on the state

16. Which procedure in Illinois allows an authority to acquire possession of a landowner's property before having to pay just compensation?

   a. Taxation
   b. Condemnation
   c. Escheatment
   d. A quick-take
   e. None of the above

17. Sam and Martha have just returned from the closing on their new home. One of the many documents that they were given was the deed. What is the purpose of the seller giving the deed to Sam and Martha?

    a. Provide legal vesting of the property in the buyer's name
    b. To provide the buyer with suitable clothing attire for both of them to wear when they celebrate having taken ownership
    c. To create a scenario whereby the King of England has provided Sam with knighthood
    d. To provide Sam's and Martha's children with the legal right of ownership during the lifetime of Sam and Martha

18. Which entity or entities have the power to initiate eminent domain in Illinois?

    a. Illinois Department of Transportation
    b. Illinois counties
    c. Tax Assessor's office
    d. A and B
    e. A, B, and C

19. Concerning the topic of condemnation, "just compensation" is required by the _____.

    a. County law
    b. State law
    c. Municipal law
    d. None of the above because just compensation is prohibited.

20. What is "the inherent power of a government to exercise reasonable control over persons and property within its jurisdiction in the interest of the general security, health, safety, morals, and welfare except where legally prohibited" known as?

    a. Police state
    b. Condemnation
    c. Curfew law
    d. Police power

CHAPTER 12:

REAL PROPERTY OWNERSHIP INTEREST II

LEARNING GOALS:

By the end of this lesson, you will:

- Recognize the four categories of estates in land
- Understand related terms like fee simple and future interest
- Increase your comprehension about legal life estates
- Know the four types of wastes and their implications

ESTATES IN LAND DEFINITION AND CATEGORIES

First off, it's important to know that the terms "estate" and "estates in land" are not interchangeable. They have different and distinct meanings. The term estate often references the assets that a person possesses that can be inheritable by their heirs upon the owner's death. In contrast, "estates in land" refers to the ownership interest, specifically the bundle of rights, that an individual may possess whether they have interest by virtue of a deed or a lease. As discussed earlier, the bundle of rights consists of five elements: possession, quiet enjoyment, exclusion, control, and disposition. When ownership has been granted by a deed, the recipient is said to have an estate in land that is inheritable. When a right to occupy the space by virtue of a lease, the law does extend to the tenant an estate in land by virtue of having rights of possession, control, exclusion, and quiet enjoyment. In contrast with property owners, a tenant does not generally have the right of disposition. An overarching insight to know is this. The characteristic that distinguishes the different types of estates in land always comes down to duration.

Leasehold estates are as they sound. There is no ownership for the tenant. However, there are rights of possession and use of the estate. The owner or landlord (known as the lessor) legally grants this right of use and possession to the tenant (known as the lessee). These are not forever or for a lifetime. Instead, tenantship is granted for a defined period of time. In total, there are four primary types of leasehold estates. They are: 1) Estate for years also known as fixed-term tenancy, 2) Periodic tenancy, which is a rolling tenancy that's generally month to month, 3) Estate at will which is sometimes called tenancy at will, and finally 4) Estate at sufferance, which at times is called tenancy at sufferance. Each type has specific traits and characteristics concerning the lease time frame and the legal relationship between the tenant and owner/landlord. (We will get into greater detail about leasehold estates in Chapter 23.)

FREEHOLD ESTATE

Freehold estates are estates that have and feature an indefinite and indeterminate duration of time. Essentially, this means that they can exist forever, or for a lifetime. The three categories of freehold estates are:

- Fee simple absolute

- Fee simple defeasible

- Life estates

Fee simple absolute and **fee simple defeasible** have no defined termination point. Upon the death of the owner, it may be distributed in accordance with his or her will, such as given to one or more heirs, donated to the city or state, etc.

Life estates are exactly how they sound. A life estate endures as long as a designated life exists. This is what makes it indeterminate. When the designated life ceases to exist, the life estate is over and the ownership will transfer to the defined party, as detailed in the life estate agreement.

Freehold estates have a small variety of types. Diagram 12.1 illustrates what you'll learn next.

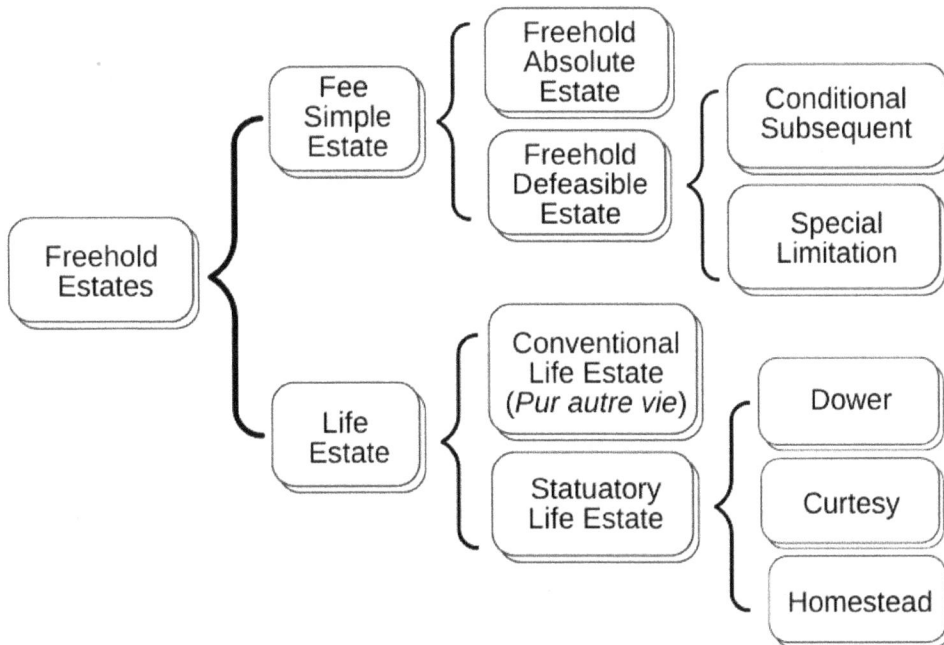

Diagram 12.1

FEE SIMPLE

This is an ownership interest that provides the least number of restrictions and yet encompasses the greatest rights of ownership. Fee simple ownership provides you with the most inclusive form of ownership because it is inheritable. It refers to the ownership that has been granted to you by a deed, which grants the bundle of rights. There are two forms of fee simple estates:

- Fee simple absolute

  - This provides the greatest level of protection for the owner as it establishes the least number of restrictions with regard to how the property can be used, and most of all, enjoyed.

  - The easiest way to determine if you have a fee simple absolute is to compare the ownership of your property to that of your neighbors. If you both have the same level of restrictions (such as taxes), then you possess fee simple absolute ownership. The rights one has as a single-family owner cannot be adequately compared to the rights that a condominium owner possesses. This is because living in a condominium configuration requires the inclusion of a monthly assessment fee that many single-family homeowners do not have to contend with.

- Fee simple defeasible

  - Also called fee simple determinable, this is a form of ownership that incorporates a condition or restriction into the ownership. This means it limits you to something that must be completed or must never be completed.

  - Regardless of whether it is a condition or a restriction, it is of a nature that it will be embedded into the deed, such that the current and all future owners of the property will be subjected to the compliance of the condition. The two different forms of fee simple defeasible interest are:

  - Condition subsequent—This is a condition that prevents someone from undertaking a specific action. For example, John Smith is selling his home, and he does not enjoy the taste of coffee. He can place into the deed a restriction that whoever purchases this property shall be restricted from consuming coffee during the duration of ownership. While this may seem like a ridiculous condition, as long as the limitation does not violate any aspect of the law, it is permitted until it is either removed by the party that created the condition or dismissed by a court of law. Violating this condition does not directly result in the loss of ownership, but can involve a court order mandating the property owner comply with the restriction.

  - Special limitation—This is a condition that is found in the deed that requires the owner of the property to perform a certain task. Every successive owner is subjected to its existence, and it could result in the loss of ownership should a court of law find the current owner is violating the obligation to perform the defined task. While this may seem to be harmful, as long as the task is legal, the potential loss of ownership will exist. In order to reduce the negative impact from the potential loss, Illinois law limits the loss of ownership to only the first 40 years. This does not remove the condition from the title, but eases the negative impact the owner of record may face. For example, John Smith is looking to sell his home. John owns a coffee shop and is a strong believer that coffee is beneficial to one's health. He puts a provision in the deed that whoever shall own this property must consume not less than 24 ounces of coffee daily. This would be a special limitation that the owner of record must comply with if they wish to retain ownership. Once again, it may not be a logical condition. Throughout history, there have been many times conditions placed on ownership did not seem logical. However, even today, as long as they are legal, they can exist.

LIFE ESTATE

Commonly known as a conventional life estate, this is an ownership interest in property that is tied to the existence of a life. Legally speaking, a life estate is the ownership of immovable property for the entirety of a designated life. This form of ownership can be created by deed or by will. It is sometimes referred to as life tenancy.

During the lifespan that has been selected, the life estate owner of the property shall have full ownership rights, including the right of disposition. However, the right to dispose of the property, either by sale or lease, has a limitation. As the ownership is limited to the duration of a life, so is the disposition. If Martha has a life estate for so long as she shall live, and upon her passing the estate shall go to her brother Mark, if Martha sells the property to Sam, Sam's rights of ownership exist so long as Martha remains alive. When Martha passes away, Mark now gets the ownership of the property and can have Sam evicted. That's why it is imperative this form of ownership is established in the deed or will such that future potential owners or tenants are aware of their limitations.

The selected lifespan can be that of either the designated life estate holder or a disinterested third party. (This is known as *pur autre vie.* You'll read about this concept soon.) Disinterested means the designated life has no ownership interest in the specific property. Life estates, although tied to a designated life, are not necessarily tied to a human life. Many times, a life estate is based upon the life duration of a dog, cat, and, to get ridiculous, even that of an earthworm. As long as the designated life is animate, it can be used as the basis for this relationship. The lifespan of a tree does not qualify. You cannot use an inanimate life to base the duration of ownership upon.

Do specific benefits come with ownership of the property? Absolutely. However, the life estate holder does not have absolute rights. The life estate holder has the right to:

1. Enjoy the right of occupancy. This means the life estate holder has the legal right to live at (occupy) the property for the duration of the designated life.

2. Rent out the whole estate, entire house, all or parts of the land, rooms, and/or space as he/she desires while he/she has possession. Tenant occupancy is subject to the designated life continuing to exist.

3. Sell or give away the estate in Illinois. However, the recipient must understand that their rights of ownership will also be limited to the duration of the designated life.

The life estate holder does not have the right to bequeath the estate as part of his or her will. Additionally, the life estate holder is not permitted to destroy, injure, deface, or harm the estate in any way.

Upon the individual's death, the ownership of the property may revert to the creator of the life estate (reversion), or it may pass to another designated entity (remainder).

Reversion and Remainder

Before you read about reversion and remainder, a foundational term to understand is future interest. **Future interest** is the legal *future* right an entity may have in a property. However, the property ownership does not include *present* possession, use, or enjoyment of the property. Keep in mind that possession does not mean or imply ownership. It comes down to the terms contained within the deed.

In US property law, **reversion** is a future interest in property granted under a life estate, resulting in the ownership returning to the prior grantor of the estate at the conclusion of the designated life. This takes place once all interests in the said property that were held by the life estate holder have been fully terminated.

A **remainder** is the individual other than the life estate holder or the prior grantor that has the future rights to the property. At times, it's called remainder interest. This happens when a property owner creates a transfer of property to another individual. However, the owner does not want to retain future rights to the property, and conveys those rights through a third party. This third party is called the "transferee" or "remainderman." This individual will become the property owner when the designated life comes to a close. Only a deed or a will can create a remainder. Here's an example: Wanda deeds the Shackleton Estate to her brother Rolland for the duration of his life. When Rolland's life comes to an end, the estate conveys to either the previous grantor (Wanda) or to the remainder. If Rolland's daughter, Jenna, is the named remainder, Wanda can also name Jenna's children as *contingent remainders* should Jenna pass away before Rolland.

Only two types of remainders exist: vested and contingent. A **vested remainder** is created when property is granted to two people or parties. The second type of remainder, a **contingent remainder**, is generated at the time of the granting when a remainder cannot be fully vested. This most typically happens in two different situations: 1) when the beneficiary is unknown or unable to be located and thus the property cannot be vested, and 2) when the known beneficiary is subject to one or more specific conditions which have not yet happened.

To summarize, both remainder and reversion are a type of future interest. If Mr. Jones gives Susan one of his estates for the duration of her life, then Mr. Jones retains the future interest called reversion. If Mr. Jones defines a third party (and not Susan) as the future recipient of ownership following Susan's passing, the party to whom the ownership will pass upon Susan's death is called the remainder.

CONVENTIONAL LIFE ESTATE WITH PUR AUTRE VIE

Pur autre vie is a French legal term. It means "for the life of another." This term describes how long the life estate ownership interest lasts. As you know, it is determined by the *lifespan* of a human being, an animal, or some other type of animate entity. The ownership interest is dependent on the duration of the designated lifespan. When the designated life ends, the ownership interest ends.

For example, Richard is granted ownership rights of the family estate so long as his father remains alive. For the duration of his father's life, Richard owns the house. When his father dies, his ownership rights to the family estate cease to exist. Thus, *pur autre vie* is what gives Richard ownership rights until the death of his father.

LEGAL LIFE ESTATE

A legal life estate is not created at will or intentionally by the owner/s. A legal life estate is created by a statute or law. As such, they're also referred to as "statutory life estates." Every state has its own requirements and parameters when it comes to legal life estates. While most states recognize the three basic types of legal life estates, not all states do. The three basic types of legal life estates in no particular order are:

1. Dower

2. Curtesy

3. Homestead

A **dower** is a common law right. The purpose of a dower is to protect a wife's interest once her husband dies and there is no will. It refers to her legal rights to the property once he has passed. Most commonly, the dower is what empowered the new widow to meet her own needs, as well as the needs of her late husband's children that he had with her. When the husband is alive, he cannot transfer his wife's dower rights without her written permission. In short, dower is the wife's future interest in the husband's estate.

Curtesy is, in many ways, the opposite of a dower because its focus is on the husband. This is the husband's future interest in the wife's estate. Curtesy is another common law right to the property and estate of his deceased wife.

However, in 1975, Illinois discontinued the use of the common law terms of dower and curtesy. Instead, Illinois adopted the **Uniform Probate Code** (UPC). It is a uniform act drafted by the National Conference of Commissioners on Uniform State Laws (NCCUSL). This body governs the probate process in all US states. Its main focus is to speed up the probate process. Another main goal of UPC is to simplify, standardize and update the ways in which state laws govern intestacy, wills, and trusts. Intestacy, or intestate, means a person died without having a legal will in place. If someone says, "He died in intestacy," it simply means he died without a legal will. When this happens, how do the deceased's assets get distributed? This is done by a probate court. At times, a will presented in court is deemed invalid. Likewise, when this happens, the estate is now deemed intestate. Intestacy law focuses on who is entitled to the property in light of no valid will being present. Which courts oversee probate cases? Circuit courts. Illinois' bigger counties feature a specific division for probate within the circuit court. The county in which the deceased person lived is the county where the probate case will take place. Typically in Illinois, if there are no contests and/or disputes, probate will be finalized in less than twelve months.

Every death must go through probate. There are four purposes for the utilization of probate:

1. Verify the existence of a will.

2. Define the precise assets of the deceased.

3. Define who the heirs are.

4. Identify outstanding debts.

Homestead is a type of legal life estate in Illinois. While homestead is most commonly used in everyday language as a place where one lives, in this context, it's a legal term. A homestead is a freehold estate. It was created in order to shield and protect individuals who declare bankruptcy from unsecured creditors. A secured creditor is one who has defined the asset that is the target of the claim, such as a mortgage. Unsecured creditors have the right to pursue all of the assets of the debtor. Homestead, in this case, is designed to protect the individual that is faced with total financial devastation as a result of a claim from an unsecured creditor.

For example, let's say I just left the grocery store. I'm getting ready to pull out of my parking spot and I do not look behind me. Is it possible a man called Mike might be walking behind my vehicle? Yes. Could I accidentally hit Mike? Absolutely. At that point, could Mike sue me? Yes. Next, let's say Mike tries to convince the court that I have to give him forty million dollars for pain and suffering. (An astronomical amount of money is intentionally being used.) In this context, does Mike have the right to take everything I own, including my home, car, clothing, furniture, and food? The answer is yes! Mike does have the right. This is the result of a general lien. (A lienholder has the right to seize all of a person's assets as a result of a lawsuit.) By court order, the lien allows the injured person, Mike, to take everything from me. Could he theoretically be putting me in a cardboard box tonight, since I won't have a home? Yes. At this crucial juncture is where homestead comes into play. It's a protection against claims from unsecured creditors under a general lien. If I am going to be financially devastated because of this claim, Mike will be able to take what I own. However, Mike must return something to me so I can start my life over again. If I am a single person, Mike must return $15,000. For married couples, $30,000 must be returned. That's the application of the word homestead in this particular realm.

To summarize, conventional and *pur autre vie* life estates are created by way of conveyance or through grants to another individual. A legal life estate, in contrast, is created and dictated by a law or statute.

ESTATES AND THE FOUR TYPES OF WASTE

Waste is the proper legal term that describes harm, destruction, or injury to the property. Waste entails a cause of action that can turn into a lawsuit or other legal matter. These lawsuits are referred to as a "lawsuit for waste." The lawsuit's focus is on the condition of real property. Specifically, it's about how the life estate holder damages or injures the property, which results in a decrease in demand and property value. Who can bring up the charges? Either the remainder or the original creator of the life estate can hold the life estate holder responsible for the damage and subsequent loss of value.

Waste falls inside one of these four types. They are:

1. Voluntary waste

2. Permissive waste

3. Ameliorative waste

4. Equitable waste

Voluntary waste is also known as affirmative waste. Within this concept is any type of change or changes done to the estate that negligently or intentionally cause injury and harm to the estate. Additionally, it can be any type of harm or damage that depletes, diminishes, and/or robs the estate of its resources. The exception would be that the depletion had already been set in motion due to some type of preexisting use.

Permissive waste is caused by a type of failure or negligence. In this circumstance, the owner intentionally or unintentionally does not maintain the estate. This includes failing to facilitate both the physical health and the financial health of the estate. In most cases, the owner is required to pay for repairs or make financial reparations . . . whatever it takes to restore the estate back to its original condition.

Ameliorative waste is an upgrade or improvement to an estate that changes the character or personality of the estate itself. What's fascinating is that even if the change increases the estate value, it is still considered ameliorative waste. Once again, financial reparations must be made by the life tenant to undo the changes that were done. Why is this? Usually, the main reason is that the life tenant is legally required to keep the property in good condition based on society's expectations at that moment.

Equitable waste is some type of action, or possibly negligence, that could decrease the value of the property in the future. For example, let's say you are the remainderman in a life estate. One day, the life tenant decides to remove twenty apple trees from the property because he wants a clear view of the Pacific coastline. Does this action, without the remainderman's consent, constitute potential financial harm? It possibly can. If so, legal action may be sought by the remainder and may result in monetary damages. As you can see, this is an area where legal advice is recommended.

Without reviewing, take a moment to do the chapter quiz below.

CHAPTER 12 QUIZ

1. The terms "estate" and "estate in land" are interchangeable.

    a. True
    b. False

2. Michael has an interest in real property that he will possess in the future. Which term describes what he has?

    a. Estate in land
    b. Estate
    c. Leasehold estate

3. When ownership has been granted by a deed, the recipient is said to have _____ that is inheritable.

    a. An estate in land
    b. A leasehold estate
    c. Reversionary rights
    d. None of the above is correct.

4. What are the three types of freehold estates?

    a. Fee simple estates, leasehold estates, and current estates
    b. Fee simple absolute, fee simple defeasible, and life estates
    c. Leasehold estates, fee simple defeasible estates, and concurrent estates
    d. Leasehold estates, fee absolute estates, and equitable estates

5. A new licensee is still confused about the four general types of estates. What can you tell him to focus on that can help him remember what makes them different?

    a. Focus on who the owner is
    b. Focus on the deed
    c. Focus on the duration
    d. None of the above

6. Which type of estate has an indefinite and indeterminate duration of time? Essentially, this means that it can exist forever, or for a lifetime.

    a. Freehold estates
    b. Leasehold estates
    c. Concurrent estates
    d. Equitable estates
    e. All of the above

7. What makes fee simple absolute different from fee simple defeasible?

    a. Fee simple absolute defines a definitive period of time for ownership while fee simple defeasible grants unlimited ownership duration.
    b. Fee simple absolute provides the least number of restrictions regarding the property ownership while fee simple defeasible defines a specific condition that you must comply with or ignore.
    c. Fee simple remainder, fee simple defeasible, and life estates all refer to the same legal concept.
    d. None of the above

8. In a leasehold estate, can tenantship be granted indefinitely by the grantor?

    a. Yes
    b. No. It's only granted for a defined period of time.
    c. No. It's only for the lifetime of the tenant.
    d. None of the above

9. Janet is the tenant of a leasehold estate. Does this mean she is also the owner?

    a. Yes
    b. No
    c. Not enough information is given.

10. Which of the following can be rolling tenancy?

    a. Week to week
    b. Month to month
    c. Year to year
    d. All of the above

11. James and Rolland are not related. However, they both own the same property and are both occupants. Which type of estate do they have?

    a. Freehold estate
    b. Leasehold estate
    c. Concurrent estate
    d. Equitable estate

12. Which of the following freehold estates feature an indefinite and indeterminate duration of time?

    a. Life estates and fee simple defeasible
    b. Simple derivative
    c. Fee simple and fee simple defeasible
    d. All of the above

13. In the context of real estate, which of the following best describes a fee?

    a. One's legal right to the ownership of land
    b. One's legal right to sell his or her land
    c. One's legal right to possess the land
    d. None of the above

14. Loretta is a chronic worrier. She has experienced bankruptcy twice as well as a divorce. She is risk-averse. Which type of estate would give her the greatest level of protection and arguably the most peace of mind?

    a. Fee simple absolute
    b. Fee simple defeasible
    c. Life estate
    d. Legal life estate

15. Jim is a no-nonsense type of guy who does not like being tied down to a lot of restrictions. If Jim is selling his personal residence, which of the following estates would establish a level of ownership with the least number of restrictions?

    a. Fee simple absolute
    b. Fee simple defeasible
    c. Life estate
    d. Legal life estate

16. Tasha wants to sell her land. She has a sprawling, beautiful estate that includes numerous peach trees. As peach orchards have been in her family for generations, she places a restriction that the peach orchards must be maintained. What is this type of arrangement called?

    a. Owner's prerogative
    b. Special limitation
    c. Fee simple determinable
    d. Condition subsequent

17. The ownership of a life estate includes which of the following?

    a. A limited period
    b. An indefinite period
    c. An agreed-upon duration of time that varies case by case
    d. Any of the above

18. Brian is a life tenant. His nephew had a horrible financial setback and Brian is considering gifting the estate to his nephew so he will at least have a foundation for his life. Does Brian have the right to transfer the estate?

    a. Yes, but with limited rights
    b. Yes, with full fee simple absolute rights
    c. No
    d. More information is needed

19. A legal life estate is conventionally and always created by a will or testament.

    a. True
    b. False

20. What are the four types of waste?

    a. Volitionary, negligence, ameliorative, and equitable
    b. Voluntary, permissive, ameliorative, and equitable
    c. Voluntary, permissive, ameliorative, and erosive
    d. None of the above

CHAPTER 13:

MOTHER NATURE AND REAL ESTATE

LEARNING GOALS:

By the end of this lesson, you will:

- Realize the unique relationship Mother Earth has with real estate
- Know the implications of riparian rights and littoral rights
- Understand easements and their implications
- Know how easements are created and terminated
- Be able to articulate the difference between an easement and a license

PEOPLE ALWAYS HAVE PLANS and expectations for their property. As much as they want their plans to go smoothly, that is not always how it happens. Why? Because real estate cannot exist without the Earth and Mother Nature. In other words, real estate and Mother Nature do not always play well together. Issues come up. Obstacles arise. These could be anything from natural disasters and annual floods to neighbors arguing over water or mineral rights. The bottom line is that both Mother Nature and Earth science are always connected to real estate.

MOTHER NATURE: WATER RIGHTS

What water rights exist when you are a property owner adjacent to a waterway? Most of the time, property owners have the unfettered and unrestricted right to use the waterway as they see fit. However, they are not permitted to change the course of the water and, understandably, cannot contaminate or pollute the water. Most commonly, water rights are equated with the type of waterway and the way the water is used, which could be for a variety of purposes.

Riparian rights are commonly held by property owners when their land has a border with any type of natural waterway and/or contains water. At times, you may hear these property owners referred to as riparian owners. Additionally, riparian rights include water that naturally flows through his or her property as well. The water must touch his or her property. What happens if the property is close to the water but does not actually touch it? In this case, the property owner does not have riparian rights.

Riparian rights can apply to waterways that are navigable and not navigable. This includes rivers, streams, creeks, ponds, lakes, and similar waterways. When is the waterway navigable versus non-navigable? You can discount and exclude kayaks, canoes, and rowboats. This concept specifically focuses on the utilization of motorboats or sailboats. Is the waterway deep enough to avoid impaling the propeller or fin keel into the soil? Is the waterway wide enough to provide for a U-turn without the boat capsizing? If the answer to both questions is yes, the waterway is deemed to be navigable. Non-navigable waterways cannot handle motorboats and sailboats. This is how we define where the **lot line** of a property that borders the waterway is. If the waterway is not navigable, the lot line is in the middle of the waterway. This means a portion of your property is underwater. For example, Jane owns a large number of acres and a river flows around the property. If the waterway is not navigable, Jane owns to the center point of the waterway. If the river that surrounds Jane's land is navigable, in order to keep the waterway open to public use, Jane's lot line would extend to the shoreline of the waterway. Here is another example. A kayaker is floating down a thirty-foot-wide river and is five feet off the shoreline. Technically, he or she is trespassing on private property.

Littoral rights specifically refer to property adjacent to an ocean or other large body of water.

Property owners who own such property have littoral rights. Specifically, their land borders a waterway that has a tide and can be navigated by boat. When a landowner has littoral rights, she has unrestricted access to the lake or ocean. At a certain distance from the shore, she is no longer the owner. The ownership belongs to the government. To get detailed, she only owns up to what is called the "mean high water mark." Also called MHW at times, this is known as a tidal datum. It's a standard elevation that is defined by a certain phase of the water's tide. It shows the average of 100% of the daily tidal high water heights, which have been observed over several years' time. The tide is a function of the gravitational pull of the moon. Therefore, we typically experience high tide during the evening hours when the moon is directly overhead. This is the point at which we define the edge of your property. During daylight hours, when the moon is on the other side of the planet, the exposed shoreline is public ground. Although the homeowner did purchase an oceanfront property, the reality is that a good portion of the land along the shoreline is available for public access. This means consumers have the right to stroll along the water's edge without trespassing on the property. Keep in mind that governmental restrictions can limit access to the public grounds exposed by low tide.

Scenario: Whether a property owner's rights are riparian or littoral, what about animals in the water? If a beaver creates a dam in front of the property, can it divert water on the property? Yes. If so, then the owner has to suffer with that. The owner cannot destroy the beaver's habitat. There are provisions of law that dictate that an owner cannot destroy natural habitats. Could the owner ask for assistance from the local government to relocate the beaver and its dam? Yes. However, it will cost time and money.

There are three geological ways in which water can interact with the whimsical nature of shorelines and coasts. They are: 1) accretion, 2) erosion, and 3) avulsion.

1. **Accretion**: This is the gradual deposit of sediment by the actions of a waterway that increases the land mass. After a submersion (under water) occurrence, accretion is the process of sand returning to the visible portion of a beach or shoreline. A healthy beach or shoreline will almost always experience a period of submersion during mild and strong storms and subsequent accretion during calmer and more tranquil times. Can landowners gain and legally own any "new" land due to accretion? Yes.

2. **Erosion**: To erode simply means for something to be worn away over time by natural agents. Erosion has two parts. The first is the removal of soil, rock, and/or dissolved material from one position or location on land. The second part is that the soil, rock, or other elements are transported to another location. This occurs by way of different surface processes from Mother Nature, such as the flow of water or the consistency or strength of the wind. Erosion differs from weathering because weathering does not include movement. For example, if a large boulder changes over time or even gets

broken but stays in the same place, that is weathering. Simply put, erosion includes movement and weathering does not. Can landowners lose land due to erosion? Yes. It is a common occurrence.

3. **Avulsion**: This is a sudden, easily perceived, and many times dramatic loss of land that happens because of the force and power of water. Most commonly, hurricanes, nor'easters (a powerful extratropical cyclone), and other storms cause avulsion. When hurricanes happen, it is common to see before and after images chronicling how a shoreline has changed.

MOTHER NATURE: LAND AND ENCUMBRANCES

Now that you've learned how water rights work, let's explore the other half of the equation, which is land. Like water, land also brings up many questions and, at times, dilemmas or confusion. This brings us to the next important and related term, encumbrances.

An **encumbrance** is a restriction or claim levied on a parcel of land that limits what the current owner can do. It is a right to, a legal liability for, and/or an interest in property. An encumbrance does not preclude the property owner from transferring title, but it can affect the property's transferability. Because of the restrictive nature of an encumbrance, it could negatively impact the property's desirability and value. Mortgages, easements, and property tax liens are the most well-known and common forms of encumbrances on real estate. There are different types of encumbrances: 1) liens (most commonly financial charges), 2) encroachments, 3) easements, 4) leases, 5) mortgages, 6) restrictive covenants, and 7) deed restrictions. (You will read about the first three now and learn more about the rest in the chapter about deeds.)

1. **Liens**: As you recall, a lien is a claim against property to enforce the payment of money. All liens are encumbrances. However, not every encumbrance is a lien.

2. **Encroachments**: An encroachment is a physical intrusion that is unwelcome or unwanted by a property owner. It is when a piece of real estate extends from one property over, under, or onto the property's surface or air space of another landowner's property. Examples include but are not limited to a tree, a stairway, a garden, bushes, a bay window, a garage, a fence that is leaning, or any part of a house. Keep in mind that the encroachment illegally passes one property owner's land boundary and enters the land of someone else..

3. **Easements**: An easement allows an individual or an organization (who does not own the land) to use the land of a property owner for a specific purpose. It is a non-possessory right to use and/or enter into someone else's real property, although he/she does not actually own the property. Easements are very useful for linking or connecting

two or more pieces of land. This allows people to gain access to other properties and/or facilities. For example, many students who are reading this book have, at one point or another, gone to a public beach. How did they access that public beach? Most likely, they followed a path on land that is privately owned. Another common example is gaining access to a privately owned lake for the purpose of ice skating or fishing. An easement is usually considered a property right of non-owners in common law.

Rights and privileges of an easement holder can differ significantly. It all comes down to the jurisdiction in which he/she owns property. In the past, these four forms of easements were enforced by common law courts:

- Right-of-way, (also called easements of way)

- Easements of support (related to excavation projects)

- Easements of light (solar easement), and air

- Rights connected to artificial waterways

Related terms include:

- **Positive and negative easements:** A positive easement is the right to use another person's property for a particular purpose. A negative easement is the right to prohibit and stop anyone from doing anything that is otherwise legal on their own land. A positive easement could be that a plumbing company can fix pipes in a neighborhood without needing to obtain permission from anyone. A negative easement, for example, can restrict James from putting up a tall fence on his property because it would block Sarah's beach view. This means James is subject to a negative easement from Sarah.

- **Dominant tenement and servient tenement:** The land that receives the benefit is called the dominant tenement. The land that does not receive the benefit is called the servient tenement. It is sometimes also called the "burdened land" as it is subject to the easement's existence.

- **Public and private easements:** The difference between these easements is quite simple. All you have to do is ask, "Who benefits?" Thus, a public easement is one in which the public benefits. Examples include public streets and highways, public libraries, and public facilities. A private easement is one whose enjoyment is limited to certain people. It is not public. An example would be an estate that has a lake. The lake is private and not open to the public. Said another way, the public has no right to enjoy the lake.

- **Easement in gross:** It is a right to use the land of another for a specific purpose. It is granted to the person. It is not attached to the land. By not attaching it to the land, the person that receives the right does not have the right to transfer the ability to someone else. Thus, an easement in gross benefits a person or a legal entity instead of benefiting the dominant estate. Can an easement in gross be for personal or commercial usage? Yes, this type of easement can apply to either context. A personal use example would be that of Jack being able to use a boat ramp. A commercial use example is a local utility company running overhead high-tension cables over a commercial building. An easement in gross could be granted in the absence of a utility easement.

- **Easement appurtenant:** An easement appurtenant is one that usually favors the dominant estate. It transfers automatically when the dominant estate itself is transferred and is included with the estate ownership. An appurtenant easement enables individuals the ability to gain access to land (such as a beach or lake) that is only available by entering the land owned by another person.

- **Floating easement:** This is an easement as usual except with one key difference. The reason "floating" is in its name is because the easement dimensions and location are not clearly defined. This type of easement is fluid and changeable. Additionally, the owner can change the access route if he/she chooses to do so.

- **Party wall:** Every time you stay at a hotel, most likely your room is boxed in by one or two party walls. A party wall is simply a shared wall. It separates and divides two different and separate houses or properties (rented or owned). The most common occurrences for party walls are commercial properties, such as hotels, condos, office complexes, and apartments. Multiunit residential properties also have party walls. Party walls are essentially anywhere in which different tenants or owners share or cohabitate a structure together. Local laws and/or state laws outline requirements for party walls. They state exactly how party walls must be constructed and which specifications are required. Specifications may include soundproofing, insulation that is fire retardant, and other safety features.

EASEMENT CREATION

How are easements created? The primary ways are:

1. Express grant

2. By implication

3. By necessity

4. By prescription

5. By condemnation

In an **express grant**, an easement is created by written or verbal consent. When it is written, it can be made by contract or deed. When done well, the written agreement will outline the exact location, along with the dimensions of the easement. Doing so bypasses problems that may arise from verbal agreements and floating easements.

Easement created by implication exists when there is no recorded or documented easement. However, the circumstances, details, and/or history reveal that an easement was the intention. This type of easement is also called an "easement by prior use."

Easement created by necessity means that the individual claiming an easement needs to show evidence that the easement is necessary. For example, everyone has the right to access their property from a public thoroughfare. If your property is landlocked (surrounded on all sides by private property), the law will intervene and grant you the right to trespass (cross over) the land of another property owner so you can access your property.

Easement by prescription, also known as prescriptive easement, grants an individual the right to use your property for a particular purpose because they have been doing so for a lengthy period of time without restriction. In order for someone to seek a claim for a prescriptive easement, they must be able to prove to the satisfaction of the court that their actions have been done:

- Continuously (in Illinois 20 consecutive years)

- Open (visible to the property owner)

- Hostile (without first securing consent from the owner)

- Notorious (every step on the property is a violation of the law known as trespass)

- Adverse (not in the best interest of the property owner).

Easement by condemnation: Although not very common, this type of easement exists. If the government feels there is a need to use a portion of your property for the benefit of the public, the local municipality can exercise condemnation proceedings that result in an easement appurtenant. This creates a permanent easement for public benefit and use on your property. The government has the power to do this by way of eminent domain. If property value decreases because of this action, the government is required to compensate the property owner.

EASEMENT TERMINATION

Any one of the following methods is the process to terminate an easement:

1. **Not needed**: The necessity for the easement no longer exists.

2. **Quiet title**: Someone can initiate legal action to "quiet title." This legal action is taken against the person who claims to have a right to an easement.

3. **Building demolition**: If there is an easement to use a particular structure, once the building does not exist, the easement does not exist.

4. **Abandonment**: This easement termination takes place when the use of the easement has been abandoned and is no longer being accessed by the party to whom it was granted.

5. **Release**: This means both the easement's grantor and grantee agree to legally terminate the easement.

6. **Expiration**: The easement reaches its formal expiration date as set forth by a previous legal agreement.

7. **Merger**: This occurs when one property owner gains the title to both dominant and servient tenement. This is also called termination by merger.

8. **Condemnation**: The government exercises its right of eminent domain to cease the property for the public good. This claim supersedes any easement rights that currently may exist on the property.

EASEMENT IN GROSS VERSUS LICENSE

By now, you understand the definition and meaning of easement in gross. A related term is called a license. A license verbally grants someone permission to use someone else's land for a specific reason or purpose. The licensor has the right to alter or revoke a person's right to the license at will. Licenses are easily confused with easements in gross because both involve using someone else's land. The key difference is a license grants informal consent and an easement in gross grants formal consent. A license is not an interest in the land itself like an easement in gross.

For example, a father and son want to hunt on a portion of land that they do not own. In this circumstance, they can request permission from the landowner to hunt on his or her land. The permission is given and exists as a license. When the father and son have completed their hunting outing, their licenses terminate. In contrast, an easement in gross continues on into the future.

Now it's time to take your chapter quiz.

CHAPTER 13 QUIZ

1. Which of the following cannot be separated from real estate?

   a. Earth science

   b. Nature

   c. Hurricanes

   d. Nor'easters

   e. All of the above

2. A new licensee, Frank, is showing an oceanfront property. The lady who is interested begins asking him about her water rights if she chooses to purchase the property. Which specific topic below will Frank talk about with her?

   a. Riparian rights

   b. Sovereignty of land

   c. Littoral rights

   d. None of the above

3. Riparian rights in Illinois are simple and easy to understand because of the state's statutory provisions.

   a. True

   b. False

4. Jocelyn just purchased a property that has a stream and a lake. What is she not allowed to do?

   a. Divert or change the stream's course

   b. Put waste in the lake

   c. Build a small dam

   d. All of the above

   e. Only A and B

5. Shannon and Mike are newlyweds and recently purchased a beautiful sprawling property that has everything they were searching for. The property is adjacent to a creek. Do they have riparian rights?

   a. Yes

   b. No

   c. More information is needed.

6. Are human-made and artificial waterways or bodies of water included with riparian rights?

    a. Yes
    b. No
    c. More information is needed.

7. If people are limited to the use of kayaks, canoes, and rowboats in a body of water, where do the property owner's riparian rights end?

    a. At the water's edge
    b. The middle of the body of water
    c. At the high tide mark
    d. None of the above

8. Frank and Martha have lived on their property for 20 years. They were shocked last month when they discovered that beavers were building a dam on what they call "their creek." They noticed that it was diverting the course of the water. They know that if they do not break the dam or do something to run off the beavers, they will lose land. Since they want to sell in five years, they do not want their property value to decrease. What can they do?

    a. They can remove the beavers, or hire someone to do so.
    b. They can destroy the dam, or hire someone to do so.
    c. Legally, they cannot do anything.
    d. They can ask for local government assistance to relocate the beavers, and the dam, although it will cost time and money.

9. Can beachfront property landowners gain and legally own "new" land due to the geological phenomenon of accretion?

    a. Yes
    b. No

10. Erosion is only defined as the loss of land caused by natural agents.

    a. True
    b. False

11. Large batches of sediment and rocks are flowing from John's shoreline down two miles to his neighbor Sarah's shoreline. What is this called?

    a. Erosion
    b. Accretion
    c. Avulsion
    d. Encumbrance

12. Which of the following is the broadest term that affects the transferability of a property?

   a. Easement
   b. Encumbrance
   c. Encroachment
   d. Liens
   e. Deed restrictions

13. Every encumbrance is a lien.

   a. True
   b. False
   c. Not enough information is given.
   d. All of the above

14. Bob is a veteran who has lived at his coastal residence with his wife since 1988. His wife has always wanted an upstairs balcony. For their anniversary this year, Bob decided that he and his sons are going to build it for her. Garry is Bob's neighbor. While Garry and his family are on a two-week vacation, Bob and his sons get to work building the balcony. The balcony blocks Garry's bedroom window view of the beach. When Garry returns, he is livid. Whether intentionally planning to build it when Garry was gone or not, which term describes what Bob has created?

   a. Negative easement
   b. Encumbrance
   c. Encroachment
   d. Easement appurtenant

15. What do you call the right to use another person's property for a particular purpose?

   a. Servient tenement
   b. Private easement
   c. Easement in gross
   d. None of the above

16. The Thacker family is upset because they do not understand an easement that is on their property. After purchasing, they discovered that the easement has no exact dimensions or location. Which term best describes the type of easement they have?

   a. Negative easement
   b. Public easement
   c. Private easement
   d. Floating easement

17. The burdened land is the land that is subject to the easement. It does not receive the benefit. Which term best describes this?

    a. Dominant tenement
    b. Servient tenement
    c. Negative easement
    d. None of the above

18. Phil and Lois are a young couple who just signed up for a two-year lease in a homeowners association. Between working full-time jobs and having three kids, they are always busy. During some of their sessions with the leasing agent, they were tired. Sometimes, they simply nodded their heads in agreement, not fully understanding what was being said. Upon moving in, they reviewed their paperwork. One folder was dedicated fully to HOA rules and regulations. Lois had wanted to plant marigolds in the front yard but according to the rules, and learned that she cannot. Phil wanted to put a small shed in the backyard, and likewise, that would be against the rules. They're both frustrated. Which of the following is in place that creates this type of scenario?

    a. Deed restrictions
    b. Title restrictions
    c. HOA restrictions
    d. Condemnation

19. In which way can an easement appurtenant not legally be terminated?

    a. Demolition
    b. Abandonment
    c. Condemnation
    d. Sale of the property

20. Monica is now in her late 70s. Her husband, who passed away three years ago, was a lifelong fisherman. She and her husband owned their property together for more than 35 years. The acreage is sprawling and has five lakes. They granted fishing licenses to countless individuals through the years. Many of them her husband knew, but she had only met a handful of them. Nowadays, she no longer feels comfortable with strangers on her property. What can she do?

    a. Nothing. She has to wait for each license to expire.
    b. She has to talk to an accountant about the topic of estoppel.
    c. She needs to create a negative easement.
    d. She can revoke their licenses when she sees fit.

CHAPTER 14:

ALL ABOUT LIENS AND REAL ESTATE TAXES

LEARNING GOALS:

By the end of this lesson, you will:

- Know the wide variety of liens that make up the world of real estate
- Understand the process of property valuation
- Discover why and when equalization is implemented

LET'S START WITH A FEW POINTS about liens that you've already read. A lien is a claim or charge against property to enforce the payment of money. Written another way, a lien is a type of security interest. It's a legal claim or charge against property. Its goal is to drive and dictate payment. A lien is granted on an item of property in order to secure the payment of a debt. At times, it secures the fulfillment of some other type of obligation. The property owner who grants the lien is called the lienee. The individual who reaps the benefit of the lien is the lienholder or lienor. Liens are most commonly financial charges.

Security is referred to as collateral at times. In lending agreements, having security (collateral) is a borrower's promise and duty to the lender to repay the loan in full. The collateral can be viewed as a type of protection for the lender in case the borrower defaults on the loan. If the borrower fails to pay in accordance with the lending agreement (contract), the collateral, in most cases, is seized from the borrower.

SPECIFIC AND GENERAL LIENS

First of all, there are specific and general liens. A **specific lien** is directly connected to a specific and particular asset. For example, the mortgage and the property taxes are examples of a specific lien, because the real property is the collateral for the debt. Specific liens are tied to specific assets.

For example, mortgage foreclosure takes place in the context of a specific lien. As you know, foreclosure is the loss of real property due to the failure to meet the loan payment obligation. It is not the loss of everything that the debtor owns.

Another example of a specific lien involves property taxes that are owed on the debtor's real property. It does not include the debtor's personal property. Since local governments have the authority to foreclose on unpaid property taxes, the majority of lenders require real estate property tax payments to be escrowed. Why? Because the government's claim to the property supersedes the lender's claim.

A **general lien** is obviously not specific. It's the other side of the coin. A general lien is a lien against the entirety of one's property. This means it includes both personal property and real property. In other words, the debtor does not just lose the house. He/she also loses any vehicles, furniture, clothing, electronics, and so forth.

An example of a general lien would be an IRS tax lien. No doubt you've heard of celebrities getting in trouble with the IRS because of unpaid taxes. Perhaps one of the most famous cases was that of legendary country music singer Willie Nelson. In 1990, he was slammed with a large bill of back taxes from the IRS. The total owed? A whopping $32 million! The total was later reduced. Regardless, as the story goes, he was unable to pay. In light of that, the government seized the majority of his assets. With this type of infraction, the IRS had a hold over his personal and real property, including bank accounts, vehicles, and more.

Consensual and Non-consensual Liens

Liens can be consensual (voluntary) or non-consensual (involuntary). Consensual liens are created by a legal contract between the lienee and the lienholder. Non-consensual liens most commonly are created by statute, or because of the presence of common law. What allows the lienholder the right to impose a lien in the first place? It is the law. The lien can be on real property or a chattel.

Consensual liens include:

- Mortgage liens: This is a lien against real property, rather than personal property. As a real estate broker, this is the type of lien you will most frequently encounter.

- Chattel mortgages: This is a lien against personal property, rather than real property.

Non-consensual liens include:

- Tax liens: These are implemented to secure tax payments.

- Mechanic's liens: This type of lien secures payment for labor that is done on someone's property or land. Have you ever heard of a property owner failing or refusing to pay a contractor who worked on his real property? I'm sure you have. When this occurs, a mechanic's lien comes into play. It is a lien focused on securing payment for the services rendered by the contractor. The service provider wants his or her unpaid compensation to be paid in full. Can this also include materials? Absolutely. It can include both services and materials provided, depending on the context. Although called a mechanic's lien, it applies to any type of service provider who did work on an owner's property. Most often, mechanic's liens are filed by contractors, subcontractors, companies that lease equipment, design professionals, and different types of suppliers. The state of California has gone so far as to make mechanic's liens a state constitutional right. The Act weighs in heavily on this and has an entire section dedicated to this topic. It's called the Mechanics Lien Act and is located in 770 ILCS 60. A mechanic's lien takes precedence over all other liens except for government liens.

Less common non-consensual liens include:

- Weed liens: These are also known as "demolition liens." They occur when a property is a public hazard or a nuisance in some form or fashion. The government does an assessment in order to figure out how to fix or improve the problematic property, or whether it is best to demolish it.

- Attorney's liens: This is a lien against an individual who refuses to compensate an attorney for legal services rendered. It allows the attorney to seize and hold the assets of the individual as collateral until the debt is paid. Most often, the assets are documents and paperwork.

- Judgment liens: These liens are imposed to secure payment of a court-ordered judgment.

- Maritime liens: Admiralty law, also known as maritime law, imposes this type of lien on ships in order to secure payment.

- Homeowner association (HOA) liens: These liens exist in order to secure payment from current or previous HOA members or property owners for one or more of the following: late charges, unpaid assessments, lawyer or attorney fees, interest accrued, and related costs or fees.

At this juncture, it's important to understand what is known as the priority of liens. Some liens have more weight and influence than others. For example, government-based liens, such as property taxes, have a higher priority than all other claims on a property. Illinois grants contractors, subcontractors, and material handlers a unique privilege in that their claim (a mechanic's lien) can only be superseded by a government lien. All other liens become subordinate first to government liens, and second to mechanic's liens. This is oftentimes why lenders want to be notified if you are undertaking capital improvements that could result in the placement of a mechanic's lien.

TAX ASSESSMENT AND EQUALIZATION

Tax assessment, or **assessment**, is the job of determining the value of a property (i.e., valuation). It is done to calculate property tax. This task is usually overseen and managed by the assessor's office. At times, you'll hear this individual referred to as the county tax assessor.

The tax assessor is the government official that is charged with the responsibility of reviewing the property values throughout the entire county. After completing this task, he/she determines how much property tax needs to be acquired to meet the financial needs of the county and municipalities within the county. The assessor takes a look at the total financial needs and correlates that to total property values to come up with a tax rate. Applying the tax rate to your property's value establishes your contribution to the support of governmental services. If you wish to learn how your county determines your property taxes, the best source is to visit your county tax assessor's website. Most of those websites will clearly set forth how property taxes are determined for their respective counties.

Here is an overview of the process of tax assessment along with details:

- The assessor is responsible for determining the market value (MV) of your property. This number is used by the county treasurer in order to calculate your property taxes. The assessor neither sets tax rates or levies, nor decides the dollar amount of your tax bill. He or she only determines the market value of your property.

- For taxation purposes, the county must determine the assessed value. Most counties in the state of Illinois use an assessed value (AV) of 33.33%. Cook County, on the other hand, assesses value at 10% of its market value.

- This brings us to a concept called the equalization factor. Equalization refers to the process of making things (in this context, taxes) equal, and/or fair across the board. It is a fluctuating number defined by each county to help ensure equalization of taxes on different properties when there are shared governmental benefits. In other words, its purpose is to fix tax inequities. Equalization is impacted by a number of different variables, none of which is consistent in every county. Keep in mind that market value is the foundation of calculating property taxes.

  - For example, let's say that you have two homeowners living in identical homes within the same subdivision. The only difference is the two homes are in two different counties. Both homes have children attending the same school. Can the difference in the assessed values cause each homeowner to disproportionately contribute support to their children's school? Yes. This is the reason for the use of the equalization factor. It equalizes the assessed values so that each homeowner contributes equitably to the school. What if the houses are in the same county? Once again, equalization is used.

- Next in the formula, the equalization factor is applied to the AV. This creates the equalized assessed value (EAV) for the property.

- After any qualified property tax exemptions are deducted from the EAV, your local tax rate and levies are applied to compute the dollar amount of your property taxes. As a reminder, each tax year's property taxes are billed and due the following year. For instance, 2022 taxes are billed and due in 2023.

The following images and corresponding text are from the DuPage County Illinois government website. Each number in the small circle on the images is explained below.

MAKE CHECK PAYABLE TO: DU PAGE COUNTY COLLECTOR – *SEND THIS COUPON* WITH YOUR 1ˢᵗ INSTALLMENT PAYMENT OF **2021 TAX**

MAIL PAYMENT TO P.O. BOX 4203, CAROL STREAM, IL 60197-4203
PAY ON LINE AT treasurer.dupageco.org
SEE REVERSE SIDE FOR ADDITIONAL INFORMATION

❶ 01-23-456-789
JOHN DOE
❷ 1234 E KNOWN ST
WHEATON, IL 60189

ON OR BEFORE: ❹ PAY:
JUNE 1, 2022 **$4,942.45**

PAYING LATE? PAY THIS AMOUNT
JUN 2 THRU 30 ❺ 5,016.59
JUL 1 THRU 31 5,090.72
AUG 1 THRU 31 5,164.86
SEP 1 THRU 30 5,239.00
OCT 1 THRU 31 5,313.13
NOV 1 THRU 16 5,387.27

U.S. POSTMARK IS USED TO DETERMINE LATE PENALTY.
PAYMENT OF THIS 2021 TAX BILL AFTER OCTOBER 28, 2022 REQUIRES A CASHIER'S CHECK CASH OR MONEY ORDER

CHECK BOX AND COMPLETE CHANGE OF ADDRESS ON BACK

NO PAYMENT WILL BE ACCEPTED AFTER NOV. 16, 2022

1010110000881019000049424541

MAKE CHECK PAYABLE TO: DU PAGE COUNTY COLLECTOR – *SEND THIS COUPON* WITH YOUR 2ᴺᴰ INSTALLMENT PAYMENT OF **2021 TAX**

MAIL PAYMENT TO P.O. BOX 4203, CAROL STREAM, IL 60197-4203
PAY ON LINE AT treasurer.dupageco.org
SEE REVERSE SIDE FOR ADDITIONAL INFORMATION

❶ 01-23-456-789
JOHN DOE
❷ 1234 E KNOWN ST
WHEATON, IL 60189

ON OR BEFORE ❼ PAY:
SEP 1, 2022 **$4,942.45**

PAYING LATE? PAY THIS AMOUNT
SEP 2 THRU 30 ❽ 5,016.59
OCT 1 THRU 31 5,090.72
NOV 1 THRU 16 5,174.86

*INCLUDES $10 COST. SEE BACK OF BILL FOR EXPLANATION

U.S. POSTMARK IS USED TO DETERMINE LATE PENALTY.
PAYMENT OF THIS 2021 TAX BILL AFTER OCTOBER 28, 2022 REQUIRES A CASHIER'S CHECK CASH OR MONEY ORDER

CHECK BOX AND COMPLETE CHANGE OF ADDRESS ON BACK

NO PAYMENT WILL BE ACCEPTED AFTER NOV. 16, 2022

2010110000881019000049424542

1. Parcel Number: Also known as PIN (Property Index Number). This unique number identifies your property.

2. Billing Name and Address: To change Billing Name or Address contact the County Clerk at 630-407-5540.

3. First installment payment coupon: Payment due on or before June 1, 2022. One tax bill is sent per year with two coupons attached for your first and second real estate installment payments.

4. Total Amount Due: Payment due on or before June 1, 2022.

5. Pay this amount if paying after the due date: U.S. Postmark is used to determine late payment penalty.

6. Second installment payment coupon: Payment due on or before September 1, 2022. One tax bill is sent per year with two coupons attached for your first and second real estate installment payments.

7. Total Amount Due: Payment due on or before September 1, 2022.

8. Pay this amount if paying after the due date: U.S. Postmark is used to determine late payment penalty.

Rate 2020 ⑨	Tax 2020 ⑩	Taxing District ⑪	Rate 2021 ⑫	Tax 2021 ⑬
		** COUNTY **		
.0975	108.78	COUNTY OF DU PAGE	.0966	107.75
.0202	22.53	PENSION FUND	.0196	21.86
.0308	34.36	COUNTY HEALTH DEPT	.0298	33.24
.0124	13.83	PENSION FUND	.0127	14.16
.1128	125.85	FOREST PRESERVE DIST	.1102	122.92
.0077	8.59	PENSION FUND	.0075	8.36
.0148	16.51	DU PAGE AIRPORT AUTH	.0144	16.06
		** LOCAL **		
.0846	94.38	WAYNE TOWNSHIP	.0857	95.59
.0058	6.47	PENSION FUND	.0042	4.68
.0706	78.76	WAYNE TWP ROAD	.0695	77.52
.0022	2.45	PENSION FUND	.0029	3.23
.7426	828.51	VLG OF BARTLETT	.7237	807.28
.1640	182.97	PENSION FUND	.1688	188.29
.4533	505.74	HANOVER PK PARK DIST	.4470	498.62
.0229	25.54	PENSION FUND	.0389	43.39
.5816	648.89	BARTLETT FIRE DIST	.5865	654.24
.1072	119.60	PENSION FUND	.1045	116.56
.2643	294.87	BARTLETT LIBR DIST	.2712	302.52
.0287	32.02	PENSION FUND	.0306	34.13
		** EDUCATION **		
5.4108	6,036.82	UNIT SCHL DIST U-46	5.3911	6,013.77
.2258	251.92	PENSION FUND	.1911	213.17
.4581	511.10	COMM COLLEGE 509	.4548	507.32
.0001	0.23	PENSION FUND	.0001	0.24
8.9188	9,950.72	TOTALS	8.8614	9,884.90

Mailed to ⑭
JOHN DOE
1234 E KNOWN ST
WHEATON, IL 60189

Property Location ⑮
1234 E KNOWN ST
WHEATON, IL 60189

Township Assessor
WAYNE ⑯
630-231-8900

Tax Code
1019 ⑰

Property Index Number
01-23-456-789 ⑱

CHANGE OF NAME/ADDRESS
CALL: 630-407-5900

* S OF A FACTOR 1.0309

TIF Frozen Value ⑲		
Fair Cash Value ⑳		
Land Value ㉑	61,050	
+ Building Value ㉒	50,500	
= Assessed Value ㉓	111,550	*
x State Multiplier ㉔	1.0000	
= Equalized Value ㉕	111,550	
- Residential Exemption ㉖		
- Senior Exemption ㉗		
- Senior Freeze ㉘		
- Disabled Veteran ㉙		
- Disability Exemption ㉚		
- Returning Veteran Exemption ㉛		
- Home Improvement Exemption ㉜		
- Housing Abatement ㉝		
= Net Taxable Value ㉞	111,550	
x Tax Rate ㉟	8.8614	
= Total Tax Due ㊱	9,884.90	
- Less Advance Payment ㊲	0.00	
= Net Tax Due ㊳	9,884.90	
+ PACE Reimbursement ㊴		
= Net Due ㊵		

2021 DuPage County Real Estate Tax Bill
Gwen Henry, CPA, County Collector
421 N County Farm Road
Wheaton, IL 60187

Office Hours – 8:00 am–4:30 pm, Mon–Fri
Telephone – (630) 407-5900

2020 $111,570   Assessed Value   2021 $111,550

1. Rate 2020: 2020 tax rates shown for comparison.

2. Tax 2020: The amount of tax for the previous year for comparison

3. Taxing District: Listing of all taxing districts that receive your tax dollars, sorted by County, Local, Education and TIF District.

4. Rate 2021: 2021 tax rate is determined by the combined spending of all taxing districts, including the County, the Forest Preserve District, townships, community colleges, schools, villages, fire districts, libraries, parks, etc. Each taxing district prepares a budget, requests the revenues needed, and submits the request to the County Clerk. The County Clerk calculates the tax rate based on their requests.

5. Tax 2021: The amount of tax for 2021.

6. Mailed to: Billing name and address. To change billing name or address contact the County Clerk at 630-407-5540.

7. Property Location: Property address if available.

8. Township Assessor: Township is the area in which the property is located. Assessment questions should be directed to your Township Assessor.

9. Tax Code: Tax code identifies the taxing districts that receive your tax dollars.

10. Property Index Number: Parcel Number also known as PIN (Property Index Number). This unique number identifies your property.

11. TIF Frozen Value: The frozen value that determines how much tax will be distributed to the TIF district.

12. Fair Cash Value: The value the assessor places on each residential parcel of real estate.

13. Land Value: The assessed valuation of the land only.

14. Building Value: The assessed valuation of the building only.

15. Assessed Value: The total value for land and building.

16. State Multiplier: Multiplier which equalizes assessed value. If assessed values are too low or too high, the State will apply a multiplier to all assessments to equalize the assessments to one-third of the fair market value. This value is known as the Equalized Value.

17. Equalized Value: One-third of the fair cash value of your property. The assessor is required by law to assess properties at one-third of their market value.

18. Residential Exemption: Lowers the taxable value of the property up to $6,000. To qualify for this exemption, a homeowner must live in the home on or before January 1 of the tax year.

19. Senior Exemption: Lowers the taxable value of the property up to $5,000. To qualify for this exemption, a homeowner must have lived in the home and reached 65 years of age during the tax year.

20. Senior Freeze: Freezes the assessed value on your property. To qualify for this exemption, a homeowner must apply and establish age, ownership, residency and have a total household income of $65,000 or less.

21. Disabled Veteran: Returning Veteran Exemption provides an annual reduction in the assessed value of the primary residence occupied by a disabled veteran each year depending on the percentage of the veteran's service connected disability.

22. Disability Exemption: Provides an annual $2,000 reduction in the assessed value of the property owned and occupied on January 1 of the assessment year by the disabled person who is liable for the payment of the property taxes.

23. Returning Veteran Exemption: Provides a one-time $5,000 reduction in the assessed value of the veteran's primary residence for the taxable year that the veteran returns from active duty in an armed conflict involving the armed forces of the United States.

24. Home Improvement Exemption: Homestead Improvement Exemption provides an exemption of up to $25,000 of assessment increase due to home improvement.

25. Housing Abatement: Provides a reduction in value for qualified units of section 8 housing.

26. Net Taxable Value: The equalized value minus any exemptions.

27. Tax Rate: The sum of the rates in the "Rate 2021" column.

28. Total Tax Due: Total current tax due.

29. Less Advance Payment: Prepaid tax payments.

30. Net Tax Due: Net tax due.

31. PACE Reimbursement: Property Assessed Clean Energy (PACE) program for commercial properties.

32. Net Due: Combined amount due, property tax and PACE payment. (Source: DuPage County government)

Property tax bill configuration can vary from county to county. As a licensee capable of representing clients in multiple counties, you may find it beneficial to look at each county's property tax bill so you familiarize yourself and your clients with the documentation they are going to receive.

Frequently Asked Questions

- How often are property tax bills mailed? They are mailed twice a year in all counties in Illinois.

- When is the first installment due? Your first installment is due June 1 in all counties, except Cook County. Cook County accelerated the due date to March 1.

- When is the second installment due? It is due September 1 in all counties, except Cook County. Cook County accelerated the due date to August 1.

- As a property owner, what can you do if you believe your home's assessed value should be lower? You have the right to file an appeal.

- Who actually calculates the property taxes? Although many people mistakenly believe it is the county assessor, this official does not calculate taxes, collect taxes, generate tax bills, or establish tax rates. The assessor focuses specifically on property values, not taxes. The property taxes are calculated and collected by the county treasurer, sometimes referred to as the county collector.

A unique caveat that you need to know involves what is called the *Senior Citizens Assessment Freeze Homestead Exemption*. This exemption does exactly what it says. It freezes the taxable assessment on the homeowner's property. However, it does not freeze the tax rate. This exemption allows sixty-five-plus-year-old homeowners to freeze the assessed value of the home at a base year value, along with preventing any increase due to inflation. This applies during the assessment year and the homeowner must be able to prove that he/she has a total household income of $65,000 or less. What is the base year? It is the calendar year before the first year the homeowner applies and qualifies for this exemption. The owner must file an application by September of each year if he/she expects to receive this exemption. Note that if improvements are added, then the "base amount" will change.

SPECIAL ASSESSMENTS

Another type of tax is a special assessment tax. Special assessments are typically involuntary liens. Many times, these tax assessments are referred to as improvement taxes. Its purpose is to finance and fund infrastructure projects that are specific and local. Only certain property owners who live close to the improvements and benefit from them are required to pay these taxes. What types of infrastructure improvement projects are implemented? There can be any variety of improvements. They can include anything from road maintenance and better street lighting to construction and sewer line improvements. Much of the time, a special assessment is not tax deductible unless it involves maintenance and/or repairs.

There are two methods of calculating a special assessment.

1. Perceived percent of benefit. One or more government officials decide how much you will benefit from the improvement and use that to determine how much you will pay.

2. Front foot. Your contribution to the improvement is determined by the front footage of your lot. As you will learn later, the front footage is the width of your lot that borders the street.

REAL ESTATE TAX LIENS

Are real estate taxes a lien? The answer is yes. The government has the right to tax your property. Your tax money is used for a variety of reasons, including but not limited to: paying government employees, creating state and country infrastructure, and creating places and spaces from which the public can benefit like public libraries and public parks. Two important terms in this chapter include:

- Tax levy: A tax levy is the seizure of property to pay taxes owed to the IRS. Usually, the tax levy becomes a factor after a tax lien has been made known. Levies can include seizing bank accounts, garnishing wages, etc.

- Tax sale: A tax sale is an enforced and mandatory sale of real estate property by the government. The cause of this is the property's owner's delinquent taxes.

What happens when an Illinois property owner does not pay his or her property taxes? A tax sale may be implemented. This is an enforced and mandatory sale of real estate property by the government. The cause of this is the property owner's delinquent (unpaid) taxes. It is the government's effort to collect the owed money. The three types of tax sales in Illinois in no particular order are:

1. **Annual sales**: You must remember that the government operates like a business. Just like any other corporation, it needs revenue to survive. If the annual property taxes are not paid, the government is unable to provide you with the services that you have come to expect. When the property taxes are unpaid, the government has the right to seize the property and put it up for a tax sale. Annual sales generally occur toward the end of the calendar year.

2. **Forfeiture sales**: When nobody bids at the annual sale, a property moves into a forfeiture sale. What happens to the lien for taxes? The county where the property resides gets stuck with it. At that point, it's possible that someone may want to buy the forfeited lien from the county.

3. **Scavenger sales**: When a property does not sell at an annual tax sale or the forfeiture sale, it moves to a scavenger sale. These sales occur every two years in odd-numbered years. A scavenger sale is for properties that have unpaid taxes for three or more years.

JUDGMENTS AND JUDGMENT LIENS

A judgment is a court order concerning a civil matter. It's a decision resulting from a lawsuit. It is the judge's official answer as to the outcome of a lawsuit.

A **non-monetary judgment** is a court order that entitles the plaintiff to something other than money. For example, Mary engaged a contractor to install hardwood floors in her home. She paid in full to incentivize the contractor at the beginning of the project. The contractor started the project but failed to complete it. After numerous calls, emails, and texts from Mary, she had had enough. She decided to seek a court order, a judgment against the contractor. This way, the court will force the contractor to complete the project.

A **money judgment** (monetary judgment) is a court order that entitles the plaintiff to some amount of money. Examples are far and wide and include, but are not limited to, the following: rental unit damage, money borrowed, service provider bills, unpaid rent, and so forth. For example, Michael is being sued for debts owed. After months of hearings, financial burden, and stress, the judge decides in the creditor's favor. Meaning, the creditor won the court case, and a judgment has been entered against Michael. When this happens, most likely Michael will have to pay his creditor back in a specific manner, as outlined by the court.

What happens when an individual is served a judgment? Generally, it means that a debt collector will have the court's support in securing full payment of the outstanding debt. Also, most creditors have advanced tools and methods that they can use as a means to collect unpaid debts. The two most popular tools are wage garnishment and placing a lien on the individual's property. When someone is unable or unwilling to pay a judgment, the amount owed may be altered by interest and penalties, as defined by the court. The debtor may also have to pay the creditor's legal fees and/or other costs that went into getting the debt collected.

A judgment and a judgment lien are not the same thing. However, a judgment can serve to create a lien if and when a state's law allows it to do so. A judgment lien is an involuntary lien that is sometimes called an "abstract of judgment." It is filed and gives constructive notice. Constructive notice is a notification to the public of the court decision, as it has been recorded in public records with the county recorder's office. A judgment lien is a court ruling specifically attached to the debtor's assets and/or property. If the debtor fails to satisfy and fulfill his or her signed contract, the creditor has the right to take possession of the property of the debtor. What makes a judgment lien non-consensual? It is the fact that the judgment lien is attached to the property, with *no* consent or agreement from the property owner. The majority of states require creditors to record liens by way of state filing or county filing. Can this type of lien be attached to personal property, real property, or both? The answer is it can be attached to both. In fact, if the debtor, for whatever reason, has no real property or personal property, the lien can be attached to what he/she purchases in the future.

What about the time in between A) when a lawsuit is filed, and B) when a judgment is rendered? This unique and precarious time when the lawsuit is pending is referred to as "**lis pendens**." This Latin term means "suit pending." In everyday language, it means the case is undecided and up in the air. Lis pendens is a written public notice of litigation making it known that a real estate-related lawsuit has been filed. Typically, the issue is either about claimed ownership interest or the property title. It won't surprise you that when this happens, the property, if it were for sale, instantly becomes less attractive at best. At worst, it will repel potential buyers. If someone buys the property during a pending lawsuit, that pending lawsuit transfers to the new property owner.

Attachments is another related topic. An **attachment lien** is a lien that is ordered against someone's personal or real property. Its purpose is to stop and prevent him/her from disposing of the asset/s while the lawsuit is still ongoing. If the plaintiff wins, the court issues what is known as a "writ of execution" or "execution." This allows the property to be taken and sold in order to pay the money owed by the debtor. What if the debtor is up to no good and decides to do something with his real or personal property? For example, if he has a collection of diamonds, what is to prevent him from selling the collection for thousands of dollars and then hiding the money? This is where a writ of attachment comes in.

> "A writ of attachment is a form of prejudgment process in which the court orders the seizure or attachment of property specifically described in the writ. Such property is seized and maintained in the custody of a designated official, usually the U.S. Marshal, under order and supervision of the court" (U.S. Marshals Service)

Liens show up in other ways as well. Here's a breakdown:

- **Landlord's lien:** This lien is typically placed on a property. Much of the time, the landlord owns an apartment building, small complex, or house that he/she is renting out. This lien gives the landlord the ability to recover and receive the unpaid rent from his or her tenant/s.

- **Utility lien:** Yes, even a utility company can place a lien on the property that has unpaid bills. If a property owner refuses or is unable to pay his or her utility bills (such as gas, electricity, water, and so on), the utility company can issue a lien against the property owner. This can possibly lead to foreclosure. The foreclosure revenue is paid to the utility company in order to get the account paid in full and settled.

- **Corporate franchise tax lien:** Corporate franchises include companies like RE/MAX, H&R Block, Circle K, Subway, Marriott International, KFC, and Anytime Fitness Inc. Usually, state governments charge each franchise taxes for the opportunity to create, run, and manage businesses in their state. If a franchise does not pay, this lien can be issued in order to collect the money owed. As of 2022, there are fifteen states total that assess a franchise tax on corporations. (The number of states may change at any time. For the most up-to-date stats, please check online). Currently, Illinois is one of those states. On top of franchise tax, Illinois also requires franchises to pay income taxes.

- **Bail bond lien:** Bail is the monetary payment to the court system in order to be able to secure release from jail. When a property owner is charged with a crime and is subject to face trial, he/she usually has the option of posting bail. Posting bail usually means paying a specific amount of money as bail. However, if the property owner cannot use cash, he/she may have the option to post bail via the real estate he/she owns. A bail bond itself is a legal agreement by the defendant to be present for the trial and to pay what the court orders. You can think of a bail bond as a surety bond. A surety bond is a commitment or promise to be liable for the money owed. The contract is a three-party contract. The surety is the party who guarantees that the second party (the defendant) will pay what is owed to the plaintiff. This type of bail bond creates a bail bond lien against the defendant's property.

- **Federal tax lien:** The IRS website explains a federal tax lien as the following. "A federal tax lien is the government's legal claim against your property when you neglect or fail to pay a tax debt. The lien protects the government's interest in all your property, including real estate, personal property, and financial assets. A federal tax lien exists after the IRS puts your balance due on the books (assesses your liability), and sends you a bill that explains how much you owe (Notice and Demand for Payment). You neglect or refuse to fully pay the debt in time. The IRS files a public document, the Notice of Federal Tax Lien, to alert creditors that the government has a legal right to your property." A federal tax lien is sometimes referred to as an IRS tax lien.

- **Estate tax lien:** When a United States citizen who owns property passes, an estate tax lien is created. This lien attaches to the entirety of the deceased's assets. This lien enables the IRS to collect unpaid estate taxes on the deceased's property. What happens if the property is transferred? The lien transfers to the new owner. This makes him/her liable to pay the estate tax lien in full.

- **Inheritance tax lien:** Inheritance tax, not to be confused with estate tax, is a tax paid by the individual who inherits and receives money and/or property of the deceased. Said another way, it is the tax levied on the person/s who inherit assets from the departed. This is a state tax. No federal inheritance tax exists. However, inherited assets can be taxed in certain states. If the tax is not paid, a state can issue an inheritance tax lien. Illinois does not have inheritance tax. However, it is one of twelve states that does impose a death tax. It is wise to refer your clients to their accountants to better understand the implication that this tax may have on an estate.

CHAPTER 14 QUIZ

1. What is the most common goal of a lien?

    a. To gain possession of a property
    b. To receive money that is due
    c. To gain collateral
    d. None of the above

2. What do lenders use to protect themselves financially in case the borrower defaults on the loan?

    a. Collateral
    b. Security
    c. All of the above
    d. None of the above

3. David had a difficult year financially. His business almost went under. This past week, he learned that the contractor who was installing a new asphalt roof had placed a lien on the property. What type of lien is this?

    a. Specific
    b. General
    c. Consensual
    d. Judgment lien

4. Consensual liens are created by a legal contract between the lienee and the lienholder.

    a. True
    b. False

5. Jane was a subcontractor on a new home. She did an outstanding job. Two months have passed, and she has not received payment. The homeowner has not answered multiple phone calls and emails. What type of lien does Jane have the right to issue?

    a. Self-employment lien
    b. Unpaid compensation lien
    c. Contractor's lien
    d. Mechanic's lien

6. Special assessments are liens designed to gather the public's assistance in paying for a community improvement project. Which of the following statements would apply to a special assessment tax lien?

   a. An infrastructure lien is covered exclusively by local commercial property owners.
   b. Special assessments are used exclusively for the installation of new roadways.
   c. The most logical means of assessing the public's participation is through using the front foot method.
   d. Special assessments are always voluntary liens wherein the local municipality hopes for the community's monetary participation.

7. Which lien is a lien against documents and monies/funds in order to secure payment of fees owed for legal services?

   a. Attorney's lien
   b. Litigious lien
   c. Legal lien
   d. None of the above

8. The tax assessor sets tax rates and levies, and also decides the dollar amount of the tax bills of property owners who live in his or her county.

   a. True
   b. False

9. Bob and Jane are homeowners in Kendall County, Illinois. They just received the paperwork, which states their home's assessed value. They believe it is very high. What can they do?

   a. Nothing
   b. File a lawsuit
   c. File an appeal
   d. Sue the seller for providing incorrect information

10. The Senior Citizens Assessment Freeze Homestead Exemption freezes the tax rate as well as the taxable assessment on the homeowner's property.

   a. True
   b. False

11. A special assessment is which of the following?

    a. An improvement tax
    b. A way to fund local, specific infrastructure projects
    c. All of the above
    d. None of the above

12. All property taxes are real estate taxes.

    a. True
    b. False

13. Which of the following describes a judgment lien?

    a. Abstract of judgment
    b. It gives constructive notice
    c. Court ruling
    d. All of the above
    e. None of the above

14. Is it possible for a judgment to transform into a lien?

    a. Yes
    b. No

15. A lawsuit has been filed against Kelly. She knows that it may be a year or more before the court case is settled. What is that period of time between filing and securing a judgment called?

    a. Attachment
    b. Bond
    c. Interim
    d. None of the above

16. A plaintiff is worried that a defendant will take actions that either harm the defendant's real estate or sell assets for cash and hide the cash in an effort to not pay the plaintiff. Which lien can the plaintiff issue?

    a. Landlord's lien
    b. Bail bond lien
    c. Attachment lien
    d. Mechanic's lien

17. John died a few months ago. He had a lien on his property. His neighbor Ronald wants to buy John's property. What happens to the lien if Ronald purchases the property?

    a. The entire lien is forgiven.

    b. The lien becomes Ronald's responsibility.

    c. Fifty percent of the lien goes to Ronald and the remaining fifty percent is forgiven.

    d. None of the above

18. Sam has engaged a general contractor to lay new hardwood floors in his house. Sam is not satisfied with the quality of workmanship and has refused to pay the contractor. In order to protect himself, the contractor has the right to file what type of lien?

    a. A property tax lien to complement the tax lien provided by the government and ensure payment is made.

    b. A customized lien commonly known as a "weed lien."

    c. A mechanic's lien that provides the contractor with a higher priority subject only to a tax lien.

    d. A sinister lien designed to allow the contractor to enter the home and recapture all of the improvements that have been placed in the property.

19. Judgment liens exist as a result of a court order. Such liens give the claimant the right to seize any and all assets of the defendant in order to satisfy the debt. Judgment liens are commonly referred to as:

    a. A voluntary specific lien that protects the claimant.

    b. An involuntary general lien to provide the claimant with the ability to seize all assets to cover the debt.

    c. An involuntary lien specifically that has no relevance or presence when looking at the priority of liens.

    d. A statutory lien that limits the claimant's rights.

20. John and Martha recently purchased their new home in Romeoville. Their current tax bill amounts to $13,258. They're interested in knowing the market value that was used by the county assessor. They've learned that the equalization factor is 1.76 with an assessed value amounting to 35% of the market value. The current tax rate used by the county is $7.50 per $250 of value. What would the current market value be per county records?

    a. $717,424

    b. $710,416

    c. $737,025

    d. $1,717,275

REAL ESTATE OWNERSHIP

LEARNING GOALS:

By the end of this lesson, you will:

- Learn different types of real estate ownership and their implications
- Understand how individuals and corporate entities own property
- Discover the meanings of severalty, co-ownership, and trusts

REAL ESTATE OWNERSHIP is not a one-size-fits-all solution for individuals or corporate entities. Whether it's an individual or a corporation, the party can have a wide variety of dreams, goals, backgrounds, and net worths. It is important that licensees stay committed to their buyers and help them achieve what they need if at all possible. Consider all the scenarios that individual buyers can potentially bring to the table. Many times, but not always, their needs or wants focus on some type of life stage or season. These include examples such as buying a dream home, purchasing a retirement home, investing in a rental property, buying a larger house because one's family is growing, and/or wanting to downsize because you're going to be empty nesters. (An empty nester is a parent whose children have grown up and no longer live at home.)

The type of ownership chosen by buyers can have a variety of implications, either for the present, future, or both. Questions to be answered in advance possibly include: 1) How are the rights to future claims decided? 2) What are the tax implications for buying a specific property? 3) Can the property easily be transferred in the future? It is in the licensee's best interest not to delve into this realm directly, but to provide the client with basic questions to ask his or her attorney as this can be construed as a direct violation of the Quinlan-Tyson Accord. (Per the Quinlan-Tyson Accord, licensees are only allowed to fill in blanks on a preprinted contractual form with factual information. They may not change or alter forms. Licensees are prevented from giving any interpretation of contract law that should only be handled by a licensed attorney. Refer to **Chapter 18** for more information about the Quinlan-Tyson Accord.) When a buyer begins asking you questions like those listed above, you need to advise him or her to speak with an attorney. It's critical to know that as a licensee you are not to give legal advice in any way, shape, or form. You're not a lawyer or an attorney. Leave legal matters and legal discussions to lawyers and attorneys. If a licensee does give legal advice, he/she may be subject to disciplinary action.

LEGAL ENTITIES AND REAL ESTATE OWNERSHIP

Contrasted with individuals owning real estate, it's also important to understand how legal entities own real estate. Legal entities include businesses, associations, societies, and so on. A legal entity can be any organized group of individuals with a specific purpose and/or common goal.

Businesses are required to register with a state, although some businesses register outside of the US. Much of their information is available online to the public. The business, or company, always has a specific objective. The business most often exists despite the fact that members usually come and go. Who owns a corporation's real and personal property? As a legal entity, a corporation is the owner of all corporate assets. Shareholders own shares of the corporation. The shares are considered personal property. Shareholders do not own the direct assets of a corporation like real property.

There are different types of business structures. When someone starts a business, he/she or the group can usually decide which type of business structure they want. The structure is the type of business entity. These types of business ownership vary by jurisdiction and/or by state. Each type has its own benefits and disadvantages.

The IRS states the following and shares this list.

The most common forms of business are the sole proprietorship, partnership, corporation, and S corporation. A Limited Liability Company (LLC) is a business structure allowed by state statute. Legal and tax considerations enter into selecting a business structure.

- Sole Proprietorships

- Partnerships

- Corporations

- S Corporations

- Limited Liability Company (LLC) (IRS)

Business structures can also include nonprofit organizations (NPOs) and cooperatives.

When it comes to real estate ownership, the most commonly used business types in no particular order are:

1. Corporation

2. Partnership

3. LLC

A **corporation** is a business structure, organization, and legal entity. If a corporation is created or founded in the state of Illinois, it is required to follow Illinois state laws. When created, the corporation is authorized by Illinois to function and act as one entity. The corporation is created out of statute. Federal law views and treats a corporation as its own independent and legal entity.

Corporations come in a wide variety of categories. Their options are dictated by the jurisdiction and/or the state in which the corporation is created and registered. The benefits of registering as a corporation include, but are not limited to, the following:

1. Corporation owners receive limited liability protection. This means that most often, they are not personally liable or responsible for the corporation's debt. They do not live in fear of creditors coming after their assets on behalf of the corporation. While owners appreciate this type of protection, a corporation is more complicated to set up and maintain than other business structures.

2. Corporations usually receive tax breaks and gain tax advantages. For example, health insurance premiums and life insurance can be written off.

3. Fund transfers are usually easier than other business structures because banks often favor borrowers who are incorporated.

4. The corporation has the potential to outlive its owners. This can build credibility and attract new clients and/or investors.

5. Corporation ownership can be simple to transfer, although S corporations (S-corps) do have some restrictions.

6. Owners can establish retirement funds and other plans that qualify if they want to do so.

Possible disadvantages do exist. They include the possibilities of constant and ongoing fees, being taxed twice (double taxation), and more recordkeeping required. Double taxation means you pay income taxes two times on the exact same source of earned income. C corporations (C-corps) get taxed twice because of corporate profiles if the income is allocated out as dividends. (S-corps avoid this.) Ongoing fees include state fees which are paid to the Secretary of State, along with any applicable and additional fees. For corporations, these fees are usually higher than registering as a different business type. Finally, corporations are required to meet all recordkeeping and bookkeeping requirements by the state in which it is registered. Many times, this includes filing annual and/or quarterly reports.

A **partnership** is a legal business entity that is exactly as it sounds. Two or more people own and are involved in the business together. As with any type of relationship of this nature, a partnership agreement needs to be written and signed. While less complicated and expensive than a corporation, a partnership sometimes is the best choice for partners, depending on their financial power, goals, and circumstances. There are two types of partnerships: 1) general partnerships and 2) limited partnerships.

- A **general partnership** must have two general partners (GP) at minimum. The business's partners (who number two or higher) share the business's assets and liabilities together. Each partner has unlimited liability. This means their personal assets are possibly subject to seizure if financial or legal business problems occur.

- **Limited partnerships** (LPs) can be organized in two ways:

  - A **limited partnership** requires at least one general partner and one limited partner. Each general partner has unlimited liability for the business debts. As you have already guessed, limited partners only have limited liability, which is most commonly the amount of their investment. In an LP, a limited partner cannot be part of managing the business.

- A **limited liability partnership** (LLP) is required to have two or more partners. It is sometimes called a registered limited liability partnership (RLLP). All partners are permitted to operate and manage the business. In an LLP, all partners have limited personal liability. In contrast with a limited partnership, LLP partners have more control over how the partnership is operated.

Partnerships are mostly ongoing and focus on long-term collaborative business relationships. They may last a few years or several decades.

A **limited liability company** (LLC) is a private limited company. You can think of it as a hybrid legal entity. Why? Because it has characteristics of partnerships, sole proprietorships, S-corps, and C-corps. This means the owner or owners of the LLC can benefit from the unique advantages of those business structures. LLCs in Illinois may be member-managed or manager-managed. Illinois LLC owners are referred to as members.

Historically, LLCs are newer. They were first available in Wyoming in the late 1970s. Many states did not allow LLCs until the '90s. The Illinois Limited Liability Company Act, which is also called the "LLC Act" was enacted in 1993. It became effective on January 1, 1994.

Benefits of an LLC include but are not limited to the following:

- An LLC has limited liability similar to a corporation.

- Like a partnership, an LLC has the option of pass-through income taxation. An LLC gives the owner/s liability protection without double taxation like that of a C-corp.

- LLCs are more flexible than corporations and are less complicated to register and maintain.

- If you're an LLC owner and a lawsuit is filed against you or if you file bankruptcy, your personal assets are usually safe, sound, and unaffected.

- Most banks and investors view an LLC as more favorable than a sole proprietorship.

Disadvantages of an LLC include but are not limited to the following:

- As an LLC owner, you do not receive a salary. However, it is expected that you compensate yourself as an expenditure directly out of the LLC's profit. This is as simple as writing yourself a check from the LLC's business account and depositing it into your personal bank account.

- If you are an LLC owner, you are required to pay self-employment tax. Unless you are working with a bookkeeper or CPA, you are responsible for knowing the quarterly tax deadlines and paying on time. "The law sets the self-employment tax rate as a percentage of your net earnings from self-employment. This rate consists of 12.4% for social security and 2.9% for Medicare taxes." IRS

Beyond real estate ownership by way of corporations, partnerships, and LLCs in Illinois, from time to time, you may hear about joint ventures and syndicates.

A **joint venture** (JV) is a business arrangement and form of partnership in which two or more organizations or individuals focus on completing one specific project. It is not a long-term or lifetime partnership or relationship, but rather it ends when the specific project is completed. The partners pool their resources together in order to make a real estate investment happen. Who is liable and responsible for costs, losses, and profit associated with the specific project? Every partner is. Many times, a joint venture is distinct and separate from other businesses or projects that the partner has. In other words, it's usually not their primary business. Likewise, legally, their primary business is not involved, connected with, or related to the project, although the project may be in the same industry. Can a joint venture take on any legal structure? Yes. Is it a fiduciary relationship? Yes. When compared to a partnership, a joint venture features a limited scope and duration.

A **syndicate** is a self-organized group of two or more people, entities, companies, or corporations. Their shared pursuit and goal revolve around one or more real estate investments. A syndicate appeals to investors because they know that they will have more buying power together as a whole rather than each investor operating separately. Much of the time, they not only combine their money for investment purposes but also draw on their total combined resources, connections, and skill sets. Is a syndicate a legal entity recognized by the state and Secretary of State? The answer is no, not inherently. However, a syndicate may create an ownership interest as a corporation, LLC, or partnership.

SEVERALTY, CO-OWNERSHIP, AND LAND TRUSTS

When it comes to ownership, there are three common ways a fee simple estate can be held. These are:

1. Severalty

2. Co-ownership

3. Land trust

Severalty simply means the condition or state of being separate. Many people see the word *several* in the word. As you know, several means two or more. However, the key to the definition is actually the root word *sever*. It is a Latin derivative that means to make one. Think of the word severed, meaning cut off (or distinct). In real estate, severalty means separate and exclusive ownership. The title is held by a single individual or entity, such as a company or organization. Said another way, there is only one property owner. The single property owner possesses the complete bundle of related legal rights. He/she has the right to use and enjoy the property within the confines of the law, to sell, transfer ownership by gift, lease the property, encumber the property with a mortgage, leave it as an inheritance, and more rights. State laws have an effect on severalty. It does not look the same for every single state in the US. In Illinois, severalty is commonplace.

Co-ownership is exactly as it sounds. Two or more individuals or entities own the property together. This is also referred to as concurrent ownership, co-owners, or cotenancy. Legal professionals usually use the term *cotenants*, as that word is in line with legal terminology. Generally, there are four forms of co-ownership recognized.

1. Tenancy in common

2. Joint tenancy

3. Tenancy by the entireties

4. Community property

Of the four forms, Illinois only recognizes the first three categories as a legal means of property ownership.

Tenancy in common, sometimes abbreviated as TIC, is a form of concurrent estate. It's where each owner or "tenant in common" legally owns distinct and separate shares of the exact same property. Do all of the co-owners own equal shares? No. Can they own equal shares? Yes. Can their interests differ in size? Yes.

TIC owners do not own specific units or apartments. Instead, each owns a percentage in an undivided property. This percentage is called undivided fractional interest (UFI).

What about the deed? First, every co-owner has their own individual deed which outlines their individual interests. Second, all co-owners have what is commonly called unity of possession. Here's an example. A property has seven co-owners. Six co-owners share 50% of the ownership while Mike retains the remaining 50%. Does this mean Mike owns 50% of the physical property? The answer is no. The percentage of tenancy in common ownership does not equate to physical possession of the land and/or structure to the exclusion of the other co-owners.

Illinois requires the percentage of ownership (fractional interest) to be stated on each co-owner's deed. However, not all states have this requirement. What happens when no fractional interest is indicated on a co-owner's deed? In this circumstance, the ownership is split equally among the total number of co-owners. For example, if there are eight co-owners and the deeds fail to define the individual percentage of ownership, each co-owner owns 1/8 share (12.5%).

In Illinois, tenancy in common is considered to be the base ownership form. In the absence of defining either of the two alternative forms recognized by Illinois, the form of ownership between individuals will always defer to a tenancy in common. In other words, if the deed does not state that the co-ownership is either a joint tenancy or tenancy by entirety, it automatically defaults to a tenancy in common relationship.

Most of the time, the co-owners are not married. They may or may not be related by blood. The majority of the time, co-owners have invested different amounts of money in order to buy the property. Do tenants in common have the **right of survivorship**? No. The right of survivorship means that when a co-owner dies, the surviving co-owners, will equally share the deceased's co-owner's interest in a property automatically. For example, in a tenancy in common relationship, if James owns ¼ of the property and dies suddenly, his share of the property will pass on to his heirs or devisees by way of inheritance. It will not pass on to the other co-owners.

Joint tenancy is another category of shared ownership of property. In joint tenancy, each owner owns an undivided interest. A key factor that makes joint tenancy different from tenancy in common is the concept of unity of interest, which is equal ownership interest among all co-owners.

Unlike tenancy in common, joint tenancy does include the right of survivorship. Using the earlier scenario, if James owns ¼ of the property and dies suddenly, his property interest will pass on to the other co-owners. They automatically receive James' share of the property. This brings us to two points.

- James' heirs will not inherit his share of the property.

- A joint tenancy will always cycle into an ownership in severalty. This means that the last owner surviving will own 100% of the interest in the property.

Joint tenancies are created by what is referred to as the "four unities." These are:

1. **Unity of possession**: Each co-owner has equal unrestricted right of access to the entire property as well as full possession of the same.

2. **Unity of interest**: Each co-owner has equal interest (ownership) in the property. This makes the math very simple. Examples: Two co-owners means each one has 50%. Three co-owners means 33.33% each. Four co-owners means 25% each.

3. **Unity of time**: Each co-owner is required to take (acquire) his or her share at the exact same time. In other words, ownership begins at the same point in time.

4. **Unity of title**: Unlike a tenancy in common where there is one deed per owner, in a joint tenancy there is one deed with all co-owners listed. For example, in a tenancy in common, if there are fifty co-owners, there are fifty deeds. In a joint tenancy, if there are fifty co-owners, there is only one deed.

The easiest way to remember this is an acronym that has been used by licensees for years. The acronym is "P.I.T.T." It stands for possession, interest, time, and title.

Tenancy by entirety has a right of survivorship and requires a legal marriage. It provides equal undivided interest in the property as well as protection from unsecured creditors seeking a claim on the primary residence. Tenancy by entirety only applies to the primary personal residence. It does have drawbacks. For example, a couple recently celebrated their wedding. However, this is a second marriage for both of them. Each has children from their prior marriages. If they acquire their new residence as tenancy by entirety, it is best that they both recognize these two conditions in advance:

- They cannot add the names of the children to the title.

- If one spouse passes away, under the premise of right of survivorship, the surviving spouse acquires full ownership in severalty. The children of the deceased spouse are not entitled to any inheritance from the primary residence.

When recognized by state law, the concept of **community property** provides two levels of property ownership:

1. Separate property

2. Community property

First, let's define **separate property**. In a community property state, any property that a spouse acquires prior to getting married can be labeled separate property. This is accurate as long as the other spouse does *not* receive any financial benefit from the property's existence. This includes the benefit of occupying the property. As long as the property is distinctly separate from marital assets, the property will remain separate and are the assets of the spouse who legally owns the said assets. If it can be shown that the spouse who is not on the property title has received financial benefit in some manner, a court will generally convert the property from separate property to community property. This means both spouses are co-owners and entitled to financial benefit. For example, prior to getting married, each individual acquired their own condo. If the new wife moves into the husband's condo, although his name is the only name on the title, by virtue of her occupancy, the wife is entitled to one half of his condo. If they kept her condo as a rental property and the husband can show he received financial benefit from the rental income, then he can claim one half of the ownership of her condo. Examples where one spouse receives financial benefit from the other spouse's property are numerous. For example, the rental income may:

- Pay for a shared vacation for the married couple

- Cover several household expenses

- Pay off joint credit card debt

Second, we have **community property**. These are assets that are equally shared and owned by the spouses where both receive financial benefit. Examples can include the primary residence (that they both occupy), their weekend cottage, and the joint bank accounts. Said another way, community property is a state-specific law that explains and designates the assets of each married person.

Illinois is not a community property state. It is an *equitable division* state. It can also be called an *equitable distribution* state. For example, if two co-owners are dissolving their relationship and seeking the court's direction on asset distribution, a key consideration by the court is going to be each party's current financial situation and future needs. This is the guide to determining distribution rather than relying simply on a 50/50 split.

A **trust** is a legal device whereby the trustor who initially acquires the property conveys ownership to a trustee (disinterested entity) to hold for the benefit of a third party.

There are two types of trusts:

1. Living trust

2. Land trust

A **living trust** is a legal mechanism that allows an individual to provide for his/her personal financial future as well as his/her family's financial future. It's a way for an individual's assets (possessions) to be distributed after he or she has passed away. Many times, this process is used instead of a will. A will is only implemented once the individual dies, while a living trust exists during the lifetime of the individual. This is why it's called a *living* trust.

A **land trust** is a unique form of ownership that places the ownership of real estate into the hands of the trustee (disinterested third party) for the benefit of a beneficiary. The trustor has the legal right to name him/herself or a third party as the beneficiary. The trustee holds legal title to the *real estate* (not real property) that was acquired by the trustor.

Creating a land trust is a common practice for investors as it allows the investor all the benefits of property ownership without having legal title to the property. In Illinois, this process provides two direct benefits. First, it provides a bit of distance between the investor and the property that may be a claim in a potential lawsuit. Second, the name of the beneficiary does not appear in public records. When a purchaser acquires a property directly from the seller, the purchaser is given a deed. That deed is recorded in the public record. If the purchaser subsequently wants to convey the property into a land trust, although the trustee will be noted as the legal title holder, the purchaser's name will still be visible in the public record. When an investor prefers autonomy, he or she has the sales contract stipulate that the seller is to convert ownership into a land trust before the closing. Thus, the purchaser does not receive a deed but receives the beneficial interest associated with the land trust. This method keeps the purchaser's name from being recorded in the public record.

A land trust can be used in a financial arrangement with the lender, commonly known as a deed of trust. (A deed of trust is a financial concept that deals with the financing of real estate. It will be explained in Chapter 21.)

REAL ESTATE INVESTMENT TRUST (REIT)

A real estate investment trust is a financial concept that allows an investor to purchase investment real estate and securitize it. This concept allows the REIT to offer shares in an investment to other smaller investors who want ownership interest in real estate without the obligation or stress of owning or managing the real estate. A REIT allows multiple investors to pool their money together and purchase shares or securities. This method provides the individual investors with the ability to diversify their investment portfolios. Why? Because a REIT provides access to commercial real estate they may not have been able to purchase separately. Frequently, these types of investments are ideal for long-term investment strategies and are not suited for short-term "quick and flip" approaches.

A REIT may or may not operate and/or finance its real estate. Examples include, but are not limited to, apartment complexes, high-rises, shopping centers, and office buildings. What makes REITs unique is that they are modeled after and inspired by mutual funds. They also enjoy similar tax advantages as investors who invest in mutual funds. Consequently, an investor can earn dividends on his or her real estate investments without the stress and hassle of actually financing, buying, and/or managing the property or properties. This hands-off nature creates an inviting and appealing aspect when it comes to a REIT. An investor can create an ongoing stream of income with no need to be on-site or physically involved with the investment property. The majority of REITs are publicly traded like stocks. Unlike physical real estate investments, they are very much liquid.

OWNERSHIP OF CONDOS, CO-OPS, AND MORE

Real estate is a broad field with a variety that never seems to end. As a licensee, ownership does not revolve only around single-family one-owner homes and commercial buildings. As you read about earlier, it's much broader than that. Currently, more than 27% of the US population is residing in some form of condominium ownership. How does ownership work with condos? How does ownership work with townhouses and timeshares? Here are the answers.

Condominiums

Condominium ownership has evolved over the last few decades. It can now be found in commercial structures. Nowadays, you have condominium offices, retail centers, industrial centers, and more. For example, many shopping centers today are shifting to a condominium model. If you want to run a store, you have to purchase the space. Concerning condominiums, The Act states:

    a. The legal description of the parcel.

    b. The legal description of each unit, which may consist of the identifying number or symbol of such unit, as shown on the plat.

    c. The name of the condominium, which name shall include the word "Condominium" or be followed by the words "a Condominium."

    d. The name of the city and county or counties in which the condominium is located.

    e. The percentage of ownership interest in the common elements allocated to each unit. Such percentages shall be computed by taking as a basis the value of each unit in relation to the value of the property as a whole, and having once been determined and set forth as herein provided, such percentages shall remain constant unless otherwise provided in this Act or thereafter changed by agreement of all unit owners.

    f. If applicable, all matters required by this Act in connection with an add-on condominium.

    g. A description of both the common and limited common elements, if any, indicating the manner of their assignment to a unit or units.

    h. If applicable, all matters required by this Act in connection with a conversion condominium.

    (h-5) If the condominium is a leasehold condominium, then:

        1. The date of recording and recording document number for the lease creating a leasehold interest as described in item (x) of Section 2;

2. The date on which the lease is scheduled to expire;

3. The legal description of the property subject to the lease;

4. Any right of the unit owners to redeem the reversion and the manner whereby those rights may be exercised, or a statement that the unit owners do not have such rights;

5. Any right of the unit owners to remove any improvements within a reasonable time after the expiration or termination of the lease, or a statement that the unit owners do not have such rights;

6. Any rights of the unit owners to renew the lease and the conditions of any renewal, or a statement that the unit owners do not have such rights; and

7. A requirement that any sale of the property pursuant to Section 15 of this Act, or any removal of the property pursuant to Section 16 of this Act, must be approved by the lessor under the lease.

i. Such other lawful provisions not inconsistent with the provisions of this Act as the owner or owners may deem desirable in order to promote and preserve the cooperative aspect of ownership of the property and to facilitate the proper administration thereof. (765 ILCS 605/4)

How does the law typically view a condo? Each condo is a separate parcel of real estate. Every condo owner holds a fee simple title to his or her unit. Does a condo owner have a deed to their property? The answer is yes. In this way, they are like people who own a single-family home or some other category of real estate. What about the common areas? Common areas do not feature a single owner. Therefore, each owner has an undivided interest in the common areas. The most popular common areas are places like stairs, stairwells, driveways, parking lots, yards, elevators, and lobbies. Potential amenities like pools, playgrounds, courtyards, sports courts, and gyms are also potentially included in the common areas.

Like single-family homeowners, condo owners pay property taxes and mortgage payments. In addition to those expenses, they also pay monthly dues. These dues pay for repairs and maintenance of common areas. Condominium communities are governed by HOAs (Homeowner Associations). Those elected leaders have a variety of responsibilities. Their main duties are to brainstorm ways to improve the community, explore possible solutions, and make decisions with regard to updates, improvements, and repairs. Condo associations in Illinois are regulated by the IDFPR. Usually, a condo owner has the right to sell, transfer and use his or her unit as he/she wants. However, this comes down to the HOA's legal paperwork and rules.

Townhouse ownership is a type of condominium ownership. Townhouses are a type of narrow, terraced, medium-density housing with common (communal) walls. They're almost always multilevel. They're popular in urban areas. In large cities where single-family homes are less common like Washington D.C., Philadelphia, Toronto, San Francisco, and similar cities, townhouses can be very expensive. However, single-family houses boost higher prices. A townhouse is also called a townhome, and it can greatly vary from city to city and region to region. Each townhouse is allotted a small lot. Most townhouses are run by HOAs. Most often, each townhouse owner is responsible for interior repairs and maintenance while the many HOAs take responsibility for exterior maintenance and repairs. However, there can be exceptions. As a licensee, you want to verify each HOA's responsibility for exterior maintenance and repairs as a service to your buyers. Like condos and co-ops, townhouses have common areas. These usually include driveways, walkways, sidewalks, open areas, pet relief areas, and exercise facilities.

Townhouse ownership is more similar to the ownership of a detached single-family home than it is to an apartment-style condo. What does townhouse ownership include? It usually includes the structure and the land on which the townhouse sits. The declaration establishes the extent of ownership. It clarifies what portion of the ground the townhouse owner will individually own. Each townhouse owner has his or her own deed to the townhouse, as well as a portion of the lot.

Cooperative Ownership

Cooperatives, also known as co-ops, are owned and managed by a nonprofit corporation. Co-ops share many characteristics with condos and condo ownership. However, co-op ownership is different. Co-op occupants do not own the real property and do not have a deed or title. Rather, they buy shares of stock in the nonprofit corporation. Being a shareholder gives them the right to live in a specific unit in the building. Does a condo owner have interest in real property? Yes. Does a co-op occupant have interest in real property? No. Co-op ownership is actually considered personal property. The occupant's rights are created by a proprietary lease. You can think of it as a long-term lease. To summarize, co-op owners do not own property. They own interest in the company that owns the property. Do co-op owners acquire fee simple interest? The answer is no. Their units are not assessed separately for tax purposes. Who directly pays the real estate property taxes? As you've probably already guessed, it is the corporation. Each co-op shareholder is then billed and required to pay for his or her share of the taxes. In other words, the shareholders pay the corporation, and the corporation directly pays the government. Can a condominium owner deduct their payment of real estate property taxes from their income? Yes. Can a co-op shareholder who contributes to the single tax bill that the nonprofit corporation pays deduct their tax contribution from their income? No. Do co-ops have HOAs? No. Instead of an HOA, each co-op has its own board of directors which provides management for the co-op.

Timeshare Ownership

As you read earlier, a **timeshare** is referred to as vacation ownership which is a type of real estate featuring shared rights. Timeshares have numerous purchasers who are entitled to a specific period of time each year that allows them the ability to enjoy the property. Most commonly, they are resort facilities. A timeshare can be constructed in two ways:

1. Ownership: Timeshares are fee simple, meaning that they are deeded. Fee simple or deeded is most commonly viewed as the most favored type of vacation ownership. As in condominium ownership, you will be able to participate and vote in important decisions that affect all of the owners.

2. Long-term lease: Sometimes, an individual will lease a timeshare. When it is leased, he/she has no right of ownership and there is no deed. Since these are long-term leases, they may exist for more than twenty years. In addition, since you are a tenant, you have no control concerning the amount of yearly fees you're required to pay, have no say in updates or changes to the rules of the complex, and have no control over the management.

Timeshare holders either purchase or lease a one-week or two-week interest per year. Timeshare laws in Illinois were repealed in 2017. At the present time, Illinois does not regulate timeshare developers and their plans and sales agents. The Timeshare Act of 1999 (765 ILCS 101/) has been repealed. Timeshare laws can be confusing and complex. Any licensee who sells timeshares must work diligently to stay up to date on all applicable laws. The best practice is to have your client use a lawyer during the process.

Now, it's time for your chapter quiz.

CHAPTER 15 QUIZ

1. When working with a buyer, what does a licensee need to know?

    a. The buyer's needs

    b. The buyer's wants

    c. The buyer's financial ability

    d. All of the above

2. Licensees are allowed to change or alter forms and agreements for clients as needed.

    a. True

    b. False

3. What is another way to say separate and exclusive ownership?

    a. Severalty

    b. Co-ownership

    c. Joint tenancy

    d. Tenancy in common

4. Sarah, a sponsoring broker, is explaining co-ownership to Mike, who is a new licensee. Which of the following terms also means co-ownership?

    a. Concurrent estate

    b. Co-owner/s

    c. Cotenancy

    d. All of the above

    e. Only A and B

5. Bob and Jane are getting a divorce. During their marriage, Jane consistently earned more than double what Bob made. They were married in Illinois and have always lived in Illinois. What will happen when their assets are divided up?

    a. Jane will receive more because she earned more money.

    b. Marital property, along with debts will be divided up by 50/50.

    c. The court will focus on "equitable division."

    d. None of the above.

6. Jane is talking to her sister on the phone about her divorce from Bob. Her sister says she thinks that Bob had one or more affairs. Jane feels the same way. She does not have proof but thinks it will be possible to find some evidence of the adultery. If Bob did cheat on Jane, will the court take this into consideration?

   a. Yes
   b. No

7. What is the best word below to describe when each owner legally owns distinct and separate shares of the exact same property?

   a. Timeshare
   b. Co-ownership
   c. Tenancy in common
   d. Undivided fractional interest
   e. None of the above

8. George owns ¼ of a large property on the outskirts of Chicago as a joint tenant. Yesterday, he tragically died in a car wreck. His wife and children are mourning, but know they have to talk about what happens next. Concerning this large property George owns, will it automatically go to his wife and children?

   a. Yes, survivorship is commonplace for tenants in common.
   b. It is possible, but a legal battle will have to take place.
   c. No, it's impossible. Right of survivorship prevails.
   d. More information is needed

9. Emmett owns a large property via joint tenancy. There are six other joint tenants. Today, he heard that one joint tenant, John, has received a judgment. Can this potentially affect Emmett negatively?

   a. Yes
   b. No

10. Along with nine other tenants in common, Breonna owns 30% interest in the property. Does that mean she owns 30% of the physical property?

    a. Yes
    b. No
    c. Need more information

11. In 1980, a specific piece of property was purchased by four joint tenants. Through the years, two of them died. Now, there are only two joint tenants left, Paul and Peter. Sadly, it looks like Peter is on his deathbed. When he passes, what happens to the land?

    a. Paul has to purchase Peter's portion and interest.

    b. Paul automatically receives Peter's portion and interest.

    c. Paul will own 100% of the property.

    d. A and B

    e. B and C

    f. None of the above

12. Which "four unities" create joint tenancies?

    a. Partial interest, investment, time, and tax deed

    b. Possession, interest, time, and taxation

    c. Percentage, interest, time, and title

    d. None of the above

13. Which type of business organization allows its owners to know that creditors cannot come after their personal assets and property on behalf of their business entity?

    a. Sole proprietorship

    b. Partnership

    c. Limited partnership

    d. Corporation

    e. Limited liability company (LLC)

    f. Cooperative

14. Which of the following describes a judgment lien?

    a. Abstract of judgment

    b. It gives constructive notice

    c. Court ruling

    d. All of the above

    e. None of the above

15. Is it possible for a judgment to become a lien?

    a. Yes

    b. No

16. What are the most common business types used for purchasing commercial real estate?

    a. Corporations, partnerships, and LLCs
    b. Corporations and partnerships
    c. Corporations, cooperatives, and LLCs
    d. Corporations, sole proprietorships, and LLCs

17. A plaintiff is worried that a defendant will take actions that either damage the defendant's real estate, or sell targeted assets for cash and hide the cash in an effort to avoid payment to the plaintiff. Which type of lien can the plaintiff issue?

    a. Landlord's lien
    b. Bail bond lien
    c. Attachment lien
    d. Mechanic's lien

18. Each timeshare owner is entitled to a specific time period when they can enjoy the benefits of the timeshare. Which answer shows the most common annual time frames?

    a. Five days
    b. One month
    c. One or two weeks
    d. None of the above

19. Which concept of company below is modeled after and inspired by mutual funds?

    a. Partnership
    b. Limited partnership
    c. A real estate investment trust (REIT)
    d. Corporation
    e. Cooperative

20. Which of the following is true about condominiums?

    a. It is viewed as a separate parcel of real estate.
    b. Each condo owner holds a fee simple title to his or her unit.
    c. Each condo owner has a deed to his or her property.
    d. All of the above
    e. None of the above

WHAT ARE BROKERAGE AGREEMENTS?

LEARNING GOALS:

By the end of this lesson, you will:

- Understand brokerage agreements and their implications
- Know the four main listing agreements
- Become aware of potential listing agreement problems
- See the buyer's broker responsibilities
- Know how termination and expiration work with a brokerage agreement

BROKERAGE AGREEMENTS are like a world unto themselves in the business of real estate. What is a **brokerage agreement**? It is a special relationship between the sponsoring broker and the client. A brokerage agreement is the same as a representation agreement and a listing agreement. They are a commitment of the sponsoring broker to provide guidance and brokerage services when a client is interested in either buying or selling real estate. Oftentimes, brokerage agreements are interpreted as employment agreements. However, they are not employment agreements under the traditional concept of employment. For all licensees, whether they represent buyers, sellers, landlords, or tenants, the brokerage agreement, is the most important, foundational element of the client/licensee relationship.

There are a variety of brokerage agreements. Each one's purpose is to establish and fortify the basic relationship between each party. They also provide varying levels of responsibilities and rights for the sponsoring broker. The most critical ingredient of each brokerage agreement is centered on compensation and exclusivity. They must show the required minimum services that will be provided to the client. These minimum services are given in return for what the clients pay, or for the right to compensation from someone else.

The Act states that all exclusive brokerage agreements must be in writing. Most other states require brokerage agreements in writing as well. Although oral agreements are still legal in Illinois, the issue is that oral agreements are not enforceable in a court of law because of the Statute Of Frauds provision. Only written exclusive brokerage agreements are enforceable in court.

The Illinois Human Rights Act plays a strong role in each brokerage agreement. Can a sponsoring broker or a sponsored licensee refuse to show property to a prospective client who falls under one of the defined protected classes found in the Illinois Human Rights Act? The answer is no. Sponsoring brokers and sponsored licensees may not discriminate on the basis of a person's color, race, gender, religion, national origin, order of protection status, marital status, physical or mental disability, ancestry, age, sexual orientation, military status, familial status, or criminal history. You will read more about protected classes in the following chapters.

LISTING AGREEMENTS

The listing agreement is the relationship agreement established between the sponsoring broker and the seller. Listing agreements include:

1. Exclusive right to sell listing agreement

2. Exclusive agency listing agreement

3. Open listing agreement

Exclusive right to sell listing agreement: In this agreement, a single sponsoring broker is designated as the seller's sole agent. This specific sponsoring broker has the exclusive right to market the property of the seller. Only one authorized sponsoring broker receives compensation. This takes place regardless of whether the sponsoring broker or the seller makes the sale. For example, say that the property sells while the listing is still live. If that happens, the seller is required to pay commission to the sponsoring broker. In Illinois, the majority of residential listings are exclusive right to sell listings.

There is a variation of the exclusive right to sell known as a **net listing agreement**. In this agreement, the property seller sets a minimum price for which he/she is willing to accept the specified property. This price includes the minimum net proceeds (the pocketable profit) due to the seller, plus sufficient funds to satisfy the outstanding mortgage and cover the closing costs that are incurred. The commission due to the licensee is the difference between the funds due to the seller and the sales price. In other words, the licensee keeps all funds that are in excess of the net proceeds plus mortgage and closing costs as commission. A net listing is legal in Illinois but is commonly viewed as unethical. They are illegal in several states. In Illinois, net listings are highly discouraged due to the fact that there is a high potential for fraud to take place.

Exclusive agency listing agreement: This agreement is similar to the exclusive right to sell agreement. However, the biggest difference is that while the sponsoring broker represents the seller and may be entitled to compensation if he/she or another broker acquires the purchaser, the seller has the right to market and sell the property independently without the obligation of paying a commission. If the seller successfully sells the property independently, then the seller will not pay commission to the agent. With the seller's consent, the listing broker can cooperate with other brokerages who potentially represent a ready, willing, and able buyer. Most of the time, the listing broker is paid the listing commission, which is then shared with the selling broker.

What's the main difference between exclusive right to sell and exclusive agency? The exclusive right to sell gives the licensee a commission regardless of who sells the property. Whether the property is sold by the property owner or the licensee, the licensee receives a commission. Under an exclusive agency, no compensation is due when the seller finds the buyer.

Open listing agreement: This type of listing is also called a nonexclusive listing in some areas. This agreement means that the sellers have the right to open up the listing to as many brokers as they want. However, the seller is not obligated to pay any of the brokers if the seller happens to sell the property without any aid or support from any of the brokers. If a broker successfully secures a ready, willing, and able buyer who tends an offer that is accepted by the seller, the seller is obligated to pay commission to the broker.

What information is needed on a listing agreement? At the very least, each listing agreement will include:

1. A description of the property

2. Sales terms

3. Compensation information

4. Scope and limits of the licensee's authority and rights

The most thorough answer comes from the Rules And Regulations. It's found in Section 1450.770, which is titled Brokerage Agreements and Listing Agreements. It is as follows:

a. Exclusive brokerage agreements, including exclusive listing agreements and exclusive buyer brokerage agreements, shall be in writing and shall indicate the minimum services that must be provided as set forth in Section 15-75 of The Act. Failure to include language in a brokerage agreement providing for minimum services as set forth in Section 15-75 of The Act or language in the brokerage agreement waiving those minimum services provided for in Section 15-75 of The Act will, under the definition of "exclusive brokerage agreement" in Section 1-10 of The Act, result in the brokerage agreement being considered to be nonexclusive. For purposes of this Section, "in writing" or "written" means physical or electronic writing.

b. Written buyer brokerage agreements, whether exclusive or nonexclusive, shall contain the following:

   1. Agreed basis or amount of compensation and time of payment

   2. Name of the sponsoring broker and the buyers

   3. Signatures of the sponsoring broker and the buyers or an authorized signator on behalf of the buyers

   4. Duties of the buyer's broker

   5. One of the following, clearly set forth:

      a. The duration of the buyer brokerage agreement

      b. The buyers' right to terminate the agreement annually by giving no more than 30 days prior written notice

c. Written listing agreements, whether exclusive or nonexclusive, shall contain the following:

1. List price

2. Agreed basis or amount of commission and the time of payment of the commission

3. Name of the sponsoring broker and owners

4. Identification of the real property involved (address or legal description)

5. Signatures of the sponsoring broker and owners or an authorized signator on behalf of the owners

6. Duties of the listing broker

7. One of the following, clearly set forth:

   A. The duration of the listing agreement; or

   B. The owners' right to terminate the agreement annually by giving no more than 30 days prior written notice.

   C. Written brokerage agreements shall expressly provide that no amendment or alteration to the terms, with respect to the amount of commission or with respect to the time of payment of commission, shall be valid or binding unless made in writing and signed by the parties.

   D. No licensee shall use real estate contract forms to change previously agreed commission payment terms.

   E. If a listing agreement states that, in the event of a default by a buyer, the sponsoring broker's full commission or fees will be paid out of an earnest money deposit, with any remaining earnest money to be paid to the seller, the provision shall appear in the listing agreement in letters larger than those generally used in the listing agreement.

   F. Each brokerage agreement shall clearly state that it is illegal for either the owner or any licensee to refuse to show, display, lease or sell to any person because of, race, color, religion, national origin, sex, ancestry, age, marital status, physical or mental disability, familial status, pregnancy, sexual orientation, including but not limited to gender identity, unfavorable discharge from the military service, military status, order of protection status, an arrest record, or any other class protected by Article 3 of the Illinois Human Rights Act.

   G. Each brokerage agreement for a residential property of 4 units or less that provides for a protection period subsequent to its termination date shall also provide that no commission or fee will be due and owing pursuant to the terms of the brokerage agreement if, during the protection period, a valid, written brokerage agreement is entered into with another sponsoring broker.

H. A licensee may discuss a possible future brokerage agreement with a consumer whose property is exclusively listed with another sponsoring broker or who is subject to a written exclusive buyer brokerage agreement only if:

1. The consumer initiates the contact; or

2. The following occurs:

    a. The licensee makes a request, in writing, mailed or emailed, to the broker or sponsoring broker who has the listing agreement for the type and expiration date of the brokerage agreement between the consumer and the broker or sponsoring broker who has the listing agreement;

    b. The licensee who has the listing agreement fails to provide a response in writing, mailed or emailed, within 10 calendar days;

    c. The information from the broker or sponsoring broker who has the listing agreement is not received within 14 calendar days; and

    d. The requested information cannot be obtained by the licensee from another source of shared broker information. (Section 1450.770)

Note: It is important to recognize that not everyone will know how to define certain terms. These terms include ones such as sex, gender, sexual identity, and sexual orientation. As a licensee, it's important to clearly be able to distinguish between those terms and know the definitions.

The section above uses the term familial status. It's the first time the term has been used in this book, so let's define it. **Familial status** means the presence of an individual who is under eighteen years of age. The individual is the focus. It is not relevant whether the adult is a biological parent, grandparent, foster parent, stepparent, designee, or some other type of adult who has been granted legal custody of the individual. Additionally, the marital status of the adult is not relevant. Adults or couples who are pregnant and/or working on adopting are also protected. For example, when a landlord refuses to rent to a couple who have a two-year-old daughter or treats potential tenants differently if they have a child, then the landlord may be violating federal/state law.

MULTIPLE LISTING SERVICES AND MULTIPLE LISTING PROVISION

A **multiple listing service** can also be called a multiple listing system. An MLS is a cooperative relationship amongst licensees to share product information with each other in an effort to increase the exposure of the sellers' properties. The intent is to market the properties to a wider number of potential buyers. Each MLS is a private system and therefore is not available to the public. For example, can a property owner who is going to do a "for sale by owner" (FSBO) list his or her home on an MLS? The answer is no, unless he/she is a licensee. Only a licensee can access an MLS database.

Certain listing agreements may include what is called a **multiple listing provision**. As you've probably guessed, this provision gives the broker permission and the right to list a client's property on a multiple listing service (MLS). Without this provision, a broker who lists his or her client on an MLS will be subject to disciplinary action.

Not all MLSs operate in the same manner. You need to verify with your local MLS as to what types of listing formats they allow to be uploaded to their system.

How many multiple listing services are there in the US? The Real Estate Standards Organization says there are between 600 and 700. The specific number fluctuates from time to time since these services merge, and new ones are created and released.

To expand your knowledge of MLS, it's important to know that Illinois law requires a licensee to exercise fiduciary duties when authorized to represent the interest of the client. If the client happens to be a seller, under the concept of care, the broker needs to use every marketing tool legally available to position the property for exposure to potential buyers. In the residential sector, an MLS is viewed as an essential tool. This marketing tool allows licensees to increase the exposure of a seller's property to as many potential purchasers as possible. The average licensee usually only represents five to seven "A-quality" buyers at a given moment in time. The MLS can represent upwards of 150,000 buyers through the use of cooperating brokers. In the residential realm, this has proven to be a tremendous asset in assisting consumers with the marketing of their homes. This is why you generally find a larger percentage of homes sold through the utilization of two brokerage companies.

Generally, a sponsoring broker decides which MLS or MLSs his/her licensees are allowed to use. While there are over 600 MLSs, each of them works independently. Placing a listing on one MLS does not automatically place it on another MLS.

LISTING APPOINTMENTS AND LISTING PROCEDURES

The listing appointment is the cornerstone and hallmark point of your work as a licensee. This is when a licensee has his or her first meeting with a potential client (the seller). While listing appointments can look somewhat different for different licensees across the US, there are a few basics that are covered during this critical time. In no particular order, these key components of a listing appointment include:

1. A discussion focusing on the seller's goals and needs

2. A conversation about how the licensee can make the seller's goals happen

3. A tour or walk-through of the property that will go on sale in the future

4. A document that shows what comparable properties near the potential client's property have sold and closed for

5. An up-to-date CMA (comparative market analysis, also known as "comps")

A **comparative market analysis** shows an estimate of the potential client's property value. This opinion of value is based on similar properties in the immediate area (neighborhood) that have sold and closed recently. If he/she becomes the client of the licensee, keep in mind that the seller has the final say as to the asking price of the property. A licensee can advise on the asking price, but cannot dictate, force, or manipulate the seller into the asking price that the licensee wants. The CMA is a research-based and data-driven document that can help you guide the potential client toward arriving at a smart and reasonable asking price.

The Act is very clear and strict about CMAs. Keep in mind that this is the law. The following is from section 225 ILCS 454/10-45.

> Section 10-45. Broker price opinions and comparative market analyses.
>
> a. A broker price opinion or comparative market analysis may be prepared or provided by a real estate broker or managing broker for any of the following:
>
>> 1. an existing or potential buyer or seller of an interest in real estate;
>>
>> 2. an existing or potential lessor or lessee of an interest in real estate;
>>
>> 3. a third party making decisions or performing due diligence related to the potential listing, offering, sale, option, lease, or acquisition price of an interest in real estate; or
>>
>> 4. an existing or potential lienholder or other third party for any purpose other than as the primary basis to determine the market value of an interest

in real estate for the purpose of a mortgage loan origination by a financial institution secured by such real estate.

b. A broker price opinion or comparative market analysis shall be in writing either on paper or electronically and shall include the following provisions:

1. a statement of the intended purpose of the broker price opinion or comparative market analysis;

2. a brief description of the interest in real estate that is the subject of the broker price opinion or comparative market analysis;

3. a brief description of the methodology used to develop the broker price opinion or comparative market analysis;

4. any assumptions or limiting conditions;

5. a disclosure of any existing or contemplated interest of the broker or managing broker in the interest in real estate that is the subject of the broker price opinion or comparative market analysis;

6. the name, license number, and signature of the broker or managing broker that developed the broker price opinion or comparative market analysis;

7. a statement in substantially the following form: "This is a broker price opinion/comparative market analysis, not an appraisal of the market value of the real estate, and was prepared by a licensed real estate broker or managing broker who was not acting as a State certified real estate appraiser."; and

8. such other items as the broker or managing broker may deem appropriate. (225 ILCS 454/10-45)

A CMA must always be based upon the physical characteristics of the property being appraised, as it compares to the physical characteristics of similar properties that have recently sold and closed. Never base the interpretation of value on factors that violate fair housing law. As you will shortly see, there are fifteen protected classes named in federal and state fair housing law. They consist of race, color, religion, national origin, gender (sex), disability, familial status, ancestry, age, marital status, military service, sexual orientation, order of protection, criminal history, and source of income.

At this juncture in a listing appointment, depending on the groundwork that a licensee has already done, here is how a licensee can be highly effective. If the potential client wants time to consider working together, ask him or her when a good time to follow up is. Be sure to have their correct contact information. Additionally, ask them which communication method they prefer. Do not use social media for this communication, as social media accounts are hacked on a regular basis and those platforms are not built for privacy or confidentiality. Furthermore, it's smart to know the potential client's schedule. This could be related to work, children, and so on. A smart licensee will know when a potential client (and a regular client for that matter) has the best availability and is able to: 1) receive calls and/or 2) respond to emails and/or 3) have follow-up visits or meetings.

Disclosure: Finally, keep in mind that a licensee must: 1) disclose agency relationships, 2) disclose his or her financial interest, 3) disclose the condition of the property, and 4) disclose material facts, including any known latent defects. As a reminder, you read about the Residential Real Property Disclosure earlier. With this in mind, it's important that a licensee encourages his or her client to fully disclose information about property conditions. In fact, it is safer to err on the side of disclosure. A lack of disclosure can create numerous problems, including time-consuming and finance-draining litigation. Simply put, a seller needs to know that honesty is the best policy.

LISTING AGREEMENT FORMS

There are several versions and types of listing agreement forms in the marketplace available to licensees. Ask your designated managing broker which forms your office recognizes and are approved to be used.

Potential Listing Agreement Problems and Broker Protection

Procedures do not always go as planned. Inevitably, at times, there are issues and problems in some form or fashion with or related to listing agreements. There are several scenarios. Here are a few common ones:

1. The seller wants to back out of the listing agreement. This could be due to any type of reason or combination of reasons, not limited to financial concerns or setbacks, health reasons, issues with an immediate family member, and so on. When a client wants to terminate the contract, he/she potentially can do so but taking this action may produce consequences. Most listing agreements allow some type of payment to the licensee if this occurs. The licensee may also receive a type of payment of commission if the client prohibits, hinders, or blocks the work going into selling the property.

2. The licensee may take an action that is not permitted in the listing agreement and that is not in the scope of his or her work for the client. Questions to answer in advance in a listing agreement include: 1) Can the licensee post product information organically on social media? (This is not a paid social media ad.) 2) Does the licensee have written consent to place a for sale sign in the client's front yard or some other visible area?

3. A listing agreement must include everyone with ownership interest. A smart action each licensee can take upfront is to see if there are multiple owners on the property. When a property is co-owned, it's imperative that: 1) the licensee knows this, and 2) he/she must ensure all of the co-owners' names are present on the listing agreement, and 3) he/she must secure every co-owner's signature on the listing agreement. Without doing so, the licensee is functioning without the full authority that he/she needs. Problems will ensue and the licensees' efforts will be wasted.

4. Information required by the state of Illinois is missing, inaccurate, or incomplete on the listing agreement. Questions like these must be addressed in advance and answered by way of an accurate and complete listing agreement: 1) Are any items fixtures? 2) Is everyone's information correct? 3) Is there proof of title? 4) Are there any encumbrances or zoning issues? 5) Is the wording nondiscriminatory? 6) And so on.

Concerning minimum services, as you read earlier, according to The Act, all exclusive brokerage agreements must be in writing and must show the required minimum services which will be provided to the consumer. These minimum services are given in return for what the consumers pay, or for the right to get compensated by someone else.

225 ILCS 454/15-75 of The Act outlines minimum services. It reads as follows:

Section 15-75. Exclusive brokerage agreements. All exclusive brokerage agreements must be in writing and specify that the sponsoring broker, through one or more sponsored licensees, must provide, at a minimum, the following services:

1. accept delivery of and present to the client offers and counteroffers to buy, sell, or lease the client's property or the property the client seeks to purchase or lease;

2. assist the client in developing, communicating, negotiating, and presenting offers, counteroffers, and notices that relate to the offers and counteroffers until a lease or purchase agreement is signed and all contingencies are satisfied or waived; and

3. answer the client's questions relating to the offers, counteroffers, notices, and contingencies.

Both a licensee and the principal have specific duties and responsibilities in regard to each other. The key duties of the principal are to follow the brokerage agreement and work with the licensee. The principal is expected to cooperate with the licensee on good terms and in good faith. He/she must not impede or interfere with the licensee's work. It is also the responsibility of the principal to compensate the licensee in accordance with the brokerage agreement's terms.

Broker protection: Sellers generally pay commission fees to the listing sponsoring broker who then can share the commission fees with the cooperating broker. However, have you ever wondered what occurs when a licensee's listing expires without a successful sale? During the listing period, the licensee presented the property to a number of buyers. What would happen if one of those buyers returns to directly negotiate with the seller? If the listing agreement provided a broker protection clause, and the licensee becomes aware of the seller negotiating directly with the buyer that the licensee physically presented the property to, the licensee may be entitled to full commission although he/she was not directly involved in the negotiations.

How long does a broker protection clause last? Its duration is not defined by the law but rather is outlined within the listing agreement. This provision is not required by the law. Therefore, it may not exist in all listing agreements. It is the licensee's responsibility to know if the provision does exist in order to be eligible for a commission. It's critical that the licensee recognizes that he/she cannot claim a commission unless the licensee continually remains in contact with that specific client to know whether or not the property was sold to a buyer the licensee physically presented the property to. However, there is a caveat. If the property is truly residential (four units or less) and is subsequently listed by another licensed broker within the protection period, the broker protection clause is automatically terminated. If the initial licensee physically showed the property to a buyer in the past and that same buyer returns to purchase, either directly through the seller or current listing broker, the initial licensee loses all rights to commission. If the same circumstances occur with a commercial building that has five or more residential units, then the initial licensee can potentially receive a commission.

THE THREE TYPES OF BUYER AGENCY AGREEMENTS AND RESPONSIBILITIES OF THE BUYER'S BROKER

You've learned about listing agreements, which represent the seller. Now, let's look at the other side of the coin, the buyer. Sellers have seller (or listing) agreements, and buyers have buyer agreements. A buyer agreement can also be called a buyer agency agreement, buyer's broker agreement, or buyer-broker agreement. Just like a listing agreement, a buyer agreement is also an agency relationship. What are the three types of buyer agency agreements? They are:

1. **Exclusive buyer agency agreement (or exclusive right to represent)**: This is a fully exclusive agreement between the licensee and buyer. Legally, the buyer is required to compensate the licensee. This compensation is paid out to the licensee at the time the buyer buys a property, which fits the description in their agreement. If the buyer locates the property, does the licensee still get compensated? The answer is yes. He/ she is still entitled to compensation as laid out by the contract.

2. **Exclusive agency buyer agency agreement**: This agreement shares similarities with an exclusive buyer agency agreement. How so? Both are exclusive contracts between the licensee and the buyer. What makes this agreement different, however, is that it

places a limit on the licensee's right to be compensated. The licensee only gets compensated if she or he discovers the property that the buyer chooses to purchase or if the property is acquired through another sponsoring broker. If the buyer locates the property that he/she wants to purchase, he/she owes no compensation to the licensee.

In Illinois, all exclusive agency agreements must be written and signed in order to be enforceable in court.

3. **Open buyer agency agreement**: This is a nonexclusive agency contract and verbal relationship that exists between a buyer and a licensee. This means that the buyer has the right and liberty to enter into another representation agreement with another licensee. Who gets compensated? As you already guessed, it's only the licensee who locates the property that the buyer actually purchases.

Before proceeding with the relationship, the licensee and buyer must have an in-depth conversation. This conversation is sometimes referred to as a counseling session or exploratory session. In essence, the law must be followed, and figuratively speaking, both the buyer's and licensee's cards are laid out on the table. In other words, there is full transparency. The goal is clear communication and arriving at a conclusion, which is whether they choose to sign and move forward or not. This invaluable time together gives the buyer an opportunity to ask questions and kick the tires. It gives the licensee the opportunity to educate the buyer, showcase his or her expertise, and potentially win a new client.

While there is a perception that the seller pays the commission that is shared between the different sponsoring brokers involved in the transaction, this is not a function of law, nor is it guaranteed. With the use of the MLS in the residential industry, it has become common practice for the listing office to share the commission provided by the seller with the selling office (office representing the buyer). It is not necessarily common practice in the commercial industry. In the commercial industry, you'll frequently have to negotiate the selling broker's commission with the listing agent. Regardless of which industry you are addressing, the payment of commission will never dictate an agency relationship. By state regulation, you represent the party with whom you are working unless there is a separate written declaration.

The buyer's licensee is responsible for several tasks throughout the process of securing the buyer a new property. Along with following The Act and his or her brokerage's policies, the licensee is responsible for several components. The main responsibilities upfront and throughout the property viewing process include: 1) Vision and reality: What is the vision of the buyer? What are his or her goals? What does the buyer want? What does the buyer need? How much financial power does he/she have? Confirm that the buyer is pre-approved with a mortgage lender. 2) In the field: The licensee needs to search for properties that match the buyer's description.

The licensee must communicate with the buyer and share what is available that fits his or her description. When a buyer wants to see a property, train the buyer on how to compare the properties being viewed. Share your expertise. Do not tell them what to think. Show them how to think about the properties. Next up as a responsibility of the buyer's agent comes a large multifaceted aspect of his or her work, negotiation.

THE SCIENCE AND ART OF NEGOTIATION

Learning the science and art of negotiation is paramount. It's perhaps one of the most important, essential ingredients to being an agent and having a successful career. Most real estate agents have never been provided with proper instruction on how to negotiate efficiently. Becoming masterful at negotiation will help you become a stronger communicator and better listener. Doing so will also empower you to close more deals, avoid conflicts and arguments, and grow your career faster. When you read the word negotiation, you may feel an emotional response to some extent. It may excite you, or it may worry you. Maybe you've been a part of bad negotiations in your life at some point. Perhaps when someone was negotiating with you, it felt tacky, rude, or heartless. Licensees have experienced negotiation differently. Regardless, it's important to look at the heart of negotiation; what it is and why it is used. Negotiation is simply a discussion aimed at reaching an agreement. It's a strategic conversation focused on finding one solution that is acceptable for two or more parties. While sometimes the negotiation can become a win/win, most of the time there is some type of compromise for both parties, which allows the agreement to be created and decided.

Why is negotiating sometimes viewed negatively? Because unfortunately, people can easily get caught up in the emotion of the moment. They can get emotionally hijacked. Reason and logic go out the door. It's been said in the past that everyone is rational until it comes to money. In other words, anytime money is part of the conversation (and it always is in real estate), people can quickly become irrational, rude, defensive, and/or emotionally triggered. A healthy and productive negotiation entails clear communication, exploration, empathy, and commitment. Negotiation done well does not tolerate and has no room for things like emotions, luck, magic, and wishful thinking. Yet, negotiation is the exact vehicle that opens up new opportunities, new doors, bigger paydays, and even bigger dreams. And that's exactly why you must choose to become a lifelong learner when it comes to the art of negotiation. Everything about negotiation comes down to context. Context includes who, what, where, when, and why. One technique may win in one context, yet fail miserably in another context. Thus, you must be aware of the context in which the negotiation will take place. Learning negotiation cannot be done by reading one chapter or even one book. Learning how to negotiate and mastering the skill is a lifelong learning process. With that in mind, here are several negotiation tips.

NEGOTIATION TIPS

Cultivate a win/win perspective. Do not view negotiation like you're going into battle or with an "Us versus Them" mentality. You can negotiate clearly and be honest, polite, and respectful at the same time. When an issue comes up, focus on getting to a solution. Keep in mind, people are people, and issues are issues. They are not one and the same.

Preparation is king. Who will be at the negotiation table? What do they want? What are their goals? What are their strengths and weaknesses? What type of history do they have? Do you know anyone who has dealt with this agent/party before? If so, he/she can be a wealth of information for you. Ask smart questions and do your research. Your preparation will pay off.

Be 100% responsible for being a fiduciary. If you truly want to live up to your fiduciary duty to your client, you need to make every effort possible to meet the needs of the client. This could include aspects such as pricing, timing, or other factors. Focus on protecting the clients' interest, especially during the negotiation process.

Use silence as a tool. Perhaps one of the difficult aspects of negotiation to learn while building your career in this industry is learning the art of silence. There is an old negotiation philosophy and approach that goes "He who speaks first loses." When there is silence, there is empty space. Many times, the other party will have a desire to fill the empty space by *speaking*. Let them.

Have clients be binding commitment-ready. Make sure your party is fully authorized and able to make a binding commitment. You do not want to be at the negotiation table and suddenly learn something new from your client/s that surprises you or throws everything on its side. "Let's sign" makes things happen. "Let me get back to you on that" or "Let me check with so-n-so (the real decision-maker)" will halt all of your hard work and result in wasted time and stress.

Insert a red herring (decoy) if appropriate. A red herring is something meant to be distracting. All mystery novels have red herrings intentionally in the story to throw the reader off. In other words, it's a false trail or decoy. How does this apply to negotiating in real estate? Prepare to have something to give away in advance. This is something that does not hurt your ultimate goal or negotiating position. Maybe at a certain point, when you need the party to move closer to a decision, share that you will offer something else that's nice to have. For example, you might say something like this: "If we can (ask for what you want), my seller will throw in their (yard equipment, hot tub, etc.)." A red herring can help you get closer to the deal you want. It can serve to keep the other party from going after your main goal.

Play the detective. Pay close attention to the other parties' reactions, body language, and speech patterns. When you say something, do they raise their eyebrows? Did someone purse their lips? Did they loosen up and seem to get more comfortable? If you have children, you know how to do this to an extent. You know when they're lying, when they're withholding information, and more . . . all because of their voice and body language. You may also consider the game of poker. It's not only a card game. It's also a game of "reading" the other players. Reading people and playing the detective is what you want to do during negotiations. This gives you real-time information and you can quickly make decisions on the information that they freely give you.

Be okay with however much time is required. Don't be slow. Don't be in a hurry. Be 100% present and in the moment. You don't want the other party to think that you're stalling or that you want to hurry and get the deal done so you can move on with your life. People can sense those types of energy. Instead, be in the moment. Be an empathetic listener. The time it takes is the time it takes. Be okay with that.

Have confidence in your offers. An offer will be met with: 1) acceptance, 2) rejection, or 3) a counteroffer. As you know, a counteroffer means that a previous offer or offers have been rejected. The benefit of a counteroffer is that the conversation is still on the table. If your offer is the last one on the table, do not allow your fears or emotions to cause you to change your offer. Doing so can open the door for the other party to tender another counteroffer because they most likely sensed your uncertainty and hesitation.

Look for leverage. A key way to create leverage is to use your strengths. Your strengths are important assets that create an advantage for you and your client. The other side of leverage is making use of the other party's weaknesses.

Be the alpha. Another negotiation method is being the alpha, the dominant person in the group. Start strong and start first. You initiate the meeting and lay the groundwork. You set the tone and create a solid foundation. Furthermore, you also show your knowledge and expertise. This is no time to be bashful. You've paid your dues. You're trained and you're smart. Do not play small. This gives you an advantage because you're the first person to put a stake in the ground and cast a vision for the meeting. This can instantly elevate you over the other party's agent. It also puts them in a position to play catch-up. Being the alpha does not mean being rude, mean, or unprofessional. In sports, for example, a player can be the alpha and maintain a high level of professionalism. You can do the same.

Make a trade. Making a trade is almost always an option when you're in a real estate transaction. You might view these as bargaining chips, or as a factor to move the deal forward or help finalize the deal. This generally looks like this question: "If we (do this), are you willing to (do that)?" Keep in mind that it is all open to change during a negotiation. Do not allow parties to hide behind phrases like "We've always done it this way" or "We always use . . ." etc. Negotiation inherently means it's all up for discussion. Before the meeting, be sure you identify your bargaining chips, anything you can trade in order to solidify the deal. Remember, your party may value something more than you do. You'll never know if you don't ask.

Present the offer in writing. By now, you know almost everything in the real estate industry has to be in writing. The purpose of it being in writing is to maintain clarity and transparency for all parties. It's in everyone's best interest to have the offer in writing. The written word helps you avoid misunderstandings and confusion. The offer must include all elements, nothing left out. In your mind, you want to understand each element of the offer. What's the purpose? Why is it there? Why is something left out? Knowing the ins and outs can help you recalibrate if the negotiating starts to go amiss.

Be empathetic. Empathy is showing an ability to understand and share the feelings of another. This is important in negotiations. All humans want to be seen, be heard, and feel like they are understood. Being empathetic helps facilitate a healthy atmosphere for the negotiation. What would you do if you were in their shoes? Answering that question can help you see things from their viewpoint and help you relate. It may be entirely possible to satisfy some of the other party's goals, while not sacrificing your top goals. Always be ready to let go of small goals in order to protect your main goal (your end game).

Be a good human. Negotiating is not cutthroat. You do not want the other party leaving like they've been wounded, hurt, exploited, or used. At the end of every transaction, we are still people who want to live good lives. Do you want to go after a great deal? Yes. Do you want to do it with an "at all costs" mentality? No. Remember, you may be negotiating with the same agent again two months from now. Be honest, sincere, and committed to your client. Being good to others (as well as yourself) will take you far in your career. The goal is to burn brightly for years, not to burn out quickly.

Keep crafting your negotiation skills. No two negotiations will ever be the same. Sure, they'll have similar characteristics. However, their dynamics and the contexts will come in a wide variety of shapes and sizes. Craft your sense of timing. Distinguish between when to listen, when to be silent, and when to speak. Negotiation is more art than science. That means creativity is required. You might think of it as improvisation. You will constantly be thinking on your feet and adapting in the moment. Don't be hard on yourself. Nobody learns this in a few weeks. Like anything, your negotiation skills will grow through time and your commitment.

During the negotiation, also keep these points in mind:

1. The offer is not merely a financial figure. It's more than that. The offer pulls everything together and includes all of the elements of the transaction. Not everything the other party wants is always or solely connected to the price point either. Always make sure all of the details are nailed down, clear, and out in the open for all parties to see and know. Leave no room for assumptions. Leave no questions unasked. Clarity is paramount.

2. With some negotiations at certain points, know that compromise is required in order to move a deal forward. Do not view compromise as good or bad. It's simply a tool to help you achieve a result.

The final responsibility of a buyer's broker is a commitment to follow up. A successful licensee prioritizes follow-up and always follows through. In fact, a follow-up is one of the most essential and critical jobs of any agent. For a buyer's agent, this means he/she must stay in communication with the buyer. The communication must be clear, articulate, and timely. Going a layer deeper, ideally, the buyer's broker understands the communication style of the buyer and communicates accordingly. What matters most to the buyer? Is it the numbers? Is it understanding details? Smart agents are cognizant of the communication styles of others. A buyer's agent must communicate and take any related actions to make sure the closing moves forward. If anything is slowing the process or hindering the process, he/she must take action accordingly. Finally, email is exceptionally useful for a follow-up method as it consistently gives you ongoing records and evidence of all communication. While it's possible for a licensee to see a list of phone numbers called from his or her business phone, since phone calls are verbal, there is no evidence of what was discussed on the call. Some licensees keep an ongoing journal or log of topics covered together on phone calls.

CONTEMPORANEOUS OFFERS AND DISCLOSURE OF CONTEMPORANEOUS OFFERS

Contemporaneous means existing or occurring during the same period of time. How do we define contemporaneous offers? Contemporaneous offers exist when a single licensee actively represents the interest of either two separate purchasers or two separate tenants simultaneously pursuing the same property. When the licensee finds themselves in this position, the law requires that there be written disclosure of the representation to all parties. The intent is to provide the parties with an understanding that the licensee is now going to have limitations on what they can do in assisting the clients. The primary limitation is the lack of ability to discuss financial issues, including what price the buyers or tenants should offer. A buyer, assuming the parties are working on a sale, needs to be aware that while the licensee can assist them in all phases of preparation and presentation of an offer, the licensee is restricted in providing any suggestions regarding the financial aspect. Illinois law states that before preparing a contemporaneous offer, the licensee is required to disclose this fact in written form to all clients. He/she must also refer the client to another licensee if and when the request is made. This law also provides that the disclosure of the existence of contemporaneous offers is not in conflict or breach of the agent's responsibility of confidentiality to each of the respective clients. Section 1450.830 of the Rules And Regulations defines "Disclosure of Contemporaneous Offers."

Forms related to this chapter's topics are usually called:

1. Exclusive Buyer Representation/Exclusive Right to Purchase Contract

2. Disclosure of Contemporaneous Offer

Once again, ask your designated managing broker which forms your office recognizes and are approved to be used.

BROKERAGE AGREEMENT TERMINATION

By now, you've learned how brokerage agreements are created. However, there are times when brokerage agreements cease to exist. The three most logical means by which this occurs are:

1. Both parties fulfill the agreement

2. One party (either the buyer or the seller) fails to fulfill their end of the agreement

3. Both parties fail at fulfilling the agreement

A client's licensee does his or her absolute best to fulfill the client's goals. However, there are a number of provisions that could cause a termination of the agency relationship. In Illinois, agency may be terminated when one of the following circumstances occurs:

1. The agreement is fulfilled and thus complete

2. The agreement expires

   - Expiration of brokerage agreement. No licensee shall obtain any written brokerage agreement that does not either provide for automatic expiration within a definite period of time or provide the client with a right to terminate the agreement annually by giving no more than 30 days' prior written notice. Any written brokerage agreement not containing such a provision shall be void. When the license of any sponsoring broker is suspended or revoked, any brokerage agreement with the sponsoring broker shall be deemed to expire upon the effective date of the suspension or revocation. (225 ILCS 454/10-25)

3. Death of principal

   - If there are two or more principals, the death of one does not terminate the agency relationship.

4. Mental incapacity of the principal to make rational decisions

   - If there are two or more principals, the mental incapacity of one does not terminate the agency relationship.

5. Mutual agreement among all involved parties

- The mutual agreement is between the client and the designated managing broker. The designated agent is not authorized to cancel a listing agreement because the agreement is actually with the sponsoring broker.

6. The property suffered substantial destruction

7. The government condemns the property

   - The government determines that the property is unsafe for the property owner to occupy and has the obligation to protect the property owner's safety by preventing further entry and use.

8. Operation of law

   - Bankruptcy

   - Foreclosure

9. Breach of contract by one of the parties (in which the party guilty of breach could suffer liability and/or damages)

What happens if a designated agent dies during the term of his/her representation agreement? The sponsoring broker assigns the designated agent's responsibilities to another licensee in the office.

You've finished this chapter. Well done! Now, it's time for your chapter quiz.

CHAPTER 16 QUIZ

1. In which listing agreement is the seller only obligated to pay a commission to the licensee who successfully secures a buyer?

    a. Open listing agreement
    b. Net listing agreement
    c. Exclusive agency listing agreement
    d. Exclusive right to sell listing agreement

2. In which agreement does the seller set a minimum monetary amount that he/she is willing to accept that allows the broker's commission to be anything in excess of the seller's minimum monetary needs?

    a. Open listing agreement
    b. Net listing agreement
    c. Exclusive agency listing agreement
    d. Exclusive right to sell listing agreement

3. Which marketing tool allows licensees to work in cooperation with other brokers in order to provide greater exposure of properties to potential buyers?

    a. His or her CRM (customer relationships management system)
    b. Estate for years
    c. Multiple listing service
    d. None of the above

4. Designated agents in Illinois have flexibility and options when it comes to how they want to create and present a comparative market analysis to clients.

    a. True
    b. False

5. What is a licensee required to disclose?

    a. Agency relationship
    b. His or her interest
    c. Condition of the property
    d. Material facts
    e. Only A and B
    f. A, B, C, and D

6. Agent Jane tried to sell the Rutherford estate for six months. She showed the property to over forty interested parties, but nobody purchased it. It is now sixty days later, and Jane is no longer representing the Rutherfords. However, she just learned that one of the interested parties who Jane physically presented the property to has decided to purchase it. What does Jane need to check in order to confirm that she has a right to compensation?

    a. The broker protection clause contained within the listing agreement
    b. Nothing because she has no right to compensation
    c. Her brokerage handbook
    d. None of the above

7. Which type of agreement is where the broker only gets paid if she or he discovers the property that the buyer chooses to purchase? (If the buyer locates the property that he/she wants to buy, he/she owes no compensation to the broker.)

    a. Exclusive buyer agency agreement
    b. Open buyer agency agreement
    c. Exclusive agency buyer agency agreement
    d. None of the above

8. What is a negotiation?

    a. A discussion aimed at reaching an agreement
    b. A strategic conversation
    c. A lifelong study
    d. All of the above

9. Which term below best describes what exists when a single licensee actively represents the interest of either two separate purchasers or two separate tenants simultaneously pursuing the same property?

    a. Simultaneous offers
    b. Conflict of interest
    c. Liability
    d. Contemporaneous offers

10. At times, a licensee and client will prepare to have something to give away in advance during a negotiation. What they give away will not hurt their ultimate goal or negotiating position. This type of negotiation technique is intentionally designed to be distracting. What is it called?

   a. Squirrel
   b. Red herring
   c. Advance diversion
   d. Strategic accommodation

11. In Illinois, agency may not be terminated when which of the following circumstances occurs?

   a. Mental incapacity of the principal
   b. Mutual agreement among all involved parties
   c. Lack of interest or initiative of either party
   d. The agreement expires

12. The Act reads, "No licensee shall obtain any written brokerage agreement that does not either provide for automatic expiration within a definite period of time or provide the client with a right to terminate the agreement annually by giving no more than 45 days' prior written notice. Any written brokerage agreement not containing such a provision shall be void." Is this true or false?

   a. True
   b. False

13. Sponsored licensee Mike has one listing right now. Yesterday, Mike's wife received an offer for her dream job. It's in another city that is two hundred and fifty miles away. She will make triple what she makes now. As a couple, they want her to say yes. This means they need to move soon. Is there a potential outcome that would allow the listing agreement to be terminated amicably?

   a. No. Mike is bound to the terms of his contract.
   b. Mike can explain what's going on and see if the seller is willing to terminate the agreement.
   c. No, the listing would simply be assigned to another agent.
   d. None of the above

14. Which of the following can or may need to be used during a negotiation?

    a. Improv

    b. Silence

    c. Empathy

    d. All of the above

15. When money is part of a real estate conversation, people can quickly become which of the following?

    a. Interested

    b. Irrational

    c. Defensive

    d. Emotionally triggered

    e. Any of the above

16. Which of the following is not required by The Act on written buyer brokerage agreements, whether exclusive or nonexclusive?

    a. Agreed basis or amount of compensation and time of payment

    b. Name of the sponsoring broker and the buyers

    c. Cell number or business phone numbers of the sponsoring broker and the buyers

    d. Signatures of the sponsoring broker and the buyers or an authorized signator on behalf of the buyers

17. No licensee shall use real estate contract forms to change previously agreed commission payment terms.

    a. True

    b. False

18. If a lack of disclosure is present, what might consequently happen?

    a. Litigation

    b. Disciplinary action for the licensee

    c. A potential deal can collapse

    d. The reputation of the client and/or licensee can be damaged

    e. All of the above

    f. Only A and B

19. Is social media messaging a secure practice when a licensee is communicating with a client?

    a. Yes

    b. No

    c. Depends on the brokerage handbook and policies

20. To expand your knowledge of MLS, it's important to know that Illinois law requires a licensee to exercise fiduciary duties when authorized to represent the interest of the client. If the client happens to be a seller, under the concept of care, the broker needs to use every marketing tool legally available to position the property for exposure to potential buyers.

    a. True

    b. False

CHAPTER 17:

LEGAL DESCRIPTIONS OF LAND

LEARNING GOALS:

By the end of this lesson, you will:

- Understand the purpose of legal descriptions
- Learn the three methods for defining real estate locations
- Understand commonly used measurements and terms

A **legal description** is the meticulous geographical description of real estate. Each one accurately identifies the precise location and size of a specific parcel of land. They're also called land descriptions. Legal descriptions are used in the transfer of property. They are included and depicted in the deed, survey, mortgage contract, and title insurance policy.

A legal description is not to be confused with a survey. A licensed surveyor uses a legal description to locate a specific parcel and create a written survey. The survey depicts the shape of a parcel of land as well as the locations of all easements, encroachments, and human-made improvements. It also includes bodies of water and other geographical features. A legal description does not depict that type of information.

DEFINITIONS

As a foundation for this chapter, we're going to start with a variety of important definitions that relate to legal descriptions.

- Bureau of Land Management: Also called BLM, this is the successor agency to the General Land Office. The Bureau of Land Management was established in 1946. It is responsible for administering federal lands. According to its website, its mission is to "sustain the health, diversity, and productivity of public lands for the use and enjoyment of present and future generations."

- Datum: Any time you measure on land, the elevation may be a factor. "A vertical datum is a surface of zero elevation to which heights of various points are referenced. Traditionally, vertical datums have used classical survey methods to measure height differences (i.e., geodetic leveling) to best fit the surface of the earth" (National Geodetic Survey). It can also be referred to as an altimetric datum or height datum. In other words, it is the reference point for elevation measurement, which is used for legal descriptions of property. The general datum for the US is defined as the sea elevation of New York Harbor. Because the water elevation can fluctuate from year to year, the Federal Government adopted the North American Vertical Datum of 1988 as the standard reference point from which elevation is defined.

- Bearing: This is the compass direction of a survey line. This is found in everyday language when people say phrases like "I need to get my bearings straight" and "I lost my bearings." Although used figuratively, it relates to compass direction.

- Benchmark: This is a point whose position is known to a high degree of accuracy and is normally marked in some way. The marker is often a metal disk made for this purpose, but it can also be a church spire, a radio tower, a mark chiseled into stone, or a metal rod driven into the ground.

- Principal meridian: A principal meridian is tied to a very specific longitudinal line and only runs north-south. It is a key reference point for measuring townships east to west. This is the principal north-south line, which is used for and relied upon for survey control in a large-sized region. The US has a total of thirty-seven principal meridians.

- Baseline: A baseline is tied to a very specific latitudinal line and runs east-west. It is a key reference point for measuring townships north to south. Combined with a principal meridian, this creates the means for defining a precise location of a township.

- Range lines: Range lines are lines that go north to south and mark the east-west boundaries of each township. They are six miles apart.

- Township lines: These lines run east to west and mark the north-south boundaries of the township. They are six miles apart.

- Township: A township is created by range lines and township lines. A township is a square parcel of land that contains 36 square miles. It is arranged in a square that measures six miles by six miles. In a township, there are 36 sections.

- Section: A section is a block of land that is one square mile (one mile by one mile). Each section has 640 acres.

METHODS FOR DEFINING REAL ESTATE LOCATIONS

To define real estate locations, there are three basic systems and methods. In no particular order, they are:

1. Lot and block method

2. Metes and bounds method

3. Rectangular survey method

Lot and Block Method

The lot and block survey is commonly implemented for lots in highly populated metropolitan areas and the suburbs. It's also known as the recorded plat survey or recorded map survey system. The lot and block system identifies parcels of land by the utilization of lot numbers and block numbers. The general concept has been to create communities that are geometrical in nature. Primarily, this is implemented by using squares and rectangles. Many subdivisions are geometrical, which is why their streets tend to run east to west and north to south. Each block is created by the intersection of these streets and needs to be defined and identified. The block number is usually a three-digit number found within an oval placed at the center of the block. Each block contains lots. A two-digit number is assigned to each lot. By utilizing the lot number and the block number within a given defined area, we are able to identify a specific parcel of land. The given defined area is determined by the utilization of the metes and bounds or rectangular survey methods.

Metes and Bounds Method

This method focuses on the boundaries of the property and the area inside of the boundaries. How is this determined? The surveyor starts at the point of beginning (POB). This is a designated point on the property. From the POB, he/she delineates the sides and angles (boundaries) of the property. The surveyor continues to what is called the point of ending (POE). The POE is also the POB. You might view this as physically going full circle, start to finish. It works this way because the property has to be enclosed. Think of high school or university track for runners. The starting point is the ending point.

Look at the image below. The states that do not have any grayscale or shading (the east coast and Texas) use metes and bounds as their primary means of legal description. The remaining states (shaded in gray) came about after the Louisiana Purchase and use the rectangular survey method.

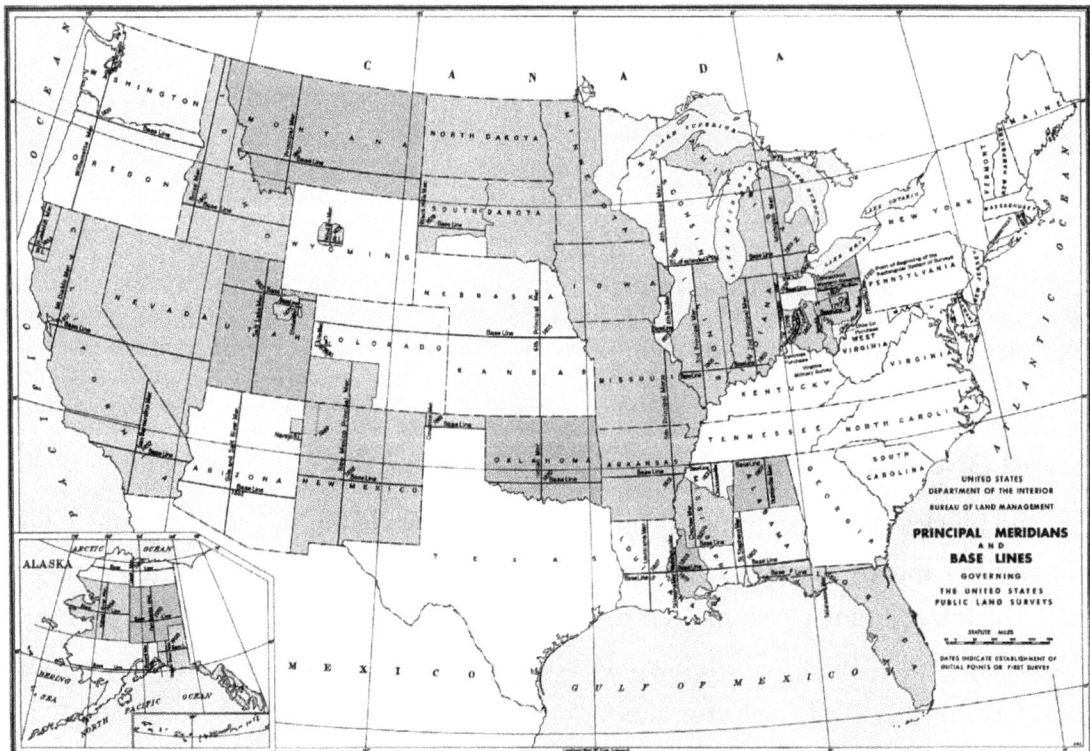

Image credit: U.S. Department of the Interior-Bureau of Land Management

Rectangular Survey Method

Back in the 1790s, the US was negotiating with France to buy a large piece of land. They finalized the purchase in 1804. This was known as the Louisiana Purchase. This pivotal action was literally what opened the door to migration from the east coast to the west coast. All of that land became United States land. It gave citizens the opportunity to relocate and the chance to own something of value for themselves. The Louisiana Purchase is what prompted the creation and implementation of the rectangular survey method. The intent was and is to provide a simple, easy-to-use way to define individual parcels.

Image credit: This work is in the public domain because it is a work of the United States Federal Government. From Frank Bond, Louisiana and the Louisiana Purchase. Washington, Government Printing Office, 1912. Map No. 4.

Before we cover this method, it's important to know two foundational definitions used in geography:

1. Longitude: These are lines on a globe or map that run north to south from the North Pole to the South Pole.

2. Latitude: These are lines on a globe or map that run east to west and are parallel to the equator.

A rectangular survey is also known as the government survey system, the Public Land Survey System (PLSS), and the geodetic survey system. Geodetic comes from geodesy, which is an

Earth science that focuses on measuring and understanding our planet's geometric shape, its orientation in space, and its gravitational field. For easy reference, keep a rectangular grid in mind with this topic. What does this type of survey use? A surveyor uses longitude (principal meridian) and latitude (baseline) lines. Using those bearings, he/she will divide the land into six-by-six square mile parcels, commonly referred to as a township. (You'll read the full definition of a township further below.) From there, they're divided into thirty-six smaller parcels, commonly known as sections. A section of land is one square mile in size, consisting of 640 acres.

Illinois is a rectangular survey state. However, depending on the nature of the property, the legal description may require the use of both the rectangular survey and the metes and bounds.

Look at the image below. The black square is a township. Although most townships have common names, the legal name of the township is comprised of two parts. Part 1 is T3N: Township row 3, north of the baseline. Part two is R5E: Range column 5, east of the principal meridian. Thus, the abbreviated name of the township below is T3N R5E.

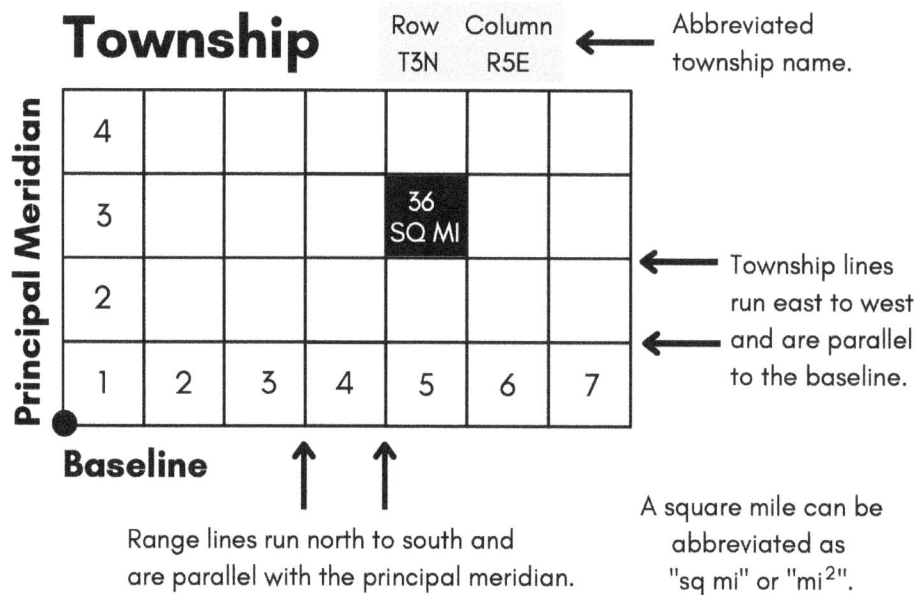

Let's review how a principal meridian and a baseline are used in defining a township. As you saw in the image above, the intersection of a principal meridian and a baseline is typically defined as the starting point (the black circle in the lower-left-hand corner of the image). From that intersection, we can define the exact location of a corresponding township. Range lines are subordinate lines that run parallel to the principal meridian and create columns that are consistently six miles apart. Township lines are also subordinate lines that run parallel to the baseline and are also consistently six miles apart. The grid pattern that originates from the overlay of these two sets of lines is what creates the townships.

How many principal meridians does Illinois have? Within its boundaries, the state has two. Which two? The third and fourth principal meridians. Note that the second principal meridian is physically located in Indiana. It is referred to when describing property along the eastern border of Illinois, just south and east of Kankakee.

As you recall, a township consists of 36 square miles. However, the parcels of land typically owned are smaller than that. This means we need to be able to break down the township into smaller, more manageable components. These components are called sections. As you read earlier, one section is the equivalent of one square mile (640 acres). Each section is numbered, starting in the northeast corner of the township. As you can see from the image below, the sections go from right to left across the first row at the top. Then, they come down a row, going left to right. This pattern repeats until you arrive at section 36 in the southeast corner of the township.

Section Numbering

6	5	4	3	2	1
7	8	9	10	11	12
18	17	**16**	15	14	13
19	20	21	22	23	24
30	29	28	27	26	25
31	32	33	34	35	36

Section 16 of every township is specifically designated to benefit education. It does not have to contain a school. There is no hard definition of what education is required. It is merely for the benefit of education.

The image below shows how the numbers run as well as the location of section 16.

Different Divisions in a Section

NW 1/4 of NW 1/4 (40 acres)	NE 1/4 of NW 1/4 (40 acres)	W 1/2 of NW 1/4 of NE 1/4 (20 acres)	E 1/2 of NW 1/4 of NE 1/4 (20 acres)	N 1/2 of NE 1/4 of NE 1/4 (20 acres)	
				S 1/2 of NE 1/4 of NE 1/4 (20 acres)	
SW 1/4 of NW 1/4 (40 acres)	SE 1/4 of NW 1/4 (40 acres)	10 acres	10 acres	5 acres / 5 acres	5 acres / 5 acres
		10 acres	SE 1/4 of SW 1/4 of NE 1/4 (10 acres)	10 acres	10 acres
SW 1/4 (160 acres)		W 1/2 of SE 1/4 (80 acres)		E 1/2 of SE 1/4 (80 acres)	

Left vertical labels: 1,320 feet | 1,320 feet (1/4 mile) | 2,640 feet (1/2 mile)

Bottom label: ← 5,280 feet (1 mile) →

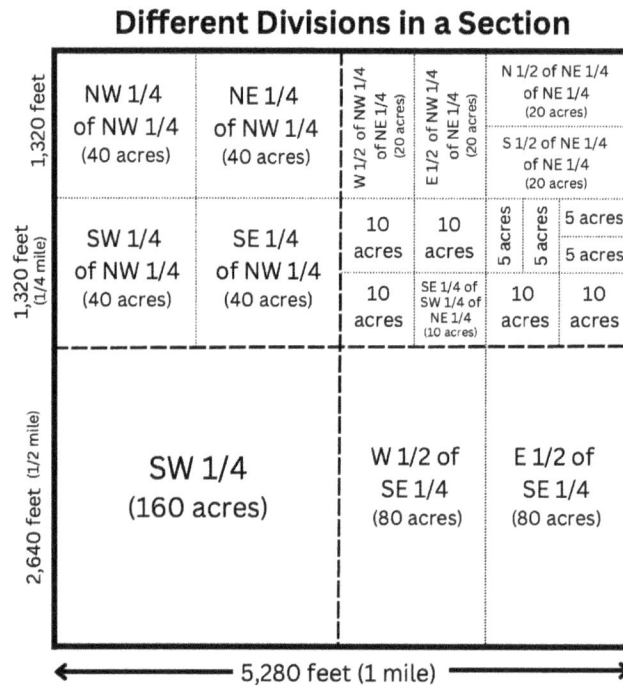

How do we break down a section? The image below details how a section can be broken into smaller, more manageable components. This process precisely defines where a designated parcel can be found within a section of land. Take a few moments to look at the details in the image below. This knowledge will help you define the size of a parcel of land based on its legal description.

LEGAL DESCRIPTIONS AND THE EARTH'S SHAPE

In practice, a licensee must use extreme care when using a legal description. Due to the Earth's shape, the reality is that it is not uncommon for townships and sections to differ from the standard measurements of area. To account for these discrepancies, the practice is to implement a system of fractional sections and government lots.

Related terms include:

1. **Correction lines**: As you read, measurements to land are done on grids. However, there is a problem that must be addressed. That problem is that while the land is surveyed via grids, the world is not a square. It's round. If you begin at the equator and go north or south, the distance between longitudinal lines decreases as these lines tend to converge on either of the two poles. Therefore, how does surveying solve that issue? The answer is correction lines. These are necessary adjustments (corrections) to address this issue. Said another way, correction lines help take the curvature of the Earth into account. It is impossible to put perfect rectangles on a round surface. Given this information, you can see that it's rare for every township to be a perfect 36 square

miles as you go further north or south. Law dictates that there must be a correction to the distance between longitudinal lines every four townships (every 24 miles).

2. **Fractional section**: A fractional section is often created when a body of water extends into a portion of land, leaving less than one square mile available. The water creates an irregular boundary which results in the creation of a government lot.

To illustrate a fractional section, look at the image below. The square is a section. As you can see, a lake extends into the section. This obviously causes a portion of the section to be underwater. Instead of the image showing four 40-acre squares along the western border, because of the lake, there is only one complete 40-acre square. The other three are impacted by the lake, thereby creating a fractional section. From the top left moving down, here is how the math works.

- 37.2 acres: The water covers 2.8 acres of this portion. 40 acres minus 2.8 acres equals 37.2 acres.

- 8.8 acres: The water covers 31.2 acres of this portion. 40 acres minus 31.2 acres equals 8.8 acres.

- 15.5 acres: The water covers 24.5 acres of this portion. 40 acres minus 24.5 acres equals 15.5 acres.

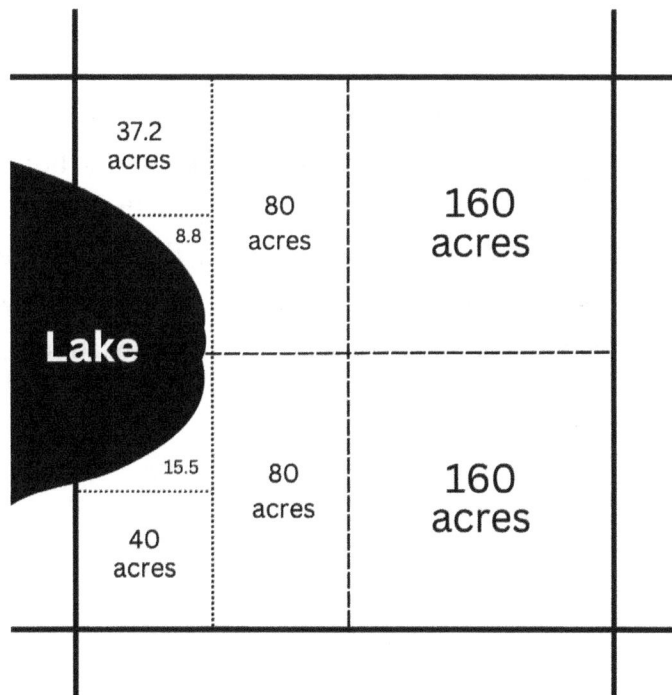

3. **Government lot**: When using the rectangular survey or government survey system, any fractional section that is less than a quarter section (160 acres) in area is called

a government lot. Government lots are generally labeled by number. The shape of government lots can be regular or irregular. Much of the time, meandering bodies of water are adjacent to government lots.

4. **Lot**: A lot is a term used to reference individual parcels of land. Frequently, for identification purposes, a lot will be assigned a two- or three-digit number to differentiate the individual lots within a subdivision.

Irregular Lot Example:

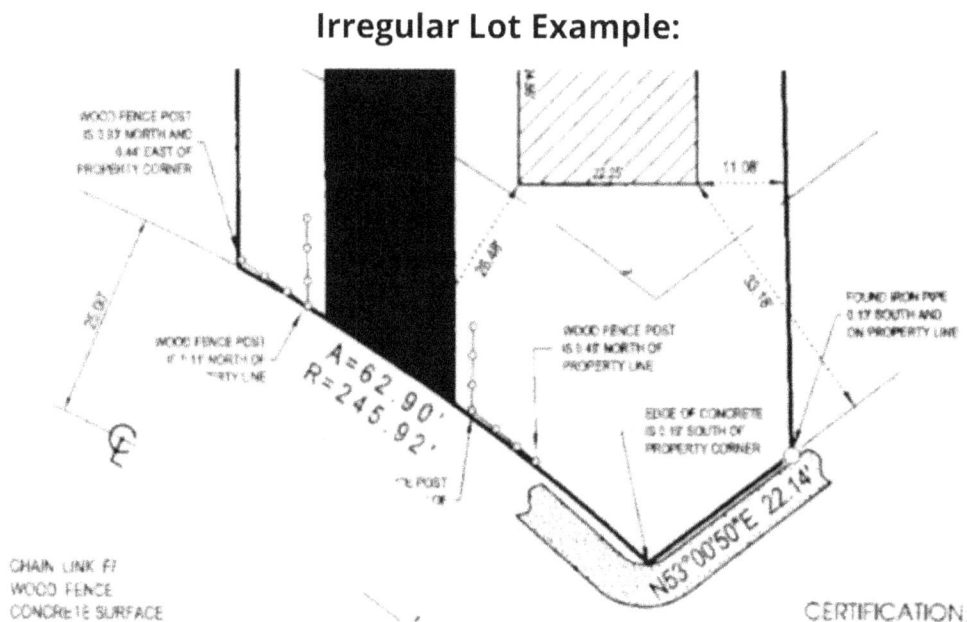

The rectangular survey method was designed to recognize rectangles and squares when it comes to defining the location of a parcel of land. However, with the introduction of cul-de-sacs, many parcels are now irregular in shape. The rectangular survey method is not equipped to define these irregular parcels. As you can see in the image below, the southern edge of the parcel is irregular. It sits on a cul-de-sac. As a result, this is an example of when we need to use both rectangular survey and metes and bounds to clearly define the location and size of the parcel.

Take your chapter quiz below now.

CHAPTER 17 QUIZ

1. Which of the following is not provided as a component when using the rectangular survey?

    a. The name of the property owner
    b. The property's exact location
    c. The size of the parcel
    d. The relationship to a defined principal meridian

2. Which measurement system focuses on the boundaries of the property and the area inside of the boundaries?

    a. Lot and block system
    b. Metes and bounds
    c. Rectangular survey
    d. None of the above

3. Sarah is a real estate investor. She is considering purchasing a large apartment building that includes its own private gym and park. It is located in a highly populated metropolitan area. Which of the following measuring systems is most likely to be used considering those details?

    a. Rectangular survey
    b. Metes and bounds
    c. Lot and block system
    d. None of the above

4. A lot and block survey is sometimes also called which of the following?

    a. Recorded plat survey
    b. Recorded map survey system
    c. Meets map
    d. A and B
    e. None of the above

5. A rectangular survey is also known as which of the following?

    a. Public Land Survey System (PLSS)
    b. Government survey system
    c. Geodetic survey system
    d. All of the above
    e. None of the above

6. Jill is a surveyor. Every day, she works with longitude and latitude lines. In legal descriptions, they are also known as which of the following, respectively?

    a. Principal meridian and baseline
    b. Prime meridian and baseline
    c. POB (point of beginning) and POE (point of ending)
    d. B and C

7. Juan is a surveyor. Currently, he is surveying a new university running track. He starts at the point of beginning (POB), then delineates the sides and angles (boundaries) of the property. Juan continues to the point of ending (POE). Which measurement system is he implementing?

    a. Geodetic survey system
    b. Lot and block system
    c. Metes and bounds
    d. Rectangular survey

8. A township is divided into 36 smaller parcels, commonly known as sections. A section of land is one square mile in size, which consists of 660 acres.

    a. True
    b. False

9. A principal meridian only runs north to south.

    a. True
    b. False

10. Mike is explaining townships to his young daughter. It does not surprise him, as she has always loved geography and math. She asks him what a principal meridian does concerning townships. How would he answer?

    a. It divides a township between east and west.
    b. It divides a township between east and west.
    c. It divides a township down the middle.
    d. None of the above.

11. How many principal meridians does Illinois have within its boundaries?

    a. One
    b. Two
    c. Three
    d. Four

12. How many principal meridians are within the US?

    a. 12 principal meridians
    b. 24 principal meridians
    c. 37 principal meridians
    d. 48 principal meridians

13. What is a bearing?

    a. A baseline
    b. The way range lines are divided
    c. A compass direction
    d. None of the above

14. What is the distance between range lines that are east or west of the principal meridian?

    a. 4 miles
    b. 6 miles
    c. 8 miles
    d. 10 miles

15. Township lines create rows. What do you call the lines that create the columns?

    a. Range lines
    b. Quarter sections
    c. Township tiers
    d. Bearing lines

16. Morris was a high school assistant principal who recently became a licensee. He is still getting acquainted with the wide variety of terms and phrases in the world of real estate. In the past, when someone said the word benchmark, he commonly thought of the strengths and weaknesses of students, along with state exams. However, in the world of surveyors and legal descriptions, what are benchmarks?

    a. Temporary reference points used to define the location of a given parcel of land
    b. Permanent reference points used to define the location of a given parcel of land
    c. The inaugural bench installed in the local park
    d. Details about the minimum requirements to be a surveyor

17. Why is it rare for a township to be a perfect 36 square miles? Which of the following is the best answer? This is due to . . .

    a. Rivers and other waterways
    b. Because of the Earth's curvature
    c. Most townships are naturally larger than 36 square miles
    d. Township lines

18. John Adams is considering buying a parcel of land with plans to construct his new home there. The legal description states that the parcel is the north half of the southeast quarter of the southwest quarter of the northeast quarter of section 21. If he purchases the property at $98,000 per acre and the commission payable is 6%, what is the commission due to John's broker?

    a. $31,250
    b. $29,400
    c. $28,700
    d. $32,100

19. What makes it possible for surveyors to adjust the width of a township because of the curvature of the Earth when doing a land description?

    a. Township lines
    b. Correction lines
    c. Fractional sections
    d. Datum

20. In a legal description, what is the reference point for elevation measurement?

    a. Benchmarks
    b. Correction lines
    c. Township lines
    d. Datum

CHAPTER 18:

REAL ESTATE CONTRACTS

LEARNING GOALS:

By the end of this lesson, you will:

- Know the four essential elements of real estate contracts
- Understand the four types of contracts
- Recognize the difference between a valid contract and an enforceable contract
- Learn related concepts and commonly used terms

ESSENTIAL ELEMENTS OF REAL ESTATE CONTRACTS

As discussed previously, a contract is a written or spoken agreement that is designed and intended to create a binding relationship between two or more parties. The purpose of the contract is to facilitate real estate being purchased, sold, exchanged, or some other type of conveyance. Conveyance is the legal act or process of transferring or conveying ownership or interest in real estate from one individual (grantor) to another (grantee). The **Statute of Frauds** (SOF) exists in US common law and requires that certain contracts be written and signed to be enforceable in a court of law. In the real estate industry, this includes all sales contracts and representation contracts (listing, buyer representation, property management agreements). A contract is designed to protect both parties. Contracts and agreements (express or implied) are governed by US contract law. The law of contracts does vary depending on the state.

A valid contract includes four essential elements. They are:

1. **Offer and acceptance**:

   - **Contractual offer:** This is what is being offered. It is not the contract yet. The offer is a proposal that details what the offeror (the giver) is willing to provide to the offeree (the receiver). When the offer is accepted and signed by all parties, it becomes a binding contract, which is legally enforceable in court.

   - **Acceptance:** This occurs when an offer tendered is agreed to by the other party. This creates a contractual relationship. Here's an example. A home seller's agent places the details of the property on an MLS. This action constitutes a request for an offer. An interested buyer who learns about the property's availability will then tender an offer through their agent, which will ultimately be presented to the seller for review. The seller has the right to accept, reject, or counter the offer.

     - If rejected, the potential sale and the business relationship come to an end. The seller looks for other buyers. The buyer looks at other houses.

     - If the seller accepts and signs the document, upon notification of acceptance to the buyer, the parties have created a legally binding contract.

     - If the seller counters the offer presented by the buyer, the seller will make a proposed modification that is then given to the buyer for review. The buyer then has the right to accept the modification, reject the entire offer, or create another counteroffer. It's important to recognize that acceptance may be the result of a compromise between the original offer and what is actually agreed to. There is almost always room for compromise.

- The term **mutual consent** comes in at this point. It is also known as "mutual assent" and "meeting of the minds." Mutual consent defines an agreement between both parties, thereby creating a contractual relationship. It also means each party enters into the agreement of their own free will. There are no outside influences dictating either of the parties' actions when entering into the agreement. No buyer or seller should be coerced, forced, or manipulated into signing.

2. **Consideration**: In the contract, what is being offered and exchanged? That is what consideration means. What is being offered and exchanged must have legal value. The most common practice in real estate is that money is the consideration. The contract must outline the consideration. There are two basic forms of consideration that have been deemed acceptable for the conveyance of real estate. They are:

   - Valuable consideration—This is anything that can be the equivalent of money.

   - Good consideration—This is generally considered as love and affection.

3. **Legality**: Everything must follow the law. Specifically, any valid contract in real estate must be for a legal purpose. In short, a contract cannot violate any aspect of the law in order to be legally recognizable.

4. **Capacity**: The parties must have the legal capacity to enter into a contract. This is also called competency. Simply put, each person in the contract is able to think rationally and is legally capable of entering into the contract. For example, a drunk seller does not have the capacity or competency at that moment to enter into a contract.

Agents in Illinois are required by law to deliver true copies. A true copy is an accurate depiction of the original document. It is a true reflection of the documentation executed by all parties to the agreement. All of the true copies must be initialed or executed, and delivered to everyone who has signed or initialed them. They must be delivered within a reasonable period of time. The key legal concept is *time is of the essence*. Failure to deliver the documentation in a timely manner might provide a means for one party to withdraw from the contract.

What happens if there are multiple offers? First, when multiple offers have been tendered, the listing broker must notify all buyers' agents of the situation. This gives each potential buyer the opportunity to revise their offer in light of the competition. The listing broker must take precautionary steps not to share any of the content within the submitted offers with the other brokers. Doing so could harm the negotiating position of each of the potential buyers. Second, the listing broker must recognize that all offers must be presented simultaneously. He/she is expected to present all offers to the client, unless prior instructions from the client state otherwise. This provides the seller with the opportunity to compare each offer side by side in order to select the best option.

FOUR MAIN TYPES OF CONTRACTS

They are:

1. Express

2. Implied

3. Bilateral

4. Unilateral

Express contract: Also called an express agreement, this is when terms and conditions are clearly and directly expressed. The terms and conditions are intentionally communicated between the parties, either orally or written. As you can see, an express contract does not have to be written. As long as the relationship has been clearly established, an express contract has been created. In other words, promises are clearly communicated. Most people are familiar with express contracts because they are widely used.

Implied contract: An implied contract is indirect because it is created by the actions, behaviors, or circumstances of the involved parties. There is no written or verbal agreement. Simply stated, this is a contract created by the implied actions of the parties.

Bilateral contract: Bilateral contracts are a promise for a promise. In this agreement, the involved parties agree to perform a specific act or group of acts. Each party is required to take a certain action. Example: In real estate, the seller promises to sell her property for a certain amount. The buyer promises to pay the specified dollar amount for the property that the seller is asking, thus creating a promise for a promise. In Illinois, all exclusive representation agreements are viewed by law as a bilateral contract. Bilateral contracts can be created either by expression or implication.

Unilateral contract: The prefix "uni-" means one. In a unilateral contract, one party accepts an offer by doing or fulfilling a specific action. For example, a seller is selling their home FSBO. A broker approaches the seller and inquires if they are interested in listing. The seller acknowledges their intent to continue as an FSBO. However, if the broker has a potential buyer who wishes to view the seller's home, and if the buyer tenders an offer that is acceptable to the seller, the seller will pay the broker a commission. In this scenario, the seller is making a promise to compensate the broker only if the broker takes the action to procure a ready, willing, and able buyer. This scenario creates a promise for an action, also known as a unilateral contract. In Illinois, open representation agreements are viewed by law as unilateral contracts. Unilateral contracts can also be created either by expression or implication.

EXECUTORY CONTRACTS VERSUS EXECUTED CONTRACTS

A contract can also be categorized as either an executed contract or an executory contract. While the terms are similar, they are different.

1. An **executory contract** means that either one, both, or all parties still have performance and an obligation to complete. There is still work to do. An executory contract is incomplete. For example, a lease agreement is an executory contract. It is fulfilled over time. Once the lease agreement hits its expiration point (perhaps a "move out" date) and all the payments have been made, at that point, it is an executed contract.

2. An **executed contract** simply means each and every party has completed and fulfilled their promises and obligations. What each party said they would do has been done. For example, if you're the seller's agent and the house is sold, at the point when the transaction closes, the contract becomes executed. An executed contract is complete.

TYPES OF CONTRACTS BASED ON VALIDITY

Another category in which all contracts fit inside pertains to the realm of validity. Concerning validity, there are four types of contracts:

1. **Void contracts** do not exist. A void contract may be the result of a valid contract having been changed. For example, maybe the previously agreed-upon sales price has been changed and the parties are not in full agreement, or an essential element never existed from the beginning. The end result? The contract does not exist.

2. **Valid contracts** are the cornerstone of real estate transactions because they are legally binding agreements that are enforceable in a court of law. They possess all the essential elements required by law.

3. **Unenforceable contracts** come across as valid, but a court will not enforce them. For example, in Illinois, if a real estate contract is not in writing, it is unenforceable. If each party agrees to perform according to the contract, it seems valid. However, the court cannot compel either party to comply with the terms.

4. **Voidable contracts** are many times the "almost but not quite" contracts. Is a voidable contract enforceable? It depends. In a voidable contract, while it may look valid and binding on the surface, in reality, one or both of the parties have been taken advantage of. Basically, they're placed in a position where they either lack essential information and/or are unable to make a rational decision. The law would grant the injured party the right to cancel the relationship upon realizing what has happened. For example, if you sign a contract while you are inebriated, mostly likely a court of law will view it

as a voidable contract. The end result is that the court will cancel the relationship so that neither party is obligated to perform. There are a number of legal reasons and/or circumstances that can make a contract voidable. These include, but are not limited to, the following:

- One or more material facts has failed to be disclosed by one or both parties

- Within the contract there exists one or more errors, fraud, or misrepresentation

- One party is legally incapable of entering the contract

- Duress, manipulation, threat, and/or something forcing a party to take an action involuntarily under influence or duress

- A line, phrase, or section of the contract is deemed unreasonably excessive, not right, or unreasonable

- There is a breach of contract by one or both parties

ELEMENTS OF CONTRACTS AND RELATED TERMS

Addendum: What happens when you do not need to change the existing contract, but you do need to add a new condition to the terms? This is an addendum. It is added to the existing contract. Nothing is changed in the original contract. You can remember this by the word "add." You're adding to the existing contract without changing it.

Amendment: Amend means to modify or change. What happens when a contract has been agreed to by all parties, but one or both parties want some type of change made to specific terms within the contract? When this occurs, the solution is to use an amendment. This is a change made to the wording in the original contract. For example, if a buyer wants an oil tank removed from the property prior to closing but that is not in the original terms, an amendment is prepared. It states exactly what needs to be done, by whom, and by when. Amendments are very common in real estate transactions.

Assignment: Assignment in the context of a real estate contract is a legal term. An assignment is the transfer of an individual's duties, rights, or property to another individual or entity. Assignment is laid out in the contract. For example, you are a well-known entrepreneur, and you want to create an entertainment venue in a destination state. Let's say you approach the owners of the property you wish to acquire. If they know of your wealth, they may try to inflate the sales price. If that happens, what can you do? One option is to create a shell corporation and name a third party as its president. Let the president approach the seller and inquire about the sales price. In this scenario, can we expect the seller to be more realistic with regard to the sales price? Likely, the answer is yes. Most importantly, if the president includes the phrase "*and/or* *my assignee*" in the sales contract and the seller accepts the contract with this provision, the seller has granted the president the legal right to transfer the power of buying this property to you, the well-known entrepreneur.

Breach of contract: In this context, a breach occurs when either party violates the terms of the agreement. For whatever reason, either one or both parties fail to live up to the terms of their agreement. The party guilty of the breach can suffer liability and/or damages. It may relate to nonperformance, interference, misrepresentation, or any number of causes. Examples include: 1) a seller failing to deliver a clean title to the buyer, or 2) the buyer failing to acquire their mortgage commitment within the time allotted.

Compensatory damages: Sometimes called additional damages, these damages are economic losses incurred due to a breach of contract. This could include, but is not limited to, issues like a loss of a party's earnings, damage to property, medical costs, and so on.

Contingencies: As you learned earlier, a contingency is a clause in a contract. A clause can be a specific or separate article or stipulation found within the contract. A proviso is a condition attached to an agreement. In a typical contract, there will always be specific components that need to be met in order to complete the transaction. These are referred to as contingencies. These are one or more conditions that must be met prior to the delivery of the deed. In other words, the contingency defines one or more conditions and/or actions that must be fulfilled in order for the contract to become binding.

Types of contingencies are listed and defined below in alphabetical order:

1. **Alternative contingencies**: This is essentially a category to capture contingencies that are not one of the contingencies listed below. Alternative means that it is not a common contingency. There is always potential for unique circumstances to arise. When they do, sometimes an alternative contingency is implemented. For example: A young buyer looking to acquire their first home wants their mom and dad's approval. There may be a contingency inserted into the offer that is subject to the parents' approval. Although not a common contingency, it is an example of some unique contingencies that a buyer and/or seller may want inserted into the contract.

2. **Attorney contingency**: Real estate licensees are not attorneys. While a licensee can give a client direction on how to fill in the blanks on contracts, should there be a question on the legal application of a specific entry, the client's question must be deferred to his or her attorney. This contingency gives the buyer and seller the choice of consulting with their attorneys before/after signing the contract. In most cases, the attorney's approval or disapproval can either solidify or disavow the contract.

3. **Appraisal contingency**: Although the appraisal is typically ordered by the lender, there may be circumstances when a buyer may want to order their own appraisal. Regardless of who orders the appraisal, should the property fail to appraise at or above the sales price, the buyer has the option to cancel the agreement without penalty. This option must be exercised within the time frame allocated to acquire a firm loan commitment.

4. **Home close contingency**: Occasionally a buyer will find the home they wish to acquire before they have been able to close on their existing home. This assumes that the buyer has already acquired a sales contract on their existing home. This contingency allows the buyer to cash out on their current home to complete the purchase of the new home. This provision grants the buyer a period of time to close on their existing home prior to closing on the new home.

5. **Home sale contingency**: Occasionally a buyer will find the home they wish to acquire before they have been able to sell their existing home. A licensee can present an offer on behalf of the buyer under the condition that the seller grants the buyer a period of time to secure a written contract from a purchaser. Should a seller grant this option to the buyer, the buyer generally grants the seller the right to continue showing the property to other perspective buyers. If another offer is tendered, the first buyer will be given an opportunity to cancel this contingency and purchase the property or release the seller to accept the second offer.

6. **Inspection contingency**: Also called home inspection contingency, this is the most common contingency according to a variety of sources. It gives the buyer the chance to formally have the property inspected. Based on the findings, it's possible that the purchase price will be renegotiated, that repairs will have to be made by the seller, or, if nothing else, the buyer can leave the contract unscathed. The offer is only valid if the inspection is acceptable and "passes." This inspection can be a home inspection, pest inspection, septic, and so on.

7. **Kick-out clause contingency**: A kick-out contingency provides for the buyer or the seller to terminate the relationship at any time without penalty.

8. **Mortgage/financing contingency**: This contingency provides the buyer some time, so he/she can work toward securing financing in order to purchase the property. If the buyer secures funding, it is a common courtesy to communicate this important update to the seller. What happens if a buyer does not provide written notification of their inability to secure financing with the time allotted per the contract? The seller may have the right, depending on how the contract is written, to presume that the buyer will do an all-cash purchase.

9. **Right to assign contingency**: Widely used for wholesale real estate investors, this contingency gives the option to exit the contract if he/she cannot assign the contract to another buyer within a specific time frame.

10. **Title contingency**: In the event of problems with the title, such as a lien, this contingency gives the buyer the right to exit the contract if the issue with the deed cannot be resolved by the seller prior to the closing.

Digital signature: In today's world, digital signatures are common. The Electronic Commerce Security Act found within The Act defines this term.

> "Digital signature" means a type of electronic signature created by transforming an electronic record using a message digest function and encrypting the resulting transformation with an asymmetric cryptosystem using the signer's private key such that any person having the initial untransformed electronic record, the encrypted transformation, and the signer's corresponding public key can accurately determine whether the transformation was created using the private key that corresponds to the signer's public key and whether the initial electronic record has been altered since the transformation was made. A digital signature is a security procedure." (5 ILCS 175/5-105)

To get detailed, know that a digital signature is not the same as an "electronic signature." This is a common misconception. Only digital signatures use asymmetric cryptography. In general terms and with technology moving so quickly, this could change next week. Here's a simple contrast for you: 1) Electronic signatures will prove the person who signed it and what type of agreement or form was signed. It also shows consent and intent. 2) Digital signatures can be viewed as a level higher. They secure any sensitive and confidential data through encryption. They can usually detect hackers and anyone trying to tamper with the document. If the document gets altered in some form or fashion that is out of line with the system's protocols, a red flag or digital alarm will be issued and parties will be notified. Comparatively, digital signatures are safer. In order to preserve the integrity of confidential information, it is preferred that licensees use digital signatures as a means of acquiring clients' consent.

Discharge: When a licensee successfully completes his or her real estate obligation on behalf of a client, he/she is discharged. In general terms, to discharge someone is to officially tell him/her that their services are no long necessary. It means to come out of an agreement, like when a soldier is discharged from his or her military service. In the context of real estate contracts, a discharge is the end of the licensee's relationship with a client.

Earnest money: Earnest money is a part of the transaction that is to be taken very seriously. Why? Because it is generally considered a part of the offer intended to show the seller that the buyer is acting in good faith with every intent to fulfill the terms of the contract. Failure of the buyer to perform under the terms of the contract, other than those conditions cited within the contract, may be sufficient cause for the seller to be able to retain the earnest money as liquidated damages. Earnest money has been referred to as the buyer having "skin in the game." It shows that they are serious. When this money is deposited, it is proof of the buyer's intention. A sales contract is the first step. The sales contract is where the amount is recorded. Following having a sales contract in place, the check can be delivered to the listing sponsoring broker. Earnest money is a specific sum of money. This sum is negotiated between the buyer and the seller as part of the negotiating process. Usually, the earnest money is held by the sponsoring broker of the firm that represents the seller. At the closing, this deposit is credited back to the buyer. The more earnest money in the account, the more it demonstrates to the seller that the buyer has financial power. Usually, the higher the house price, the larger the sum of earnest money. Earnest money deposits are not legally required in Illinois. However, it is common and customary. Most earnest money deposits are done via a check. Although there is no "right or wrong" amount of earnest money, the amount should be enough to encourage the buyer to stay committed, and sufficient to cover any expenses the seller has to pay if the buyer does default. In Illinois, both parties' signatures are required by law in order to release earnest money. Earnest money is to be deposited in a financial institution that is federally insured. All managing brokers must execute a document entitled "Consent To Audit" and submit this to IDFPR at the time they are initially licensed. This declaration provides the state with knowledge of the financial institution that holds the earnest money, including all account information.

Equitable title: Equitable title references an individual's future right to gain full ownership of a property or property interest while the other party holds the legal title. Legal title means owning the land. When a property transaction is executed, equitable interest passes from the property owner to the buyer. When the closing takes place and everything is signed and completed, at that point, the legal title passes on to the buyer.

Land contract: A land contract is a legally binding contract between the seller of real estate and the buyer, where the seller makes available some type of financing for the buyer. The buyer agrees to pay the loan following an installment plan. In this circumstance, the seller (owner) retains legal title, and the buyer (or renter) can take possession of the property. Once paid in full, the legal title of the property goes to the buyer, who is, at that moment, the new property owner.

Letter of intent: Also shortened to LOI, a letter of intent is a preliminary agreement in document form that declares and outlines one party's intention to enter into a valid contract. In other words, it's a formal and usually non-binding method to communicate, "I want to do business with you." It generally states proposed terms and details about the proposed agreement. In this way, the other party who is the recipient can evaluate the letter of intent to see if he/she wants to take action toward securing a legally binding contract. A letter of intent may be one page or several pages and may be physical or digital.

Liquidated damages: Also called LDs, the purpose of liquidated damages is to bypass any related legal costs as well as the stress of determining actual damages. When a party breaches the contract, that party may be sued by the other party for damages. Some states have a rule that liquidated damages cannot exceed a certain percentage of the purchase price. Why? To be enforceable, a liquidated damage clause is required to be reasonable. As you read earlier, in some circumstances, failure of the buyer to perform under the terms of the contract, other than those conditions cited within the contract, may be sufficient cause for the seller to retain the earnest money as liquidated damages. The liquidated damages clause in a contract is a way of financially protecting each party in a way that is guaranteed.

Novation: Novation is the substitution of a new contract in place of an existing contract. For example, a seller and buyer have agreed in writing on a sales price. The lender that the buyer is using orders an appraisal. Upon receipt, the parties realize that the appraiser underappraised the property by $20,000. This could be sufficient cause for the buyer to cancel the transaction. However, the buyer's agent meets with the seller and the seller's agent and presents the appraisal. The buyer's agent suggests modifying the sales price, reducing it by $20,000 in order to match the appraisal. If the seller accepts the reduction in price, it will allow the buyer to finance the purchase and fulfill the terms of the agreement. This retains the original buyer and creates a new contract that supersedes the prior agreement.

Operation of law: This phrase, which is also called "by operation of law," is a legal term. In some scenarios, duties outlined in a contract can be discharged or terminated by operation of law. These scenarios include:

- exceeding the statute of limitations

- impossibility to perform

- bankruptcy

- foreclosure

- one party materially altering the contract without written permission from the other party

Option/s (or real estate option): In a real estate contract, an option is a designed contract provision that exists between a buyer and a seller, or a renter and the owner. The seller or owner gives the buyer or renter the option to purchase an asset within a specific time frame. Usually, this is at a fixed price, although there can be a lot of variety in the world of real estate options. The buyer/renter must decide whether to purchase or not by the end of the time limit. Most of the time, the option is exclusive to the buyer or renter. An option is not an obligation to buy.

Rescission: In simple terms, this means the cancellation of the sale/lease by the parties. This often results in the buyer/tenant receiving his or her earnest money/security deposit back, although it is not guaranteed. Rescission occurs when a contract becomes null and void. The contract moves from being legally binding to having zero legal implications.

Specific performance: This is legal action exercised by the court to force the defaulting party to comply with the terms of the contract.

Statute of limitations: This type of statute defines a set period of limitation for initiating specific types of legal action. If a party has a dispute with a contract, he/she has a set number of years in which he/she can initiate legal proceedings. After the time limit is up, he/she has no rights in the matter and cannot instigate litigation. In Illinois, and specifically speaking about contracts, oral and written contracts have different statutes of limitation. In Illinois, the statute of limitations on oral contracts is five years, and for written contracts it is ten years. It is always important for each party to be aware of these time constraints.

Termination of contract: As you read earlier, there are several ways a contract can be terminated or discharged. We will not review those here. You can refer back to the earlier definitions in this chapter (such as novation and rescission) as well as the section called "Brokerage Agreement Termination" in Chapter 16.

Timing: You probably remember at some point during your K-12 education when you learned about interrogatives. These are also known as "question words." These words are who, what, where, when, how, and why. When there is a contract, the contract should answer the essential questions that start with who, what, where, when, how, and why. Who is the brokerage, licensee, and client. What is the goal, such as the client wanting to acquire his or her retirement home. While most of those details are clear, *when* can be a bit problematic. Knowing *when* is essential. The *when* is the time frame in which all the expectations and responsibilities are to be fulfilled. Most contracts lay out deadlines for specific actions. Each party is expected to honor those deadlines. The underlying principle of law that must be considered is *time is of the essence*.

Residential real estate purchase and sales contract: General provisions in the preprinted residential real estate purchase and sales contract contain legal clauses related to but not limited to the following:

- Affidavit of title

- Broker(s) compensation

- Business days and times (All days in contract refer to business days)

- Code violations (And code violation notices)

- Disposition of earnest money

- Escrow closing

- Flood insurance (If required)

- Insulation disclosure requirements

- Legal description

- Notice (Must be in writing)

- Operational systems (In working order)

- Patriot Act (Compliance with federal law)

- Prorations

- RESPA (Compliance with federal law)

- Removal of personal property

- Surrender of possession of real property

- Survey

- Time (Time is of the essence.)

- Title (Delivery of commitment for title insurance from seller to buyer at least five days prior to closing)

- Transfer taxes

- Uniform Vendor and Purchaser Risk Act (Compliance with Illinois law)

SAMPLE LETTER OF INTENT

September 20, 2023

Mrs. Devon Thompson, Broker
The Thomson Group
555 Main Street
Dealstown, Illinois 12345

Subject: Main Street Forever 3000

Dear Mrs. Thompson:

On behalf of The Elite 88 By Design Corporation, I am excited and pleased to present this Letter of Intent to Main Street Forever 3000. Hereafter, referred to as Tenant. Thank you for your review and consideration of this Letter of Intent.

BUILDING:	1818 Main Street Plaza
LANDLORD:	Main Street Forever 3000 owners and operators of 1818 Main Street Plaza
PREMISES:	Suite 3000, with 2000 rentable SF
SPACE REQUIREMENTS:	Requirements of 2000 rentable square feet. Tenant shall have the right to measure the space based on the most recent BOMA standards.
LEASE TERM:	Three years (3 years)
RENT AND LEASE COMMENCEMENT:	October 1, 2022. Rent shall escalate every 12 months.
GROSS RENTAL RATE:	$22.00 USD per rentable SF
GROSS RENTAL RATE ESCALATION:	The gross rental rate will increase annually by $0.65 cents per square foot, beginning at the first annual anniversary.
SECURITY DEPOSIT:	Tenant shall pay one month's gross rent upon the time of the lease execution.
ELECTRICITY:	Tenant shall receive a monthly electric bill. Each premise is metered separately for both outlets and lighting.
TENANT IMPROVEMENT:	Tenant understands and shall accept the premises in "AS IS" condition. Should the tenant need to make physical modifications to the space they occupy, they must first seek consent of the landlord and clarify who is financially responsible for the modifications. In addition, there needs to be clarification as to whether or not the tenant must return the space at the conclusion of lease to the original condition when they first received it.
AMENITIES:	The premises features several amenities including high-speed Internet, 10 covered parking for disabled individuals, a break room, and employees-only cafe area.

PARKING: Landlord to designate 20 uncovered regular parking spots exclusively for the tenant.

SECURITY: Security is generally the responsibility of the tenant. However, as a service of the building, the landlord may provide common area security 24 hours a day 365 days a year.

JANITORIAL: Landlord provides professional cleaning by a highly rated cleaning service six nights per week and carpet cleaning every quarter.

BUILDING HOURS: 7 a.m. to 11 p.m. every day

TELECOMMUNICATIONS FACILITIES: The tenant may choose his or her telephone vendor.

LEASE COMMISSION: The commission earned on a leasing assignment varies based on the type of property. For example, residential leases tend to be the equivalent of one month's rent. However, commission on a commercial lease tends to be a percentage of gross rental income received during the term of the lease. Example: The licensee helps to put a commercial tenant into an office structure. The licensee may receive a percentage of the first year's rent, plus a reduced percentage for each of the remaining years of the lease.

CONFIDENTIALITIES: This Letter of Intent is a non-binding indication of interest and is confidential in nature. It may not be disclosed other than to you and Main Street Forever 3000 advisors. This information is on a strictly need-to-know basis. It does not create a binding obligation in any way, shape, or form.

EXPIRATION: Forty-five (45) days from the date hereof

OPTION TO RENEW: Many commercial leases are written with a defined right of the tenant to renew the lease for a specified period of time. By placing this option into the lease, it is generally considered the tenant's right to renew the lease even if the landlord would prefer not to do so.

Thank you for your consideration.

Warmly,

Jane Doe, The Elite 88 By Design Corporation

QUINLAN/TYSON DECISION: UNLICENSED PRACTICE OF LAW AND ROLE OF BROKER IN TRANSACTION

One famous Supreme Court case in Illinois in the past changed something that all licensees need to be aware of, know, and practice. The case was called Chicago Bar Association versus Quinlan and Tyson, Inc.

> "Quinlan and Tyson, Inc. (defendant) employs licensed real estate brokers and salesmen who, during the course of their duties, prepare offers to purchase property, contracts of purchase and sale, deeds, and other instruments used to clear and transfer title. The documents originate as standard forms initially drawn up by licensed attorneys, which the brokers complete by filling in with relevant facts and information about the parties. The Chicago Bar Association (the association) (plaintiff) brought suit to enjoin Quinlan and Tyson from continuing this practice, contending that such actions constituted the unauthorized practice of law by individuals who are not licensed attorneys. The trial court agreed with the association, except that it permitted Quinlan and Tyson to fill in offer for purchase forms, which the court determined were a necessary component of Quinlan and Tyson's business. The appellate court reversed the exception, concluding that none of the activities could be performed by non-lawyers. Quinlan and Tyson appealed, contending that their filling in of standardized forms is a simple task requiring only ordinary business intelligence." Quimbee: https://www.quimbee.com/cases/chicago-bar-association-v-quinlan-and-tyson-inc

The Illinois Supreme Court's decision implemented specific limitations on real estate licensees regarding how to draft or modify a contract. The ruling states that licensees must use pre-printed form contracts, approved by the REALTOR® organizations and the bar associations in that geographical area. The forms are legal documents that have been created by attorneys and/or law firms. In a sense, it's a one-two punch from two different professions, in order to draft or modify documents that are legal, practical, and relevant. And of course, they're in line with the Illinois Supreme Court ruling. Licensees are only authorized to fill in the blanks in these forms with factual information. They are never to change or alter forms and/or content and are not to give legal advice in any way. When they do, they may be subject to disciplinary action. Real estate licensees must keep a clear line between what they are and what they are not licensed to do, such as practice law.

CONTRACT FORMS USED IN REAL ESTATE

A wide variety of contract forms are used in the world of real estate. The most popular and commonly used forms in no particular order are the following:

1. Buyer agency agreements

2. Listing agreements

3. Lease agreements

4. Power of attorney agreements

5. Purchase agreement contracts

6. Deed contracts

7. Land contracts

8. Escrow agreements

9. Real estate sales contracts

10. Options agreements

Disclaimer: As a real estate licensee, these are not documents that you are allowed to create. Always refer to legally approved forms customarily used in your area.

Ask your designated managing broker which forms your office has approved to be used. Familiarize yourself with each form.

Counteroffers: To end this chapter, it's important you learn about counteroffers. In the world of real estate transactions, first offers are not always accepted. Counteroffers are very common. As you know, a counteroffer is an offer made in response to an initial offer. The reasons and reasoning for counteroffers are exceptionally varied. A counteroffer means that the initial offer was not accepted. The counteroffer replaces the initial offer. Both the initial offer and a counteroffer create one of three possible outcomes from the other party: 1) acceptance, 2) rejection, or 3) further negotiations. Counteroffers can continue until an offer is accepted, if the parties choose to do so. Sometimes they continue until one party chooses to exit the negotiation process.

THE ROLE OF THE BROKER

Once a contract is signed, the role of the broker, whether representing the buyer or the seller, is to primarily help coordinate the events to fulfill the contract terms. This activity can include but is not limited to the following tasks:

- Represent the clients and provide moral support

- Remain in contact with all parties involved to assist in the coordination of the closing.

- Assist in making arrangements for:
- Buyer
- Coordinate a meeting with the loan officer
- Engage and meet with the home inspector
- Accept the delivery of earnest money, and forward it to the responsible parties to be held on file
- Meet with any other specialists as applicable
- Follow up with the lender to ensure the processing is on track with the closing date
- Follow up with the attorney
- Keep the buyer informed of current status and progress
- Seller
- Meet with the land surveyor
- Assist in the coordination the home inspector's visit
- Get earnest money deposited in a timely fashion
- Meet the appraiser on-site
- Participate in a final walk-through with clients
- Submit a commission statement to the settlement agent/attorney
- Participate in the closing

You may want to review this chapter as you learned a wide variety of terms. When you're ready, take the chapter quiz below.

CHAPTER 18 QUIZ

1. A real estate contract is which of the following?

    a. Agreement between two or more parties
    b. Enforceable by law if signed by all parties
    c. Able to be edited by licensees
    d. Only A and B
    e. Only A and C

2. Which are governed by US contract law?

    a. Express contracts
    b. Implied contracts
    c. Express or implied contracts
    d. None of the above

3. Is an offer a legally binding contract?

    a. Yes
    b. No

4. Which statement is false concerning mutual consent?

    a. The seller has the right to accept or reject the offer.
    b. No buyer should be coerced into signing.
    c. Each party enters the agreement of their own free will.
    d. None of the above.

5. Can valuable goods be used as consideration in a real estate offer in Illinois?

    a. Yes
    b. No

6. Which type of contract encapsulates all terms and conditions, either verbally (orally) or written?

    a. Express contracts
    b. Implied contracts
    c. Express or implied contracts
    d. None of the above

7. Michael is a seller. He promises to sell his property for $300,000. Janissa is the buyer. She promises to pay $300,000 for the property. They have entered into a written agreement. What type of contract is this?

   a. A bilateral contract

   b. A unilateral contract

   c. Exclusive right to sell

   d. None of the above

8. Which of the following is viewed as a unilateral contract in Illinois?

   a. Exclusive right to sell listing agreement

   b. Open listing agreement

   c. Exclusive buyer agency agreement

   d. Exclusive property management agreement

9. The Walden Family worked with Deborah as their broker. They wanted to sell their estate outside of Chicago so they could live full time in Colorado. The estate sold and closed within four weeks. Fortunately, the whole process went as smoothly as possible. The sellers were pleased and so was Deborah. Which type of contract best describes this transaction at this point in time?

   a. Unilateral contract

   b. Executory contract

   c. Implied contract

   d. Executed contract

10. Which type of contract is neither enforceable in nor outside of a court of law?

   a. Exclusive agency contract

   b. Valid contract

   c. Voidable contract

   d. Unenforceable contract

11. Licensee Brian just discovered that his seller failed to disclose a handful of material facts. The buyer will find out within the hour. Because of this, it's likely that their contract will go from valid to which of the following?

   a. Void

   b. Valid

   c. Voidable

   d. Unenforceable

12. In Illinois, if a real estate sales contract is not in writing, it is not enforceable.

    a. True
    b. False

13. At what point is a broker discharged from his or her contract?

    a. When the broker breaches the contract
    b. When the contract is successfully fulfilled
    c. If the seller's lender files a foreclosure action
    d. All of the above

14. Which legal term is used when a contract moves from being legally binding to having zero legal implications?

    a. Novation
    b. Assignment
    c. Rescission
    d. None of the above

15. Broker Williams had an exclusive right to sell listing on seller Caitlin's home. However, her lender filed a foreclosure action against her. What is the provision of law that caused the listing contract to be terminated?

    a. Novation
    b. Operation of law
    c. Rescission
    d. None of the above

16. Earnest money deposits are not legally required in Illinois.

    a. True
    b. False

17. Fill in the blank with the correct answers below. In Illinois, the statute of limitations on oral contracts is _____ years, and for written contracts, it is _____ years.

    a. One and three
    b. Two and four
    c. Five and ten
    d. Five and seven

18. Sarah and her husband have equitable title in their dream house. Once the property transaction is executed and completed, what happens?

   a. They continue to have equitable title.
   b. They have legal title.
   c. They legally own the land.
   d. Both B and C
   e. Both A and B

19. James wants to buy property. Due to a divorce a few years ago, lending institutions see him as high risk. He showed evidence of his career, but nothing he seemed to do helped. A few banks did offer a loan, but the APR was exceptionally high. James told the property owner about his situation. Rebecca, the property owner, has known James for years and says that she can help with financing. What is this arrangement known as?

   a. Owner/lender option
   b. An illegal form of lending
   c. Property contract
   d. Land contract

20. What is a contingency?

   a. A clause in a contract
   b. A specific condition that needs to be met in order to complete the transaction
   c. A clause that protects the buyer and/or seller
   d. All of the above
   e. None of the above

CHAPTER 19:

DEEDS

LEARNING GOALS:

By the end of this lesson, you will:

- Know what is required for a deed to be valid
- Have learned the different types of common deeds
- Understand court-order deeds
- Know how to record a deed and its importance

THIS BOOK HAS TOUCHED ON THE TOPIC of deeds here and there throughout many of the chapters you have read. In this chapter, we will dive more thoroughly into deeds. Let's begin.

With real estate transactions, a deed is a cornerstone document. It is a signed legal document that conveys ownership. The deed is transferred from the previous property owner (the grantor) to the new owner (the grantee). A deed conveys interest, right, and title of real property. (It is not used for personal property. That would be done by way of a bill of sale.) As you know, conveyance is the legal act or process of transferring or conveying ownership or interest in real estate from one individual (grantor) to another (grantee). A deed is evidence of ownership and gives the grantee specific rights to an asset, which in this case is real estate property.

VALID DEED REQUIREMENTS

Below is a summary of key elements from the Conveyances Act (765 ILCS 5).

In order to have a valid deed that is enforceable in a court of law, the minimum requirements are:

- The deed must be in writing with the grantor or grantors' signature/s.

- The deed must contain conveyance language, which communicates the intention to transfer the present title to another person. The statutory phrase "conveys and warrants" is commonly used in this regard.

- The names of the grantee/s and grantor/s are required to be on the deed.

- The seller(s) must have the legal capacity to sign the deed and must do so voluntarily, uncoerced, and manipulated by other influences.

- A legal description that is complete and accurate of the property that will be conveyed via the real estate transaction.

- A grantor has the right to set aside a selection of parts of the property and/or of the estate that he/she is conveying. These are referred to as exceptions and reservations. Each and every exception and reservation, if any, are required to be present in the deed.

  - A deed exception is literally a condition within the deed that provides for additional limitations the new owner may be obligated to recognize. Examples of such exceptions might consist of:

    - A life estate, as previously defined in Chapter 12.

- Retention by the seller to some portion of the former estate, such as the continued right to use the private beach (easement appurtenant).

- Retention of the right to use the property by the seller even after the deed has been delivered.

- Reservation of how the property can be used, which shares information about what can be done to the property or on the property.

  - Example: The buyer must maintain the original color scheme on the exterior of the home. It was applied when first constructed. This is a fee simple defeasible.

- Reservation to certain elements within the property, such as the retention of the ownership of gold or oil deposits still in the ground.

- The deed must be delivered as well as accepted in order for a valid conveyance to take place. In other words, the grantor delivers the deed, and the grantee accepts the deed. The deed changes owners and hands, so to speak. This does not have to be completed in person. It can be done using a third party, who has been granted power of attorney by either the buyer or the seller. When this occurs, delivery and acceptance has been achieved.

- In the county where the property is located is where the deed must be recorded. (765 ILCS 5)

IMPORTANT TERMS AND CONCEPTS RELATED TO DEEDS

Adverse possession: This type of possession is commonly referred to as squatter's rights. A squatter is an individual that takes up possession and occupancy without the legal right to do so. Adverse possession is a type of *involuntary* transfer. If a period of years passes and someone is squatting on the property, it's possible that the squatter can become the legal and valid owner of the property. In most circumstances, the owner is not present in person and is unaware that there is anyone residing on his or her property. In order for a squatter to acquire legal title in Illinois, they must occupy the property for twenty consecutive years. It does not matter if the possession was intentional (purposeful illegal trespass) or unintentional (innocent accident). Courts generally view squatting less as a criminal offense and more of a civil matter. With land owned by the government, adverse possession does not apply. Simply put, if you squat on a piece of land in Yellowstone National Park for twenty or even thirty years, it still isn't yours. The government is still the owner. Requirements for the squatter to claim ownership of the land include showing that their actions were done:

- Continuously (in Illinois 20 consecutive years)

- Open (visible to the property owner)

- Hostile (without first securing consent from the owner)

- Notorious (every step on the property is a violation of the law known as trespass)

- Adverse (not in the best interest of the property owner)

If those words sound familiar, it's because you read them when you learned about creating an easement by prescription in Chapter 13.

Consideration: A deed must spell out that the grantor has received consideration from the grantee. The majority of the time, the consideration is monetary.

Granting clause: Also called words of conveyance, this clause that must be included in a valid deed clearly states that the grantor has the intention of conveying the title to his or her land. Commonly used conveyance language includes words like give, sell, grant, and so on. Although rules and provisions can vary from state to state, usually different types of deeds contain different granting clauses.

- A general warranty deed may use a phrase like "warrant generally" or "convey and warrant."

- A special warranty deed may use a phrase like the grantor "remises," "releases," "alienates," and "conveys."

- A bargain and sale deed may use a phrase like "bargain," "grant," or "sell."

- A quitclaim deed may use a phrase like "quitclaim" or "release."

Voluntary alienation: A voluntary alienation is the unforced and uncoerced transfer of a title. The grantor voluntarily grants the property to the grantee. Involuntary alienation is the opposite and means a transfer of title to real property happens without the owner's consent, such as foreclosure.

REQUIREMENTS FOR RECORDING A DEED

In order to be recorded, the deed must first be valid. This means that those requirements must be met in order to actually record the deed. As you learned earlier, those are in the Conveyances Act. In no particular order, each deed is to have all of the following in order for the recording to take place:

1. Names of the grantor and the grantee.

2. Below the grantor's signature, his or her name must be present (written or typed).

3. A blank space of at least 3 ½ inches by 3 ½ inches. The recorder of the deed will use this space to enter the pertinent information when the deed is recorded. This space has to be large enough for the recording date and also to show the transfer tax stamps.

4. The grantee's complete address.

5. The individual who prepares the deed, his or her name and address must be on the deed itself.

6. Depending on if it's a county requirement or not, the property's common address.

7. The real estate transfer declaration completely filled out and signed. (Confidential record).

8. State and county transfer tax evidence (receipt) of payment, or evidence of any exemption that applies to the property.

- If applicable, municipal transfer tax evidence (receipt) of payment.

Below is a copy of the Illinois Real Estate Transfer Declaration.

PTAX-203
Illinois Real Estate
Transfer Declaration

Please read the instructions before completing this form.
This form can be completed electronically at **tax.illinois.gov/retd**.

Step 1: Identify the property and sale information.

1 _____
Street address of property (or 911 address, if available)

_____
City or village   ZIP

_____
Township

2 Write the total number of parcels to be transferred. _____

3 Write the parcel identifying numbers and lot sizes or acreage.

Property index number (PIN)	Lot size or acreage
a _____	_____
b _____	_____
c _____	_____
d _____	_____

Write additional property index numbers, lot sizes or acreage in Step 3.

4 Date of instrument: ____ / ____ ____ ____ ____
                    Month   Year

5 Type of instrument (Mark with an "X."): ____ Warranty deed
____ Quit claim deed ____ Executor deed ____ Trustee deed
____ Beneficial interest ____ Other (specify): _____

6 ____ Yes ____ No Will the property be the buyer's principal residence?

7 ____ Yes ____ No Was the property advertised for sale?
                   (i.e., media, sign, newspaper, realtor)

8 Identify the property's current and intended primary use.
  Current Intended   (Mark **only one item per column** with an "X.")
  a ____ ____ Land/lot only
  b ____ ____ Residence (single-family, condominium, townhome, or duplex)
  c ____ ____ Mobile home residence
  d ____ ____ Apartment building (6 units or less) No. of units: _____
  e ____ ____ Apartment building (over 6 units) No. of units: _____
  f ____ ____ Office
  g ____ ____ Retail establishment
  h ____ ____ Commercial building (specify): _____
  i ____ ____ Industrial building
  j ____ ____ Farm
  k ____ ____ Other (specify): _____

9 Identify any significant physical changes in the property since January 1 of the previous year and **write the date of the change.**
Date of significant change: ____ / ____ ____ ____ ____
                          Month   Year
(Mark with an "X.")
____ Demolition/damage ____ Additions ____ Major remodeling
____ New construction ____ Other (specify): _____

10 Identify only the items that apply to this sale. (Mark with an "X.")
a ____ Fulfillment of installment contract —
       year contract initiated : ____ ____ ____ ____
b ____ Sale between related individuals or corporate affiliates
c ____ Transfer of less than 100 percent interest
d ____ Court-ordered sale
e ____ Sale in lieu of foreclosure
f ____ Condemnation
g ____ Short sale
h ____ Bank REO (real estate owned)
i ____ Auction sale
j ____ Seller/buyer is a relocation company
k ____ Seller/buyer is a financial institution or government agency
l ____ Buyer is a real estate investment trust
m ____ Buyer is a pension fund
n ____ Buyer is an adjacent property owner
o ____ Buyer is exercising an option to purchase
p ____ Trade of property (simultaneous)
q ____ Sale-leaseback
r ____ Other (specify): _____
_____
s ____ Homestead exemptions on most recent tax bill:
       1 General/Alternative $_____
       2 Senior Citizens $_____
       3 Senior Citizens Assessment Freeze $_____

Step 2: Calculate the amount of transfer tax due.

Note: Round Lines 11 through 18 to the next highest whole dollar. If the amount on Line 11 is over $1 million and the property's current use on Line 8 above is marked "e," "f," "g," "h," "i," or "k," complete Form PTAX-203-A, Illinois Real Estate Transfer Declaration Supplemental Form A. If you are recording a beneficial interest transfer, do not complete this step. Complete Form PTAX-203-B, Illinois Real Estate Transfer Declaration Supplemental Form B.

11	Full actual consideration	11	$ _____
12a	Amount of personal property included in the purchase	12a	$ _____
12b	Was the value of a mobile home included on Line 12a?	12b	____ Yes ____ No
13	Subtract Line 12a from Line 11. This is the net consideration for real property.	13	$ _____
14	Amount for other real property transferred to the seller (in a simultaneous exchange) as part of the full actual consideration on Line 11	14	$ _____
15	Outstanding mortgage amount to which the transferred real property remains subject	15	$ _____
16	If this transfer is exempt, use an "X" to identify the provision.	16	____b ____k ____m
17	Subtract Lines 14 and 15 from Line 13. **This is the net consideration subject to transfer tax.**	17	$ _____
18	Divide Line 17 by 500. Round the result to the next highest whole number (e.g., 61.002 rounds to 62).	18	_____
19	Illinois tax stamps — multiply Line 18 by 0.50.	19	$ _____
20	County tax stamps — multiply Line 18 by 0.25.	20	$ _____
21	Add Lines 19 and 20. **This is the total amount of transfer tax due.**	21	$ _____

PTAX-203 (R-10/10)

This form is authorized in accordance with 35 ILCS 200/31-1 *et seq*. Disclosure of this information is REQUIRED. This form has been approved by the Forms Management Center.   IL-492-0227

Page 1 of 4

Step 3: Write the legal description from the deed. Write, type (minimum 10-point font required), or attach the legal description from the deed. If you prefer, submit an 8¹/₂" x 11" copy of the extended legal description with this form. You may also use the space below to write additional property index numbers, lots sizes or acreage from Step 1, Line 3.

Step 4: Complete the requested information.

The buyer and seller (or their agents) hereby verify that to the best of their knowledge and belief, the full actual consideration and facts stated in this declaration are true and correct. If this transaction involves any real estate located in Cook County, the buyer and seller (or their agents) hereby verify that to the best of their knowledge, the name of the buyer shown on the deed or assignment of beneficial interest in a land trust is either a natural person, an Illinois corporation or foreign corporation authorized to do business or acquire and hold title to real estate in Illinois, a partnership authorized to do business or acquire and hold title to real estate in Illinois, or other entity recognized as a person and authorized to do business or acquire and hold title to real estate under the laws of the State of Illinois. Any person who willfully falsifies or omits any information required in this declaration shall be guilty of a Class B misdemeanor for the first offense and a Class A misdemeanor for subsequent offenses. Any person who knowingly submits a false statement concerning the identity of a grantee shall be guilty of a Class C misdemeanor for the first offense and of a Class A misdemeanor for subsequent offenses.

Seller Information (Please print.)

Seller's or trustee's name ___ Seller's trust number (if applicable - **not** an SSN or FEIN)

Street address (after sale) ___ City ___ State ___ ZIP ( )

Seller's or agent's signature ___ Seller's daytime phone

Buyer Information (Please print.)

Buyer's or trustee's name ___ Buyer's trust number (if applicable - **not** an SSN or FEIN)

Street address (after sale) ___ City ___ State ___ ZIP ( )

Buyer's or agent's signature ___ Buyer's daytime phone

Mail tax bill to:

Name or company ___ Street address ___ City ___ State ___ ZIP

Preparer Information (Please print.)

Preparer's and company's name ___ Preparer's file number (if applicable)

Street address ___ City ___ State ___ ZIP ( )

Preparer's signature ___ Preparer's daytime phone

Preparer's e-mail address (if available)

Identify any required documents submitted with this form. (Mark with an "X.") ___ Extended legal description ___ Form PTAX-203-A
___ Itemized list of personal property ___ Form PTAX-203-B

To be completed by the Chief County Assessment Officer

1 ___ County ___ Township ___ Class ___ Cook-Minor ___ Code 1 ___ Code 2

2 Board of Review's final assessed value for the assessment year prior to the year of sale.
Land ___
Buildings ___
Total ___

3 Year prior to sale ___ ___ ___ ___
4 Does the sale involve a mobile home assessed as real estate? ___ Yes ___ No
5 Comments

Illinois Department of Revenue Use | **Tab number**

Page 2 of 4 ___ PTAX-203 (R-10/10)

Instructions for Form PTAX-203, Illinois Real Estate Transfer Declaration

General Information

The information requested on this form is required by the Real Estate Transfer Tax Law (35 ILCS 200/31-1 *et seq.*). All parties involved in the transaction must answer each question completely and truthfully.

What is the purpose of this form?

County offices and the Illinois Department of Revenue use this form to collect sales data and to determine if a sale can be used in assessment ratio studies. This information is used to compute equalization factors. Equalization factors are used to help achieve a state-wide uniform valuation of properties based on their fair market value.

Must I file Form PTAX-203?

You must file either (1) Form PTAX-203 and any required documents with the deed or trust document **or** (2) an exemption notation on the original deed or trust document at the County Recorder's office within the county where the property is located. File Form PTAX-203 for all real estate transfers except those qualifying for exempt status under (a), (c), (d), (e), (f), (g), (h), (i), (j), or (l) listed below.

Which property transfers are exempt from real estate transfer tax?

The following transactions are exempt from the transfer tax under 35 ILCS 200/31-45.

(a) Deeds representing real estate transfers made before January 1, 1968, but recorded after that date and trust documents executed before January 1, 1986, but recorded after that date.

(b) Deeds to or trust documents relating to (1) property acquired by any governmental body or from any governmental body, (2) property or interests transferred between governmental bodies, or (3) property acquired by or from any corporation, society, association, foundation or institution organized and operated exclusively for charitable, religious or educational purposes. However, deeds or trust documents, other than those in which the Administrator of Veterans' Affairs of the United States is the grantee pursuant to a foreclosure proceeding, shall not be exempt from filing the declaration.

(c) Deeds or trust documents that secure debt or other obligation.

(d) Deeds or trust documents that, without additional consideration, confirm, correct, modify, or supplement a deed or trust document previously recorded.

(e) Deeds or trust documents where the actual consideration is less than $100.

(f) Tax deeds.

(g) Deeds or trust documents that release property that is security for a debt or other obligation.

(h) Deeds of partition.

(i) Deeds or trust documents made pursuant to mergers, consolidations or transfers or sales of substantially all of the assets of corporations under plans of reorganization under the Federal Internal Revenue Code (26 USC 368) or Title 11 of the Federal Bankruptcy Act.

(j) Deeds or trust documents made by a subsidiary corporation to its parent corporation for no consideration other than the cancellation or surrender of the subsidiary's stock.

(k) Deeds when there is an actual exchange of real estate and trust documents when there is an actual exchange of beneficial interests, except that that money difference or money's worth paid from one to the other is not exempt from the tax. These deeds or trust documents, however, shall not be exempt from filing the declaration.

(l) Deeds issued to a holder of a mortgage, as defined in Section 15-103 (now Section 15-1207) of the Code of Civil Procedure, pursuant to a mortgage foreclosure proceeding or pursuant to a transfer in lieu of foreclosure.

(m) A deed or trust document related to the purchase of a principal residence by a participant in the program authorized by the Home Ownership Made Easy Act, except that those deeds and trust documents shall not be exempt from filing the declaration.

PTAX-203 (R-10/10)

Can criminal penalties be imposed?

Anyone who willfully falsifies or omits any required information on Form PTAX-203 is guilty of a Class B misdemeanor for the first offense and a Class A misdemeanor for subsequent offenses. Anyone who knowingly submits a false statement concerning the identity of a grantee of property in Cook County is guilty of a Class C misdemeanor for the first offense and a Class A misdemeanor for subsequent offenses. The penalties that could be imposed for each type of misdemeanor are listed below (35 ILCS 200/31-50 and 730 ILCS 5/5-8-3 and 5/5-9-1).

Misdemeanor	Prison Term	Maximum Fines
Class A	less than 1 year	$2,500
Class B	not more than 6 months	$1,500
Class C	not more than 30 days	$1,500

Line-by-line Instructions

The sellers and buyers or their agents must complete Steps 1 through 4 of this form. For transfers of a beneficial interest of a land trust, complete the form substituting the words "assignor" for "seller" and "assignee" for "buyer."

Step 1: Identify the property and sale information.

Line 1 — Write the property's street address (or 911 address, if available), city or village, zip code, and township in which the property is located.

Line 3 — Write all the parcel identifying numbers and the properties' lot sizes (*e.g.*, 80' x 100') or acreage. If only the combined lot size or acreage is available for multiple parcels, write the total on Line 3a under the "lot size or acreage" column. If transferring only a part of the parcel, write the letters "PT" before the parcel identifying number and write the lot size or acreage of the split parcel. If transferring a condominium, write the parcel identifying number and the square feet of the condominium unit. If surface rights are not being transferred, indicate the rights being transferred (*e.g.*, "minerals only"). If transferring right-of-way (ROW) property that does not have a parcel identifying number, write "ROW only." If five or more parcels are involved, use the space provided on Page 2, Step 3. The parcel identifying number is printed on the real estate tax bill and assessment notice. The chief county assessment officer can assist you with this information.

Line 4 — Write the month and year from the instrument.

Line 5 — Use an "X" to identify the type of instrument (*i.e.*, deed, trust document, or facsimile) to be recorded with this form. For a deed-in-trust, limited warranty, special warranty, trust deed, or other deed types not listed on this form, select "Other" and write the deed type. "Joint tenancy" and "tenants-in-common" identify ownership rights and **cannot** be used as a deed type.

Line 6 — Select "Yes" if the property will be used as the buyer's principal dwelling place and legal residence.

Line 7 — Select "Yes" if the property was sold using a real estate agent or advertised for sale by newspaper, trade publication, radio/electronic media, or sign.

Line 8 — Use an "X" to select **one** item under each of the column headings "Current" and "Intended." "Current" identifies the current or most recent use of the property. "Intended" identifies the intended or expected use of the property after the sale. If the property has more than one use, identify the **primary** use only.

Line 8h, Commercial building — Write the type of business (bank, hotel/motel, parking garage, gas station, theater, golf course, bowling alley, supermarket, shopping center, *etc.*).

Line 8k, Other — Choose this item only if the primary use is not listed and write the primary use of the property.

Note: For Lines 8h and 8k, if the current and intended categories are the same but the specific use will change, (*i.e.*, from bank to theater), write the **current** use **on** the line provided and write the **intended** use **directly below** the line provided.

Page 3 of 4

Line 9 — Use an "X" to identify any significant physical changes in the property since January 1 of the previous year. Write the date the change was completed or the property was damaged.

Line 10 — Select only the items that apply to this sale. A definition is provided below for all items marked with an asterisk.

Line 10a, Fulfillment of installment contract — The installment contract for deed is initiated in a calendar year prior to the calendar year in which the deed is recorded. Write the year the contract was initiated between the seller and buyer. Do **not** select this item if the installment contract for deed was initiated and the property was transferred within the same calendar year.

Line 10c, Transfer of less than 100 percent interest — The seller transfers a portion of the total interest in the property. Other owners will keep an interest in the property. Do **not** consider severed mineral rights when answering this question.

Line 10d, Court-ordered sale — The property's sale was ordered by a court (e.g., bankruptcy, foreclosure, probate).

Line 10g, Short sale — The property was sold for less than the amount owed to the mortgage lender or mortgagor, if the mortgagor has agreed to the sale.

Line 10h, Bank REO (real estate owned) — The first sale of the property owned by a financial institution as a result of a judgment of foreclosure, transfer pursuant to a deed in lieu of foreclosure, or consent judgment occurring after the foreclosure proceeding is complete.

Line 10k, Seller/buyer is a financial institution — "Financial institution" includes a bank, savings and loan, credit union, Resolution Trust Company, and any entity with "mortgage company" or "mortgage corporation" as part of the business name.

Line 10o, Buyer is exercising an option to purchase — The sale price was predicated upon the exercise of an option to purchase at a predetermined price.

Line 10p, Trade of property (simultaneous) — Buyer trades or exchanges with the seller one or more items of real estate for part or all of the full actual consideration (sale price) on Line 11.

Line 10r, Other — Explain any special facts or circumstances involving this transaction that may have affected the sale price or sale agreement or forced the sale of the property. This includes property that is subject to an existing lease or property that is part of an IRC §1031 Exchange.

Line 10s, Homestead exemptions on most recent tax bill — Write the dollar amount for any homestead exemption reflected on the most recent annual tax bill.

Step 2: Calculate the amount of transfer tax due.

Round Lines 11 through 18 to the next highest whole dollar.

Note: File PTAX-203-B, Illinois Real Estate Transfer Declaration Supplemental Form B, when filing instruments other than deeds, or trust documents. (Do **not** complete Step 2, of the PTAX-203 when filing the PTAX-203-B).

Line 11 — Write the full actual consideration (sale price). Full actual consideration is the amount actually paid, excluding any amount credited against the purchase price or refunded to the buyer for improvements or repairs to the property. Include the amount for other real estate transferred in a simultaneous exchange from the buyer to the seller, even if the transfer involves an even exchange. Also include the amount of outstanding mortgages to which the property remains subject at the time of the transfer.

Note: File PTAX-203-A, Illinois Real Estate Transfer Declaration Supplemental Form A, if the amount on Line 11 is over $1 million and the property's current use on Line 8 is marked "Apartment building (over 6 units)," "Office," "Retail establishment," "Commercial building," "Industrial building," or "Other."

Line 12a — Write the amount of personal property items included in the sale price on Line 11. Do **not** include the value of a beneficial interest of a land trust. Personal property items are generally listed on the "bill of sale." If you are uncertain as to whether an item is real estate or personal property, consult your attorney, tax advisor, or the chief county assessment officer.

On 8½" x 11" paper, submit an itemized list of personal property (include values) transferred from the seller to the buyer if this sale meets either of the following conditions:

- residential property — if the amount of personal property (not including the value of a mobile home) on Line 12a is greater than 5 percent of the sale price on Line 11, **or**
- non-residential property — if the amount of personal property on Line 12a is greater than 25 percent of the sale price on Line 11.

Residential personal property — Generally, "personal property" includes items that are **not** attached (built-in) to the home and that are normally removed by the seller when vacating the property. Examples include artwork, automobiles and boats, draperies, furniture, freestanding appliances (e.g., refrigerators, stoves, washers and dryers, but **not** built-in appliances), lawn mowers, tractors, snow blowers, rugs (excludes wall-to-wall carpets), and window air-conditioners (excludes central air). Include the value of a mobile home as personal property on Line 12a if it meets **all** of the following conditions:

- The value of the mobile home was included on Line 11.
- The value of the mobile home was not included on the real estate tax bill.

Commercial/Industrial personal property — Generally, "personal property" is any item that is **not** a permanent improvement to the land and includes, but is not limited to, intangibles such as goodwill, licenses, patents, franchises, business or enterprise values; and certain tangibles such as inventories, cash registers and shopping carts, free-standing shelving and displays, furniture, office equipment and supplies, vehicles, and machinery and equipment not assessed as real estate.

Generally, "personal property" does **not** include building components (e.g., wiring and lighting, heating, air-conditioning, plumbing, fire protection); foundations, pits and other building components for specialized or heavy machinery; permanent fixtures including, but not limited to, machinery and equipment and cranes assessed as real estate, craneways, and non-portable tanks; and site improvements such as paving and fencing.

Line 14 — Write the amount of other real estate transferred from the buyer to the seller that was included in the sale price on Line 11. This value only applies to a **simultaneous** exchange between the parties involved in this transaction. Do **not** include the value of property involved in a deferred exchange under IRC §1031.

Line 15 — Write an amount **only** if the deed or trust document states that the transferred property remains subject to a mortgage at the time of the transfer.

Line 16 — Use an "X" to identify the letter of the provision for the exemption from the transfer tax (i.e., (b), (k), or (m)) that applies to this transfer. See "Which property transfers are exempt from real estate transfer tax?" in these instructions.

Step 3: Write the legal description from the deed.

Write the legal description from the deed. Use a minimum 10-point font if the legal description is typed. If the legal description will **not** fit in the space provided, submit an 8½" x 11" copy of the extended legal description from the deed with this form.

Step 4: Complete the requested information.

Write the requested information for the seller, buyer, and preparer.

Write the addresses and daytime phone numbers where the seller and buyer can be contacted **after** the sale.

The seller and buyer (or their agents) and preparer **must** sign this form. By signing the form, the parties involved in the real estate transfer verify that

- they have examined the completed Form PTAX-203,
- the information provided on this form is true and correct, and
- they are aware of the criminal penalties of law associated with falsifying or omitting any information on this form.

Use an "X" to identify any required documents submitted with this form.

As a short summary concerning deeds, always keep in mind that there are two lists with requirements to be followed. The first list is for a valid deed. Without those requirements met, the deed is not valid and thus it's not eligible for recording. The second list is for recording a deed. In order to record the deed, the requirements of a valid deed must be met first. That is the legal foundation. On top of that, all of the requirements to record the deed must be met as well. Concerning fee simple determinable estates, their deeds must include some type of durational word or phrase. These include, but are not limited to, the following: as long as, until, so long as, during, and/or while.

RECORDING A DEED AND ITS IMPORTANCE

Recording a deed means filing the deed so it is on public record. Each state's laws dictate the process of recording documents. This is a declaration to the world that demonstrates and proves that the grantee (buyer) is the legal owner of a property. Obtaining a deed does not mean the person owns property until he/she tells the world by the recording of the deed. It is recorded in public records so it's accessible to everybody. When a buyer purchases a home, generally the title agent or escrow agent extends the service of recording the buyer's original deed in the appropriate government office (Recorder of Deeds) within the county in which the property is located. A benefit is that it secures the buyer's rights to the property against any legal claims that might come up in the future.

Generally, the purpose of the county recorder's office is to record and store property records as well as other official documents. On the recorder's website, many times it's possible for you to take any number of actions. Usually, you can: 1) check your deed, 2) search recordings, 3) learn about recording fees, 4) learn about fraud, 5) download forms for recording, and more.

The ability to record the deed necessitates having the grantor notarize the deed. Acknowledgment is another way of saying notarized. A deed needs to be notarized in order to be recorded.

CONSTRUCTIVE NOTICE AND ACTUAL NOTICE

Let's say that Janet purchased a property and received the deed from the seller. She must provide notice to the world of her interest. There are two foundational types of notice. They are:

1. **Constructive notice** is the act of recording. Recording the deed legally provides notification to the world of your interest, but who actually knows that? The presumption is that by giving a copy of the deed to the Recorder's Office, you are literally giving a copy to everyone. This technically is known as "legal fiction." Legal fiction is a fact that is assumed by the consumer without having factual knowledge. For example, let's say your neighbor of two years is Virginia. You think that she owns the house. Do you really know? Most likely the answer is no. You're *assuming* she owns the house. Unless you have seen her deed, you do not know with certainty. If you do not have direct knowledge, then it's legal fiction.

2. **Actual notice** is the other side of the coin. It provides actual notice of an interest you have in the property. For example, Janet occupies the property next to you. Her living there does not define her interest. Is her interest that of an owner or renter? Her occupancy does not clearly set forth which type of interest she has acquired. Without further clarification, her interest is uncertain. However, by occupying the property, she is telling the world she has some form of interest.

A related term is **priority**. Imagine a property that has existed for 130 years. Pretend you can see a timeline from day one of the property to the present day. Next, imagine the variety of owners and consider how the property has been conveyed several times. Finally, imagine the timeline showing the exact date of events concerning giving notice, actual notice, constructive notice, deed recordings, and so on. Priority revolves around the chain of events concerning the involved parties' rights to the property. In situations like this, it is best to refer clients to their respective attorneys, as they can be very complicated.

TYPES OF DEEDS

Deeds are their own small and unique world. There are several types of deeds. The most common deeds are listed below and go from the most favorable ones to least favorable ones for the buyer:

1. **General warranty deed**: Also called a warranty deed, this deed is when the grantor (seller) establishes that he/she, in fact, holds a clear title to the property acceptable to the grantee (buyer) and legally has the right to sell it. This deed protects the grantee and future heirs against title defects, which possibly could come to light at any point. This protection can be viewed as comprehensive because it covers the present ownership back to the first recorded ownership of the property.

2. **Special warranty deed**: This deed is related to the general warranty deed; however, it only protects the buyer against known title defects. These title defects could originate from the seller's actions, omissions, or both.

3. **Bargain and sale deed**: With this deed, the seller has implied that they have legal title and subsequently can convey the ownership to a buyer. However, with this conveyance, the buyer also receives any accompanying and related encumbrances, defects, and liens (if the property does, in fact, have any or all of those). The transferor of the title gives no assurances about the history of the title. Since this deed is a type of non-warranty deed, getting title insurance coverage to safeguard against future claims can be difficult and problematic.

- Illinois has modified the traditional interpretation of the bargain and sale deed so it provides greater protection for the buyer. There are three benefits that this deed provides:

- The seller establishes that they do have a fee simple interest with the right to convey

- The seller warrants quiet enjoyment which has previously been established as protection from interference of third parties

- There are no encumbrances on the title other than those already made known to the buyer

4. **Quitclaim deed**: With a quitclaim deed, the grantor quits (terminates) his or her claim and/or right to the property, whether the claim is real or not. A quitclaim deed releases an individual's interest in a property without outlining or declaring the nature of the individual's rights or interest. This deed gives no confidence or assurances that the grantor truly has ownership of the property. The grantee receives no warranty concerning the property title status. This deed has the least protection for the grantee of all of the different deeds defined thus far.

5. **Deed in trust**: This is the conveyance used to transfer ownership from a trustor to a trustee when creating a land trust.

6. **Trustee's deed**: This deed is initiated by a trustee and is used when the property is being conveyed out of the trust and back to the beneficiary.

7. **Reconveyance or release deed**: This deed is initiated by a trustee and is used when the property is being conveyed out of the trust and back to the trustor.

- Example: A piece of real estate has been conveyed to a minor. Since the child lacks the capacity to make rational decisions regarding the property, the designated guardian would need to assume that responsibility. If there is a need to dissolve the trust on behalf of the minor, the guardian can invoke the right of revocation and order the trustee to deliver the deed to the trustor.

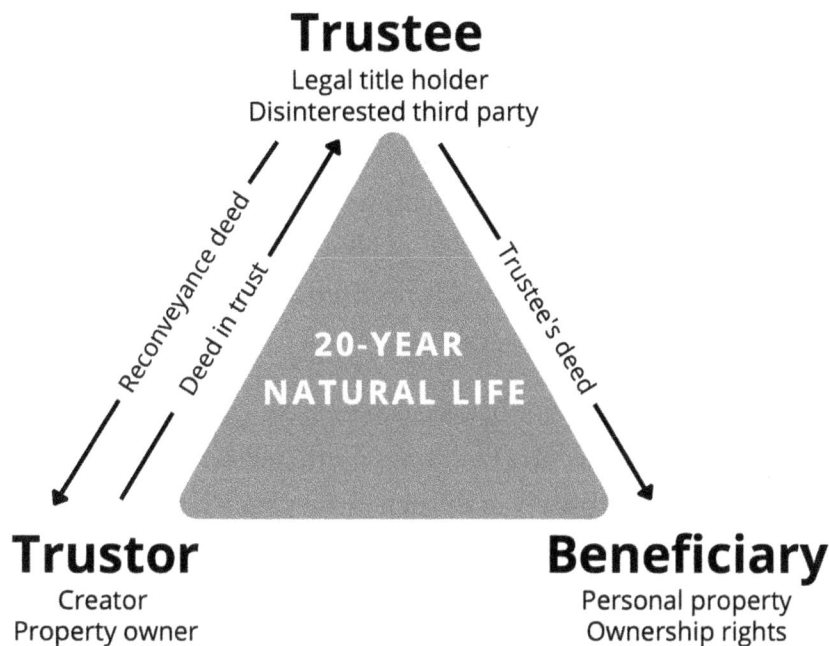

8. **Grant deed**: This deed is implemented so an individual can legally transfer ownership of real property. It gives evidence that the title is clear. A clear title means that there are no claims or liens on the property. A grant deed has less protection than a general warranty deed. Unlike the general warranty deed, this deed, while it does establish a clean title is being conveyed, does not provide ownership protection for future heirs that may ultimately inherit the property.

9. **Master deed**: A master deed is used when creating a condominium environment, whether it is new construction or conversion. It conveys ownership of the individual condominium units to the condo developer or converter. This document defines the individual airspace that each unit will consist of. Basically, you're taking a parcel of land that currently exists under a single deed and converting the airspace into individual blocks of air, which creates condominium units. Each unit requires its own individual deed. Note: Do not confuse "master deed" with a "master's deed." Although almost identical, they are different. A master deed relates to condominiums. The master's deed is an alternative phrase for a court-ordered deed, as explained below.

10. **Court-order deed**: Also called a "deed executed pursuant to court order," this is a special category of deeds that originate during a legal proceeding. Deeds in this category include: 1) administrator's deed, 2) executor's deed, 3) sheriff's deed, and 4) tax deed. What each of these deeds shares in common is that they are court ordered. This means they are executed legally without the owner's consent, or at times via a will, with an executor's deed being the primary example. Each court-order deed must

follow the laws of the state in which the property is located, and may be different in different jurisdictions within the same state. Here are details about each of the court-order deeds mentioned:

- Administrator's deed: This deed is how property is transferred when a property owner dies without a legal will. As a reminder, when someone dies without a legal will, the deceased is referred to as an intestate individual. Usually, the property goes to the next of kin by using an administrator's deed. Legal proceedings are how the estate of the deceased is resolved and how the estate is distributed. This deed involves probate proceedings.

- Executor's deed: This type of deed can be used when an individual dies with a legal well (testate). The executor of the estate will transfer the deceased's legal ownership of his or her real property to the beneficiary, who is named in the deceased's will. This deed involves probate proceedings.

- Sheriff's deed: This is a hybrid deed issued by the court system when there is a successful bidder on a mortgage foreclosure. It is also used when there is a successful claim by an individual under the banner of adverse possession.

- Tax deed: A tax deed is issued by the courts following a tax foreclosure that is the result of a property owner failing to pay their property taxes. Under a court order, the county will put the property up for auction. The successful bidder will receive a tax deed, after the statutory period of redemption expires.

TRANSFER TAX

Transfer tax is the commonly used phrase concerning real estate transfer tax. Sometimes, it is also referred to as deed transfer tax or stamp tax. When title to property or ownership is transferred (conveyed), this is the charge that is levied. You can view it as a property transaction fee. In the US, this tax can be set forth by municipalities, counties, and states, depending on the type of property that is being transferred. Some municipalities have transfer tax stamps. Before recording a deed, transfer tax must be paid. Evidence of the payment must be affixed to the deed. Many times, it is simply a small piece of paper glued to the deed.

Is transfer tax deductible on state or federal income taxes? Usually, it is not. The basis of transfer tax is usually the property's value. Who pays? Most of the time, sellers pay. In different locations in Illinois, such as Chicago for example, both the buyer and seller pay transfer tax.

The Act contains a piece of legislation called the Real Estate Transfer Tax Law (35 ILCS 200). What is the cost of the transfer tax? Here is one excerpt: "The Department (state) shall charge at a rate of 50¢ per $500 of value in units of not less than $500. The recorder or registrar of titles of the several counties shall sell the revenue stamps at a rate of 50¢ per $500 of value or a fraction of $500."

For example, if a home sells for $500, the fee for state transfer tax is 50¢. However, what if the home sells for $1,000? The fee would be $1.00. Therefore, a simple rule of thumb for calculating state transfer tax would be $1.00 per $1,000. This is only a rule of thumb. If the property sells for $100,000, simply divide the sales price by 1,000 and the resulting answer would be $100, which is the amount of the state transfer tax.

The county rate is 25¢ per every $500, or any part thereof. Example: A property costing $100,000 is conveyed. The state transfer tax is $100, and the county transfer tax is $50. (In all counties, the county transfer tax is exactly half of the state transfer tax.)

What about local transfer taxes for municipalities? It is important to research to see what each municipality charges, if anything.

In Illinois, this form is always required, unless the party is claiming an exemption. All information can be found in The Act, Section 120.5, which is titled Transfer Declaration and Supplemental Information.

HOW IS A DECEASED PERSON'S PROPERTY TRANSFERRED?

Probate court involves the legal process of administering a deceased individual's estate. When a legal will is present, the process can be fairly quick and smooth. When a person dies and has a legal will in place, assets are distributed in alignment with his or her wishes, pending any unforeseen circumstances. The steps involve showing evidence that the will is valid legally, following the will's instructions, and finally, paying any applicable taxes and fees.

As you read earlier, intestacy or intestate means a person died without having a legal will in place. When this happens, how do the deceased's assets get distributed? This is done by a probate court and follows the Uniform Probate Code. Since there is no will, the estate is now deemed intestate. Instead of following a legal will's wishes, the probate court must follow the state's intestate law in order to distribute assets. Intestacy law focuses on who is entitled to the property in light of no valid will being present. Which courts oversee probate cases? Circuit courts. Illinois' bigger counties feature a specific division for probate within the circuit court. The county in which the deceased person lived is the county where the probate case will take place. Typically in Illinois, if there are no contests and/or disputes, probate will be finalized in less than twelve months. Probate proceedings can be expensive, long, and confusing for those involved. Many individuals who plan ahead before dying help their families avoid probate court completely. It spares their loved ones the stress and hassle that often comes with probate proceedings. There is a deed in Illinois called a "transfer on deathbed" (TOD). It makes it possible for a property to be transferred to the heir or heirs when the current owner dies. This method bypasses probate court. It transfers all legal rights to the heir/s.

TRANSFERRING TITLE BY A WILL AND BY DESCENT

By will: A will is one of the most important legal documents. It communicates the wishes and desires of the deceased regarding paramount decisions, such as who will care for children under the age of eighteen years old and how assets will be distributed. Parties, such as children and/or heirs, have no legal right to assets listed in a parent's will or any individual's will until that person passes. The person who creates the will is called the testator. A devise is a gift of real property. The beneficiary is called the devisee or legatee. A bequest (related to the word bequeath) is also called a legacy. It is generally a gift of personal property and/or cash. The probate process can take several months to several years before being finalized.

By descent: When someone dies without a legal will, what law dictates how the outcome will be reconciled? It comes down to each state's laws concerning descent. In Illinois, it is called the Illinois Law of Descent and Distribution. Its rules are covered in The Act in 755 ILCS 5, which is referred to as the Probate Act of 1975. Note that the word "stirpes" means by root or by branch.

Here is an excerpt:

1. Section 2-1. Rules of descent and distribution. The intestate real and personal estate of a resident decedent and the intestate real estate in this State of a nonresident decedent, after all just claims against his estate are fully paid, descends and shall be distributed as follows:

   a. If there is a surviving spouse and also a descendant of the decedent: 1/2 of the entire estate to the surviving spouse and 1/2 to the decedent's descendants per stirpes.

   b. If there is no surviving spouse but a descendant of the decedent: the entire estate to the decedent's descendants per stirpes.

   c. If there is a surviving spouse but no descendant of the decedent: the entire estate to the surviving spouse.

   d. If there is no surviving spouse or descendant but a parent, brother, sister or descendant of a brother or sister of the decedent: the entire estate to the parents, brothers and sisters of the decedent in equal parts, allowing to the surviving parent if one is dead a double portion and to the descendants of a deceased brother or sister per stirpes the portion which the deceased brother or sister would have taken if living.

   e. If there is no surviving spouse, descendant, parent, brother, sister or descendant of a brother or sister of the decedent but a grandparent or descendant of a grandparent of the decedent: (1) 1/2 of the entire estate to the decedent's maternal grandparents in equal parts or to the survivor of them, or if there is none surviving, to their descendants per stirpes, and (2) 1/2 of the entire estate to the decedent's paternal grandparents in equal parts or to the survivor of them, or if there is none surviving, to their descendants per stirpes. If there is no surviving paternal grandparent or descendant of a paternal grandparent, but a maternal grandparent or descendant of a maternal grandparent of the decedent: the entire estate to the decedent's maternal grandparents in equal parts or to the survivor of them, or if there is none surviving, to their descendants per stirpes. If there is no surviving maternal grandparent or descendant of a maternal grandparent, but a paternal grandparent or descendant of a paternal grandparent of the decedent: the entire estate to the decedent's paternal grandparents in equal parts or to the survivor of them, or if there is none surviving, to their descendants per stirpes.

f. If there is no surviving spouse, descendant, parent, brother, sister, descendant of a brother or sister or grandparent or descendant of a grandparent of the decedent: (1) 1/2 of the entire estate to the decedent's maternal great-grandparents in equal parts or to the survivor of them, or if there is none surviving, to their descendants per stirpes, and (2) 1/2 of the entire estate to the decedent's paternal great-grandparents in equal parts or to the survivor of them, or if there is none surviving, to their descendants per stirpes. If there is no surviving paternal great-grandparent or descendant of a paternal great-grandparent, but a maternal great-grandparent or descendant of a maternal great-grandparent of the decedent: the entire estate to the decedent's maternal great-grandparents in equal parts or to the survivor of them, or if there is none surviving, to their descendants per stirpes. If there is no surviving maternal great-grandparent or descendant of a maternal great-grandparent, but a paternal great-grandparent or descendant of a paternal great-grandparent of the decedent: the entire estate to the decedent's paternal great-grandparents in equal parts or to the survivor of them, or if there is none surviving, to their descendants per stirpes.

g. If there is no surviving spouse, descendant, parent, brother, sister, descendant of a brother or sister, grandparent, descendant of a grandparent, great-grandparent or descendant of a great-grandparent of the decedent: the entire estate in equal parts to the nearest kindred of the decedent in equal degree (computing by the rules of the civil law) and without representation

h. If there is no surviving spouse and no known kindred of the decedent: the real estate escheats to the county in which it is located; the personal estate physically located within this State and the personal estate physically located or held outside this State which is the subject of ancillary administration of an estate being administered within this State escheats to the county of which the decedent was a resident, or, if the decedent was not a resident of this State, to the county in which it is located; all other personal property of the decedent of every class and character, wherever situate, or the proceeds thereof, shall escheat to this State and be delivered to the State Treasurer pursuant to the Revised Uniform Unclaimed Property Act.

In no case is there any distinction between the kindred of the whole and the half blood. (755 ILCS 5)

DEED COVENANTS

Restrictive covenants: Although not used in everyday language, a covenant means an agreement or restriction. In this context, a restrictive covenant is a legal agreement. In a restrictive covenant, some type of restriction is imposed. The purpose of the restriction is to limit the use of land. By doing so, both the land and its value can be preserved.

Deed restrictions: A deed restriction allows you as the property owner to place one or more limitations on how future owners can use the property. It can limit both the actions they are permitted to take as well as what can be constructed on the land. A fee simple defeasible restriction can limit their ability to use the property if the restriction has been recorded in the deed. One of the reasons for deed restrictions is the intention to preserve the property value and/or the ways in which the property will be used.

Now it's time for your chapter quiz.

CHAPTER 19 QUIZ

1. Which is true concerning a deed?

    a. It is a signed legal document that conveys ownership.
    b. A deed conveys interest, right, and title of real property.
    c. A deed is used for personal property.
    d. It gives the grantee specific rights to a real property asset.
    e. All of the above
    f. Only A, B, and D
    g. Only A, C, and D

2. Which of the following are required for a deed to be valid?

    a. The deed must be in writing with the grantor or grantors' signature/s.
    b. The names of the grantee/s and grantor/s are required to be on the deed.
    c. A legal description that is complete and accurate of the property that will be conveyed via the real estate transaction.
    d. All of the above
    e. None of the above

3. A grantor has the right to set aside a selection of parts of the property and/or of the estate that he/she is conveying. What are these called?

    a. Exceptions
    b. Reservations
    c. Hold-backs
    d. A and B
    e. A and C

4. Acceptance of a deed is required to be done manually in person in the state of Illinois.

    a. True
    b. False
    c. Depends on the type of property

5. How is personal property transferred?

    a. Deed
    b. Bill of sale
    c. Probate
    d. None of the above

6. Through an inheritance, George receives his deceased grandmother's property. It includes 30 acres, a large house, and a barn. He decided to sell the property and quickly received a highly qualified buyer. George is planning the transfer of title to real property to the buyer within the week. This is George's personal decision that he is making independently of anyone else. What is this exact term called in the world of real estate?

   a. Consideration
   b. Voluntary alienation
   c. Involuntary alienation
   d. None of the above

7. What is another way to say words of conveyance?

   a. Granting clause
   b. Consideration
   c. Conveyance agreement
   d. None of the above

8. Twenty-two years ago, James moved into an abandoned property that he discovered in an unincorporated area of Kankakee County Illinois. The small property with a tiny house was tucked away at the end of a dead-end dirt road. Now, James is being challenged in court for the ownership. Is James the owner or not, and why?

   a. James is not the owner because of Illinois state law.
   b. At this point, James has a legal right to the ownership because of adverse possession.
   c. James is a squatter who will most likely be evicted.
   d. The next of kin to the previous property owner will be contacted and will receive the property. James will have to move out.

9. Ricky has been living off the grid for over two decades. He has lived on a small hidden plot of land in Rocky Mountain National Park. After that many years, does he legally own the small plot of land?

   a. Yes, after twenty years, he is the owner.
   b. Yes, because of adverse possession.
   c. No. He can never own the land because it's government land.
   d. Yes, because of A and B.
   e. More information is required to answer the question.

10. Is a real estate transfer declaration required for a valid deed?

    a. Yes
    b. No

11. Which of the following is not a requirement for a valid deed?

    a. A blank space of at least 3 ½ inches by 3 ½ inches. The recorder of the deed will use this space to enter the pertinent information when the deed is recorded.

    b. The grantee's notarized signature.

    c. The individual who prepares the deed, his or her name and address must be on the deed itself.

    d. An accurate legal description

12. Cynthia wants to record her deed. She is worried that she is getting incomplete information. Which of the following is false concerning recording her deed?

    a. Recording the deed proves that the grantee (buyer) is the legal owner of a property.

    b. It secures her property rights against any legal issues that might come up in the future.

    c. She can buy a title insurance policy prior to recording the deed.

    d. Recording makes it accessible to everybody.

13. A best practice is for a deed to be acknowledged. Acknowledgment is also known as notarization and is an Illinois law requirement.

    a. True

    b. False

14. Which word does this definition match? The courts assume that a party who is interested in a property has knowledge that they, in fact, may not have. This legal presumption is that the party should have known about a legal action that took place because the action was recorded in public records.

    a. Giving notice

    b. Direct knowledge

    c. Actual notice

    d. Constructive notice

15. Jake has just relinquished any and all claims and rights (whether real or not) to a former property of his. Most likely, which type of deed was used to convey this ownership?

    a. Quitclaim deed

    b. Deed in trust

    c. Special warranty deed

    d. Bargain and sale deed

    e. None of the above

16. Which deed is issued by the court system when there is a successful bidder on a mortgage foreclosure or when we have a successful claim by an individual under the banner of adverse possession?

    a. Mortgage deed
    b. Master deed
    c. Bargain and sale deed
    d. Sheriff's deed

17. The Jackson family lives a short drive from Grant Park in Chicago. They're in the process of selling their home. Who will pay the county transfer tax?

    a. The buyer
    b. The Jackson family (the seller)
    c. Both buyer and seller
    d. More information is needed.

18. Concerning transfer taxes in Illinois, the state rate is 50¢ per every $1000 dollars. The county rate is 25¢ per every $500, or part thereof. Is that accurate?

    a. Yes
    b. No. The state rate is $1 for every $500.
    c. No. The state rate is 50¢ for every $500.
    d. No. The country rate is 50¢ per every $500 dollars.

19. What is done when a person dies with a legal will?

    a. Probate court is involved.
    b. Evidence is shown that proves the will is valid legally.
    c. Actions follow the will's instructions.
    d. Heirs have to pay any applicable taxes and fees.
    e. Only A and C
    f. A, B, C, and D

20. Shannon's great-aunt died recently. Her aunt left her both personal property and $15,000 cash. Which of the following did Shannon receive?

    a. Bequest
    b. Legacy
    c. Devise
    d. A and B
    e. A and C

CHAPTER 20:

TITLES AND
TITLE RECORDS

LEARNING GOALS:

By the end of this lesson, you will:

- Know the difference between a title and a deed
- Understand how public records work
- Know the difference between marketable titles and insurable titles
- Discover other terms related to titles

IN THIS CHAPTER, YOU WILL LEARN details and insights about titles. Let's start with defining the word and then you will see the concept applied in the realm of real estate. In its most common form, a title is a type of document that demonstrates legal ownership to property or any other kind of asset. One of the most common everyday examples is a car title, which names the person who legally owns a car.

DEEDS VERSUS TITLES

A title is not a deed. A deed is not a title. While they do overlap in areas, each one is separate and distinct. A deed is a signed legal document that conveys ownership and is evidence of real property ownership. It conveys interest, right, and title of real property. Deeds are the vehicle by which title is transferred to another person or entity. A title is a legal right to ownership of personal property. Ownership may come in the form of legal interest or equitable interest. When a buyer purchases a house, he/she receives both the deed and the title. In real estate, title is simply a *concept.* The deed is the physical evidence of ownership being conveyed. Holding a deed to a home means the owner has ownership control and the bundle of accompanying legal rights. The ownership showcases the owner's legal rights, which include using the property, changing the property however the owner wants (within the confines of the state and local laws), the right to sell the property, and the right to transfer interest by way of a deed. A deed can be in one person's name (severalty), or two or more people's names (concurrent). Similarly, a deed can be held by an individual or a type of entity such as a corporation, partnership, organization, trust, and so on. In those instances, the ownership rights are shared among the property owners. The ownership embodies more of the concepts and intangibles of rights that are conveyed with the deed.

PUBLIC RECORDS

A public record is a record filed in a public office. Anyone, whether via private sector or public sector, has the right to access, read, and view public records. Public records help generate transparency as well as accountability in the US. The information is recorded and stored by a government agency. More specifically, this work is done by people with the following job titles: recorder of deeds, county treasurer, city clerk, county clerk, collectors, and so on. What types of documents are stored in public records? The documents include a wide variety, including but not limited to property records, title records, probate records, tax records, judgments, and marriage records.

Title records are most commonly found in every county courthouse in every state within the US. These records can help anyone learn who owns a particular property, as well as if the property has any encumbrances, liens, and/or other issues. One can discover whether or not a title is free and clear by doing a title record search.

When it comes to real estate, all real estate transactions are public record. For example, if you want to search for a specific real estate transaction in a certain county in Illinois, you can do so through the County Recorder's Office website. You can search recorded land records by using the PIN (property identification number), grantor or grantee name, or by other indexed details.

TITLE SEARCH

In the world of real estate, a title search is the action and process of retrieving and examining public records that show the historical events related to a specific piece of real property. It's also called a property title search. It is done in order to confirm the legal owner/s of the property, as well as to discover whether or not any liens, claims, or clouds are on the property. A cloud on the title is defined as an uncertainty, whether it be in the realm of ownership, or other specific restrictions. These clouds must be resolved most often by a court of law. A title search can help the individual understand any unique and relevant interests in the property, as well as see what regulations apply to the property. When someone is wondering if a title is clean, the first action to take is to do a title search. The title search itself is usually done by a title company, lender, or attorney. Most individuals will not attempt to do a title search on their own. The reason being is that it can be a complicated process. Wading through public records and reading countless legal documents is challenging for someone not trained and practiced in the process. He/she could easily miss an important fact due to his or her inexperience.

Chain of title is the *complete chronological history* and sequence of ownership transfers for a piece of property. It is the timeline of the title changing hands to new owners through the years. The chain starts at the first recorded claim of ownership (original grant) and continues to the present day. The chain of title lists all documents in the public record that have affected the title to the property. This document shows all information about all recorded liens, grants, title transfers, pending building code violations, all subsequent conveyances, and encumbrances that have ever affected the property even if the encumbrance has been removed or satisfied

At times, families, cities, or courts need to reconstruct the chain of title in order to solve a problem or inquiry. When a chain of title has a period of time with no recorded information, this is many times called a "gap in the chain" or a "cloud on the title." What action can a property owner take when the chain of title is incomplete? At this point, an action to quiet the title (also called a suit to quiet title) comes into play. Its goal is to "quiet" any claims or challenges to the title. This is a lawsuit brought in a court that has the power to resolve property disputes. The goal of the lawsuit is to establish the party's rights to the title, and accurately fill in the gaps within the chain.

Usually, a chain of title is found through the registry office or civil law notary. The data in a chain of title could include liens, encumbrances, lawsuits, claims, or anything of that nature that may have an impact on ownership.

Abstract of title is a *condensed summary* and record of the title. It shows all recorded legal actions that are related in some way to the property. It also lists the public records that were searched, as well as the public records that were not searched. However, an abstract of title does not reveal encroachments on the property, which would need to be documented through a property survey, not through public records. It is one of the most important documents for buyers and investors. They want assurance that the property title is clear.

The abstract of title is prepared by a professional known as a title examiner or an abstractor. Along with compiling all the information, he/she also certifies that the summary is accurate as well as complete. What might the abstractor discover during the course of his or her work? Possibilities include, but are not limited to, the following: outstanding mortgages, liens, dower interests, future interests of others in the property (a reverter), as well as restrictive covenants, encumbrances, easements, claims of adverse possession, and/or zoning violations. Ideally, the best discovery is made . . . the title *is* free and clear.

In Illinois, it reflects the history of ownership for the last forty years, unless an unresolved claim is recorded against title. At this point, the research is required to go back a total of seventy-five years.

Neither the abstract of title nor the chain of title ensures the title's validity. Rather, each one establishes the quality of the ownership intended to be conveyed.

MARKETABLE TITLES AND INSURABLE TITLES

Marketable title: Sometimes called a merchantable title, this is a title (chain of ownership) that is unaffected by any litigation threats and concerns as well as free from reasonable doubt. The title means the property is free and clear of defects, to the extent that it compels the buyer to accept. Could there be a defect? Yes, it's possible. However, a marketable title is one in which a reasonable and prudent person would accept as being good, clean, and valid. At the closing, the seller is expected to deliver a marketable title to the buyer.

Insurable title: This type of title is one in which the title insurance company finds little to no risk and therefore is willing to insure the title against future claims. These types of claims could challenge the property title holder's right of ownership. If and when a claim does occur, the title insurance company steps in to protect the purchaser's ownership.

WHAT IS USED TO ESTABLISH THE QUALITY OF OWNERSHIP?

It's common for people to think that a property owner can simply show his or her deed to someone to establish ownership. This is not accurate in Illinois as well as many other states. The deed itself is not considered sufficient evidence of ownership. Why is this? It's because a new deed is prepared with each transfer of ownership. This means that a deed presented as evidence may reflect ownership of a property that was sold and conveyed years ago. Let's say I bought a house in 2000 and then sold it in 2010. It's very possible I still have the original deed. Showing this document to an individual gives the appearance that I have ownership because I'm named as the buyer. However, I obviously do not have ownership because the property was sold. A new deed was created and given to the buyer back in 2010.

There are three commonly used methods to establish the quality of ownership that is about to be conveyed to the buyer. The buyer must recognize that not all three methods provide the same level of protection if a future claim arises.

Certificate of title: This is a professional opinion on the quality of title that is prepared by a title examiner. Does a certificate of title mean that the title is free and clear? No. It merely presents evidence of what the title examiner was able to determine from the public records. In the absence of title insurance, it does not provide for any protection if the title examiner missed an essential component concerning the property ownership. Should a future claim arise as a result of the title examiner's error, the seller bears the responsibility for compensating the buyer upon loss of ownership.

Abstract and Attorney's opinion: Another way of establishing the quality of ownership, which adds more credibility, is to take the title examiner's opinion (certificate of title) and have an attorney (typically the seller's attorney) review the content and render a legal opinion on the quality of ownership.

Title insurance: As you read earlier, title insurance is a form of indemnity insurance. Indemnity is security or protection against a loss or other financial burden. It protects both buyers and sellers from financial loss in the event of defects in a title. The most common claims filed against a title are the result of unresolved clouds on the title. These may include but are not limited to claims such as failure to record a previous deed or other encumbrances such as deed restrictions. Generally speaking, the seller acquires the title insurance that protects the buyer. However, if the purchaser has secured a mortgage on the property, the lender will generally require to be named co-beneficiary.

What happens if a claim against ownership does arise? What is the role of the title insurance carrier? As noted above, title insurance is a form of indemnity, and the title insurance carrier will take the responsibility to protect their client's interest. However, in order for the title insurance carrier to be able to fight the claim in court, they may require the insured party to **subrogate** their interest. (Subrogation is the process by which we can subordinate one issue to another issue.) With the client's consent, the title insurance carrier now has the right to go to court and negotiate a settlement on behalf of the client.

Now, it's time for your chapter quiz.

CHAPTER 20 QUIZ

1. Which document is a signed legal document that conveys interest, right, and title of real property?

    a. Title
    b. Deed
    c. Abstract of title
    d. Chain of title

2. Which document can include a complete list of potential liens, encumbrances, lawsuits, claims, or anything of that nature which may have an impact on ownership?

    a. Title
    b. Deed
    c. Abstract of title
    d. Chain of title

3. Through what means is ownership transferred from one person or entity to another person or entity?

    a. Title
    b. Deed
    c. Abstract of title
    d. Chain of title

4. Are all real estate transactions in the US public record?

    a. Yes
    b. No
    c. Depends on the state
    d. Depends on the county where the property is located

5. Jaqueline is interested in purchasing a property. She wants to see the history of the property as related to the sequence of ownership transfers that have taken place over the years. You're her broker. When she asks for this, what is she asking to receive?

    a. Title history
    b. Title report
    c. Abstract of title
    d. Chain of title
    e. C or D

6. What is the condensed and summarized history and record of the title?

    a. Title history
    b. Title report
    c. Abstract of title
    d. Chain of title

7. The Baker family moved to Illinois and acquired a property on October 15th, 1922. For the creation of an abstract of title, initially how far back in the time would the title examiner search to show the quality of ownership to be conveyed today?

    a. October 15th, 1922
    b. October 15th, 1941
    c. 75 years from the current date of conveyance
    d. 40 years from the current date of conveyance

8. Cynthia wants to record her deed to ensure she is giving notice to the world of her interest. She is worried that she has incomplete information. Which of the following is false concerning recording her deed?

    a. Recording the deed proves that Cynthia is the legal owner of a property.
    b. It secures her property rights against any legal issues that might come up in the future.
    c. If the seller refuses to purchase title insurance, Cynthia will be barred from recording her deed because title insurance is the only legal way of establishing ownership.
    d. Recording makes it accessible to everybody.

9. Frank is an abstractor. Yesterday, he started a new project for the Baker family concerning a piece of property they want to purchase. What might Frank discover during the course of his work concerning the title?

    a. Encumbrances
    b. Zoning violations
    c. Liens
    d. All of the above
    e. Only A and B

10. Martha grants to her son Kevin a five-acre parcel of land in Grundy County. Kevin lives in LaSalle County and does not visit the land very often. When researching the entire history of ownership, which document would an interested investor look at to determine the ownership lineage?

    a. The abstract of title reflecting the ownership records of the last 40 years
    b. The chain of title tracing the ownership back to the late 1800s
    c. The plat of survey maintained by the county recorder's office
    d. A or B

11. Tom is talking with the next-door neighbor and has learned that the property both homes have been built on was formerly used as a cemetery. Lately, there has been a lot of discussion regarding the rights to the property by the descendants of individuals previously buried here. Tom is curious to know if there are any restrictions that may exist on the property that could eventually challenge his rights of ownership. Which of the following could Tom use to learn about prior ownership interests?

    a. Abstract of title
    b. Archives of the local church
    c. The local alderman
    d. There are no historical records that can provide Tom with this insight

12. Which word below best fills in the blank of the following sentence? In real estate, a title is a _____.

    a. Form of physical evidence
    b. Concept
    c. Legal right
    d. None of the above

13. A deed can be in the name of a single entity (severalty), or in the names of two or more entities (concurrent).

    a. True
    b. False

14. Licensee Ted received a title search this morning. As he is reviewing the information, he discovers that, unfortunately, the title has a gap of six years in which there are no recorded public records. Nothing accounts for the ownership during that six-year time frame. What is this gap known as?

    a. A cloud

    b. A certainty

    c. An inconsistency

    d. An encumbrance

15. What can be completed in order to confirm the list of all owners from the very first recording of the property, as well as determine if the property has any liens, claims, or clouds?

    a. Title search

    b. Claims search

    c. Abstract of title

    d. A and C

16. Emma is a client of Licensee Jane. Jane tells Emma that the next step in their process of working together is to do a title search. Emma, a natural overachiever, says that she will do it herself. However, Jane tells her that it would not be in her best interest to do this important project by herself. Who can Jane recommend for running a title search?

    a. A title company

    b. Emma's lender

    c. An attorney

    d. Any of the above

    e. None of the above

17. Which of the following is an item that an abstractor could find when doing an abstract of title?

    a. Leasehold interest

    b. Potential claims of adverse possession

    c. Life estate interest

    d. Outstanding easement in gross

18. Which statement below is true?

    a. Neither the abstract of title nor the chain of title ensures the title's validity.

    b. Only the abstract of title ensures the title's validity.

    c. Only the chain of title ensures the title's validity.

    d. Both the abstract of title and chain of title ensure the title's validity.

19. Which of the following is a professional opinion on the quality of title that is prepared by a title examiner?

    a. Attorney's opinion

    b. Certificate of title

    c. Title insurance

    d. A and B

20. Which form of title is the result when a title insurance company finds little to no risk with the title and is willing to insure the title against future claims?

    a. Marketable title

    b. Safe harbor title

    c. Certificate of title

    d. Insurable title

CHAPTER 21:

FINANCING IN REAL ESTATE

LEARNING GOALS:

By the end of this lesson, you will:

- Understand real estate financing basics
- Discover the three theories of mortgage law
- Discover provisions and clauses in mortgages
- Have a thorough overview of foreclosure
- Know the types of loans, loan programs, ratios used, and understand qualified mortgages

TODAY'S LICENSEE MUST BE financially savvy. Real estate is a game of financial transactions. Financing is inseparable from real estate transactions because the majority of transactions require financing. Very few transactions are cash only. Financing is a broad and nuanced topic that requires an in-depth exploration. Any transaction can have unique circumstances and/or surprises. More than knowing the lingo and real estate financial vocabulary, the focus is for the licensee to stay up to date with his or her current working knowledge. This chapter will serve to extend your financial know-how and savviness so you're equipped for the business of real estate.

Concerning financing, let's begin with mortgage law. All financial transactions are to take place under the law and follow the law. Every mortgage is a kind of legal instrument. It creates a security interest in real property. The real property is held by a lending institution or private lender as a security for a debt, most commonly a specific amount of money. Mortgages, however, are not debts. In fact, a mortgage is the lender's security for the said debt. A lender-borrower relationship is contractual in nature and is subject to state and federal laws.

THE THREE THEORIES OF MORTGAGE LAW

Property law contains unique elements called legal theories. Pertaining to mortgages, there are three theories related to who holds legal title to a mortgaged property. Their purpose is to establish a lender's position when providing the purchaser with the necessary funds to acquire a property.

1. **Title theory:** In this theory, the seller of the property conveys the legal ownership to the lender, providing the funds needed by the buyer to purchase the property. The lender (mortgagee) has legal title. The purchaser (mortgagor) holds equitable title. When the mortgage debt is paid in full, the mortgagor receives the legal title and thus is the legal owner of the property. In other words, the title is held in the name of the lender up until the point at which the last payment is paid. At that point, the title is passed to the borrower. What happens when the borrower defaults? Since the lender already has legal ownership, the lender has the right to sell the property and evict the borrower prior to conveying title to the successful bidder. Title theory is implemented in the following states as of this publication being written: Alaska, Arizona, California, Colorado, Washington D.C., Georgia, Idaho, Mississippi, Missouri, Montana, Nebraska, Nevada, North Carolina, Oregon, South Dakota, Tennessee, Texas, Utah, Virginia, Washington State, West Virginia, and Wyoming.

2. **Lien theory:** In this theory, the borrower holds both the equitable and legal title. The deed remains in the hands of the borrower. The lender puts a lien on the property by way of the mortgage. When the loan is paid in full, the lien is terminated. However, it

is the borrower's responsibility to record the evidence that the lien has been satisfied. Typically, this evidence is completed by way of a **satisfaction of mortgage**. This form is the legal documentation provided by the lender and proves that the debt has been paid in full. What happens when the borrower defaults? The mortgagee must file a foreclosure suit in order force the property into a public auction. This allows the property to be sold to the highest bidder. Lien theory is implemented in the following states as of this publication being written: Arkansas, Connecticut, Delaware, Florida, Indiana, Iowa, Kansas, Kentucky, Louisiana, Maine, New Mexico, New York, North Dakota, Ohio, New Jersey, Pennsylvania, Puerto Rico, South Carolina, and Wisconsin.

3. **Intermediate theory**: In this theory, the title is retained by the borrower. There is an agreement in which the lender can regain the title if and when the borrower defaults. A formal foreclosure process is required, like lien theory, in order to obtain the legal title. The key advantage to this theory is that it is a less complicated approach to the foreclosure process than with a lien theory state. Intermediate theory is implemented in the following states as of this publication being written. Those states include: Alabama, Hawaii, Maryland, Michigan, Minnesota, New Hampshire, Montana, Massachusetts, Oklahoma, Rhode Island, and Vermont.

What about Illinois? On most websites, you'll see Illinois listed as a lien theory state. However, Illinois does not adamantly adhere to either title theory or lien theory. Thus, the most accurate category would be intermediate theory.

FOUNDATIONAL TERMS

- **Assignment of rents:** This phrase is also known as "assignment of leases, rents, and profits." It is a clause in a mortgage contract that allows the lender to collect rent payments in the event of the borrower defaulting on mortgage payments. Let's say George owns a 10-unit apartment building. He defaults on the loan. In this circumstance, who do the tenants make their rental payments to? When this happens, the tenants are notified in writing with instructions to begin paying the rent directly to the lender. The lender will retain the monies due and any money in excess of the monthly mortgage payment will be sent to George.

- **Assumability:** These are existing mortgage loans on a property that a buyer can assume responsibility for, oftentimes as the result of having a lower interest rate. On a conventional loan, the right of assumability is at the discretion of the lender. Under federal regulation, all FHA and VA mortgages are fully assumable if the buyer qualifies for the monthly debt obligation.

- **Debt instrument:** Commonly known as a promissory note, IOU ("I owe you"), note payable, or simply a note, it is a negotiable financial and legal instrument. Party A (the issuer) makes a promise in writing (which is signed), saying that he/she will pay a specific amount of money to Party B (the payee). Can notes be sold? Yes. Notes can legally be sold to a third party. The terms of the note remain unchanged. The third party is usually some type of investor, such as Fannie Mae. A debt instrument is the negotiable interest sold to investors on the secondary mortgage market, which you'll read about later in this chapter.

- **Discount points:** Also called mortgage points or points, these are a type of prepaid interest available when generating and creating a mortgage. One point is 1% of the total loan amount. One point means $1,000 for every $100,000. These help the borrower lower the interest rate because he/she has paid an upfront fee. The fee is paid directly to the lender. You might hear people use the term "buying down the rate" when talking about points. You can view this as paying more interest upfront in order to pay less interest over the life of the loan.

- **Escrow:** This is an account maintained by a financial institution. Its purpose is to provide the broker with a secure environment to hold and protect earnest money or security deposits on behalf of the client. The broker must recognize that there are provisions of law they must comply with when it comes to the maintenance and disbursal of these monies. The disbursement is dependent on conditions agreed to by the transacting parties.

- **Hypothecation:** This is the practice in which a borrower "pledges" real property in order to secure a debt for the loan. The debt is secured by the real property, which is also known as collateral in this context. The borrower receives equitable rights. As you know, if the borrower defaults on the loan, the creditor has a legal right to the property.

- **Interest:** Interest is the profit the lender earns on providing you with the cash (loan) you need in order to meet your objective. You can view it as money charged (what you pay) in order to borrow money. It is the amount that is paid on top of the total amount of money borrowed. Interest is commonly expressed as an annual percentage rate (APR). Interest charged on a mortgage is paid annually.

- **Loan origination:** This process is the method by which a borrower applies for a new loan. The lending institution processes and oversees his or her application. Origination most commonly includes every step in the process. This includes answering questions the client has about the loan application itself to the submission of the application, approval (or not), to finally disbursing the funds. A loan origination fee is what the lender charges in order to manage the process and see it through.

- **Mortgage:** A mortgage is the act of granting the lender consent to use the real property as collateral for a debt. In return, the lender provides the money. Surprisingly, most consumers believe that they actually get the mortgage from the bank. However, as we just defined, the mortgage is the act of granting consent to the lender to use the property as collateral. The mortgagor (buyer) is the giver of the mortgage. The mortgagee (lender) is the receiver of the mortgage.

- **Negotiable instrument:** This is a document that guarantees the payment of a certain sum of money. It is assigned and passed from one party to another. The end result is that money is paid. Examples include but are not limited to checks, mortgage promissory notes, bills of exchange, and government promissory notes.

- **Prepayment:** This term is exactly how it sounds. The total loan amount is paid in advance of its official due date. Although this accounting term applies to endless topics, in real estate, it is most commonly used when a home loan is paid off early. This brings up a related topic, prepayment penalties. This is a penalty for paying off a loan early. In some contracts, there is a prepayment clause. Prepayment for a lender means the lender will not receive the full interest revenue that was expected over the life of the loan. In other words, while prepayment can be financially advantageous for the borrower, it can be a disadvantage for the lender, as they will receive less interest revenue. The penalty can take a wide variety of forms. It all comes down to what the specific clause states. Prepayment penalties are tax deductible because they are considered to be a form of interest.

- **Security instrument:** This document grants the lender the rights to the property if the buyer falls into default. Like any contract, it is a binding agreement between the parties. When making an application for a mortgage loan, the contractual relationship between the lender and the borrower can take two different forms:

  - **Mortgage contract:** This contract is a two-party relationship agreement. It is a contractual relationship that the borrower has with the lender. This is the most common relationship that borrowers have with their lenders in Illinois. In this relationship agreement, the legal ownership is in the name of the borrower.

  - **Deed of trust:** This contract is a three-party relationship agreement composed of a trustor, trustee, and beneficiary. When used in financing property, the legal ownership is held in trust until the loan is fully paid off. This relationship agreement places the legal ownership in the name of the trustee. The borrower is the trustor and retains the legal bundle of rights. The lender assumes the role of the beneficiary. What happens if the trustor stops making payments? The lender has a claim to the property. Many times, the trust agreement features a power of sale clause. This clause, in the event of a borrower defaulting on payments, gives the lender the power and right to seize the property and sell it. Why? So, the lender can recover the remainder of the loan that was originally slated to be paid by the borrower. This clause means the lender is not required to take the borrower to court.

- **Subject to:** When selling property under a subject to provision, the seller typically conveys ownership and possession of the property to the buyer but does not pay off the existing mortgage loan. The buyer is assuming the ownership under the premise that the seller will continue making regular monthly payments. This is most often seen when the relationship between the buyer and the seller is a land contract.

- **Subrogation:** This is a legal principle of insurance law. Subrogation is the process by which we can subordinate one issue to another issue. An example is when there are two mortgages on one property. The mortgage that was taken out first, by agreement, can be subordinate to the second mortgage. This is done frequently when there is an existing mortgage on vacant land that you now want to improve, requiring a second mortgage to cover the cost of the construction. The second lender may require the first lender to agree to a subordination, as the construction would likely be more valuable than the land alone.

- **Usury:** Usury is the illegal practice of a lender charging an interest rate in excess of the legal limits. These loans are unfairly and immorally engineered to benefit the lender. The person who practices usury in the past was called an usurer. Nowadays, the term "loan shark" is more commonly heard. To combat usury, many states have set laws that allow a maximum legal rate. A lender who employs a usurious loan in some states can possibly be penalized or face litigation. Illinois has abolished usury limits, allowing the marketplace to control the interest rates the consumer is subject to.

PROVISIONS AND CLAUSES IN MORTGAGES

Mortgage contracts and deeds of trust can have a variety of clauses. Here are five primary different types of clauses that every licensee needs to understand.

1. Acceleration clause

2. Alienation clause

3. Prepayment penalty clause

4. Release clause

5. Subordination clause

Acceleration clause: This clause states and stipulates that the full amount of debt is due ASAP in the event of the borrower defaulting on the contract's terms. Usually, it outlines the circumstances in which a lender can demand a complete repayment of the loan. A series of missed payments by the borrower can initiate the acceleration clause being acted upon. These clauses are common in both residential and commercial real estate.

Alienation clause: This clause is also called a due-on-sale clause. This provision requires the borrower to pay off the full balance of the loan, along with accrued interest, to the lender before the owner can transfer the property to either a buyer or a tenant. Why do lenders use this clause? It prevents the borrower from conveying the collateral into the control of a third party without the lender's consent. This provides the lender with assurances that the original borrower will retain control of the property, which preserves the lender's financial interest. This is the provision in a conventional loan that makes it less probable that a potential buyer can assume the loan.

Prepayment penalty clause: This clause protects lenders against some of the loss of interest revenue that would have been generated over the full and expected lifetime of the loan. If Jane is a homeowner and pays her home off ten years earlier than expected, this clause will impose a penalty on her. The point of the penalty is to allow the lender to recoup some of the lost interest revenue.

Priority of liens: As you learned earlier, the date a lien is recorded establishes its position in terms of priority. The old adage is *first in, first out*. It basically states that the older liens will be satisfied first and newer liens will be satisfied last. The exception to this rule involves government liens and mechanic's liens. The order of priority is to satisfy government liens first, mechanic's liens second, and all remaining liens based on the date of each one's recording (first in, first out).

Release clause: This clause liberates a property, in whole or in part, from creditors' claims after a certain amount of the mortgage has been paid off.

Subordination clause: This means that a lender states that its lien takes precedence over any other liens on a borrower's property, whether current liens or ones that occur in the future. For example, if a property has three liens and a lender comes in with a subordination clause, that lender's lien becomes the superior debt instrument. It's the alpha and the other liens are the subordinates. This clause is common in home refinances and new construction. Example: Let's say that Eric wants to construct a new home on a recently acquired piece of land to meet his growing family's needs. He purchased the parcel for $75,000. Three months after the land acquisition, it's time to begin home construction. He secures a new construction loan for $400,000 with a second lender. Which lien has higher priority if this project goes to foreclosure? In accordance with the law, the concept is *first in, first out*. The lien on the land would take priority over the lien on the new construction loan. Could this prevent the second lender from granting the construction loan? Yes. This is why the second lender would insist on having a subordination clause (which the first lender must agree to) that makes the new construction loan the superior lien to be satisfied first in the event of a foreclosure.

FORECLOSURE DEFINITION, FACTS, AND TYPES

Foreclosure is a legal process at its core. It's the means by which a lender works to recover a loan balance from a borrower who quits submitting payments. The lender seizes and assumes control of the mortgaged property and attempts to sell it in order to generate revenue. Generally, a certain number of payments must be missed in order to trigger the foreclosure process. This number varies between different lenders. In most cases, a lender will implement the acceleration clause, which is outlined in the contract. Generally, a foreclosure involves five stages. They are: 1) payments are missed, 2) the mortgagor is notified (public notice), 3) pre-foreclosure, 4) attempt to sell / auction, and 5) post-foreclosure. In some states, public notice is known as "Notice of Default" (NOD), resulting in a placement of a *lis pendens* on the title.

There are three types of foreclosure: 1) judicial 2) nonjudicial, and 3) strict. Judicial and strict foreclosures must be approved by a court of law. In judicial and strict foreclosures, the mortgagee is required to go to court and show evidence that the mortgagor (owner/buyer) is delinquent under the terms of the mortgage contract, thereby permitting the mortgagee (lender) to pursue an order of foreclosure.

In a **judicial foreclosure**, the lender files a civil suit against the mortgagor. Although details and steps can be different from state to state, it usually works like this. The mortgagor is served with notice of their delinquency and the lender's intent to pursue a foreclosure. The claim of foreclosure is filed in the county in which the property is physically located. Public notice is usually provided by way of legal notification in a newspaper and/or other media outlets found in the geographical location of the property. The notice communicates the hour, date, and location of the auction so interested parties are aware. It's possible a mortgagor can stop the foreclosure by exercising either of the two redemption options that you'll learn about next, which are the statutory right of reinstatement and equitable right of redemption. Either of these options will terminate the foreclosure process, allowing the mortgagor to retain ownership of the property. If the mortgagor fails to meet either of those options, the lender proceeds with the foreclosure. The entire process with a judicial foreclosure can take a year or several years. If legal objections arise, the foreclosure will take that much longer. Illinois is a state that adheres only to judicial foreclosure, as per Illinois Mortgage Foreclosure Law found in 735 ILCS 5 of The Act.

Nonjudicial foreclosures are common in deed of trust states. Although details and steps can be different from state to state, it usually works like this. A third party is the trustee who has interest in the real estate, which is collateral for loan repayment. It is the beneficiary/lender who has the authority to start the foreclosure process. This is done by his or her power of sale clause, which is in either the deed of trust or mortgage contract. Next, he/she records a Notice of Default at the county clerk's office. This means there is a notice of an upcoming and impending foreclosure sale. The beneficiary/lender gives the trustor/mortgagor notification of the foreclosure process along with a period of time to pay the full debt off. There is no state-mandated time frame. It is merely what the beneficiary/lender feels is reasonable. If the debt is not satisfied, the beneficiary/lender is free to bypass the court system and sell the property directly to an interested party.

In a **strict foreclosure**, the mortgagor is given a defined period of time to satisfy the debt in its entirety. If he/she is unable to do so, the courts will award the ownership to the lender, without providing for an auction sale. This type is only lawful in Connecticut and Vermont as of writing this book. Both Connecticut and Vermont have their own established laws and processes in order for a strict foreclosure to take place.

It is possible for homeowners to avoid foreclosure by way of a short sale or a deed in lieu of foreclosure. Understandably, whichever route they choose, their credit scores take a severe hit.

1. **Short sale**: This term means that a homeowner who is behind on mortgage payments is willing to sell his or her property for less than what he/she owes on the mortgage loan. It relates to the phrase "coming up short," as in not producing the necessary money for something. It's less commonly known as a pre-foreclosure sale. Many times, the borrower is not able to sell the house for the total amount owed on the loan. As you can guess, if the property sells, 100% of the proceeds less closing costs are allocated to the lender. At that point, the lender has a few options. The lender can: 1) forgive the loan difference due or 2) generate a deficiency judgment (a suit) against the borrower. (A deficiency judgment is a court ruling against a borrower who has defaulted on a secured loan. It means that selling the property is not going to cover the full cost of the loan and associated expenses and fees. It's a method a lender uses to collect all the money owed to them.) Short sales work differently in different states. They can be an exhausting and long-drawn-out process for licensees. Not only are there multiple variables, including property law and taxes, but also there are the difficult feelings and stress being experienced by the seller/s and his or her family. When executing a short sale, the buyer is likely to submit earnest money as part of the offer. The lender is required to approve any short sale. This brings up the question, when is a broker required to deposit the earnest money into the special account? Since the lender is not a co-owner and the law dictates the earnest money must be deposited by the close of the next business day following acceptance of the contract, the trigger for the deposit of earnest money is when the *seller* accepts the offer, not the lender.

2. **A deed in lieu of foreclosure**: This concept and document is also called a friendly foreclosure. Why? Because it is managed by agreement, rather than a requirement of a lawsuit. The document transfers the property's title from the borrower to his or her lender in consideration of being relieved of the mortgagor's loan debt. It helps the borrower bypass foreclosure proceedings. Generally, it is the borrower's last resort before foreclosure. He/she can attempt a short sale prior to this option. If a short sale is not possible, this could be their last option. Being able to bypass sluggish and tedious foreclosure proceedings is a huge benefit for both borrower and lender.

EQUITY OF REDEMPTION

If a borrower is in the process of foreclosure, he/she can possibly redeem the mortgage. In this context, redeem means to buy back or pay off and recover. This can be done by making delinquent payments as well as paying any other accumulated costs, fees, and interest. In any foreclosure setting, there are potentially three different rights of redemption that the borrower may be entitled to. The choice is set by state provision.

1. **Statutory right of redemption**: This is a specified period of time, by law, that grants the individual losing the property a second chance to retain it. Typically, this occurs after the foreclosure auction has taken place and before the successful bidder receives a sheriff's deed. The time frame is set by state statute, and thus, can vary from state to state. Illinois is an example of a state that does not recognize the statutory right of redemption in a mortgage foreclosure. (While this is not recognized in Illinois as relief in a mortgage foreclosure, it is recognized as relief for the property owner in a tax foreclosure.)

2. **Equitable right of redemption**: This is a method by which a borrower can keep his or her property that has entered into the foreclosure process. The equitable right of redemption begins after the foreclosure notice is received. Not including a few exceptions, a borrower has seven months (redemption period) from the day he/she is served (notice received) to pay off the full amount of the loan that is due. Redemption takes place once the mortgage debt has been discharged. This means the debt is satisfied in its entirety. Not all states have equitable right of redemption. Illinois does.

3. **Statutory right of reinstatement**: Illinois has a statutory right of reinstatement which is outlined in the Illinois Mortgage Foreclosure Law. Let's say you're the borrower. To reinstate your loan, you are required to pay all missed payments as well as other costs and expenses associated with the loan. At that point, you are no longer in default and your relationship with the lender is reinstated. You will continue to make the monthly payments as originally agreed from that point forward. The right of reinstatement

gives you ninety days to make up all missed payments and pay off any fees and penalties. Day one is the day you are served by the process server. Day ninety is the final day and deadline, and the only relief you will possess is the remaining time available under the equitable right of redemption.

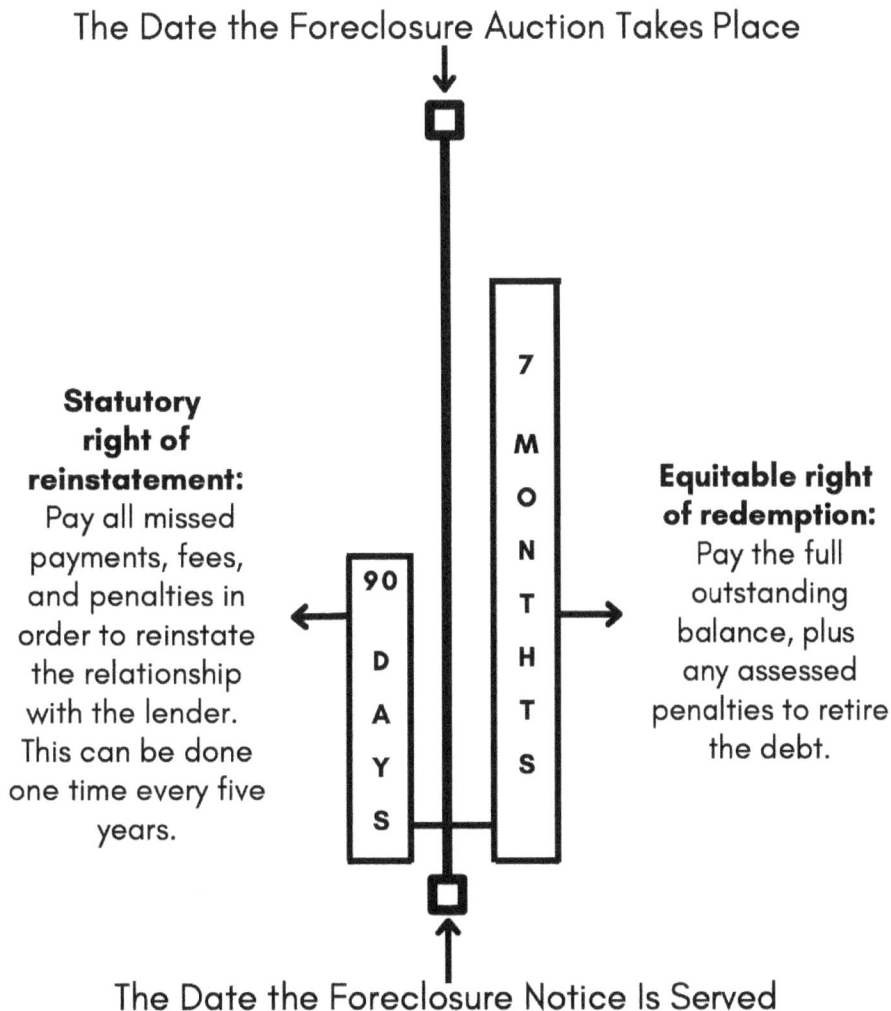

The Date the Foreclosure Auction Takes Place

Statutory right of reinstatement:
Pay all missed payments, fees, and penalties in order to reinstate the relationship with the lender. This can be done one time every five years.

7 MONTHS

90 DAYS

Equitable right of redemption:
Pay the full outstanding balance, plus any assessed penalties to retire the debt.

The Date the Foreclosure Notice Is Served

As you can see from Diagram 21.1 above, in Illinois, the two rights of redemption run simultaneously. Day one is the day the notice is served.

CAN BANKRUPTCY BE CLAIMED DURING A FORECLOSURE?

The simple answer is yes, it can be claimed. The better question is, should it be claimed in the first place? At this difficult and complicated intersection of property law, taxes, and finances, it is best to have anyone considering bankruptcy talk with highly trained professionals. Bankruptcy is not a "get out of jail free" card and it's not a hall pass. Furthermore, it is a complicated and emotional topic that can easily trigger people.

There are six different types of bankruptcies in total. However, only two are applicable to foreclosures. They are Chapter 13 and Chapter 7. A Chapter 13 bankruptcy can possibly allow the borrower to keep the house. Basically, some type of payment plan is set up. There are requirements, like showing proof of income. Essentially, the borrower pays current payments, along with delinquent payments, enabling him/her to keep the home. A Chapter 7 bankruptcy differs from a Chapter 13 because a Chapter 7 requires the sale of your property to pay off some debts and then discharges the remaining eligible debt. However, the discharge of the debt will not prevent a foreclosure. Since banks use the property as the security for the debt, they can seize the property in a foreclosure process in order to recoup the outstanding funds due.

THE FEDERAL RESERVE

As you read earlier, you cannot separate the real estate industry from government policies. With government policies in the context of real estate, usually, the topic focuses on the Federal Reserve (also known as the Federal Reserve System or the Fed). It is the US's central banking system. Overseen by a board, it regulates and supervises the practices of lending and banking institutions. You can instantly and easily see how decisions made there can impact the real estate industry. Their changes are most commonly in response to laws that have been enacted by the US government's legislature. Its ultimate goal is to generate and produce banking system stability. The Federal Reserve defines what it does as, "Supervising and regulating banks and other important financial institutions to ensure the safety and soundness of the nation's banking and financial system and to protect the credit rights of consumers. Maintaining the stability of the financial system and containing systemic risk that may arise in financial markets."

> "When the Federal Reserve decides to increase the federal funds rate, it puts upward pressure on mortgage interest rates as well. Higher mortgage interest rates increase the overall cost of purchasing a home, by increasing mortgage payments" (Congressional Research Service: Introduction to U.S. Economy: Housing Market https://crsreports.congress.gov)

The Federal Reserve requires a reserve requirement for its member banks. Reserve requirement is also called cash reserve ratio. This is the minimum amount of cash reserves that is required to be held by a commercial bank. This percentage is set by the Federal Reserve. In fact, the Fed sets both the primary rate and the discount rate. The prime rate is a short-term federal interest rate. The discount rate is an even shorter term rate. Many times, it's an overnight rate and fluctuates regularly. The prime rate applies to the public. The discount rate is non-public and applies only to the Fed's member banks and is used for discount loans. A member bank can borrow money from the Fed in order to fund more mortgage loans.

PRIMARY AND SECONDARY MORTGAGE MARKETS

There is a primary real estate mortgage market and a secondary real estate mortgage market. The primary mortgage market focuses on properties sold to the public. Thus, loan origination takes place in the primary mortgage market. Borrowers receive loans from a primary lender. These loans could come from banking institutions, credit unions, insurance companies, mortgage bankers, pension funds, mortgage brokers, endowment funds, and similar. The Secure and Fair Enforcement for Mortgage Licensing Act of 2008 is also referred to as the SAFE Act. It required all states to implement a Mortgage Loan Originator (MLO) licensing and registration system. Subject to strict federal standards, each state can manage and oversee its own systems for licensing and registrations. The other option is joining the Nationwide Mortgage Licensing System and Registry (NMLS), which is sometimes simply called the Registry or the System. What happens if a state's licensing and registration system fails to meet the strict minimum standards? HUD has the authority to intervene and make the state use the Nationwide Mortgage Licensing System and Registry. The NMLS neither grants nor denies license authority.

Most likely, you have heard of Fannie Mae, Freddie Mac, and/or Ginnie Mae. If so, you've already heard of the secondary mortgage market. This market focuses on entities like private lenders, lending institutions, and investors that buy and sell existing mortgage promissory notes (previously issued mortgages) and/or securities that are mortgage-backed. Loans are not originated here, rather they are bought and sold. It's like a market for reselling promissory notes. This means that the new lender now can earn revenue from mortgage fees and interest. These mortgages are organized in pools or blocks. Many times, mortgages in the same pool or block share one or more similar characteristics.

FANNIE MAE, FREDDIE MAC, AND GINNIE MAE

Fannie Mae is the nickname for the Federal National Mortgage Association. Fannie Mae originates from the acronym FNMA. It is an enterprise sponsored by the government that was founded in 1938 through the New Deal by President Franklin D. Roosevelt. In 1968, it became a publicly traded company. Fortune Global 500 reports that Fannie Mae was ranked 33 in 2022.

Freddie Mac is the nickname for the Federal Home Loan Mortgage Corporation (FHLMC) and is similar to Fannie Mae. It is an enterprise sponsored by the government. Congress initiated its creation in 1970 as a means of supporting middle-income Americans' dreams of homeownership. In 2022, the Fortune 500 list ranked Freddie Mac as 56.

Freddie Mac and Fannie Mae share many similarities. Both. . .

- Are publicly traded
- Facilitate the growth of the secondary mortgage market

- Purchase promissory notes from the primary market

- Pull the promissory notes together

- Sell the notes as mortgage-backed securities to private and corporate investors, as well as foreign governments

- Feature different programs and requirements

- Provide additional funding in the hands of the primary lender to generate additional mortgage loans

Ginnie Mae is the nickname for the Government National Mortgage Association (GNMA). It is fully owned by a government-owned corporation as opposed to being government-sponsored. It was founded in 1968 and is a self-financing corporation within HUD. Its goal is to expand budget-friendly and affordable housing by reducing the financial burden that buyers would face when using a conventional loan. Its investors are guaranteed an on-time payment of mortgage-backed securities even if homeowners default and even if homes are foreclosed. The official Ginnie Mae website shares the following as its mission:

> "Our mission is to bring global capital into the housing finance system—a system that runs through the core of our nation's economy—while minimizing risk to the taxpayer. For over fifty years, Ginnie Mae has worked to make affordable housing a reality for millions of Americans through providing liquidity and stability, serving as the principal financing arm for government loans, and ensuring that mortgage lenders have the necessary funds to provide loans to consumers. Ginnie Mae delivers mortgage securitization programs for mortgage lenders and attractive offerings for global investors. Ginnie Mae developed the nation's first mortgage-backed securities (MBS) in 1970. It is the only federal agency tasked with the administration and oversight of an explicit, paid-for, full-faith-and-credit guarantee on MBS. Even in difficult times, an investment in Ginnie Mae MBS has proven to be one of the safest an investor can make, as evidenced by the demand for these securities from investors worldwide."

Which mortgage-backed securities of loans does Ginnie Mae guarantee? They include the FHA (Federal Housing Administration) Veterans Affairs (VA), Office of Public and Indian Housing (PIH), and Rural Development (RD). Because it is government owned, it does not qualify to enter lists like Fortune 500.

CREDIT SCORE AND CREDIT HISTORY

Inseparable from loans are the topics of credit history and credit scores. This is only one of many factors at play when a lender is considering issuing a loan to an applicant.

A credit score is a number or numerical expression that shows a lender an applicant's financial capacity to repay a loan. It's a statistical analysis based on the applicant's credit files. A credit score is a three-digit number that demonstrates creditworthiness. Most commonly, a credit score range is between 300 and 850. The information is sourced from credit bureaus, the largest three being Experian, TransUnion, and Equifax. A general overview of credit score ranges and what they mean are as follows:

- 300 to 579: Poor

- 580 to 669: Fair

- 670 to 739: Good

- 740 to 799: Very good

- 800 to 850: Excellent

A FICO (Fair Isaac Corporation) score is the most widely used type of credit score. According to myFICO, the average credit score (as of April 2022) for Americans is 716. Lenders use credit score as a measurement of how much credit risk they can extend to each applicant. Additionally, lenders use them as guides for determining interest rates, credit limit, and which applicants qualify for a loan. "How likely is this person to pay his or her bills?" is the question a credit score answers. The higher the credit score, the more favorable credit terms an applicant receives. Are income or employment history factors related to how high or low a credit score is? No. The interest rates of most mortgage loans are based largely on one's credit score.

How does the loan process work? The loan originator takes the application from the consumer. The loan processor then gathers all of the information concerning the applicant's financial status. The information is organized and given or presented to the mortgage underwriter. He/she takes an in-depth look at and studies an applicant's finances, credit score, and any necessary assessments in order to determine how much of a risk the applicant is to the lender. The underwriter also looks for any information or evidence concerning current or previous foreclosures, judgments, and bankruptcies. Ultimately, it is a mortgage underwriter who will make the final decision in offering or denying the applicant a loan.

TYPES OF LOANS

Most real estate purchases require a loan. There are a wide variety of financing options available. Here is a list of the most common types of loans.

Conventional Mortgages

This home loan is not insured by the Federal Government. It includes two types of conventional loans, which are conforming loans and nonconforming loans.

Conforming loans are considered to be the most secure for lenders as they fall below the conforming loan limits established by the Federal Housing Finance Agency (FHFA). Reviewed annually, the conforming loan limit is a reflection of the maximum average price in a geographical area. Because of the inconsistencies in the market, to understand the limits in your geographical area, you may want to check with your local loan officer.

Consider this: A lender has $1,000,000 of available cash to loan out. Financially, would it be best for the lender to provide one loan with for $1,000,000 or five loans worth $200,000? From Freddie Mac or Fannie Mae's perspective, which is a better business decision? The answer is granting five loans. Why? If one of the $200,000 loans goes bad, the lender as well as Fannie Mae or Freddie Mac still has four remaining good loans. If the single $1,000,000 loan goes bad, they share in a total loss. The five loans hold less risk as compared to the single loan, which makes it more advantageous.

Jumbo loans are used when the purchase price of a home exceeds the conforming values established by FHFA. This is a nonconforming loan as it does not fit within the FHFA's defined mortgage guidelines.

Nonconforming loans are loans where the mortgage value exceeds the maximum value established for a conforming loan; and/or the buyer does not meet the minimum requirements. Jumbo loans place a greater level of risk on the lender because they are providing the consumer with more than the average cash amount. This results in the lender's ability to charge a higher interest rate.

Subprime loan: This type of loan has higher interest rates and fees because the borrower usually has a credit score of 600 or below. The higher rates and fees are how the lender compensates for increased risk due to the borrower's low credit score. Note that there is no standard definition in the US for a subprime loan.

Private mortgage insurance (PMI): PMI is an insurance policy the lender requires on a conventional loan when the down payment falls below the 20% threshold. This policy, by federal regulation, must be dropped when the consumer reaches a 22% equity level based on the original purchase price of the home. History has established that the minimum down payment should be 20%. This results in an 80% LTV (loan-to-value ratio) for the lender. This ratio is the percent of the purchase price provided by the lender. When the purchaser puts down 20%, the lender typically considers the loan to be a reasonable risk. Therefore, the lender does not require an insurance (PMI) backup. However, the economy has evolved to the point that consumers want to put as little money down as possible when purchasing a home. This has resulted in down payments as low as 3% on some conventional loans. The end result puts greater risk on the lender. As such, to protect themselves, lenders require the borrower to take out an insurance policy (PMI) to cover any losses a lender may incur as a result of a future foreclosure. Once a foreclosure sale has taken place, should the sale result in a financial loss to the lender, PMI makes up the difference. This enables the lender to bypass financial losses that it otherwise would have experienced. PMI gives the lender the ability to take on a riskier borrower.

FHA Government-Insured Loans

FHA-insured loans are a type of federal assistance. These loans are backed by the Federal Government and are provided through an FHA-approved lender. FHA loans repay the bank or lending institution if the borrower defaults on his or her mortgage payment. From the inception of the FHA concept in the 1930s, the intent was to provide for owner-occupied housing. It is not geared toward real estate investors or investment products. Historically, the original intent was to provide housing assistance to lower-income Americans; however, this payment structure is not limited to low-income purchasers. As long the individual meets the minimum financial requirements, he/she is eligible. Regardless of the loan structure, a financial institution is a for-profit entity. Its goal is to protect its investments. When a down payment falls below the 20% threshold, as you saw earlier, the lender requires the borrower to acquire an insurance policy. This policy will pay for any losses the lender might incur as a result of a foreclosure sale. On FHA, this is commonly known as **mortgage insurance premium (MIP)**. Unlike a conventional loan when the lender requires private mortgage insurance (PMI), MIP is permanent and will exist for the full life of the debt.

FHA-approved banks and lending institutions evaluate the borrowers' financial qualifications for the loans. Requirements to get approved are strict. Understandably, some of these borrowers have lower than average credit scores. When a borrower is approved, the money used is issued by qualified lenders. While the money comes from a traditional lender, FHA insures the loan to protect the lender's investment should there be a default by the purchaser.

The most popular loan package that FHA offers is called the 203(b) fixed-rate loan. It's a standard single-family home loan. The HUD website shares more information about this loan:

- What is the purpose of this program?

    - To provide mortgage insurance for a person to purchase or refinance a principal residence. The mortgage loan is funded by a lending institution, such as a mortgage company, bank, savings and loan association and the mortgage is insured by HUD.

- What are the eligibility requirements?

  - The borrower must meet standard FHA credit qualifications.

  - The borrower is eligible for approximately 96.5% financing *(3.5% down payment). The borrower is able to finance the upfront mortgage insurance premium into the mortgage. The borrower will also be responsible for paying an annual premium.

  - Eligible properties are one-to-four unit structures. (HUD)

The MIP premium is comprised of two elements. The first element is an upfront payment consisting of 1.75% of the mortgage amount. It is due at the closing. However, this fee can be added to the original mortgage balance and paid off over time. The second element of MIP is approximately 0.45% of the original mortgage balance and is calculated annually. This portion is broken into monthly increments and added to the monthly payment.

Along with the 203(b) fixed-rate loan, FHA offers other types of loans. This is not a complete list of available products. In no particular order, they are:

- Home Equity Conversion Mortgage (HECM) program

  - "Reverse mortgages are increasing in popularity with seniors who have equity in their homes and want to supplement their income. The only reverse mortgage insured by the U.S. Federal Government is called a Home Equity Conversion Mortgage (HECM), and is only available through an FHA-approved lender. The HECM is FHA's reverse mortgage program that enables you to withdraw a portion of your home's equity." HUD (You will read about reverse mortgages later in this chapter.)

- 203(k) Improvement loan

  - "FHA's Limited 203(k) program permits homebuyers and homeowners to finance up to $35,000 into their mortgage to repair, improve, or upgrade their home. Homebuyers and homeowners can quickly and easily tap into cash to pay for property repairs or improvements, such as those identified by a home inspector or an FHA appraiser. Homeowners can make property repairs, improvements, or prepare their home for sale. Homebuyers can make their new home move-in ready by remodeling the kitchen, painting the interior or purchasing new carpet." HUD

- Section 245(a) loan

  - "This program facilitates early homeownership for households that expect their incomes to rise. Initially, monthly payments are smaller than payments in a level-payment mortgage. Later, the payments gradually increase. The program is limited to principal residences. Only one-family dwellings are eligible." HUD

- Energy Efficient Mortgage program loan:

  - "FHA's Energy Efficient Mortgage program (EEM) helps families save money on their utility bills by enabling them to finance energy efficient improvements with their FHA-insured mortgage. The EEM program recognizes that an energy-efficient home will have lower operating costs, making it more affordable for the homeowners. Cost-effective energy improvements can lower utility bills and make more income available for the mortgage payment." (HUD)

Two attractive benefits of FHA loans are that there is no prepayment penalty (the consumer is not penalized if he or she pays off the loan before the maturity date), and the loan is fully assumable as long as the purchaser qualifies for the monthly obligation.

VA-Guaranteed Loans

A VA-guaranteed loan, also called a VA loan or VA-backed loan, is a mortgage loan that is guaranteed by the US Department of Veterans Affairs (VA). Guaranteeing the loan means that the guarantor (VA) will reimburse the lender any monies lost should the property go into foreclosure and be sold at a price less than the outstanding mortgage debt.

The VA website offers this information:

> VA helps Servicemembers, Veterans, and eligible surviving spouses become homeowners. As part of our mission to serve you, we provide a home loan guaranty benefit and other housing-related programs to help you buy, build, repair, retain, or adapt a home for your own personal occupancy. VA Home Loans are provided by private lenders, such as banks and mortgage companies. VA guarantees a portion of the loan, enabling the lender to provide you with more favorable terms.

Minimum active-duty service requirements:

- For service members: If you've served for at least 90 continuous days (all at once, without a break in service), you meet the minimum active-duty service requirement.

- For Veterans, National Guard members and Reserve members: The minimum active-duty service requirements depend on when you served.

A VA-backed purchase loan often offers:

- No down payment as long as the sales price isn't higher than the home's appraised value (the value set for the home after an expert reviews the property)

- Better terms and interest rates than other loans from private banks, mortgage companies, or credit unions (also called lenders)

- The ability to borrow up to the Fannie Mae/Freddie Mac conforming loan limit on a no-down-payment loan in most areas—and more in some high-cost counties. You can borrow more than this amount if you want to make a down payment.

- No need for private mortgage insurance (PMI) or mortgage insurance premiums (MIP)

  - PMI is a type of insurance that protects the lender if you end up not being able to pay your mortgage. It's usually required on conventional loans if you make a down payment of less than 20% of the total mortgage amount.

  - MIP is what the Federal Housing Administration (FHA) requires you to pay to self-insure an FHA loan against future loss.

- Fewer closing costs, which may be paid by the seller

- No penalty fee if you pay the loan off early

If you qualify for a VA-backed purchase loan*, you can use the loan to:

- Buy a single-family home, up to 4 units

- Buy a condo in a VA-approved project

- Buy a home and improve it

- Buy a manufactured home or lot

- Build a new home

- Make changes or add new features (like solar power) to make your home more energy efficient (VA)

Personal residence/owner-occupied only

What are the loan limits?

Eligible Veterans, servicemembers, and survivors with full entitlement no longer have limits on loans over $144,000. This means you won't have to pay a down payment, and we guarantee to your lender that if you default on a loan that's over $144,000, we'll pay them up to 25% of the loan amount. You have full entitlement if you meet any of these requirements.

At least one of these must be true:

- You've never used your home loan benefit, or

- You've paid a previous VA loan in full and sold the property (in this case, you'd have your full entitlement restored), or

- You've used your home loan benefit, but had a foreclosure or compromise claim (also called a short sale) and repaid us in full (VA)

For more information, visit the VA government website and download their free resource called "VA Home Loan Guaranty Buyer's Guide."

Payment Structures

- **Amortized:** This is also known as direct reduction. This pay structure results in paying the lender off in its entirely by the end of the loan's term. Amortization references the process of lowering or paying off a debt with regular ongoing payments of principal and interest. In an amortized loan, the loan's principal is paid down throughout the life of the loan. In other words, it is amortized. This sequence follows an amortization schedule. Most of the time, the loan is paid off by way of equal monthly installments. To be clear, this is not a loan, it's actually a payment structure. Below are two types of commonly used payment structures.

  - **Fixed-rate:** This payment structure is fully amortized. The interest rate on the note remains consistent throughout the loan's term. Consequently, the payment amounts as well as the duration of the loan are fixed, and thus do not change. The borrower benefits from a consistent, single payment and the ability to plan a budget based on this fixed cost.

  - **Adjustable-rate:** As you read in Chapter 1, these mortgages are sometimes called ARMs, variable-rate mortgages, or tracker mortgages. In this type of payment structure, the interest rate periodically adjusts based on an index that shows the lender's cost of borrowing on the credit markets. (Basically, if the lender had to borrow money themselves, what interest rate would the lender have to pay?). Although commonly based on a one-year period, the interest rate can change more frequently. There are some hybrid ARMs that may allow for interest adjustment in as short as six-month intervals. These hybrids can also provide for a combination of a fixed interest rate for a specified period of time, and a conversion to an annual adjustment. (Example: The 5/25 means that for the first five years of the loan's interest, the APR is fixed. However, starting in the sixth year, the interest rate converts to an annual adjustable rate.) The loan may be offered at the lender's standard variable rate/base rate. However, as the lender is entitled to a profit beyond the base rate, there is likely going to be an additional fee to cover that. This is commonly known as the margin. The combination of the lender's base rate (index), plus the lender's profit (margin), defines the new interest rate the consumer will be charged for the next period of time. During the loan term, by nature, the interest rate will fluctuate up and down (increase and decrease). As you know, the lender is a for-profit institution. They need to be conscientious of making a profit not only on the day they grant you the loan but also ten to thirty years into the future. Therefore, the interest rates they charge today are intended to provide a profit now and ten-plus years from now too. Because of this expectation, the fixed-rate loan provides the lender with that security. What if you grant the lender consent to alter the interest rates every twelve months? If you do, they only have to look toward the next twelve months with regard to their profitability. By granting the lender the right to alter the rate every twelve months based upon the then-current cost of funds (the index), they can charge a lower interest rate recognizing that if they need to increase it within twelve months, they can do so. Like the fixed-rate loan, an ARM is also an amortized mortgage loan.

- **Interest-only:** Also called straight loans or straight-term loans, these payment structures only require interest to be paid during the loan's term. Since the consumer has only been paying interest for the life of the loan, the entire loan debt will be due as a single payment at the end of the loan's term. This payment is usually referred to as a balloon payment. Often, when it is time for the consumer to pay off the debt in its entirety, they may be forced to either refinance the house or sell it if they lack the available capital. Commonly, an interest-only loan is used for construction and land financing. It's safe to write that interest-only loans have mostly been replaced by amortized loans.

Other Financing Options

Other loans available to consumers include the following:

- **Balloon payment loan:** This loan does not completely amortize over the note's term. There is a balance that is due at the loan's maturity. The loan maturity date is the date when the borrower's final payment is due. The last payment is referred to as a "balloon payment" because it is generally a large sum of money. The interest rate on balloon payment loans might be fixed or floating. These types of mortgages are utilized more in commercial real estate than residential.

- **Growing-equity mortgage:** Also called a GEM or rapid payoff mortgage, it's another kind of fixed-rate mortgage. The monthly payments increase over time and are credited against the outstanding principal. The intent is to reduce the outstanding debt at a much faster rate than the typical thirty-year mortgage. The increase takes place in alignment with a set schedule known by all parties. Does the interest rate on the loan change? No. It's fixed for the life of the loan.

- **Non-recourse loan:** "A non-recourse debt (loan) does not allow the lender to pursue anything other than the collateral. For example, if a borrower defaults on a non-recourse home loan, the bank can only foreclose on the home. The bank generally cannot take further legal action to collect the money owed on the debt." IRS. He or she has no personal responsibility concerning the loan. These loans are not common in the residential sector.

- **Package loan:** This is a loan that is used to finance the purchase of both real property and also personal property. The personal property may include furniture, major and/or minor appliances, and more. Thus, it's a "package deal." This is commonly used in the acquisition of new construction when the buyer wants to upgrade the appliances instead of the standard appliances offered by the developer. Using a package loan, the buyer is able to finance the acquisition of both the real property and the personal property.

- **Recourse loan:** "A recourse debt holds the borrower personally liable." IRS. This allows the lender to protect itself. Should the borrower go into default, the lender is capable of not only pursuing the real property as collateral but also personal assets as well.

- **Reverse mortgage:** "With a reverse mortgage, you borrow money from the lender, based on the amount of equity you have in your home. The lender may send you the funds from the reverse mortgage in one lump sum payment, a series of monthly payments, or some combination of those. But no matter how the money gets distributed to you, the lender adds interest each month to the balance you owe (the principal). That means your balance goes up over time, increasing the amount you have to pay, and you have less and less equity in your home." FTC

OTHER PATHS TO FINANCING

Just as there is a wide variety of borrowers with different financial capabilities and circumstances, not only is there a wide variety of loans, but there is also a myriad of different financing techniques.

Agricultural loan programs: Agricultural real estate property includes farmland, forestry, orchards, and ranches.

"Farm Ownership Loans offer up to 100 percent financing and are a valuable resource to help farmers and ranchers purchase or enlarge family farms, improve and expand current operations, increase agricultural productivity, and assist with land tenure to save farmland for future generations. With a maximum loan amount of $600,000 ($300,150 for Beginning Farmer Down Payment), all FSA Direct Farm Ownership Loans are financed and serviced by the Agency through local Farm Loan Officers and Farm Loan Managers. The funding comes from Congressional appropriations as part of the USDA budget." (FSA)

Blanket loan: This loan can be implemented to fund the purchase of two or more pieces of real property. Blanket loans are popular with and commonly used by developers and builders who purchase big tracts of land. Their goal is to subdivide the land they purchase in order to create several individual parcels. Those parcels can be sold off one by one over time. This helps them bypass securing a new mortgage for each parcel. It simplifies the process and avoids time wasted with multiple loans. Thus, the blanket loan purchases all of the land where the parcels will be. With each parcel sold, a part of the mortgage gets released. This is allowed by way of what is called a partial release clause in the contract. How is a blanket mortgage secured? By the property being bought (or refinanced). The property, like several other types of loans, serves as collateral.

Buydown: This financing technique involves the borrower working to secure a lower APR on a mortgage loan or deed of trust. The lower APR may be temporary or permanent. At the closing, the lender receives a lump sum paid in cash.

Construction loan: Also called a self-build loan or interim financing, this short-term loan is used specifically to finance a real estate construction project, whether a home or some other type of build. Its goal is to cover the costs during the actual period of construction, not post-project. Lenders view these loans as risky. Accordingly, they have higher interest rates. The borrower receives draws (funds) from the lender during the construction work. Lenders reserve the right to observe, monitor, and/or inspect the build because they want the project to be completed so that repayment starts. The borrower pays only on disbursed funds, not the full amount of the loan. Since these are short-term loans, at the conclusion of the project it is common for the borrower to refinance the loan into a traditional payment structure.

Home equity loan: This highly popular type of loan is a loan in which a borrower's home equity (ownership) is used as collateral. The property value dictates the loan amount. Most of the time, the lender will send an appraiser to do an appraisal. As you know, this determines the home's fair market value. The lien is against the borrower's residence. Does it reduce the actual home equity? Yes. Home equity loans can be used for a wide variety of expenses, including, but not limited to, the following: home projects, house repairs, home upgrades, paying medical bills, paying for a college education, and so on. To receive this loan, the borrower needs to have a high credit score, along with acceptable loan-to-value ratios. With a home equity line of credit (HELOC), the borrower may use some or all of the credit as he/she chooses. A home equity loan is commonly called a second mortgage because it is a junior lien. (The first mortgage on a specific property is the senior mortgage. All other mortgages are known as subordinate or junior liens.)

Open-ended/closed-ended loans: Loans can be open-ended or closed-ended. With an open-ended mortgage, the borrower has the authority and right to increase the amount of the outstanding mortgage principal in the future. In contrast, a closed-ended loan is an installment loan that has a set term, amount, and interest rate. An open-ended mortgage allows the borrower to return to the lender and borrow more money like a line of credit. Generally, there is a maximum amount (limit) that can be borrowed. This loan has similarities with delayed draw term loans. Any new funds borrowed go toward investing in the property.

Purchase money mortgage (PMM) loan: This type of loan is generally sought out when the borrower cannot qualify for more traditional and common loans. PMM is sometimes called seller or owner financing. The seller is the issuer of the loan, thus he/she functions as the lender. This type of mortgage program emulates the land contract as it is a form of seller financing. However, it differs from a land contract because in a land contract, the seller retains legal ownership until the buyer satisfies the debt. In a PMM, the seller conveys legal ownership to the buyer immediately and simply retains a lien on the property until the debt is repaid.

Wraparound loan: This is a type of creative seller financing sometimes called a wrap for short. It is secondary financing. The original (senior) mortgage loan stays in place when the property sells. The seller offers a junior mortgage to the borrower/buyer. A junior mortgage is the same as a second mortgage. It uses the home value as collateral. In circumstances of a foreclosure, the senior (first) mortgage is required to be paid first. Then the junior mortgage is to be paid. Thus, the junior mortgage wraps around the superior mortgage, which is also secured by the property. A wrap note is secured by a (new) wraparound deed of trust.

QUALIFIED MORTGAGES AND FINANCIAL TERMS

Each loan will exist within a certain category. Loan programs many times come down to questions and decisions regarding:

- Fixed mortgage or adjustable-rate mortgage

- Government-insured or conventional loans

The **loan-to-value (LTV) ratio** is a financial term. It is commonly used by lending institutions, enabling them to communicate the ratio of a loan to the value of a purchase. It assesses the risk involved in lending. The LTV is examined before a mortgage loan is approved. A high LTV means high risk. Most likely, the lender will decline to offer the loan. A low LTV means low risk, which increases the probability that the applicant will be approved.

Another important ratio is the **debt-to-income ratio (DTI)**. It's the percentage of an applicant/consumer's monthly gross income that is allocated to pay down debts. This ratio is important to lenders because it enables them to see how much risk is involved with lending money to a specific applicant.

A **qualified mortgage** is one that meets or exceeds specific requirements for lender protection and secondary market trading. This traces back to a law called the Dodd-Frank Wall Street Reform and Consumer Protection Act. It serves to regulate the financial markets while protecting consumers. Built into its design are elements to avoid something like the 2008 financial crisis from happening again. A government organization that is a major player in this regard is the Consumer Financial Protection Bureau (CFPB). Their mission, as per their website, reads as follows:

> "We aim to make consumer financial markets work for consumers, responsible providers, and the economy as a whole. We protect consumers from unfair, deceptive, or abusive practices and take action against companies that break the law. We arm people with the information, steps, and tools that they need to make smart financial decisions. In a market that works, the prices, risks, and terms of the deal are clear upfront so that consumers can understand their options and comparison shop. Companies all play by the same consumer protection rules and compete fairly on providing quality and service." (CFPB)

What does this have to do with qualified mortgages? The Dodd-Frank regulation defines the requirements for a qualified mortgage. It initiates that a lender invests the time to make an effort in good faith to ascertain whether or not an applicant honestly has the financial ability to repay the residential mortgage loan. Said another way, it helps borrowers not take on a loan that is too big or overwhelming for their budget and income level.

> "The **Ability-to-Repay/Qualified Mortgage Rule** (ATR/QM Rule) requires a creditor to make a reasonable, good faith determination of a consumer's ability to repay a residential mortgage loan according to its terms. Loans that meet the ATR/QM Rule's requirements for qualified mortgages (QMs) obtain certain protections from liability." (Federal Register)

WHICH LEGISLATION GOVERNS FINANCING IN REAL ESTATE?

Mortgage lending practices are regulated by the government through several important acts. Although there are more, these are the largest ones. In no particular order, they are:

1. Truth in Lending Act (TILA)

2. Real Estate Settlement Procedures Act (RESPA)

3. TILA-RESPA Integrated Disclosure Rule (TRID)

4. Secure and Fair Enforcement for Mortgage Licensing Act (SAFE)

5. Equal Credit Opportunity Act (ECOA)

6. Homeowners Protection Act (HPA)

7. Community Reinvestment Act (CRA)

The Truth in Lending Act (TILA) is also called Regulation Z. It is a federal law. TILA requires lenders and creditors to simply and clearly disclose how much purchasers are going to pay for credit. In other words, this provision requires the lender to disclose to the purchaser *exactly* what it will cost them in acquiring their mortgage. This gives the purchaser the ability to shop the loan with various lenders in order to make an informed, rational decision concerning which lender is the best choice.

Advertising is an aspect that TILA works to guard. There are strict requirements. Here is an excerpt from the government website called Consumer Finance:

1026.24 Advertising.

A. Actually available terms. If an advertisement for credit states specific credit terms, it shall state only those terms that actually are or will be arranged or offered by the creditor.

B. Clear and conspicuous standard. Disclosures required by this section shall be made clearly and conspicuously.

C. Advertisement of rate of finance charge. If an advertisement states a rate of finance charge, it shall state the rate as an "annual percentage rate," using that term. If the annual percentage rate may be increased after consummation, the advertisement shall state that fact. If an advertisement is for credit not secured by a dwelling, the advertisement shall not state any other rate, except that a simple annual rate or periodic rate that is applied to an unpaid balance may be stated in conjunction with, but not more conspicuously than, the annual percentage rate. If an advertisement is for credit secured by a dwelling, the advertisement shall not state any other rate, except that a simple annual rate that is applied to an unpaid balance may be stated in conjunction with, but not more conspicuously than, the annual percentage rate.

1. Triggering terms. If any of the following terms are set forth in an advertisement, the advertisement shall meet the requirements of paragraph (d)(2) of this section:

a. The amount or percentage of any down payment.

b. The number of payments or period of repayment.

c. The amount of any payment.

d. The amount of any finance charge.

2. Additional terms. An advertisement stating any of the terms in paragraph (d)(1) of this section shall state the following terms, as applicable (an example of one or more typical extensions of credit with a statement of all the terms applicable to each may be used):

a. The amount or percentage of the down payment.

b. The terms of repayment, which reflect the repayment obligations over the full term of the loan, including any balloon payment.

c. The "annual percentage rate," using that term, and, if the rate may be increased after consummation, that fact. (Consumer Finance website)

Complete details concerning advertising can be found here: https://www.consumerfinance.gov/rules-policy/regulations/1026/24/

Real Estate Settlement Procedures Act (RESPA): This law was passed by Congress in 1974. RESPA's main objective is to protect homeowners by helping them become better educated about real estate services. Another focus is the elimination of referral fees and kickbacks. Each of those practices adds an extra financial burden to settlement services. Lenders, according to RESPA, are required to provide borrowers with timely and applicable disclosures. The goal is to make the real estate settlement process clear and understandable. RESPA applies to mortgage-secured loans for residential properties for one to four families. You will see sample forms at the end of the chapter.

TILA-RESPA Integrated Disclosure Rule (TRID): TRID informs consumers applying for a mortgage and defines compliance rules for lenders. TRID is a combination of TILA and RESPA. TRID's guidelines outline which information mortgage lenders must provide to borrowers, along with when the information must be provided. Rules from TRID regulate the fees that lenders can charge, as well as how these fees can shift as the loan matures. The goal is to empower borrowers to better understand the mortgage options available to them and make an informed, smart decision regarding which option to select. As of 2015, all mortgage lenders are required to follow TRID rules when offering estimates and issuing mortgages. A nickname for TRID rules is the "Know Before You Owe" rules.

Secure and Fair Enforcement for Mortgage Licensing Act (SAFE): HUD explains the SAFE Act as:

"The SAFE Mortgage Licensing Act is designed to enhance consumer protection and reduce fraud by encouraging states to establish minimum standards for the licensing and registration of state-licensed mortgage loan originators and for the Conference of State Bank Supervisors (CSBS) and the American Association of Residential Mortgage Regulators (AARMR) to establish and maintain a nationwide mortgage licensing system and registry for the residential mortgage industry. The SAFE Act sets a minimum standard for licensing and registering mortgage loan originators. Specific state licensing requirements can be found at the Nationwide Mortgage Licensing System Registry (NMLSR). Mortgage loan originators employed by a federally regulated depository or a regulated subsidiary can learn the registration requirements on the NMLSR website or from their employer's federal bank regulator." (HUD)

Equal Credit Opportunity Act (ECOA):

"The ECOA was enacted October 28th, 1974. The FTC, the nation's consumer protection agency, enforces the Equal Credit Opportunity Act (ECOA), which prohibits credit discrimination on the basis of race, color, religion, national origin, sex, marital status, age, or because you get public assistance. Creditors may ask you for most of this information in certain situations, but they may not use it when deciding whether to give you credit or when setting the terms of your credit. Not everyone who applies for credit gets it or gets the same terms: Factors like income, expenses, debts, and credit history are among the considerations lenders use to determine your creditworthiness. (FTC)

Additionally, something very important that is also conveyed on the website is this:

"Know why your application was rejected. The creditor must tell you the specific reason for the rejection or that you are entitled to learn the reason if you ask within 60 days. An acceptable reason might be: 'your income was too low' or 'you haven't been employed long enough.' An unacceptable reason might be 'you didn't meet our minimum standards.' That information isn't specific enough." (FTC)

Homeowners Protection Act (HPA):

"The Homeowners Protection Act of 1998 became effective in July 1999. The act, also known as the PMI Cancellation Act, addresses the difficulties homeowners have experienced in canceling private mortgage insurance (PMI) coverage. It establishes provisions for the cancellation and termination of PMI, sets forth disclosure and notification requirements, and requires the return of unearned premiums. It allows prospective buyers who cannot, or choose not to, make a significant down payment to obtain mortgage financing at an affordable rate." (Federal Reserve)

The Community Reinvestment Act (CRA):

> "The Community Reinvestment Act (CRA), enacted in 1977, requires the Federal Reserve and other federal banking regulators to encourage financial institutions to help meet the credit needs of the communities in which they do business, including low- and moderate-income (LMI) neighborhoods (Federal Reserve).
>
> The Community Reinvestment Act, or CRA, became law in 1977 and remains one of the seminal pieces of legislation to address systemic inequities in access to credit." (Office of The Comptroller of The Currency)

One goal of the CRA was to eliminate the unfair practice of redlining. Redlining, in its broadest sense and definition, is withholding services (financial or other) from residents of specific geographical areas. Most common, the practice is based on ethnicity or race. Also, it is usually done systematically. It is not random. It's intentional. Redlining has nothing to do with the applicant's financial qualifications or creditworthiness. In the real estate industry, redlining is a form of lending discrimination. It is the unethical practice of denying mortgage loans (or insurance policies) to residents of a certain race or in specific geographical areas. As mentioned before, it commonly revolves around skin color or cultural background. Generally, it is minority neighborhoods that experience the majority of redlining. Although redlining has been illegal for decades, its scars are still present in communities throughout the US. Who is responsible for the CRA? This duty lies with the Federal Deposit Insurance Corporation (FDIC), Federal Reserve Board (FRB), and the Office of the Comptroller of the Currency (OCC).

Although other laws and regulations can also apply, these apply *specifically* to FDIC-supervised institutions:

- Truth in Lending Act

- Ability-to-Repay/Qualified Mortgage Rule

- Real Estate Settlement Procedures Act

- TILA-RESPA Integrated Disclosure Rule

- Flood Insurance

  - Part 339—Loans in Areas Having Special Flood Hazard

- Servicing

  - Mortgage Servicing Rules provides access to the details on the sections of Regulation X—Real Estate Settlement Procedures and Regulation Z—Truth in Lending that apply to mortgage servicing.

- Homeowners Protection Act

- Secure and Fair Enforcement for Mortgage Licensing Act

    - Part 1008—SAFE Mortgage Licensing Act (Regulation H) provides access to regulatory information regarding the secure and fair enforcement for the Mortgage Licensing Act (FDIC)

REAL ESTATE SETTLEMENT TIMELINE

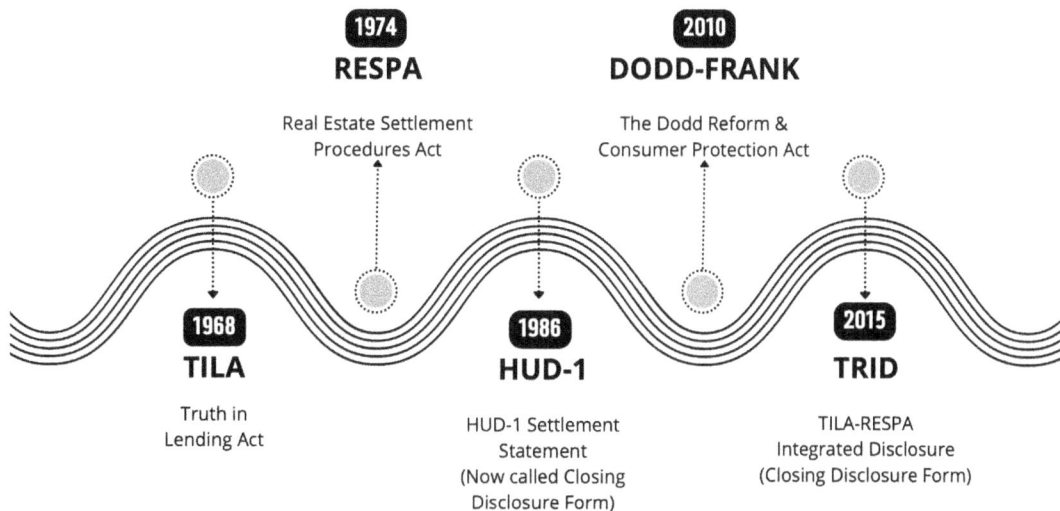

1974
RESPA
Real Estate Settlement
Procedures Act

2010
DODD-FRANK
The Dodd Reform &
Consumer Protection Act

1968
TILA
Truth in
Lending Act

1986
HUD-1
HUD-1 Settlement
Statement
(Now called Closing
Disclosure Form)

2015
TRID
TILA-RESPA
Integrated Disclosure
(Closing Disclosure Form)

At the end of this chapter before your quiz, you will see a sample closing disclosure form provided by the Consumer Financial Protection Bureau. It is called "TILA RESPA Integrated Disclosure: H-25(B) Mortgage Loan Transaction Closing Disclosure – Fixed Rate Loan Sample."

FRAUD IN THE MORTGAGE INDUSTRY

The topic of fraud is one that cannot be ignored or avoided when talking about mortgage financing. Here is what the FBI says about mortgage fraud.

"It is crime characterized by some type of material misstatement, misrepresentation, or omission in relation to a mortgage loan which is then relied upon by a lender. A lie that influences a bank's decision—about whether, for example, to approve a loan, accept a reduced payoff amount, or agree to certain repayment terms—is mortgage fraud. The FBI and other entities charged with investigating mortgage fraud, particularly in the wake of the housing market collapse, have broadened the definition to include frauds targeting distressed homeowners." FBI

With that context in mind, read the related definitions below.

- **Bait and switch:** A deceptive sales technique that dishonestly advertises a particular product or rate to the consumers in order to attract them (i.e., bait). Then, the lender persuades and/or manipulates the consumer to agree to less favorable terms (i.e., switch). By doing so, the lender is able to generate more profit by earning a much higher fee. The majority of states have consumer protection laws that make this strategy illegal.

- **Collusion:** Secret agreement or cooperation between people, especially for deceitful or fraudulent purposes.

- **Equity skimming:** Any scam, scheme, or deceptive practice that is designed to steal equity from a homeowner.

- **Extreme lending:** Lending to a borrower who has extremely high debt in relation to income.

- **Flipping (legal):** Purchasing a piece of property, and immediately reselling it for a profit, usually after making strategic improvements to the property.

- **Flipping (illegal):** Purchasing a piece of property at a low price with the intention of reselling it for an unrealistic price so you can make a large profit. Generally, only small improvements are made, if any at all.

  - "A con artist buys a property with the intent to re-sell it an artificially inflated price for a considerable profit, even though they only make minor improvements to it." FBI

- **Identity theft:** A crime that occurs when someone uses another person's identity in order to commit fraud and/or other crimes. Generally, the information used includes the victim's personally identifying information (such as name, debit card number, credit card number, social security number, etc.). A criminal may use this information for any variety of actions, including but not limited to applying for loans, making small and/or large purchases, paying medical bills and opening an account in the victim's name.

- **Inflated appraisal:** Valuing property higher than it's actually worth, resulting in lenders issuing loans for more than a home's real value.

- **Loan flipping:** Refinancing a property over and over again.

- **Material misstatement:** False statement of facts.

- **Misrepresentation:** False or altered information which may include but is not limited to a borrower's income, credit history, credit rating, and/or the buyer's identity.

- **Omission:** There are two types of omission.

  - Intentional omission: Purposefully not reporting information that would disqualify someone for a loan.

  - Innocent omission: Accidentally failing to report information that may impact a person's ability to qualify for a loan.

- **Packing a loan:** "The term 'packing' in this case refers to the practice of automatically including optional insurance in the loan amount without the consumer's request; as a result, some consumers may perceive that the insurance is a required part of the loan, and others may not be aware that insurance has been included" Federal Register.

  - Note: This could include health, disability, accident, and/or unemployment insurance although it is not limited to those.

- **Phishing:** This happens when a cybercriminal or hacker pretends to be a legitimate business or other institution in order to steal confidential and/or sensitive information from the victim. It can also be a way to place ransomware on the victim's laptop or network. Most commonly, phishing is done through legitimate-looking and professionally designed emails.

- **Straw buyer:** Straw buying may be legal or illegal. It comes down to intent. This term can also be called a straw owner or straw purchaser.

  - Legal: When done legally, it falls under the concept of assignment. It is a business action that authorizes one person to tender an offer to buy real estate with the intent to transfer the buying power to an unnamed third party.

  - Illegal: When done illegally, a person receives payment for the use of another person's name and credit history to apply for a loan, generally as part of a mortgage fraud scheme.

- **Triggering term:** Words or phrases that require a disclosure when used in advertising are referred to as "trigger terms." These disclosures are required by the Truth in Lending Act (TILA), which is intended to safeguard consumers against inaccurate and misleading financial terms. Triggering terms can also be called trigger phrases. Examples include "No interest", "No prepayment penalty" and "Zero APR."

MORTGAGE FRAUD

Mortgage fraud can and does happen even today. It is a criminal offense and can be classified as bank fraud, wire fraud, mail fraud, and/or money laundering. Mortgage fraud occurs when a party in a mortgage loan transaction misrepresents material facts and/or conceals important information in order to obtain a mortgage loan. It may result in significant financial losses. Penalties can be steep and can include jail time. This type of fraud impacts lenders. As you will see below, not all perpetrators have the same objective. The FBI website shares that mortgage loan fraud is divided into two primary categories.

1. Fraud for housing

Fraud for housing, also called fraud for property and mortgage fraud, is motivated by the desire to gain access to property or housing. Using fraud to obtain tangible goods, such as cars, electronics, or jewelry, usually falls into this category as well. This type of fraud is usually done by borrowers. It occurs when a person intentionally misrepresents facts or deceives another person in order to obtain property or some other type of benefit. Fraud can take many forms and may involve a variety of people who scheme together.

Examples of fraud for property include identity theft, mortgage fraud, and embezzlement. Identity theft is employed in order to steal someone's personal information in order to gain access to their property or bank accounts.

This type of fraud is typically represented by illegal actions taken by a borrower motivated to acquire or maintain ownership of a house (FBI).

Examples of mortgage fraud include but are not limited to the following:

- A buyer intentionally lies on a loan application.

- A false statement is purposefully made on a loan application.

- A borrower misrepresents his/her income or assets.

- An appraiser artificially increases the property value, although he/she knows the property is not worth how much the appraisal report states it is worth.

- A borrower submits a loan application on behalf of a different person without their permission.

- A scammer obtains a loan under false pretenses, such as using someone else's identity to take out a loan, or taking out a loan for a property that does not actually exist.

With the increase of electronic banking and other forms of e-commerce, we are warned of the dangers of personal data becoming public. The threat of someone taking possession of a social security, bank account, or credit card number has led to many forms of security measures, privacy policies, and protection programs.

Examples of identity theft include:

- Stealing a customer's identity.

- Using false names and other information with the purpose of securing a loan.

- An appraiser using another individual's name to submit falsified reports.

How can a licensee or other party know that he/she is being targeted for fraud? What are the red flags and indicators? Here are a few:

- Fraudulent loan applications. A borrower may be coached by the loan officer into lying on the application. The false information may include a stolen social security number or non-reporting of credit card debt.

- A statement that coerces the buyer, claiming he/she will personally live in the home, when in fact, they intend to make it a rental property.

- Bogus supporting loan documentation. This may include employment verification, gift letters, credit reports, and so on. This may enable a risky borrower to secure a loan that would not have been possible otherwise.

- Higher-than-market appraisals. Higher appraisal values are frequently associated with housing bubbles. This occurs when the demand for housing increases exponentially but the supply is low. Limited supply coupled with high demand causes housing values to increase. This frequently is enhanced by low interest rates. Inflated values are typically much higher than the normal sale prices for comparable homes. This wide difference should alert the researcher to a potentially inflated value.

2. Fraud for profit

Fraud for profit is a criminal activity in which individuals and organizations manipulate the mortgage loan process in order to obtain some type of financial benefit. Its purpose is *not* to secure a property or housing. Cash and/or equity are the focus. Greed is usually the main driver. Generally, fraud for profit involves activities such as money laundering, investment scheme fraud, identity theft, false advertising, loan fraud, insurance fraud, and credit card fraud. It is common for these criminals to target vulnerable individuals and/or organizations.

"Those who commit this type of mortgage fraud are often industry insiders using their specialized knowledge or authority to commit or facilitate the fraud. Current investigations and widespread reporting indicate a high percentage of mortgage fraud involves collusion by industry insiders, such as bank officers, appraisers, mortgage brokers, attorneys, loan originators, and other professionals engaged in the industry. Fraud for profit aims not to secure housing, but rather to misuse the mortgage lending process to steal cash and equity from lenders or homeowners. The FBI prioritizes fraud for profit cases." FBI

Real Estate Brokers and Fraud

There are many ways a real estate broker can knowingly participate in mortgage fraud schemes, including:

1. Inventing straw buyers

2. Falsifying MLS records

3. Preparing false appraisal reports themselves

These are all examples of unethical practices that are strictly prohibited and punishable as violations under the law. Let's look at the details of each malicious practice.

Inventing straw buyers: An unethical real estate agent may assist the lender by inventing a fictitious buyer, known as a straw buyer. Often, the straw buyer is the real estate broker or even the lender. Buyers who are commonly named as an "LLC" or "LTD" often are found to be straw buyers; the company name hides that of the real borrower. This type of fraud may occur as part of an illegal flipping scheme.

Falsifying MLS records: Illegal flipping schemes often involve properties in disrepair. Unscrupulous real estate brokers may falsify MLS records to indicate a home has been repaired and remodeled when, in fact, it has not been. Another example is a broker who intentionally deceives potential buyers by showing property images that have been virtually staged while purposefully hiding the true condition of the property.

Preparing bogus appraisal reports: Some documented instances of appraiser identity theft have involved real estate brokers using appraisal software to prepare the appraisal report. Then, a licensed appraiser's name and signature are stolen and applied to the report.

HOW ARE LAND SALES REGULATED?

Joe and Shannon live in Lexington, Kentucky. They are moving to Peoria, Illinois, and want to purchase property there. How does a scenario with out-of-state buyers work? The answer comes in the form of legislation called the Interstate Land Sales Full Disclosure Act of 1968. It's sometimes referred to as ILSFDA or ILSA.

ILSA's goals are to oversee the regulation of interstate land sales for out-of-state buyers and to protect and safeguard consumers from abuse and fraud from unscrupulous salespeople and/ or developers. This applies to both selling/buying land and leasing. It most commonly covers large-scale developments. Non-compliance with ILSA can currently result in fines of $10,000 or more, and/or prison time, which is usually five years or fewer. The Consumer Financial Protection Bureau is responsible for overseeing and administering the Interstate Land Sales Full Disclosure Act.

> "The Interstate Land Sales Full Disclosure Act prohibits developers and their agents from selling or leasing, by mail or by means of interstate commerce, any lot in any subdivision of 100 or more nonexempt lots unless a Statement of Record is filed with HUD that discloses and documents current information about the ownership of the land; the state of title; physical characteristics; planned availability of roads, services and utilities; and other matters and the information in the Statement of Record is delivered to each purchaser or lessee in advance of signing the contract or agreement. The Act also contains antifraud provisions, applicable to subdivisions with 25 or more lots, which prohibit developers from engaging in misleading sales practices. Any willful violation of The Act is subject to criminal penalties of imprisonment or fine, civil damages, civil money penalties, or suspension of registration." (HUD)

The Illinois Mortgage Fraud Task Force

In response to fraud, the Illinois Mortgage Fraud Task Force was formed in 2006. It is composed of investigators, managers, and attorneys representing the three IDFPR divisions, which are Financial Institutions, Banking, and Professional Regulation. Its mission is to investigate and stop mortgage fraud. It has the authority to examine every aspect of a residential real estate transaction, from listing a property for sale to the closing of the purchase and sale transaction. According to a press release published on May 13, 2009, by the IDFPR:

> "The Mortgage Fraud Task Force (MFTF) has taken disciplinary action against more than 70 persons and entities and assessed fines in excess of $200,000 since its inception." In 2008, "the MFTF conducted a regulatory sweep of more than 150 mortgage companies to ensure that they were complying with a new law that established stricter underwriting standards for mortgage companies." IDFPR

There is also the Illinois Consumer Fraud and Deceptive Business Practices Act (815 ILCS 505/7). It is patterned after Section 5 of the Federal Trade Commission Act. This act allows the Attorney General to bring actions. It also allows the court to exercise all powers necessary, including injunctive relief, restitution, and/or civil penalties. The Illinois Consumer Fraud and Deceptive Business Practices Act states the following:

- Whenever the Attorney General or a State's Attorney has reason to believe that any person is using, has used, or is about to use any method, act or practice declared by this Act to be unlawful, and that proceedings would be in the public interest, he or she may bring an action in the name of the People of the State against such person to restrain by preliminary or permanent injunction the use of such method, act or practice. The Court, in its discretion, may exercise all powers necessary, including but not limited to: injunction; revocation, forfeiture or suspension of any license, charter, franchise, certificate or other evidence of authority of any person to do business in this State; appointment of a receiver; dissolution of domestic corporations or association suspension or termination of the right of foreign corporations or associations to do business in this State; and restitution.

- In addition to the remedies provided herein, the Attorney General or State's Attorney may request and the Court may impose a civil penalty in a sum not to exceed $50,000 against any person found by the Court to have engaged in any method, act or practice declared unlawful under this Act. In the event the court finds the method, act or practice to have been entered into with the intent to defraud, the court has the authority to impose a civil penalty in a sum not to exceed $50,000 per violation.

- In addition to any other civil penalty provided in this Section, if a person is found by the court to have engaged in any method, act, or practice declared unlawful under this Act, and the violation was committed against a person 65 years of age or older, the court may impose an additional civil penalty not to exceed $10,000 for each violation.

  - A civil penalty imposed under this subsection (c) shall be paid to the State Treasurer who shall deposit the money in the State treasury in a special fund designated the Department on Aging State Projects Fund. The Treasurer shall deposit such moneys into the Fund monthly. All of the moneys deposited into the Fund shall be appropriated to the Department on Aging for grants to senior centers in Illinois.

  - An award of restitution under subsection (a) has priority over a civil penalty imposed by the court under this subsection.

  - In determining whether to impose a civil penalty under this subsection and the amount of any penalty, the court shall consider the following:

    - Whether the defendant's conduct was in willful disregard of the rights of the person 65 years of age or older.

- Whether the defendant knew or should have known that the defendant's conduct was directed to a person 65 years of age or older.

- Whether the person 65 years of age or older was substantially more vulnerable to the defendant's conduct because of age, poor health, infirmity, impaired understanding, restricted mobility, or disability, than other persons.

- Any other factors the court deems appropriate.

- This Section applies if: (i) a court orders a party to make payments to the Attorney General and the payments are to be used for the operations of the Office of the Attorney General or (ii) a party agrees, in an Assurance of Voluntary Compliance under this Act, to make payments to the Attorney General for the operations of the Office of the Attorney General.

- Moneys paid under any of the conditions described in subsection (d) shall be deposited into the Attorney General Court Ordered and Voluntary Compliance Payment Projects Fund, which is created as a special fund in the State Treasury. Moneys in the Fund shall be used, subject to appropriation, for the performance of any function pertaining to the exercise of the duties of the Attorney General including but not limited to enforcement of any law of this State and conducting public education programs; however, any moneys in the Fund that are required by the court or by an agreement to be used for a particular purpose shall be used for that purpose. (815 ILCS 505/7)

Predatory Lending

Predatory lending is an illegal practice that includes unethical and intentional methods implemented by lending institutions during a loan origination process. These practices are deceptive, misleading, unfair, and fraudulent. The FDIC says predatory lending means "posing unfair and abusive loan terms on borrowers." Predatory lending methods may include coercion, manipulation, shaming, and more. The borrower could potentially be stripped of equity. The sales tactics can be very aggressive and/or intentionally confusing.

"Predatory lending typically affects senior citizens, lower income and challenged credit borrowers. Predatory lending forces borrowers to pay exorbitant loan origination/settlement fees, subprime or higher interest rates, and in some cases, unreasonable servicing fees. These practices often result in the borrower defaulting on his mortgage payment and undergoing foreclosure or forced refinancing." (FBI Archives)

According to two online publications by the Illinois Attorney General, red flags and warning signs of predatory lending include:

- **False or misleading promises.** Be wary of claims that sound too good to be true. Common terms include ones like:

    - "Easy credit!"

    - "We say yes to anybody!"

    - "No out-of-pocket expenses."

    - "Easy payment terms."

    - "No payment for 60/90/120 days or more."

    - And other enticing come-ons.

- **Excessive fees.** Loan fees should be no more than 3% (e.g., $3,000 on a loan of $100,000). Fees over 5% of the loan amount are excessive. A best practice is to ask the broker or lender for an itemization of the loan amount with all fees explained. When dealing with a mortgage broker, find out how the broker will be paid.

- **Excessive mortgage broker compensation (yield spread premiums).** Brokers may receive extra compensation from lenders called a yield spread premium; the extra compensation is earned when the *broker signs the borrower to a loan with a higher interest rate that is excessive. (Note: *mortgage broker.)

- **High or adjustable interest rates.** Use caution if a loan interest rate is adjustable. Ask how much the rate can increase over the life of the loan. A loan with an adjustable rate often starts out with reasonable monthly payments, but the adjustable rate can increase over time, making it unaffordable. A low introductory interest rate that can increase during the loan term is known as a teaser rate.

- **Excessive prepayment penalties.** Prepayment penalties are fees charged by lenders to the borrower for paying off a loan early. Prepayment penalties can negatively impact a borrower's options in the future to refinance for better loan terms or pay off a loan early because the borrower will be required to pay an excessive fee. A best practice is to find out whether a mortgage includes a prepayment penalty, how much it is, and how long it will be in place.

- **"End of Loan" features.** Be aware of loan terms that do not come into play until the end of the loan. These features can include balloon payments (a large payment due at the end of a loan, typically following lower monthly payments).

- **Equity stripping.** A predatory lender may loan more than you can pay every month and wait for you to default on your loan. The predatory lender can then foreclose on your house and strip you of your equity. Be suspicious if a lender makes the decision to offer a mortgage on the equity in a borrower's home instead of her income.

- **Loan flipping or repeated refinancing.** When a loan is refinanced, the lender charges fees that increase the amount the borrower owes, but the borrower does not realize any actual benefit from the refinance. Beware if a borrower has been making payments and a broker or lender encourages the borrower to refinance without realizing any real benefits.

- **Misstated income.** An unethical lender may suggest that a borrower could qualify for a higher loan amount by including income on the loan application that doesn't exist, or by inflating the borrower's income on the loan application. This practice is an example of mortgage fraud. Pay attention if a broker or lender changes any of the income information a borrower has provided. This practice could qualify the borrower for a loan his income may not support. (Illinois Attorney General)

Sources: "Predatory Lending" and "Looking for a Home Loan? How To Avoid Predatory Mortgage Lending and Get A Loan You Can Afford" PDFs by the Illinois Attorney General.

Targets of predatory lending can include but are not limited to the following:

- Older adults who have paid off their home loan.

  - They may have no real need for a loan. However, the terms being offered appear to be irresistible and very tempting. The older adult may be convinced that the loan terms are a once-in-a-lifetime offer and may possibly feel pressured to take action quickly.

- Middle-income consumers.

  - Many times, this category of consumers is interested in paying off high interest credit card balances. They may want to consolidate medical debts or other debts, or they might be tempted to make a dream purchase.

- Borrowers who have lower incomes and/or weak credit, and/or who have experienced bankruptcy.

  - They may be made to feel lucky to receive a loan and may form a bond with the lender who is "helping them." They may be misinformed, low-income, and/or hard-to-finance individuals who become easy targets for high-pressure tactics or mortgage fraud scams.

- Desperate borrowers.

- They possibly might be on the verge of foreclosure, have a large IRS tax problem, be dealing with the financial aftermath of a death in the family, feel buried in medical debt, and/or be confronting some type of personal emergency. They might be vulnerable to marketing terms like "last chance offer" and other types of scare tactics.

A related piece of legislature that was created to combat fraud is called the **Home Ownership Equity Protection Act (HOEPA).**

"The Home Ownership and Equity Protection Act was enacted in 1994 as an amendment to the Truth in Lending Act (TILA) to address abusive practices in refinances and closed-end home equity loans with high interest rates or high fees. Since HOEPA's enactment, refinances or home equity mortgage loans meeting any of HOEPA's high-cost coverage tests have been subject to special disclosure requirements and restrictions on loan terms, and consumers with high-cost mortgages have had enhanced remedies for violations of the law." CFPB

"The Home Ownership and Equity Protection Act of 1994 (HOEPA) amended the TILA. The law imposed new disclosure requirements and substantive limitations on certain closed-end mortgage loans bearing rates or fees above a certain percentage or amount. The law also included new disclosure requirements to assist consumers in comparing the costs and other material considerations involved in a reverse mortgage transaction and authorized the Federal Reserve Board to prohibit specific acts and practices in connection with mortgage transactions." CFPB

These consumer protection tips about predatory lending come from the FDIC and can be helpful to you, your clients, friends, and family.

- Ask yourself: Do I really need this loan?

- Deal with a reputable lender.

- Ask questions and shop around.

- Understand the importance of credit reports and credit scores.

- Know what you are signing.

- Speak up if you think you've been treated improperly.

Source: "High-Cost 'Predatory' Home Loans: How to Avoid the Traps" PDF by the FDIC.

Illinois High Risk Home Loan Act

The purpose of the Illinois High Risk Home Loan Act (815 ILCS 137) reads as follows.

> "The purpose of this Act is to protect borrowers who enter into high risk home loans from abuse that occurs in the credit marketplace when creditors and brokers are not sufficiently regulated in Illinois. This Act is to be construed as a borrower protection statute for all purposes. This Act shall be liberally construed to effectuate its purpose." (815 ILCS 137)

A wide variety of provisions and restrictions related to high-risk home loans include but are not limited to topics such as:

- Verification of the borrower's ability to repay the loan and the minimum requirements for verification

- Good faith dealings and fraudulent or deceptive practices

  - "A lender must act in good faith in all relations with a borrower, including but not limited to, transferring, dealing in, offering, or making a high risk home loan. No lender shall employ fraudulent or deceptive acts or practices in the making of a high risk home loan, including deceptive marketing and sales efforts." (815 ILCS 137/25)

- No prepayment penalty

  - "A high risk home loan may not contain terms under which a consumer must pay a prepayment penalty for paying all or part of the principal before the date on which the principal is due." (815 ILCS 137/30)

- Bona fide discount points

  - "Bona fide discount points" means loan discount points that are knowingly paid by the consumer for the purpose of reducing, and that in fact result in a bona fide reduction of, the interest rate or time price differential applicable to the mortgage." (815 ILCS 137/10)

- No balloon payments

- Pre-paid insurance products and warranties

- Certain cases in which refinancing is prohibited

- Financing of points and fees

- Payments to contractors

- Negative amortization (which is not allowed)

- Negative equity (which is not allowed)

- How late payment fees work

- What happens when a borrower fails to make his/her installment payment

- Compounding payments (which is not allowed)

  - No lender shall transfer, deal in, offer, or make a high risk home loan that includes terms under which more than 2 periodic payments required under the loan are consolidated and paid in advance from the loan proceeds provided to the borrower. (815 ILCS 137/85)

- Call provision

  - No lender shall transfer, deal in, offer, or make a high risk home loan that contains a provision that permits the lender, in its sole discretion, to accelerate the indebtedness, provided that this provision does not prohibit acceleration of a loan in good faith due to a borrower's failure to abide by the material terms of the loan. (815 ILCS 137/90)

- Modification and deferral fees (which are prohibited)

  - A lender, successor in interest, assignee, or any agent of any of the foregoing may not charge a consumer any fee to modify, renew, extend, or amend a high risk home loan or to defer any payment due under the terms of the loan. (815 ILCS 137/90.5)

- Disclosure prior to making a high risk home loan

- Counseling prior to perfecting foreclosure proceedings and the right to cure

- Report of default and foreclosure rates on conventional loans (815 ILCS/137)

The Illinois High Risk Home Loan Act defines the **Mortgage Awareness Program** (MAP) as follows.

"The Mortgage Awareness Program is a counseling and educational component that must be provided in Illinois by the Director of Financial Institutions and the Commissioner of the Office of Banks and Real Estate." (815 ILCS 137/110)

Created to protect consumers, the goal of MAP is to provide a comprehensive and objective explanation of a high-cost loan to each prospective borrower. The core curriculum of the Mortgage Awareness Program is required to give clear information about the amount financed,

APR, total payments, right of rescission, significant debt ratios, credit options, and much more.

To further protect consumers, the IDFPR website shares the following information.

> "Understand your contract: When purchasing a new home or refinancing an existing mortgage, consumers must make important financial decisions. Be sure that you are well informed and aware of all your options. Listed below are several terms that are frequently used in the lending industry.

> - Knowing them is the first step to understanding a loan contract and making an educated borrowing decision. Before you sign any loan document, be sure to review the following terms in the contract:

> - Know the annual percentage rate (APR)—This is the cost of your credit as a yearly rate. When shopping for a loan, compare the APR offered by various lenders.

> - Know the finance charge—The finance charge is the dollar amount the credit will cost you. It is based on the APR, the amount borrowed, and the length of the loan. Beware of hidden charges!

> - Know the amount financed—This is the dollar amount of the credit that is provided to you by your lenders.

> - Know if you are paying "points"—"Points" are fees you pay to a lender to obtain a real estate secured loan. These prepaid finance charges are not refundable.

> - Know the total number and exact dollar amount of each payment—This will help you determine if the loan is within your budget. It is important to also consider other possible contract terms, such as "balloon payments," when examining the cost and affordability of the loan.

> - Know the payment date—This is the date the payment must be received by the lender.

> - Know about collateral—Collateral is property that is used to secure a loan. If a borrower defaults on the loan, the lender may take your collateral. In a real estate loan your home is your collateral.

> - Know the total dollar amount of payments—The total amount paid over the term of the loan after you have made all payments as scheduled."

Source: A MAP to Home Ownership—Don't Fall Prey to Predatory Lending.

Every licensee must do his or her due diligence in only referring clients to reputable and trustworthy lending institutions, especially considering that each licensee is a fiduciary.

Types of Fraud

As you know, fraud is a planned and intentional deception, misrepresentation, lie, or a series of lies done in order to unfairly win or gain something. Hiding and concealing information (such as material facts) and making false and/or misleading statements are considered fraud. There are two types of fraud:

1. Actual fraud

2. Constructive fraud

Actual fraud is intentional. It involves intentional lies or misrepresentations made by a licensee to a consumer. It involves a licensee making false or misleading statements and/or omitting key facts in order to manipulate a consumer into a transaction. Actual fraud can occur when facts are intentionally ignored, hidden, and/or altered. This kind of fraud occurs when a licensee uses his/her superior knowledge of the market and industry to take advantage of a customer without disclosing all relevant and pertinent information.

Constructive fraud is unintentional. There is no plan or goal to deceive or mislead the consumer. This occurs when a licensee accidentally lies or omits (leaves out) some type of important information or makes a misleading statement, usually due to a lack of knowledge. If a licensee omits important information and that causes the licensee to benefit in some way, he/she may be guilty of constructive fraud.

Both types of fraud can occur in real estate transactions and can have serious and costly consequences for customers. When a licensee fails to disclose the information required, it can be a form of fraud.

There are three primary ways in which intentional fraud can be committed:

1. **Material misrepresentation**

   - This is an intentional false statement of fact (assertion) that pressures, entices, and/or manipulates a party to say yes to a contract. When this type of fraud occurs, the buyer may be entitled to compensation if they can prove that the seller intentionally misled them in order to influence their decision to enter the contract. It is important for buyers and sellers to be aware of these potential risks, and to make sure all information disclosed is accurate and honest.

   - Material misrepresentation can take many forms in real estate. Examples include but are not limited to:

- A seller misrepresents the square footage of their property to make it appear more desirable in order to increase the asking price.

- A licensee or seller can fail to disclose a known defect or issue with the property.

2. **Material misstatement**

- This intentional action occurs when a seller or licensee presents wrong or misleading information about any aspect of the property, such as its size or condition. An inaccurate statement can lead to an unfair or illegal transaction, or some other type of backlash and consequences. Licensees must be aware of potential material misstatements and take steps to confirm the accuracy of any information given.

- Examples include but are not limited to:

  - A home seller may misrepresent the size of a home in order to secure a higher rental rate.

  - A property owner may misstate the amount of debt on the property to get a lower interest rate on a loan.

  - A condominium seller claims that their property is free of termites, when in fact it has a history of termites.

3. **Omission**

- As you recall, intentional omission means leaving out or not communicating something important. Omission is a type of fraud in which one party knowingly and willfully fails to disclose information that would have an impact on the other party's decision.

- Examples include but are not limited to:

  - A seller fails to disclose that the property has experienced flooding in the past and knows that this will impact the property's future. If the seller fails to disclose this fact, and the buyer purchases the property unaware of the flooding, this would be considered a material omission. In some cases, this may entitle the buyer to damages or even a rescission of the contract.

  - A licensee fails to communicate that the city council intends to rezone the property, resulting in a reduced market value in the near future.

Material misrepresentation, material misstatement, and omission are all terms used to describe the intentional or unintentional act of misrepresenting facts.

Closing Disclosure Form

The Closing Disclosure is the document that shows the detailed and complete accounting for a real estate transaction. It is the balance sheet where all of the money that a buyer or seller owes/pays at closing is shown. It itemizes each party's debits and credits by showing the amount each party will receive and/or be required to pay at the closing. It is most often prepared by the settlement agent (closing agent) but can be prepared by the lender. This document is the standardized form required for all 1-4 family dwellings under RESPA. The form must be available to the borrower at least three business days prior to the closing, per RESPA requirements. Note that the bottom line for a buyer is how much money he or she is required to bring to settlement. The bottom line for a seller is how much money he or she will leave the transaction with, although sometimes it shows what he or she is required to bring to settlement. The Closing Disclosure is also called the settlement statement. It was previously called the HUD-1 Settlement Statement.

> "This is a sample of a completed Closing Disclosure for the fixed rate loan illustrated by form H-24(B). The purpose, product, sale price, loan amount, loan term, and interest rate have not changed from the estimates provided on the Loan Estimate. The creditor requires an escrow account and that the consumer pay for private mortgage insurance for the transaction." Consumer Financial Protection Bureau

Take a moment and review the Loan Estimate and Closing Disclosure forms below. Then, take the quiz.

FICUS BANK
4321 Random Boulevard · Somecity, ST 12340

Save this Loan Estimate to compare with your Closing Disclosure.

Loan Estimate

DATE ISSUED	2/15/2013
APPLICANTS	Michael Jones and Mary Stone
	123 Anywhere Street
	Anytown, ST 12345
PROPERTY	456 Somewhere Avenue
	Anytown, ST 12345
SALE PRICE	$180,000

LOAN TERM	30 years
PURPOSE	Purchase
PRODUCT	Fixed Rate
LOAN TYPE	☒ Conventional ☐FHA ☐VA ☐_____
LOAN ID #	123456789
RATE LOCK	☐ NO ☒ YES, until 4/16/2013 at 5:00 p.m. EDT

*Before closing, your interest rate, points, and lender credits can change unless you lock the interest rate. All other estimated closing costs expire on **3/4/2013** at 5:00 p.m. EDT*

Loan Terms

		Can this amount increase after closing?
Loan Amount	$162,000	**NO**
Interest Rate	3.875%	**NO**
Monthly Principal & Interest *See Projected Payments below for your Estimated Total Monthly Payment*	$761.78	**NO**
		Does the loan have these features?
Prepayment Penalty		**YES** · **As high as $3,240** if you pay off the loan during the first 2 years
Balloon Payment		**NO**

Projected Payments

Payment Calculation	Years 1-7	Years 8-30
Principal & Interest	$761.78	$761.78
Mortgage Insurance	+ 82	+ —
Estimated Escrow *Amount can increase over time*	+ 206	+ 206
Estimated Total Monthly Payment	**$1,050**	**$968**

		This estimate includes	In escrow?
Estimated Taxes, Insurance & Assessments *Amount can increase over time*	**$206** a month	☒ Property Taxes	YES
		☒ Homeowner's Insurance	YES
		☐ Other:	
		See Section G on page 2 for escrowed property costs. You must pay for other property costs separately.	

Costs at Closing

Estimated Closing Costs	$8,054	Includes $5,672 in Loan Costs + $2,382 in Other Costs – $0 in Lender Credits. *See page 2 for details.*
Estimated Cash to Close	$16,054	Includes Closing Costs. *See Calculating Cash to Close on page 2 for details.*

Visit **www.consumerfinance.gov/mortgage-estimate** for general information and tools.

Additional Information About This Loan

LENDER	Ficus Bank
NMLS/__ LICENSE ID	
LOAN OFFICER	Joe Smith
NMLS/__ LICENSE ID	12345
EMAIL	joesmith@ficusbank.com
PHONE	123-456-7890

MORTGAGE BROKER	
NMLS/__ LICENSE ID	
LOAN OFFICER	
NMLS/__ LICENSE ID	
EMAIL	
PHONE	

Comparisons — Use these measures to compare this loan with other loans.

In 5 Years	$56,582	Total you will have paid in principal, interest, mortgage insurance, and loan costs.
	$15,773	Principal you will have paid off.
Annual Percentage Rate (APR)	4.274%	Your costs over the loan term expressed as a rate. This is not your interest rate.
Total Interest Percentage (TIP)	69.45%	The total amount of interest that you will pay over the loan term as a percentage of your loan amount.

Other Considerations

Appraisal
We may order an appraisal to determine the property's value and charge you for this appraisal. We will promptly give you a copy of any appraisal, even if your loan does not close. You can pay for an additional appraisal for your own use at your own cost.

Assumption
If you sell or transfer this property to another person, we
☐ will allow, under certain conditions, this person to assume this loan on the original terms.
☒ will not allow assumption of this loan on the original terms.

Homeowner's Insurance
This loan requires homeowner's insurance on the property, which you may obtain from a company of your choice that we find acceptable.

Late Payment
If your payment is more than *15* days late, we will charge a late fee of *5% of the monthly principal and interest payment.*

Refinance
Refinancing this loan will depend on your future financial situation, the property value, and market conditions. You may not be able to refinance this loan.

Servicing
We intend
☐ to service your loan. If so, you will make your payments to us.
☒ to transfer servicing of your loan.

Confirm Receipt

By signing, you are only confirming that you have received this form. You do not have to accept this loan because you have signed or received this form.

_____ _____   _____ _____
Applicant Signature   Date   Co-Applicant Signature   Date

Closing Disclosure

This form is a statement of final loan terms and closing costs. Compare this document with your Loan Estimate.

Closing Information

Date Issued	4/15/2013
Closing Date	4/15/2013
Disbursement Date	4/15/2013
Settlement Agent	Epsilon Title Co.
File #	12-3456
Property	456 Somewhere Ave
	Anytown, ST 12345
Sale Price	$180,000

Transaction Information

Borrower	Michael Jones and Mary Stone
	123 Anywhere Street
	Anytown, ST 12345
Seller	Steve Cole and Amy Doe
	321 Somewhere Drive
	Anytown, ST 12345
Lender	Ficus Bank

Loan Information

Loan Term	30 years
Purpose	Purchase
Product	Fixed Rate
Loan Type	☒ Conventional ☐ FHA ☐ VA ☐ _____
Loan ID #	123456789
MIC #	000654321

Loan Terms

		Can this amount increase after closing?
Loan Amount	$162,000	**NO**
Interest Rate	3.875%	**NO**
Monthly Principal & Interest *See Projected Payments below for your Estimated Total Monthly Payment*	$761.78	**NO**
		Does the loan have these features?
Prepayment Penalty		**YES** • As high as **$3,240** if you pay off the loan during the first 2 years
Balloon Payment		**NO**

Projected Payments

Payment Calculation	Years 1-7	Years 8-30
Principal & Interest	$761.78	$761.78
Mortgage Insurance	+ 82.35	+ —
Estimated Escrow *Amount can increase over time*	+ 206.13	+ 206.13
Estimated Total Monthly Payment	**$1,050.26**	**$967.91**

		This estimate includes	In escrow?
Estimated Taxes, Insurance & Assessments *Amount can increase over time* *See page 4 for details*	**$356.13** a month	☒ Property Taxes	YES
		☒ Homeowner's Insurance	YES
		☒ Other: Homeowner's Association Dues	NO
		See Escrow Account on page 4 for details. You must pay for other property costs separately.	

Costs at Closing

Closing Costs	$9,712.10	Includes $4,694.05 in Loan Costs + $5,018.05 in Other Costs – $0 in Lender Credits. *See page 2 for details.*
Cash to Close	$14,147.26	Includes Closing Costs. *See Calculating Cash to Close on page 3 for details.*

Closing Cost Details

Loan Costs		Borrower-Paid		Seller-Paid		Paid by Others
		At Closing	Before Closing	At Closing	Before Closing	
A. Origination Charges		**$1,802.00**				
01 0.25 % of Loan Amount (Points)		$405.00				
02 Application Fee		$300.00				
03 Underwriting Fee		$1,097.00				
04						
05						
06						
07						
08						
B. Services Borrower Did Not Shop For		**$236.55**				
01 Appraisal Fee	to John Smith Appraisers Inc.					$405.00
02 Credit Report Fee	to Information Inc.		$29.80			
03 Flood Determination Fee	to Info Co.	$20.00				
04 Flood Monitoring Fee	to Info Co.	$31.75				
05 Tax Monitoring Fee	to Info Co.	$75.00				
06 Tax Status Research Fee	to Info Co.	$80.00				
07						
08						
09						
10						
C. Services Borrower Did Shop For		**$2,655.50**				
01 Pest Inspection Fee	to Pests Co.	$120.50				
02 Survey Fee	to Surveys Co.	$85.00				
03 Title – Insurance Binder	to Epsilon Title Co.	$650.00				
04 Title – Lender's Title Insurance	to Epsilon Title Co.	$500.00				
05 Title – Settlement Agent Fee	to Epsilon Title Co.	$500.00				
06 Title – Title Search	to Epsilon Title Co.	$800.00				
07						
08						
D. TOTAL LOAN COSTS (Borrower-Paid)		**$4,694.05**				
Loan Costs Subtotals (A + B + C)		$4,664.25	$29.80			

Other Costs

		Borrower-Paid		Seller-Paid		Paid by Others
E. Taxes and Other Government Fees		**$85.00**				
01 Recording Fees	Deed: $40.00 Mortgage: $45.00	$85.00				
02 Transfer Tax	to Any State			$950.00		
F. Prepaids		**$2,120.80**				
01 Homeowner's Insurance Premium (12 mo.) to Insurance Co.		$1,209.96				
02 Mortgage Insurance Premium (mo.)						
03 Prepaid Interest ($17.44 per day from 4/15/13 to 5/1/13)		$279.04				
04 Property Taxes (6 mo.) to Any County USA		$631.80				
05						
G. Initial Escrow Payment at Closing		**$412.25**				
01 Homeowner's Insurance $100.83 per month for 2 mo.		$201.66				
02 Mortgage Insurance per month for mo.						
03 Property Taxes $105.30 per month for 2 mo.		$210.60				
04						
05						
06						
07						
08 Aggregate Adjustment		– 0.01				
H. Other		**$2,400.00**				
01 HOA Capital Contribution	to HOA Acre Inc.	$500.00				
02 HOA Processing Fee	to HOA Acre Inc.	$150.00				
03 Home Inspection Fee	to Engineers Inc.	$750.00			$750.00	
04 Home Warranty Fee	to XYZ Warranty Inc.			$450.00		
05 Real Estate Commission	to Alpha Real Estate Broker			$5,700.00		
06 Real Estate Commission	to Omega Real Estate Broker			$5,700.00		
07 Title – Owner's Title Insurance (optional) to Epsilon Title Co.		$1,000.00				
08						
I. TOTAL OTHER COSTS (Borrower-Paid)		**$5,018.05**				
Other Costs Subtotals (E + F + G + H)		$5,018.05				
J. TOTAL CLOSING COSTS (Borrower-Paid)		**$9,712.10**				
Closing Costs Subtotals (D + I)		$9,682.30	$29.80	$12,800.00	$750.00	$405.00
Lender Credits						

Calculating Cash to Close

Use this table to see what has changed from your Loan Estimate.

	Loan Estimate	Final	Did this change?
Total Closing Costs (J)	$8,054.00	$9,712.10	**YES** · See **Total Loan Costs (D)** and **Total Other Costs (I)**
Closing Costs Paid Before Closing	$0	– $29.80	**YES** · You paid these Closing Costs **before closing**
Closing Costs Financed (Paid from your Loan Amount)	$0	$0	**NO**
Down Payment/Funds from Borrower	$18,000.00	$18,000.00	**NO**
Deposit	– $10,000.00	– $10,000.00	**NO**
Funds for Borrower	$0	$0	**NO**
Seller Credits	$0	– $2,500.00	**YES** · See Seller Credits in **Section L**
Adjustments and Other Credits	$0	– $1,035.04	**YES** · See details in **Sections K and L**
Cash to Close	$16,054.00	$14,147.26	

Summaries of Transactions

Use this table to see a summary of your transaction.

BORROWER'S TRANSACTION

K. Due from Borrower at Closing	$189,762.30
01 Sale Price of Property	$180,000.00
02 Sale Price of Any Personal Property Included in Sale	
03 Closing Costs Paid at Closing (J)	$9,682.30
04	
Adjustments	
05	
06	
07	
Adjustments for Items Paid by Seller in Advance	
08 City/Town Taxes to	
09 County Taxes to	
10 Assessments to	
11 HOA Dues 4/15/13 to 4/30/13	$80.00
12	
13	
14	
15	

L. Paid Already by or on Behalf of Borrower at Closing	$175,615.04
01 Deposit	$10,000.00
02 Loan Amount	$162,000.00
03 Existing Loan(s) Assumed or Taken Subject to	
04	
05 Seller Credit	$2,500.00
Other Credits	
06 Rebate from Epsilon Title Co.	$750.00
07	
Adjustments	
08	
09	
10	
11	
Adjustments for Items Unpaid by Seller	
12 City/Town Taxes 1/1/13 to 4/14/13	$365.04
13 County Taxes to	
14 Assessments to	
15	
16	
17	

SELLER'S TRANSACTION

M. Due to Seller at Closing	$180,080.00
01 Sale Price of Property	$180,000.00
02 Sale Price of Any Personal Property Included in Sale	
03	
04	
05	
06	
07	
08	
Adjustments for Items Paid by Seller in Advance	
09 City/Town Taxes to	
10 County Taxes to	
11 Assessments to	
12 HOA Dues 4/15/13 to 4/30/13	$80.00
13	
14	
15	
16	

N. Due from Seller at Closing	$115,665.04
01 Excess Deposit	
02 Closing Costs Paid at Closing (J)	$12,800.00
03 Existing Loan(s) Assumed or Taken Subject to	
04 Payoff of First Mortgage Loan	$100,000.00
05 Payoff of Second Mortgage Loan	
06	
07	
08 Seller Credit	$2,500.00
09	
10	
11	
12	
13	
Adjustments for Items Unpaid by Seller	
14 City/Town Taxes 1/1/13 to 4/14/13	$365.04
15 County Taxes to	
16 Assessments to	
17	
18	
19	

CALCULATION

Total Due from Borrower at Closing (K)	$189,762.30
Total Paid Already by or on Behalf of Borrower at Closing (L)	– $175,615.04
Cash to Close ☒ From ☐ To Borrower	**$14,147.26**

CALCULATION

Total Due to Seller at Closing (M)	$180,080.00
Total Due from Seller at Closing (N)	– $115,665.04
Cash ☐ From ☒ To Seller	**$64,414.96**

Additional Information About This Loan

Loan Disclosures

Assumption

If you sell or transfer this property to another person, your lender

☐ will allow, under certain conditions, this person to assume this loan on the original terms.

☒ will not allow assumption of this loan on the original terms.

Demand Feature

Your loan

☐ has a demand feature, which permits your lender to require early repayment of the loan. You should review your note for details.

☒ does not have a demand feature.

Late Payment

If your payment is more than *15* days late, your lender will charge a late fee of *5% of the monthly principal and interest payment.*

Negative Amortization (Increase in Loan Amount)

Under your loan terms, you

☐ are scheduled to make monthly payments that do not pay all of the interest due that month. As a result, your loan amount will increase (negatively amortize), and your loan amount will likely become larger than your original loan amount. Increases in your loan amount lower the equity you have in this property.

☐ may have monthly payments that do not pay all of the interest due that month. If you do, your loan amount will increase (negatively amortize), and, as a result, your loan amount may become larger than your original loan amount. Increases in your loan amount lower the equity you have in this property.

☒ do not have a negative amortization feature.

Partial Payments

Your lender

☒ may accept payments that are less than the full amount due (partial payments) and apply them to your loan.

☐ may hold them in a separate account until you pay the rest of the payment, and then apply the full payment to your loan.

☐ does not accept any partial payments.

If this loan is sold, your new lender may have a different policy.

Security Interest

You are granting a security interest in
456 Somewhere Ave., Anytown, ST 12345

You may lose this property if you do not make your payments or satisfy other obligations for this loan.

Escrow Account

For now, your loan

☒ will have an escrow account (also called an "impound" or "trust" account) to pay the property costs listed below. Without an escrow account, you would pay them directly, possibly in one or two large payments a year. Your lender may be liable for penalties and interest for failing to make a payment.

Escrow		
Escrowed Property Costs over Year 1	$2,473.56	Estimated total amount over year 1 for your escrowed property costs: *Homeowner's Insurance Property Taxes*
Non-Escrowed Property Costs over Year 1	$1,800.00	Estimated total amount over year 1 for your non-escrowed property costs: *Homeowner's Association Dues* You may have other property costs.
Initial Escrow Payment	$412.25	A cushion for the escrow account you pay at closing. See Section G on page 2.
Monthly Escrow Payment	$206.13	The amount included in your total monthly payment.

☐ will not have an escrow account because ☐ you declined it ☐ your lender does not offer one. You must directly pay your property costs, such as taxes and homeowner's insurance. Contact your lender to ask if your loan can have an escrow account.

No Escrow		
Estimated Property Costs over Year 1		Estimated total amount over year 1. You must pay these costs directly, possibly in one or two large payments a year.
Escrow Waiver Fee		

In the future,

Your property costs may change and, as a result, your escrow payment may change. You may be able to cancel your escrow account, but if you do, you must pay your property costs directly. If you fail to pay your property taxes, your state or local government may (1) impose fines and penalties or (2) place a tax lien on this property. If you fail to pay any of your property costs, your lender may (1) add the amounts to your loan balance, (2) add an escrow account to your loan, or (3) require you to pay for property insurance that the lender buys on your behalf, which likely would cost more and provide fewer benefits than what you could buy on your own.

Loan Calculations

Total of Payments. Total you will have paid after you make all payments of principal, interest, mortgage insurance, and loan costs, as scheduled.	$285,803.36
Finance Charge. The dollar amount the loan will cost you.	$118,830.27
Amount Financed. The loan amount available after paying your upfront finance charge.	$162,000.00
Annual Percentage Rate (APR). Your costs over the loan term expressed as a rate. This is not your interest rate.	4.174%
Total Interest Percentage (TIP). The total amount of interest that you will pay over the loan term as a percentage of your loan amount.	69.46%

Questions? If you have questions about the loan terms or costs on this form, use the contact information below. To get more information or make a complaint, contact the Consumer Financial Protection Bureau at **www.consumerfinance.gov/mortgage-closing**

Other Disclosures

Appraisal
If the property was appraised for your loan, your lender is required to give you a copy at no additional cost at least 3 days before closing. If you have not yet received it, please contact your lender at the information listed below.

Contract Details
See your note and security instrument for information about
- what happens if you fail to make your payments,
- what is a default on the loan,
- situations in which your lender can require early repayment of the loan, and
- the rules for making payments before they are due.

Liability after Foreclosure
If your lender forecloses on this property and the foreclosure does not cover the amount of unpaid balance on this loan,
- ☒ state law may protect you from liability for the unpaid balance. If you refinance or take on any additional debt on this property, you may lose this protection and have to pay any debt remaining even after foreclosure. You may want to consult a lawyer for more information.
- ☐ state law does not protect you from liability for the unpaid balance.

Refinance
Refinancing this loan will depend on your future financial situation, the property value, and market conditions. You may not be able to refinance this loan.

Tax Deductions
If you borrow more than this property is worth, the interest on the loan amount above this property's fair market value is not deductible from your federal income taxes. You should consult a tax advisor for more information.

Contact Information

	Lender	Mortgage Broker	Real Estate Broker (B)	Real Estate Broker (S)	Settlement Agent
Name	Ficus Bank		Omega Real Estate Broker Inc.	Alpha Real Estate Broker Co.	Epsilon Title Co.
Address	4321 Random Blvd. Somecity, ST 12340		789 Local Lane Sometown, ST 12345	987 Suburb Ct. Someplace, ST 12340	123 Commerce Pl. Somecity, ST 12344
NMLS ID					
ST License ID			Z765416	Z61456	Z61616
Contact	Joe Smith		Samuel Green	Joseph Cain	Sarah Arnold
Contact NMLS ID	12345				
Contact ST License ID			P16415	P51461	PT1234
Email	joesmith@ ficusbank.com		sam@omegare.biz	joe@alphare.biz	sarah@ epsilontitle.com
Phone	123-456-7890		123-555-1717	321-555-7171	987-555-4321

Confirm Receipt

By signing, you are only confirming that you have received this form. You do not have to accept this loan because you have signed or received this form.

_____   _____   _____   _____
Applicant Signature   Date   Co-Applicant Signature   Date

CLOSING DISCLOSURE

PAGE 5 OF 5 · LOAN ID # 123456789

Take the quiz below.

CHAPTER 21 QUIZ

1. In which theory is the title held in the name of the lender up until the point at which the last payment is paid?

    a. Title theory
    b. Lien theory
    c. Intermediate theory
    d. None of the above

2. In this theory, the title is retained by the borrower. There is an agreement in which the lender can regain the title if and when the borrower defaults. A formal foreclosure process is required in order to obtain the legal title. Which theory is being described?

    a. Title theory
    b. Deed in lieu of foreclosure
    c. Intermediate theory
    d. None of the above

3. Jane makes a promise in writing and signs it. In the agreement, she says that she will pay a specific amount of money to Michael. What is this agreement known as?

    a. Negotiable instrument
    b. Hypothecation
    c. Usury
    d. Promissory note

4. Ray is down on his luck. He took multiple financial hits over the last year and the setbacks have pushed him into a financial corner. Currently, he knows he cannot pay his mortgage next month. Embarrassed, he finds himself at a business that does personal loans. After a 30-minute conversation, Ray is looking down at the numbers in front of him. It would be a relief to have the money, but the rates seem astronomical to him. He cannot ever remember seeing an APR so high. Additionally, on page 2, he sees other upfront fees he has to pay. Most likely, what is the best way to describe what he is experiencing?

    a. Logical business principles
    b. Hypothecation
    c. Predatory lending
    d. Lis pendens

5. Jean took out a loan for her home. She pledged the real property in order to secure the debt for the loan. If she defaults on her payments, she knows the lender has a legal right to seize her property. Which provision of the mortgage contract gives the lender the right to claim the property when the borrower is in default?

    a. Hypothecation
    b. Security and debt
    c. Mortgage
    d. Usury

6. Tom and Jerri are planning to purchase their first house. They're nervous and excited. However, they're also somewhat disoriented by all the new terms and phrases that come along with buying a house. How would you explain what loan origination is and/or what it includes?

    a. Filling out the application.
    b. Submitting the application.
    c. Funds being disbursed.
    d. All of the above.
    e. None of the above.

7. Concerning discount points, to whom is the fee paid? Which is the best answer?

    a. The lender
    b. The broker
    c. The trustee
    d. The title company

8. Which answer best fills in the blank? A _____ is used when Party A takes out a loan from Party B in order to buy a property and the property is conveyed into a trust.

    a. Land contract
    b. Mortgage document
    c. Lis pendens
    d. Deed in trust

9. David is severely behind on his mortgage payments. He is reading his contract now. Which clause gives the lender power to initiate a foreclosure?

    a. Acceleration clause
    b. Alienation clause
    c. Prepayment penalty clause
    d. Release clause
    e. Subordination clause

10. Fred is at a licensee training with you. The trainer keeps using the term "due-on-sale clause." Fred cannot figure out what that is. He leans over to you and asks you. You tell him that it's another phrase for which of the following?

    a. Prepayment penalty clause
    b. Acceleration clause
    c. Subordination clause
    d. Alienation clause
    e. Release clause
    f. None of the above

11. Jack initiated his mortgage loan six years ago. He has fallen on hard times and is no longer able to make his monthly mortgage payment. Which foreclosure philosophy would allow the lender to sell the property without first securing court authorization?

    a. Judicial foreclosure
    b. Nonjudicial foreclosure
    c. Strict foreclosure
    d. None of the above

12. What do we call a legally binding contract between the seller of real estate and the buyer when the seller is providing the financing?

    a. Hypothecation
    b. Lis pendens
    c. Land contract
    d. Deed of trust
    e. Property contract

13. In which ways might it be possible for a homeowner who is in default to avoid foreclosure?

    a. A short sale
    b. A deed in lieu of foreclosure
    c. Chapter 13 bankruptcy
    d. Any of the above
    e. None of the above

14. A borrower in default, Nancy received notice of foreclosure today. She was served. She now has seven months to pay off the full amount of the loan that is due. What is this known as?

    a. Equitable right of redemption
    b. Statutory right of reinstatement
    c. Right of redemption
    d. Statutory right of redemption

15. Which type of bankruptcy can possibly allow a borrower in default to pay what is owned by allowing him/her to pay the ongoing current payments, along with delinquent payments?

    a. Chapter 7
    b. Chapter 13
    c. Neither. It's not possible.

16. Which market works with entities like private lenders, lending institutions, and investors that buy and sell existing mortgage promissory notes (previously issued mortgages) and/or securities that are mortgage-backed?

    a. Primary mortgage market
    b. Secondary mortgage market
    c. Tertiary mortgage market
    d. None of the above

17. Will is applying for a home loan. His application is being reviewed by a mortgage underwriter this week. What will the underwriter be doing? He/she will . . .

    a. Look up Will's credit score
    b. Research to see whether or not Will has any current or previous foreclosures, judgments, and bankruptcies
    c. Decide whether or not to approve or deny the application
    d. All of the above
    e. Only B and C

18. What provision within the mortgage contract provides lenders with a method to recoup some of the lost interest revenue that would have been generated over the full and expected lifetime of the loan, when the loan is paid off early?

    a. Release clause
    b. Premature loan termination
    c. Prepayment penalty clause
    d. A and C
    e. None of the above

19. Which type of foreclosure, often referred to as a friendly foreclosure, is a managed agreement between the parties, rather than a requirement of a lawsuit?

    a. A deed in lieu of foreclosure
    b. Judicial foreclosure
    c. Nonjudicial foreclosure
    d. Strict foreclosure
    e. None of the above

20. Donald is buying a three-unit building to use as an income property. He does not intend to live on the premises. However, he tells the lender that he will. Donald is most likely engaging in which of the following?

   a. An act of blockbusting
   b. An act of mortgage fraud
   c. An antitrust violation
   d. An unethical yet not illegal practice

CHAPTER 22:

APPRAISALS IN REAL ESTATE

LEARNING GOALS:

By the end of this lesson, you will:

- Learn how The Act defines appraisal and related terms
- Understand comparative market analysis and broker price opinion
- Learn about elements of value, market value, and market price
- Understand economic principles that affect valuation
- Learn the three approaches to value and more

APPRAISAL TERMS AND THE ACT

An appraisal is a professional appraiser's opinion of value and his or her estimate of the home's current market value. The estimation is calculated by comparing recently sold comparable properties in the same area in which the property being appraised is located. Mortgage lenders require an appraisal. They want assurance that it's a fair and just amount of money for the property, and that their lenders are not overpaying or falling victim to malicious practices.

Although having existed for over 50 years, appraisal management companies were created to facilitate the ordering, tracking, and quality assurance of residential appraisals. The need for such oversight became far more relevant with the recession of 2007. Because of some unethical and questionable practices, lenders are now required to coordinate the acquisition of an appraisal through the utilization of appraisal management companies. Here is how the **Appraisal Management Company Registration Act** found in The Act in 225 ILCS 459/10 defines an appraisal management company:

> "Any corporation, limited liability company, partnership, sole proprietorship, subsidiary, unit, or other business entity that directly or indirectly: (1) provides appraisal management services to creditors or secondary mortgage market participants; (2) provides appraisal management services in connection with valuing the consumer's principal dwelling as security for a consumer credit transaction (including consumer credit transactions incorporated into securitizations); (3) within a given year, oversees an appraiser panel of any size of State-certified appraisers in Illinois; and (4) any appraisal management company that, within a given year, oversees an appraiser panel of 16 or more State-certified appraisers in Illinois or 25 or more State-certified or State-licensed appraisers in two or more jurisdictions shall be subject to the appraisal management company national registry fee in addition to the appraiser panel fee. "Appraisal management company" includes a hybrid entity." (225 ILCS 459/10)

In Illinois, the Appraisal Management Company Registration Act establishes the foundation of the appraisal industry. Its intention is to:

- Protect the public

- Maintain high standards of professional conduct by those registered as appraisal management companies in one to four family real estate transactions

- Ensure appraisal independence in the determination of real estate valuations

The Appraisal Management Company Registration Act also states:

"Appraisal management companies or employees of an appraisal management company involved in a real estate transaction who have a reasonable basis to believe that an appraiser involved in the preparation of an appraisal for the real estate transaction has failed to comply with the Uniform Standards of Professional Appraisal Practice, has violated this Act or its rules, or has otherwise engaged in unethical conduct shall report the matter to the Department. Any registrant, employee, or individual acting on behalf of a registrant, acting in good faith, and not in a willful and wanton manner, in complying with this Act by reporting the conduct to the Department shall not, as a result of such actions, be subject to criminal prosecution or civil damages." (225 ILCS 459/160)

Here are selected definitions from the Appraisal Management Company Registration Act found in The Act in 225 ILCS 459/10.

"**Appraisal**" means (noun) the act or process of developing an opinion of value; an opinion of value (adjective) of or pertaining to appraising and related functions.

"**Appraisal firm**" means an appraisal entity that is 100% owned and controlled by a person or persons licensed in Illinois as a certified general real estate appraiser or a certified residential real estate appraiser. An appraisal firm does not include an appraisal management company.

"**Appraisal report**" means a written appraisal by a licensed appraiser to a client.

"**Appraisal practice service**" means valuation services performed by an individual acting as an appraiser, including, but not limited to, appraisal or appraisal review.

"**Appraiser**" means a person who performs real estate or real property appraisals. (Note: He/she must possess a state-issued appraiser's license.)

"**Assignment result**" means an appraiser's opinions and conclusions developed specific to an assignment.

"**Valuation**" means any estimate of the value of real property in connection with a creditor's decision to provide credit, including those values developed under a policy of a government-sponsored enterprise or by an automated valuation model or other methodology or mechanism.

"**Written notice**" means a communication transmitted by mail or by electronic means that can be verified between an appraisal management company and a licensed or certified real estate appraiser.

"**USPAP**" means the Uniform Standards of Professional Appraisal Practice as adopted by the Appraisal Standards Board under Title XI. (225 ILCS 459/10) Note: The USPAP is a collection of national standards for US appraisers to ensure that quality controls and assurances are met when providing an opinion of value.

Are appraisers in Illinois required to be licensed? Yes. In fact, licensure or certification is mandatory in every US state. Illinois requires appraisers to possess a state-issued license if the intent is to provide an opinion of value to federally regulated lenders. There may also be an obligation to be certified as a licensed appraiser for other venues as well. It is illegal to act as an appraiser or give an appraisal unless the person holds a current appraisal license.

Can a CMA be used as an appraisal? No. The Act answers:

> "A comparative market analysis shall not be considered an appraisal within the meaning of the Real Estate Appraiser Licensing Act of 2002, any amendment to that Act, or any successor Act." (225 ILCS 454/1-10)

That being the case, what is the role of the broker? Real estate licensees do render opinions of value, commonly known as CMAs. They do *not* need to possess an appraiser's license to do so. The appraisal act does not restrict real estate licensees from rendering opinions of value. However, it does restrict them from using the phrase "appraisal report."

Legislation in The Act includes the Real Estate Appraiser Licensing Act of 2002 (225 ILCS 458). The beginning reads as follows:

> The intent of the General Assembly in enacting this Act is to evaluate the competency of persons engaged in the appraisal of real estate and to license and regulate those persons for the protection of the public.

Types of Appraisers in Illinois

States have different classifications of appraisers and types of appraisals. For example, California has four different types of appraisers while Illinois has three different types of appraisers. In 225 ILCS 458/1-10, The Act defines each type of appraiser:

1. **Associate Real Estate Trainee Appraiser**. The Act defines this role. It "means an entry-level appraiser who holds a license of this classification under this Act with restrictions as to the scope of practice in accordance with this Act."

2. **Certified Residential Real Estate Appraiser**. This means "an appraiser who holds a license of this classification under this Act and such classification applies to the appraisal of one to four units of residential real property without regard to transaction value or complexity, but with restrictions as to the scope of practice in a federally

related transaction in accordance with Title XI, the provisions of USPAP, criteria established by the AQB, and further defined by rule." Note: AQB means the Appraiser Qualifications Board.

3. **Certified General Real Estate Appraiser**. The Act defines this role. It means "an appraiser who holds a license of this classification under this Act and such classification applies to the appraisal of all types of real property without restrictions as to the scope of practice." (225 ILCS 458/1-10)

Requirements for Associate Real Estate Trainee Appraiser:

The Act says:

Application for associate real estate trainee appraiser. Every person who desires to obtain an associate real estate trainee appraiser license shall:

1. apply to the Department on forms provided by the Department, or through a multi-state licensing system as designated by the Secretary, accompanied by the required fee;

2. be at least 18 years of age;

3. provide evidence of having attained a high school diploma or completed an equivalent course of study as determined by an examination conducted or accepted by the Illinois State Board of Education;

4. (blank); and

5. provide evidence to the Department, or through a multi-state licensing system as designated by the Secretary, that he or she has successfully completed the prerequisite qualifying and any conditional education requirements as established by rule. (225 ILCS 458/5-20)

Requirements for Certified Residential Real Estate Appraiser:

The Act says:

Application for State certified residential real estate appraiser. Every person who desires to obtain a State certified residential real estate appraiser license shall:

1. apply to the Department on forms provided by the Department, or through a multi-state licensing system as designated by the Secretary, accompanied by the required fee;

2. be at least 18 years of age;

3. personally take and pass an examination authorized by the Department and endorsed by the AQB;

4. prior to taking the examination, provide evidence to the Department, or through a multi-state licensing system as designated by the Secretary, of successful completion of the prerequisite classroom hours of instruction in appraising as established by the AQB and by rule; evidence shall be in a Modular Course format with each module conforming to the Required Core Curriculum established and adopted by the AQB; and

5. prior to taking the examination, provide evidence to the Department, or through a multi-state licensing system as designated by the Secretary, of successful completion of the prerequisite experience and educational requirements as established by AQB and by rule. (225 ILCS 458/5-15)

How much experience is essential to become a Certified Residential Real Estate Appraiser? Meeting the requirement entails having accumulated no less than 1,500 hours of acceptable residential appraisal experience. These hours must be gained within a timeframe of a maximum of 12 months.

Requirements for Certified General Real Estate Appraiser:

The Act says:

Application for State certified general real estate appraiser. Every person who desires to obtain a State certified residential real estate appraiser license shall:

1. apply to the Department on forms provided by the Department, or through a multi-state licensing system as designated by the Secretary, accompanied by the required fee;

2. be at least 18 years of age;

3. personally take and pass an examination authorized by the Department and endorsed by the AQB;

4. prior to taking the examination, provide evidence to the Department, or through a multi-state licensing system as designated by the Secretary, in Modular Course format, with each module conforming to the Required Core Curriculum established and adopted by the AQB, that he or she has successfully completed the prerequisite classroom hours of instruction in appraising as established by the AQB and by rule; and

5. prior to taking the examination, provide evidence to the Department, or through a multi-state licensing system as designated by the Secretary, that he or she has successfully completed the prerequisite experience and educational requirements as established by AQB and by rule. (225 ILCS 458/5-10)

How much experience is essential to become a Certified General Real Estate Appraiser? Meeting the requirement entails having accumulated no less than 3,000 hours of acceptable appraisal experience. These hours must be gained within a timeframe of at least 18 months. Additionally, candidates must have completed a minimum of 1,500 hours of non-residential appraisal work (within the 3,000 hours) to satisfy the experience criteria.

The appraisal industry in Illinois is regulated by the IDFPR. It is the only body that issues appraisal licenses in the state. As per their website:

Real Estate Appraisal Professions and Entities Licensed or Registered with IDFPR:

1. Associate Real Estate Trainee Appraiser

2. Certified Residential Real Estate Appraiser

3. Certified General Real Estate Appraiser

4. Appraisal Management Companies (IDFPR)

All information, as well as updates and changes, can be found on their official site here: https://idfpr.illinois.gov/profs/appraisal.html

COMPARATIVE MARKET ANALYSIS AND BROKER PRICE OPINION

Both a Comparative Market Analysis (CMA) and a Broker Price Opinion (BPO) reflect a real estate licensees' opinion of value. However, a licensee is not allowed to utilize the term "appraisal" written or verbally. Neither a CMA nor a BPO is an appraisal. However, the composition of a licensee's CMA or BPO needs to emulate exactly what an appraiser would do.

The CMA is typically given to the consumer who may have an interest in either listing their home for sale, or a purchaser looking to acquire property that needs direction on pricing.

The BPO is typically given to a financial institution that has recently taken a property into inventory as a result of a foreclosure and wants to dispose of it quickly.

Regardless of the product you are creating, there are three primary components that both you, as the broker and the appraiser, are going to be focused on:

1. **Recently sold properties**: Recent sales provide us with direction on what the consumers have been doing with regard to this type of property. In preparing your analysis, you want to use minimally five recent sales that have closed within the last six months. Only use six months as the economy can easily change in a very short span of time. You're going to use recent sales in the same geographical area of similar types of

properties. While no two properties are ever identical, we need to find a way of being able to use those sales as guidance. We do such by making characteristic adjustments to the comp in order to create a match for our subject. The fewer the modifications, the better the choice of comp. The reason for selecting minimally five recent sales is that this is going to create a range with two of the comps acting as the high and low parameters, and the remaining three or more comps giving you (hopefully), a grouping to provide a more accurate reflection of values.

2. **Currently listed properties**: While the recent sales provide us with direction on what the consumers have done, we also want to know what consumers are trying to accomplish today. Looking at recent sales, you might have come up with an average sale price of $650,000, but looking at homes currently on the market, the average asking price is $800,000. This difference indicates current sellers are trying to press the envelope and secure higher sales prices for their homes.

3. **Expired listings**: What current listings may indicate is that the sellers are trying to challenge the market. Expired listing occurs when an active listing period expires, which allows the seller client to pursue alternative representation. Expired listings are going to provide us with two important concepts:

   - An indicator as to how the buying public has responded to the seller trying to increase the potential sales price; and

   - What may have been some of the marketing mistakes other brokers had encountered in attempting to market similar homes in that geographical location.

Some states have no specific format requirements concerning CMAs and BPOs. Like legal documents, either one of these that an agent uses should be in writing.

ELEMENTS OF VALUE

Appraisals, CMAs, and BPOs all center around and focus on one primary factor—value. However, how is value determined? What achieves value? Generally, there are four essential elements or ingredients that show us whether or not a real property has value. Keep the acronym D.U.S.T. in mind. Those elements are:

1. **Demand**: This focuses on the need or desire within the marketplace, along with the financial ability of someone to purchase.

2. **Utility**: This focuses on usefulness. Is the property being sold going to satisfy a need and/or fulfill a desire?

3. **Scarcity**: What's available is limited in supply. Its time on the market can have a short shelf life. This creates urgency in the marketplace.

4. **Transferability**: This focuses on how easy and simple it is to transfer the property from the seller to the buyer. Is the title clean? Is there a lien on the property? The easier the transferability, the better it is for the buyer and the seller.

There are several forces that can influence value. These can be, but are not limited to, the following:

1. **Government and legal forces**: This includes items such as building codes, zoning, health protection services, new or amended environmental legislation, and regulations related to the use of land.

2. **Economic forces**: This includes employment levels, price levels, credit opportunities, interest rates, and housing supply and demand.

3. **Physicality**: These include topographical and environmental forces such as climate, climate change, highway systems, natural resources, and erosion.

4. **Sociology**: This includes how cultures shift, how people's attitudes and/or actions evolve, social changes, family relationships and dynamics, family size, and social causes.

MARKET VALUE AND MARKET PRICE

Market value is a data-based opinion of the value of a specific property. It conveys what a property would most likely sell for in a competitive market. This opinion is founded on a variety of statistics and information, such as the real estate market as a whole, property features, property, supply and demand, and as you read earlier, what similar properties have sold for in the same condition and geographical area. When you hear the term market value, think of the word opinion.

Adding to this unique concept is the reality that it is very common for buyers and sellers to view value differently. For example, let's say a property has a hot tub. The buyer may view the hot tub as something unwanted and may be making plans to remove it if and when he/she moves in. For the seller, the hot tub may be viewed as an asset that complements the property and makes it more attractive. Sometimes value is in the eye of the beholder.

Market price is what a willing, ready, and able buyer would agree to pay for a property on the market and the price at which a seller will sell the property. Ideally, the buyer would feel like it was purchased for a fair, reasonable price and that he/she was not taken advantage of. Market price is the real selling price, not the asking price, and not an opinion of value. It is evidenced by a closing, which as you know is the result of the transfer of the deed from the seller to the buyer. When you hear the term market price, know that it is a fact and an event in time.

Market value is much more nuanced and complicated than market price. Why? Because market value is influenced by subjective factors. It is not entirely based on facts and data. Different people view a property as having varying degrees of market value.

ECONOMIC PRINCIPLES THAT AFFECT VALUATION

Specific economic principles influence and affect the value of property. The most common ones are the following.

Principle of anticipation: This principle focuses on the anticipated future benefits that would be derived from the property. A buyer sees the purchase as a decision that will create and generate benefits to be enjoyed and experienced in the future. This anticipation can help the value of the property rise. The buyer expects that certain things will take place after purchasing the property. The person looks to the future for the value, not the present. For example, if a community is going to have a new park, recreation center, and elementary school built by the following year, people anticipate that the value of those properties in the community will increase.

Principle of balance: This is the dynamic relationship that exists and evolves between cost, added costs, and return on value. When a seller improves their home, this has a strong impact on potentially improving the desirability of that house. However, what happens when the seller over-improves the property? While the seller may feel that it adds to the overall value of the property, it may actually be harming the value as potential buyers may not see the benefits and therefore avoid the property.

Principle of change: Change is the only constant. This principle recognizes the evolving and lively nature of the real estate market. Change affects one-family properties, apartment buildings, condos, communities, neighborhoods, cities, and even regions. Value is affected by both social changes and economic changes. A qualified appraiser knows this and views change through its four different stages: 1) growth, 2) stability, 3) decline, and 4) rebirth. The stages work like this. Growth is a time period of healthy social and economic dynamics. The area is viewed as favorable and desirable. Stability means the growth has stabilized. It is not increasing or decreasing to any large margin. There are no significant losses or gains. There are no advancements and no setbacks. Decline is obvious when one or more factors destabilize the area. Demand and desirability decrease. Public perception goes from positive, to apathetic, or perhaps negative. Rebirth means a time of renewal, life, and vibrancy. There is rejuvenation. The market begins experiencing demands once again. This is referred to frequently as regentrification.

Principle of competition: This principle focuses on the competition that originates from supply and demand and their fluctuations. When demand for property increases, competition gets harder. More homes are being built and purchased. Things are happening! However, where there is too much building occurring, it creates an oversupply of housing. This makes the demand decrease. The fluctuation in supply and demand has a direct impact on the valuation of real estate. As demand goes up and supply becomes short, housing values will increase. As demand dwindles and we have an oversupply of housing, the values will decrease.

Principle of conformity: This principle states that a property's maximum value is realized when it fits in well with its structural and natural surroundings. The property is compatible and similar to the area in which it is located. This tends to generate and maintain value because there is harmony and conformity. By nature, humans like conformity in their lives. That is why you'll frequently see a specific style of house constructed in a given area.

Principle of contribution: Sometimes called the principle of marginal productivity, it relates to the increasing and decreasing returns on components to the property. This principle focuses on how the value of one part of the property is measured by its overall effect on the property as a whole. An item's cost does not always equal its contributory value to the property. For example, an apartment owner pays $25,000 for a new pool to be installed in his small apartment complex. However, it may only result in an increase of the property value by $18,000. Obviously, although the pool may be a desirable feature to some guests, it is not a major contributor to the overall value of the property. On the other hand, a vintage homeowner completely remodels the front porch and modernizes the kitchen. It cost her $30,000. Because these improvements increase the desirability of the property, her property value could increase by $42,000.

Principle of highest and best use: Sometimes shortened to HBU, this principle relates to property being appraised in the context of the property's highest and best use. This concept defines the HBU regardless of whether the property is currently being used in such a manner. It is the use that would generate the highest value for the property. The principle indicates the most probable market value within a specific market. The use must be: 1) legally permissible, 2) physically possible, 3) financially feasible, and 4) maximally productive.

Principle of progression and regression: A property's price can increase or decrease according to the perceived value of its location.

Progression: For example, Mary is selling her house. It is very old, does not have many updates, and is in need of repairs. At first, someone may think the property would not be worth buying. However, if Mary's house is located in a quickly growing neighborhood where the surrounding houses are being renovated, Mary's property value will increase because of its location and proximity to other homes that are increasing in value. Perhaps you've heard the phrase, "Buy the worst house in the best neighborhood." If so, that is progression. The house value will naturally increase because of the proximity to the more valuable homes.

Regression: Regression is the opposite of progression. It's when a property's price decreases because there is less perceived value of its location. For example, Jane has a gorgeous two-story house with well-kept grounds. However, over time, if the properties surrounding her house have decreased in value as a result of undesirable features or circumstances, the value of her house decreases by way of association.

Principle of substitution: A property's value is usually set at a similar price level as an equally desirable substitute property. For example, if Condo A has a close amount of square footage, features, and perks as Condo B, they can be substituted. Thus, they should have similar prices since they are similar. For example, if Condo A had a price that was 40% higher than Condo B despite their similarities, buyers would shy away and most likely select Condo B.

Principle of supply and demand: When housing demand is high and supply is low, house prices usually increase. This is known as a "seller's market" because the market favors sellers at that point in time. When the housing supply is high, it is common for homeowners to decrease their asking prices because there is less demand in the market. This is known as a "buyer's market." There are a number of components that impact supply and demand for real estate.

Plottage is the increase in value that is generated by combining adjacent separately owned parcels of land into a larger parcel. As you would expect, the value of the new whole and larger parcel is larger than the total of the smaller individual parcels. Instead of selling two parcels separately, the two can be combined and sold for a larger amount of money. For example, two adjacent lots may be valued at $50,000 each. However, once combined, they may be valued at $120,000. Plottage is the added and higher value that's generated by combining the parcels together. Assemblage is the process and act of combining two or more separately owned parcels together.

APPRAISALS AND THE THREE APPROACHES TO VALUE

Value is not a one-size-fits-all scenario when it comes to the work of an appraiser. The three approaches to value that appraisers use are:

1. The sales comparison approach

2. The income capitalization approach

3. The cost approach

Each method works best with a different type of property.

Sales comparison approach to value: This procedure arrives at an opinion of property value by comparing and contrasting it with similar properties that have been sold and closed recently.

It relies on recent sales data and stats from similar properties. The procedure makes proper adjustments for time, along with differences in size, square footage, acres, and other different conditions. A requirement for this approach is an active market for similar properties. Ideally, market conditions locally and nationally should be stable. This approach is primarily based on the principle of substitution.

A variety of factors can create price differences between comparable properties. These include, but are not limited to the following and in no particular order:

1. Ownership interest

2. Cash equivalency

3. Market conditions

4. Conditions of sale

5. Physical characteristics

6. Location characteristics

7. Economic characteristics and differences

8. Components of value outside of realty

9. Use

The income approach to value: This is sometimes called the income capitalization approach. This approach is used when the appraisal is for a property that produces income such as apartment buildings, strip malls, office buildings, shopping centers, and so on. The real property's valuation is determined by one primary question: How much net income will this property produce over its expected lifetime? To get to the net income, you have to start with the gross income. The gross income is the total rents collected from tenants along ancillary revenue sources like parking fees, laundry fees, etc.). Net income is the result of subtracting the building's expenses (like taxes, maintenance, and utilities) from the gross income. Simply put, the net is the revenue that the investor keeps. The result is the profit that the investor can claim from the ownership of the property.

The formula for income approach is: Net Annual Income (NAI) = % Rate (cap rate, short for capitalization rate) x Value. (I = R x V). The math works like this:

1. Start with the net annual income.

2. Next, divide the net annual income by the cap rate. (A cap rate is the anticipated percentage of the market value the investor expects to acquire every year as their

net income. In other words, the money they can put in their pockets. A cap rate is a percentage that the individual investor is anticipating. The cap rate is not a fixed number but rather a percentage decided by each investor. It changes from investor to investor.)

3. The end result is the expected value of the property.

Here's another way of looking at this. If an investor knows how much they're willing to spend for a building, by establishing a desired cap rate, the investor can identify how much net income they likely are going to receive annually owning this investment. (Value x Cap Rate = Net Annual Income).

Cost approach to value: This appraisal method takes the approach that the value should equal what it would cost today to build a similar structure.

The formula for cost approach is: Property Value = RCN (Replacement Cost New) - Depreciation + Land. Replacement Cost New is the estimated cost of the improvement if it were constructed today, using today's costs and methods. The math works like this:

1. Start with the value of the improvement as though it was constructed brand new, using today's construction standards and costs.

2. Estimate the amount of depreciation lost over the time the building has actually existed. As you will shortly learn, there are three different components to depreciation; physical, functional, and external. (Depreciation is the decrease of the fair value of a physical asset such as a house over its life expectancy compared to what it would cost to replace the asset today with today's prices. It shows how much value of the asset has been used or consumed.) Once you have determined the level of depreciation, looking at all three factors, you now have the depreciated value of the current physical structure.

3. At this point, add in the value of the land. (As you recall, land is indestructible and therefore does not depreciate.)

4. Looking at the depreciated value of the building and the current value of the land, you now have the estimated value of the property using the cost approach.

Although this approach may be the best to take in specific circumstances like a unique house that has few to no comparables or doing a new construction evaluation, in general, this method is viewed as less dependable. Why is it viewed like this? It's because the amount of depreciation recognized is subjective. It varies from person to person. This results in an inconsistent approach to value.

Reproduction Costs and Replacement Costs

The cost approach to value has two perspectives concerning a building's construction costs. They are the reproduction method and the replacement method. The reproduction method takes into consideration what an exact replica (model/copy) of the property would cost if it were built. This uses current construction cost pricing. The replacement method is what it would cost to construct a similar property with the same use/utility. However, it is not an exact duplicate. Appraisers will compare the replacement cost with the reproduction cost. How are these costs determined? They are determined by using one of four methods.

1. **Square footage method**: Also called the comparison method, it calculates the construction cost by multiplying the structure's external square footage by the total construction cost that would be required for that specific type of structure. This is one of the most popular and commonly used methods by appraisers when estimating replacement or reproduction costs. It's also the easiest.

2. **Unit-in-place method**: At times referred to as the segregated cost method, it gives the appraiser the total cost to build a structure by estimating construction costs. The costs are individually calculated and include materials, labor, profit, as well as fees, interest, and overhead.

3. **Quantity survey method**: This is a highly detailed method that requires the appraiser to break down each and every building component. Then, he/she does two cost estimations:

   A. A materials cost estimation

   - This is oftentimes referred to as direct costs and are also called hard costs. These are project expenses that do not vary. Examples include materials, profit, and labor.

   B. An installation cost estimation

   - This could include indirect costs such as building permits, taxes, and other miscellaneous charges. Indirect costs, also known soft costs, are expenses that vary. They include all of the costs minus materials, profit, and labor. They're indirect because they're not directly associated with the construction of the structure.

3. **Index method**: In this method, the appraiser learns the original cost of construction (minus the land) of the specific building. Then he/she multiplies the original total cost by a number that factors in how construction costs have risen since the original building was constructed. This is widely seen as the most inaccurate method because

it holds several opportunities for mistakes. At times, it is used as a check against the other three methods above.

Depreciation

Depreciation has three different forms:

1. Physical deterioration

2. Functional obsolescence

3. External obsolescence

Physical deterioration: This is the value a property loses as a result of use, wear, and tear. Usually, this is due to the property aging. Wear and tear can come from nature and people. Examples of nature include wind, water, natural disasters, termites, and similar. Examples of people causing physical deterioration refer to everyday usage that causes physical elements of the property to simply wear down or wear out. For example, a house with a family of seven will wear and tear faster than that of a couple enjoying retirement. Properties age faster or slower depending on the types of uses and how often. Most of the time, the physical deterioration is what is visible and observable such as paint, wood, carpet, and so on. At times, it may take an inspection. For example, you cannot see what's going on inside of a heating system simply by looking.

Functional obsolescence: (Note: Obsolescence is the process of becoming obsolete and no longer usable.) This means that the value decreases because the market is not responding in the way it used to respond. This could come from a type of flaw or stem from outdated characteristics and features or undesirable qualities. At times, this relates to trends. Either usefulness, desirability, or both have decreased, and with it, the value of the property has diminished. Sometimes this is due to a design feature that would be expensive and/or difficult to change, update, or renovate. In short, this obsolescence focuses on what society is looking for and willing to accept. It does not necessarily look at the functionality (that is, whether or not the item actually works), but rather on how it is accepted.

External obsolescence: This has also been called economic obsolescence. In this circumstance, a property's value decreases because of factors outside of the property. These are factors that the property owner cannot control. These forces can be social, environmental, and/or economic in nature. Examples include rising crime rates, new highway construction, a shift in airplane flight patterns, high voltage towers being constructed close to the property, or a gas station being built across the street from the property.

When looking at depreciation, there are two factors we have to take into consideration. Specifically, the factors are whether or not the depreciation being recognized is curable or incurable.

Curable depreciation means it is a form of deterioration that can be repaired. It's financially feasible to repair it and the repair will increase the value and desirability of the property. In other words, it is possible to be repaired and financially worth doing so. Examples include a fresh coat of interior paint, updated tile in bathrooms, and minor or major kitchen updates.

Incurable depreciation has two different definitions:

1. It is not possible to repair something.

2. If something is able to be repaired, the increase in value (if there is one) will not exceed the cost of repair. Commonly, this is a type of defect.

There is no financial perk or benefit to making the repair/s. Many times, incurable depreciation is related to the building's structure. For example, large problems in the foundation could be called incurable. While they could be fixed, the repairs would cost more than the value they add.

How does this affect depreciation?

Curable versus Incurable		
	Curable	**Incurable**
Physical depreciation	X	X
Functional obsolescence	X	X
External obsolescence		X

Depreciation Calculation	
Formula	**Variations**
Annual Depreciation = Original Acquisition Price - Land Value ÷ Economic Life	No variations

Economic life is the number of years the building is expected to produce a financial return to the owner.

RECONCILIATION

In general terms, reconciliation means making one view, belief, aspect, or study compatible with another. In appraisal terms, it is a detailed process by which an appraiser looks at value derived from all three appraisal methods. He/she will review all the data and different figures in order to come to a conclusion of a final value estimation. This is a complicated process because he/she is reconciling different comparables. It's not an average. Each method is viewed individually. Data is reviewed. Research is done. Items are adjusted for differences. All of this effort works to reconcile the conclusions of the three different methods.

Each appraiser defines each of the three methods of value in his or her reports. Furthermore, the appraiser has to be able to show and communicate why he/she ruled two methods out and chose his or her selected method (approach to value).

APPRAISALS FOR RESIDENTIAL RENTAL PROPERTIES

Four units or fewer: When a buyer or investor is aiming to purchase a residential rental property consisting of four units or fewer, a ratio called the gross rent multiplier (GRM) is implemented. It is the ratio of the property's price to its gross annual rental income, before expenses like property taxes, utilities, and insurance are factored in. Notice it is gross rent multiplier, not net rent multiplier. For investors, a lower GRM is more attractive as it represents a smarter opportunity. Although GRM is used as a quick way of estimating the property value, it is not considered a formal method for coming up with a value that can be used for financing the purchase.

Five units or more: When a buyer or investor is aiming to purchase a residential rental property consisting of five units or more, a ratio called the gross annual income multiplier is commonly implemented. Also called the gross annual rent multiplier, it is a means of estimating value by using the gross income multiplied by a factor defined by the investor. How does the investor come up with this factor? By taking an average of factors used with similar buildings in the same geographical area and applying the average to the current building that is being appraised.

Both the gross rent multiplier and the gross annual income multiplier have the same flaw. Neither one takes into account the property's expenses. Expenses could have a devastating impact on the bottom-line value.

APPRAISALS FOR COMMERCIAL RENTAL PROPERTIES

The most common method used in developing the value of non-residential commercial structures is the income approach. As you learned above, the income approach uses the gross annual income divided by a capitalization rate in order to determine the current market value of the property.

The cap rate indicates the direction property values are taking. It is common to see children on a playground playing on a seesaw (teeter-tooter). As one child goes up, the other child comes down. They continue in this motion to have fun. Like a seesaw, the cap rate and the property values flow in opposite directions. If the cap rate climbs, the property values decline. In reverse, if the cap rate declines, property values increase.

THE APPRAISAL PROCESS

The general steps an appraiser takes are as follows. These apply to residential and commercial properties.

1. Identify the target property to be appraised. Sometimes this is referred to as identifying the problem. He/she determines the client, property characteristics, property use, and so on.

2. Create an outline of the scope of work. He/she determines the type and amount of information that is required to be sought out, recorded, and researched, along with analyses and methods to be applied. Everything is outlined, so there is a clear view of the scope of work.

3. Start and finish data collection. Next is collecting different types of data from a variety of sources including but not limited to market area research, comparable properties, improvements, variables that cause property value fluctuations, subject site, along with data on sales, income and expense, and cost.

4. Analyze the data. At this point, the appraiser takes a deep dive into all of the data collected and does an in-depth and comprehensive analysis. This is not all math and statistics. Also included in the analysis are aspects like desirability, scarcity, utility, and more.

5. Determine the property's highest and best use.

6. Estimates the total land value by looking at and comparing similar land parcels that have sold and closed.

7. Form an opinion of value by reviewing each of the three different approaches to value. Along with data and analyses, the appraiser leans into his or her expertise and experiences.

8. Reconcile the values so a final opinion of value can be rendered.

9. Prepare an appraisal report and submit it. The report is expected to be in one of the formats defined by The Uniform Standards of Professional Appraisal Practice. Many

government entities require the use of the Uniform Residential Appraisal Report (URAR). The most recent version of the URAR is called "Fannie Mae Form 1004. It was updated in March 2005 and is currently viewable at this link: https://singlefamily. fanniemae.com/media/12371/display

Appraisal reports are required to include the following information.

1. The client's name and identity (as well as any other recipients, if applicable)

2. The appraisal report's intended use, including the appraisal's purpose and type of value

3. Identity of the property being evaluated

4. The date the appraiser viewed the property

5. The ownership interest that is being valued

6. Any specific assignment conditions that impact or influence the appraisal

7. The extent of work completed, commonly referred to as the script of work, which includes data collection, confirming data validity, and reporting the discoverable data

8. Information about common approaches to value that were left out

9. The highest and best use of the property being appraised, if that information is deemed essential and applicable

10. Information about which data was reviewed, the evaluation methods utilized, and the logic that the appraiser employed

11. An official certification that includes the appraiser's signature that follows the guidelines and requirements of USPAP (The Uniform Standards of Professional Appraisal Practice) Standards Rule 2-3

Take this chapter's quiz now.

CHAPTER 22 QUIZ

1. Which best describes what an appraisal is in terms of value?

    a. A proven fact
    b. A guess
    c. An opinion
    d. None of the above

2. Only certain states require appraisers to be licensed.

    a. True
    b. False

3. How many different types of appraisers does Illinois have?

    a. Two
    b. Three
    c. Four
    d. Five

4. Which of the following is false?

    a. A CMA is not an appraisal.
    b. A BPO reflects a real estate licensee's opinion of value.
    c. A licensee can use the term appraisal written or verbally.
    d. Neither a CMA nor a BPO is a formal appraisal.

5. Dustin, a new licensee, has been asked to render an opinion of value on a potential listing. To ensure that Dustin's opinion matches that of an appraiser, which three components will both Dustin and the appraiser use in rendering their opinions?

    a. Recently sold properties, current listings, expired listings
    b. Recently sold properties, current listings, the neighborhood demographics
    c. Recently sold properties, expired listings, property history
    d. Expired listings, property history, current listings

6. Maxine is studying to become a licensed real estate agent. She has just read the chapter you just completed. You're studying with her. She asks you which of the following is true. How do you respond?

    a. Some states require no specific format requirements for CMAs and BPOs.
    b. Like legal documents, both of these should be in writing.
    c. All of the above
    d. None of the above

7. Appraisals, CMAs, and BPOs focus on value. What are the four essential elements or ingredients that show us whether or not a real property has value?

    a. Transferability, demand, use, and scarcity
    b. Transferability, desirability, use, and scarcity
    c. Transferability, desirability, utility, and scarcity
    d. Transferability, utility, demand, and scarcity

8. Which of the following sources of information is used in developing an opinion of value used by both an appraiser and a real estate licensee?

    a. Market price
    b. Market value
    c. Reasonable price
    d. None of the above

9. Market value is influenced by subjective factors.

    a. True
    b. False

10. Steve and Nancy have been house hunting and have narrowed their choices to two. One costs $30,000 more than the other. The large loan it would require makes them a bit uncomfortable. The less expensive house provides greater flexibility as they believe they can do a number of projects to make the home their dream home. What is at work during their conversation and decision-making?

    a. Principle of contribution
    b. Principle of highest and best use
    c. Principle of change
    d. Principle of anticipation

11. Which principle applies when a property's maximum value is realized because it fits in harmoniously with its structural and natural surroundings?

    a. Principle of highest and best use
    b. Principle of contribution
    c. Principle of substitution
    d. Principle of conformity

12. Which one word correctly completes both of the following blanks? Less _____ means higher value. More _____ means lower value.

    a. Demand
    b. Supply
    c. Competition
    d. Change
    e. None of the above

13. Which principle is the main point of the following story? This past summer, Jonathan and Robin decided to invest money into their backyard area. They added a beautiful brick patio with a firepit and a medium-sized pool surrounded by updated landscaping. The total cost will be $45,000. However, they spoke with three advisors and each one shared data showing that it would increase the value of the property from $420,000 to at least $500,000. The reason for this investment is that next summer, the couple is moving to Nashville because Robin's mom lives there. Their oldest son is graduating a month prior, so they will be empty nesters. They think it will be the best time to put the house on the market and move.

    a. Principle of contribution
    b. Principle of change
    c. Principle of progression and regression
    d. Principle of anticipation

14. This appraisal method generates an opinion of property value by comparing and contrasting it with similar properties that have been sold and closed recently. It relies on recent sales data and stats from similar properties that have sold. The procedure makes proper adjustments for time, along with differences in size, square footage, acres, and other different conditions. Which approach to value is this describing?

    a. Cost approach
    b. Income capitalization approach
    c. Sales comparison approach
    d. Gross rent multiplier

15. Lucas is a property owner who is working with an appraiser. The appraiser tells him about replacement costs and reproduction costs. To calculate those, which method below is most likely to be used by the appraiser?

    a. Unit-in-place method
    b. Quantity survey method
    c. Index method
    d. Square footage method

16. Joyce wants to sell her house. She has never sold a house before but is confident she will receive a good price. With her Type A personality, she has always had regular repairs and maintenance performed. Everyone in her neighborhood knows that she also keeps the inside of the house sparkling clean. The house has a large wraparound porch, a large backyard, five bedrooms, one bathroom, and beautiful landscaping. Erica, a local real estate agent, has been invited by Joyce to look at the house in person for the first time. The neighborhood has been in high demand by parents with growing families. Erica's one concern, which will cause the house to have less value, is caused by which of the following?

    a. Physical deterioration
    b. Functional obsolescence
    c. External obsolescence
    d. Economic obsolescence

17. Karen is an investor. She has an eye on a residential property that has four units. Which ratio would be used for an appraisal?

    a. Gross income multiplier
    b. Net income multiplier
    c. Gross rent multiplier
    d. None of the above

18. Which of the following is required to be included in an appraisal report?

    a. Intended use and purpose of the appraisal report
    b. The assignment's purpose and type of value
    c. Effective date when the opinion was rendered
    d. All of the above

19. What is the name of the most commonly used appraisal form for government institutions like Fannie Mae?

    a. Uniform USPAD appraisal report
    b. USPAE appraisal report
    c. Conventional appraisal report
    d. Uniform residential appraisal report

20. A gross rent multiplier measures the investment property's value by dividing the property's selling price by its annual gross rental income.

    a. True
    b. False

CHAPTER 23:

LEASES

LEARNING GOALS:

By the end of this lesson, you will:

- Understand lease agreements and common terms
- Know the four types of leasehold estates
- Be able to differentiate types of leases

INFORMATION ABOUT LEASES

Statista reports that in 2020 there were forty-three million renter-occupied properties in the US. The majority of those rental properties are managed by professionals. While owners can manage a property if they choose, it is the exception. Given the fact that there are forty-three million properties rented, it stands to reason that the topic of leases can be broad in its scope. Every licensee needs to know the basics about leases, landlord and tenant dynamics, and related topics.

A **lease** can be called a leasing agreement or a tenant agreement. In real estate, a lease is a legally binding contract and relationship between two or more parties, a tenant/s and a landlord. It may be written, or oral. The Statute of Frauds dictates that certain contracts must be written to be enforceable. In Illinois, the current premise of law dictates that leases with terms of one year (365 days) or less are enforceable in a court of law even if verbal. If the lease term exceeds 365 days, then the lease must be written to be recognizable and enforceable in a court of law.

The tenant (lessee) agrees to pay the owner or property management company (lessor) for use of a rental unit/property (the asset). Common assets that are leased include buildings, vehicles, and industrial equipment. The lessor is the legal owner of the rental property. The owner also retains what is called reversionary right. This means that once a tenant's contract expires and his or her lease is up, the ownership and property revert automatically back to the original owner. The tenant pays regular rental payments for the right to use and enjoy the rental property and thus has possessory rights. The lessor's interest is known as a leased fee estate plus reversionary right. Additionally, in the agreement are guidelines and conditions that the renter is expected to follow concerning rental property use. The contract is enforceable by each party and does involve qualities found in the deed.

What's the difference between a renter and a tenant? Here's an easy way to remember. A renter is someone who rents on a short-term verbal basis. It's typically period to period. A tenant usually signs a lease that is for a designated period of time, such as a one-year or two-year lease.

LEASE AGREEMENTS

A lease is a legal document. By nature, it will have legal terms. Here are the most common ones:

1. **Capacity to contract**: Each party entering into the lease agreement has the legal capacity to do so. Factors such as age, mental competency, and so on are considered.

2. **Consideration**: For a valid lease contract, the most common consideration is money by way of rental payments. The amount of the periodic rent is usually set for the duration of the contract. The rental amount can only be increased or decreased if both parties agree in writing to make such a change. Additionally, money is not the

only form of consideration. It can be something else, such as labor. For example, a college student may bypass paying for room and board by maintaining a property in accordance with the landlord's wishes and goals. The landlord gets work done and does not have to pay cash for it. The college student pays with his time instead of his money. This creates a win/win scenario.

3. **Legal objective**: The purpose and objective of a lease must be legal. For example, if a property is leased in order to perform an illegal activity, upon discovery, the lease is terminated. The owner will suffer no penalties or issues given a crime was committed—it's a matter of police enforcement and applicable laws at that point.

4. **Offer and acceptance**: Both parties agree on the contract's terms. They have mutual agreement. The foundational proof of mutual agreement is that both parties have signed the leasing agreement.

At a minimum, a written lease agreement usually includes the following:

- Full names of each party

- Start date and end date

- Location of rental property

- Information about what is being rented (apartment, house, room, etc.)

- Outlines and describes the rights, responsibilities, and obligations of both the landlord and tenant/s

- Outlines all financial details including but not limited to payments, frequency of payments, method of payment, additional fees, late payment fees, etc.

- Describes expectations and responsibilities concerning property use, rental improvements, maintenance, social gatherings, etc.

- Renewal and cancellation conditions (steps, requirements)

- Security deposit information

- Required conditions (sometimes called default conditions and specific remedies)

- Any use restrictions

- Any required insurance

- Termination clause (This shows how terminating the contract early works, outlines any penalties and/or fees, tenant rights and obligations, etc.)

Concerning residential leases, preprinted lease agreements are commonly used. Why? Generally, residential leases are simpler, and more people are familiar with them. When it comes to commercial leases, they can be complex. They may include difficult rent calculations and challenging maintenance cost calculations, and many times, they feature any variety of legal requirements. Because of this, licensees prepare letters of intent ahead of time for commercial leases. A commercial letter of intent establishes the basic agreement between the parties. From this letter of intent, respective attorneys can draft and/or verify the information they put on the lease forms. Only licensed attorneys should create drafts of commercial leases. A letter of intent is a document that outlines the understanding between two or more parties. This is an understanding that they have plans to formalize through using and signing a legally binding agreement. The LOI paints a picture of and outlines the basic terms of the agreement, along with general information. By signing this document, both parties can ensure that they both agree to the fundamental agreement/lease terms before they actually invest time together and incur the expense/s of preparation and negotiation. Generally, a letter of intent is not a legally binding contract. However, if it has been improperly worded, courts have been known to bind the parties to the agreement even though it was not the original intent.

FOUR TYPES OF LEASEHOLD ESTATES

By definition, an estate defines a form of ownership. In a leasehold estate, the tenant is granted four of the five elements that comprise the bundle of rights. As you know, the bundle of rights consists of the following:

1. Possession

2. Quiet enjoyment

3. Exclusion

4. Control

5. Disposition

Disposition is the only element that is retained by the property owner. A leasehold estate is a tenant's exclusive right to occupy and possess the real estate for the time period outlined in the lease. It is not ownership. The tenant's rights do not include real property or real estate but are considered personal property rights.

Two terms for a leasehold estate are a non-freehold estate and less than a freehold estate. Both terms imply that the tenant has fewer benefits than someone who has legal ownership by way of a freehold estate.

The four types of leasehold estates include:

1. Estate for years

2. Estate from period to period

3. Estate at will

4. Estate at sufferance

Each of these is a legal circumstance. Here is what each one means.

Estate for years: This is a written agreement that allows tenant occupancy during two specified dates: the start date and end date. It is a defined period of time. These periods can be days, weeks, months, or years. Examples include a one-year lease, a three-month lease, and a two-week lease. At the end of the agreement, the tenant is required to vacate the property. No notice is necessary as the end date (the tenant's last day of occupancy) is outlined in the contract. Can the termination date be changed to an earlier date? Yes, if both parties are in agreement, it can be changed. What happens if the property is sold between the start and end dates? The tenant and the new landlord are obligated to follow the contract and complete its terms. Estate for years is also known as fixed-term tenancy and tenancy for years.

Estate from period to period: Also called periodic tenancy, it is a type of tenancy created when a tenant and landlord create an agreement that has no end date. Most often, this is a verbal relationship. It might be week to week, month to month, and year to year. The most common time period is month to month. To terminate the contract, notice must be given. The tenancy continues until notice of termination is given.

How does **notice of termination** work in Illinois? Let's cover this now as it directly relates to estate from period to period. In 735 ILCS 5, called Code of Civil Procedure, The Act answers this question in detail. Below are paraphrased answers that apply to both the tenant and the landlord.

- Year to year tenancy

  - In all cases of tenancy from year to year, a written 60 days' notice is sufficient to terminate the tenancy at the end of the year. The notice may be given at any time within 4 months preceding the last 60 days of the year.

- Less than a year tenancy

  - Month to month

    - In all cases of tenancy for any term less than one year but greater than one week, a written 30 days' notice must be given. If the tenant ignores the termination notice issued by the landlord, the landlord may maintain an action for eviction or ejectment should the tenant fail to vacate.

- Week to week

- In all cases of tenancy from week to week, a written 7 days' notice must be given. Once again, if the tenant ignores the termination notice issued by the landlord, the landlord may maintain an action for eviction or ejectment should the tenant fail to vacate.

- Farm tenancy

  - In order to terminate tenancies from year to year of farm lands, occupied on a crop share, livestock share, cash rent, or other rental basis, the notice to terminate shall be given in writing not less than 4 months prior to the end of the rental period.

  - The notice to termination may be substantially in the following form: To A.B.: You are hereby notified that I have elected to terminate your lease of the farm premises now occupied by you, being (here describe the premises) and you are hereby further notified to quit and deliver up possession of the same to me at the end of the lease year, the last day of such year being (here insert the last day of the lease year).

- **Holdover tenancy**: When a tenant stays beyond the termination date and the landlord keeps accepting the payments, this creates holdover tenancy. The landlord willfully "holds over" the lease term expiration. In this circumstance, the landlord has the option to keep accepting rent payments, or he/she may choose to evict the tenant. If the landlord accepts the rent payment, it's considered proof of acceptance showing that holdover tenancy has been created. In Illinois, holdover tenants have limited rights. Eviction is possible. It's also possible they will have to pay double rent. When this happens in Illinois, it becomes period to period tenancy and the original lease terms are still in effect.

Estate at will: Also called a tenancy at will, estate at will allows the tenant to occupy a space because of the landlord's free will. This relationship does not provide a specific termination date. It has an indefinite duration. Either party, the landlord or tenant, can terminate with proper notice given. Upon receipt of the notice, if the tenant refuses to surrender the space and vacate within the communicated timeframe, the landlord will need to evict the tenant. Estate at will can be created by operation of law or by an express agreement between the parties. There is no written agreement. Courts do not look favorable at estates at will in light of no written agreement. The court is commonly skeptical and doubtful in such circumstances. However, it is possible for courts in Illinois to view an estate at will as an estate from period to period. The deciding factor is whether or not the tenant contributed to the household by either paying rent or providing labor, which is compensation that can be considered a form of rent. Since this is a verbal relationship, should one of the parties die, the relationship is terminated.

Estate at sufferance: Often used with leases, this is when a tenant retains possession of leased space without a current lease and without paying the rental fee. The landlord tends to suffer, thereby establishing an estate at sufferance. In other words, this is when a tenant chooses to stay past the lease's last day, regardless of whether or not he/she has permission from the landlord. It's a holdover. Consent to stay longer has not been given from the landlord to the tenant. It is possible that the tenant will have to pay double rent. Estate at sufferance is also referred to as tenancy in sufferance.

TYPES OF LEASES

Below is a variety of leases. The most common types of leases are a gross lease, net lease, and percentage lease.

Gross lease: A gross lease is a lease format where the landlord covers all the expenses of operating the building, which usually includes property taxes, property insurance, common area utilities, maintenance, and other general building expenses. The tenant pays a flat rental rate. Depending on the lease contract, the payment may be due weekly, monthly, or annually. A gross lease has a definitive period of time and specified monthly payment. The benefit for the tenant is that he/she consistently knows what the rental payment will be. The detriment to the landlord is if his or her bills increase, such as property taxes, the landlord can do nothing until the lease expires. In other words, the landlord is stuck with the situation. A broker working in a residential rental office will use a gross lease as the agreement that binds a tenant to a landlord.

Net lease: Typically a commercial real estate lease, a net lease is one where the tenant pays for all or a portion of the expenses associated with owning and operating the property. There are three ways a net lease can be constructed.

- Single net (N): The landlord pays approximately 66% of the property's operational expenses. The tenant pays 34%.

- Double net (NN): The landlord pays approximately 34% of the property's operational expenses. The tenant pays 66%.

- Triple net (NNN): The landlord pays approximately 0% of the property's operational expenses. The tenant pays 100%.

Operational expenses may include but are not limited to property taxes, property insurance, maintenance, and repairs. The tenant is responsible for the operational expenses outlined in the lease contract in addition to their ongoing rental payments. Most often, a net lease is created as a triple net. This requires the tenant to pay 100% of the operational expenses. A property with a triple net lease is usually very appealing to landlords because they retain 100% of rental payments as revenue.

Percentage lease: A percentage lease means the tenant pays a base rent along with a percentage of any revenue earned above a given threshold while leasing a space. This may be done on a monthly basis or annual basis. This lease is typically used in retail environments when dealing with smaller boutique types of tenants. The rent could have an impact on the retailer's survival. For example, assuming the tenant is on a monthly rental plan, if the tenant's gross sales do not surpass the given threshold for the month, the tenant pays only the base rent. If the sales exceed the threshold, the tenant pays the base rent plus a percentage of gross revenue in excess of the threshold. Simply stated, if the tenant is making more money, the landlord should be making more money too. The intent is to provide the landlord with a variable source of income that increases with rental income as the tenant becomes more profitable. This agreement usually decreases the lessee's initial base rate and also may offer the lessor some type of benefits and perks.

The leases listed below are used to a lesser extent.

Agricultural lease: It is very common for agricultural landowners to lease their land to tenant farmers. A tenant farmer is someone who farms on land that he/she rents from a property owner. In this scenario, a landowner can get paid a monthly rate from the tenant farmer, or receive a percentage of profit from the tenant farmer's crops that were sold.

Ground lease: The circumstance that creates a ground lease is this. Let's say a landowner has land that he has not used for anything up to this point. It has just been sitting there. If someone comes along and says that they want to lease the land because they want to build a building on the land and the owner is open to leasing to him/her, this is a ground lease. It is most common for the land and the building to be owned separately. Written another way, the building owner's structure is built on land he/she does not own, but rather leases. The building owner develops the property during the lease period. At the conclusion of the lease term, the land as well as the building revert to the landowner. Ground leases are generally written for 50+ year terms to give the tenant sufficient time to recapture the initial investment of constructing the improvement. This is typically a triple net lease. Once they construct the building, is that going to cause the property to be worth more money? Yes. As a result, we want the tenant to pay the property taxes.

Lease with option to purchase: This lease type is frequently called a rent to own or a lease purchase. The tenant wants to purchase, but he/she is not able to do so right now. Usually in this lease type, the property owner will set the monthly rental rate slightly higher than the market rent. Why? Because there is a higher level of risk to the property owner. The benefit to the tenant is that he/she has the option to purchase during or at the end of the lease agreement.

Since the property owner has already entered into an agreement with the current tenant, the property owner is restricted from offering the property to other potential tenants and/or buyers until the current tenant makes a formal decision. When the lease term is close to ending, the tenant must decide whether to vacate or to purchase. If the tenant decides to buy, a portion of the monthly rental payments may be credited toward the purchase price. The purchase price is generally negotiated at the end of the lease term. Should the tenant elect not to purchase the property, the landlord can keep the full rents paid as rental income.

Sale and leaseback: Also called a leaseback for short or sale/leaseback, in this transaction, the property owner sells the property and then will lease it back from the buyer for a specific period of time. In this manner, the transaction shares similarities with a loan. This is a method to generate quick capital.

Variable lease: When creating a long-term lease, to provide the landlord with a reasonable return on their investment, a variable lease is an agreement for a tenant to pay specified rent increases. These increases are based on a predetermined index (Consumer Price Index or CPI) at set dates in the future.

RELATED CONCEPTS AND TERMS

Below is a variety of concepts and terms related to leasing a building or property.

Abatement: Abatement is the act of eliminating or reducing an obligation the consumer may be facing. Abatement in this context is a lease clause. It allows for the reduction of rent or possibly free rent in applicable circumstances for a duration of time that is to be determined. Abatement is commonly used when there is storm damage, water damage, fire, faulty electric work, and so on.

Accessibility: The Fair Housing Act prohibits discrimination in housing because of disability. "+ protects people from discrimination when they are renting or buying a home, getting a mortgage, seeking housing assistance, or engaging in other housing-related activities. Additional protections apply to federally assisted housing" (HUD). Furthermore, the Americans with Disabilities Act of 1990 (ADA) is a civil rights law. It prohibits discrimination based on a person's disability. Thus, what is being offered for rent must be accessible to people with disabilities. Someone who has a physical disability must be able to safely reach, enter, and occupy the rental property. If the person uses a wheelchair, this often includes necessities such as larger doors, ramps, bathroom modifications (if applicable), lower light switches, and similar modifications. Is the tenant allowed to make certain updates or modifications to the unit? Yes, he/she may do so. The changes must be reasonable changes, and he/she will pay for the expense/s. The landlord has the right to have him/her undo the changes once the term lease is up. Why? Because leaving the changes intact could interfere with someone else renting the property/unit in the future.

Arrears: This term means the tenant is behind on his or her payments. This could apply to rent payments, the property's utility bill, and/or similar bills. It's a debt that is owed and one that should have been paid at an earlier time.

Assignment: This legal term is the process by which a person (assignor) transfers his or her leasehold interests, rights, and benefits to another person (assignee). For example, Mike (Tenant A) is moving out of his apartment Friday, six months prior to his lease's expiration date. Robin (Tenant B) is moving into Mike's apartment on Monday. Mike's landlord will legally transfer Mike's interest in the apartment lease over to Robin. Mike's responsibility and benefits of the apartment are passed on to Robin. This is an assignment. It's also called lease takeover and lease transfer.

Certificate of occupancy: Jonathan is in an apartment building's rental office talking with an agent. He sees a certificate on the wall and asks what it is. The agent responds, "That is our certificate of occupancy. It means that the property and units that we rent here have been inspected and approved for occupancy." A certificate of occupancy is a local government-issued document that certifies a building's compliance with local and applicable laws and building codes. It is evidence that the structure is in a healthy, suitable, and livable condition for occupants.

Destruction of premises: This applies to any damage left behind by the tenant that goes beyond normal wear and tear. Examples include holes in the drywall, burnt carpeting, damage from pets, and so on.

Estoppel: Estoppel is a legal principle that prevents an individual from making a claim that is contradictory to the truth or written facts. One of the areas where we use this concept in real estate involves leases. Consider this: a seller wishes to sell their investment property and must convey to the purchaser the nature of all commercial leases. In order to ensure that the landlord is providing accurate information regarding the content of the leases, the investor may ask for an estoppel certificate. An estoppel certificate is written verification from all the tenants. It shows each tenant's perspective regarding the lease content and nature.

Right of first refusal: Existing tenants have rights. Frequently, landlords may include a provision in the lease document that grants the existing tenant the right to renew their lease or even purchase the property at the conclusion of the current lease term. For example, Barbara has been renting a house for two years. The lease is almost up so it's time to renew or let it expire. A prospective tenant, Joyce, is interested in renting the house and hopes that Barbara moves out. However, in her current lease agreement, Barbara has right of first refusal. This means Barbara can renew the lease and continue living there, or refuse to renew and vacate. This option can also be constructed in such a way that may grant Barbara the right to purchase the property at the conclusion of the lease term. Until Barbara makes a decision (within the given timeframe), neither Joyce nor other interested parties have rights or influence because Barbara's rights have priority. The landlord cannot make a deal with Joyce or anyone else currently because Barbara is protected by the terms of the lease.

Improvements: An improvement is a modification or addition made to property. The intent is to enhance the property value and its desirability. There are two types of property improvements.

1. **On-site improvements** are enhancements or additions to the buildings and/or lots that will be sold or leased. The goal is to increase the property value. Examples include landscaping, pools, garages, service buildings, drainage improvements, stairs, walkways, driveways, accessory buildings, walls, site grading, and even new buildings.

2. **Off-site improvements** include aspects like sidewalks, access roads, curbs, sewers, etc. They're labeled off-site because these improvements are outside the property boundaries.

When it comes to leasing, is the tenant or the landlord expected or required to make improvements? The answer is no. It's not a requirement for lease property. If a landlord gives a tenant permission, the tenant may make improvements. Who pays for it? It depends. It can go either way. However, if the tenant pays for the improvement, most of the time, the improvement stays when the tenant leaves. The tenant, in most cases, receives no compensation in any form from the landlord.

Lease term: The lease term is the period of time that defines the tenant's rights to occupy the space in question. Lease periods can be fixed or periodic depending upon the landlord and tenant agreement. The lease establishes the timeframe the tenant is expected to occupy the rental property. When a lease term is complete, the terms can almost always be renewed, withstanding extenuating circumstances. If a tenant wants to terminate the lease early, there are penalties that are outlined within the leasing agreement.

Maintenance: Maintenance is the process of maintaining a property to keep it in habitable condition. Landlords are expected to make necessary property repairs, such as fixing broken sidewalks, updating ramps, elevator maintenance, and so on. For apartment buildings, landlords are expected to maintain sprinklers, pools, hot tubs, gym equipment, lighting, landscaping, and so on. Tenants are expected to do regular and reasonable interior maintenance to their units. For a rental house, the lease will typically define the extent of the tenant's responsibility for maintaining the physical structure and grounds. It is always important for a tenant to clearly understand what is included and what is not included in maintenance. Generally, tenants do not have to make or pay for major repairs. However, there are lease arrangements that may place this obligation on the tenant's shoulders. Minor repairs are commonly handled in accordance with the lease terms. Upon lease expiration, if the tenant chooses not to renew, he/she is expected to hand over the rental property in the same condition in which it was received, minus normal wear and tear.

Implied warranty of habitability: Notice the word *implied* in this phrase. This guarantee is one that is not stated or written the majority of the time. It means a rental meets the basic standards of safety and means it is habitable. The expectation is these standards are accurate prior to the tenant moving in and that they will continue as he/she lives in the rental. In Illinois, the right to a habitable rental is established through case law. It is not established by a specific statutory provision. This concept was affirmed in a 1972 decision by the Illinois Supreme Court.

Nondisturbance clause: This clause exists in mortgage contracts. It says that the landlord and tenant agreement will continue, regardless of any other circumstances. For the most part, this protects the tenant in case the landlord faces foreclosure. A foreclosure by the lender will not terminate the agreement the tenant has with the landlord. If this clause is not present, the tenant could be evicted by the lender.

Notice to quit: This is a formal notice used by a landlord. It communicates to the tenant that the landlord plans to terminate the lease and move toward evicting the tenant. Sometimes, the formal notice shows how the tenant can remedy the situation and avoid eviction. Many times, the tenant's payments are in arrears. In that scenario, getting rent payments up to date (and paying any penalties or fees, if applicable) may enable the tenant to avoid eviction and continue occupying the rental.

Options: While the term options has a variety of applications, in the context of renting a house or apartment, it generally refers to a rent-to-own concept or is sometimes referred to as a lease purchase. In this framework, the tenant leases a specific space for a specified period of time, and at the conclusion of that period, the tenant will be given the opportunity to purchase the property. All terms of the purchase are defined at the moment the tenant makes the decision to buy the property. This is not an obligation to buy, but simply an option to buy. The right of first refusal is an example of another option. It is one of the most common options in leasing agreements. This is different from a lease option.

Possession of premises: When a landlord and tenant enter into and sign the leasing agreement, the tenant receives possession of premises. The tenant is the temporary keeper of the rental property and is entitled to the right to quiet enjoyment. The agreement states that the landlord will not interfere, meddle, or impede the tenant's ability to experience quiet enjoyment of the property he/she is renting. For the landlord to enter the premises, usually the tenant must grant permission. For example, the tenant and landlord may agree that the landlord will come to the property on Saturday at noon to replace a broken faucet. However, the landlord cannot show up ready to do the repair whenever he/she wants without having a conversation with the tenant.

Proration: As you read earlier, proration is the mathematical approach necessary to be able to identify what portion of the expense belongs to each party. For example, Alexei recently graduated from college and landed a dream job in Atlanta. His job starts July 1st. He wants to move into his new apartment by June 25th, so he has a few days to unpack and get settled in. At the time he moves in, he will pay the July rent along with whatever else is required, such as a security deposit. However, the question remains, does he owe rent for the six days of June when he will occupy the unit? The answer is yes. How much rent will Alexei owe for that portion of June? Using the concept of proration is how we calculate the June rent due. If his apartment is $1000 per month, those six days will cost him $200 (rounded). $1000 divided by 30 days equals $33.33 rental cost per day. $33.33 multiplied by six equals $200. There can be different variables in different situations; however, that is generally how proration works.

Quiet enjoyment: As you learned earlier, this term, as well as the concept, are a commonly accepted standard typically found in leasing agreements. It means that the tenant has the right to an enjoyable and peaceful experience while renting the landlord's property or unit. For example, if a landlord knocks on a tenant's door five times every week, this action may be deemed as interfering with the tenant's right to quiet enjoyment. Another example of quiet enjoyment being interrupted could be a landlord who starts mowing grass or weed-eating at 4:30 a.m. Ultimately, the landlord cannot intrude on, impede, or hinder a tenant's quiet enjoyment of the property.

Recording a lease: Do leases have to be recorded? For the most part, leases do not need to be recorded. The majority of states have no requirement for short-term leases to be recorded. If a lease is long-term, such as three-plus years, some states do require the lease to be recorded. This is done at the Register of Deeds office in the county where the rental property is located. In certain states, a memorandum of lease is required to be filed. Sometimes called a memo of lease, this recordable instrument puts third parties on notice. It communicates a lease interest that is encumbering real property. It outlines the specific terms and conditions of a lease agreement. The information included depends on the state and local laws in which the property is located.

Security deposit: This deposit is an additional amount of money that a tenant pays the landlord near the time of signing the lease and/or moving into his or her new rental. This deposit's purpose is to cover any damage incurred due to the tenant's actions or inaction and to act as a penalty if the tenant abandons the space prior to the expiration date. They are almost always required in leasing agreements, whether residential or commercial. When a tenant has one or more pets, at times, the security deposit is higher than those of non-pet owners. Security deposits are like a type of insurance for the owner. The money is commonly held in escrow. When the tenant moves out, if there is no damage and the rent is paid in full, he/she is refunded the full security deposit. If there is minor damage, the cost to repair it will be deducted from the security deposit before it is refunded. Security deposits and deductions from a security deposit are expected to be reasonable.

What does Illinois state law say regarding the return of security deposits? If a building or complex is five or more units, when a tenant vacates the space and surrenders the keys to the landlord, the landlord has 30 days to inspect the property and create a detailed list of all damage (if any) beyond normal wear and tear left by the tenant. If there is no damage, the landlord has 45 days from the date the tenant vacated, to return the security deposit. However, if there is damage, the landlord will have an additional 30 days to make the repairs. After repairs are completed, the cost of services and repairs is deducted from the security deposit, and the remaining balance is then returned to the tenant.

Subleasing: To sublease or sublet means the original tenant is renting all or some of the rental property to a third party. This means the original tenant is both leasing and subleasing the rental simultaneously. The original tenant is now a sublessor. A portion of the original tenant's leasehold interest is transferred to the new tenant, known as a sublessee. Ultimately, the original tenant is responsible for the sublessee and collection of his/her rental payments. The property owner has a leasing agreement with only the original tenant, not with the sublessee. The original tenant (sublessor) has a leasing agreement with the new tenant (sublessee). The majority of the time, subletting is not allowed without permission from the property owner. Permission needs to be in writing. A common way this happens today is a tenant is renting a house or apartment building and wants to make extra money. He/she lists a room or space on Airbnb or a similar service in order to generate more income. However, without written permission from the property owner, subletting can potentially lead to legal problems, fees, a terminated leasing agreement, and/or eviction.

Summary possession: This is another word for eviction. Depending on the jurisdiction, eviction might be called unlawful detainer, ejectment, summary dispossess, repossession, summary process, and forcible detainer. Regardless, the result is the same. The tenant, by the authority of the court, is legally removed from the rental property.

Use of premises: Sometimes this is referred to as permitted use of premises. In the lease, the use of premises outlines the ways in which the property can be used. Anything outside of this description and scope is not permitted. This is most common in commercial leases. For example, if the leasing contract says that the rental can only be used for a laundromat, then that is the only legal use. The tenant cannot decide to open a cafe in the rental space. Furthermore, it's a best practice that the use of space is highly defined. For example, if it were a cafe, there could be more questions to answer, such as: 1) Can a portion be used as a bakery? 2) How much seating is allowed? 3) Can there be a drive-thru window?

Vacancy rate: This is the number of vacancies as compared to the total number of units/spaces available. For example, there are 24 units within the building and 18 are currently occupied. The vacancy factor would be a percentage, determined by dividing the occupied units by the total available units. 18 units ÷ 24 units = 75%. Therefore, this particular building has a 75% occupancy rate. This translates into a 25% vacancy rate. This concept is used both in residential and commercial structures to reflect the percentage of available units for rent.

LEASES: DISCHARGE AND BREACH

As a reminder, **discharge** means to end. When the contract ends, the lease is discharged. The final day of the lease will be in the leasing agreement. For lease termination to take place, one of two events will generally occur: 1) Both parties successfully fulfill and complete their duties and obligation and the lease runs its course naturally, or 2) both parties chose to cancel the leasing agreement. When the rental property is sold or if the owner/lessor passes away, the leasing agreement usually continues. Although this is a general rule, two exceptions do exist: 1) A death of either the lessor or the lessee will terminate a tenancy at will, and 2) if the lease is from the owner of a life estate, then the lease ends when the tenant's life comes to an end. In other cases, when a deceased lessor has an heir (or heirs), they are required to follow the terms of the current lease.

A **breach of lease** happens when either the owner/landlord or tenant breaks one or more agreements in the leasing agreement. When a court determines that a tenant is in breach of the lease, the court might require the tenant to pay for the landlord's legal costs, pay for damages, and/or settle any other fees and charges. A breach does not allow a landlord to break the rule of quiet enjoyment or to behave differently than when the tenant was in compliance. A tenant may be evicted for violation of lease terms and holdover tenancy. However, the most common breach is nonpayment of rent. This could impose the concept of late fees.

In 770 ILCS 95/7.10 of The Act, it covers a section called late fees. It reads as follows:

> "(a) A reasonable late fee may be imposed and collected by an owner for each service period that an occupant does not pay rent when due under a rental agreement, provided that the due date for the rental payment is not earlier than the day before the first day of the service period to which the rental payment applies. No late payment fee shall be assessed unless the rental fee remains unpaid for at least five days after the date specified in the rental agreement for payment of the rental fee.

> (b) No late fee may be collected pursuant to this Section unless the amount of that fee and the conditions for imposing that fee are stated in the rental agreement or in an addendum to that agreement.

> (c) For purposes of this Section, a late fee of $20 or 20% of the rental fee for each month an occupant does not pay rent, whichever is greater, is deemed reasonable and does not constitute a penalty.

(d) Any reasonable expense incurred as a result of rent collection or lien enforcement by an owner may be charged to the occupant in addition to the late fees permitted by this Section. If any such expenses are charged, they shall be identified on an itemized list that is available to the occupant." (770 ILCS 95/7.10)

The first notice a tenant in arrears will receive is called a Notice to Terminate. After five days of having given that notice in Illinois, the landlord has the right to start eviction proceedings with the tenant. Before a lawsuit starts, the landlord is required to give the tenant notice. This notice is called Forcible Entry and Detainer. The purpose of this notice is to be granted an Order for Possession from the court. As you would expect, this grants the landlord the right to retake and resume possession of the rental property/unit. When this eviction period expires (the date that the tenant is required by law to vacate the premises), it's possible that physical eviction will take place. The act of physically removing a tenant from a rental property is called actual eviction. It's the physical dispossession of the tenant. On average, it takes anywhere from two weeks to five months for a landlord to evict a tenant in Illinois. Eviction actions are fully governed by the Forcible Entry and Detainer Act (735 ILCS 5/9-101) and must be overseen by the court through the sheriff's office.

RENTAL INDUSTRY REGULATION AND RENTAL FINDING SERVICES

The rental industry is a highly regulated industry that has been growing in recent years. Section 1450.785 of the Rules And Regulations is called Rental Finding Services. It defines rental finding services as the following and gives information about contracts, disclosure, and more.

a. Definition and Application

    1. A rental finding service is any business that finds, attempts to find, or offers to find, for any person who pays or is obligated to pay a fee or other valuable consideration, a unit of rental real estate or a lessee to occupy a unit of rental real estate not owned or leased by the rental finding service.

    2. Any person, corporation, limited liability company, partnership, limited partnership, or limited liability partnership that operates a rental finding service shall be considered a licensee, obtain the appropriate license, and comply with this Section.

    3. This Section shall not apply to persons exempted by Section 5-20 of The Act.

b. Contract. A rental finding service shall, prior to accepting a fee or other valuable consideration for services, enter into a written contract with the person for whom services are to be performed and deliver to the person a physical or electronic copy of the contract. The contract shall include, in the case of a rental finding service that finds, offers or attempts to find a unit of rental real estate for a person, at a minimum, the following:

1. The term of the contract;

2. The total amount to be paid for the services to be performed and a clear designation of the amount, if any, paid in advance of the performance of the services;

3. A statement regarding whether the fee paid in advance is refundable or nonrefundable, including the following in uniform type of a size larger than that used for the balance of the contract:

   A. Precise conditions, if any, upon which a refund is based;

   B. The conditions shall occur within 90 days from the date of the contract; and

   C. The refund shall be paid no later than 10 days after demand, provided the payment of the fee has been honored;

4. The type of rental unit desired, the geographical area requested, and the rent the prospective tenant is willing to pay;

5. A detailed statement of rental finding services to be performed by the licensee, which shall include, at a minimum, the delivery to the prospective tenant of all rental information set forth in subsection (c);

6. A statement that the contract shall be null and void if information concerning possible rental units or locations furnished by the licensee is not current or accurate with respect to the type of rental unit desired and as set forth in subsection (b)(4). A listing for a rental unit that has not been available for rent for over two days shall be prima facie proof of not being current;

7. A statement that information furnished by the licensee concerning possible rental units may be up to two days old; and

8. A statement requiring the licensee to refund all fees paid in connection with the contract if the contract is null and void for any reason. The licensee shall not impose any condition for the refund, and the contract shall state when the refund will be paid.

c. Disclosure. As required by subsection (b)(5), the following information for each rental unit the rental finding service is listing shall be provided, in writing, to the person with whom the contract is entered:

1. The name, address, email address, and telephone number of the owner of each rental unit or the owner's authorized agent;

2. A description of the rental unit;

3. The amount of rent requested;

4. The amount of security deposit required;

5. A statement describing utilities that are located in the rental unit and included in the rent;

6. The occupancy date and the term of lease;

7. A statement setting forth the source of the information disclosed (i.e., owner, owner's authorized agent); and

8. All other conditions that may reasonably be expected to be of concern to the prospective tenant.

d. Permission of Owner. A rental finding service shall not list or advertise any rental unit without the express written authority of the owner or owner's authorized agent of each unit. (Section 1450.785)

REFERRAL FEES

Can tenants earn referral fees from their landlords? The Act answers:

"Any resident lessee of a residential dwelling unit who refers for compensation to the owner of the dwelling unit, or to the owner's agent, prospective lessees of dwelling units in the same building or complex as the resident lessee's unit, but only if the resident lessee (i) refers no more than three prospective lessees in any 12-month period, (ii) receives compensation of no more than $5,000 or the equivalent of two months' rent, whichever is less, in any 12-month period, and (iii) limits his or her activities to referring prospective lessees to the owner, or the owner's agent, and does not show a residential dwelling unit to a prospective lessee, discuss terms or conditions of leasing a dwelling unit with a prospective lessee, or otherwise participate in the negotiation of the leasing of a dwelling unit." (225 ILCS 454/5-20)

Can residential leasing agents earn referral fees? They may be able to earn referral fees on *leasing* residential real estate. However, they cannot earn a referral fee or commission on a real estate *sale*, whether residential or commercial.

"Residential leasing agent" means a person who is employed by a broker to engage in licensed activities limited to leasing residential real estate who has obtained a license. (225 ILCS 454/1-10).

In other words, a residential leasing agent is simply not authorized to collect a commission or referral fee from a real estate sale. They are only authorized to possibly receive referral fees for services performed in direct connection with the *leasing* of real property, not the sale of real property. Why might some residential leasing agents make a referral fee for leasing while others do not? It all comes down to the terms and conditions found in the employment/independent contractor agreement.

Section 1450.780 of the Rules And Regulations is called Referral Fees and Affinity Relationships. As a real estate licensee in Illinois, you cannot pay a referral fee to someone who is not a licensee. Referral fees can only be paid to a licensed residential leasing agent (on residential leases only), broker, or managing broker in Illinois, or to someone with an equivalent license from another state. When requesting a referral fee, you must have reasonable cause for the payment. Reasonable cause for payment means that an actual introduction of a client was made to a licensee or a contractual referral fee relationship exists with the licensee. Residential leasing agent licensees may only request, or be paid, a referral fee from the lease or rental of residential real estate. Just because there is reasonable cause to request a referral fee doesn't necessarily mean that the licensee has a legal right to the referral fee. As you may recall, it is illegal to interfere with the agency relationship of another licensee in order to obtain a referral fee. This includes, but is not limited to, demanding a fee without reasonable cause, threatening to take harmful action against the client of another licensee, and counseling the client of another licensee on how to terminate or amend an existing contractual relationship.

Now it's time for your quiz.

CHAPTER 23 QUIZ

1. In terms of renting, a lease can be called which of the following?

    a. Leasing agreement
    b. Tenant agreement
    c. Rental agreement
    d. All of the above
    e. Only A, B, and C

2. What does the owner (lessor) retain when he/she rents a property to a tenant?

    a. Reversionary right
    b. Quiet enjoyment
    c. Disposition
    d. None of the above

3. Louisa is a new tenant in a beautiful residential property. What do her monthly rental payments and the contract grant her?

    a. Right to use the property
    b. Possessory rights
    c. Quiet enjoyment
    d. Leased fee estate plus reversionary right
    e. All of the above
    f. A, B, and C

4. James leased a residential single-family home to two brothers who intended to live there. He did not have the best feeling about them, but the property had been sitting vacant for months with no inquiries. Despite his intuition telling him otherwise, he decided to accept the two brothers as tenants. Their tenancy just hit month three and James discovers that they have been manufacturing an illegal drug on site. He calls his lawyer and agent. Most likely, what would they tell him?

    a. The lease must run its course.
    b. The lease can be immediately terminated based upon the illegal activity.
    c. James can file for immediate eviction based upon the illegal activity.
    d. B and C
    e. None of the above

5. Janet recently moved from Argentina to Illinois. Her friend, Agnus, has a guest house in Illinois and told her she can live there if she agrees to do specific chores, cooking and maintenance. Janet agreed. Although this is not the norm, it's not uncommon. Agnus will not receive cash rent as payment for Janet to stay there. However, Janet's labor is her rental payment. What is the most accurate term to describe what is happening here?

   a. Illegal activity
   b. Rental compensation
   c. Allowance
   d. A Fair Housing violation

6. Leasehold estate is a tenant's exclusive right to occupy and possess the real estate for the time period outlined in the lease. It is not ownership. A leasehold is usually considered personal property. What are the different types of leasehold estates?

   a. Estate for years, estate from period to period, freehold estate
   b. Estate for years, estate from period to period, life estate, and estate at sufferance
   c. Estate for years, estate from period to period, estate at will, and estate at sufferance
   d. None of the above

7. Which type of leasehold estate is a type of tenancy created when a tenant and landlord create an agreement that has no end date?

   a. Estate at sufferance
   b. Continuous estate
   c. Estate from period to period
   d. Periodic tenancy
   e. C and D
   f. A, C, and D

8. Suzie has passed the date of her lease terms. As a nursing student, she is constantly busy. When she's not working or studying, she is sleeping. The leasing agreement said that her last day was June 30th and now it's September 1st. She has kept paying rent, and the landlord has consistently accepted the payment. What is this called?

   a. Undefined tenancy
   b. Estate at will
   c. Extended tenancy
   d. Holdover tenancy

9. Which of the following is false concerning estate at will?

    a. It's also called tenancy at will.

    b. It has a specific end date or period of time.

    c. In order to end the estate at will, it's possible that the landlord will need to evict the tenant.

    d. Either party can terminate with proper notice given. If one of the parties dies, the agreement is terminated.

    e. Estate at will can be created by operation of law or by an express agreement between the parties.

10. When creating a long-term lease, to provide the landlord with a reasonable return on their investment, this type of lease is an agreement for a tenant/renter to pay specified rent increases. These increases are based on a predetermined index (CPI) at set dates in the future. What type of lease is this?

    a. Gross lease

    b. Net lease

    c. Percentage lease

    d. Variable lease

11. Peter is a disabled veteran. He is downsizing and has decided to move into an apartment building. It's hard to try and maintain his current house and the move will put him a few blocks away from his grandkids. He has been in a wheelchair for over 15 years. He really likes a specific apartment building. The apartment is on the ground floor and the assigned parking space is close. He would like to make a few modifications given his disability. More than likely, who will have to pay for those modifications?

    a. Peter

    b. Landlord

    c. Both pay 50% of the cost

    d. His grandchildren

12. This legal term is the process by which Tenant A transfers his or her leasehold interests, rights, and benefits to Tenant B. For example, Frank (Tenant A) has six months remaining on his current lease. He is moving out on June 15th. Heather (Tenant B) is assuming the responsibility of the remaining six months of Frank's lease and is moving in on July 1st. Frank's landlord will legally transfer Frank's interest, rights, and benefits over to Heather. What is this known as?

    a. Lease takeover
    b. Lease transfer
    c. Transference
    d. Assignment
    e. A and B
    f. A, B, and D

13. Ted and Terry are a married couple. Terry works at the hospital and received notice last month that they are transferring her to a different hospital in a different town. They have no choice but to move. One benefit is that Ted, an architectural engineer, will also be closer to work. As they are looking for a new apartment in the new city, they are not finding any that they like. They finally found one apartment they like, but both Ted and Terry have concerns about the structural integrity of the property. Which official document can they request to see that can ease their mind, so they have reassurance if they choose to rent there?

    a. Inspection certificate
    b. Certificate of occupancy
    c. Safety certificate
    d. A, B, and C

14. Which of the following is not an on-site improvement?

    a. Curb along the parkway
    b. Landscaping
    c. Pool
    d. Drainage improvement

15. A tenant is expected to make improvements.

    a. True
    b. False

16. Dr. Brenner is a popular therapist in Chicago. He has just learned that the owner of the office building where he rents his office is facing foreclosure. He knows nothing about real estate or how this works, so he is talking to a friend who is a licensee. After his friend explains it, Dr. Brenner feels relieved. Why is it that he will be able to retain his office space despite the owner facing foreclosure? What is inside the lease contract that offers and outlines this protective measure?

    a. Severability clause
    b. Nondisturbance clause
    c. Use of premises clause
    d. Continuity clause

17. What is the best answer to the following question? Do leases have to be recorded?

    a. Yes
    b. No
    c. If a lease is long term like three-plus years, certain states require the lease to be recorded

18. When a tenant and landlord are in an eviction situation, which notice is the landlord required by law to give the tenant that states a lawsuit is commencing?

    a. Notice to Terminate
    b. Order for Possession
    c. Forcible Entry and Detainer
    d. Eviction Notice

19. Eddie is a busy intern at a tech startup. He leaves his apartment at 6 a.m. every day and does not get home until eleven p.m. or later. He realized he forgot to pay his rent. It was due three days ago. How many more days does Eddie have, according to 770 ILCS 95/7.10 of The Act before late payment fees begin?

    a. None
    b. Two
    c. Four
    d. Seven

20. Residential leasing agents can earn a commission on a real estate sale.

    a. True
    b. False

CHAPTER 24:

THE WORLD OF PROPERTY MANAGEMENT

LEARNING GOALS:

By the end of this lesson, you will:

- Have a clear overview of property manager responsibilities
- Know how property managers set rental rates and collect rent
- Understand laws and rules that must be followed
- See the difference between property managers and community association managers
- Understand risk management, insurance, and more

PROPERTY MANAGEMENT

The owner of a property which can be leased/rented may decide to hire a property manager (PM). The property manager will be given the responsibilities to lease, manage and market the owner's rental property.

Property management is the overseeing and management of residential, retail, commercial, industrial, and/or agricultural real estate. It can include properties of any size. Almost every building you walk inside of has a property manager. Property managers manage shopping centers, strip malls, large and small office buildings, industrial parks, medical buildings, warehouses, storage facilities, retail locations, specialty properties, and more.

Although the owner can act as his/her own property manager, they frequently hire a professional property manager. The goal of a property manager is to:

- Always act effectively on behalf of the owner

- Preserve the owner's interests

- Work toward achieving the owner's goals

- Maintain the property value

- Generate profit

Are property managers required to have a real estate license? In Illinois, the answer is yes. In most other states, they're required as well. However, not all states have this as a requirement. Currently, no real estate broker license is required to be a property manager in Vermont, Maine, Massachusetts, and Idaho. Washington D.C., Montana, South Dakota, and South Carolina require only a property management license. In Oregon, one can have either a property management license or a real estate broker license.

Unless the designated property manager is also the designated managing broker under a sponsoring broker, he/she must provide their services under the direction and supervision of his or her sponsoring broker. The property management agreement designates the sponsoring broker as the property owner's agent. This forms an official business relationship with a legally-binding contract. This also means the sponsoring broker has entered into a fiduciary relationship with the property owner. However, the sponsoring broker has the right to delegate agency responsibility to one or more of the licensees within the office, naming them as the designated agent.

E&O insurance (Errors and Omissions), as you recall, is a unique type of insurance commonly used by countless licensees. This type of professional liability insurance may exclude negligent acts other than errors and omissions, commonly called mistakes. E&O coverage is not required for property management, although it is a valuable tool and a best practice.

Property management agreement: A property management agreement is a bilateral contractual relationship between the client (landlord) and the property manager (real estate licensee). This agreement is a legal document that sets up and defines the relationship between the property manager and the client (landlord). It is the first step taken before a property manager can assume the responsibility of managing a defined property. It generates a general agency relationship. The provisions of the agreement will generally contain information such as equal opportunity in housing policies, property description, contract duration, termination clause, liability/limited liability, the property owner's purpose and objectives, the parameters defining property manager's authority, allocation of costs, each party's rights and responsibilities, ongoing reporting, services and fees, and possibly more.

All exclusive written representation agreements (residential, commercial, and property management) must have a defined expiration agreement. The law does not regulate the time duration of a representation agreement. It leaves that to the mutual agreement of the client and the sponsoring broker. However, the law also states that should the representation agreement exceed one year in length, there must also be a provision that grants the client the right to terminate the agreement every twelve months with an advance thirty-day notice. In addition, the law stipulates that the agreement cannot have an automatic extension provision. Once the expiration date passes, the obligations of the licensee in representing the client come to a close. Should the client wish to retain the services of the licensee, the parties must enter into a new written representation agreement.

Property owners employ property managers so they can avoid involvement in the daily property management responsibilities and tasks, as well as those tasks involved with having an office on-site. These tasks may include any variety of these tasks but are not limited to: marketing, open houses, maintenance, tenant issues, paperwork, opening/closing the office, ordering repairs, coordinating schedules, etc. Each property manager's responsibilities depend on the terms of the agreement.

Property managers are fortunate in that they can benefit from membership in several professional real estate organizations. Although you read about these earlier in the book, here is a review of some of the most well-known organizations for PMs:

- Building Owners and Managers Association International (BOMA)

- Certified Commercial Investment Institute (CCIM)

- Commercial Real Estate Women (CREW)

- Institute of Real Estate Management (IREM)

- International Council of Shopping Centers (ICSC)

- National Multifamily Housing Council (NMHC)

- Society of Industrial and Office REALTORS® (SIOR)

- The Appraisal Institute

- Urban Land Institute (ULI)

This is not a comprehensive list of real estate trade organizations for property managers. There are countless online and in-person options. For more information about each of the organizations above, you can visit their websites.

PROPERTY MANAGEMENT BUSINESS PLANS

Similar to how startups and new entrepreneurs create business plans, property managers create and prepare property management business plans. Prior to drafting this plan, the PM will need a wide variety of property-related documents from the owner. These will include annual tax documents/records, insurance premiums, information about special assessments on the property (if applicable), and so on.

A property management business plan is an operating plan. Its purpose is to maximize return on investment, increase the property's potential, and serve as a compass in achieving the owner's goals. Its foundation is research and data, and no surprise, it should always be in writing. Research includes but is not limited to: 1) a neighborhood market analysis, 2) a regional market analysis report, 3) a comprehensive property assessment, and 4) any other analysis or assessment that is specifically relevant and related to the property. The research will have a variety of factors possibly including but not limited to boundaries, land usage, neighborhood amenities, neighborhood facilities, population information, trends, the largest employers in the city/area, supply and demand trends, building codes and regulations, along with data about the property's interior and exterior, comparable value to similar properties that are nearby, average operating costs estimate, and so on.

Financial reports are also included in a management plan. These usually include an annual operating budget and a comparative income and expense report with a three- or five-year forecast. The plan is not carved in stone, it's adaptable. It's usually constantly reviewed and revised or updated as needed.

FINANCE REPORTING RESPONSIBILITIES AND POPULAR FINANCIAL STATEMENTS

A timeless quote related to this topic is "Know your numbers to grow your numbers." This is referencing numbers on financial documents and statements. When a business owner and manager do not understand the numbers, they do not understand the business. That is a dangerous place to be. Many businesses go out of business because those in charge do not understand their financial statements.

A property manager must have a strong understanding of how financial documents work and what they mean. While a PM does not have to be a bookkeeper or CPA, he/she must understand the numbers, and also understand how to communicate what the numbers mean and what they're saying.

The most commonly used financial reports include the following in alphabetical order:

1. **Accounts payable report**: This report shows money that is owed by the property (business) to its suppliers. It includes every payment made during the reporting period for debts and any other financial obligations and agreements. This report provides a clear audit trail.

2. **Balance sheet**: This financial report shows a snapshot of the financial position of the property on the exact date the report is run/printed. It summarizes liabilities, assets, and owner equity. A balance sheet is helpful because, with one easy glance, the reader can see bank account balances, security deposits held, money owed to others, and more. Out of all four basic financial statements, a balance sheet is the only one that shows the financial condition of a business at a single point in time.

3. **Cash flow statement**: Also called a statement of cash flows, this document shows how changes in balance sheet accounts and income impact and affect cash. The focus is to show how cash is flowing in and out of the business. A cash flow analysis is broken down into the following activities: operating, investing, and financing.

4. **General ledger**: Also called a nominal ledger, this report shows a detailed record of individual transactions broken down by accounts. These are the same accounts that are listed in the chart of accounts. The journals and subledgers used include accounts payable, accounts receivable, cash management, purchasing, fixed assets, and so on. Each account requires a ledger account. Categories are classified as income, expense, assets, liabilities, or equity. Each entry is designed to be self-explanatory.

5. **Income and expense statement**: Also called a profit and loss statement (P&L), this monthly report shows a month-to-date and year-to-date featuring a detailed breakdown of income, along with itemized expenses with a comparison to the numbers that were budgeted. This statement is like a financial compass of the rental property. It also shows if the business is under, on, or over budget.

6. **Monthly bank statement copies that include reconciliations**: Reconciliation is essentially proof that the numbers in the office match the numbers the bank has. In other words, everything matches up and nothing is missing. This substantiates the bank account balances that show on the balance sheet. It also substantiates debits (like checks written) and deposits that show on the general ledger. A reconciliation report is commonly used and is generated monthly.

7. **Operating budget**: This report outlines the projected expenses and revenues of a business (or organization) for a specific period of time. It is a tool that helps a business plan, monitor, and control its financial resources. The operating budget commonly includes the day-to-day business operations, such as compensation, salaries, supplies, rent, and other costs associated with running the business. By utilizing an operating budget, organizations anticipate and plan for future expenses, track costs and revenue, and adjust their spending and operations as needed. The goal of this report is to allow the business to manage its resources and achieve its goals. This report shows and describes the income and expenses for the property.

8. **Tenant receivables and prepaid report/s**: As you can tell by the report's title, this report shows and lists tenants who are delinquent on payments, and tenants who are prepaid. When rent is paid on time, there is no balance due for rent receivable.

RECORDKEEPING AND ESCROW

Section 1450.755 of the Rules And Regulations is titled Recordkeeping. Here is an excerpt related to keeping records in property management.

Records relating to transactions shall be retained by the sponsoring broker in hard copy or electronically.

A. These records might include copies of:

1. Residential Property Transactions: Signed contracts, including offers and counteroffers, written release of escrow funds, Dual Agency Authorization, notices of designated agency or no agency, written direction for deposit into an interest-bearing special account, power of attorney, disclosures (e.g., lead paint, radon, seller disclosure), closing statements and other transaction records required to be retained by The Act.

2. Property Management/Leasing: Any rental finding agreement, property management agreements, leases, periodic accounting or statement to the owner regarding the receipts and disbursements, and any other documents set forth in subsection (a)(3)(A)(i) that are relevant to the transaction. (1450.755)

Escrow requires several responsibilities and duties. It's a topic that has many details that a licensee must remember. Section 1450.750 of the Rules And Regulations covers Special Accounts. Here is an excerpt related to keeping records in property management.

a. Escrow Moneys Defined.

1. "Escrow moneys" means all moneys, promissory notes, or any other type or manner of legal tender or financial consideration deposited with any person for the benefit of the parties to the transaction. A transaction exists once an agreement has been reached and an accepted real estate contract is signed, or a lease is agreed to by the parties. Escrow moneys include without limitation earnest moneys and security deposits, except those security deposits in which the person holding the security deposit is also the sole owner of the property being leased or sold and for which the security deposit is being held.

2. As set forth in the terms of a written agreement between a licensee and a client, such as a property management agreement, rent moneys paid to a licensee for transmittal to the licensee's client (e.g., the owner) shall not be considered to be "escrow moneys." In addition, other monies held in a custodial account by a licensee for transmittal to a licensee's client, as set forth in the terms of a written agreement, such as a contract for deed, shall not be subject to this Section.

3. Earnest money constitutes escrow money whether in the form of personal checks, cashier's checks, money orders, cash, or any other forms of legal tender.

Section 1450.750 also shares this:

Escrow Requirements for Property Management Activities. Security deposits shall be maintained in an escrow account for the duration of the lease, unless the tenant waives this requirement in writing and except if prohibited by State laws and local ordinances. The waiver, if included in the lease, shall appear in bold print.

DUTIES AND OBLIGATIONS

The duties and obligations of the property manager, whether commercial or residential, can vary greatly between properties. While there may be similarities, each property manager must recognize the landlord's purpose and goals. Some landlords like to have a more hands-on position, while others simply want to release the full responsibility to the property manager. Some of the more common responsibilities include:

1. **Maintenance**: This is the oversight of the day-to-day functions of maintaining the property. The tenants are going to expect the property to be kept clean and safe.

Should a repair need to be made, regardless of the severity, the tenant will consider it a major issue. It's smart for a property manager to walk the property regularly looking for problematic areas. The issues he/she finds may be small or large. Regardless, they need his or her attention to make the property more desirable, convenient, and enjoyable for the tenants.

2. **Expenses**: A property manager needs to watch all of the expenses, both fixed and variable. The owner acquired the property with the intent to make money. He/she expects a positive ROI (return on investment). Allowing the expenses to run out of control defeats that purpose. In conjunction with the owner, the property manager created a target budget at the start of the year. He/she needs to assess whether or not he/she is working within the budget. No budget is ever perfect. Unexpected expenses will arise. That is common and they cannot be controlled. However, attentive and smart financial management can help offset unexpected expenses.

3. **Janitorial**: Like the other aspects of our industry, it's important for a property manager to know his or her limitations. Most property managers are not maintenance specialists. A best practice is to select maintenance staff well. They actually are ambassadors, both of the property manager and of the landlord. Chances are the tenants will have greater contact with the maintenance staff than with the property manager or the landlord. Their personality and demeanor, along with the little things, can make a huge difference. More than likely, they will be entering tenants' apartments from time to time in order to access problems and make necessary fixes. It means the world to tenants when maintenance specialists are professional, kind, and respectful.

Negotiating Leases

Whether commercial or residential, the property manager needs to know the market rental rates. He/she must research what other similar properties are charging tenants. Like a CMA in negotiating a sale, the property manager should have a similar analysis of the rental market in which he/she is involved. With that market knowledge, the property manager can begin negotiating the rent between landlord and tenant. This creates a firm platform from which to work. A property manager who goes into this blindly is not sufficiently protecting the interests of his or her respective client. Going into the negotiation well-prepared and having done the research positions the property manager for the best outcome possible.

PROPERTY MAINTENANCE

Maintenance is paramount because it protects the owner's investment. It also ensures the property is well-kept, functional, and as attractive as possible for current and potential tenants.

There are four categories of property maintenance. They are routine maintenance, preventive maintenance, corrective maintenance, and emergency maintenance.

1. **Routine maintenance**: This maintenance is done on a regular basis, whether it is daily, weekly, bimonthly, monthly, quarterly, or annually. For example, a breakdown can include sweeping the sidewalks daily, checking the PH level of the pool twice a week, the lawn being mowed once a week, trimming bushes twice a month, a yearly furnace inspection, and so on.

2. **Preventive maintenance**: The purpose of this type of maintenance is to extend the life of what is being maintained. Its aim is to prevent breakdowns and failures from occurring. In the long run, it reduces expenses. Preventive maintenance makes sure that small problems do not grow into large expensive problems. If water leaks into an apartment for a day, it can most likely easily and cheaply be fixed. If water leaks into an apartment for two months, it will cost more to fix. Examples of preventive maintenance include pest control, replacing AC and furnace filters, painting, refreshing shower caulk and grout, inspecting the roof, cleaning out the gutters, patching cracks in drywall, and so on.

3. **Corrective maintenance**: These are ordinary repairs that are not an emergency. Usually, they are not a major inconvenience to the tenant. Most of the time, something has failed and has to be fixed or replaced. For example, it could be that an AC unit died. It worked for as long as possible thanks to preventive maintenance and now it is beyond the state of repair. It must be replaced. Corrective maintenance can be as simple as replacing a faulty faucet or as complex as replacing an entire heating plant.

4. **Emergency maintenance**: This type of maintenance is obviously the most urgent and important type of repair. It cannot be ignored or postponed. It includes emergencies such as broken water lines, frozen pipes, fire, broken door locks, gas leaks, broken heaters during cold winter months, and similar emergencies.

Tenant improvements is a related topic. Sometimes it's referred to as leasehold improvements. These are most common in the realm of industrial and commercial rental properties, not residential. What makes these different from repairs and maintenance is that tenant improvements are customized alterations done to the rental unit/property. They are part of a leasing agreement. Why are they done? The goal is to meet the specific needs of the client renting the space. The leasing agreement defines who will pay for the improvements. Sometimes it's the tenant. Sometimes it's the landlord or rental company. At times, the expense may be shared. The leasing agreement also outlines who will complete the improvement. Examples of tenant improvements include but are not limited to wall changes, lighting changes, installing partitions, adding a break room, drop ceilings, installing certain specialty equipment required by the tenant's business, and installing a bathroom or adding another bathroom. The majority of the time, tenant improvements are negotiable.

SETTING RENTAL RATES AND COLLECTING RENT

For the most part, rental rates are subject to fluctuations in supply and demand. It is mostly an external factor that gives property owners a reasonable range in which to set the rent. If an owner charges high rent, it's very likely potential renters will opt for a different and less expensive property if it has similar features. No owners want to price themselves out of business at worst, or into financial problems at best. Other factors in setting the rent focus on the worth of the property, what similar properties are charging (i.e., local rent), and how easy it is to cover property expenses. Obviously, the rental income must be enough to cover expenses. On top of that, the rental rate should be comparable to similar properties that are nearby (in the town, city, or region). The goal of the owner is to receive a reasonable return on investment.

One factor to consider is rental vacancy. Low vacancy is a good sign for the owner as it is proof of having most of the units occupied by tenants. In that scenario, it's possible that the owner can increase the rental rates. If there is high vacancy, the property manager's main goal is to rent more units so more revenue is generated. High vacancy can be an indicator that the rent is viewed as too expensive by potential tenants. High vacancy possible is not about the rent, however. It may be that tenants are having a bad experience, complaining to friends, and leaving negative and mediocre reviews online.

Property managers rely highly on standard operating procedures (SOPs) and systems. An essential system is one for rent collection from tenants. When a property manager is assessing an application from a potential tenant, one of the most important elements is whether or not he/she has the financial capacity to consistently pay his or her rent. Methods to collect rent include an automated online system, in person, drop box, or mail. Mail is rarely used since it's the most unreliable. Automated online systems are the most common nowadays. Generally, it's attached to the tenant's checking or savings account. The system automatically pulls out the rent each month on a set date. It's very common for tenants to be able to set this up. Each one has a profile and can check their account, understand any extra charges (if applicable) and print out a full rental payment history document. The lease agreement should include all the steps about how a tenant pays rent. At a minimum, the steps included will have a monthly due date, payment method (how to pay), information about bounced checks and late payment penalties/fees, along with nonpayment damages information, and the lease termination process. All rent payments, along with a property manager's system, must follow state and local laws. If a tenant is late on rent, a PM's goal is to successfully collect the rent without moving into the realm of legal action. A PM will usually try to avoid legal action to the extent possible. He/she knows that it can be expensive and create a lot of wasted time, hassle, and stress. When a PM has no option but to pursue legal action, he/she must follow a clear and set course of legal procedures.

Both landlords and tenants have specific legal rights and responsibilities. These are based on state laws, along with judicial decisions. It is important for each party involved in legal action to know his or her rights. It's best for them to directly consult with their local municipality and understand the ordinances that regulate their rights. Both parties need to stay up to date and be well informed about their rights, responsibilities, and options.

Section 765 ILCS 705 of The Act is called the Landlord and Tenant Act. It lays out information about liability exemptions, class X felony by lessee or occupant, changing or rekeying of the dwelling unit locks, the rights of military personnel in military service and their right to terminate the lease, and more. You can read the full section at this link.

https://www.ilga.gov/legislation/ilcs/ilcs3.asp?ActID=2201&ChapterID=62

An interesting caveat is the topic of interest on security deposits. How is interest on security deposits maintained? As you know, property managers are required to have a license. They are required by law to place security deposits into a defined escrow account. Sound familiar? If so, it's because that's exactly how residential and commercial licensees are required to handle and oversee earnest money. How does interest on a security deposit work? A PDF titled "Landlord and Tenant Rights and Laws" by the current Illinois Attorney General answers. "State law requires your landlord to pay you interest on your security deposit if it is held for at least six months and there are at least 25 units in your building or complex. Your landlord must pay you the interest or apply the interest as a credit to your rent every 12 months. You may sue your landlord for willfully failing to pay interest and recover an amount equal to your security deposit, court costs, and attorney's fees." You can read the PDF in its entirety here: https://www.illinoisattorneygeneral.gov/Page-Attachments/LandlordAndTenantRightsLaws.pdf

Keep in mind that real estate licenses are not only issued to individuals. They are also issued to LLCs, corporations, and partnerships. Any one of those business organizations that has a real estate license has the authority to engage potential tenants in terms of leasing transactions. How do sponsoring brokers collect rental compensation for these leasing services? Frequently, the property manager compensation is a fixed fee defined by the management agreement. The fee the sponsored licensee is entitled to is defined in the employment/independent contractor agreement each licensee must have with his/her sponsoring broker. As you recall from our prior discussion, Illinois Real Estate License Law does not allow the sponsored licensee to receive or collect rental compensation directly from the public or from sponsoring brokers, other than their own sponsoring broker.

By definition, a residential leasing license only permits residential leasing. Anything beyond that, unless the licensee holds a broker or managing broker license, is not permitted or authorized. For example, a residential leasing agent cannot lease a retail space in a shopping center to a potential tenant. It is outside of the scope of his or her license.

TENANT SELECTION

How is it that property managers select and approve tenants? As you know, no tenant is to experience discrimination. Fair housing laws also apply. The majority of the time, a tenant will be selected if he/she has an acceptable credit score (or credit report), good references, and no prior evictions. Property managers are looking for those people who are financially qualified and moral to the extent that is searchable. This helps them avoid potential tenants who are a financial risk. PMs want to build long-term relationships with tenants. They want a client to stay in Apartment 15 for multiple years, not just one year or less. PMs know it's easier to keep a tenant happy than it is to find a new tenant.

When it comes to commercial rental businesses, the property manager is looking at other variables as well. With a strip mall, for example, it makes sense to have a nail salon beside or close to a cafe. They are complimentary. However, having businesses that do not mesh well together like a low-end dollar store beside a boutique clothing store can be a poor decision. Complimentary businesses feed off of each other. They equally encourage foot traffic. More people mean more sales. Those sales mean that these businesses keep consistently making their rental payments. Additionally, adding competitors to the same location can create issues. For example, a shopping area with two large office stores can be problematic. Neither owner of one of the office stores will be pleased if a direct competitor is only a short walk away from his or her store.

TENANT RELATIONSHIP BUILDING

> "Trust is the glue of life. It's the most essential ingredient in effective communication. It's the foundational principle that holds all relationships." Stephen Covey

Building and maintaining relationships with tenants is critical to tenant retention. Ideally, property managers are skilled with both projects and people. This can be a rare trait, although it can be developed. Since they interact with people on a daily basis, building relationships is of the utmost importance. A simple way to build relationships with tenants is to use the W.I.N. acronym. (The original source is unknown.) W.I.N. works for building relationships in any context and capacity. **W.I.N.** stands for Wants, Interests, and Needs.

Here are examples of what a property manager can ask a tenant to stimulate conversation and build the relationship.

1. **Wants:**

    - What are you planning this weekend?

    - Any plans this summer?

    - When you've finished your MBA, what's next?

2. **Interests:**

    - How's the dog?

    - What's new with your painting project?

    - How are the yoga classes going?

3. **Needs:**

    - How is everything working with your rental?

    - Do you need anything right now?

    - Do you need anything repaired?

The benefits produced by building relationships include, but are not limited to, the following:

1. There is less tenant turnover. Simply put, happy tenants always rent longer than disgruntled tenants. It's easier and more cost-effective to keep current tenants than it is to secure new tenants.

2. Tenants feel seen, heard, and appreciated and that creates connectedness.

3. Tenants grow to know, like, and trust the property manager.

4. Tenants are more likely to tell friends and family that they're having a positive experience where they're renting.

5. There is a greater probability of good to great online reviews.

6. Tenants who feel heard and cared for are more likely to take care of the rental property, set good examples, and put positive pressure on other tenants to follow the rules and guidelines.

7. Tenants are less likely to complain and more likely to be compliant with rent payments and expectations when they have a good relationship with the property manager.

Building relationships is not only about listening and talking. It's also about how quickly repairs are made. It's about keeping tenants informed, whether verbally and/or via email newsletters or printed newsletters. Being attentive to what tenants need shows them that they are valued and appreciated. If you've ever had a bad landlord and later a good landlord, you completely understand the difference. The bad landlord is only interested in collecting rent. He/she is not concerned about chitchat or building the relationship. He/she is in no hurry to make repairs or updates to your rental. A good landlord, on the other hand, is the opposite and it makes all the difference. It's more important that a PM *shows* a tenant that he/she cares, instead of merely telling a tenant. Attention and action make a huge difference in relationships with tenants. As always, actions speak louder than words.

PROPERTY MANAGEMENT AND THE ENVIRONMENT

As awareness and information about the environment grow and deepen, a property manager's responsibilities increase as well. Real estate is inseparable from its environment. Some environmental-friendly steps may be simple. These include using energy-efficient light bulbs, installing eco-friendly dishwashers in each unit, using eco-friendly laundry systems (in an on-site laundry room for example), adding recycling canisters in convenient locations on the property, purchasing only green products for maintenance, installing a leak detection device/service, and similar options. Other environmental-friendly steps or precautions can be complex. In this category are topics like radon, asbestos, hazardous wastes, and/or related health hazards that are directly related to the rental living conditions.

The Radon Awareness Act requires sellers and landlords of residential property to provide a radon disclosure to the current and prospective buyers and tenants. The Radon Awareness Act states the following.

> "(a) A lessor of a dwelling unit shall disclose to lessees the existence of a radon hazard consistent with the provisions of this Section. For the purposes of this Section, "dwelling unit" means a room or suite of rooms used for human habitation and for which a lessor and a lessee have a written lease agreement.
>
> (b) The provisions of this Section apply only to dwelling units located below the third story above ground level.
>
> (c) If a current lessee has provided in writing to the lessor the results of a radon test that indicate that a radon hazard exists in a dwelling unit covered by this Section, then the lessor shall disclose in writing to any individual seeking to enter into a lease of that dwelling unit that a radon test has indicated that a radon hazard may exist in the dwelling unit. After receiving a notification of a radon test that indicates a radon hazard, the lessor may choose to conduct a radon test in the dwelling unit. If the lessor's radon test indicates that a radon hazard does not exist on the premises, the lessor shall not be required to disclose that a radon hazard exists in the dwelling unit.

(d) If a lessor conducts a radon test in a dwelling unit and the radon test indicates that a radon hazard exists in the dwelling unit, the lessor shall disclose in writing to the current lessee, and any individual seeking to enter into a lease of that dwelling unit, the existence of a radon hazard in the dwelling unit.

(e) If a lessor has undertaken mitigation activities and a subsequent radon test indicates that a radon hazard does not exist in the dwelling unit, then the lessor is not required to provide the disclosure required by this Section.

(f) Nothing in this Section shall be construed to require a lessor to conduct radon testing." (420 ILCS 46/25)

Any hazardous waste on a rental site must be disposed of safely and securely, following any applicable state and local laws.

How can a property manager understand the property and its environment? One step is for an environmental audit to be completed. This is important for several reasons. The CDC states that "Building-related illnesses include asthma, hypersensitivity pneumonitis, inhalation fever, rhinosinusitis, and infection. In contrast to sick building syndrome, these building-related illnesses are less common and may result in substantial medical morbidity." Building-related illnesses are sometimes called BRIs. Many times, these issues are related to poor ventilation and indoor air quality issues. A property manager's job is to provide and facilitate a healthy place for his or her tenants. This always includes making sure that the environment is safe, unimpaired, and healthy.

RISK MANAGEMENT AND PROPERTY MANAGERS

All types of businesses face different types of risks, and the rental property business is no different. The goal of risk management is to minimize losses and maximize opportunities. Disastrous or tragic events can wreak havoc on the business financially, as well as damage the business' reputation. Risk management is about weighing the pros and cons. Is it worth it to install a pool, or are the risks heavier than the perks? Is it worth it to build a separate small building as a gym for tenants? Is having an unsupervised area with free weights and cardio equipment too risky? These questions and similar inquiries are ones that PMs and landlords are constantly asking themselves and exploring. Most commonly, risk management is taught with one of four different possible actions to be taken:

1. **Avoid the risk.** This is the simplest approach, although that does not mean it is the best in all circumstances. This approach answers with no. Examples include "We're not building the pool" or "We are not adding a daycare center." If there is no risk, then there is no related liability or financial loss that can take place.

2. **Control the risk.** Controlling the risk acknowledges that risk is present and that the decision is to manage and control the risk. How is that done? The property manager takes decisive steps to mitigate against potential risks and/or minimize potential risks. Being proactive is a key to controlling risks. Examples include installing carbon dioxide detectors in units, having a state-of-the-art fire alarm system, security cameras, and similar endeavors. The goal is to show proof of due diligence.

3. **Directly manage the risk.** In other words, the property manager accepts the risk and chooses to manage it themselves. Why would someone do this? If filing a claim potentially causes an increase in the annual premium and the property manager knows he/she can absorb the cost of the risk if it comes to fruition, he/she may decide to manage the risk in-house.

4. **Transfer the risk.** This involves shifting responsibility. The weight of the potential risk is shifted to another party. Most commonly, this is done by purchasing a comprehensive insurance policy.

COMPLIANCE WITH THE AMERICANS WITH DISABILITIES ACT OF 1990

Property managers are expected to stay in compliance with the Americans with Disabilities Act of 1990. Known as ADA, this applies regardless of whether the property was built before or after 1990. Disabled individuals must be able to access every public area on a rental property. This includes the rental office, conference room, event areas, and any public restroom on-site.

> "To be protected by the ADA, one must have a disability, which is defined by the ADA as a physical or mental impairment that substantially limits one or more major life activities, a person who has a history or record of such an impairment, or a person who is perceived by others as having such an impairment." (ADA)

Disability is a wide term that encompasses a large variety of disabilities and conditions. Some are easily observable. Some are not easily observable. A property manager must never discriminate in any way, shape, or form. A PM cannot directly ask a disabled person about his or her disability. Likewise, a PM cannot ask for proof of a disability during the rental application process. After the lease is signed, if the new disabled tenant asks for a specific type of modification or accommodation to be made, the PM may ask for proof. The goal of the proof is to show how the modification or accommodation will make the rental safer and/or more functional for the tenant.

In 2022, the CDC and the Disability and Health Data System (DHDS) reported that 1 in 4 Americans in the United States have a disability. The most common disabilities are: 1) mobility,

2) cognitive, 3) independent living, 4) hearing, 5) vision, and 6) self-care. Look at the definitions and percentages in the following chart.

MOST COMMON DISABILITIES AND CORRESPONDING INFORMATION, AS REPORTED BY THE CDC and THE DHDS		
Type Of Disability	Definition	Percentage of adults with functional disability types
Mobility	Serious difficulty walking or climbing stairs	11.1%
Cognitive disability	Serious difficulty concentrating, remembering, or making decisions	10.9%
Independent living	Difficulty doing errands alone	6.4%
Hearing	Deafness or serious difficulty hearing	5.7%
Vision	Blindness or serious difficulty seeing	4.9%
Self-care	Difficulty dressing and/ or bathing	3.0%

Review the full chart from the CDC here: https://www.cdc.gov/ncbddd/disabilityandhealth/infographic-disability-impacts-all.html

The CDC recently stated the following:

- Adults living with disabilities are more likely to be obese, smoke, have heart disease and diabetes.

- Concerning adults with disabilities from ages 18 to 44:

  - One in four adults does not have a usual healthcare provider.

- One in five adults has an unmet healthcare need because of cost in the past year.

- One in four adults did not have a routine check-up in the past year.

The CDC shared the following information in a 2018 press release.

- Two in five adults age 65 and older have a disability.

- One in four women have a disability.

- Two in five Non-Hispanic, American Indians/Alaska Natives have a disability.

The Act recognizes five types of disabilities (15 ILCS 335/4A). They are laid out in the chart below.

DISABILITY TYPES DEFINED BY THE ACT				
Type 1	**Type 2**	**Type 3**	**Type 4**	**Type 5**
Physical disability	Visual disability	Developmental disability	Hearing Disability	Mental Disability

The ADA requires landlords to make what they call "**reasonable accommodations**" for tenants with disabilities. How is that term defined?

> "A reasonable accommodation is a change, exception, or adjustment to a rule, policy, practice, or service that may be necessary for a person with disabilities to have an equal opportunity to use and enjoy a dwelling, including public and common use spaces, or to fulfill their program obligations. Please note that the ADA often refers to these types of accommodations as 'modifications'. Any change in the way things are customarily done that enables a person with disabilities to enjoy housing opportunities or to meet program requirements is a reasonable accommodation. In other words, reasonable accommodations eliminate barriers that prevent persons with disabilities from fully participating in housing opportunities, including both private housing and in federally-assisted programs or activities. Housing providers may not require persons with disabilities to pay extra fees or deposits or place any other special conditions or requirements as a condition of receiving a reasonable accommodation." (HUD)

A reasonable accommodation must obviously be reasonable. This means that the request is not outlandish or shocking. It should not create a heavy financial burden on the landlord. Many times, a reasonable accommodation is installing an access ramp, designating a priority parking spot for the disabled tenant, and similar changes. Property managers and landlords want to stay up to date with ADA compliance and be proactive about serving disabled tenants to the best of their abilities.

INSURANCE AND CLAIMS

First, let's start with tenants. Many tenants falsely believe that if something devastating happens, like a fire, their personal property inside of their unit is covered. This is not accurate. Property managers need to inform tenants that they have the option to purchase renter's insurance. In Illinois, it's called HO4 or HO-4 insurance. If a tenant decides not to purchase renter's insurance, he/she does so at his or her own risk. If someone breaks in and steals a tenant's laptop and flat screen, it is the tenant's loss. The property manager and rental company are not liable. Neither a property owner nor the property manager can insure the tenants' belongings because he/she does not own them. When a tenant secures HO4 insurance, his or her personal property is covered. Most commonly, this insurance covers what is known as the "16 perils." These are specific damages or losses listed in his or her policy. Usually, this insurance will cover specific legal expenses, fees, and temporary living expenses. It also includes personal liability and medical payment coverage.

THE 16 PERILS			
Accidental and sudden damage caused by short-circuiting	Explosion	Hail or windstorm	Vandalism
Accidental and sudden tearing apart, burning, bulging and/or cracking	Falling object	Non-intentional water overflow or steam	Vehicles
Civil commotion or riot	Fire and/or lightning	Smoke and/or ash	Volcanic activity or eruption
Damage from aircraft	Freezing weather	Theft	Weight of sleet, ice, or snow

Note: The original source of the 16 perils is unknown.

Next, let's move to insurance for the rental property. Property managers have the goal of protecting the property against damages and losses. A wide variety of insurance types are available in order to fulfill this goal. Common types of coverage for rental properties like apartment complexes include the following in no particular order:

1. **Fire and hazard**: This common insurance policy generally provides coverage for fire and hazards. However, hazards may include damages due to fire, thunderstorms, hail, smoke, theft, civil insurrections, and an act of war. In the coverage, it's common for the property manager to cover the property's total replacement cost and not only its current cash value.

2. **Flood**: This coverage protects the property from direct damage by flooding.

3. **Business interruption insurance**: Also known as loss of rent and previously known as use and occupancy insurance, this coverage handles business costs that have occurred due to damaged equipment or facilities. For example, if an area suffers from an extended power outage, this insurance covers this type of disaster. Other examples include mudslides, flooding, and similar disasters. This also covers lost revenue (whether rent or non-rent revenue) that the business incurs because of the disaster.

4. **Contents insurance**: Also called personal property insurance, this coverage covers contents and personal property when the items are not physically located on the property. For example, a property manager and her assistant are doing a presentation in a different part of town. They took all of their AV equipment, including two new laptops. While they were looking at the space where they'd be setting up, someone broke the SUV window and stole all the equipment. This coverage covers the replacement costs of the equipment.

5. **Liability**: Liability refers to someone being responsible for one or more specific things. Every time there is a person on a rental property, it's possible that something can happen. This coverage comes to the rescue when a tenant or someone from the public gets injured on the rental property. This insurance covers loss and damages. For example, say Jan is touring a unit on the second floor. Upon leaving the unit, she steps down on a wooden stair. The stair breaks and she tumbles down the stairs. If this happens, the property owner is liable, and this insurance covers Jan's injuries and expenses.

6. **Worker's compensation**: Related to liability—if an employee falls off a ladder while painting the side of Building C and is injured, if it's determined the landlord is liable, then it is classified as worker's compensation.

7. **Casualty**: Casualty coverage is a very broad term and can encompass different coverages. In the world of property management, this policy includes liability coverage and helps protect property owners if they are found legally liable for an accident that injures a person or damages another person's belongings. This coverage is usually not all-inclusive. Usually, it involves specific risks that are highly relevant to the property. It covers damage and theft. Worker's compensation is a type of casualty insurance.

8. **Surety bonds**: What happens if a property manager discovers that an employee has been involved in criminal activity and/or negligence during his or her work hours? This coverage protects against these types of difficult circumstances and provides protection against related financial losses. Surety bonds are not insurance, although it's commonly talked about with insurance in this context.

Actual cash value and replacement cost value are two methods of insurance coverage options for rental properties. They determine how much money an insurance company will pay for a claim. Actual cash value (ACV) is also called depreciated cash value. This is the amount of money required to fix a damaged rental property minus the decrease in its value (due to use and age). It is the cost to replace the damaged property with like kind, less the depreciation. As you recall, the IRS defines like-kind as "property of the same nature, character, or class. Quality or grade does not matter. Most real estate will be like-kind to other real estate." Replacement cost value (RCV) is the sum of money required to repair and/or replace the damaged rental property at today's prices. This includes building supplies and replacing damaged items and belongings with similar items and belongings. Depreciation is not a factor in RCV. The policy will define and explain replacement costs. Both methods are based on today's costs. The key difference is that ACV factors in depreciation and RCV does not.

COMMUNITY ASSOCIATION MANAGERS

A common mistake is for people to think that property managers and community association managers are the same. They are not. While there is some overlap in responsibilities, they are separate and distinct jobs. In a nutshell, community association managers manage communities. Property managers manage property. While property managers obviously work with people, the primary focus is the property. There are a variety of communities that can be managed by a community association manager. These include but are not limited to HOAs, resort communities, condominium associations, and commercial tenant associations. Community association managers work directly and closely with homeowners and the complex board of directors. They are only responsible for common areas like pool areas, gyms, and so on. They are not responsible for, nor do they maintain, individually owned units.

Does a real estate managing broker or broker license supersede the need to acquire this license? No, in Illinois, anyone that manages a condominium complex consisting of more than 10 units is required to acquire this license. Your real estate managing broker or broker license will exempt you from the required education, but not from having to take the state exam.

Section 225 ILCS 427 of The Act is called the Community Association Manager Licensing and Disciplinary Act. It regulates and safeguards community association managers. Its legislative intent is as follows.

> "It is the intent of the General Assembly that this Act provide for the licensing and regulation of community association managers and community association management firms, ensure that those who hold themselves out as possessing professional qualifications to engage in the business of community association management are, in fact, qualified to render management services of a professional nature, and provide for the maintenance of high standards of professional conduct by those licensed to provide community association management services." (225 ILCS 427)

This section covers definitions, requirements for holding a license, and more. You can read it here: https://ilga.gov/legislation/ilcs/ilcs3.asp?ActID=3152&ChapterID=24

Now it's time to take your quiz about property management.

CHAPTER 24 QUIZ

1. Are property managers required to have a real estate license?

   a. Yes, for every state
   b. Depends on the state
   c. In Illinois, yes
   d. Only B and C

2. In which of the following scenarios can E&O coverage protect agents and brokers?

   a. Closing transaction delays as a result of the broker's mismanagement
   b. Discrimination, libel, or slander
   c. Failure of the licensee to advise on a reasonable price
   d. Failure of the licensee to inspect property
   e. Mishandling earnest money, security deposits, or other monies
   f. All of the above
   g. A, C, D, and E
   h. A, B, and D

3. Does the law regulate the time duration of a commercial property management representation agreement?

   a. Yes
   b. No

4. Suzie is a property manager. Her assistant left her a message saying that the owner wants a printout of a financial document that gives a snapshot in time. It's a financial document that shows bank account balances, security deposits held, money owed to others, and more. Which report is being requested?

   a. Accounts payable report
   b. Balance sheet
   c. Cash flow statement
   d. Income and expense statement
   e. None of the above

5. Which financial document shows a month-to-date and year-to-date featuring a detailed breakdown of income, along with itemized expenses with a comparison to the numbers that were budgeted?

    a. Accounts payable report

    b. Balance sheet

    c. Cash flow statement

    d. Income and expense statement

    e. Tenant receivables and prepaid report

6. Terry is a new property manager. She is learning about setting rental rates. Which of the following are true considering what she is learning about?

    a. They mostly revolve around supply and demand.

    b. It's important to learn what similar properties in the city/region are charging.

    c. The owner must receive a reasonable ROI.

    d. All of the above.

    e. Only A and C.

7. Eddie paid a security deposit of $1400 to lease his apartment 11 months ago. Since he was just promoted at work, he will be staying there at least one more year if not longer. The apartment complex where he rents a unit has over 50 units. Is Eddie's landlord required to pay Eddie interest on his security deposit?

    a. Yes

    b. No

    c. Yes, or the landlord has to apply the interest as a credit to Eddie's rent every 12 months.

8. Earnest money constitutes escrow money in which of the following forms?

    a. Personal checks

    b. Cashier's checks

    c. Money orders

    d. Cash

    e. Any form of legal tender

    f. All of the above

    g. Only A, B, C, and E

9. What are the categories of property maintenance?

    a. Routine, preventive, corrective, and emergency
    b. Mandatory, proactive, reparative
    c. Everyday, electrical, structural, and emergency
    d. None of the above

10. Dimitri commercially manages a small shopping center outside of Chicago. A small consulting firm wants to rent a space. They are requesting a few things to be added, including partitions, another restroom, and lowered ceilings. What is the best way to describe these additions?

    a. Updates
    b. Tenant improvements
    c. Tenant renovations
    d. Specialized updates

11. Mikey is a community association manager. He wants to move from Boise to Naperville. He is looking online for job openings that he qualifies for. In which of the following communities can Mikey work?

    a. HOAs
    b. Apartment complexes
    c. Resort communities
    d. Condominium associations
    e. Commercial tenant associations
    f. All of the above
    g. All of the above except for B
    h. All of the above except for A and C

12. Tina is crafting her first property management business plan. Which of the following is not going to be part of her research?

    a. Neighborhood market analysis
    b. Regional market analysis report
    c. Race research
    d. Comprehensive property assessment

13. Which of the following is the least likely to be on a list of building-related illnesses?

    a. Asthma
    b. Hypersensitivity pneumonitis
    c. Stomach flu
    d. Inhalation fever
    e. Rhinosinusitis

14. To be protected by ADA, a person must have a disability. How does ADA define this?

    a. A person with a physical or mental impairment that substantially limits one or more major life activities.
    b. A person who has a history or record of such an impairment.
    c. A person who is perceived by others as having such an impairment.
    d. All of the above

15. Phil and Robin have been living in their apartment building in Illinois for over a year. Over the weekend, they were visiting Robin's mom in another state. That Saturday, they received a call saying that their building had caught on fire. Their unit was destroyed. Everything inside was consumed by the fire. They were devastated. They decided to leave early. On the way back, they discovered that they did not really know if their belongings were covered and would be replaced or not. Phil thought this insurance was included when they signed the lease. Robin thought it was an additional insurance. Neither remembered if it was a monthly expense they have. Which of the following is correct?

    a. This insurance is commonly included in leases, and their belongings will be replaced.
    b. Nothing will be replaced unless they have HO4 insurance.
    c. The property owner is personally liable to replace their belongings.
    d. None of the above

16. Which type of insurance covers civil insurrections?

    a. Fire and hazard
    b. Business interruption insurance
    c. Contents insurance
    d. Casualty

17. Bill is a property manager. He has just learned that an employee has been embezzling funds. Bill is worried about how this will affect the property's future. Which type of insurance or coverage will assist in this type of unfortunate event?

   a. Business interruption insurance
   b. Contents insurance
   c. Casualty
   d. Surety bonds

18. What is depreciated cash value also known as?

   a. Actual cash value
   b. Replacement cost value
   c. A and B
   d. None of the above

19. Jenna is a property manager. She hired a DJ for an evening event for the benefit of the tenants. At the conclusion of the event, the DJ stores his equipment temporarily in a utility closet in the complex. The property manager locks it, and they go to the office. When they finish talking in the office, they both go back to get his equipment. Unfortunately, they found the lock broken on the ground and all of the DJ's equipment is gone. Since the property owner is most likely to be liable or responsible for the DJ's equipment that was stored on-site, what type of insurance will cover the DJ's stolen equipment?

   a. Contents insurance
   b. Business interruption insurance
   c. Surety bonds
   d. Casualty
   e. According to the CDC, what are the top three most common disabilities?

20. Mobility, vision, and independent living

   a. Hearing, vision, and self-care
   b. Cognitive, vision, and independent living
   c. Mobility, cognitive, and independent living

CHAPTER 25:

THE ENVIRONMENT AND REAL ESTATE

LEARNING GOALS:

By the end of this lesson, you will:

- Understand common environmental hazards
- Know the role and goals of the Illinois Environmental Protection Agency (IEPA)
- Deepen your understanding of the most common hazards
- See how landfills and waste management works

IN THE PREVIOUS CHAPTER about property management, you read some about environmental issues affecting professionals in the property management field. In this chapter, you will see how the environment affects all real estate transactions. The majority of states understand that there is a dynamic balancing act between real estate and the environment. How can a city grow while at the same time preserving or enhancing its air, soil, and water quality? How do cities and states focus on sustainability? There are no easy answers to these questions or similar ones. Nowadays, it is not simply a property that wins over homebuyers and causes them to purchase. Many homebuyers also heavily consider the environment in which the property is located. How is the air quality? Are any parks close? Is a walk in nature to get fresh air an easy option? How is the soil quality if a homeowner wants to grow a small garden? As said earlier, real estate is inseparable from the environment.

How does hazard discovery work? The EPA website describes the process of an ecological risk assessment (ERA) as follows:

- Planning: As described in the Guidelines for Ecological Risk Assessment (U.S. EPA, 1998), planning is the initial phase of an ecological risk assessment (ERA). During planning, risk managers and risk assessors define the goals, scope, and timing of a risk assessment. These may include government officials, politicians, ecologists, toxicologists, wildlife biologists, chemists, statisticians, and engineers. They also identify the resources that are available and necessary to achieve the goals. After the planning phase, the problem formulation process begins.

- Problem formulation: Problem formulation is a process for generating and evaluating preliminary hypotheses about why ecological effects have occurred, or may occur, from human activities (U.S. EPA, 1998). During problem formulation,

  - the purpose of the assessment is articulated,

  - the problem is defined, and

  - a plan for analyzing and characterizing risk is determined.

- **Phase 1 of the ERA: Planning and problem formulation**

  - Goal: Articulate the purpose for the assessment, define the problem, and make a plan for analyzing and characterizing risk.

  - Who is involved?

    - Risk assessors and other professionals who bring expertise relevant to the locations, stressors, ecosystems, scientific issues, and other expertise as needed, depending on the type of assessment.

- Risk managers—individuals and organizations who have the responsibility or authority to take action or require action to mitigate an identified risk.

- Other interested parties, or "stakeholders" that may include Federal, State, tribal, and municipal governments, industrial leaders, environmental groups, small-business owners, landowners, and other segments of society concerned about an environmental issue at hand or attempting to influence risk management decisions.

- Approach and planning

  - Identify the interested parties: risk assessors, risk managers, and stakeholders.

  - Begin the planning dialogue between risk assessors and risk managers.

  - Determine if a risk assessment is the best option for supporting the decision.

  - Come to an agreement on the goals, scope, and timing of a risk assessment and the resources that are available and necessary to achieve the goals.

- Problem formulation

  - Refine objectives for the risk assessment.

  - Evaluate the nature of the problem: gather available information on stressor sources and characteristics, exposure opportunities, characteristics of the ecosystem(s) potentially at risk, and ecological effects.

  - Select assessment endpoints that identify specific receptors to be protected and characteristics of the receptors that are important to protect.

  - Develop conceptual models that describe predicted relationships among stressors, exposures, and assessment endpoints.

  - Develop an analysis plan that includes a delineation of the assessment design, data needs, and uncertainties. The plan also includes measures that will be used to evaluate the risk hypotheses, and methods that will be used for conducting the analysis.

  - Describe pathways and relationships identified during problem formulation that will be pursued during the analysis phase of the ERA. Ensure that the planned analyses will meet risk manager needs. (EPA)

- Products

  - Planning

- Clearly established and articulated management goals.

- Characterization of decisions to be made within the context of the management goals.

- Description of scope, complexity, and focus of the risk assessment, including the expected output and the technical and financial support available to complete the assessment.

- Problem formulation

  - Site description that defines the scale and site boundaries, describes the habitat, and identifies species that are present. Site description may be based on an actual site, conceptual site, or generic site.

  - Assessment endpoints that adequately reflect management goals and the ecosystem they represent.

  - Conceptual models that describe key relationships between a stressor and assessment endpoint or between several stressors and assessment endpoints.

- Analysis plan

- **Phase 2 of the ERA: Analysis**

  - Goal: Provide the information necessary for determining or predicting ecological responses to stressors under exposure conditions of interest. Analysis connects problem formulation with risk characterization.

  - Who is involved?

    - Risk assessor(s) (in consultation with Risk Manager)

    - Approach

  - Exposure Characterization

    - Describe sources of stressors, their distribution in the environment, and their contact or co-occurrence with ecological receptors.

  - Ecological Effects Characterization

    - Evaluate stressor-response relationships or evidence that exposure to stressors causes an observed response.

- Products

  - Exposure Characterization

  - Exposure profile that describes source(s) of the stressors, receptors, fate and transport of the stressor and exposure pathways, extent of exposure, impact of variability and uncertainties in exposure estimates, and conclusions about the likelihood that exposure will occur.

  - Ecological Effects Characterization

  - Stressor-response profile that describes the effects to receptors, the cause-and-effect relationships, how fast the receptor recovers, relationships between the assessment endpoints and measures of effect, and the uncertainties and assumptions associated with the analysis. (EPA)

Types of Hazards

There are several categories of hazards. A hazard is a risk and may include, but are not limited to, the following:

Physical hazards: These are physical aspects of the property that may cause harm or even death to individuals. They include faulty electrical outlets, exposed live wires, heights, fire, noise, radiation, low-hanging entryways, spills on floors, unsafe machinery, rotting wood, and so on. Even something as common as damaged carpet can cause someone to trip and get hurt.

Biological hazards: Viruses, bacteria, mold, dust, animals (especially vermin), insects, and the like are biological hazards. Humans are also included in this category. It is anything biological that can cause harm, adverse health conditions, or even death. Sewage is also commonly placed in this category, although it is also a physical hazard.

Cultural hazards: These relate to an individual's practices and habits. These rarely directly relate to real estate, although they are helpful to know. Cultural hazards include excessive smoking, excessive consumption of alcohol, overeating, excessive use of legal drugs, use of illegal drugs that are usually very addictive, and working at hazardous jobs like mining, excavation, or operating large powerful equipment.

Social hazards: Poverty and illiteracy are two examples of social hazards. This also includes alcoholism, obesity, excessive smoking, and drug abuse (which are connected with cultural hazards).

Chemical hazards: This is any chemical or hazardous substance that can harm or kill an individual. These include cleaning chemicals, pesticides, acids, solvents, etc. Consequences can include skin issues, feeling unwell, respiratory problems, blindness, and more. One or more of the following properties can make a chemical harmful or dangerous: toxicity, ignitability, corrosivity, and reactivity.

ILLINOIS ENVIRONMENTAL PROTECTION AGENCY (IEPA)

What is the IEPA and what is its mission?

"The Illinois General Assembly was the first state legislature in the nation to adopt a comprehensive Environmental Protection Act. It was signed into law by Governor Richard Ogilvie and became effective on July 1, 1970. As a part of that act, the Illinois Environmental Protection Agency was created. The mission of the Illinois EPA is to safeguard environmental quality, consistent with the social and economic needs of the State, so as to protect health, welfare, property, and the quality of life. The Illinois EPA works to safeguard the state's natural resources from pollution to provide a healthy environment for its citizens. By partnering with businesses, local governments, and citizens, the Illinois EPA is dedicated to continued protection of the air we breathe and our water and land resources." (Illinois Environmental Protection Agency)

The Illinois Environmental Protection Act is Illinois' primary environment-focused statute. Its goal is to "establish a unified, state-wide program supplemented by private remedies, to restore, protect and enhance the quality of the environment, and to assure that adverse effects upon the environment are fully considered and borne by those who cause them" (415 ILCS 5). There are several acts related to the mission of a cleaner and healthier Illinois. These include the Electronic Products Recycling and Reuse Act, the Mercury-Added Product Prohibition Act, the Mercury Switch Removal Act, the Mercury Thermostat Collection Act, the Mercury Fever Thermometer Prohibition Act, and the Consumer Electronics Recycling Act (CERA). There are also federal environmental regulations in effect. Rules and other pollution control standards adopted by the Illinois Pollution Control Board or the Illinois EPA can be found and read in Title 35 of the Rules And Regulations.

HAZARDS IN REAL ESTATE

Asbestos

Asbestos is a fibrous silicate mineral. It occurs in nature and has soft, flexible fibers. The fibers are very durable and resistant to electricity, heat, and corrosion. It's an exceptional insulator. It can be used in a variety of items including cement, paper, plastic, insulation, and more. It makes other materials stronger and more durable. Asbestos was used in buildings, construction materials, and even helicopters, planes, and ships. Its positive qualities are why it was used so much in the past, before its dangers were known. Exposure is highly toxic. Asbestos mineral fibers can get trapped in someone's body. They can cause a permanent and progressive disease that worsens over time. The mineral fibers enter the body by way of ingestion or inhalation. Insulation containing asbestos generates airborne contaminants, which can be the source of respiratory diseases. Over the course of years, these captured and trapped asbestos fibers can be the source of ongoing inflammation, scarring, and ultimately, genetic damage. Mesothelioma is an uncommon combative cancer caused by asbestos. Asbestosis is also caused by asbestos. It is an interstitial and progressive lung disease. During the '70s and beyond was when U.S. culture shifted and began recognizing, studying, and becoming aware of the dangers of asbestos. Buildings made prior to the 1980s are commonly thought to have asbestos, although they may not have it.

Between 1999 and 2013, a 2015 study completed by the EWG (Environmental Working Group) Action Fund showed Illinois ranking seventh in asbestos-related deaths. The worst states for asbestos were California, Florida, Pennsylvania, New York, Texas, and Ohio.

> "The Illinois EPA Asbestos Unit protects the people of the State of Illinois and the environment from asbestos exposure. Illinois EPA (IEPA) is the USEPA delegated authority to enforce the National Emission Standards for Hazardous Air Pollutants (NESHAP) for regulated asbestos during demolition, renovation and disposal." (IEPA)

Identifying asbestos can be challenging. If it is insulating water pipes or heating pipes, it can be simple and easily visible. However, the majority of the time it is difficult because the asbestos is underneath the floor or inside of the walls. This can make people rightfully nervous when renovating and remodeling old buildings because such actions can disturb the asbestos. When it comes to asbestos in residential buildings, no guidelines exist. For commercial and public buildings, federal regulation stipulates that testing for ACMs (asbestos-containing materials) must be completed. Removal of asbestos can present a risk for those involved and close by.

> "Workers who manage or abate asbestos in schools, commercial, or public buildings must be trained and licensed. Contractors are responsible for conducting asbestos abatement projects. All contractors who conduct asbestos abatement projects must have insurance and are required to be licensed" (Illinois.gov). (Abatement means removal and disposal.)

The licensing requirement for asbestos workers comes from the Federal Government. Certain states mandate permits and licenses to conduct asbestos abatement. Asbestos removal and disposal in Illinois can only be done with a license. The license must be renewed annually. If the asbestos removal is too expensive or not preferable, a possible option is encapsulation. This process seals off asbestos-containing materials (ACMs). The sealant material surrounds and encapsulates asbestos fibers. This process prevents any release of the toxic fibers. A membrane is created over the surface and acts as a bridging encapsulant. Finally, a penetrating encapsulant permeates the material and binds all the components together. It is the owner's responsibility to systematically check the encapsulation to ensure it is whole and intact. Owners, property managers, licensees, and everyday individuals should avoid trying to check for asbestos. Only certified asbestos inspectors should do this type of job because only they have the training and the protective equipment.

Radon

You read about radon earlier. Let's start with a refresher and then you'll read new content. Remember the Radon Awareness Act? This act requires that a seller of residential property provides a radon disclosure to the buyer, prior to the buyer tendering an offer. The Radon Awareness Act states:

> "Every buyer of any interest in residential real property is notified that the property may present exposure to dangerous levels of indoor radon gas that may place the occupants at risk of developing radon-induced lung cancer. Radon, a Class-A human carcinogen, is the leading cause of lung cancer in non-smokers and the second leading cause overall. The seller of any interest in residential real property is required to provide the buyer with any information on radon test results of the dwelling showing elevated levels of radon in the seller's possession." (420 ILCS 46/10)

Radon is a gas that is radioactive, colorless, odorless, and tasteless. The World Health Organization says that "Radon is produced from the natural radioactive decay of uranium, which is found in all rocks and soils. Radon can also be found in water."

Outdoors, radon disperses rapidly and, generally, is not a health issue. Most radon exposure occurs inside homes, schools, and workplaces. Radon gas becomes trapped indoors after it enters buildings through cracks and other holes in the foundation. Indoor radon can be controlled and managed with proven, cost-effective techniques. Breathing radon over time increases your risk of lung cancer. Radon is the second leading cause of lung cancer in the United States. Nationally, the EPA estimates that about 21,000 people die each year from radon-related lung cancer. Only smoking causes more lung cancer deaths (EPA).

Where can the greatest concentrations of radon be found in the home? As it is a radioactive gas, it is a heavy gas. Therefore, you'll find the greatest concentrations in basements and crawl spaces. Oftentimes, the consumer has a radon problem and does not know it, because it is an odorless gas. Fortunately, radon detection devices are commercially available for purchase.

Resources:

1. Pamphlet version of "Radon Testing Guidelines for Real Estate Transactions" download link: https://iemaohs.illinois.gov/content/dam/soi/en/web/iemaohs/nrs/radon/documents/radontestguidelineforrealestatepamphlet.pdf

2. Page format version of "Radon Testing Guidelines for Real Estate Transactions" download link: https://iemaohs.illinois.gov/content/dam/soi/en/web/iemaohs/nrs/radon/documents/radontestguidelineforrealestate.pdf

3. Homebuyer's and Seller's Guide to Radon PDF download: https://www.epa.gov/sites/production/files/2015-05/documents/hmbuygud.pdf

Below is the Illinois radon disclosure form.

Formaldehyde

Formaldehyde is a colorless gas with a strong odor. You may have been exposed to formaldehyde back in your high school biology class if you were required to dissect a frog. Chances are that the frog was stored in liquid formaldehyde to preserve it until you were able to study it. It is commonly used to preserve and embalm bodies in preparation for burial.

DISCLOSURE OF INFORMATION ON RADON HAZARDS

(For Residential Real Property Sales or Purchases)

Radon Warning Statement

Every buyer of any interest in residential real property is notified that the property may present exposure to dangerous levels of indoor radon gas that may place the occupants at risk of developing radon-induced lung cancer. Radon, a Class-A human carcinogen, is the leading cause of lung cancer in non-smokers and the second leading cause overall. The seller of any interest in residential real property is required to provide the buyer with any information on radon test results of the dwelling showing elevated levels of radon in the seller's possession.

The Illinois Emergency Management Agency (IEMA) strongly recommends ALL homebuyers have an indoor radon test performed prior to purchase or taking occupancy, and mitigated if elevated levels are found. Elevated radon concentrations can easily be reduced by a qualified, licensed radon mitigator.

Property Address: _____

Seller's Disclosure (initial each of the following which applies)

(a)_____ Elevated radon concentrations (above EPA or IEMA recommended Radon Action Level) are known to be present within the dwelling. (Explain)

(b) _____ Seller has provided the purchaser with the most current records and reports pertaining to elevated radon concentrations within the dwelling.

(c)_____ Seller either has no knowledge of elevated radon concentrations in the dwelling or prior elevated radon concentrations have been mitigated or remediated.

(d) _____ Seller has no records or reports pertaining to elevated radon concentrations within the dwelling.

Purchaser's Acknowledgment (initial each of the following which applies)

(e)_____ Purchaser has received copies of all information listed above.

(f) _____ Purchaser has received the IEMA approved Radon Disclosure Pamphlet.

Agent's Acknowledgment (initial) (if applicable)

(g) _____ Agent has informed the seller of the seller's obligations under Illinois law.

Certification of Accuracy

The following parties have reviewed the information above and each party certifies, to the best of his or her knowledge, that the information he or she provided is true and accurate.

Seller _____ Seller _____
       Printed Name   Printed Name

Seller _____ Date _____ Seller _____ Date _____
       Signature   Signature

Purchaser _____ Purchaser _____
          Printed Name   Printed Name

Purchaser _____ Date _____ Purchaser _____ Date _____
          Signature   Signature

Agent _____ Agent _____
      Printed Name   Printed Name

Agent _____ Date _____ Agent _____ Date _____
      Signature   Signature

In real property in the past, formaldehyde was used in the production of building materials and countless household products. It can be found in plywood, particle board, glues, fiberglass, adhesives, permanent-press fabrics, molded plastics, lacquers, some insulation materials, and more. People can use it to manufacture other chemicals. Additionally, formaldehyde occurs naturally in the environment. The main method of exposure is inhalation. It's classified as a volatile organic compound (VOC) and one of the most common VOCs in the world. Other examples of VOCs include ethylene glycol, benzene, methylene chloride, and tetrachloroethylene. Many words ending with -ene are unsaturated hydrocarbons that contain a double bond.

> "Formaldehyde is a sensitizing agent that can cause an immune system response upon initial exposure. It is also a cancer hazard. Acute exposure is highly irritating to the eyes, nose, and throat and can make anyone exposed cough and wheeze. Subsequent exposure may cause severe allergic reactions of the skin, eyes and respiratory tract. Ingestion of formaldehyde can be fatal, and long-term exposure to low levels in the air or on the skin can cause asthma-like respiratory problems and skin irritation, such as dermatitis and itching. Concentrations of 100 ppm are immediately dangerous to life and health (IDLH). Note: The National Institute for Occupational Safety and Health (NIOSH) considers 20 ppm of formaldehyde to be immediately dangerous to life or health." OSHA (Ppm stands for parts per million.)

The Clean Air Act Amendments of 1990 listed formaldehyde as 1 of 187 hazardous air pollutants that are currently on their air pollutants list. Federal agencies like the FDA and EPA have set limits on formaldehyde use. The Federal Register in Part 3280 called Manufactured Home Construction and Safety Standards shares the following:

Formaldehyde emission controls for composite wood products.

a. Definitions. For purposes of this section, the definitions found in 40 CFR 770.3 apply.

b. Formaldehyde emission levels. The following maximum formaldehyde emission standards apply whether the composite wood product is in the form of a panel, or is incorporated into a component part or finished good:

1. For hardwood plywood made with a veneer core or composite core, the maximum level is 0.05 parts per million (ppm) of formaldehyde

2. For medium density fiberboard, the maximum level is 0.11 ppm of formaldehyde

3. For thin medium density fiberboard, the maximum level is 0.13 ppm of formaldehyde

4. For particleboard, the maximum level is 0.09 ppm of formaldehyde. (Federal Register)

Lead Hazards

Lead-based paint is a hazard. Exposure to lead paint can cause a variety of symptoms and health problems, including but not limited to headaches, fatigue, dizziness, diminished motor skills, high blood pressure, nervous system damage, learning disabilities, kidney damage, diminished height, stunted growth, hearing issues, and even delayed development.

Lead is especially dangerous to babies and kids because it has a sweet taste. This sweet taste is why it was common in the past for children to put lead chips in their mouths and/or chew and suck on toys with lead dust. Lead-based paint is sometimes found on surfaces that children can put their mouths on or even chew. For adult men and women, lead paint can cause reproductive problems.

Making it more problematic, lead can also be found on surfaces that get a lot of everyday use, like doors, door frames, windows, windowsills, railings, stairs, and so on. Lead can be found in water, lead-glazed pottery, the soil, lead-soldered garbage cans, lead-based painted toys, and more items. It's possible for lead to infiltrate drinking water by way of plumbing pipes and materials that are eroding and deteriorating. This is most common in places where the water has high acidity. It also occurs when there is low mineral content because that also corrodes pipes. Homes constructed prior to 1986 are more likely to have installed and be using lead pipes. Lead may not only be found in pipes, but it can also be found in fixtures and solder. It can even be airborne. Lead is considered a possible and likely carcinogen. High levels of lead paint may result in death.

Because of the numerous dangers, the government responded by creating the Lead Disclosure Rule. The HUD website shares the following:

Congress passed the Residential Lead-Based Paint Hazard Reduction Act of 1992, also known as Title X, to protect families from exposure to lead from paint, dust, and soil. Section 1018 of this law directed HUD and EPA to require the disclosure of known information on lead-based paint and lead-based paint hazards before the sale or lease of most housing built before 1978.

The HUD website also states the following.

Before ratification of a contract for housing sale or lease, sellers and landlords must:

- Give an EPA-approved information pamphlet on identifying and controlling lead-based paint hazards (Protect Your Family From Lead In Your Home pamphlet, currently available in English, Spanish, Vietnamese, Russian, Arabic, Somali).

- Disclose any known information concerning lead-based paint or lead-based paint hazards. The seller or landlord must also disclose information such as the location of the lead-based paint and/or lead-based paint hazards, and the condition of the painted surfaces.

- Provide any records and reports on lead-based paint and/or lead-based paint hazards which are available to the seller or landlord (for multi-unit buildings, this requirement includes records and reports concerning common areas and other units, when such information was obtained as a result of a building-wide evaluation).

- Include an attachment to the contract or lease (or language inserted in the lease itself) that includes a Lead Warning Statement and confirms that the seller or landlord has complied with all notification requirements. This attachment is to be provided in the same language used in the rest of the contract. Sellers or landlords, and agents, as well as homebuyers or tenants, must sign and date the attachment.

- Sellers must provide homebuyers a 10-day period to conduct a paint inspection or risk assessment for lead-based paint or lead-based paint hazards. Parties may mutually agree, in writing, to lengthen or shorten the time period for inspection. Homebuyers may waive this inspection opportunity.

- Effective Dates: The regulations became effective on September 6, 1996, for transactions involving owners of more than four residential dwellings and on December 6, 1996, for transactions involving owners of one to four residential dwellings. (HUD)

Types of housing covered include most private housing, public housing, federally owned housing, and housing receiving federal assistance.

"Lead poisoning, the number one environmental illness of children, is caused primarily by lead-based paint in older homes. While Illinois has made great progress in recent years, we maintain one of the highest rates in the nation for the number of children with elevated blood lead levels. The most common exposure to lead by children is through the ingestion of paint chips and contaminated dust from deteriorated or disturbed lead-based paint in homes built before 1978. About 75% of Illinois homes built before 1978 contain some lead-based paint. Other exposures may be from imported goods or food containing lead." Illinois Department of Public Health

Under Public Health, in response to the dangers of lead paint, the Illinois General Assembly created the Lead Poisoning Prevention Act. (410 ILCS 45/).

Mitigation notices come from the Illinois Department of Public Health. The notice communicates that a lead hazard has been discovered on a specific property and that it must be taken care of. The definition of mitigate is to correct the defect.

What happens when a residential property owner gets a mitigation notice?

1. The owner needs to take action to eliminate the lead hazard (and/or)

2. If the owner is in the process of selling the property, he/she must give notice of this development to potential buyers.

What happens if the property owner is renting the property? Likewise, the owner by law must inform the renters/tenants about the presence of a lead hazard.

A new lease cannot be entered into until the lead hazard is no longer present. Only mitigation makes it possible for a new lease or sale to take place.

Millions of houses today have lead paint. At times, the lead paint is under newer paint. If the paint remains in good condition, usually the lead paint does not cause any problems. However, when lead-based paint deteriorates, it can be problematic. Deterioration can be in one or more of these forms: chipping, peeling, chalking, damaged, cracking, and/or damp. When these circumstances are present, the lead paint is a hazard. Immediate attention must be taken.

In Illinois, if a building contains lead paint (or lead hazards), here are the timetables for the building owner to eliminate the hazard.

1. 90 days: Eradicate the lead hazard, in a way that follows the state law guidelines.

2. 30 days: If the occupants have a child or children under the age of six years and/or if an occupant is a pregnant woman.

HOMEBUYERS AND RENTERS: KNOW YOUR RIGHTS BEFORE YOU PURCHASE OR LEASE REAL ESTATE DISCLOSURES ABOUT POTENTIAL LEAD HAZARDS FROM THE EPA	
HOMEBUYERS	RENTERS

Federal law requires that before being obligated under a contract to buy target housing, including most buildings built before 1978, buyers must receive the following from the home seller:

- An EPA-approved information pamphlet on identifying and controlling lead-based paint hazards Protect Your Family From Lead In Your Home (PDF).

- Any known information concerning the presence of lead-based paint or lead-based paint hazards in the home or building.

  - For multiunit buildings, this requirement includes records and reports concerning common areas and other units when such information was obtained as a result of a building-wide evaluation.

- An attachment to the contract, or language inserted in the contract, that includes a "Lead Warning Statement" and confirms that the seller has complied with all notification requirements.

  - Sample Seller's Disclosure of Information (PDF) in English (PDF) and in Spanish (PDF).

- A ten-day period to conduct a paint inspection or risk assessment for lead-based paint or lead-based paint hazards. Parties may mutually agree, in writing, to lengthen or shorten the time period for inspection. Homebuyers may waive this inspection opportunity. If you have a concern about possible lead-based paint, then get a lead inspection from a certified inspector before buying.

Federal law requires that before signing a lease for target housing, including most buildings built before 1978, renters must receive the following from their landlord:

- An EPA-approved information pamphlet on identifying and controlling lead-based paint hazards, Protect Your Family From Lead In Your Home (PDF).

- Any known information concerning the presence of lead-based paint or lead-based paint hazards in the home or building.

  - For multiunit buildings, this requirement includes records and reports concerning common areas and other units when such information was obtained as a result of a building-wide evaluation.

- An attachment to the contract, or language inserted in the contract, that includes a "Lead Warning Statement" and confirms that the landlord has complied with all notification requirements.

  - Sample Lessor's Disclosure of Information in English (PDF) and in Spanish (PDF).

If you have a concern, ask your landlord to get a lead hazard inspection from a certified inspector before signing your lease.

—EPA.gov

As owners, landlords, agents, and managers of rental property, you play an important role in protecting the health of your tenants and their children. Buildings built before 1978 are much more likely to have lead-based paint. Federal law requires you to provide certain important information about lead-based paint and/or lead-based paint hazards before a prospective renter is obligated under lease to rent from you (EPA).

If a homebuyer does not receive a Disclosure of Information on Lead-Based Paint and/or Lead-Based Paint Hazards form when he/she bought or leased pre-1978 housing, he/she can contact 1-800-424-LEAD (5323) or the HUD website.

(https://www.hud.gov/program_offices/healthy_homes/enforcement/disclosure)

In real estate transactions, a lead-based paint inspection is the buyer's responsibility. To review the Disclosure of Information on Lead-Based Paint and/or Lead-Based Paint Hazards, use this link: https://www.epa.gov/sites/production/files/documents/selr_eng.pdf

Removal or encapsulation of lead-based paint must be done by certified or licensed individuals according to federal law.

HOUSING LESSORS AND SELLERS:
KNOW YOUR RESPONSIBILITIES BEFORE YOU SELL OR LEASE

Property Managers and Landlords.	Real Estate Agents and Home Sellers.
Landlords must give prospective tenants of target housing, including most buildings built before 1978:	As real estate agents and home sellers, you play an important role in protecting the health of families purchasing and moving into your home. Buildings built before 1978 are much more likely to have lead-based paint. Federal law requires you to provide certain important information about lead-based paint and/or lead-based paint hazards before a prospective buyer is obligated under a contract to purchase your home.

Landlords must give prospective tenants of target housing, including most buildings built before 1978:

- An EPA-approved information pamphlet on identifying and controlling lead-based paint hazards, Protect Your Family From Lead In Your Home (PDF).

- Any known information concerning lead-based paint or lead-based paint hazards pertaining to the building.

  - For multi-unit buildings this requirement includes records and reports concerning common areas and other units when such information was obtained as a result of a building-wide evaluation.

- A lead disclosure attachment to the lease, or language inserted in the lease, that includes a "Lead Warning Statement" and confirms that you have complied with all notification requirements.

  - Sample Lessor's Disclosure of Information in English (PDF) and in Spanish (PDF).

As real estate agents and home sellers, you play an important role in protecting the health of families purchasing and moving into your home. Buildings built before 1978 are much more likely to have lead-based paint. Federal law requires you to provide certain important information about lead-based paint and/or lead-based paint hazards before a prospective buyer is obligated under a contract to purchase your home.

Real estate agents must:

- Inform the seller of his or her obligations under the Real Estate Notification and Disclosure Rule. In addition, the agent is responsible, along with the seller or lessor, if the seller or lessor fails to comply; unless the failure involves specific lead-based paint or lead-based paint hazard information that the seller or lessor did not disclose to the agent. Read the regulations that include these requirements.

- Provide, as part of the contract process, an EPA-approved information pamphlet on identifying and controlling lead-based paint hazards, Protect Your Family From Lead In Your Home (PDF). Attach to the contract, or insert language in the contract, a "Lead Warning Statement" and confirmation that you have complied with all notification requirements.

  - Sample Seller's Disclosure of Information (PDF) in English (PDF) and in Spanish (PDF).

- Provide a ten-day period to conduct a paint inspection or risk assessment for lead-based paint or lead-based paint hazards. Parties may mutually agree, in writing, to lengthen or shorten the time period for inspection. Homebuyers may choose to waive this inspection opportunity. —EPA.gov

Disclosure of Information on Lead-Based Paint and/or Lead-Based Paint Hazards

Lead Warning Statement

Housing built before 1978 may contain lead-based paint. Lead from paint, paint chips, and dust can pose health hazards if not managed properly. Lead exposure is especially harmful to young children and pregnant women. Before purchasing or renting pre-1978 housing units, sellers (lessors) must disclose the presence of known lead-based paint and/or lead-based paint hazards in the dwelling. Buyers (lessees) must also receive a federally approved pamphlet on lead poisoning prevention.

SELLER (LESSOR) DISCLOSURE

(a) Presence of lead-based paint and/or lead-based paint hazards (check (i) or (ii) below):

(i) _____ Known lead-based paint and/or lead-based paint hazards are present in the housing (explain).

_____

_____

(ii) _____ Seller (lessor) has no knowledge of lead-based paint and/or lead-based paint hazards in the housing.

(b) Records and reports available to the seller (lessor) (check (i) or (ii) below):

(i) _____ Seller (lessor) has provided the buyer (lessee) with all available records and reports pertaining to lead-based paint and/or lead-based paint hazards in the housing (list documents below).

_____

_____

(ii) _____ Seller (lessor) has no reports or records pertaining to lead-based paint and/or lead-based paint hazards in the housing.

BUYER (LESSEE) ACKNOWLEDGMENT (INITIAL)

(c) _____ Buyer (lessee) has received copies of all information listed above.

(d) _____Buyer (lessee) has received the pamphlet *Protect Your Family from Lead in Your Home.*

AGENT'S ACKNOWLEDGMENT (INITIAL)

(e) _____ Seller's agent has informed the seller (lessor) of the seller's (lessor's) obligations under 42 U.S.C. 4852(d) and is aware of his/her responsibility to ensure compliance.

CERTIFICATION OF ACCURACY

The following parties have reviewed the information above and certify, to the best of their knowledge, that the information they have provided is true and accurate.

Seller (Lessor)	Date	Seller (Lessor)	Date
Buyer (Lessee)	Date	Buyer (Lessee)	Date
Agent	Date	Agent	Date

Above is a sample lead paint disclosure form.

Source: The HUD provides a lead disclosure form. The image above is adapted from the HUD's *lead disclosure form.*

Carbon Monoxide

Carbon monoxide (CO) is an odorless, poisonous, and colorless gas that is capable of killing people. It is exceptionally dangerous. CO is generated from fuel combustion. Potential sources of carbon monoxide include open fires that are created by oil, coal, wood or gas, and household appliances. Even charcoal produces CO. If a chimney is not clear or if the flue is blocked, it can cause CO to enter the house instead of escaping outside. Other sources of CO in a home include but are not limited to furnaces, gas clothes dryers, boilers, fireplaces, tobacco smoke, grills, generators, water heaters, both gas and wood-burning ovens, stoves, vehicles, wood stoves, gasoline-powered tools, and lawn equipment/machinery. Recreational and camping sources of CO include but are not limited to fuel-burning lanterns, camp stoves, space heaters, and boat exhausts. When there is proper and adequate ventilation and when machinery and systems are working correctly, CO is not usually a problem.

Symptoms of carbon monoxide poisoning are especially problematic because they share many of the same symptoms as the flu. This includes fatigue, headache, confusion, aches and pains, and possibly nausea. With more exposure to carbon monoxide, a human body can experience loss of consciousness, vomiting, heart irregularities, problems breathing, muscle weakness, brain damage, and death. Since some of these symptoms can easily masquerade as other ailments, it is easy for a doctor to make a misdiagnosis.

> "Carbon monoxide is harmful when breathed because it displaces oxygen in the blood and deprives the heart, brain and other vital organs of oxygen. Large amounts of CO can overcome you in minutes without warning — causing you to lose consciousness and suffocate." (OSHA)

> "Every year, at least 430 people die in the U.S. from accidental CO poisoning. Approximately 50,000 people in the U.S. visit the emergency department each year due to accidental CO poisoning." (CDC)

A helpful and insightful Fact Sheet from OSHA can be found at this link: https://www.osha. gov/sites/default/files/publications/carbonmonoxide-factsheet.pdf

Federal law does not regulate the placement of carbon monoxide detectors (CO detectors) with residences. It allows each state to determine the placement and distance from any room used for sleeping. In Illinois, as of January 1, 2007, each and every homeowner, building owner, and landlord is required by law to install carbon monoxide detectors within fifteen feet of any room that is used for sleeping.

Mold

Mold is a type of fungus. It is composed of small organisms that are found practically everywhere. Colors of mold can be green, orange, black, white, and green. Molds require moisture to grow and reproduce, which makes places with moisture the most likely place to see mold. Mold thrives best in moisture, especially when it's a dark and warm location. All humans are exposed to mold to some extent every day. Small amounts are harmless, the majority of the time. Mold releases spores into the air. If someone is sensitive to mold, he/she may experience health problems if exposed. Mold can be found in countless places in a house, including on walls, furniture, beds, appliances, basements, attics, behind walls, and so on. The most common locations of mold in a house are wet or damp locations. This means laundry rooms, bathrooms, kitchens, crawl spaces, and basements commonly have mold. Mold can grow around window leaks, roof leaks, and pipe leaks. If there has been flooding anywhere in a house, mold can begin growing if the moisture is not removed quickly. There are thousands of known mold species. When mold is growing on something, it means that the mold is feeding off of that object. This can cause mild to irreversible damage depending on the object/s, locations, and how long the mold persists. Stachybotrys chartarum is known as black mold and usually causes health problems for people exposed.

> "Exposure to damp and moldy environments may cause a variety of health effects, or none at all. Some people are sensitive to molds. For these people, exposure to molds can lead to symptoms such as stuffy nose, wheezing, and red or itchy eyes, or skin. Some people, such as those with allergies to molds or with asthma, may have more intense reactions. Severe reactions may occur among workers exposed to large amounts of molds in occupational settings, such as farmers working around moldy hay. Severe reactions may include fever and shortness of breath." (CDC)

Electromagnetic Fields

Also called an EM field, electromagnetic fields are an invisible field of energy that are made up of electric and magnetic components. It is radiation. They are generated when charged particles like electrons accelerate. The Earth's magnetic field generates EM fields. Human activity also generates EM fields primarily by the use of electricity. Electric current flowing through live wires and electronic devices causes a magnetic field. The stronger the current, the stronger the field. The farther away from its source, the weaker it becomes. Electric and magnetic fields together are referred to as an electromagnetic field (EMF).

There are two categories of EMF frequencies: 1) higher frequencies by X-rays and gamma rays and 2) low to mid frequencies, which are produced by smartphones, appliances, microwaves, electric power lines, radio waves, infrared radiation, and other sources. For example, magnetic fields are continuously produced by working power lines because current is constantly flowing through them.

High-frequency EMFs can damage DNA and/or cells. Low- to mid-frequency EMFs are currently considered to not cause direct cell or DNA damage, although this is still controversial and disputed. Cancer is the main health concern of electromagnetic fields. Pollution is the most common non-health concern. In the US, EMF emissions are not regulated by the government. In some countries, they are.

EMF awareness has grown over the years and now it's a conversation in real estate circles. It is something that licensees do not have the luxury of avoiding or dismissing. Why? Because property value can be affected by EMFs. Some buyers include an EMF test in requirements for the home inspection. Individual EMF meters for testing are available, but generally, they are not thought to be very reliable or comprehensive. A total residential EMF home testing panel currently costs between $150 and $350, although it depends on where the property is located. It's best to have experts do the EMF test.

Chlorofluorocarbons and Hydrochlorofluorocarbons

Chlorofluorocarbons (CFCs) are chemicals that are composed of carbon, chlorine, and fluorine. Hydrochlorofluorocarbons (HCFCs) are chemicals composed of carbon, chlorine, fluorine, hydrogen, and hydrocarbons. Where are they found? In refrigerants, solvents, and aerosol sprays. People commonly use aerosol sprays daily. From shaving cream and bathroom cleaners to hair spray and automotive products, they are commonplace. In the late 70s, the US banned the use of CFCs in aerosol cans. Freon is one example. It was commonly used as a refrigerant in air conditioner units made before 2003. Freon was also used in freezers and dehumidifiers. Realizing that CFCs were depleting the ozone layer prompted the US to ban CFCs in aerosol cans.

How does this apply to licensees? It is possible this topic will come up if a real estate transaction involves older appliances. These could include ACs, freezers, and/or refrigerators that still use CFCs. For example, if a refrigerator was discarded and placed in an old shed in the backyard on the property years ago, it could still contain refrigerants. When it comes to an AC unit, it's fairly common to see a nameplate or sticker on the unit, which tells which coolant is used.

Removing and disposing of appliances containing CFCs and HCFCs is no simple or quick task. First, the appliance needs to be recognized and defined as a potential health hazard. Second, it needs to be safely disposed of in accordance with the EPA, IEPA, and local environmental regulations. Lack of compliance can result in jail time as well as monetary fines. It's the responsibility of licensees to understand the implications of CFCs and HCFCs. It's the responsibility of the seller to disclose all related information regarding CFCs and HCFCs.

WATER AND WATER-RELATED HAZARDS

Water is one of Earth's most precious resources because it's an essential requirement for life. Guarding against contamination and other hazards is supremely important. Groundwater is the water under the surface of our planet. It is present underground in spaces and cracks in sand, soil, and rock. The water is stored inside the spaces and cracks and gradually flows through its surroundings. The sand, soil, and rocks through which the water passes are called aquifers. An aquifer is a body of enterable and porous rock that is able to hold and/or transmit groundwater. Groundwater forms the water table. This is the boundary and border between the unsaturated zone and the saturated zone. Underneath the water table, groundwater fills up any spaces and cracks. The water table can be close to the surface or extremely deep, depending on the location. When nature's filtering system does not function correctly because of nature itself or because of humankind's actions or lack of action, contamination may be a result. The availability of pure water can be jeopardized. This can cause contamination in public water systems and/or private wells. Because of this, it's in humankind's best interest to protect groundwater from contaminants. In response, the EPA created the Safe Drinking Water Act (SDWA) in 1974. It is "the main federal law that ensures the quality of Americans' drinking water. Under SDWA, EPA sets standards for drinking water quality and oversees the states, localities, and water suppliers who implement those standards" (EPA website). The EPA is responsible for overseeing the nation's drinking water regulation. The SDWA applies to each and every public water system (PWS) in the US. It was amended in 1986 and again in 1996. Other federal laws similar to SDWA exist and their goal is to protect groundwater. These laws include the Resource Conservation and Recovery Act (RCRA), the Comprehensive Environmental Response, Compensation, and Liability Act (CERCLA), the Federal Insecticide, Fungicide, and Rodenticide Act (FIFRA), the Toxic Substances Control Act (TSCA) and finally, the Clean Water Act (CWA). According to the CDC, our country currently has over 155,000+ public water systems that provide healthy drinking water.

> "Sources of drinking water are subject to contamination and require appropriate treatment to remove disease-causing contaminants. Contamination of drinking water supplies can occur in the source water as well as in the distribution system after water treatment has already occurred. There are many sources of water contamination, including naturally occurring chemicals and minerals (for example, arsenic, radon, uranium), local land-use practices (fertilizers, pesticides, concentrated feeding operations), manufacturing processes, and sewer overflows or wastewater releases. The presence of contaminants in water can lead to adverse health effects, including gastrointestinal illness, reproductive problems, and neurological disorders. Infants, young children, pregnant women, the elderly, and people whose immune systems are compromised because of AIDS, chemotherapy, or transplant

medications, may be especially susceptible to illness from some contaminants." (CDC)

How does this apply to licensees? You may recall that a designated agent has a duty to care for the best interest of their clients. As such, it is the licensee's responsibility to ensure that the buyer/client is aware of the status of the septic system and water supply on the property he/she is considering purchasing. Full disclosure by the seller is a requirement under the Residential Real Property Disclosure Report.

It's a good practice for all parties to understand what causes groundwater contamination. They need to learn this for both the property itself and the land/area surrounding the property. If a water supply is not part of a city or town, a best practice is to have the water tested. Many county health departments are available to help test for nitrates, coliform bacteria, sulfate, chloride, fluoride, pH, sodium, iron, manganese, hardness, and total dissolved solids. When the county where the property is located is not able to perform a water test, the licensee or buyer will need to get the test done by a state-certified laboratory. There is a "Safe Drinking Water Hotline" available at 800-426-4791 if their assistance is necessary.

The EPA provides a free resource called "The Citizen's Guide To Ground-Water Protection." It can be found at this link. https://www.epa.gov/sites/production/files/2015-10/documents/2006_08_28_sourcewater_guide_citguidegwp_1990.pdf

Underground Storage Tanks

What is an underground storage tank (UST)?

> "A tank and any underground piping connected to the tank that has 10% or more of its volume (including pipe volume) beneath the surface of the ground. USTs are designed to hold gasoline, other petroleum products, and hazardous materials." (EPA)

A UST can be made of steel, fiberglass, aluminum, or a combination of those and other materials. Some are single-walled, and others feature double-wall construction. The EPA states that there are 542,000 USTs throughout the US that store petroleum or hazardous substances. A UST that has a leak can present a great threat to groundwater. Any leak from a UST has the potential to create a lot of contamination in groundwater, as well as health issues in people who drink the contaminated water. USTs are commonly found in commercial and industrial businesses such as gas stations, chemical plants, paint factories, paper mills, and similar establishments. These facilities are regulated under federal, state, and local legislation. However, in the residential realm, a UST is commonly an oil tank used for heating the house (consumptive use). These are not required to follow federal regulations. However, there may be local and/

or state regulations that must be followed. While other states may define an oil tank as a UST, Illinois does not consider an oil tank to be a UST by Illinois state law.

A UST that has a leak is called a LUST (leaking underground storage tank). The leak means it is compromised. This unfortunate scenario means that the fuel product that was being stored is now infiltrating the surrounding area. It has the power to contaminate not only the soil and water but also indoor air spaces.

Is every UST required to meet federal EPA regulations? The answer is no. According to the CDC, the following USTs do not need to meet federal requirements:

- Farm and residential tanks of 1,100 gallons or less capacity holding motor fuel used for noncommercial purposes;

- Tanks storing heating oil used on the premises where it is stored;

- Tanks on or above the floor of underground areas, such as basements or tunnels;

- Septic tanks and systems for collecting stormwater and wastewater;

- Flow-through process tanks;

- Tanks of 110 gallons or less capacity; and

- Emergency spill and overfill tanks. However, some state and local regulatory authorities may regulate these types of tanks so check where your USTs are located. (EPA)

For safety requirements, any consumer interested in properties with a UST should research any federal, state, and local regulations that may impact the ownership and use of the property.

Licensees need to be aware of the existence of USTs so they can bring it to their clients' attention if necessary.

The most current reports about USTs can be found at this link: https://www.epa.gov/ust/ust-performance-measures

Brownfields

"Brownfield is a term applied to a property where its expansion, redevelopment, or reuse may be complicated by the presence or potential presence of a hazardous substance. A petroleum brownfield is a type of brownfield where the contaminant is petroleum," stated by the EPA. At times, it is referred to as "brownfield land." Many times, the land was used for industrial or commercial purposes in the past. A brownfield means there is either known contamination, like toxic waste, at worst, or suspected pollution, at best.

The EPA estimates that there are over 450,000 brownfields in the US. These properties are quite possibly risky, unsafe, hazardous, or threatening. Brownfields decrease the beauty and attractiveness of any community in which one is located. Not only can they be frustrating or annoying to look at, but they additionally also are a time bomb waiting to go off. It goes without saying that these derelict locations decrease property value and appeal. What about cleaning up brownfields and reinvesting in the properties? While this is possible, it can potentially be very expensive depending on the size of the property and circumstances. However, the perks of transforming a brownfield into a useful and attractive property can increase property values, increase local tax bases, help increase job growth, and more. This type of project is called a brownfield redevelopment. These redevelopments can be very impressive.

For example, let's consider Berry Lane Park in Jersey City, New Jersey. In the past, this area was a sprawling property made up of eleven industrial sites. The area had rail yards, warehouses, auto repair shops, and industrial facilities. This toxically contaminated land contained lead, hexavalent chromium, and PCBs. For its redevelopment, over 700,000 tons of hazardous waste were safely removed. Extensive work was done to the area. Nowadays, Berry Lane Park is a fun, vibrant, and safe playground. The revitalized 17.5 acres are enjoyed every single day by hundreds of Jersey City kids and their families. Along with a playground, the park features two tennis courts, two basketball courts, a baseball field, a soccer field, a splash pad water park, and 600 trees.

To read more transformational redevelopments, read this online document called "Brownfields: Properties With New Purpose": https://www.epa.gov/sites/production/files/2019-06/documents/bf_booklet.pdf

For a full overview from the EPA, read this online document called "Anatomy of Brownfields Redevelopment": https://www.epa.gov/sites/production/files/2015-09/documents/anat_bf_redev_101106.pdf

LANDFILLS AND WASTE MANAGEMENT

Real estate cannot ignore the presence of waste and how it affects the environment and land. Here are some stats from the EPA:

- In 1960, the total municipal waste (MSW) was around 100 million tons.

- In 1990, the total municipal waste was around 200 million tons.

- In 2018, the total municipal waste was 292.4 million tons, which is 4.9 pounds of garbage every day per person in the US.

- Over 146 million tons of MSW in 2018 were landfilled. (2018 is the most current year with data from the EPA on this topic.)

There are three primary sources of waste.

1. **Domestic waste** is any waste from personal residences, including apartment buildings.

2. **Municipal waste** is waste from offices, retail, and schools.

3. **Industrial waste** originates from industrial plants and factories.

A landfill is a designated site used for the disposal of waste materials like everyday trash and garbage. Landfills are commonly confused with garbage dumps or dumping grounds.

A **dump** is an open hole in the ground, usually quite large. The trash is dumped in the hole and buried. Commonly, birds, mice, rats, and other vermin are found in and around dumps. Sometimes, they're called open dumps. While both a landfill and a dump are excavated pieces of land, a landfill is not a dump. Dumps are smaller and have no treatment system.

A **landfill** is a vital type of garbage containment strategy that is regulated by the government. Sometimes called a sanitary landfill, it's also one of the most common and oldest types of waste disposal methods. Carefully designed, a landfill has a type of liner at the bottom. Dumps do not. The purpose of the liner is to catch and contain the liquids that are produced by the enormous amounts of waste. The liner creates a boundary between the waste and the surrounding environment, thereby creating or implementing a system of layers that allows the waste to safely decompose. Landfills are covered by soil or mud. This is called capping or soil capping. A cap of soil is placed over the waste to encapsulate and contain it. Capping cannot remove or destroy the contaminants. Capping helps prevent bad odors from infiltrating the air and drifting for miles and miles. It also creates a barrier between wildlife and people entering the area and being exposed to the numerous contaminants held inside the landfill. Much of the time, the byproduct of the waste's decomposition is methane. Methane hurts the environment because it contributes to climate change. The majority of sanitary landfills are equipped to safely collect methane. Instead of being released and harming the environment, by capturing it, it can be used to generate electricity. Most sanitary landfills include a leachate tank, a groundwater monitoring well for leachate, a soil monitoring well for gas and leachate, pipes to collect methane gas, a methane gas recovery well, a ventilation pipe, and a building for electricity generation. Leachate is the liquid that forms when waste breaks down inside the landfill and water filters through the waste. It is usually highly toxic.

As you know, CERCLA stands for the Comprehensive Environmental Response, Compensation, and Liability Act. CERCLA grants the Federal Government the authority and power to impose taxes on any chemical and/or petroleum company that is found guilty of releasing hazardous waste into unregulated areas whether intentionally or by accident. Informally, it is called SuperFund. This is because it is a federal "super fund" that helps clean up and improve hazardous waste sites that have been abandoned or are not controllable. The SuperFund also assists financially with spills, other accidents, and emergencies that have released contaminants and pollutants into the open.

> "Superfund's goals are to protect human health and the environment by cleaning up contaminated sites, make responsible parties pay for cleanup work, involve communities in the Superfund process and return Superfund sites to productive use." (EPA)

The Superfund Amendments and Reauthorization Act (SARA) amended CERCLA on October 17, 1986. This generated several changes. Here are a few. The trust fund amount increased to 8.5 billion. More importance was placed on permanent solutions and not Band-Aid solutions. Innovative treatment technologies moved into the picture and were implemented. State involvement was increased. Citizens were encouraged and invited to participate in cleanup efforts.

One problem the EPA is faced with is orphan sites. These are toxic waste areas where:

1. the responsible party cannot be identified

2. the responsible party refuses to pay for cleanup, or

3. there is no viable party who caused or contributed to the contamination.

> "When there is no viable responsible party, Superfund gives EPA the funds and authority to clean up contaminated sites." (EPA)

CERCLA "imposes liability on parties responsible for, in whole or in part, the presence of hazardous substances at a site. Superfund Liability is:

- Retroactive—Parties may be held liable for acts that happened before Superfund's enactment in 1980.

- Joint and Several—Any one potentially responsible party (PRP) may be held liable for the entire cleanup of the site (when the harm caused by multiple parties cannot be separated).

- Strict—A PRP cannot simply say that it was not negligent or that it was operating according to industry standards. If a PRP sent some amount of the hazardous waste found at the site, that party is liable" (EPA).

What happens if a piece of contaminated land is purchased without the buyer knowing about the contamination? Is he/she liable? If a property buyer had no knowledge of the toxicity when purchased, it's possible he/she is eligible for the innocent landowner defense. To be eligible, the buyer must have followed all appropriate inquiries and also have complied with pre-purchase and post-purchase conditions. There are strict requirements and steps to qualify. The Superfund defines three different types of landowners:

- "Purchasers who acquire property without knowledge of contamination on the property.

- Governments acquiring contaminated property involuntarily or through the exercise of eminent domain authority by purchase or condemnation.

- Inheritors of contaminated property" (EPA).

Federal and state laws need to be on the minds of everyone involved in real estate transactions, not only the licensees. A responsible licensee will inform his/her clients about environmental issues. The licensee can easily share relevant links and PDFs with the client as a way to make sure the client is up to date. Who deals with the most legal liability in a transaction? Most often, it is the seller. Still, it's possible for someone who purchased contaminated property to be held accountable if he/she is not eligible for innocent landowner protection. As you can see, there are not only environmental risks, but there are also financial risks. One of those factors alone should be enough to convince each individual involved to do his or her due diligence. Licensees are not experts on environmental issues and contamination. Regardless, they are responsible for staying involved and knowing when they need to reach out for assistance or professional services.

Questions a licensee can ask him/herself include:

- Are there any known contaminants? How can I be sure?

- Do I need to order a test or assessment?

- Does anything in, on, or around the property look suspicious?

- What potential contaminants and/or threats might exist on this property or surrounding properties?

- Is the property in compliance?

Once again, a licensee should be an expert at real estate. Additionally, he/she needs to know when to seek professional assistance in terms of technical experts. Many times, the best professional to reach out to is an environmental auditor. This highly specialized type of auditor is able to ensure that environmental standards are currently met, or being exceeded. They can search for and identify any environmental management deficiencies as well as point out any compliance issues. Ordering an environmental assessment can go a long way in avoiding litigation, ensuring all parties are informed, and generating peace of mind, which leads the way for a smoother real estate transaction.

A percolation test ("perc test") may also be advantageous. Percolation is the process of liquid passing slowly through some type of filter. It refers to the movement and filtering of liquids through porous and permeable materials. In real estate, a percolation test is used to measure the rate at which water passes through soil. It is used to determine the suitability of soil for constructing septic tanks, as well as other real estate projects. A percolation test involves measuring the amount of time it takes for a specific amount of water to pass through a sample of soil. This is done by collecting data from several points in the soil and then calculating an average rate at which water percolates through the sample. The results are then compared against established standards in order to determine whether or not the soil is suitable for a certain use. Using data from a percolation test ensures a properly designed septic system.

As you can see, real estate is inseparable from the environment. Now, it's time for your chapter quiz.

CHAPTER 25 QUIZ

1. Which of the following does the IEPA not do?

    a. Provide grants for safe housing
    b. Work to protect the health of Illinois residents
    c. Safeguard environmental quality
    d. Fight against pollution

2. Trevon discovered that a crawl space in his house has asbestos. He is telling his family about it. Which of the following is something he would not say because it is not accurate?

    a. Asbestos was commonly used in buildings years ago.
    b. Exposure is highly toxic.
    c. If asbestos mineral fibers can get trapped in an individual, they can be safely removed by a doctor.
    d. Mineral fibers enter the body by way of ingestion or inhalation.

3. The licensing requirement for asbestos workers comes from the state in which they reside.

    a. Yes
    b. No

4. Which of the following is false concerning the topic of radon in the state of Illinois?

    a. A seller of residential property must provide a radon disclosure to the buyer.
    b. Radon is a Class-B human carcinogen.
    c. Radon is the leading cause of lung cancer in non-smokers.
    d. Radon is a radioactive, colorless, odorless, and tasteless gas.

5. Which of the following is true concerning formaldehyde?

    a. It is a colorless gas with a strong odor.
    b. It was used mostly in the past for building materials and countless household products.
    c. It can be found in plywood, particle board, glues, fiberglass, adhesives, permanent-press fabrics, and similar products.
    d. It occurs naturally in the environment.
    e. All of the above
    f. Only A, B, and C

6. Most likely, where would radon be found in a residential property?

    a. Crawl spaces
    b. Bedrooms
    c. Kitchens
    d. Basements
    e. B and C
    f. A and D

7. As of the publishing of this book, what was listed as the number one environmental hazard that causes illness in babies and children?

    a. Radon
    b. Formaldehyde
    c. Mold
    d. Lead poisoning
    e. Asbestos

8. Reginald and Amy purchased their first home nine months ago. Amy just found out she is pregnant! After learning about the exciting news, they started talking about how to ensure that the home is 100% safe for the baby. What recommendations would you make if you were their close friend who happens to be a licensee?

    a. Review your lead paint disclosure
    b. Review the residential real property disclosure
    c. Buy a carbon monoxide detector
    d. All of the above

9. Can asbestos removal in Illinois legally be accomplished without a license?

    a. Yes
    b. No

10. Where can lead be found?

    a. In water
    b. In the air
    c. In the soil
    d. All of the above

11. Carbon monoxide poisoning has similar symptoms to which of the following?

    a. Stomach virus symptoms
    b. Flu
    c. Sinus infection
    d. None of the above

12. On a federal level, as of January 1, 2007, each and every homeowner, building owner, and landlord is required by law to install carbon monoxide detectors within 15 feet of any room that is used for sleeping.

    a. True
    b. False

13. Although mold can be found almost anywhere, which of the following locations would be the most likely place for mold to be present?

    a. Bedroom
    b. Patio room
    c. Kitchen
    d. Attic

14. Which of the following is not a health concern of electromagnetic radiation exposure?

    a. DNA damage
    b. Dementia
    c. Respiratory problems
    d. Cancer

15. Which of the following sentences describes groundwater accurately?

    a. It is the water under the Earth's surface.
    b. It is the water we can see.
    c. It is water that is naturally safe for drinking.
    d. It is the water that is stored in aquifers.
    e. All of the above
    f. Only A and D
    g. Only A, B, and C

16. Is every underground storage tank in the US required to comply with federal EPA regulations?

    a. Yes
    b. No

17. What is the primary concern of an underground storage tank?

    a. Explosion
    b. A leak
    c. That it does not have an owner or responsible party associated with it, and thus is an orphan site.
    d. None of the above

18. What are the main types of waste as related to landfills?

    a. Chemical, biological, residential, and commercial
    b. Domestic, municipal, and industrial
    c. Domestic and commercial
    d. Biological, residential, and commercial

19. Janissa purchased property last spring. After a few complaints from neighbors, she had someone do an environmental test. She was shocked and angry to discover that her newest property is contaminated. Is Janissa liable for this?

    a. Yes
    b. No
    c. Not if she is eligible and qualifies with the EPA as an innocent landowner.
    d. Yes, she could be subject to a monetary penalty equal to five times the purchase price.

20. Which of the following can produce carbon monoxide?

    a. Furnace
    b. Clothes dryers
    c. Fireplaces
    d. Generators

CHAPTER 26:

THE FAIR HOUSING ACT, ETHICS, AND BEST PRACTICES

LEARNING GOALS:

By the end of this lesson, you will:

- Learn about the Fair Housing Act details and ordinances
- Know what to do if there is a Fair Housing Act violation
- Understand more details about the Illinois Human Rights Act
- Learn the Fair Housing Act and what it says about people with disabilities, service animals, and more
- See how ethics can elevate one's career
- Know how to recognize and report sexual harassment

THE FAIR HOUSING ACT

The Fair Housing Act is the right of individuals to select housing without experiencing or being subject to unlawful discrimination. Housing laws on federal, state, and local levels protect people from discrimination. This protection not only includes real estate sales, but also transactions in housing rentals, lending, and insurance.

Here is a brief history and timeline:

- 1866: Following the American Civil War ending in April of 1865, the Civil Rights Act of 1866 was the first provision in US history to focus on discrimination. It establishes there is no selectivity in any phase of life (credit, employment, education, and housing) based on a person's race and/or color.

- 1917: Housing discrimination surfaced in 1917 after the end of slavery, particularly through the enactment of "Jim Crow laws" that encouraged racial segregation. The Federal Government took action against these laws in response to the Supreme Court's decision in Buchanan v. Warley. It ruled that any laws forbidding Black individuals from owning or residing in buildings in predominantly White neighborhoods were not constitutional.

- 1968: The Civil Rights Act of 1968 included legislation (Title VII) known as the Fair Housing Act. It was created to protect people from discrimination that stems from one's race, color, religion, or national origin. This law helps ensure that all individuals are treated fairly and equally. It prohibits anyone from refusing to rent or sell property to someone because of their race, color, religion, or national origin. By protecting individuals' civil rights and prohibiting discrimination in housing, the Civil Rights Act of 1968 works to ensure that all people have access to fair and equal treatment when it comes to renting or buying a residence. Despite this progress, housing discrimination still exists today.

- 1974: The Housing and Community Development Act reinforced the Federal Fair Housing Act by adding sex/gender to the list of protected classes.

- 1988: The Fair Housing Amendments Act, also called Title VIII, was amended to prohibit discrimination that stemmed from disability and/or familial status. It also greatly expanded the enforcement role of the Department of Housing and Urban Development.

The HUD website states:

- The Fair Housing Act protects people from discrimination when they are renting or buying a home, getting a mortgage, seeking housing assistance, or engaging in other housing-related activities. Additional protections apply to federally assisted housing.

- The Fair Housing Act prohibits discrimination because of race, color, national origin, religion, sex (including gender identity and sexual orientation), familial status, and disability. (HUD)

FEDERAL FAIR HOUSING PROTECTED CLASSES

Provision of Law	Protected Classes						
	Race	Color	Religion	National Origin	Sex	Disability	Familial Status
Civil Rights Act 1866	x	x					
Fair Housing Act 1968	x	x	x	x			
Housing & Community Dev. 1974	x	x	x	x	x		
Fair Housing Adm. 1988	x	x	x	x	x	x	x

FAIR HOUSING PROTECTED CLASSES: FEDERAL AND ILLINOIS

FEDERAL	ILLINOIS HUMAN RIGHTS ACT	
Race	Race	Ancestry
Color	Color	Age
Religion	Religion	Marital status
National origin	National origin	Military status
Sex	Sex	Sexual orientation
Physical or mental disability	Physical or mental disability	Order of protection
Familiar status	Familiar status	Criminal history
		Source of income

As a reminder, familial status means the presence of a child under eighteen years of age. The child is the focus. It is not relevant whether the adult is a biological parent, grandparent, foster parent, stepparent, designee, or some other type of adult who has been granted legal custody of the child. Additionally, the marital status of the adult is not relevant. This means single parents are protected. An adult or couple who is pregnant and/or in the process of securing legal custody of a person under eighteen years of age is protected, including same-sex couples. FHA protects all families with children under the age of eighteen. The discrimination can come from a licensee, landlord, or property owner.

Which types of housing does the Federal Fair Housing Act cover? HUD answers:

The Fair Housing Act covers most housing. In very limited circumstances, the Act exempts:

- owner-occupied buildings with no more than four units

- single-family houses sold or rented by the owner without the use of an agent

- housing operated by religious organizations and private clubs that limit occupancy to members (HUD).

In addition, selectivity may exist based on gender when the prospective tenant will occupy space within the landlord's principal residence.

When it comes to home sales and rentals, what is prohibited? The HUD website answers:

It is illegal discrimination to take any of the following actions because of race, color, religion, sex, disability, familial status, or national origin:

- Refuse to rent or sell housing

- Refuse to negotiate for housing

- Otherwise make housing unavailable

- Set different terms, conditions, or privileges for the sale or rental of a dwelling

- Provide a person with different housing services or facilities

- Falsely deny that housing is available for inspection, sale, or rental

- Make, print, or publish any notice, statement, or advertisement with respect to the sale or rental of a dwelling that indicates any preference, limitation, or discrimination

- Impose different sales prices or rental charges for the sale or rental of a dwelling

- Use different qualification criteria or applications, or sale or rental standards or procedures, such as income standards, application requirements, application fees, credit analyses, sale or rental approval procedures, or other requirements

- Evict a tenant or a tenant's guest

- Harass a person

- Fail or delay performance of maintenance or repairs

- Limit privileges, services, or facilities of a dwelling

- Discourage the purchase or rental of a dwelling

- Assign a person to a particular building or neighborhood or section of a building or neighborhood

- For profit, persuade, or try to persuade, homeowners to sell their homes by suggesting that people of a particular protected characteristic are about to move into the neighborhood (blockbusting)

- Refuse to provide or discriminate in the terms or conditions of homeowners insurance because of the race, color, religion, sex, disability, familial status, or national origin of the owner and/or occupants of a dwelling

- Deny access to or membership in any Multiple Listing Service or real estate brokers' organization (HUD)

If a licensee is directed by the client to be selective in showing the property to a given protected class, the license is required to educate the client and if they are still insistent on the licensee being selective, the licensee is to walk away from the client. When a licensee is silent on the matter, the silence can be interpreted as complying with the client's request.

In mortgage lending: It is illegal discrimination to take any of the following actions based on race, color, religion, sex, disability, familial status, or national origin:

- Refuse to make a mortgage loan or provide other financial assistance for a dwelling

- Refuse to provide information regarding loans

- Impose different terms or conditions on a loan, such as different interest rates, points, or fees

- Discriminate in appraising a dwelling

- Condition the availability of a loan on a person's response to harassment

- Refuse to purchase a loan (HUD)

Harassment: The Fair Housing Act makes it illegal to harass persons because of race, color, religion, sex, disability, familial status, or national origin. Among other things, this forbids sexual harassment. In addition, it is illegal discrimination to:

- Threaten, coerce, intimidate, or interfere with anyone exercising a fair housing right or assisting others who exercise the right

- Retaliate against a person who has filed a fair housing complaint or assisted in a fair housing investigation (HUD)

Every brokerage agreement is required to transparently and clearly state that it is illegal for anyone to refuse to show, rent, or sell to anybody due to the person being in a protected class.

LOCAL FAIR HOUSING ORDINANCES

As a reminder, a local ordinance is a law, regulation, or rule that is specifically for a specific town or city limits. They can be mandated in local governments, such as a municipality, county, parish, and so on. Each city can have its own unique set of ordinances. Because of this, the difference in ordinance violations can be very varied, as can the fines. Ordinances are not considered criminal matters, nor are they recorded as such. A competent licensee will know which protected classes are covered by federal and state laws. However, each agent must also stay current with local fair housing ordinances. Local fair housing ordinances might include other protected classes, in addition to those covered by federal and state laws. It's important for a licensee to check with local municipalities to learn whether or not there are any additional protected classes.

BACKGROUND CHECKS AND CRIMINAL HISTORY CONSIDERATIONS

Although the average person is familiar with background checks, it is important to give a full definition. A background check is a process a person (or company) implements in order to verify that a person is who they claim to be. It gives an opportunity for someone to check a person's criminal record, education, employment history, and other activities that happened in the past in order to confirm their validity and truthfulness.

How far back do background checks go? There is no one answer to this question because it varies from state to state. For many states, including Illinois, background checks go back seven years. If a conviction, felony, and/or misdemeanor or series of those occurred, it can go back ten years.

What about criminal history considerations? Fair Housing Project (FairHousingNC.org) states:

- "Recent federal fair housing guidance states that it may be illegal for housing providers to refuse to rent to someone because of their criminal background without considering the nature and severity of the crime(s), how old the record is, and any rehabilitative efforts since the conviction. This is because landlords who refuse to rent to anyone with a criminal record may be disproportionately limiting housing choices for people protected by the Fair Housing Act because of their race, national origin, disability, and/or sex."

- "Your criminal background is not necessarily indicative of whether or not you will be a good tenant."

The HUD website has an outstanding PDF called **FAQs: Excluding the Use of Arrest Records in Housing Decisions**. For the sake of convenience, the PDF is copied below. It includes common questions about criminal history and detailed answers directly from the HUD.

These FAQs are issued by HUD's Office of Public and Indian Housing ("PIH"), Office of Housing, and Office of General Counsel to address questions raised by *Notice PIH 2015-19 / H 2015-10*, which was issued on November 2, 2015, and is entitled *Guidance for Public Housing Agencies (PHAs) and Owners of Federally-Assisted Housing on Excluding the Use of Arrest Records in Housing Decisions*. These FAQs are intended as a supplemental resource to *Notice PIH 2015-19 / H 2015-10*.

Q1: What does Notice PIH 2015-19 / H 2015-10 do?

A1: The Notice clarifies that the fact that someone has been arrested does not itself prove that the person has engaged in criminal activity. As a result, the fact of an arrest is not itself an acceptable reason for denying that person admission, terminating their assistance, or evicting tenants in public or federally assisted housing.

The Notice also reminds PHAs and owners of HUD-assisted multifamily properties ("owners") that HUD does not require the adoption of "one-strike" policies and that PHAs and owners have an obligation to safeguard the due process and civil rights of applicants and tenants.

In addition, the Notice provides some best practices for PHAs and owners interested in revising their admissions and occupancy policies to improve housing opportunities for persons who, despite past criminal activity, do not pose a threat to the health or safety of residents or staff.

Q2: Why is the fact of an arrest not itself a permissible basis for making a housing decision?

A2: The fact that someone was arrested means only that the person was suspected of having committed an offense. Further investigation may have shown that no criminal activity actually occurred, or that the arrested individual did not, in fact, commit an offense.

Consequently, the fact of the arrest itself does not prove that a person engaged in disqualifying criminal activity, poses a threat, or has otherwise violated admission standards or lease terms relating to criminal activity.

Q3: Does Notice PIH 2015-19 / H 2015-10 completely exclude the review of arrest records in housing decisions?

A3: No. Although the fact that an individual was arrested is not grounds to deny a housing opportunity, a record of an arrest might properly trigger an inquiry by a PHA or owner into whether a person actually engaged in disqualifying criminal activity. As part of such an inquiry, a PHA or owner may continue to obtain and review the police report, record of disposition of any criminal charges, and other evidence associated with the arrest to inform its eligibility determination.

Q4: If an individual has an arrest history, what kind of evidence of criminal activity is needed before disqualifying that person from housing assistance?

A4: In determining whether a person who was arrested for disqualifying criminal activity actually engaged in such activity, PHAs and owners may consider, among other things: police reports that detail the circumstances of the arrest; statements made by witnesses or by the applicant or tenant that are not part of the police report; whether formal criminal charges were filed; whether any charges were ultimately withdrawn, abandoned, dismissed, or resulted in an acquittal; and any other evidence relevant to whether the applicant or tenant engaged in the disqualifying criminal activity. The best evidence of a person's involvement in criminal activity is an official record of the person's conviction in a court of law for disqualifying criminal activity.

Q5: In considering evidence of a person's criminal activity, what is the threshold that must be met before a PHA or owner may disqualify that person from housing assistance?

A5: Public housing and Section 8 applicants may not be denied admission or assistance based on the mere suspicion that they or a household member engaged in disqualifying criminal activity. There must be enough evidence to be able to reasonably conclude that the applicant engaged in criminal activity. Thus, the fact that an individual was arrested is not an adequate basis for disqualifying an applicant for admission or assistance.

When terminating assistance for participants of Section 8 tenant-based and moderate rehabilitation programs due to disqualifying criminal activity, HUD regulations specifically provide that disqualifying criminal activity by a tenant, other household member, or guest must be demonstrated by a "preponderance of the evidence." In other words, when taking all the evidence together and considering its reliability or unreliability, it must be more likely than not that the person in question engaged in the disqualifying criminal activity. The same preponderance of the evidence standard applies to public housing evictions as well.

As a reminder, only in limited and specific cases of criminal activity do HUD statutes and regulations require denial of admission or termination of assistance (and in only two cases—where someone has been convicted of producing methamphetamine in federally assisted housing or must register as a lifetime sex offender—is someone permanently barred). In all other cases, PHAs and owners have the discretion to consider any mitigating circumstances in making admission and eviction decisions.

Q6: What is an example of an admissions policy that complies with Section 4 of Notice PIH 2015-19 / H 2015-10?

A6: An admissions policy that complies with Section 4 of the Notice and recognizes the interests of applicants who need access to affordable housing while guarding the safety interests of current residents might include the following statement:

"The fact that an applicant or tenant was arrested for a disqualifying offense shall not be treated or regarded as proof that the applicant or tenant engaged in disqualifying criminal activity. The arrest may, however, trigger an investigation to determine whether the applicant or tenant actually engaged in disqualifying criminal activity. As part of its investigation, [the PHA or owner] may obtain the police report associated with the arrest and consider the reported circumstances of the arrest. The PHA may also consider any statements made by witnesses or the applicant or tenant not included in the police report; whether criminal charges were filed; whether, if filed, criminal charges were abandoned, dismissed, not prosecuted, or ultimately resulted in an acquittal; and any other evidence relevant to determining whether or not the applicant or tenant engaged in disqualifying activity."

Q7: Does Notice PIH 2015-19 require a PHA to rewrite its (1) Admissions and Continued Occupancy Policies (ACOP) or (2) Section 8 Administrative Plan (Admin Plan) if the ACOP or Admin Plan does not include the same language used in the previous answer's example?

A7: Maybe. All PHAs must comply with Notice PIH 2015-19. PHAs should therefore review their ACOPs and Admin Plans and revise them where a policy treats the fact that someone was arrested as a reason to deny admission, terminate assistance, or evict tenants in public or federally assisted housing.

At the same time, a PHA is not required to use the same language used in the previous example to comply with the Notice. Where a PHA's ACOP and Admin Plan are completely consistent with the example policy set forth in the previous answer and do not permit relying on the fact of an arrest (or arrests) to prove disqualifying criminal activity, it may be that no revisions are required.

HUD encourages PHAs to revise their ACOP and Admin Plans as they relate to criminal records in order to better facilitate access to HUD-assisted housing for applicants who, despite their criminal history, do not pose a threat to the health or safety of residents or staff.

Q8: If, during an applicant's admissions screening process, the applicant is arrested for violent or other disqualifying criminal activity, must a PHA or owner wait until the arrest disposition to determine the applicant's eligibility for housing?

A8: No. While it may be advisable to wait until the arrest disposition—especially if the disposition is imminent—PHAs and owners have discretion to go ahead and use the available evidence to make an eligibility determination according to the standards in the applicable written admissions policies of the PHA or owner.

Q9: Must a PHA or owner provide an applicant with notice and the opportunity to dispute the accuracy or relevance of a criminal record before denying admission on the basis of that record?

A9: Yes. Before a PHA denies admission to the public housing or Section 8 program on the basis of a criminal record, the PHA must notify the applicant of the proposed decision and provide the applicant and the subject of the record with a copy of the criminal record and an opportunity to dispute the accuracy and relevance of that record. In addition, public housing and Section 8 applicants have the right to request an informal review of the decision after their application has been denied. For further guidance, please consult 24 CFR. §§ 960.204I, 960.208(a), 982.553(d), 982.554.

Similarly, when owners make the decision to reject an applicant on the basis of a criminal record, the owner must provide the applicant with a written rejection notice. This notice must state the reason for the rejection, advise of the applicant's right to respond to the owner in writing or to request a meeting within 14 days to dispute the rejection, and advise that persons with disabilities have the right to request reasonable accommodations to participate in the informal hearing process. For further guidance, please consult HUD Handbook 4350.3, REV-1, paragraphs 4-9.

Q10: May PHAs or owners contact HUD if they have questions about Notice PIH 2015-19 / H 2015-10?

A10: Yes. If assistance is needed, PHAs and owners can contact their local field office, which can put them in touch with HUD regional counsel to answer any questions about the Notice.

(https://www.hud.gov/sites/documents/FAQEXCLUDEARRESTREC33116.PDF)

FAIR HOUSING AND SERVICE, EMOTIONAL SUPPORT, AND THERAPY ANIMALS

Agents and owners must know what the Fair Housing Act and RELA say about animals that provide service, emotional support, and therapy. Let's look at each definition.

Assistance animal:

- The Illinois General Assembly's definition is as follows: "Assistance animal" means an emotional support or service animal that qualifies as a reasonable accommodation under the federal Fair Housing Act or the Illinois Human Rights Act. (310 ILCS 120, Assistance Animal Integrity Act)

- Any animal that works, provides assistance, or performs tasks for the benefit of a person with a disability, or provides emotional support that alleviates one or more identified symptoms or effects of a person's disability (Americans With Disabilities Act).

  - What is ADA and what does it do? Here is an excerpt from the ADA website: "The ADA was signed into law on July 26, 1990, following many years of advocacy by the disability and civil rights communities. It protects people with disabilities from discrimination. Disability rights are civil rights. From voting to parking, the ADA is a law that protects people with disabilities in many areas of public life." (ADA)

  - To stay up to date or search for questions you have, visit here: https://www.ada.gov

- Individuals with a disability may be entitled to keep an assistance animal as a reasonable accommodation in housing facilities that otherwise impose restrictions or prohibitions on animals. In order to qualify for such an accommodation, the assistance animal must be necessary to afford the individual an equal opportunity to use and enjoy a dwelling or to participate in the housing service or program. Further, there must be a relationship, or nexus, between the individual's disability and the assistance the animal provides. If these requirements are met, a housing facility, program or service must permit the assistance animal as an accommodation, unless it can demonstrate that allowing the assistance animal would impose an undue financial or administrative burden or would fundamentally alter the nature of the housing program or services. (HUD)

Companion animal:

- The Illinois General Assembly's definition of a "companion animal" is an animal that is commonly considered to be, or is considered by the owner to be, a pet. "Companion animal" includes, but is not limited to, canines, felines, and equines (510 ILCS 70/2.01a).

- They generally do not have special rights or privileges as they are considered pets.

- As there are no guidelines under federal or state law, the concept of a companion animal must be clarified by the landlord or business owner.

Emotional support animal:

- As stated earlier, the Illinois General Assembly's definition of assistance animal means an emotional support or service animal that qualifies as a reasonable accommodation under the federal Fair Housing Act or the Illinois Human Rights Act (Assistance Animal Integrity Act 310 ILCS 120).

- An emotional support animal (ESA) may be a cat, dog, or any other kind of small, domesticated animal. Sometimes they are referred to as comfort animals.

- An ESA letter is documentation that comes from a licensed mental health professional where he/she states that your disability requires help from an emotional support animal. The professional who issues the ESA letter could be a counselor, doctor, psychologist, or psychiatrist. The ESA letter is proof for a landlord that you, as a tenant, have an eligible disability that requires an emotional support animal.

- Unlike a service animal, the ESA does not have to be trained on how to complete a specific task.

- The ADA does not view emotional support animals as service animals.

Service animal:

- The Illinois General Assembly's definition is an animal trained in obedience and task skills to meet the needs of a person with a disability (Humane Care for Animals Act 510 ILCS 70/2.01c).

- A service animal is any dog that is individually trained to do work or perform tasks for the benefit of an individual with a disability, including a physical, sensory, psychiatric, intellectual, or other mental disability. Other species of animals, whether wild or domestic, trained or untrained, are not service animals for the purposes of this definition. The work or tasks performed by a service animal must be directly related to the individual's disability. Examples of work or tasks include, but are not limited to, assisting individuals who are blind or have low vision with navigation and other tasks, alerting individuals who are deaf or hard of hearing to the presence of people or sounds, providing non-violent protection or rescue work, pulling a wheelchair, assisting an individual during a seizure, alerting individuals to the presence of allergens, retrieving items such as medicine or the telephone, providing physical support and assistance with balance and stability to individuals with mobility disabilities, and helping persons with psychiatric and neurological disabilities by preventing or interrupting impulsive or destructive behaviors. The crime deterrent effects of an animal's presence and the provision of emotional support, well-being, comfort, or companionship do not constitute work or tasks for the purposes of this definition (Americans with Disabilities Act 1990 Section 35.136).

- If the dog's mere presence provides comfort, it is not a service animal under the ADA. But if the dog is trained to perform a task related to a person's disability, it is a service animal under the ADA. For example, if the dog has been trained to sense that an anxiety attack is about to happen and take a specific action to help avoid the attack or lessen its impact, the dog is a service animal (ADA).

- To summarize, the ADA states:

  - Service animals are:

    - Dogs

    - Any breed and any size of dog

    - Trained to perform a task directly related to a person's disability

  - Service animals are not:

    - Required to be certified or go through a professional training program

- Required to wear a vest or other ID that indicates they're a service dog

- Emotional support or comfort dogs, because providing emotional support or comfort is not a task related to a person's disability (ADA)

Therapy animal:

- The Illinois General Assembly does not have a specific definition for "therapy animal" that is found in The Act.

- Generally, a therapy animal is trained to provide comfort and affection to specific people and/or communities. They are part of an emotional, therapeutic, and/or physical treatment and/or recovery plan. The locations where a therapy animal is present include but are not limited to: hospitals, hospices, schools, disaster zones, retirement homes, nursing homes, and similar locations and communities.

- They are usually better socially adjusted than service animals.

- A therapy animal is a type of animal-assisted intervention in which there is a goal-directed intervention in which an animal meeting specific criteria is an integral part of the treatment process. Animal-assisted therapy is provided in a variety of settings and may be group or individual in nature (Air Carrier Access Act and CFR Part 382; AVMA).

Under Title II and Title III of the ADA, *none* of the following are considered service animals:

1. Comfort animals

2. Emotional support animals

3. Therapy dogs

How does The Act define a therapeutic relationship?

'Therapeutic relationship' means the provision of medical care, program care, or personal care services, in good faith, for and with actual knowledge of, an individual's disability and that individual's disability-related need for an assistance animal by: (1) a physician or other medical professional, (2) a mental health service provider, or (3) a non-medical service agency or reliable third party who is in a position to know about the individual's disability. Therapeutic relationship does not include an entity that issues a certificate, license, or similar document that purports to confirm, without conducting a meaningful assessment of a person's disability or a person's disability-related need for an assistance animal, that a person (a) has a disability, or (b) needs an assistance animal." (310 ILCS 120/5).=

Under federal law, disability is a protected class. If an individual who is disabled under the definition of the law needs the assistance of an animal, such as a dog, and the animal has been certified as a support animal, whether that be as the result of a mental or physical disability or even an emotional disability, the landlord and even the seller of a residential structure is not allowed to inquire about the animal. If the disabled person brings up the existence of the animal, the landlord or seller can acknowledge the animal's existence, but cannot question further the necessity of the animal. Under the Fair Housing provisions, the landlord or seller should inquire as to whether or not the animal is certified under federal and/or state law. The disabled individual may have to produce evidence that the animal is certified under federal, and/or state law, to perform in accordance with the individual's physical, mental, and/or emotional needs.

Are landlords in Illinois required by law to allow service dogs or support animals on the properties they own and/or oversee? The first answer comes from the Illinois Human Rights Act. It states that it is illegal to decide not to sell or rent housing to an individual who is hearing impaired, blind, and/or has some other type of a physical disability based on the fact that he/she has a support animal such as a guide dog, hearing dog, or another type of support dog. This provision specifically applies to individuals with physical disabilities.

Another factor is the Federal Fair Housing Act. It is broader and defines the obligations of housing providers as follows.

> Individuals with a disability may request to keep an assistance animal as a reasonable accommodation to a housing provider's pet restrictions. Housing providers cannot refuse to make reasonable accommodations in rules, policies, practices, or services when such accommodations may be necessary to afford a person with a disability the equal opportunity to use and enjoy a dwelling. The Fair Housing Act requires a housing provider to allow a reasonable accommodation involving an assistance animal in situations that meet all the following conditions:
>
> - A request was made to the housing provider by or for a person with a disability
>
> - The request was supported by reliable disability-related information, if the disability and the disability-related need for the animal were not apparent and the housing provider requested such information, and
>
> - The housing provider has not demonstrated that:
>
>   - Granting the request would impose an undue financial and administrative burden on the housing provider
>
>   - The request would fundamentally alter the essential nature of the housing provider's operations

- The specific assistance animal in question would pose a direct threat to the health or safety of others despite any other reasonable accommodations that could eliminate or reduce the threat

- The request would not result in significant physical damage to the property of others despite any other reasonable accommodations that could eliminate or reduce the physical damage. (HUD)

Here is a helpful question-and-answer section directly from the ADA website.

1. What does "do work or perform tasks" mean?

   - The dog must be trained to take a specific action when needed to assist the person with a disability. For example, a person with diabetes may have a dog that is trained to alert him when his blood sugar reaches high or low levels. A person with depression may have a dog that is trained to remind her to take her medication. Or, a person who has epilepsy may have a dog that is trained to detect the onset of a seizure and then help the person remain safe during the seizure.

2. Are emotional support, therapy, comfort, or companion animals considered service animals under the ADA?

   - No. These terms are used to describe animals that provide comfort just by being with a person. Because they have not been trained to perform a specific job or task, they do not qualify as service animals under the ADA. However, some State or local governments have laws that allow people to take emotional support animals into public places. You may check with your State and local government agencies to find out about these laws.

3. If someone's dog calms them when having an anxiety attack, does this qualify it as a service animal?

   - It depends. The ADA makes a distinction between psychiatric service animals and emotional support animals. If the dog has been trained to sense that an anxiety attack is about to happen and take a specific action to help avoid the attack or lessen its impact, that would qualify as a service animal. However, if the dog's mere presence provides comfort, that would not be considered a service animal under the ADA.

4. Does the ADA require service animals to be professionally trained?

   - No. People with disabilities have the right to train the dog themselves and are not required to use a professional service dog training program.

5. Are service-animals-in-training considered service animals under the ADA?

- No. Under the ADA, the dog must already be trained before it can be taken into public places. However, some State or local laws cover animals that are still in training. (ADA)

Next, read the article called *Disability Rights: Service Animals: A Guide for Individuals with Disabilities and Illinois Businesses*. It is from the Illinois Attorney General. Pay special attention to the FAQ section. Click below to read now. https://illinoisattorneygeneral.gov/Page-Attachments/service animals.pdf

The Illinois' Humane Care for Animals Act can be found at this link. Take time and read it now by clicking here: http://www.ilga.gov/legislation/ilcs/ilcs3.asp?ActID=1717

Once you have read the content from both links above, continue reading this chapter.

Reasonable Accommodations

Reasonable accommodations can be a confusing or difficult topic for licensees. Staying within the boundaries of the law and ensuring up-to-date practices can cause licensees to experience stress, worry, and fear.

Although you read about this topic in an earlier chapter, to enhance your understanding, we want to highlight a PDF called "Reasonable Accommodations and Modifications: A Guide for Housing Professionals." The PDF comes from the Illinois Department of Human Rights working in partnership with Access Living.

> "The Guidebook on Reasonable Accommodations and Modifications offers clarification on which accommodations and modifications must be made in housing for persons with disabilities, in accordance with the Federal Fair Housing Act." (Illinois.gov)

> "This Guidebook provides general legal guidance to housing professionals on reasonable accommodations and reasonable modifications for residents with disabilities and their family members. This guidance may not be appropriate in all situations and is not a substitute for legal advice. Further, federal and state law is subject to change, so it is recommended that housing professionals contact a housing attorney in their community for further information or legal advice." (Illinois.gov)

Read the following quoted excerpts from a PDF called "Reasonable Accommodations and Modifications: A Guide for Housing Professionals." The content in the following charts is directly from the PDF. If you want to read it in its entirety, the complete 41-page document is available online. Note that none of this information is a substitute for acquiring your own legal advice.

Source: https://www.illinois.gov/content/dam/soi/en/web/dhr/publications/documents/idhr-reasonable-accommodations-and-modifications-2-0.pdf

REASONABLE ACCOMMODATIONS AND MODIFICATIONS: A GUIDE FOR HOUSING PROFESSIONALS		
EXAMPLES OF DISABILITY	A REQUEST IS NOT REASONABLE IF	EXAMPLES OF REASONABLE MODIFICATIONS
A person who has visible scarring may be considered disabled if treated differently because of that trait.

Someone with a hearing aid or someone who uses a wheelchair as an apparent disability.

People with intellectual disabilities, chronic pain or fatigue, mental health disabilities, and learning disabilities have non-apparent disabilities. | Providing a reserved accessible parking space near a resident's unit for someone with a mobility or respiratory disability.

Providing documents in alternate formats such as large print or in electronic form for a person with a vision disability.

Allowing a resident with a disability to have an assistance animal in a "no pets" building.

Waiving guest fees or guest rules for a live-in aide for a resident with a disability. | Installing grab bars in the bathroom.

Changing doorknobs to levers for easier access.

Installing a ramp to the front door of the building.

Installing a doorbell with a light instead of sound.

Winding the doorways in a unit for easier access. |

The chart above is a quoted segment from "Reasonable Accommodations and Modifications: A Guide for Housing Professionals," created and released by the Illinois Department of Human Rights.

EXAMPLES: DETERMINING THE NEED FOR AN ACCOMMODATION	A REQUEST IS NOT REASONABLE IF:	EXAMPLE OF REASONABLE ACCOMMODATION COSTS:
Hae Jung's landlord requires tenants to pay rent in person at the rental office that is three blocks away from the apartment building. Hae Jung has a psychiatric disability that makes her afraid to leave her unit. She requests permission to mail her rent payment. Hae Jung's disability creates a need for her to mail her rent check and, therefore, the accommodation request should be granted. Kwane has epilepsy. Kwane works late and asks permission from the condominium association to use the pool after hours. There is no distinguishable disabilityrelated need for Kwane to use the pool after hours and, therefore, the accommodation request can be denied.	A request for an *accommodation* is not reasonable if it imposes an undue financial and administrative burden on the housing provider; or fundamentally alters the basic operation or nature of a housing provider's services or programs by significantly modifying, eliminating, or adding to the services it provides. A request for a **modification** is not reasonable if: the resident fails or refuses to provide the proper assurances the housing provider has requested regarding the workmanship, permits, and restoration of the property, as more fully explained in Section 6-Associated Costs and Section 7-Complex Issues.	A housing provider must usually pay for a sign language interpreter or the creation of an accessible parking space.

The chart above is a quoted segment from "Reasonable Accommodations and Modifications: A Guide for Housing Professionals," created and released by the Illinois Department of Human Rights.

EXAMPLES OF IMPROPER DENIALS

- Sasha has a personal attendant assisting her daily with chores, such as cooking and cleaning. As a reasonable accommodation, Sasha requests that the personal attendant be allowed to use the laundry facility. The accommodation is denied because the housing provider believes the resident should live in a nursing facility. This would be improper.

- Rita's landlord filed an eviction action because of clutter in her apartment. The clutter results from Rita's psychiatric disability. As a reasonable accommodation, she requests that her landlord give her more time to clean. It would be improper for the landlord to continue with the eviction without considering her request for a reasonable accommodation.

- Donald's landlord gives him a notice that his lease will not be renewed. Donald's son lives with him and he uses a wheelchair. Donald looks for a new accessible unit but is unable to find one and overstays his tenancy. His landlord files an eviction action. As a reasonable accommodation, Donald requests additional time to find a new accessible place for him and his son. It would be improper for the landlord to continue with the eviction without considering Donald's request for a reasonable accommodation.

The chart above is a quoted segment from "Reasonable Accommodations and Modifications: A Guide for Housing Professionals," created and released by the Illinois Department of Human Rights.

COMMUNICATION TIPS FOR HOUSING PROVIDERS

- Do not assume a person with a speech disability has difficulty hearing or understanding.

- Ask the person to identify the preferred method of communication, such as email or online chat.

- Be patient. A conversation with someone with a communication disability may take longer and the housing provider should not cut off the communication (e.g., hang up the phone).

- If necessary, ask the person to repeat or clarify statements. Generally, a person with a communication disability will not be offended.

- Speak directly to the person with a disability and not to an interpreter assisting the person (e.g., state, "I want to talk to you about …" rather than "Tell her [the person with a disability] that …").

The chart above is a quoted segment from "Reasonable Accommodations and Modifications: A Guide for Housing Professionals," created and released by the Illinois Department of Human Rights.

INVALID REASONS FOR DENYING AN ACCOMMODATION		EXAMPLES OF SOLUTIONS FOR RESERVED PARKING
The accommodation would violate rules or policies: An accommodation is an exception to the housing provider's rules. Sheer reluctance to allow an exception to the rules is not a valid reason to deny an accommodation.	*Dislike of the resident:* A housing provider's opinion of a resident's character or behavior, or a bad relationship with the resident, is generally not relevant as to whether the accommodation is needed.	Ask the user/owner of the leased or deeded space to voluntarily exchange the space.
The resident already received an accommodation: More than one accommodation may be needed if a resident's needs have increased, the previous accommodation request proves to be insufficient, or if the new accommodation addresses a different need.	*Housing provider's perception of what is best:* A housing provider may not deny a person with a disability an accommodation because the housing provider believes the housing is unsafe, the person needs more care, or the person should live in a different environment, such as a nursing home.	Modify the terms of the lease to allow the housing provider to exchange spaces.
Allowing the accommodation will open the floodgates: An accommodation cannot be denied because of fear that others will want something similar. If an accommodation is granted to a resident with a disability, a similar arrangement is not required for a person without a disability or need for the accommodation.	*Requests made during evictions:* A person may request an accommodation at any time during the application process and throughout the tenancy, even after the housing provider files for an eviction.	Reserve the space specifically for the resident with a disability once the current lease expires. If spaces cannot be exchanged, create new space from unused space in the parking lot, such as where the garbage bins or maintenance equipment is kept.
Impair aesthetics and property values: A housing provider may not deny an accommodation because of speculation that it may affect the aesthetics or property value of the building.		

The chart above is a quoted segment from "Reasonable Accommodations and Modifications: A Guide for Housing Professionals," created and released by the Illinois Department of Human Rights.

FAIR HOUSING AND PEOPLE WITH DISABILITIES

Although the Americans with Disabilities Act (ADA) of 1990 was not specifically created because of real estate, it fully applies to the real estate industry. As you read earlier, ADA is a civil rights law and prohibits discrimination based on one's disability. Properties and units for rent must be accessible to people with disabilities. A person who has a physical disability must be able to safely reach, enter, and occupy the rental property. If the person uses a wheelchair, this often includes necessities such as larger doors, ramps, bathroom modifications (if applicable), lower light switches, and similar modifications. ADA applies to what is called public life. This term encompasses job sites and places of employment, transportation, schools, and other educational centers, and all private and public places that are open to the public. For example, the rental office in an apartment building is considered a public space. It must adhere to ADA requirements. A brokerage is also considered a public space. The Fair Housing Act is what governs and covers the apartments and rental units, not ADA.

VIOLATIONS OF FAIR HOUSING

Violations of Fair Housing can come in many forms. Those most common violations are advertising, blockbusting, redlining, and steering. Concerning advertising and Fair Housing, the HUD website states:

> "Discriminatory housing advertisements are illegal under the Fair Housing Act and other federal civil rights laws. Note that in HUD's housing programs, certain types of affirmative fair housing marketing are required by federal law." (HUD)

The HUD website goes on to ask two common questions and answer them.

1. What is prohibited?

    - In nearly all housing, including private housing, public housing, and housing that receives federal funding, the Fair Housing Act prohibits the making, printing, and publishing of advertisements that indicate a preference, limitation, or discrimination because of race, color, religion, sex, disability, familial status, or national origin. The prohibition applies to publishers, such as newspapers and directories, as well as to persons and entities who place real estate advertisements in newspapers and on websites. It also applies where the advertisement itself violates The Act, even if the property being advertised may be exempt from the provisions of The Act. Other federal civil rights laws may also prohibit discriminatory advertising practices. Examples of advertising that may violate The Act include phrases such as "no children," which indicates discrimination on the basis of familial status, or "no wheelchairs," which indicates disability discrimination.

2. What type of affirmative fair housing marketing may be required?

- Federal law requires that applicants for participation in HUD's subsidized and unsubsidized housing programs pursue affirmative fair housing marketing policies. This is to help ensure that individuals of similar income levels in the same housing market area have a like range of housing choices available to them regardless of their race, color, religion, sex, disability, familial status, or national origin. (HUD)

In this short excerpt below, the Federal Fair Housing Act states:

"Discrimination in sale or rental of housing and other prohibited practices. As made applicable by section 803 of this title and except as exempted by sections 803(b) and 807 of this title, it shall be unlawful:

(a) To refuse to sell or rent after the making of a bona fide offer, or to refuse to negotiate for the sale or rental of, or otherwise make unavailable or deny, a dwelling to any person because of race, color, religion, sex, familial status, or national origin. (b) To discriminate against any person in the terms, conditions, or privileges of sale or rental of a dwelling, or in the provision of services or facilities in connection therewith, because of race, color, religion, sex, familial status, or national origin. (c) To make, print, or publish, or cause to be made, printed, or published any notice, statement, or advertisement, with respect to the sale or rental of a dwelling that indicates any preference, limitation, or discrimination based on race, color, religion, sex, handicap, familial status, or national origin, or an intention to make any such preference, limitation, or discrimination. (d) To represent to any person because of race, color, religion, sex, handicap, familial status, or national origin that any dwelling is not available for inspection, sale, or rental when such dwelling is in fact so available. (e) For profit, to induce or attempt to induce any person to sell or rent any dwelling by representations regarding the entry or prospective entry into the neighborhood of a person or persons of a particular race, color, religion, sex, handicap, familial status, or national origin." (Sec. 804 of 42 U.S. Code 3604)

To read the Federal Fair Housing Act or review details, go to this link:

https://www.ilga.gov/legislation/ilcs/ilcs4.asp?DocName=077500050HArt.+3&ActID=2266&ChapterID=64&SeqStart=1393750&SeqEnd=2200000

Advertising

The following portion comes directly from HUD in a PDF download called "Part 109—Fair Housing Advertising."

"109.20 Use of words, phrases, symbols, and visual aids.

The following words, phrases, symbols, and forms typify those most often used in residential real estate advertising to convey either overt or tacit discriminatory preferences or limitations. In considering a complaint under the Fair Housing Act, the Department will normally consider the use of these and comparable words, phrases, symbols, and forms to indicate a possible violation of the act and to establish a need for further proceedings on the complaint, if it is apparent from the context of the usage that discrimination within the meaning of the act is likely to result.

a. Words descriptive of dwelling, landlord, and tenants. White private home, Colored home, Jewish home, Hispanic residence, adult building.

b. Words indicative of race, color, religion, sex, handicap, familial status, or national origin—

- Race—Negro, Black, Caucasian, Oriental, American Indian.

- Color—White, Black, Colored.

- Religion—Protestant, Christian, Catholic, Jew.

- National origin—Mexican American, Puerto Rican, Philippine, Polish, Hungarian, Irish, Italian, Chicano, African, Hispanic, Chinese, Indian, Latino.

- Sex—the exclusive use of words in advertisements, including those involving the rental of separate units in a single or multi-family dwelling, stating or tending to imply that the housing being advertised is available to persons of only one sex and not the other, except where the sharing of living areas is involved. Nothing in this part restricts advertisements of dwellings used exclusively for dormitory facilities by educational institutions.

- Handicap—crippled, blind, deaf, mentally ill, retarded, impaired, handicapped, physically fit. Nothing in this part restricts the inclusion of information about the availability of accessible housing in the advertising of dwellings.

- Familial status—adults, children, singles, mature persons. Nothing in this part restricts advertisements of dwellings which are intended and operated for occupancy by older persons and which constitute housing for older persons as defined in Part 100 of this title.

- Catch words—Words and phrases used in a discriminatory context should be avoided, e.g., restricted, exclusive, private, integrated, traditional, board approval, or membership approval.

c. Symbols or logotypes. Symbols or logotypes which imply or suggest race, color, religion, sex, handicap, familial status, or national origin.

d. Colloquialisms. Words or phrases used regionally or locally that imply or suggest race, color, religion, sex, handicap, familial status, or national origin.

e. Directions to real estate for sale or rent (use of maps or written instructions). Directions can imply a discriminatory preference, limitation, or exclusion. For example, references to real estate location made in terms of racial or national origin significant landmarks, such as an existing black development (signal to blacks) or an existing development known for its exclusion of minorities (signal to whites). Specific directions which make reference to a racial or national origin significant area may indicate a preference. References to a synagogue, congregation, or parish may also indicate a religious preference.

f. Area (location) description. Names of facilities that cater to a particular racial, national origin, or religious group, such as country club or private school designations, or names of facilities that are used exclusively by one sex may indicate a preference. "(HUD)

Source: "Part 109—Fair Housing Advertising" PDF by HUD. https://www.hud. gov/sites/dfiles/FHEO/documents/BBE%20Part%20109%20Fair%20Housing%20 Advertising.pdf

To extend your learning and grasp of this topic, read the two sections below. Each one gives more examples of which words and phrases are most likely to be acceptable and ones where you must exercise caution. The words and phrases below build upon the HUD requirements you just read and are derived from "Part 109—Fair Housing Advertising" of HUD. The two sections below are not all-inclusive. These are only a sample. There is *no guarantee* that they are current, accurate, or complete, as each section can change at any time. They are provided as a reminder when preparing any marketing materials. For the most current information, visit the HUD website and refer to your brokerage handbook. Whether flyers, signs, newspaper advertising, and/or Internet-based, the HUD's list of unacceptable terms is considered to be discriminatory and should not be used in any form or manner. As a general rule of law, real estate licensees should promote the *features* of the property and avoid any language that may describe a specific type of buyer or tenant. This information is not an attempt to offer legal advice. Should you have any questions regarding the acceptability of a specific word or phrase, you should seek legal counsel. *Please note that some words in the sections below may trigger, frustrate, or upset you as the reader.*

Examples of acceptable words and phrases:

- Features of the property

    - Number of bedrooms

    - Number of bathrooms

    - Total square feet

    - Guesthouse

- Close to the property

    - Parks, playgrounds

    - Golf course

    - Mass transit

    - Bus route

    - Easy access to transportation hubs.

- Amenities

    - Gated community

    - Guest parking

    - Clubhouse

    - Swimming pool

    - Workout facilities

    - Dog park

Examples of words and phrases that indicate you must exercise caution:

- Age:

    - Retirees

    - Senior community

    - Senior citizens

    - Senior housing

- Grandparents
- Gender:
  - Female only
  - Male only
  - Bachelor
  - Bachelorette
- Other:
  - Prestigious
  - Gentleman's farm
  - Membership approval required
  - Board approval required

Examples of unacceptable words and phrases:

- Community
  - Adult community
  - Adult living
  - Couples only
  - Quiet tenants
  - Newlyweds.
- Disability
  - No wheelchairs
  - Not wheelchair accessible
  - No handicap parking
  - No mentally handicapped
  - No blind people.
- Other:

- Number of children

- No children

- Only singles may apply

- Physically fit only.

For a more complete list of unacceptable words and phrases along with specific guidelines, refer to the HUD excerpt above.

In addition to the HUD's information and our example sections noted above, the law also considers the following terms to be discriminatory: Catholic only, near religious centers, name of (religious organization), and Mormon only. Members of society that do not believe in any religious concept are also protected under the Fair Housing laws.

Here is what HUD states about housing for older persons:

What Are the Fair Housing Act's "Housing for Older Persons" Exemptions?

The Fair Housing Act specifically exempts three types of housing for older persons from liability for familial status discrimination. Such exempt housing facilities or communities can lawfully refuse to sell or rent dwellings to families with minor children *only* if they qualify for the exemption. In order to qualify for the "housing for older persons" exemption, a facility or community must comply with *all* the requirements of the exemption.

The Housing for Older Persons exemptions apply to the following housing:

1. Provided under any state or federal program that the Secretary of HUD has determined to be specifically designed and operated to assist elderly persons (as defined in the state or federal program);

2. Intended for, and solely occupied by persons 62 years of age or older; or

3. Intended and operated for occupancy by persons 55 years of age or older.

The 55 or older exemption is the most common of the three.

How to Qualify for the "55 or Older" Exemption

In order to qualify for the "55 or older" housing exemption, a facility or community must satisfy *each* of the following requirements:

- At least 80 percent of the units must have at least one occupant who is 55 years of age or older; and

- The facility or community must publish and adhere to policies and procedures that demonstrate the intent to operate as "55 or older" housing; and

- The facility or community must comply with HUD's regulatory requirements for age verification of residents.

"The "housing for older persons" exemption does not protect such housing facilities or communities from liability for housing discrimination because of race, color, religion, sex, disability, or national origin." (HUD).

Note: This particular framework is designed to allow couples, whether they're married or not, to continue to live together even if only one is 55 years of age or older.

Blockbusting, Redlining, and Steering

Blockbusting is an illegal process in which licensees and developers use manipulative tactics in order to pressure property owners to sell their houses, potentially at low prices. How? By telling the homeowners that some type of minority will be moving into the neighborhood soon. This practice is also called panic selling and panic peddling. The licensee will say that the neighborhood is "changing" in an effort to instill fear in the homeowners that their property value is drastically going to decrease in the near future.

Example: Both licensee Rick and homeowner Bob are Caucasian. Rick tells Bob that minorities are moving into the neighborhood and that it's best to sell as soon as possible before Bob loses a lot of equity. Rick may say directly or indirectly that crime will increase, that unemployment will go up, and/or any other type of story in order to manipulate Bob. Bob caves into the manipulation. The purchaser, a friend of Rick, buys Bob's property for $140,000 and turns around and immediately sells it for $190,000. He splits the profits with Rick. Did Rick actively work in Bob's best interest?

By the time the '80s had hit, blockbusting had disappeared for the most part, but not entirely. This practice can be related to racism, religion, sexuality, and more.

Redlining, as you recall, means a service provider is withholding services (financial or other) from residents of specific geographical areas. The practice is usually based on ethnicity or race. Also, it is commonly done systematically. It is not random. It's intentional. Redlining has nothing to do with the applicant's financial qualifications or creditworthiness. In the real estate industry, redlining is a form of lending discrimination. It is the unethical practice of denying mortgage loans (or insurance policies) to residents of a certain race or in specific geographical areas. Generally, it is minority neighborhoods that experience the majority of redlining. (Note: At one time in history, redlining was backed by the US government.)

Steering is a discriminatory practice. It is when a licensee, by his/her own choice, works toward guiding or routing home seekers to specific areas or neighborhoods and away from others. This discrimination can be based on race, religion, sexuality, and/or something else.

Examples: Licensee Suzie tries to sell Latino families on neighborhoods with lots of Latinos and where Spanish is commonly spoken. A leasing agent at a large apartment complex tries to only have Muslim occupants in Building D, which is the furthest away from the leasing office. This illegal practice can cause a civil lawsuit.

Steering is grounds for discipline. The Act states the following:

> "Influencing or attempting to influence, by any words or acts, a prospective seller, purchaser, occupant, landlord, or tenant of real estate, in connection with viewing, buying, or leasing real estate, so as to promote or tend to promote the continuance or maintenance of racially and religiously segregated housing or so as to retard, obstruct, or discourage racially integrated housing on or in any street, block, neighborhood, or community." (225 ILCS 454/20-20)

THE ILLINOIS HUMAN RIGHTS ACT

The Illinois Department of Human Rights is also known as IDHR. It administers the Illinois Human Rights Act. This act prohibits discrimination related to employment, public accommodations, financial credit, and real estate transactions on the basis of a person's race, color, religion, national origin, gender, disability, familial status, ancestry, age (40+), marital status, military service, sexual orientation, order of protection status, criminal history, and source of income. It also prohibits sexual harassment in education and discrimination because of citizenship status. This act applies to both owners and licensees. Violating the rights of a person based on any of the protected classes constitutes a civil rights violation and may be subject to penalties. As you can see, there is a common thread that all boils down to three guidelines:

1. Treat all people the same.

2. Treat each person fairly.

3. Never display favoritism.

Are there exemptions to the Illinois Human Rights Act? Yes. They are found in section 775 ILCS 5/3-106. It states the following:

Exemptions. nothing contained in Section 3-102 shall prohibit:

A. Private Sales of Single-Family Homes.

1. Any sale of a single-family home by its owner so long as the following criteria are met:

    a. The owner does not own or have a beneficial interest in more than three single-family homes at the time of the sale;

    b. The owner or a member of his or her family was the last current resident of the home;

    c. The home is sold without the use in any manner of the sales or rental facilities or services of any real estate broker or salesman, or of any employee or agent of any real estate broker or salesman;

    4. The home is sold without the publication, posting, or mailing, after notice, of any advertisement or written notice in violation of paragraph of Section 3-102.* *(See note below.)*

    5. This exemption does not apply to paragraph (F) of Section 3-102.

B. Apartments. Rental of a housing accommodation in a building which contains housing accommodations for not more than four families living independently of each other, if the owner resides in one of the housing accommodations. This exemption does not apply to paragraph (F) of Section 3-102.

C. Private Rooms. Rental of a room or rooms in a private home by an owner if he or she or a member of his or her family resides therein or, while absent for a period of not more than twelve months, if he or she or a member of his or her family intends to return to reside therein.

D. Reasonable local, State, or Federal restrictions regarding the maximum number of occupants permitted to occupy a dwelling.

E. Religious Organizations. A religious organization, association, or society, or any nonprofit institution or organization operated, supervised, or controlled by or in conjunction with a religious organization, association, or society, from limiting the sale, rental or occupancy of a dwelling which it owns or operates for other than a commercial purpose to persons of the same religion, or from giving preference to such persons, unless membership in such religion is restricted on account of race, color, or national origin.

F. Sex. Restricting the rental of rooms in a personal residence to persons of one sex.

G. Persons Convicted of Drug-Related Offenses. Conduct against a person because such person has been convicted by any court of competent jurisdiction of the illegal manufacture or distribution of a controlled substance as defined in Section 102 of the federal Controlled Substances Act (21 U.S.C. 802).

H. Persons engaged in the business of furnishing appraisals of real property from taking into consideration factors other than those based on unlawful discrimination or familial status in furnishing appraisals.

    a. (H-1) The owner of an owner-occupied residential building with four or fewer units (including the unit in which the owner resides) from making decisions regarding whether to rent to a person based upon that person's sexual orientation.

I. Housing for Older Persons. No provision in this Article regarding familial status shall apply with respect to housing for older persons.

    1. As used in this Section, "housing for older persons" means housing:

    a. intended and operated for occupancy by persons 55 years of age or older and:

        1. at least 80% of the occupied units are occupied by at least one person who is 55 years of age or older; or

        2. *the housing facility or community publishes and adheres to policies and procedures that demonstrate the intent required under this subdivision (a); and

        3. *the housing facility or community complies with rules adopted by the Department for verification of occupancy, which shall:

            1. provide for verification by reliable surveys and affidavits; and

            2. include examples of the types of policies and procedures relevant to a determination of compliance with the requirement of clause (ii).

    b. intended for, and *solely occupied by, persons 62 years of age or older; or

        1. at least 100% of the occupied units are occupied by at least one person who is 62 years of age or older; or

        2. *the housing facility or community publishes and adheres to policies and procedures that demonstrate the intent required under this subdivision (b); and

        3. *the housing facility or community complies with rules adopted by the Department for verification of occupancy, which shall:

            a. provide for verification by reliable surveys and affidavits; and

b. include examples of the types of policies and procedures relevant to a determination of compliance with the requirement of clause (ii).

c. intention to make any such preference, limitation, or discrimination.

Note: Above, in Section I.1.a and b parts ii and iii, here is what you need to know about the asterisks. Those bullet points are applicable whether the age bracket is 55 or 62.

*Section 3-102 (F) Publication of Intent. Make, print, circulate, post, mail, publish or cause to be made, printed, circulated, posted, mailed, or published any notice, statement, advertisement or sign, or use a form of application for a real estate transaction, or make a record or inquiry in connection with a prospective real estate transaction, that indicates any preference, limitation, or discrimination based on unlawful discrimination or unlawful discrimination based on familial status or an arrest record, or an intention to make any such preference, limitation, or discrimination." (775 ILCS 5/3-102)

These surveys and affidavits shall be admissible in administrative and judicial proceedings for the purposes of such verification.

1. Housing shall not fail to meet the requirements for housing for older persons by reason of:

    a. persons residing in such housing as of the effective date of this amendatory Act of 1989 who do not meet the age requirements of subsections (1)(b) or (c); provided that new occupants of such housing meet the age requirements of subsections (1)(b) or (c) of this subsection; or

    b. unoccupied units; provided that such units are reserved for occupancy by persons who meet the age requirements of subsections (1)(b) or (c) of this subsection.

(a) A person shall not be held personally liable for monetary damages for a violation of this Article if the person reasonably relied, in good faith, on the application of the exemption under this subsection (I) relating to housing for older persons.

(b) For the purposes of this item (3), a person may show good faith reliance on the application of the exemption only by showing that:

    1. the person has no actual knowledge that the facility or community is not, or will not be, eligible for the exemption; and

    2. the facility or community has stated formally, in writing, that the facility or community complies with the requirements for the exemption.

Note: An important detail to acknowledge about this part of The Act is that the phrase "housing for older persons" means housing intended for, and occupied by 1) 80% or more if the age bracket is set at 55, or 2) 100% if the age bracket is set at 62 years of age. Regardless of the age bracket, nobody under the age of eighteen may reside in a senior community.

B. Child Sex Offender Refusal to Rent. Refusal of a child sex offender who owns and resides at residential real estate to rent any residential unit within the same building in which he or she resides to a person who is the parent or guardian of a child or children under 18 years of age.

Scenario: Can a landlord refuse to rent a unit to a registered sex offender if there are children in the building, or if the unit is within a certain distance from a school? The answer is yes. This is not considered discrimination.

C. Arrest Records. Inquiry into or the use of an arrest record if the inquiry or use is otherwise authorized by State or federal law.

Read the Illinois Human Rights Act. You may want to break the reading into two segments. This extensive portion can be found in 775 ILCS 5/. The link is here: http://www.ilga.gov/legislation/ilcs/ilcs5.asp?ActID=2266&ChapterID=64

WHAT IF THERE IS A VIOLATION OF THE FEDERAL FAIR HOUSING ACT?

Any individual may file a complaint to the Office of Fair Housing and Equal Opportunity (FHEO). If filed online, currently only English and Spanish are available. The HUD website also provides a nationwide toll-free phone number for those who need to call. The caller will speak with a FHEO intake specialist. Calling a regional FHEO office is another option. The final option is to print a form, fill it out, and mail it to the regional FHEO office. Printable forms are available in Arabic, Cambodian, Chinese, Korean, Russian, Somali, Spanish, and Vietnamese. Assistance is available for persons with disabilities. If someone is not sure if his or her rights have been violated, he/she is encouraged to submit a complaint. Due to time limits, complaints need to be filed quickly.

"It is illegal to retaliate against any person for making a complaint, testifying, assisting, or participating in any manner in a proceeding under HUD's complaint process at any time, even after the investigation has been completed. The Fair Housing Act also makes it illegal to retaliate against any person because that person reported a discriminatory practice to a housing provider or other authority. If you believe you have experienced retaliation, you can file a complaint." HUD

For example, if Janet filed a complaint against Bob, her property manager, it is illegal for Bob to retaliate in any form, even once the investigation is closed. If Janet believes that Bob has retaliated, she can file a second complaint.

Full details and procedures can be found here: https://www.hud.gov/program_offices/fair_housing_equal_opp/online-complaint

THE IMPORTANCE OF ETHICS

Ethics are moral principles. A principle is a belief-based rule of conduct concerning what is right and wrong and what is acceptable and unacceptable. Ethics are based on personal values. Ethics govern a person's behavior and speak to how someone conducts him/herself in the world. Many times, an individual's ethics are at a higher standard than the law. For example, Jane is sitting in a line of traffic in a popular congested area at five p.m. Drivers are frustrated and honking their horns. Michael is trying to enter the street Jane is on from a side street. Nobody is allowing him to enter. They're not allowing him to enter is not illegal. However, Jane allows Michael to enter in front of her vehicle. It's her choice. She is following her own ethics. While laws govern society, a person's ethics are what he/she uses to govern him/herself.

The National Association of REALTORS® has its own code of ethics. Similarly, different real estate associations and brokerages may also have their own code of ethics. If so, the expectation is that the code is followed. A strong code of ethics helps licensees build a solid foundation for fulfilling and financially thriving careers. If you have ever had someone over-deliver or "go above and beyond" the common level of service, that is prompted many times from his or her code of ethics. It makes a huge difference in business because it builds trust. Many professional fields have codes of ethics. What sets real estate apart is that it is one of the few industries in which a licensee can face disciplinary actions if he/she breaks the code of ethics.

Regardless of whom a licensee interacts with, it's important to treat everyone fairly, justly, and indiscriminately. There should be no body language that communicates disdain or hate. Furthermore, people share their experiences in person and online. Although there can be unjust and unfair reviews written online, there can be valid reviews written where those discriminated against speak up and share their experiences. While licensees are to adhere to Fair Housing practices and applicable laws, ethics takes customer service, care, and experience to a whole new level.

HARASSMENT

Harassment covers a wide variety of behaviors that are viewed as offensive in nature. Commonly, this behavior is viewed as any action that humiliates, demeans, embarrasses, or devalues another human being. These behaviors are or seem to be troubling, inappropriate, harmful, or threatening. Harassment usually comes from a foundation of discrimination, and it blocks and inhibits another person from fully experiencing the rights afforded to them for simply being a human being. Harassment can lead victims to be manipulated, feel controlled, want to shut down, and/or feel stuck emotionally. Harassment may be a one-time event, like an insult. However, when it becomes a pattern, it moves into the realm of bullying.

Sexual harassment is a type of harassment that involves the use of sexual overtones and meanings that may be implicit, explicit, direct, or indirect. It can occur anywhere where there are two or more people. It can also occur digitally, via emails, texts, social media messages, and so on. Harassers and victims may be of any profession, age, gender, sexual orientation, and so on.

The U.S. Department of Health and Human Services shares the following:

Sex-based harassment includes sexual harassment (including sexual violence) and gender-based harassment. The definitions below have been developed by the Office for Civil Rights at the U.S. Department of Education. Because of the overlap between Section 1557 and Title IX and to ensure consistency for entities covered by both statutes, these definitions will be used for both statutes to describe prohibited behavior.

- **Sexual harassment** is unwelcome conduct of a sexual nature. It includes unwelcome sexual advances, requests for sexual favors, and other verbal, nonverbal, or physical conduct of a sexual nature. Sex-based harassment can happen to people and be perpetrated by people of any sex.

- **Sexual violence** is a form of sexual harassment. Sexual violence refers to physical sexual acts perpetrated against a person's will or where a person is incapable of giving consent (e.g., due to the victim's age or use of drugs or alcohol, or because an intellectual or other disability prevents the victim from having the capacity to give consent). A number of different acts fall into the category of sexual violence, including rape, sexual assault, sexual battery, sexual abuse, and sexual coercion.

- **Gender-based harassment** is unwelcome conduct based on an individual's actual or perceived sex. It includes slurs, taunts, stereotypes, or name-calling as well as gender-motivated physical threats, attacks, or other hateful conduct. (HHS)

The U.S. Department of Health and Human Services elaborates on these themes and states the following:

- What are some examples of sexual harassment?

  - Physician at a health center in a university engages in inappropriate touching of female students and others who receive examinations.

- Professor sexually assaults male students during a research internship in an isolated setting, requiring them to share a bedroom.

- Researcher repeatedly makes lewd and sexually demeaning comments in the laboratory.

- What are some examples of gender-based harassment?

- Male graduate students sabotage the results of female graduate students' research.

- Hospital denies student an internship in its training and outreach program after an initial interview. Supervisor of internships remarked to colleagues that the student did not look sufficiently feminine for the role.

- What are some examples of both sexual harassment and gender-based harassment?

- Male Primary Investigator in research lab demeans and calls out the mistakes of female employees of the lab, but not of male employees who make similar errors. Women are not promoted into supervisory positions under the Primary Researcher. He also makes sexually inappropriate remarks about female researchers at a laboratory that was being considered for collaboration. (HHS)

Harassment is serious. In Section 10-40 of The Act, it states that "every brokerage company or entity, other than a sole proprietorship with no other sponsored licensees, shall adopt a company or office policy dealing with topics . . ." One of the key topics is harassment.

When it comes to the topic of sexual harassment and prevention in the workplace, Illinois' authority is the IDFPR. All licensed professionals in Illinois are required by the IDFRP to receive sexual harassment prevention training. This course gives the student one hour of Continuing Education credit. Each Illinois licensee is required to complete Sexual Harassment Prevention training prior to renewing their license (even if this is their first time to renew).

Read the hand-selected excerpts from the document called "**New Sexual Harassment Prevention Training Continuing Education requirement to renew licenses issued by the Division of Real Estate beginning January 1, 2020.**" The excerpts are followed by the link below so you can read the entire document.

"Sexual harassment prevention training is now required of all persons who hold a license issued by the Division of Real Estate ("DRE") for professions that require Continuing Education ("CE") to renew. The new law requires licensees to complete a one-hour CE course in sexual harassment prevention training and is effective for all renewals on or after January 1, 2020, where CE is required.

How do I know if the CE provider or sponsor is accepted or approved?

Licensees can take this CE course from any CE provider or sponsor that is authorized to provide CE for any profession regulated by IDFPR. This includes businesses or entities that have active CE provider licenses for any profession. For example, any licensee (appraiser, broker, home inspector, etc.) can take a class offered by a company that has a Nurse CE provider license.

Is there a list of approved sexual harassment prevention training CE providers or sponsors? For real estate professionals, a list of approved CE providers and their courses is available on the IDFPR website, DRE section. https://idfpr.illinois.gov/dre/education/rececourselist.html

There is no list or special license specifically for sexual harassment prevention training courses. If you are considering a class, please contact the CE provider or sponsor in advance to confirm that they have a CE provider license issued by IDFPR.

Will I have to send proof that I completed the sexual harassment prevention training CE course to the Department? No. However, like all other CE, you must receive a Certificate of Completion and retain it for your records. The certificate must include information such as the number of hours completed, the name of the CE provider or sponsor, and the date the CE was completed. You will not need to provide a certificate if you renew on time, but you may be asked to confirm that you have completed the training. You may need to provide a certificate if you renew late, need to restore an expired license, or if you are included in a CE audit.

Is this training required each time I renew my license? Yes. Sexual harassment prevention training will be required for every renewal after January 1, 2020.

Will I need to complete sexual harassment prevention training to restore or reinstate my license? Yes. Depending on when your next renewal period is after January 1, 2020, for which you must take CE, you are required to take the sexual harassment prevention training."

To read the full PDF release, click the link here: https://idfpr.illinois.gov/profs/realest.html

Take the chapter quiz below and test how well you have learned concepts from this chapter.

CHAPTER 26 QUIZ

1. On which levels do housing laws protect people from discrimination?

    a. Federal

    b. State

    c. Local

    d. All of the above

    e. Only state and local

2. Which act added sex/gender to the list of protected classes?

    a. The Civil Rights Act of 1968

    b. The Housing and Community Development Act of 1974

    c. The Fair Housing Amendments Act of 1988

    d. None of the above

3. The Fair Housing Act protects individuals from discrimination in which of the following scenarios?

    a. Renting a condo

    b. Buying a home

    c. Getting a mortgage

    d. Seeking housing assistance

    e. All of the above

    f. Only A, B, and C

4. James moved from Wyoming to Illinois. He is 31 years old. When he was 25, he was convicted of criminal conduct and thus has a criminal record. He wants to rent a room in a small town. Michael owns a large house and has a room for rent within his primary dwelling. Can he deny James the room because of his criminal record?

    a. Yes, he is within his rights to do so.

    b. No, he may not.

5. Concerning emotional support animals (ESAs), which of the following is true?

    a. ESAs do not qualify as service animals under the Americans with Disabilities Act (ADA), but they may be permitted as reasonable accommodations for persons with disabilities under the Fair Housing Act.
    b. ESAs do qualify as service animals under the Americans with Disabilities Act (ADA)
    c. An ESA can only be a dog.
    d. None of the above.

6. Dean is a residential leasing agent for a small apartment complex. Sarah came into the office this morning. She is blind and has a service animal. Dean is concerned it will be a hassle to accept Sarah as a resident because the service animal is a large dog. While pets are allowed, no large dogs are allowed. Does Dean have to accept Sarah if she qualifies financially for the apartment?

    a. Yes
    b. No

7. Jean owns a small construction company. She is in the process of drawing up blueprints for a small apartment building with eight units. The location is a small town in Illinois. The land sits on a hill. Is Jane required by law to make the leasing office for the new building accessible to those with disabilities, in wheelchairs for example?

    a. No
    b. Yes

8. Which advertisement would be appropriate under the Federal Fair Housing rules for advertising units in a small apartment building?

    a. Catholic applicants only
    b. English speaking only
    c. Near parks
    d. No wheelchairs

9. Licensee Robert tells the Jones family that it's in their best interest to move. They are a Caucasian devout Latter-day Saints family. He tells them that the neighborhood is changing because of a lower cost of living as compared to other neighborhoods. Robert also shares that the people buying properties in their neighborhood represent a mix of other religions and races, and that they are forcing the housing values to decline. What is this Fair Housing violation called?

    a. Blockbusting

    b. Redlining

    c. Steering

    d. Rerouting

10. In the 1970s, the Singh family moved from Bangalore, India, to the outskirts of Chicago. Both Mr. and Mrs. Singh had medical degrees and had been accepted by a well-known medical school in Chicago to further their education. While the Singhs were financially qualified and spoke fluent English, it took them over a year to get their purchase financed. Despite easily qualifying financially, for one reason or another, no lending institution would do business with them. It is conceivable that lenders were reluctant to finance them because of their background. Which discriminatory action was most likely taking place?

    a. Blockbusting

    b. Redlining

    c. Steering

    d. Panic peddling

11. The Huang family moved from China to Springfield, Illinois, last month. Since then, they have been staying at an Airbnb while scouting out a house to purchase. Mrs. Huang has done endless hours of research in advance. She happily brought a list of neighborhoods when she and her husband met with their first licensee. The licensee looked at the list. Out of the ten neighborhoods, he crossed off seven and said, "One of these three neighborhoods will be best for you." Later, as they toured the three neighborhoods, Mr. and Mrs. Huang noticed that the signs for the commercial businesses were predominantly in Chinese. Which type of discriminatory practice is occurring?

    a. Blockbusting

    b. Redlining

    c. Steering

    d. Panic peddling

12. A licensee named Todd has just discriminated against a lesbian couple who are clients. They were speaking with him on the sales floor inside the brokerage office. Two other licensees overheard what he said and were shocked, hurt, and disappointed. Each of them immediately went to the sponsoring broker's office to talk with her about the incident. Which of the following categorizes what Todd did?

    a. Civil rights violation

    b. Office policy that covers Fair Housing laws

    c. A and B

    d. None of the above

13. Juan, a Spanish speaker, has a complaint about his current rental situation. He knows what is happening is not fair. Nobody in the office speaks Spanish. Juan's English is limited, although he has been building his speaking and listening skills. He has heard of the Office of Fair Housing and Equal Opportunity. However, he knows he cannot clearly articulate what is happening with someone on the phone as it would be too hard to explain the situation in English. What is most likely his best option?

    a. Ignore the situation

    b. File a complaint online

    c. Talk to the property owner again

    d. Call the regional management office

14. Jane lives in a small complex and the property manager personally oversees the office, maintenance, and repairs. Her dishwasher recently broke. She submitted a repair request to the property manager. However, the property manager failed to respond for over three weeks. She reached out to him again, and he once again failed to respond. Jane's next recourse is to file a complaint against the property manager and the complex with the municipal building department. It has now been over six weeks. What can Jane do?

    a. Seek legal advice

    b. Follow up on her first complaint

    c. Jane can file a subsequent complaint

    d. Any of the above

15. If you are a licensee who is part of an industry-based organization or association that has a strict code of ethics, what can happen if you break the code?

    a. Nothing.

    b. They can penalize you.

    c. They can revoke your membership.

    d. B and C

16. To whom does the Illinois Human Rights Act apply?

    a. Property owners
    b. Property managers
    c. Licensees
    d. All of the above
    e. Only B and C

17. Age is a protected class in the Illinois Human Rights Act. At what age is an individual protected?

    a. 40 and up
    b. 50 and up
    c. 60 and up
    d. 70 and up

18. Which of the following is sexual harassment?

    a. Forwarding emails with sexual content
    b. Requesting sexual favors
    c. Inappropriate touching
    d. All of the above

19. The Thorton family has been living in an apartment building for three weeks. Mr. Thornton is a very talkative person. He has been meeting residents in his building and other buildings. He started to notice that all of the residents in his building, Building C, were Christians. He noticed several church and God stickers on vehicles before they arrived, but had assumed that was common for the complex. This week, he started talking with people who live in Building A. The majority of them are Muslim. Which violation does it look like the property manager is guilty of?

    a. Blockbusting
    b. Redlining
    c. Steering
    d. Panic peddling

20. Do emotional support animals qualify as service animals under the Americans with Disabilities Act?

    a. Yes
    b. No

CHAPTER 27:

CLOSING
THE DEAL

LEARNING GOALS:

By the end of this lesson, you will:

- Discuss how closing day works
- Responsibilities of each party at the closing
- RESPA and TRID's impact on closing

LICENSEES LOVE CLOSING DAYS! While they may be stressful, frustrating, or possibly pack a surprise, the majority of the time the closing day goes smoothly. A licensee does not generate income unless he/she closes the deal and completes a real estate action. The closing is the final phase in executing and completing a real estate transaction. Closing is also known as settlement. It involves the exchange of funds. During the negotiation phase, the parties agree on a closing date. The closing date is commonly weeks after an offer has been formally accepted. Before a real estate transaction can close, all conditions and contingencies of the sales contract must be met. When does the closing process actually begin? It starts when the seller accepts, signs, and returns the purchase agreement.

Until the closing day, the licensee has worked tirelessly managing countless tasks as well as building relationships for those involved in each and every transaction that he/she is involved in. From innumerable phone calls and emails to working with inspectors and other third parties, closing day is when the licensee sees the finish line up close in his or her mind.

Usually, the parties present on closing day include the licensee, the broker/s, the buyer, the buyer's attorney, the seller, and the seller's attorney. It's not uncommon for other parties, like a title company representative and/or mortgage lender, to be present as well.

What commonly happens on closing day? Buyers pay sellers the agreed sale price for the property as well as fees to the lender, some settlement costs, attorney fees, and perhaps commission. Sellers pay commissions, attorney fees, and some settlement costs. It's possible that buyers and sellers may have additional expenses that are not mentioned here. On closing day, the property ownership is fully and legally transferred to the buyer.

Definitions Related to Closing

Next, read the key terms below.

- **Abstract of title:** The condensed summary and record of the title. It shows all recorded legal actions that are related in some way to the property.

- **Accrued expenses:** These are costs that have occurred and are shown, but the expenses have not been paid yet. They show up on a settlement statement. The expenses are paid in arrears. The assumption is that nothing has yet been paid, so the seller's portion must be calculated so she can be debited and the buyer credited for this amount. The seller owes the money, even though the bill may not have arrived yet. If the buyer gets credited for that amount, the buyer pays the entire amount when the bill comes due, because the seller has already taken care of his obligation by giving credit to the buyer. Examples include real estate taxes, mortgage interest, and water bills.

- **Bill of sale:** This document is used to transfer title to personal property from one individual to another individual. As you know, it is not uncommon for real property purchases to include personal property (such as furniture). When personal property is included in the sale of real property, a bill of sale is used for the transfer.

- **Certificate of title:** This is a professional opinion on the quality of title that is prepared by a title examiner. In the absence of title insurance, it does not provide for any protection if the title examiner missed an essential component concerning the property ownership. Should a future claim arise as a result of the title examiner's error, the seller bears the responsibility for compensating the buyer upon loss of ownership.

- **Chain of title:** The complete chronological history and sequence of ownership transfers for a piece of property. It is the timeline of the title changing hands to new owners through the years. The chain starts at the first recorded claim of ownership (original grant) and continues to the present day. The chain of title lists all documents in the public record that have affected the title to the property.

- **Closing:** The last part of a real estate transaction when real property is transferred from the seller to the buyer.

- **Closing Disclosure:** The Closing Disclosure is the document that shows the detailed and complete accounting for a real estate transaction. It is the balance sheet where all of the money that a buyer or seller owes/pays at closing is shown. It itemizes each party's debits and credits by showing the amount each party will receive and/or be required to pay at the closing. It is most often prepared by the settlement agent (closing agent) but can be prepared by the lender. This document is the standardized form required for all 1-4 family dwellings under RESPA. The form must be available to the borrower at least three business days prior to the closing, per RESPA requirements. Note that the bottom line for a buyer is how much money he or she is required to bring to settlement. The bottom line for a seller is how much money he or she will leave the transaction with, although sometimes it shows what he or she is required to bring to settlement. The Closing Disclosure is also called the settlement statement. It was previously called the HUD-1 Settlement Statement.

"This is a sample of a completed Closing Disclosure for the fixed rate loan illustrated by form H-24(B). The purpose, product, sale price, loan amount, loan term, and interest rate have not changed from the estimates provided on the Loan Estimate. The creditor requires an escrow account and that the consumer pay for private mortgage insurance for the transaction." Consumer Financial Protection Bureau

- **Clouds on a title:** An uncertainty on the title, whether it be in the realm of ownership, or other specific restrictions. A cloud must be resolved most often by a court of law.

- **Conveyance:** This is the legal act or process of transferring or conveying ownership or interest in real estate from one individual (grantor) to another (grantee).

- **Discharge of mortgage:** Refers to when the seller's mortgage on the property is paid off. The lender issues the discharge of the mortgage contract, and the seller should record this document. Also referred to as release of lien.

- **Evidence of title:** This serves as evidence that the title is in good condition. The seller is required to provide it to the purchaser. Basically, the seller attests to the fact that the title is free and clear of any liens, restrictions, or encumbrances, unacceptable to the buyer. Evidence of title is typically provided through one of the following documents:

  - Certificate of Title (document)

  - Attorney's opinion of title (document)

  - Title insurance supplied by the title company (insurance policy)

- **Grantee:** The individual or entity who receives a conveyance of real property in a real estate transaction.

- **Grantor:** The individual or entity who transfers title to real property in a real estate transaction.

- **Homeowners insurance:** An insurance policy that generally covers a variety of specific losses and damages to the home and/or property in the event of one or more of the 16 perils you read about earlier (such as theft, explosion, freezing, etc.).

- **Loan estimate:** A loan estimate is sometimes called an "LE" and was previously called a good faith estimate. A loan estimate groups and categorizes total estimated costs, not actual costs. It does not itemize individual costs. An LE is not as precise as the settlement statement. Simply put, it provides the buyer (and/or seller) with an estimate of the total costs required to close the real estate transaction. These estimates can be compared to actual costs on the Closing Disclosure.

- **Marketable title:** Sometimes called a merchantable title, this is a title (chain of ownership) that is unaffected by any litigation threats and concerns as well as free from reasonable doubt. The title means the property is free and clear of defects, to the extent that it compels the buyer to accept. Could there be a defect? Yes, it's possible. However, a marketable title is one in which a reasonable and prudent person would accept as being good, clean, and valid. At the closing, the seller is expected to deliver a marketable title to the buyer.

- **Mortgage:** A mortgage is the act of granting the lender consent to use the real property as collateral for a debt. In return, the lender provides the money. Surprisingly, most consumers believe that they actually get the mortgage from the bank. However, the mortgage is the act of granting consent to the lender to use the property as collateral. The mortgagor (buyer) is the giver of the mortgage. The mortgagee (lender) is the receiver of the mortgage.

- **Mortgagee's policy:** This kind of title insurance protects the lender's interests in a property by covering losses that might occur if the title to the property is disputed. It usually only covers money owed on the loan at the time of claim, though it may cover other debts as well.

- **Negative amortization:** "Amortization means paying off a loan with regular payments so that the amount you owe goes down with each payment. Negative amortization means that even when you pay, the amount you owe will still go up because you are not paying enough to cover the interest. Your lender may offer you the choice to make a minimum payment that doesn't cover the interest you owe. The unpaid interest gets added to the amount you borrowed, and the amount you owe increases." CFPB

- **Opinion of value:** This is the value placed on the property by an individual at a given moment in time. As you read earlier, there are three different approaches that can be used in order to assess the value. They are the sales comparison approach, the cost approach, and the income capitalization approach.

- **Prepaid expenses** are expenses on a settlement statement that the seller has paid off in advance. Many times, this is an expense he/she pays at the start of the year which keeps the specific account paid in full until the following year. The time line may be quarterly, annually, or something else. Since the seller has already paid for these items, it is understandable that he/she will want to be credited for the portion that he/she paid but will not be using. Examples include condominium assessments and heating and oil costs. For example, if the seller pays $1200 for a certain expense for the year in January, and sells the house in late June, he/she will expect a credit for $600. This $600 reflects payments running from July to December.

- **Prepayment penalties:** These penalties are money charged by a lender when the borrower pays off his/her loan early.

- **Promissory note:** This is the basic evidence of debt, showing in writing who owes how much to whom.

- **Property inspection report:** This report is completed by a professional property inspector and documents the property conditions. The report may include inspections for termites, structural integrity, septic systems, soil, waterflow, and/or radon gas.

- **Property survey:** This is the process of measuring property boundaries in order to determine the precise area of a parcel of land. Surveys also depict easements, encroachments, and physical placement of human-made improvements. They usually show the locations of the building or buildings, parking/driveway, and fences, along with any other improvements.

- Proration is the financial process of allocating usage costs between a buyer and a seller when closing a real estate transaction. It involves the division of certain costs between the two parties based on their respective interests in the property. In other words, it is the mathematical approach necessary to be able to identify what portion of the expense belongs to each party. Proration is an important part of closing because it ensures that both parties are fairly compensated for their contributions and that no one party incurs more costs than necessary. It also helps to ensure that all taxes, fees, and other expenses associated with the transaction are properly divided among both parties in accordance with applicable laws. Sometimes, you'll hear proration referred to as adjustments.

- **Reconciliation:** Verifying the debits and credits have been added and subtracted correctly on a real estate settlement statement.

- **Title insurance:** This is a form of indemnity insurance. (Indemnity is security or protection against a loss or other financial burden.) Title insurance protects the mortgagee (lender) and sometimes the property owners (mortgagors) against loss due to disputes over ownership of a property and defects in the title that are not found in the search of the public record. It protects property owners (mortgagors) from claimants not listed in the insurance policy including forged documents, errors in a property's legal description, improper deeds, and other mistakes. Title insurance does not cure defects, but insures against losses due to title defects. The title company is required to go to court, if necessary, in order to defend its policyholder against any claim against the land ownership. Generally, it is paid for with a one-time premium at closing by the seller. Illinois recognizes two different types: 1. Owner's coverage (mortgagee), and 2. Lender's protection (mortgagor).

- **Title report:** A report issued by a title company that discloses the condition of the title to a specific piece of property.

Final Inspection

Shortly before a closing, a final inspection is scheduled. This appointment is commonly called a walk-through or a final walk-through. A final inspection is not a home inspection, nor should it be confused with one. During the final inspection, the buyer and licensee walk through the property one last time before the closing date. The buyer should verify that the property is in relatively the same condition now as it was when they first viewed it. Everything should be functional and working. If there's anything wrong or malfunctioning, the licensee should document it and bring it up to the attorneys at closing. A buyer's checklist for a final walk-through may include these tasks or more:

- Ensure any pending repairs and/or updates have been completed

- Turn on and test all sinks and check for any leaks

- Turn on and test all appliances (anything with an on/off switch)

- Test electrical outlets

- Test for hot water

- Open and close all doors, windows, cabinet drawers, and similar to ensure they're working properly

- Make sure all sinks/tubs drain properly

- Test the showers

- Flush all the toilets

- Check additional features like pool pump, hot tub, outdoor lighting, safety features, etc.

It is never a smart idea for a buyer to intentionally forgo a final walk-through, because once the closing takes place, the seller is not responsible for any unknown repairs or related issues. However, a buyer is not legally required to do a walk-through.

Closing Location and Expenses Breakdown

The closing location is usually one of the following:

- Title company office

- Lending institution

- One of the participating attorney's offices

Typical buyer expenses may include but are not limited to:

- Appraisal
- Attorney's fees
- Bank fees
- Broker's commission
- Credit report
- Home inspection fee
- Mortgage insurance
- Mortgage recording tax
- Municipality transfer taxes (Does not apply in all municipalities)
- Origination fee
- Points
- Private mortgage insurance
- Tax service fees

Typical seller expenses may include but are not limited to:

- Attorney's fees
- Broker's commission
- Existing lien payments
- Flood certification fee
- Municipality transfer taxes (Does not apply in all municipalities)
- Recording fees
- State and county transfer taxes
- Survey fees
- Title search

Typical shared expenses may include but are not limited to:

- HOA fees

- Property taxes

- Title insurance fees

TWO TYPES OF CLOSINGS AND PARTY RESPONSIBILITIES

Face-to-face closing: This method of conducting a closing in Illinois is also known as a round-table closing. A face-to-face closing is a settlement meeting between the buyer and seller. It is typically conducted by a closing officer or settlement agent. As you learned earlier, there is a high likelihood that there will be other parties present during the closing.

Here are the roles and responsibilities that different participants have on a closing day.

The buyer:

- Receives the closing statement

- Signs all necessary documents

- Pays additional funds as required

- Accepts the deed to the property

- Receives the keys (and security codes if applicable) to the property

The seller:

- Signs all necessary documents

- Conveys the property to the buyers by way of a signed deed

- Approves the settlement statement

- Hands over the house/property keys (and security codes if applicable) to the buyer

- Receives payment that they're due

The real estate brokers:

- Represent the clients

- Provide moral support for their clients

- Receive compensation

- Remain in contact with all parties involved to assist in the coordination of the closing.

- Assist in making arrangements for final utility readings prior to closing.

- Usually attend a final walk-through with clients

- Gather last-minute documentation to ensure that everything needed to close the transaction is in place

- Submit a commission statement to the settlement agent/attorney

- Whether present or not, the broker's commission is usually paid at the closing

Note: Should a modification in the sales contract be desired by the buyer and/or seller, any modification suggested *prior* to the closing will require written authorization from all parties. The broker may be involved with acquiring said authorization. Frequently, at this late stage of the transaction, any contract modifications will be addressed by the two attorneys, rather than the brokers.

The lender/mortgage company representative:

- Verifies mortgagor's employment status prior to closing day

- Provides the mortgage and promissory note for the buyer to sign

- Examines all loan documents for accuracy and completeness

- Provides the required funds to complete the transfer of ownership

The title company representative (closing officer / settlement agent):

- Conducts the closing proceedings

- Prepares and reviews the settlement statement

- Delivers the title insurance policy

- Collects and disburses all funds to the appropriate parties

The attorneys:

- Represent their clients in the transaction

- Gather all necessary closing documents

- Help ensure all the elements of the sales contract are satisfied

- Confirm all necessary documents are submitted

- Review all closing documents

- Collect their fees at settlement

Escrow Closing

Although not as popular as a traditional roundtable closing, an **escrow closing** is an alternate way of transferring ownership. The main difference is that in an escrow closing, the date of conveyance is the date the escrow account was opened. In a traditional closing, the date of conveyance is the day the deed is handed to the buyer, which could be weeks after the closing date.

An escrow closing occurs when the buyer and seller mutually agree to the use of a third party (closing/escrow agent). Diagram 27.1 below provides a visualization of what is going to happen. The seller delivers the deed, along with all other required documentation, to the escrow agent. This is generally done within days of accepting the offer from the buyer. The buyer delivers the earnest money, along with required documentation (which includes a written loan commitment from the lender) to the escrow agent.

THE DATE OF CLOSING IS THE DATE THE ESCROW IS OPEN

SELLER

- Deed
- Survey
- Bill of sale
- Title evidence
- Affidavit of title
- Payoff statement
- Transfer tax declaration

BUYER

- Available cash
- Loan documents
- Proof of hazard insurance

ESCROW AGENT

CLOSING TABLE

Closing Documents

Closing documents, in no particular order, include:

- Bill of Sale for personal property; supplied by the seller

- Checks; usually supplied by the buyer or the buyer's lender

- Deed or other title document, such as a land contract; supplied by the seller

- Discharge of Mortgage; supplied by the seller's lender

- Evidence of Title

  - Evidence of title is typically provided through one of the following documents:

    - Certificate of Title

    - Attorney's Opinion of Title

- Title Insurance supplied by the title company

- Financial documentation, such as promissory notes and mortgages; supplied by the buyer's lender

- Homeowners insurance; supplied by the buyer

- IRS Form 1099; supplied by the settlement officer or escrow officer

- Property inspection reports, such as insects, lead, occupancy permits, etc.; supplied by the seller

- Closing Disclosure; generally supplied by a settlement officer or escrow officer

- Survey; supplied by a surveyor on behalf of the buyer or the seller

Note: Title defects do not have to be removed in order to obtain title insurance. Recorded defects or claims, such as liens or easements, can show up in the title reports listed as exceptions to standard title insurance. A purchaser is responsible for any defects excluded from coverage. Extended coverage title insurance policies cover additional defects in title that may be discovered only through actual inspection of a survey.

IRS Form 1099: The Internal Revenue Service requires that every real estate transaction be reported. The closing agent is responsible for filing a Form 1099 with the IRS. If the closing agent fails to notify the IRS, the responsibility is then passed to the mortgage lender. However, any of the parties involved in the transaction could be held liable if the transaction goes unreported.

Reminder: A deed is an instrument that conveys a grantor's interest in land, real estate, or real property. It is not the same thing as a title. A deed is a *tangible* document that conveys legal ownership and can also be referred to as a conveyance. Unlike a car title, which is tangible, a title in real estate is merely an intangible *concept* of ownership.

Evidence of title:

- It must be provided by the seller at closing to prove that he/she has a marketable title.

- It has no hidden liens, encumbrances, or defects that could potentially subject the buyers to legal action, make it difficult for them to use the property as they see fit, or inhibit them from selling the property in the future.

- There is no guarantee associated with evidence of title. This means that if the home-owner or lender discovers title defects later on, there is no possibility for legal action to be instigated. Essentially, he/she is solely responsible to attempt to correct any title defects. (If there is a title defect that was known by the seller but not communicated to the purchaser, the purchaser may have legal recourse against the seller for failure to disclose.)

The essential elements of a valid deed include the following:

- Grantor: A seller with the mental capacity to make rational decisions.

- Grantee: A buyer with reasonable certainty. As you recall, a contract assignment allows one person to sign the sales contract and then assign the rights to the deed to another party. The name in the deed must reflect the party whose ownership is being granted. Whatever name is in the deed, that is the name we must be certain is getting the ownership.

- Act of conveyance: Also called a granting clause, this clause that must be included in a valid deed clearly states that the grantor has the intention of conveying the title to his or her property. Commonly used conveyance language includes words like give, sell, grant, and so on. Although rules and provisions can vary from state to state, usually different types of deeds contain different granting clauses.

- Consideration: This is the value the seller receives from the buyer in a real estate transaction. Although consideration is commonly money, consideration can be anything else of value. This includes but is not limited to services (labor), goods, a promise to take or not take a specific action, personal property, real property, and/or love and affection.

- Legal description: A complete and accurate depiction of the geographical location and size of a parcel of land that will be conveyed during the real estate transaction.

- Limitations, restrictions, exceptions, and reservations: Although four different words are used here, these are conditions listed in a deed that impact how you can use the property right now and in the future. These conditions may limit what you can do, or might establish what you are required to do in order to retain ownership. An example is a fee simple defeasible limitation.

- Signatures: Legal signatures of all grantors.

- Acknowledgment: An authorized party's or notary public's signature which acknowledges and declares that the deed signing happened in his/her physical presence and that all signatures were signed according to each person's free will.

For a deed to be valid, it must be in writing and contain necessary information on its face. In Illinois, an acknowledgment is required for a valid deed. Should the deed be used as evidence in a court of law, that deed will need to have been notarized. The buyers' attorneys are going to require that the grantor's signature be notarized.

Deed at closing:

- The grantor (seller) needs to provide a newly signed deed to the grantee (buyer).

- The title transfers from the grantor to the grantee.

- A deed has no legal effect and does not successfully transfer property from the grantor to the grantee until the deed is delivered by the grantor to the grantee.

- A deed does not fully convey ownership of the property to the grantee until the deed is accepted by the grantee.

- Once a deed is delivered and accepted, the grantee holds the title to the land. The transfer of property ownership is now complete.

- A deed does not prove ownership. All that a deed establishes is that at some point in time, the ownership had been conveyed. The deed does not reflect the subsequent resale of the property by the grantee to another purchaser.

- Simply returning the deed to the grantor or destroying the deed does not terminate the prior transfer. The grantee still has ownership because he/she accepted the deed initially.

- A deed (as it was presented by the seller) cannot be reassigned or transferred to the next owner. Each new property transfer requires a new deed because the participants' titles are going to change. Example: The purchasers, Mike and Jill, are originally the grantees. Now that they are selling the property, they are the grantors. Thus, this will be reflected in the new deed.

A title is:

- A legal right to ownership (legal interest or equitable interest) of personal property, like your vehicle for example.

- A concept and theory, rather than a physical document.

The Title Insurance Act and Good Funds Amendment

During a closing, an essential foundation is that all parties know and have assurances that the seller's title is 100% in compliance with the sales contract. As you read earlier, a lender requires title insurance. This helps if any claims are on the title and/or if encumbrances exist on the real estate property. Only a title that is clear will be issued title insurance. Its issuance signifies that encumbrances from previous years are remote and doubtful. The end game is for the new owner to receive an owner's title policy that is valid and clear. This document basically establishes the quality of ownership and signifies the property is free of previous liens or possible claims. An owner's title policy can protect him/her against several issues, including but not limited to property survey errors, encroachments, boundary disputes, property deed errors, and documents that were not recorded correctly.

In 215 ILCS 155/26 of The Act, Section 26 covers settlement funds. This was an amendment to the Title Insurance Act. It's known as the "good funds" amendment. It reads as follows:

A. A title insurance company, title insurance agent, or independent escrowee shall not make disbursements in connection with any escrows, settlements, or closings out of a fiduciary trust account or accounts unless the funds in the aggregate amount of $50,000 or greater received from any single party to the transaction are good funds as defined in paragraphs (2), (6), or (7) of subsection (c) of this Section; or are collected funds as defined in subsection (d) of this Section. For the purposes of this subsection (a), where funds in the aggregate amount of $50,000 or greater are received from any purchaser of residential real property, as defined in paragraph (14) of Section 3 of this Act, the aggregate amount may consist of good funds of less than $50,000 per paragraph, as defined in paragraphs (3) and (5) of subsection (c) of this Section and of up to $5,000 in good funds, as defined in paragraph (4) of subsection (c) of this Section. (a-5) In addition to the good funds disbursement authorization set forth in subsection (a) of this Section, a title insurance company, title insurance agent, or independent escrowee is authorized to make disbursements in connection with any escrows, settlements, or closings out of a fiduciary trust account or accounts where the funds in the aggregate amount of $50,000 or greater are received from any single party to the transaction if:

1. the funds are transferred by a cashier's check, teller's check, or certified check, as defined in the Uniform Commercial Code, that is drawn on or issued by a financial institution, as defined in this Act;

2. the title insurance company, title insurance agent, or independent escrowee and the financial institution, as defined in this Act, agree to the use of cashier's checks, teller's checks, or certified checks to disburse the loan and related closing costs being funded by the financial institution as good funds under item (3) of subsection (c) of this Section; and

3. the cashier's check, teller's check, or certified check is delivered to the title insurance company, title insurance agent, or independent escrowee in sufficient time for the check to be deposited into the title insurance company's, title insurance agent's, or independent escrowee's fiduciary trust account prior to disbursement from the fiduciary trust account of the title insurance company, title insurance agent, or independent escrowee.

B. A title insurance company or title insurance agent shall not make disbursements in connection with any escrows, settlements, or closings out of a fiduciary trust account or accounts unless the funds in the amount of less than $50,000 received from any single party to the transaction are collected funds or good funds as defined in subsection (c) of this Section.

C. "Good funds" means funds in one of the following forms:

(1) lawful money of the United States;

(2) wired funds unconditionally held by and credited to the fiduciary trust account of the title insurance company, the title insurance agent, or independent escrowee;

(3) cashier's checks, certified checks, bank money orders, official bank checks, or teller's checks drawn on or issued by a financial institution and unconditionally held by the title insurance company, title insurance agent, or independent escrowee;

(4) a personal check or checks in an aggregate amount not exceeding $5,000 per closing, provided that the title insurance company, title insurance agent, or independent escrowee has reasonable grounds to believe that sufficient funds are available for withdrawal in the account upon which the check is drawn at the time of disbursement;

(5) a check drawn on the trust account of any lawyer or real estate broker licensed under the laws of any state, provided that the title insurance company, title insurance agent, or independent escrowee has reasonable grounds to believe that sufficient funds are available for withdrawal in the account upon which the check is drawn at the time of disbursement;

(6) a check issued by this State, the United States, or a political subdivision of this State or the United States; or

(7) a check drawn on the fiduciary trust account of a title insurance company, title insurance agent, or independent escrowee, provided that the title insurance company, title insurance agent, or independent escrowee has reasonable grounds to believe that sufficient funds are available for withdrawal in the account upon which the check is drawn at the time of disbursement.

D. "Collected funds" means funds deposited, finally settled, and credited to the title insurance company, title insurance agent, or independent escrowee's fiduciary trust account.

E. A purchaser, a seller, or a lender is each considered a single party to the transaction for the purposes of this Section, regardless of the number of people or entities making up the purchaser, seller, or lender. (215 ILCS 155/26)

When the amount is less than $50,000, the requirements are significantly more user-friendly and not as strict. This means if the payment is for $49,999.99, then it is classified as good funds. It is not common for a title company to accept a personal check due to potential risk. Parties need to know what types of payment methods are acceptable when paying ahead of time.

At a closing, how are the sales proceeds distributed? Although there can be variables and differences, here is a general sequence of events:

- At the closing, the lender provides a check on behalf of the buyer in the amount of the mortgage, payable to the seller.

- The buyer presents the agreed-upon down payment, along with the monies provided by the lender.

- The title officer, as a part of the closing process, will begin to disburse the monies starting with the commission due to the broker(s).

- If the seller still has a mortgage on the property, the seller needs to supply a payoff statement from his/her lender, which shows the exact amount owed on the mortgage. The title officer will then prepare and issue a check to the seller's lender, which satisfies the outstanding balance. This action results in the discharge of the mortgage lien.

- Once the seller's lender is paid, that lender will issue a discharge of mortgage, a document that the seller should record as evidence that the lien has been released.

- After the payoff amount and commission are subtracted from the sales price of the property, the remaining funds are used at settlement to pay all other seller obligations.

- Once all of the seller's financial obligations are taken care of, any amount remaining will be the seller's profit, known as the seller's net.

RESPA AND CLOSINGS

RESPA is present in a variety of ways when it comes to a closing. As a reminder, RESPA's goals are to: 1) protect consumers from abusive lending practices, 2) provide important, accurate, and timely information, and 3) eliminate kickbacks. RESPA gives borrowers the right to obtain title insurance from a provider of their choice.

RESPA provisions include but are not limited to:

- Prohibit kickbacks and fees for settlement-related services

- Require a HUD Special Information Booklet that explains settlement costs be given to buyers

- Require a loan estimate of closing costs be given to the buyer within three business days of applying for a mortgage

- Require the use of the Closing Disclosure for all federally related residential loans (1-4 family units)

- Give the buyer the right to inspect the Closing Disclosure three business days prior to closing

- Require brokers and lenders to disclose ownership interest and/or affiliated business relationships without obligating parties to use the suggested referral (Paraphrased from HUD)

TRID TIMELINE AND CLOSINGS

From the starting point to the ending point, the timeline goes as follows:

- Buyer shops for a mortgage.

- Buyer makes a preliminary application for a mortgage.

- Buyer is given three business days to review and accept.

- The loan estimate form expires 10 days after issued.

- Buyer completes a formal application and signs an "Intent to Proceed" with the lender or the loan estimate form is void.

- A change in an essential element requires a new loan estimate form.

- The closing disclosure form must be delivered to the purchaser three business days prior to the closing.

  - "This three-day window allows you time to compare your final terms and costs to those estimated in the loan estimate that you previously received from the lender. The three days also gives you time to ask your lender any questions before you go to the closing table." CFPB

- If an essential change is required in the loan disclosure form, the purchaser must be given three business days to decide on whether to accept the change.

- Closing date.

Loan estimate (LE) form:

- "The lender must provide you a Loan Estimate within three business days of receiving your application." CFPB

- No fees, other than the fee for acquiring the credit report, may be imposed upon the consumer prior to the consumer executing the LE and Intent To Proceed document.

- A loan estimate only has a 10-day lifespan from the day it is issued to the consumer. After 10 days, the LE expires. Upon expiration, a new loan estimate form must be issued showing any new updates and changes.

- Monday through Saturday are considered business days. Sundays and legal public holidays are excluded.

Loan application is made. It is completed with the following essential information:

- The consumer's name

- Income

- Social security number

- Address of the property

- Estimated property value

- Amount of the mortgage loan being sought

Closing disclosure form:

- As you read earlier, this form is designed to assist the consumer in understanding the cost of the transaction.

- Certain changes in the closing disclosure form will require a three-day waiting period. These include:

  - The annual percentage rate has changed ⅛ of a point on fixed-rate loans or ¼ of a point for adjustable-rate loans.

  - The addition of a prepayment penalty.

  - The basic loan product has changed, switching from a fixed rate to an adjustable rate. (Paraphrased from CFPB)

FICUS BANK
4321 Random Boulevard · Somecity, ST 12340

Save this Loan Estimate to compare with your Closing Disclosure.

Loan Estimate

DATE ISSUED 2/15/2013
APPLICANTS Michael Jones and Mary Stone
123 Anywhere Street
Anytown, ST 12345
PROPERTY 456 Somewhere Avenue
Anytown, ST 12345
SALE PRICE $180,000

LOAN TERM 30 years
PURPOSE Purchase
PRODUCT Fixed Rate
LOAN TYPE ☒ Conventional ☐FHA ☐VA ☐_____
LOAN ID # 123456789
RATE LOCK ☐NO ☒YES, until 4/16/2013 at 5:00 p.m. EDT
*Before closing, your interest rate, points, and lender credits can change unless you lock the interest rate. All other estimated closing costs expire on **3/4/2013** at 5:00 p.m. EDT*

Loan Terms

		Can this amount increase after closing?
Loan Amount	$162,000	**NO**
Interest Rate	3.875%	**NO**
Monthly Principal & Interest *See Projected Payments below for your Estimated Total Monthly Payment*	$761.78	**NO**
		Does the loan have these features?
Prepayment Penalty		**YES** • **As high as $3,240** if you pay off the loan during the first 2 years
Balloon Payment		**NO**

Projected Payments

Payment Calculation	Years 1-7	Years 8-30
Principal & Interest	$761.78	$761.78
Mortgage Insurance	+ 82	+ —
Estimated Escrow *Amount can increase over time*	+ 206	+ 206
Estimated Total Monthly Payment	$1,050	$968

Estimated Taxes, Insurance & Assessments *Amount can increase over time*	$206 a month	**This estimate includes** ☒ Property Taxes ☒ Homeowner's Insurance ☐ Other: *See Section G on page 2 for escrowed property costs. You must pay for other property costs separately.*	**In escrow?** YES YES

Costs at Closing

Estimated Closing Costs	$8,054	Includes $5,672 in Loan Costs + $2,382 in Other Costs – $0 in Lender Credits. *See page 2 for details.*
Estimated Cash to Close	$16,054	Includes Closing Costs. *See Calculating Cash to Close on page 2 for details.*

Visit **www.consumerfinance.gov/mortgage-estimate** for general information and tools.

Closing Cost Details

Loan Costs

A. Origination Charges	**$1,802**
.25 % of Loan Amount (Points)	$405
Application Fee	$300
Underwriting Fee	$1,097

B. Services You Cannot Shop For	**$672**
Appraisal Fee	$405
Credit Report Fee	$30
Flood Determination Fee	$20
Flood Monitoring Fee	$32
Tax Monitoring Fee	$75
Tax Status Research Fee	$110

C. Services You Can Shop For	**$3,198**
Pest Inspection Fee	$135
Survey Fee	$65
Title – Insurance Binder	$700
Title – Lender's Title Policy	$535
Title – Settlement Agent Fee	$502
Title – Title Search	$1,261

D. TOTAL LOAN COSTS (A + B + C)	**$5,672**

Other Costs

E. Taxes and Other Government Fees	**$85**
Recording Fees and Other Taxes	$85
Transfer Taxes	

F. Prepaids	**$867**
Homeowner's Insurance Premium (6 months)	$605
Mortgage Insurance Premium (months)	
Prepaid Interest ($17.44 per day for 15 days @ 3.875%)	$262
Property Taxes (months)	

G. Initial Escrow Payment at Closing		**$413**
Homeowner's Insurance $100.83 per month for 2 mo.		$202
Mortgage Insurance per month for mo.		
Property Taxes $105.30 per month for 2 mo.		$211

H. Other	**$1,017**
Title – Owner's Title Policy (optional)	$1,017

I. TOTAL OTHER COSTS (E + F + G + H)	**$2,382**

J. TOTAL CLOSING COSTS	**$8,054**
D + I	$8,054
Lender Credits	

Calculating Cash to Close

Total Closing Costs (J)	$8,054
Closing Costs Financed (Paid from your Loan Amount)	$0
Down Payment/Funds from Borrower	$18,000
Deposit	– $10,000
Funds for Borrower	$0
Seller Credits	$0
Adjustments and Other Credits	$0
Estimated Cash to Close	$16,054

Additional Information About This Loan

LENDER	Ficus Bank	**MORTGAGE BROKER**	
NMLS/__ LICENSE ID		**NMLS/__ LICENSE ID**	
LOAN OFFICER	Joe Smith	**LOAN OFFICER**	
NMLS/__ LICENSE ID	12345	**NMLS/__ LICENSE ID**	
EMAIL	joesmith@ficusbank.com	**EMAIL**	
PHONE	123-456-7890	**PHONE**	

Comparisons	Use these measures to compare this loan with other loans.	
In 5 Years	$56,582	Total you will have paid in principal, interest, mortgage insurance, and loan costs.
	$15,773	Principal you will have paid off.
Annual Percentage Rate (APR)	4.274%	Your costs over the loan term expressed as a rate. This is not your interest rate.
Total Interest Percentage (TIP)	69.45%	The total amount of interest that you will pay over the loan term as a percentage of your loan amount.

Other Considerations

Appraisal
We may order an appraisal to determine the property's value and charge you for this appraisal. We will promptly give you a copy of any appraisal, even if your loan does not close. You can pay for an additional appraisal for your own use at your own cost.

Assumption
If you sell or transfer this property to another person, we
☐ will allow, under certain conditions, this person to assume this loan on the original terms.
☒ will not allow assumption of this loan on the original terms.

Homeowner's Insurance
This loan requires homeowner's insurance on the property, which you may obtain from a company of your choice that we find acceptable.

Late Payment
If your payment is more than *15* days late, we will charge a late fee of *5% of the monthly principal and interest payment.*

Refinance
Refinancing this loan will depend on your future financial situation, the property value, and market conditions. You may not be able to refinance this loan.

Servicing
We intend
☐ to service your loan. If so, you will make your payments to us.
☒ to transfer servicing of your loan.

Confirm Receipt

By signing, you are only confirming that you have received this form. You do not have to accept this loan because you have signed or received this form.

_____	_____	_____	_____
Applicant Signature	Date	Co-Applicant Signature	Date

Closing Disclosure

This form is a statement of final loan terms and closing costs. Compare this document with your Loan Estimate.

Closing Information

Date Issued	4/15/2013
Closing Date	4/15/2013
Disbursement Date	4/15/2013
Settlement Agent	Epsilon Title Co.
File #	12-3456
Property	456 Somewhere Ave
	Anytown, ST 12345
Sale Price	$180,000

Transaction Information

Borrower	Michael Jones and Mary Stone
	123 Anywhere Street
	Anytown, ST 12345
Seller	Steve Cole and Amy Doe
	321 Somewhere Drive
	Anytown, ST 12345
Lender	Ficus Bank

Loan Information

Loan Term	30 years
Purpose	Purchase
Product	Fixed Rate
Loan Type	☒ Conventional ☐ FHA
	☐ VA ☐ _____
Loan ID #	123456789
MIC #	000654321

Loan Terms

		Can this amount increase after closing?
Loan Amount	$162,000	**NO**
Interest Rate	3.875%	**NO**
Monthly Principal & Interest *See Projected Payments below for your Estimated Total Monthly Payment*	$761.78	**NO**
		Does the loan have these features?
Prepayment Penalty		**YES** • As high as $3,240 if you pay off the loan during the first 2 years
Balloon Payment		**NO**

Projected Payments

Payment Calculation	Years 1-7	Years 8-30
Principal & Interest	$761.78	$761.78
Mortgage Insurance	+ 82.35	+ —
Estimated Escrow *Amount can increase over time*	+ 206.13	+ 206.13
Estimated Total Monthly Payment	**$1,050.26**	**$967.91**

Estimated Taxes, Insurance & Assessments *Amount can increase over time* *See page 4 for details*	$356.13 a month	This estimate includes ☒ Property Taxes ☒ Homeowner's Insurance ☒ Other: Homeowner's Association Dues *See Escrow Account on page 4 for details. You must pay for other property costs separately.*	In escrow? YES YES NO

Costs at Closing

Closing Costs	$9,712.10	Includes $4,694.05 in Loan Costs + $5,018.05 in Other Costs – $0 in Lender Credits. *See page 2 for details.*
Cash to Close	$14,147.26	Includes Closing Costs. *See Calculating Cash to Close on page 3 for details.*

Closing Cost Details

Loan Costs		Borrower-Paid		Seller-Paid		Paid by Others
		At Closing	Before Closing	At Closing	Before Closing	
A. Origination Charges		**$1,802.00**				
01 0.25 % of Loan Amount (Points)		$405.00				
02 Application Fee		$300.00				
03 Underwriting Fee		$1,097.00				
04						
05						
06						
07						
08						
B. Services Borrower Did Not Shop For		**$236.55**				
01 Appraisal Fee	to John Smith Appraisers Inc.					$405.00
02 Credit Report Fee	to Information Inc.		$29.80			
03 Flood Determination Fee	to Info Co.	$20.00				
04 Flood Monitoring Fee	to Info Co.	$31.75				
05 Tax Monitoring Fee	to Info Co.	$75.00				
06 Tax Status Research Fee	to Info Co.	$80.00				
07						
08						
09						
10						
C. Services Borrower Did Shop For		**$2,655.50**				
01 Pest Inspection Fee	to Pests Co.	$120.50				
02 Survey Fee	to Surveys Co.	$85.00				
03 Title – Insurance Binder	to Epsilon Title Co.	$650.00				
04 Title – Lender's Title Insurance	to Epsilon Title Co.	$500.00				
05 Title – Settlement Agent Fee	to Epsilon Title Co.	$500.00				
06 Title – Title Search	to Epsilon Title Co.	$800.00				
07						
08						
D. TOTAL LOAN COSTS (Borrower-Paid)		**$4,694.05**				
Loan Costs Subtotals (A + B + C)		$4,664.25	$29.80			

Other Costs		Borrower-Paid		Seller-Paid		Paid by Others
E. Taxes and Other Government Fees		**$85.00**				
01 Recording Fees	Deed: $40.00 Mortgage: $45.00	$85.00				
02 Transfer Tax	to Any State			$950.00		
F. Prepaids		**$2,120.80**				
01 Homeowner's Insurance Premium (12 mo.) to Insurance Co.		$1,209.96				
02 Mortgage Insurance Premium (mo.)						
03 Prepaid Interest ($17.44 per day from 4/15/13 to 5/1/13)		$279.04				
04 Property Taxes (6 mo.) to Any County USA		$631.80				
05						
G. Initial Escrow Payment at Closing		**$412.25**				
01 Homeowner's Insurance $100.83 per month for 2 mo.		$201.66				
02 Mortgage Insurance per month for mo.						
03 Property Taxes $105.30 per month for 2 mo.		$210.60				
04						
05						
06						
07						
08 Aggregate Adjustment		– 0.01				
H. Other		**$2,400.00**				
01 HOA Capital Contribution	to HOA Acre Inc.	$500.00				
02 HOA Processing Fee	to HOA Acre Inc.	$150.00				
03 Home Inspection Fee	to Engineers Inc.	$750.00			$750.00	
04 Home Warranty Fee	to XYZ Warranty Inc.			$450.00		
05 Real Estate Commission	to Alpha Real Estate Broker			$5,700.00		
06 Real Estate Commission	to Omega Real Estate Broker			$5,700.00		
07 Title – Owner's Title Insurance (optional) to Epsilon Title Co.		$1,000.00				
08						
I. TOTAL OTHER COSTS (Borrower-Paid)		**$5,018.05**				
Other Costs Subtotals (E + F + G + H)		$5,018.05				

J. TOTAL CLOSING COSTS (Borrower-Paid)		$9,712.10				
Closing Costs Subtotals (D + I)		$9,682.30	$29.80	$12,800.00	$750.00	$405.00
Lender Credits						

Calculating Cash to Close

Use this table to see what has changed from your Loan Estimate.

	Loan Estimate	Final	Did this change?
Total Closing Costs (J)	$8,054.00	$9,712.10	**YES** • See **Total Loan Costs (D)** and **Total Other Costs (I)**
Closing Costs Paid Before Closing	$0	– $29.80	**YES** • You paid these Closing Costs **before closing**
Closing Costs Financed (Paid from your Loan Amount)	$0	$0	**NO**
Down Payment/Funds from Borrower	$18,000.00	$18,000.00	**NO**
Deposit	– $10,000.00	– $10,000.00	**NO**
Funds for Borrower	$0	$0	**NO**
Seller Credits	$0	– $2,500.00	**YES** • See Seller Credits in **Section L**
Adjustments and Other Credits	$0	– $1,035.04	**YES** • See details in **Sections K and L**
Cash to Close	$16,054.00	$14,147.26	

Summaries of Transactions

Use this table to see a summary of your transaction.

BORROWER'S TRANSACTION

K. Due from Borrower at Closing	**$189,762.30**
01 Sale Price of Property	$180,000.00
02 Sale Price of Any Personal Property Included in Sale	
03 Closing Costs Paid at Closing (J)	$9,682.30
04	
Adjustments	
05	
06	
07	

Adjustments for Items Paid by Seller in Advance

08 City/Town Taxes	to	
09 County Taxes	to	
10 Assessments	to	
11 HOA Dues	4/15/13 to 4/30/13	$80.00
12		
13		
14		
15		

L. Paid Already by or on Behalf of Borrower at Closing	**$175,615.04**
01 Deposit	$10,000.00
02 Loan Amount	$162,000.00
03 Existing Loan(s) Assumed or Taken Subject to	
04	
05 Seller Credit	$2,500.00
Other Credits	
06 Rebate from Epsilon Title Co.	$750.00
07	
Adjustments	
08	
09	
10	
11	

Adjustments for Items Unpaid by Seller

12 City/Town Taxes 1/1/13 to 4/14/13	$365.04
13 County Taxes to	
14 Assessments to	
15	
16	
17	

CALCULATION

Total Due from Borrower at Closing (K)	$189,762.30
Total Paid Already by or on Behalf of Borrower at Closing (L)	– $175,615.04
Cash to Close ☒ From ☐ To Borrower	**$14,147.26**

SELLER'S TRANSACTION

M. Due to Seller at Closing	**$180,080.00**
01 Sale Price of Property	$180,000.00
02 Sale Price of Any Personal Property Included in Sale	
03	
04	
05	
06	
07	
08	

Adjustments for Items Paid by Seller in Advance

09 City/Town Taxes	to	
10 County Taxes	to	
11 Assessments	to	
12 HOA Dues	4/15/13 to 4/30/13	$80.00
13		
14		
15		
16		

N. Due from Seller at Closing	**$115,665.04**
01 Excess Deposit	
02 Closing Costs Paid at Closing (J)	$12,800.00
03 Existing Loan(s) Assumed or Taken Subject to	
04 Payoff of First Mortgage Loan	$100,000.00
05 Payoff of Second Mortgage Loan	
06	
07	
08 Seller Credit	$2,500.00
09	
10	
11	
12	
13	

Adjustments for Items Unpaid by Seller

14 City/Town Taxes 1/1/13 to 4/14/13	$365.04
15 County Taxes to	
16 Assessments to	
17	
18	
19	

CALCULATION

Total Due to Seller at Closing (M)	$180,080.00
Total Due from Seller at Closing (N)	– $115,665.04
Cash ☐ From ☒ To Seller	**$64,414.96**

Additional Information About This Loan

Loan Disclosures

Assumption
If you sell or transfer this property to another person, your lender
- ☐ will allow, under certain conditions, this person to assume this loan on the original terms.
- ☒ will not allow assumption of this loan on the original terms.

Demand Feature
Your loan
- ☐ has a demand feature, which permits your lender to require early repayment of the loan. You should review your note for details.
- ☒ does not have a demand feature.

Late Payment
If your payment is more than 15 days late, your lender will charge a late fee of 5% of the monthly principal and interest payment.

Negative Amortization (Increase in Loan Amount)
Under your loan terms, you
- ☐ are scheduled to make monthly payments that do not pay all of the interest due that month. As a result, your loan amount will increase (negatively amortize), and your loan amount will likely become larger than your original loan amount. Increases in your loan amount lower the equity you have in this property.
- ☐ may have monthly payments that do not pay all of the interest due that month. If you do, your loan amount will increase (negatively amortize), and, as a result, your loan amount may become larger than your original loan amount. Increases in your loan amount lower the equity you have in this property.
- ☒ do not have a negative amortization feature.

Partial Payments
Your lender
- ☒ may accept payments that are less than the full amount due (partial payments) and apply them to your loan.
- ☐ may hold them in a separate account until you pay the rest of the payment, and then apply the full payment to your loan.
- ☐ does not accept any partial payments.

If this loan is sold, your new lender may have a different policy.

Security Interest
You are granting a security interest in
456 Somewhere Ave., Anytown, ST 12345

You may lose this property if you do not make your payments or satisfy other obligations for this loan.

Escrow Account
For now, your loan
- ☒ will have an escrow account (also called an "impound" or "trust" account) to pay the property costs listed below. Without an escrow account, you would pay them directly, possibly in one or two large payments a year. Your lender may be liable for penalties and interest for failing to make a payment.

Escrow		
Escrowed Property Costs over Year 1	$2,473.56	Estimated total amount over year 1 for your escrowed property costs: *Homeowner's Insurance Property Taxes*
Non-Escrowed Property Costs over Year 1	$1,800.00	Estimated total amount over year 1 for your non-escrowed property costs: *Homeowner's Association Dues* You may have other property costs.
Initial Escrow Payment	$412.25	A cushion for the escrow account you pay at closing. See Section G on page 2.
Monthly Escrow Payment	$206.13	The amount included in your total monthly payment.

- ☐ will not have an escrow account because ☐ you declined it ☐ your lender does not offer one. You must directly pay your property costs, such as taxes and homeowner's insurance. Contact your lender to ask if your loan can have an escrow account.

No Escrow		
Estimated Property Costs over Year 1		Estimated total amount over year 1. You must pay these costs directly, possibly in one or two large payments a year.
Escrow Waiver Fee		

In the future,
Your property costs may change and, as a result, your escrow payment may change. You may be able to cancel your escrow account, but if you do, you must pay your property costs directly. If you fail to pay your property taxes, your state or local government may (1) impose fines and penalties or (2) place a tax lien on this property. If you fail to pay any of your property costs, your lender may (1) add the amounts to your loan balance, (2) add an escrow account to your loan, or (3) require you to pay for property insurance that the lender buys on your behalf, which likely would cost more and provide fewer benefits than what you could buy on your own.

Loan Calculations

Total of Payments. Total you will have paid after you make all payments of principal, interest, mortgage insurance, and loan costs, as scheduled.	$285,803.36
Finance Charge. The dollar amount the loan will cost you.	$118,830.27
Amount Financed. The loan amount available after paying your upfront finance charge.	$162,000.00
Annual Percentage Rate (APR). Your costs over the loan term expressed as a rate. This is not your interest rate.	4.174%
Total Interest Percentage (TIP). The total amount of interest that you will pay over the loan term as a percentage of your loan amount.	69.46%

Questions? If you have questions about the loan terms or costs on this form, use the contact information below. To get more information or make a complaint, contact the Consumer Financial Protection Bureau at **www.consumerfinance.gov/mortgage-closing**

Other Disclosures

Appraisal
If the property was appraised for your loan, your lender is required to give you a copy at no additional cost at least 3 days before closing. If you have not yet received it, please contact your lender at the information listed below.

Contract Details
See your note and security instrument for information about
  • what happens if you fail to make your payments,
  • what is a default on the loan,
  • situations in which your lender can require early repayment of the loan, and
  • the rules for making payments before they are due.

Liability after Foreclosure
If your lender forecloses on this property and the foreclosure does not cover the amount of unpaid balance on this loan,

☒ state law may protect you from liability for the unpaid balance. If you refinance or take on any additional debt on this property, you may lose this protection and have to pay any debt remaining even after foreclosure. You may want to consult a lawyer for more information.

☐ state law does not protect you from liability for the unpaid balance.

Refinance
Refinancing this loan will depend on your future financial situation, the property value, and market conditions. You may not be able to refinance this loan.

Tax Deductions
If you borrow more than this property is worth, the interest on the loan amount above this property's fair market value is not deductible from your federal income taxes. You should consult a tax advisor for more information.

Contact Information

	Lender	Mortgage Broker	Real Estate Broker (B)	Real Estate Broker (S)	Settlement Agent
Name	Ficus Bank		Omega Real Estate Broker Inc.	Alpha Real Estate Broker Co.	Epsilon Title Co.
Address	4321 Random Blvd. Somecity, ST 12340		789 Local Lane Sometown, ST 12345	987 Suburb Ct. Someplace, ST 12340	123 Commerce Pl. Somecity, ST 12344
NMLS ID					
ST License ID			Z765416	Z61456	Z61616
Contact	Joe Smith		Samuel Green	Joseph Cain	Sarah Arnold
Contact NMLS ID	12345				
Contact ST License ID			P16415	P51461	PT1234
Email	joesmith@ ficusbank.com		sam@omegare.biz	joe@alphare.biz	sarah@ epsilontitle.com
Phone	123-456-7890		123-555-1717	321-555-7171	987-555-4321

Confirm Receipt

By signing, you are only confirming that you have received this form. You do not have to accept this loan because you have signed or received this form.

_____   _____   _____   _____
Applicant Signature   Date   Co-Applicant Signature   Date

Now it's time for your chapter quiz.

CHAPTER 27 QUIZ

1. Which of the following is required by RESPA?

    a. An attorney to prepare the loan estimate of closing costs.

    b. Brokers and lenders to disclose any affiliated business relationships to all parties.

    c. Brokers and lenders prepare the Closing Disclosure at least three business days prior to closing.

    d. Buyers use settlement service providers recommended by brokers and lenders.

2. Which of the following is not done by the lender/mortgage company representative at a closing?

    a. Examines all loan documents for accuracy and completeness

    b. Verifies mortgagor's employment status prior to closing day

    c. Delivers evidence that the title is insured

    d. Provides a check for the loan amount

3. In Illinois, is an acknowledgment required for a valid deed?

    a. Yes

    b. No

4. Which of the following is false concerning a title? A title . . .

    a. Is the actual lawful ownership of real property.

    b. Refers to holding the bundle of rights conveyed.

    c. Is a physical document.

    d. Is a theory of ownership.

5. Who usually performs a title search?

    a. The buyer

    b. The seller

    c. The licensee

    d. An abstractor

    e. A title company

    f. D or E

    g. C or F

6. Jane recently married. She is selling her house in Chicago and moving to Hawaii with her husband. She has no need for her furniture. It is included in the home sale. Which document below will be used to transfer the title of personal property from Jane to the buyer?

    a. Bill of sale
    b. Closing Disclosure
    c. Sales contract
    d. Title

7. Which of the following does not show evidence as to the quality of the title being conveyed?

    a. Certificate of Title
    b. Attorney's opinion of title
    c. Title insurance
    d. Quit claim deed

8. Which of the following is false concerning a loan estimate?

    a. A loan estimate is sometimes called an "LE."
    b. A loan estimate was previously called a good faith estimate.
    c. A loan estimate is just as precise as the Closing Disclosure statement.
    d. A loan estimate groups and categorizes total estimated costs.

9. Which of the following is not typically a shared expense between the buyer and the seller?

    a. HOA fees
    b. Property survey
    c. Property taxes
    d. Title insurance fees

10. Mary is a title company representative. She is responsible for preparing a particular closing document that shows every title-related event in the public record for a particular piece of property. What is Mary working on?

    a. The abstract of title
    b. Property survey
    c. Property deed
    d. Sales contract

11. If the buyer does not insist upon a professional property inspection, or inspections for termites, who would most likely request these?

    a. Buyer's attorney

    b. Closing agent

    c. Lender's representative

    d. Title company representative

    e. None of the above

12. On the settlement date, the seller is generally responsible for which of the following?

    a. Creating the abstract of opinion

    b. Issuing a letter of opinion

    c. Paying prorated expenses for the day of closing

    d. Preparing the settlement statement

13. Which type of evidence of title gives the purchaser or the lender recourse if title defects are later discovered?

    a. Abstract of title

    b. Attorney's opinion

    c. Certificate of title

    d. Title insurance

14. Closing day arrives and licensee Viola takes her buyer client on a final walk-through of the property. Viola notices a large section of flooring appears warped. It was not warped on the previous inspection. What should Viola do?

    a. Bring this to her client's attention

    b. Contact the listing agent and ask for monetary credit

    c. Not say anything to her client

    d. Suggest to her client that she cancel the transaction

    e. A and C

15. Broker Maria insists that her buyer clients review a home inspection report on a house. This is an example of which of the following?

    a. Engaging in the unauthorized practice of law

    b. Ensuring the full disclosure of pertinent material facts

    c. Misleading buyers into making false conclusions

    d. Providing a service outside her field of competence

16. Which statements are true concerning discharge of mortgage?

   a. It is also known as a release of lien.
   b. When the mortgage is paid off, the lender issues a discharge of the mortgage debt.
   c. A and B
   d. None of the above

17. Which statements are true concerning marketable title?

   a. They are only used in residential.
   b. It is sometimes called a merchantable title.
   c. It is one in which a reasonable and prudent person would accept as being good, clean, and valid.
   d. B and C

18. Which statement below is false concerning the topics of amortization and negative amortization?

   a. Amortization is the process of making regular payments to pay off a loan.
   b. Negative amortization means that your monthly payments are not sufficient to cover the interest, and this causes the total amount you owe to continue to increase.
   c. Lenders do not work with borrowers who are experiencing negative amortization and it's best for borrowers to seek legal and financial counsel.
   d. When the borrower is delinquent in making their mortgage payments, the lender may provide the borrower with the option to make a minimum payment, but if chosen, the deferred interest will be added to the outstanding debt and the borrower's overall debt obligation will increase.

19. Which law requires lenders to provide timely information about loan terms and costs?

    a. The Truth in Lending Act
    b. The Home Ownership and Equity Protection Act
    c. The Illinois High Risk Home Loan Act
    d. A and C
    e. B and C

20. Licensee Sarah was hopeful to sign up a new seller. The property was immaculate. She expected to get top dollar. However, she just found out there is a construction lien on the property. This makes real property unmarketable. Under which of the following categories does this construction lien fall?

    a. Cloud
    b. Right to rescind
    c. Curveball
    d. Hardstop

CHAPTER 28:

PROPERTY DEVELOPMENT AND LAND USE

LEARNING GOALS:

By the end of this lesson, you will:

- Understand how land-use regulation and sale regulation works
- See the importance of a municipality having a comprehensive plan
- Grasp details about zoning
- Understand how building codes and certificates of occupancy work
- Discover the implications of private land-use controls

THE FEDERAL GOVERNMENT AND REAL ESTATE

Homeownership has long been touted as the American Dream. However, real estate ownership is not all-encompassing or unconditional despite the owners having rights. Land use is regulated mostly by the authority of states and municipalities. This regulation is done by way of zoning. The Federal Government, for the most part, has granted authority to each state. Most states have granted authority to their municipalities through state constitutions and statutes. For the most part in the US, it is the local governments who primarily regulate the use of land. Specifically, this land is called public land or state land.

As you know, a real estate owner cannot do whatever he/she wants to his or her land. Personal use that creates nuisances and disturbances for neighbors will most likely get called out. Builders using unsafe or sketchy practices that can potentially harm the public and/or the environment will likewise most likely get called out and challenged.

It is important for every licensee to recognize and grasp how different government entities operate within the real estate marketplace. Land and buildings are managed, leased, owned, and sold by federal, state, and local agencies throughout the US. Some licensees will encounter a variety of circumstances and situations that involve government agencies. While some will not, it's foundational that all licensees understand the topics in this chapter.

Land-use regulation is a broad term for rules and guidelines that govern the development of land. Federal lands are lands owned by the U.S. Federal Government. The majority of federal lands are administered by:

- Bureau of Land Management (BLM)

- U.S. Fish and Wildlife Service (FWS)

- National Park Service (NPS)

- U.S. Forest Service (FS)

The first three are included in the US Department of the Interior. The Forest Service is included as part of the U.S. Department of Agriculture. It is estimated that close to 2% of all federal land is owned by the U.S. Department of Defense (DOD). Where are most federal lands located? You'll find them in Alaska and states in the Western US.

The Federal Government owns roughly 640 million acres, about 28% of the 2.27 billion acres of land in the United States. (Congressional Research Service)

The Bureau of Land Management divides the lands that it oversees into one of four primary categories:

- Public lands

- Developed recreation areas

- Wilderness areas

- Conservation lands

The primary laws that affect federal lands include:

- Alaska National Interest Lands Conservation Act of 1980

- Alaska Native Claims Settlement Act (1971)

- Endangered Species Act of 1973

- Federal Land Policy and Management Act of 1976

- Federal Land Transaction Facilitation Act (2000)

- Mineral Leasing Act of 1920

- National Environmental Policy Act (1970)

- Omnibus Public Land Management Act of 2009

- Taylor Grazing Act of 1934

- Wild and Free-Roaming Horses and Burros Act of 1971

Examples of federally-owned land and structures include, but are not limited to, the following:

- Federal Government buildings such as the White House, Pentagon, the Internal Revenue Service Building, and the Eisenhower Executive Office Building.

- National parks like Yosemite, Yellowstone, Glacier, and Haleakalā.

- Military bases such as Fort Bragg in North Carolina and Fort Campbell in Kentucky.

- Legislative offices.

- Any Federal Government buildings and/or land used for military education and training.

- Specific hospitals like the University of California Davis Medical Center and the Ronald Reagan UCLA Medical Center.

- All Veteran Affairs (VA) hospitals and medical centers.

- And more.

Is Native American land owned by the US government? The US government holds the legal title of Native American land, which is trust land. However, the beneficial title is held by the tribe or individual. As implied, a beneficial title gives the holder the legal right to use and benefit from the property. Some tribes own their own land, which is called fee land. This means the tribe has legal title under specific statutory authority. The majority of Native American land is trust land.

> "In the United States, there are three types of reserved federal lands: military, public, and Indian. A federal Indian reservation is an area of land reserved for a tribe or tribes under treaty or other agreement with the United States, executive order, or federal statute or administrative action as permanent tribal homelands, and where the Federal Government holds title to the land in trust on behalf of the tribe. Approximately 56.2 million acres are held in trust by the United States for various Indian tribes and individuals. There are approximately 326 Indian land areas in the U.S. administered as federal Indian reservations (i.e., reservations, pueblos, rancherias, missions, villages, communities, etc.). The largest is the 16 million-acre Navajo Nation Reservation located in Arizona, New Mexico, and Utah. The smallest is a 1.32-acre parcel in California where the Pit River Tribe's cemetery is located. Many of the smaller reservations are less than 1,000 acres. Some reservations are the remnants of a tribe's original land base. Others were created by the Federal Government for the resettling of Indian people forcibly relocated from their homelands. Not every federally recognized tribe has a reservation. Federal Indian reservations are generally exempt from state jurisdiction, including taxation, except when Congress specifically authorizes such jurisdiction." (Indian Affairs, U.S. Department of Interior. https://www.bia.gov/frequently-asked-questions)

In the US, "**home rule**" refers to the authority and power of a constituent part of a state to rightfully exercise its powers of governance, which are delegated to it by its own state government. Some states are referred to as home rule states. The constitution of the state gives municipalities and/or counties the legal right and ability to pass and enact laws to govern themselves as they choose. The state must also be in compliance with the federal constitution. States without home rule have limited authority from local governments. In states that are not home rule, a municipality or county must request and obtain permission from the state legislature if it wants to pass a law or ordinance. This would be for a law or ordinance that is not specifically allowed under the current state legislation.

In Illinois, this brings up the concept of "home rule" units of government. It is based on Article VII of the Illinois State Constitution. What is a home rule unit?

"In general, a home rule unit is either a county that has a chief executive officer elected by the electors of the county or a municipality that has a population of 25,001 or more. Municipalities of 25,000 or less may elect, by referendum, to become a home rule unit." (Illinois Government website)

You can view home rule as a local constitution. The residents who are voters work together to draft, adopt, and amend their own local ordinances. Home rule defines its own authority and its own limitations. It creates control on a local level. It is a way for locals to create local solutions to problems and issues that are affecting their municipality. According to the Illinois Municipal League, there are currently 221 home rule units in Illinois. These include Chicago, Aurora, West Chicago, Naperville, Willowbrook, and Springfield.

There is some flexibility with home rule authority. It is possible for a municipality with less than 25,000 people to elect, by referendum, to attain home rule status. Similarly, a home rule unit municipality can likewise elect, by referendum, to forego home rule status. Can a township be a home rule unit? No, townships are not permitted.

Finally, know that each state has police power. This defines the basic right of governments to enact laws and regulations that are for the good of the people and their benefit. In the US, a state has the right to enact laws that are based on their police power.

As you recall, enabling acts are provisions of law that grant each state and local jurisdiction the right to create laws that further enhance the objective of protecting the health, welfare, and safety of the public. Enabling acts give municipalities the power and right to establish and regulate zoning and building codes to meet the objective of protecting public safety. Several states passed their own version of the Standard State Zoning Enabling Act (SZEA). This act allows municipalities to implement and enforce local zoning laws as a method to regulate land use. First issued in 1922, this act was a major development in land-use planning throughout the US and laid a new and better foundation for the future.

PROPERTY DEVELOPMENT

Property development is also called real estate development. This multifaceted business process includes a wide variety of roles, procedures, and activities. These activities include, but are not limited to, the following:

- Building property on purchased land

- Buying land

- Converting property from one type of use to another

- Extending property

- Improving property

- Leasing property

- Raw land purchases

- Renovation

- Selling property

- And more

Those activities and more are coordinated and overseen by real estate developers. A developer can be an individual entrepreneur or an entrepreneurial company that seeks to create improvements, make updates, and add value to property. The end goal is to develop buildings and/or land into a higher use value. To make development happen, the following work is almost always included:

- Building plans

- Environmental assessments

- Feasibility studies

- Infrastructure improvements

- Land acquisition (or obtaining option rights to purchase)

- Market analysis

- Permit work

- Planning for and securing construction financing

- Property surveys

- Site plans

As you read earlier, there are two types of property improvements.

1. **On-site improvements** are enhancements or additions to the buildings and/or lots that will be sold or leased. The goal is to increase the property value. Examples include landscaping, pools, garages, service buildings, drainage improvements, stairs, walkways, driveways, accessory buildings, walls, site grading, and even new buildings.

2. **Off-site improvements** include aspects like sidewalks, access roads, curbs, sewers, etc. They're labeled off-site because these improvements are outside the property boundaries.

Note that real estate development is not the same as construction or new construction. However, many developers choose to manage the process of construction. At times, development can be discouraged or deterred because of expensive property transfer costs and/or required construction permit fees or even an increase in property taxes.

COMPREHENSIVE PLAN

Managing a single household can be challenging. Imagine managing an entire town or city. When it comes to property and land-use development, how can those in charge work to ensure that they're making great decisions? How will certain new developments impact, change, and improve the municipalities and the communities? With such staggering questions and actions that can potentially impact tens of thousands of people, it's obvious that thoughtful planning, clear communication, and strong leadership are required. To facilitate developments, what is commonly used is a comprehensive plan. A comprehensive plan is sometimes called a master plan or a municipal business plan.

This plan helps establish the guidelines and enforce policies that will help development roll out as well as possible. The plan is not set in stone. As circumstances change, such as migratory patterns, and as feedback is given by the public, elements of a master plan are edited or adapted in order to bring forth the best outcome. A master plan includes future objectives, the vision, strategies to be implemented, and timelines. Essentially, it is a business plan for a municipality. The planning covers both immediate needs as well as future use/s. The plan also includes sustainability. How does the plan protect the environment? How does it invite tourism and create good, positive experiences for residents and travelers? How does it impact the economy? How does it make the city safer and cleaner? All of those questions and more are covered in a comprehensive plan. Five key elements that are always included are:

1. Land use

2. Housing needs

3. People movement

4. Community facilities

5. Energy conservation

ZONING

Zoning is law that establishes and organizes how land is used within a defined area. It is the process of dividing a city, town, or municipality into distinct areas in order to regulate land use. Zoning laws are created by local governments to ensure that each area of a city or town is used for the purpose it was intended for and the laws outline what is allowed and what is prohibited. Zoning laws can be used to separate residential and commercial areas, as well as to limit certain types of development in certain areas. These laws also dictate how much space can be devoted to particular uses such as parks, schools, and public buildings. In addition, zoning laws can also be used to regulate the size and shape of buildings and other structures in a given area. By understanding zoning regulations and their implications on real estate development, municipalities can better plan for the future growth of their communities.

Local governments in the majority of developed nations employ zoning as a method of land-use planning and urban planning. The term originates from the process of identifying mapped zones that control the type, shape, and compatibility of development.

A zoning plan, also called a zoning map, is a highly detailed map that follows the local laws and divides municipalities into different zones such as residential, business, commercial, industrial, special use, and/or agricultural. Each zone has its own set of rules and regulations which must be followed when constructing any building or facility within it. Real estate developers must adhere to these zoning laws when they look to develop properties within a municipality's boundaries. Thus, zoning plans are used by municipalities to regulate the use of land in their jurisdiction. They also help ensure that any new construction or development is done in a way that is consistent with the municipality's vision for its future growth. This can include things like limiting the number of stories a building can have or where certain types of businesses can be located. A zoning plan is typically passed into law as a by-law using the appropriate legal processes. Zoning can give its community a sense of flavor, prestige, and/or personality. As with most things, zoning has its own pros and cons.

Zoning is achieved via:

1. Zoning ordinances

2. Zoning plans (zoning maps)

As you recall, police power is the obligation of the government to protect public health, welfare, and safety. Focusing on the concept of safety, it is the government's obligation to regulate how we use our properties to ensure that they are safe and functional, allowing us to meet our individual needs.

What else can zoning guidelines entail? They can entail the regulation of permitted activities, parking, open space requirements, floor area, height, storage, unit size, lot size, signage, building facades, and/or landscaping.

What does zoning entail? Although this is not an exhaustive list, each item below is impacted by zoning:

- Building heights

- Density

- Lot sizes

- Natural resources

- Permitted building and land uses

- Protection of natural resources

- Setback lines

- Signs

- Style and appearance

- Types of structures

Zoning maps commonly use this type of key:

- C means Commercial

- M means Manufacturing

- PD means Planned unit Development

- POS means Parks and Open Space

- R means Residential

Each of the categories listed above may have a variety of sub-categories. For example, residential may incorporate subcategories labeled R2, R3, RS3, RT4, and RM5. These are examples of how a municipality can further label and define permitted uses within a given category.

Zoning is covered in The Act under Municipalities (65 ILCS 5) of the Illinois Municipal Code in a section called Planning, Zoning and Urban Rehabilitation.

Read it here now: http://www.ilga.gov/legislation/ilcs/ilcs4.asp?DocName=006500050HArt+11+prec+Div+11&ActID=802&ChapterID=14&SeqStart=147000000&SeqEnd=155700000

There are several different types of zoning. The main types of zoning include:

- **Aesthetic zoning:** This is popular in upscale neighborhoods and locations. This can include color schemes, solar panels, mailbox styles, and more.

- **Agricultural zoning:** This zoning is used mostly to protect and ensure the future of farming communities.

- **Commercial zoning:** This includes malls, hotels, office buildings, and similar commercial buildings. Depending on where you are, commercial zoning may or may not include retail. Some municipalities distinguish the two and have separate regulations for commercial zoning (offices) and retail zoning (stores, malls).

- **Historic zoning:** This zoning includes homes and structures older than 50 years. The goal is to preserve their original look, style, and feel. The US's official list of historic buildings, districts, and more can be found online on the National Register of Historic Places.

- **Home-based business:** This zoning applies to businesses operated out of a residential home. It comes down to local zoning as to whether home-based businesses are allowed in certain communities.

- **Industrial zoning:** This zoning includes manufacturing plants, packaging locations, storage facilities, and similar structures.

- **Mixed-use zoning:** Also called combination zoning, this includes any type of combination of different uses within the same area.

- **Public zoning:** This zoning focuses on infrastructure development such as fire stations, libraries, educational facilities, and similar public buildings.

- **Residential zoning:** This zoning is one of the most common and applies to homes, single-family residences, multifamily residences, apartments, cooperatives, condos, duplexes, mobile home parks, and similar structures.

- **Rural zoning:** This zoning applies to ranches and farms.

Nonconforming use is a type of zoning variance. It's sometimes called "legal nonconforming use." You can think of it as an exception to the rule. The property in question is not compatible with the current allowable use. For example, a piece of land in a certain jurisdiction might qualify to be an exception from current zoning ordinances. Perhaps the previous owner had made improvements. Perhaps the changes were made prior to the current zoning ordinances. Let's say a building was constructed in 1980 and it was built in accordance with the zoning and building codes in existence at the time of construction. Now it's over two decades later, and the zoning laws have changed. Consequently, the building is labeled nonconforming because it is not in compliance with current zoning laws. The end result? The use of the property is allowed to continue without violating the current zoning ordinance.

BUILDING CODES AND CERTIFICATE OF OCCUPANCY

The Act defines a building code as "any municipal or county ordinance or resolution regulating the construction and maintenance of all structures within the municipality or county" (50 ILCS 810).

Said another way, a building code is a set or collection of rules and regulations that outline and specify the exact standards and minimum requirements for the construction or repair of buildings. It can also be referred to as building control and/or building regulations. The building code is written and enacted by city or county government officials. Each building is expected to conform to the building code in order to obtain planning permission and necessary permits. Four key elements of a building code are: 1) local laws, 2) construction standards, 3) how to repair or erect buildings, and 4) material requirements.

One of the main purposes of building codes is to protect residents and the public while creating an environment for good general welfare and public health. Building codes answer questions such as:

- How many evacuation points does a 10-story structure require?

- Are carbon dioxide detectors required to be in each unit?

- Which materials cannot be used in construction?

- And more

Building codes position new and existing projects and construction for long-term viability and safety. Building code violations can result in fines and/or penalties.

A wide variety of professionals work within the boundaries of building codes, including, but not limited to, the following:

- Architects

- Builders

- Business owners who rent space

- Community managers

- Environmental scientists

- Facility managers

- Government officials

- Insurance companies

- Interior designers

- Manufacturers' products and materials used for construction and buildings

- Property managers

- Real estate developers

- Regulators

- Residents

- Safety inspectors

- Structural engineers

- Subcontractors

- And more

Certificate of occupancy: Once the construction is complete, a structure is inspected. If it is found to meet or exceed the minimum requirements of the municipality in which it is located, a certificate of occupancy is issued by the municipal inspector. A certificate of occupancy is a local government-issued document that certifies a building's compliance with local and applicable laws and building codes. It is evidence that the structure is in a healthy, suitable, and livable condition for occupants. Although the list below is not comprehensive, a certificate of occupancy is commonly required when:

- A new structure is built.

- There is a change of ownership with a commercial, industrial, or multiple-family residential building.

- A structure originally built for one use is going to be used in a different way (converted use).

- The occupancy of an industrial or commercial structure changes.

Requirements and procedures for certificate of occupancy can vary greatly from jurisdiction to jurisdiction. It also varies concerning the type of structure. This inspection can be called several names including, but not limited to, the following: city presale inspection, municipal presale inspection, presale home inspection, point of sale inspection, re-occupancy inspection, and certificate of compliance inspection. Do all municipalities require this type of inspection? No. However, the trend is growing, and it is becoming a requirement in more and more municipalities each year. Who pays for this inspection? Most commonly, the seller is responsible to pay for it. He/she also arranges the inspection to take place. This inspection must be done and a certificate of occupancy must be issued before the building can be occupied, regardless of whether it's rented or sold. Keep in mind that this inspection is not a home inspection. These are two different types of inspections. A home inspector is not going to review zoning, parking compliance, permits, and so on.

LAND DEVELOPMENT REGULATIONS

Land development regulations are enacted by each state and local governing body, not by the Federal Government. The Federal Government does not implement blanket one-size-fits-all land development regulations. Just as the Federal Government has given authority to states, in most circumstances, states have given authority to local governing bodies and municipalities. Admittedly, states still do maintain considerable indirect influence on municipalities. This means that land-use controls widely vary from municipality to municipality.

How do states ensure development adheres to a specific set of guidelines? The general overview of the process in order is: 1) land development plan, 2) subdividing, and 3) plats.

Prior to subdividing, the subdivider is required to go through the steps of land development planning. This plan must adhere to the comprehensive plan of the municipality. Each state sets and maintains specific standards for subdivision developments.

Subdivision is the process of dividing a large piece of land into smaller parcels or tracts. It is a common practice used in real estate to divide a single tract of land into multiple lots, which can then be sold individually. Subdivision involves the creation of a plat, which is an official map that outlines the boundaries and dimensions of each lot. Through this process, landowners can create multiple parcels from one tract of land, thus increasing its value and allowing them to generate more revenue from it. In other words, you divide a single property into two or more smaller pieces. How subdivisions can be developed always comes down to local ordinances. A developer will draft a written diagram. It illustrates how the land is divided, plus it shows the proposed improvements to the property.

A plat map is a visual depiction of a parcel of land. It defines the size, configuration, and possibly the topography. This helps the buyer become aware of what they are about to purchase. It is drawn to scale and shows how the land is divided into parcels. Plat maps can include blocks, streets, alleys, waterways, and more. The plan must be approved by the relevant governing body. Usually this body is a zoning board or zoning office. However, at times, it may be the county commissioner's office or some other government entity. The intended use must be in alignment with the municipal comprehensive plan. The subdivision must adhere to approved density zoning. This means that only a specific number of houses are allowed to be constructed in a specific subdivision.

For example, in Chicago, the average city lot is 25 feet wide and 125 feet deep. This amounts to 3,125 square feet in total. An acre is 43,560 square feet. Doing the math, this may allow for as many as 14 lots per acre. However, if we go thirty-two miles northwest of Chicago to a city called South Barrington, it's different. Their city ordinance only allows one home per acre.

PRIVATE LAND-USE CONTROLS

Not only are there public land-use controls, but there are also private land-use controls. This means private restrictions that are commonly implemented by property owners and developers. Private land-use control is not allowed to break any type of government law that regulates land use. The use of a specific property is limited by a restrictive covenant, which is a legal agreement. In a restrictive covenant, some type of restriction is imposed. The purpose of the restriction is to limit the use of land. By doing so, both the land and its value can be preserved. Additionally, this enables the value, along with the enjoyment of any adjoining land to be preserved as well. Along with restrictive covenants, there are also conditions, covenants, and restrictions (CCRs) that also limit use. Set up by the developer, these restrictions are commonly written in subdivision bylaws, governing body bylaws, and property deeds. They set up standards for the specific subdivision. The goal is to maintain the ambience, the look and feel, of the subdivision as well as safety. This can include architectural style, methods of construction, square footage, maximum building height, and so on. It is fairly common for restrictive covenants to be more restrictive than local zoning ordinances. When it comes down to the two, the most restrictive one takes precedence.

RELATED TERMS

Related terms to this topic include the following terms and definitions:

- **Buffer zone:** A buffer is something that prevents two items or areas from coming in contact with each other. A buffer zone is most commonly a piece of land that separates two other types of land that have different uses. Buffer zones can also be used for protecting the environment. The buffer can be human-made or anything from nature, such as a river. It can be vegetation or even an open neutral space.

- **Bulk zoning:** This kind of zoning is designed to control density and prevent overcrowding and oversaturation.

- **Building permit:** This permit is written authorization from a government (or some other type of regulatory body) that must be obtained prior to an individual or company: 1) building a new or existing structure, 2) implementing some type of alteration on a property, or 3) demolishing a structure. For developers, a building permit is what makes the action of building a structure legal. When it comes to alterations, a permit may be necessary, even if it's simply adding a fence to a property. No buildings can be demolished without a building permit.

- **Conditional use permit:** Sometimes called a special use permit, this government-issued permit is generally granted to a property owner, and it allows him/her to implement a special use for his or her property. This special use is not in alignment with the location's zoning ordinance. These permits are commonly granted by way of a public hearing process and are issued by the zoning board. There are usually specific requirements or conditions that must be met in order for a property owner to obtain this permit. These permits apply to all property classifications.

- **Density zoning:** Commonly used in municipality planning, density zoning puts limitations in place on property development. It does this by controlling and restricting how many structures are located in a certain area. These efforts work to control population density and can serve to increase, maintain, or decrease it.

- **Real estate developer:** This individual works closely with an architect or architecture firm in order to design and create a blueprint for a new structure or subdivision. Then, the developer brings the vision to life by building it.

- **Setback:** A setback or setback line shows the minimum distance which a building is required to be "set back" from something else. The setback's distance can be from a road, highway, waterway, railroad tracks, shore, human-made structure, or the lot line. Sometimes, it is a certain distance from a natural feature that requires protection and/or a safe distance.

- **Subdivider:** This is an individual or company that buys undeveloped acreage, and then divides it into smaller lots and sells them to individuals and/or developers.

- **Variance:** A variance is a deviation or divergence from a municipality's zoning regulations. It is something different from the norm. For example, it is issued so an owner can use his/her property outside of the common zoning regulations. Examples of variances include placing a fence along one's property line, and building a structure taller than what zoning regulations permit. From municipality to municipality, variances can greatly differ. Each municipality's zoning authority can issue a variance. Zoning variance is not the same as a nonconforming use. These are two entirely separate legal concepts.

- **Zoning permit:** This is a government-issued permit by the municipality that allows an individual or company to use a building or property for his or her or its specific purpose. This permit must be obtained before development starts. Requirements must be met in order to obtain the zoning permit. Most commonly, building permits are obtained after being granted a zoning permit.

Now it's time to take your chapter quiz.

CHAPTER 28 QUIZ

1. Billy is a senior in high school who is considering becoming a real estate licensee. He has been learning more about the topic and what the life of a licensee is like. Recently, he wrote down several questions to ask his mentor. He is curious about how the government and states control land. What is their main method of overseeing the vast amount of land in the US? Which of the following is the topic or topics he should learn about?

    a. Local ordinances
    b. Land regulation
    c. Zoning
    d. All of the above
    e. Only B and C

2. How much land does the Federal Government own?

    a. About 640 million acres
    b. About 240 million acres
    c. About 840 million acres
    d. A little over 1000 million acres

3. A small rural town in Illinois has the authority to make and pass its own laws for its municipality as long as those laws are not in conflict with any state and federal laws. What is this called?

    a. Home rule unit
    b. Township
    c. Local authority
    d. Municipality limited sovereignty

4. Buying land, building new structures, renovating existing structures, and converting property from one type of use to another are referred to as which of the following?

    a. Property development
    b. Real estate development
    c. Land development
    d. All of the above
    e. Only A and B
    f. Only A and C

5. What are the five essential elements in a municipality's comprehensive plan?

    a. Land use, housing needs, community facilities, energy conservation, stewardship

    b. Land use, property use, people movement, community facilities, energy conservation

    c. Land use, housing needs, people movement, community facilities, energy conservation

    d. Land use, people movement, raising property taxes, community facilities, energy conservation

6. What are the two primary ways in which zoning is achieved and overseen?

    a. Municipal rulings and voting

    b. Ordinances and maps

    c. Jurisdiction meetings and local hearings

    d. Building permits and density control

7. Which of the following is not a type of zoning?

    a. Aesthetic

    b. Nonprofit

    c. Combination

    d. Home-based business

8. Local laws, construction standards, how to repair or erect buildings and material requirements are the four key elements of which of the following?

    a. Property development

    b. Land use

    c. A building permit

    d. A building code

9. Betty is a real estate developer. In a meeting with her team, the focus is a new 12-story building. It will be the largest building in a small municipality. As they talk about details, someone asks how many evacuation points will be required. This question falls best inside which of the following categories?

    a. Building permit

    b. Inspection requirements

    c. Building code

    d. Safety ordinances

10. Who generally arranges and pays for a municipal presale inspection once a building is completed?

    a. The buyer
    b. The seller
    c. Both the buyer and seller (50/50)
    d. Insurance company

11. Land development regulations are enacted by each state and local governing body, not by the Federal Government.

    a. True
    b. False

12. Which is the usual order of the land development process?

    a. Land-use development, land development plan, subdividing, plats
    b. Land-use development, subdividing, plats
    c. Land development plan, plats, subdividing
    d. Land development plan, subdividing, plats

13. Which of the following is not typically included in a plat map?

    a. Land ownership
    b. Blocks and streets
    c. Size of the parcel
    d. Configuration of the parcel

14. Licensee Gerardo moved to a new neighborhood. He is an avid jogger. He decides he wants to get to know the area more by jogging. One evening while out on a run, he sees a fence and what he suspects is a human-made stream between a school and a horse farm. For what purpose do the stream and fence exist?

    a. Separation zone
    b. Natural barrier
    c. Buffer zone
    d. Property line

15. Jill believes the municipality she lives in has one area suffering from overcrowding and nonstop building. At a town hearing, she is planning to bring this topic up with everyone. Under which category does her topic best fit?

    a. Density zoning

    b. Real estate development

    c. Setback

    d. Variance

16. Margaret and Ted always wanted to build a retirement house by a stream. As they were scoping out some land, they found a beautiful vacant spot near a stream. After two weeks, they finally tracked down the property owner and asked if she was willing to sell. They told her their plans. However, the property owner said, "Your house plans sound wonderful. However, no houses can be built by the river. In this area, the closest a house can be is 400 feet." What is the topic of this conversation?

    a. Riparian rights

    b. Density zoning

    c. Variance

    d. Setback

    e. A and C

    f. C and D

17. David wants to build a wooden fence on the north side of his property line. This is not allowed by local zoning. However, how might he possibly be able to build his fence with the permission of the municipality?

    a. Zoning permit

    b. Variance

    c. Setback

    d. Improvement

    e. Conditional use permit

18. This permit is a government-issued permit by a municipality that allows an individual or company to use a building or property for his or her or its specific purpose. This permit must be obtained before development starts. Requirements must be met in order to obtain it. Which type of permit is this?

    a. Building permit

    b. Developer permit

    c. Zoning permit

    d. Special use permit

19. Which of the following is not traditionally considered federally-owned land?

    a. Nellis Air Force Base
    b. Yosemite National Park
    c. Saint Tobias Catholic Church
    d. Ronald Reagan UCLA Medical Center

20. Which of the following is false concerning a zoning map?

    a. It is a highly detailed map.
    b. It follows the local laws and divides municipalities into zones.
    c. It shows the different zones and labels them.
    d. It defines the property owners of record with the county.

CHAPTER 29:

REAL ESTATE MATH AND CALCULATIONS

LEARNING GOALS:

By the end of this lesson, you will:

- Learn foundational math formulas and abbreviations
- Have a working knowledge of percentages, decimals, and fractions
- Learn common real estate math formulas
- Know how to calculate tax proration, mortgage interest, loan-to-value ratios, and more

JUST AS REAL ESTATE IS INSEPARABLE from the environment, it is also inseparable from math. A wide variety of calculations and ratios are commonly used in the practice of real estate. Don't worry. If you struggled with advanced math in high school or college, you can still learn the skills required. Depending on a licensee's specialization and focus, the math encountered on a daily basis can greatly vary from licensee to licensee. In this chapter, we will move forward step by step so you can see how real estate mathematics works in the real world. As with all skills, practice is key.

UNITS AND MEASUREMENTS

Inches, Feet, and Yards

- 1 foot = 12 inches long

- 1 square foot = 12 inches by 12 inches

- 1 yard = 3 feet (or 36 inches)

- 1 square yard = 9 square feet

- 1 cubic yard = 27 cubic feet (3 feet x 3 feet x 3 feet)

- Cubic yard × 27 = cubic feet

- Cubic feet ÷ 27 = cubic yard

Rods

- 1 rod = 16 ½ linear feet or 5 ½ yards

- 6.6 rods = 100 feet

Miles

- 1 mile = 5,280 feet or 1,760 yards or 320 rods

- ½ mile = 2,640 feet

- ¼ mile = 1,320 feet

- 1 square mile = 640 acres

Acres

- 1 acre = 43,560 square feet

- 1 acre = 4,840 square yards

- 1 acre = 160 square rods

Townships

- 1 township = 36 square miles

- 1 township = 36 sections

- 1 section = 1 square mile

Angles

- Angles are measured in degrees.

- The symbol ° is always used for degrees.

- 360° is a full complete circle, or a full rotation around.

- Compass headings:

- 0° (North).

- 90° is ¼ of a circle. (East).

- 180° is ½ of a circle. (South).

- 270° is ¾ of a circle. (West).

- 360° (North).

BASIC MATH FORMULAS

Shapes

- Rectangle: length x width = square footage

- Triangle: (base x height) / 2 = square footage

- Trapezoid: [(base 1 + base 2) x height] / 2 = square footage

Area and Volume

- Area of a square or rectangle = length × width

- Area of a triangle = (base x height) ÷ 2

- Volume = length × width × height

Common Math Abbreviations

- Area = A

- Base = B or (b1 / b2 if it is a trapezoid)

- Diagonal = d (d1 / d2 for a diamond shape)

- Height = H

- Length = L

- Perimeter = P

- Width = W

Whole

- Whole × Rate = Part

- Part ÷ Whole = Rate

- Part ÷ Rate = Whole

SAMPLE MATH PROBLEM

What is the square footage of triangle A below?

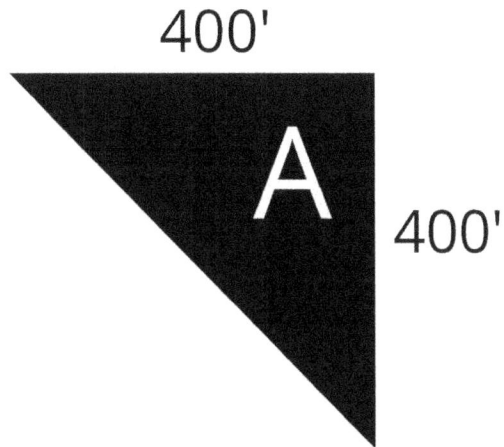

Triangle A: 400 feet x 400 feet = 160,000 square feet.

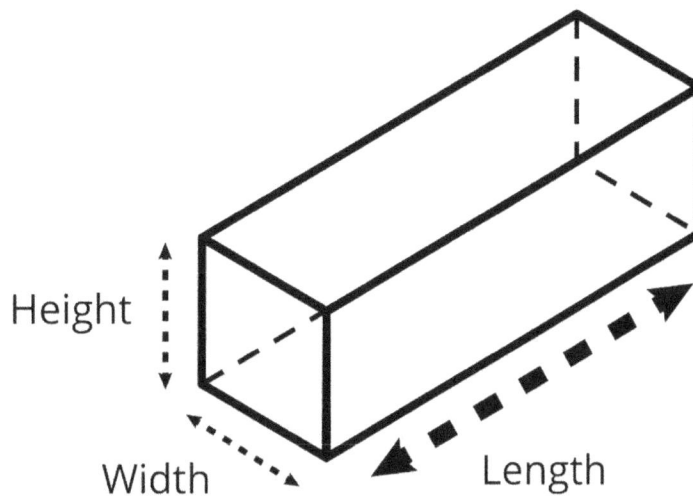

Referencing the image above, what is the total cubic feet?

34 x 34 x 130 = 150,280 cubic feet

What is the total cubic yard?

150,280 ÷ 27 = 5,565.9

Height, Depth, and Length

Length and width exist on a horizontal plane. Height exists on a vertical plane.

- **Length** is the distance from front to back.

- **Height** is the total vertical distance from the base of an object to the top. It measures up and down.

- **Width** is side to side, when you are looking straight on or at the object.

- **Depth** depends on your application. It can refer to the length of a lot, from the front to the back. It can also refer to how deep something is, such as the depth of a swimming pool or a coal mine.

- **Area** is for measuring the space inside of a two-dimensional shape. For example, area is used to measure regular size parcels of land, sidewalk areas, bedrooms, and more. Area is simply length times width. A = L x W. If a regular size lot has a length of 150 and a width of 130, then the area is 19,500. 150 x 130 = 19,500.

- **Street frontage** is the front foot that defines the width of a lot that borders the street.

- **Water frontage** is the width of a lot that borders an ocean, lake, or some other type of body of water. This is the plot's width that directly faces a waterway. How much or how little frontage can affect the value of the property.

SAMPLE MATH PROBLEM

A one-story colonial house is comprised of 3,000 square feet. This is the area. The width of the house is 40 feet. Two of the three numbers are known. How do you determine the house's length? Keep the formula L x W = A in mind. The area (A) is 3,000 square feet. The width (W) is 40 feet. 3,000 (A) ÷ 40 (W) = 75 (L). This means the length of the house is 75.

Perimeter is the line or path that outlines or surrounds a shape, whether rectangular, circular, or irregular-shaped. It's the total length of all of the sides. To find the perimeter of any shape, you add all of the sides together. If a property in a subdivision has four sides, the perimeter is the sum of all of the sides. When you think of perimeter, think of a fence. Let's say a fence entirely surrounds a property. The fence is the perimeter. How long is the fence? That's how long the perimeter is. Perimeter is not the space or area inside of the fence. That is area. When the concept of a perimeter is applied to a circle, such as a round swimming pool, it is most commonly called **circumference**.

How to Convert Feet to Acres

Let's say a parcel is 600 feet by 500 feet. To calculate the number of acres, the first step is to find the total area of the parcel. 600 feet x 500 feet = 300,000 square feet. Next, divide by 43,560 (the total number of square feet in one acre). 300,000 feet ÷ 43,560 square feet = 6.88 acres.

Legal Description

A simple way of calculating the number of acres in a specific legal description is to use the following approach.

1. You are looking at a legal description that reads out

   NW ¼ of the SE ¼ of the NW ¼ of Section 21

2. When calculating the number of acres, you always have to work right to left beginning with the word section.

3. There are only two basic fractions that you will see, which are one half (½) and one quarter (¼).

4. Look for the denominator in each fraction. The denominator is typically the lower number within a fraction. For example, if the fraction is ¼, the denominator is 4.

5. Beginning with the word section, which is always 640 acres,

   - 640 acres ÷ 4 = 160 acres. (This is the denominator of the first fraction you encounter working right to left.)

   - 160 acres ÷ 4 = 40 acres. (This is the denominator of the second fraction you encounter working right to left.)

   - 40 acres ÷ 4 = 10 acres. (This is the denominator of the last fraction you encounter working right to left.)

   - In this description, you have a total of 10 acres of land which you're dealing with.

PERCENTAGES, DECIMALS, AND FRACTIONS

Percentages, decimals, and fractions are expressions of the same number. Tip: Percent simply means out of one hundred.

A half can be written in three ways:

- As a percentage, it's 50%.

- As a decimal, it's 0.5.

- As a fraction, it's ½.

A quarter can be written in three ways:

- As a percentage, it's 25%.

- As a decimal, it's 0.25.

- As a fraction, it's ¼.

PERCENTAGE, DECIMALS, AND FRACTIONS: SIDE BY SIDE COMPARISON CHART		
Percentage	Decimal	Fraction
1%	0.01	1/100
5%	0.05	1/20
10%	0.1	1/10
15%	0.15	3/20
20%	0.20	⅕
25%	0.25	¼
33.33%	0.33	⅓
50%	0.50	½
75%	0.75	¾
87.5%	0.875	⅞
100%	1	—

Conversion reminders

- To convert from a whole number to a decimal, divide by 100. To convert from a decimal to a whole number, multiply by 100. (A whole number is any number without any fractions or decimals. It's called an integer. It is something that is complete in and of itself. Whole numbers include positive and negative numbers as well as zero).

- To convert from decimal to percentage, multiply by 100 and then add the percentage sign. For example, 0.135 x 100 = 13.5. Now, add the percentage sign. The end result is 13.5%. Alternatively, simply move the decimal point two places to the right and add a percentage sign.

- To convert from a fraction to a decimal, you will divide the numerator (top number) by the denominator (bottom number). For example, to convert ⅖ , divide 2 by 5. That gives you 0.4. That means ⅖ equals 0.4.

When solving problems focusing on percentages, it is helpful to know the concepts of whole, part, and rate.

- The whole represents the total quantity or amount that you are working with. It is generally thought of as the "big" number.

- For example, if you are working with 25 lots, then 25 is the whole.

- The part is a number smaller than the whole and represents a portion or fraction of the whole. It is a percentage of the whole and is generally thought of as the "small" number.

- Using the example above, if you want to know how many of those 25 lots are adjacent to a waterway, that would be the part.

- The rate is the percentage or fraction of the whole. It tells you how much of the whole is represented by the part.

- Continuing with the example, if 5 lots out of 25 lots are adjacent to a waterway, then the rate would be 20%. (5 ÷ 25 = 20%).

As a reminder, the formulas used are:

- Whole = Part ÷ Rate

- Part = Whole × Rate

- Rate = Part ÷ Whole

Now let's look at examples using three different variations of a similar scenario.

Example: Finding the whole

Stacy, another licensee in your brokerage, tells you that her client has put down 20% on the house they're buying. The 20% is $35,000. Before she can tell you the total of the property, there is an interruption, and she has to answer her cell. She disappears into a private office. You go back to your desk knowing you'll pick up the conversation later. How would you figure out the total cost of the property based on what she said?

The question is this. 35,000 is 20% of what number?

1. Here is the foundation for solving the problem.

    %/100 = part/whole

2. Identify the part. The part is 35,000.

3. Identify the percentage, which is 20%.

    With these two values, you can find the whole, which is the total price of the property. Now, let's update the equation above with the information we have.

    20/100 = 35000/whole

4. Next, you will cross-multiply. 20% × Whole = 35,000 × 100%.

5. Then, divide both sides by 20%. This gives you the whole.

    35,000 ÷ 20% = $175,000.

Example: Finding the part

After just two weeks on the market, Cici sold her property for $525,000. As per the contract with her agent, she pays 5.5% commission on the sale price. What is the amount of commission due to her agent?

The formula to use is Whole × Rate = Part.

- 525,000 x 5.5% = $28,875

- $28,875 is due to her agent.

Example: Finding the rate

The Remington property sold for $750,000. Big City Brokerage received $88,750 commission. What was the percentage of commission (the rate)?

The formula to use is Part ÷ Whole x 100 = Decimal.

- To convert a decimal to a rate digit, multiply by 100.

- Commission rate = $88,750 ÷ $750,000 = 0.1183

- Convert the decimal 0.1183 to a percentage by multiplying by 100.

- 0.1183 x 100 = 11.83%

Equations

Background: In equations, X is the real part. It's what we know. The letter Y is what is not yet known. It is usually used as a variable in math. Sometimes, A and B can be used as well.

Example: What is 15% of 175? Here are the steps:

- Convert the problem to an equation. Use the percentage formula which is:

    - P% x A = B

    - P is 15%. A is 175.

    - The equation is 15% x 175 = B

- Convert 15% to a decimal. How? You remove the percent sign. Then, divide by 100: 15/100 = 0.15

    - Substitute 0.15 for 15% in your equation. 15% x 175 = B changes into:

    - 0.15 x 175 = B

- Now, do the math: 0.15 x 175 = 26.25

    - B = 26.25

    - So 15% of 175 is 26.25.

REAL ESTATE MATH FORMULAS

PROFIT	
Primary Formula	**Variations**
$ Profit = $ Original Purchase Price x % Profit	% Profit = $Profit ÷ $ Original Purchase Price
	$ Original Purchase Price = $ Profit ÷ % Profit

COMMISSION	
Primary Formula	**Variations**
$ Commission = $ Sales Price x % Commission	% Commission = $ Commission ÷ $ Sales Price
	$ Sales Price = $ Commission ÷ % Commission

MORTGAGE	
Primary Formula	**Variations**
$ Annual Interest = $ of Mortgage Value x the Interest Rate	$ Monthly Interest = $ of Mortgage Value x the Interest Rate ÷ 12
	$ Points = $ Mortgage x Number of Points
	% Interest = $ Annual Interest ÷ $ Loan Amount
	$ Loan Balance = $ Annual Interest ÷ % Interest

APPRAISAL	
Primary Formula	**Variations**
Cost approach: Property Value = RCN - Depreciation + Land	No variations
Income approach: Net Annual Income = % Rate x Value. (I = R x V)	Rate = Net Annual Income ÷ Value
	Value = Net Annual Income ÷ Rate

Seller's Net Formula

When working with a seller, one of the most important figures for the seller is what they're going to net from the sale of their property. This generally takes place once the sales price is decided.

SELLER'S NET	
Primary Formula	**Variations**
Seller's Net = $ Sales Price - Mortgage - Closing Costs - Commission Paid	No variations

Improvement Age

- Actual age is the actual number of years a building has stood.

- Effective age is the perceived age of the building based on the condition.

- Economic life is the number of years the building is expected to produce a financial return to the owner.

REAL ESTATE CALCULATIONS: BASIC MATH CONCEPTS

- Mortgage interest

- Loan-to-value ratios

- Discount points

- Equity

- Down payment / amount to be financed

Mortgage Interest

Mortgage interest is simple interest. Loan-to-Value = % of purchase price provided by the lender.

MORTGAGE INTEREST	
Primary Formula	**Variations**
Mortgage Amount x % Interest = $ Interest (1 Year)	$ Annual Interest ÷ 360 = $ Interest/Day
	$ Interest/Day x of Days = Prorated $ Interest

Loan-to-Value Ratios

"The loan-to-value (LTV) ratio is a measure comparing the amount of your mortgage with the appraised value of the property. The higher your down payment, the lower your LTV ratio. Mortgage lenders may use the LTV in deciding whether to lend to you and to determine if they will require private mortgage insurance. If you have to get private mortgage insurance, it will increase your monthly costs. Be sure to compare the amounts, terms, and costs of several loans, including the cost of mortgage insurance if it will be required." Consumer Finance Protection Bureau

To calculate the LTV, divide the mortgage value by the total value of the real estate. Let's say it is a $250,000 home. The buyer receives a $135,000 loan. $135,000 divided by $250,000 equals 0.54, or 54%. The LTV is 54%. In simple terms, the LTV is the percent of the purchase price provided by the lender.

Albert is looking to acquire his first home. He has tendered an offer on a three-bedroom ranch listed for $245,000. He intends to offer the seller $210,000 with a $20,000 earnest money check in order to show the seller he is acting in good faith. Albert wants to put 15% of the sales price as a down payment and finance the balance. If the seller accepts his offer of $210,000, what will the loan-to-value ratio be?

Simple solution: 100% of the purchase price minus 15% down payment equals 85% LTV.

Discount Points

Discount points is a means of buying down the interest rate in order to make the loan affordable. Points are either service points or discount points.

- 1 point = 1/8 of a percent of interest

Samantha and Jackson have been struggling for a number of years because of the debt they currently are carrying. They want to buy their first home and found a perfect two-story colonial that meets all of their family's needs. The only issue is the current interest rate is above what they can afford. The buyers want to finance $325,000. If the current interest rate is 4.25% but the buyers need an interest rate of 3.625%, how much cash will be required to buy down the interest rate in order to allow them the ability to make this their new home?

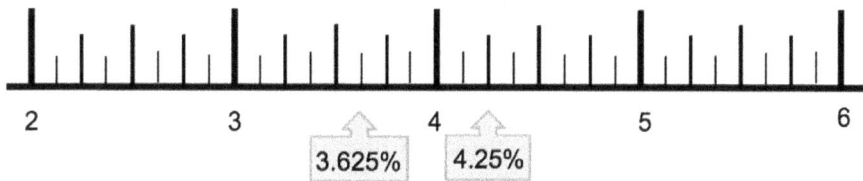

The simple solution can be determined by drawing a ruler. Refer to Diagram 29.1 above. The lender wants 4.25% (4¼) as an interest rate, but the buyer can only afford 3.625% (3⅝). Now that we have marked the two rates on the ruler, keep in mind one discount point is the equivalent of ⅛ counts the number of spaces between the two rates. In this case, there are five spaces between the rates, which is the equivalent of five discount points. One discount point equals 1% of the mortgage amount. Therefore; $325,000 x 5% = $16,250. This is the amount the buyer must bring to the closing, which they will give to the lender in order to acquire the lower interest rate and yet still give the lender the opportunity to make the same level of profit they would have made at 4¼ interest.

Equity

- Current value - Outstanding debt = Equity

- Debt + Closing Costs

Bob and Clarice are discussing selling their present home in order to purchase a newly constructed home that just came on the market. They're going to need $120,000 of equity from their current home in order to be able to finance the new purchase. Their broker has estimated their closing costs will likely run approximately $26,000 including a 6% commission. If their existing mortgage debt is $312,000, what would the current value of their existing home consist of?

- $120,000 of equity + $312,000 mortgage + $26,000 = $458,000

- $458,000 / 94% = $487,234

How did I come up with the 94%? When dealing with a seller's net, you always include the expenses such as the net, mortgage, and closing costs and then divide that total by the percent of the sales price the seller is allowed to retain after the commission has been paid. In this case, it is 94%.

Down Payment Amount Financed

- Down Payment ÷ Purchase Price = Down Payment Percentage

Christopher and Angela Hastings are looking at a three-unit apartment building that they would like to purchase and occupy one of the units. They're talking with their broker about tendering an offer. The seller is asking $435,000, but the Hastings are thinking about offering $398,000. If the Hastings and the seller ultimately agree on a sales price of $410,000 and the Hastings want to put down $60,000, what percentage of the purchase price does the down payment reflect?

- $60,000 ÷ $410,000 = 14.6%

- Down payment ÷ purchase price = percent of down payment

CALCULATIONS FOR TRANSACTIONS

These include, but are not limited to, the following:

1. Required buyer funds

2. Commissions and commission splits

3. PITI (principal, interest, taxes, and insurance) payments

4. Property tax calculations

5. Property tax prorations

6. Insurance proration

7. Closing statement example

8. Sellers proceeds

9. Transfer tax fee (Convenience tax, revenue stamps)

Before you learn each calculation, you should be aware of the basic rules of calculating prorations.

Prorations is the mathematical approach necessary to be able to identify what portion of the expense belongs to each party, that is, the seller and the buyer. Proration calculations follow four rules:

- Unless otherwise specified, use a statutory month (30 days) and statutory year (360 days).

- The day of closing is a day of expense of the seller.

- The day of closing is a day of income to the seller.

- The day of closing is a day of interest expense to the buyer.

Required Buyer Funds

Buyer Stanley is working with broker Mike and has found what Stanley considers to be the perfect house. Stanley is confident the seller will accept $402,000 for the house. But Stanley has a concern as to how much cash he is going to need in order to complete the purchase. He wants to keep his down payment low and hopes the lender will accept an 11% down payment. Stanley has estimated his closing costs at $15,200. He is also working under an exclusive buyer agency agreement requiring that he pay broker Mike 3% of the purchase price. How much cash is Stanley going to require in order to complete this purchase?

- $402,000 x 11% = $44,220 (expected down payment)

- Closing costs: $15,200

- Buyer/broker commission: $402,000 x 3% = $12,060 (buyer's agent's commission)

- $44,220 + $15,200 + $12,060 = $71,480 (required cash to close)

Commissions and Commission Splits

Roger has been working with a potential buyer Hank for six weeks. While there have been a number of properties presented to Hank, he has rejected every one of them. The house that Roger presented to Hank today appears to be the perfect home for Hank to raise his family in. If Hank tenders an offer of $423,000, and the commission payable by the seller is 6.5% with a cooperating broker's share of the commission set at 55%, and if Roger is to receive 60% of the commission earned by his office, how much commission will Roger be paid by his sponsoring broker?

- First step: $423,000 x 6.5% = $28,080 (total commission paid by seller)

- Second step: $28,080 x 55% = $15,444 (commission due Roger's office)

- Third step: $15,444 x 60% = $9,266.40 (commission due Roger)

PITI (Principal, interest, taxes, and insurance)

In order to calculate a monthly payment of principal and interest (PI), apply the following steps:

- The table is based upon $1,000 increments.

- All factors are based upon a 30-year loan term.

- The payment factor reflects the monthly payment due per $1,000 of value.

Problem 1: You are seeking a $350,000 mortgage from the lender. The term is 30 years, and the current interest rate is 4.5%.

- Go to the 4.5% line.

- Look at the factor just to the right of the interest rate (5.07).

- This is your multiplier.

- Divide the mortgage amount by 1000. $350,000 ÷ 1,000 = 350

- Multiply the result by the rate factor. 350 x 5.07 = $1,774.50

- The monthly PI (principal and interest) will be $1,774.50.

Problem 2: Oswald and Jennifer are looking to acquire a conventional loan to purchase their first townhouse. They are tendering an offer of $265,000. The lender they are working with wants to charge them 3.75% interest for a 30-year fixed-rate loan. If the amortization factor is 4.63 and the annual taxes are $9,463 with the hazard insurance annual premium of $750, what will their PITI consist of?

Answer: $265,000 / $1,000 = $265 (Amortization tables are typically created on $1,000 increments, which is what necessitates dividing the sales price by $1,000).

$265 x 4.63 (The amortization factor per $1,000 at 3.75% interest) = $1,226.95. (This is the monthly payment of principal and interest.) PITI reflects the standard monthly payment on a mortgage. It is comprised of the principal, interest, 1/12 of the annual tax bill, and 1/12 of the annual insurance bill. In order to calculate the total monthly payment, take the annual taxes and divide that by 12.

- $9,463 / 12 = $788.58

- Take the annual insurance bill and divide that by 12.

- $750 / 12 = $62.50

- Finally, add all three numbers.

- $1,226.95 + $788.58 + $62.50 = $2,078.03

- The total monthly PITI will be $2,078.03.

Below is a typical amortization table that you'll likely be given access to when you take the state exam.

Amortization Table

Rate	30 Year	Rate	30 Year	Rate	30 Year	Rate	30 Year
1	3.22	4	4.78	7	6.65	10	8.78
1-1/8	3.27	4-1/8	4.85	7-1/8	6.74	10-1/8	8.89
1-1/4	3.33	4-1/4	4.92	7-1/4	6.82	10-1/4	8.96
1-3/8	3.39	4-3/8	5.00	7-3/8	6.91	10-3/8	9.05
1-1/2	3.45	4-1/2	5.07	7-1/2	6.99	10-1/2	9.15
1-5/8	3.51	4-5/8	5.15	7-5/8	7.08	10-5/8	9.24
1-3/4	3.57	4-3/4	5.22	7-3/4	7.16	10-3/4	9.33
1-7/8	3.63	4-7/8	5.30	7-7/8	7.25	10-7/8	9.43
2	3.70	5	5.37	8	7.34	11	9.52
2-1/8	3.76	5-1/8	5.45	8-1/8	7.42	11-1/8	9.62
2-1/4	3.82	5-1/4	5.53	8-1/4	7.51	11-1/4	9.71
2-3/8	3.89	5-3/8	5.60	8-3/8	7.60	11-3/8	9.81
2-1/2	3.95	5-1/2	5.68	8-1/2	7.69	11-1/2	9.90
2-5/8	4.02	5-5/8	5.76	8-5/8	7.78	11-5/8	10.00
2-3/4	4.08	5-3/4	5.84	8-3/4	7.87	11-3/4	10.09
2-7/8	4.15	5-7/8	5.92	8-7/8	7.96	11-7/8	10.19
3	4.22	6	6.00	9	8.05	12	10.29
3-1/8	4.28	6-1/8	6.08	9-1/8	8.14	12-1/8	10.38
3-1/4	4.35	6-1/4	6.16	9-1/4	8.23	12-1/4	10.48
3-3/8	4.42	6-3/8	6.24	9-3/8	8.32	12-3/8	10.58
3-1/2	4.49	6-1/2	6.32	9-1/2	8.41	12-1/2	10.67
3-5/8	4.56	6-5/8	6.40	9-5/8	8.50	12-5/8	10.77
3-3/4	4.63	6-3/4	6.49	9-3/4	8.59	12-3/4	10.87
3-7/8	4.70	6-7/8	6.57	9-7/8	8.68	12-7/8	10.96

Property Tax Calculations

Property Taxes—$/$ Method

Process when starting with market value:

Function	Item
	Market Value
x	% Assessed
	$ Assessed Value
x	Equalization Factor
	$ Adj Assessed Value
-	Homestead
	$ Taxable Value
÷	Tax Factor
	Decimal
x	Tax Rate
	$ Property Taxes

Process when starting with taxes paid:

Function	Item
	$ Taxes Paid
÷	Tax Rate
	Decimal
x	Tax Factor
	$ Taxable Value
+	Homestead
	$ Adj Assessed Value

÷	Equalization Factor
	$ Assessed Value
÷	% Assessed
	$ Market Value

Andrea, a recent divorcée, is now responsible for the home she previously shared with her husband. She is talking to her best friend and exploring the option of selling the house. She has her recent tax bill and is looking at the way the county has calculated the property taxes, trying to figure out approximately what the house might be worth. The tax bill indicates that her paid property taxes were $14,234. It also indicates that the county is applying an equalization factor of 1.83 against the assessed value, which happens to be 38% of the current market value. Assuming there is a $5,000 owner-occupant homestead, and the tax rate is $6.34 per $350 of value. Based on these facts, what would you estimate as the market value?

Function	Item	
	Market Value	1,137,170.90
÷	% Assessed Value	38%
	$ Assessed Value	432,124.94
÷	Equalization Factor	1.83
	$ Adjusted Assessed Value	790,788.64
+	Homestead	5,000
	$ Taxable Value	785,788.64
x	Factor	350
	Decimal	2245.11
+	Tax Rate	6.34
	Property Taxes	14,234

Numbers above depicted in red are the results of the mathematical functions. You can read this from left to right moving up. Remember, this process is in reverse order.

Property Tax Prorations

PROPERTY TAX PRORATION	
Primary Formula	**Variations**
Annual Taxes ÷ 360 = $ Taxes per Day	No Variations
$Taxes per day x # days = Prorated taxes due	No Variations

Property purchased

- Annual Taxes ÷ 360 = $ Taxes per Day

- $ Taxes/Day x Days Seller Owes = $ Tax due

Rent

- $ Monthly rent ÷ 30 days = Rent per day

- Daily rent x # of days = Prorated rent

Insurance Proration

The seller acquired a three-year fire insurance policy on his current residence beginning April 15, 2019. The three-year premium was $2,075 paid on April 15, 2023. The seller is now selling his home with an anticipated closing date of May 31, 2024. If the buyer intends to assume the responsibility for the current fire insurance policy, what would be the amount of the proration and how would it be entered into the closing statement?

3-year premium was paid in advance on April 15, 2019.

3-year policy × 360 days = 1,080 days.

$2,075 ÷ 1,080 days = $1.92 per day.

Closing was scheduled for May 31, 2020.

Days in which the seller is responsible for insurance:

2023:

- April = 15 days

- 8 full months = 240 days

2024:

- 5 full months = 150 days

- 15 days + 240 days + 150 days = 405 days

- $1.92 × 405 days = $777.60

- $2,075 - $777.60 = $1,297.40

$1,297.40 will be posted on the closing statement as a debit from the buyer, and $1,297.40 will also be posted as a credit to the seller.

Buyer		Seller	
Debit	Credit	Debit	Credit
1,297.40			1,297.40

Generally speaking, closing proration problems on the state exam use the traditional four-column statements (as you see above) while many attorneys prefer the two-column statement. In the four-column statement, there is a debit and credit column for the buyer and the seller. An example is shown below. As you complete the problem, in many cases, there will be an entry on the buyer's side and the seller's side of the form. However, there are some expenditures that may reflect an expense to the buyer or the seller, but not necessarily to both.

For example, the commission the seller pays their broker on the sale is 6% of the sales price. If the sales price is $475,000, the commission will amount to $28,500. As this is an expense of the seller exclusively, it will be entered into the form as a debit to the seller.

Buyer		Seller	
Debit	Credit	Debit	Credit
		28,500	

Closing Statement Example

A debit deducts funds. Money leaves your account. A credit adds funds. Money enters your account. In a closing, the buyer and the seller both commonly have debits and credits.

Example: Let's say a house sold for $475,000. The buyer is getting an 80% mortgage for 30 years, with three points due at the closing. The interest on this new mortgage is 7%.

		Buyer		Seller	
		Debit	Credit	Debit	Credit
1	Purchase Price	475,000			475,000
2	Buyer's 1st mortgage		380,000		
3	Service points 3%	11.400			
4	Prorated interest on Buyer's first mortgage 8 days	591*			

*Prorated interest calculation:

Buyer's first mortgage

- $475,000 x 80% = $380,000

Prorated interest on buyer's first mortgage

- $380,000 x 7% = $26,600 ÷ 360 days = $73.89 (Interest per day)

The closing is set for August 23rd of this year.

Interest on mortgage payments is charged in arrears. The interest for the utilization of the lender's money is the only time that it is paid in advance. Assuming a 30-day statutory month, and recognizing the lender is entitled to interest for the day of closing, how many days in the month of August is the buyer responsible for interest? The answer is 8 days.

- 8 x $73.89 = $591.12

For this problem, we are rounding the interest charge to the nearest whole number.

Now, let's continue the problem. The buyer gave $20,000 in earnest money when the contract was accepted. It is being held by the listing broker in a non-interest-bearing account. There's no proration on earnest money calculation.

		Buyer		Seller	
		Debit	Credit	Debit	Credit
5	Earnest Money		20,000		

The seller must pay a 6% commission and $900 in title charges. There is no proration on commission or title charge.

		Buyer		Seller	
		Debit	Credit	Debit	Credit
6	Commission 6%			28,500	
7	Title Charges			900	

The seller must retire an existing first mortgage loan of $210,000 with an interest rate of 6% interest. There is no proration on the mortgage amount, but there is a proration on the interest payable.

		Debit	Credit	Debt	Credit
8	Seller's existing 1st Mortgage			210,00	
9	Unpaid Interest on 1st Mortgage 23 days			805*	

*Unpaid interest calculation

- $210,000 x 6% = $12,600 annual interest

- $12,600 ÷ 360 days = $35.00 interest per day

The interest for the month of closing has not been paid because interest is collected one month in arrears.

This is the mortgage held by the seller, so the lender will collect interest from the first of the month.

How many days in August, including the day of closing, is the seller liable for interest? The answer is 23. The seller will not deliver the deed until the 23rd of August and must pay interest up to and including the date the deed is delivered.

- $35 x 23 days = $805

The seller must also retire an existing second mortgage for $100,000 at 7½% interest.

		Debit	Credit	Debit	Credit
10	Seller's existing 2nd Mortgage			100,000	
11	Unpaid Interest 2nd Mortgage 23 days			479	

The seller must also pay the state and county transfer taxes. (Use the Illinois schedule for state and county transfer taxes).

		Debit	Credit	Debit	Credit
12	Transfer Taxes			713	

The annual real estate taxes are $13,062 and have not been paid for the year of closing.

		Debit	Credit	Debit	Credit
13	Property Taxes 233* days		8,454	8,454	

*Seven full months = 30 statutory days x 7 months = 210 statutory days

23 statutory days in the month of closing

- 210 days + 23 days = 233 days

The building is a two-unit apartment building with each unit rented out at $1,250, and a security deposit on file with the seller equal to one month rent for each unit. The seller has collected the rents for the month of close.

		Buyer		Seller	
		Debit	Credit	Debit	Credit
14	Rent for month of close 7 days		583	583	
15	Security deposits		2,500	2,500	

- $1,250 monthly per unit x 2 = $2,500 monthly rent

Remember, the day of closing is a day of income to the property owner. Therefore, the buyer's entitlement to rent does not begin until August 24th. The buyer is entitled to 7 statutory days of earned rental income in August.

- $2,500 ÷ 30 statutory days = $83.33 rental income per day

- 7 statutory days x $83.33 = $583.33 (rounded to $583.00)

Here is the final step. Add the numbers in each column as noted above to obtain the total per column and insert that total on Line 16.

		Buyer		Seller	
		Debit	Credit	Debit	Credit
16	Total for each column	486,991	411,537	352,934	475,000
17	Cash to Close		75,454		
18	Net to Seller			122,066	
19	Totals	486,991	486,991	475,000	475,000

As you will note, Line 16 (total for each column) has different numbers. When dealing with debits and credits, it is critical that the debit column equals the credit column, as the debit column and credit column for the buyer are different. You need to calculate what that difference amounts to. The difference between the buyer's debit and credit columns reflects the cash the buyer must bring to the closing to satisfy the purchase. This number is entered into the credit column of Line 17. You repeat this process with the seller, only here, you take the difference in the debit column and credit column and insert those numbers into Line 18 under the seller's debit category. This line shows the net proceeds the seller is entitled to from the sale of the property.

Seller Proceeds

Timothy is looking to sell his home. He has found a new home that he needs to move on quickly. In order to purchase the new home, Timothy must be able to net a minimum of $300,000 from his existing home. If he has an outstanding mortgage of $265,000, anticipated closing costs of $26,000, plus the 5.5% broker's commission, what would be the minimum sales price that Timothy could accept in order to be able to purchase the new house?

$300,000 (seller's net) + $265,000 (mortgage value) + $26,000 (closing costs) = $591,000 before commissions.

Remember, the buyer pays 100% of the sales price. If the seller shares part of that money with the broker (5.5%), the seller retains the remaining 94.5% of the purchase price.

Divide the $591,000 by the seller's share, after the commission has been satisfied. The end result is the minimum sales price the seller can accept.

$591,000 ÷ 94.5% (share of the sales price the seller gets to retain) = $625,396.83

This is the minimum sales price Timothy can accept to be able to supply all of his financial needs.

Transfer Tax Fee (Convenience tax, revenue stamps)

- Illinois state transfer taxes:

  - 50 cents per $500 of value or a fraction thereof payable to the state of Illinois.

  - (Note: Deduct any assumed mortgage amounts prior to calculating the transfer tax.)

  - Rule of thumb: To simplify your calculation, consider this scenario. If the seller accepts a sales price of $500, the seller will pay 50 cents to the state of Illinois as a transfer tax. If the seller accepts a sales price of $1,000, the seller will pay $1 to the state of Illinois as a transfer tax. As a result, take the sales price and divide it by 1000. The result is the transfer tax due to the state of Illinois.

- County transfer taxes in Illinois (Currently, all counties are charging the same transfer fee):

  - 25 cents per $500 of value or a fraction thereof payable to the county.

  - Rule of thumb: Divide the state transfer tax by 2. The result is the county transfer tax.

  - (Note: Deduct any assumed mortgage amounts prior to calculating the transfer tax.)

What does a fraction thereof mean? The law is written to base the transfer tax on increments of $500. If the seller accepts a price of $753,305, before the tax can be calculated, you need to round the last three digits up to the closest $500 amount. Therefore, a sales price of $753,305 gets rounded up to $753,500 before calculating the transfer tax. Ironically, let's assume the sales price is $753,500.01. In this case, the law requires rounding this amount to $754,000 before calculating the tax. Always remember to round up, never round down.

Example 1: A purchaser negotiates a sales price of $800,000 with the seller. Both are in agreement and a contract is created. At the closing, the seller needs to pay both the state and county transfer tax. How much will be required? Answer:

$800,000 ÷ 1000 = $800 payable to the state.

$800 payable to the state ÷ 2 = $400 payable to the county.

Total transfer taxes payable by the seller: $800 + $400 = $1,200

Example 2: Margo and Franklin are purchasing a home in Wheaton, Illinois. They agreed on a sales price of $785,203. At the closing, in order to allow Margo and Franklin to record the deed in their names, the sellers need to pay both the state and county transfer taxes. Using the Illinois schedule for both the state and the county taxes, what will the transfer tax consist of in order to allow the purchaser to record the deed?

To calculate the transfer taxes, you must first round the sales price upward to the next $500 increment. Therefore, $785,203 is rounded to $785,500.

$785,500 ÷ 1000 = $785.50.

Thus, $785.50 is the state-specific transfer tax.

To find the county tax, simply divide the state tax by 2.

$785.50 ÷ 2 = $392.75

Thus, $392.75 is the county transfer tax.

The total transfer tax payable by the seller would be the addition of county and state transfer taxes.

$785.50 + $392.75 = $1,178.25

This concludes calculations for transactions. Now, it's time for the final topics of this chapter.

Construction Costs

While there are different ways to estimate construction costs, the most common is the square foot method. This method requires the hard (direct) costs and soft (indirect) costs to be researched in advance. The construction cost is calculated by multiplying the building's square footage by the construction cost.

As a reminder, hard costs do not vary. Examples include materials, profit, and labor. Soft costs do vary. They include all of the costs minus materials, labor, and profit. They're indirect because they're not directly associated with the direct construction of the structure. These costs may include line items like permits, architect fees, consulting fees, and so on.

Cost per square foot can vary from city to city and region to region. Different variables can influence the price, such as the quality of the materials to be used and more. Scenario: Bob is a contractor. He has been asked to calculate how much it will cost to build a new home in a neighboring medium-sized town. The neighborhood in which it will be built is mostly upper-middle class. The living area is 2,450 square feet. It will include a 650-square-foot garage and work area. Homes in that town usually cost $140 per square foot to build. Garage and work area spaces generally cost less, clocking in at $75 per square foot.

How does Bob estimate the construction costs? Let's look.

Living area: 2,450 square feet x $140 = $343,000

Garage and work areas: 650 square feet x $75 = $48,750

$343,000 + $48,750 = $391,750 (This is total construction costs. It does not include the land.)

Income-Generating Properties and Value

When it comes to properties that generate revenue or income, how are they valued? When appraised, the main factor is the annual net operating income (NOI), along with either the capitalization rate or the current market rate. The formula for NOI is:

Net operating income = All revenue generated by the property - operating expenses.

This formula allows real estate professionals and investors to determine a particular investment's potential profitability. It brings all revenue and expenses for the property under one roof and presents the calculation in a clear way.

A capitalization rate, sometimes called a "cap rate," is a valuation measurement used in real estate. It helps real estate professionals compare and see the pros and cons of different real estate investments. A capitalization rate is generally calculated as the ratio between the net operating income that the asset generates and the current market value.

Example: A strip mall in a rapidly growing community generates $450,700 annual gross income. Its yearly expenses are $97,400. James, an appraiser, uses a 9.5 cap rate of return when he estimates the value. Given this information, what is the strip mall's estimated value?

All revenue generated by the property - operating expenses = Net operating income

$450,700 - $97,400 = $353,300 (NOI)

Using this formula, you can calculate the monthly NOI or the ROI if the focus is real estate investing.

The basic formula is: NAI (net annual income) = Cap rate x property value.

If you know the NAI and the cap rate that the investor wishes to acquire, to find the maximum dollar the investor should pay for the property, simply divide the NAI by the cap rate.

The answer to the scenario above is:

$353,300 ÷ 9.5 = $3,718,947.37

(Convert the cap rate of 9.5 to a decimal in order to properly determine the market value.)

Each licensee must know the basic math, formulas, and concepts presented. Nobody outgrows the basics or the fundamentals. They're essential. Challenging calculations are not a daily part of life for most real estate licensees, although they're important. Being familiar with the formulas and concepts can help you build trust and rapport with everyone in your circle of influence.

CHAPTER 29 QUIZ

1. Which is correct concerning the length of a mile?

    a. 5,280 linear feet and 1,760 yards
    b. 4,280 linear feet and 1426 yards
    c. 3,280 linear feet and 1093 yards
    d. None of the above

2. James is with a potential buyer. They looked at a large house for sale. Now, they are driving around the property. James boasts about the property spanning three square miles. The potential buyer says, "I really don't use those measurements much anymore. How many acres is it?" What is the correct response?

    a. 740 acres
    b. 1280 acres
    c. 1740 acres
    d. 1920 acres

3. Which formula below is incorrect?

    a. Part = whole ÷ rate
    b. Whole = part ÷ rate
    c. Part = whole x rate
    d. Rate = part ÷ whole

4. A broker agrees to a sliding scale commission. She will receive 7% on the first $175,000 and 4% on the next $200,000 and 2% on the balance. What is the sales price of the property if she is paid $28,350 in commission?

    a. $510,000
    b. $620,000
    c. $780,000
    d. $850,000

5. A two-story modern house in Chicago is 2,500 square feet. The width of the house is 45 feet. What is the house's rounded depth?

    a. 2025
    b. 112,500
    c. 56
    d. None of the above

6. Janetta is scouting out a retirement home while her husband is traveling. Today's home is a sprawling property with a high white fence enclosing the entirety of the property. She asks the licensee, "What is the linear length of the entire fence?" The licensee knows the fence is a perfect rectangle. Two sides are 300 feet and the other two are 250 feet. Which formula below would help him answer correctly?

   a. 300 x 250
   b. 300 x 2 + 250 x 2
   c. 300 + 300 + 250 + 250
   d. None of the above
   e. B and C

7. Betty sells her property for $550,000 and pays 4% commission on the sale price. If the commission is split equally between the listing office and the selling office, how much commission will the listing office retain?

   a. $11,000
   b. $18,000
   c. $22,000
   d. $26,000

8. The Smith estate outside of Chicago sold for $450,000. The listing office received $24,750 in commission. What was the brokerage's percentage of commission on this real estate transaction?

   a. 5.5%
   b. 4.5%
   c. 6.5%
   d. 5%

9. Mike and Jane are upset. They discovered that their property value has decreased. In their small town, the real estate prices have decreased by 11% over the past twelve months. They purchased the house last year for $320,000. Given the decrease in property value, what is their home currently worth?

   a. $264,800
   b. $274,800
   c. $279,800
   d. $284,800

10. Although Sarah is a well-known doctor in her community, she and her husband John have a financial obstacle. Last year, John had a horrible medical issue that drained their savings and retirement funds. They want to sell their home and downsize, but they're upset because even with doing that, the current interest rate will make it difficult for them to thrive financially. They want to finance $225,000. The current interest rate is 4.5%. However, they need an interest rate of 3.25%. How much cash will be required to buy down the interest rate in order to allow them to purchase the new home?

    a. $22,500
    b. $25,000
    c. $15,000
    d. $5,000

11. Dakota and Betty are exploring selling their current home. They are both retiring over the next six months. Their goal is to purchase a newly constructed condo. It's in a popular neighborhood and they can even walk to several stores and parks. They will need $140,000 of equity from their current home in order to be able to finance the new condo purchase. Their broker has estimated their closing costs will likely amount to $32,000 plus a 6% commission. If their existing mortgage debt is $328,000, what would be the minimum sales price they can accept in order to meet all of these expenses?

    a. $530,000
    b. $482,000
    c. $360,000
    d. $531,915

12. Daniela and Eric are searching intensely for a four-unit apartment building. Their goal is to purchase it, live in one unit, and rent out the other three units. They feel that this will help them retire soon in the future as well as have an income-producing asset. Working with their broker, they learned that the asking price is $475,000. However, they're considering offering $440,000. If the couple and the seller ultimately agree on a sales price of $455,000 and the couple wants to put down $75,000, what rounded percentage of the purchase price does the down payment reflect?

    a. 14%
    b. 15%
    c. 16%
    d. 17%

13. John, a recent divorcée, is now responsible for the home he had previously shared with his wife. He is exploring the option of selling the house. The current tax bill has recently been received and John is looking at how the county calculated the property taxes, trying to figure out approximately what the house might be worth. The tax bill indicates that the paid property taxes were $16,767. It also indicates that the county is applying an equalization factor of 1.83 against the assessed value, which happens to be 42% of the current market value. Assuming there is a $5,000 owner occupant homestead, and the tax rate is $5.34 per $350 of value. Based on these facts, what would you estimate as the market value?

   a. $1,436,327
   b. $1,336,275
   c. $1,536,254
   d. $1,245,327

14. Whitney just purchased a four-year fire insurance policy on her current residence. The start date was May 1, 2020. The four-year premium was $2,555 paid on May 1, 2020. Whitney is now selling her home with an anticipated closing date of June 15, 2021. If the buyer intends to assume the responsibility for the current fire insurance policy, what would be the amount of the proration? How would proration be entered into the closing statement? (When solving the problem, use a statutory year.)

   a. $1,903.56
   b. $1,854.15
   c. $1,776.76
   d. $1,734.95

15. Broker Viola has been working with potential buyers Alexandra and Phillip Johnson, a couple with children, for five weeks. While she has tirelessly shown the Johnsons multiple properties that were impressive, each one was rejected. Viola presented a new house today. It exceeds the list that the Johnsons had given her weeks earlier. Viola thinks it will be perfect for their growing and blended family. The Johnsons are going to tender an offer of $515,000. The commission payable by the seller is 5.5%. A cooperating broker's share of the commission is set at 55%. Viola will receive 50% of the commission earned by her office. Given those circumstances, how much commission will Viola be paid by her sponsoring broker?

   a. $9,347.38
   b. $8,265.46
   c. $7,789.38
   d. $7,354.46

16. Janet wants to sell her house. She has found a new home and due to personal circum-stances, she needs to move in ASAP. In order to purchase the new home, Janet has to be able to net a minimum of $335,000 from her existing home. Her outstanding mortgage is $298,000. The anticipated closing costs are $31,000, plus the 5.5% broker's commission. What would be the minimum sales price that Janet could accept in order to be able to purchase the new house?

    a. $698,345
    b. $705,946
    c. $711,644
    d. $702,646

17. Buyer Rebecca is working with broker Cindy. Cindy is excited because she has found what Rebecca considers to be the perfect house. Rebecca is confident the seller will accept $375,000. However, Rebecca has a concern. She is worried about how much cash she will need in order to complete the purchase. She wants to keep her down payment low. Her hope is that the lender will accept a 10% down payment. Rebecca has estimated her clos-ing costs at $12,200. She is working under an exclusive buyer agency agreement requiring that she pay broker Cindy 3% of the purchase price. How much cash is Rebecca going to require in order to complete this purchase?

    a. $62,950
    b. $60,950
    c. $65,950
    d. $49,700

18. Scotty and Christine are buying a beautiful two-story house in Rockford, Illinois. They agreed on a sales price of $820,000. At the closing, in order to allow Scotty and Christine to record the deed in their name, the sellers need to pay both the state and county transfer taxes. Using the Illinois schedule for both the state and the county taxes, what will the transfer tax consist of in order to allow the purchaser to record the deed?

    a. $1,230
    b. $820
    c. $410
    d. $1,620

19. Mickey and Rosanna want to acquire a conventional loan to purchase their first town-house. They are tendering an offer of $310,000. The lender they are working with wants to charge them 4.25% interest for a 30-year fixed-rate loan. If the amortization factor is 4.53 and the annual taxes are $11,878 with the hazard insurance annual premium of $850, what will their PITI consist of?

   a. $1,404.13
   b. $1,964.97
   c. $2,464.97
   d. $2,664.97

20. Which formula below is incorrect?

   a. % profit = $ profit ÷ $ original purchase price x 1000
   b. Net operating income = All revenue generated by the property - operating expenses.
   c. Rate = part ÷ whole
   d. Annual interest = $ mortgage x % rate

REAL ESTATE LICENSE LAW IN ILLINOIS AND WHAT IT MEANS FOR YOU

LEARNING GOALS:

By the end of this lesson, you will:

- Understand the importance and role of licenses
- Discover how license renewal and expiration works
- Learn IDFPR policies and procedures
- Know about state laws that govern the real estate industry in Illinois
- See how disciplinary action works

REAL ESTATE LICENSE ACT OF 2000 AND THE IDFPR

Section 1-5 of The Act defines the purpose or intent of the law. When the law was created, there were three distinct components that comprise the intent:

- Evaluate the competency of licensees

- Regulate the business activities of licensees

- Protect the interest of the public (225 ILCS 454/1-5)

When it comes to real estate law in the state of Illinois, all roads lead to the Real Estate License Act of 2000. Illinois real estate licensees are governed by The Act, which was amended in 2020. The IDFPR (Illinois Department of Financial and Professional Regulation) oversees The Act. The most recent version was signed into law in late 2019. It was a collaborative effort between Illinois REALTORS® and the IDFPR. By statute, The Act must be updated every ten years. The purpose of the update is to strengthen training rules, increase professionalism and knowledge, update practices, improve consumer protections, and reflect other changes in the industry. The law was enacted to protect the public. As such, there are certain actions that involve real estate representation that require a real estate license. Section 1-10 of The Act defines what actions require a real estate license. All real estate licenses in Illinois are administered and granted by the IDFPR.

What is the mission of IDFPR? They answer on their website.

> The mission of the Illinois Department of Financial and Professional Regulation, Division of Professional Regulation is to serve, safeguard, and promote the health, safety, and welfare of the public by ensuring that licensure qualifications and standards for professional practice are properly evaluated, applied, and enforced. The division regulates a variety of healthcare and occupational professionals. Some of these professions include: physicians, nurses, pharmacies, physical therapists, dentists, and veterinarians, as well as; detectives, cosmetologists, barbers, engineers, accountants, architects, and many more.

In the real estate division, the IDFPR has several responsibilities, including but not limited to:

1. Issuing and renewing real estate licenses for brokers, managing brokers, and other real estate professionals, as well as restoring revoked or suspended licenses when deemed appropriate.

2. Enforcing real estate laws and regulations in the real estate industry within Illinois. This includes conducting disciplinary hearings to determine if a licensee has violated any provision of The Act, as well as implementing necessary disciplinary action when required.

3. Maintaining records of all licensed real estate professionals in the state of Illinois. These records include relevant information about licensing, sponsorship, and disciplinary action.

4. Regulating real estate education that is available to real estate licensees and sanctioning license examinations.

The IDFPR organization has four divisions. Here is each division name, along with information as quoted from their website:

1. **Division of Banking**: The Division of Banking regulates, charters, and supervises state-chartered banks, trust companies, savings institutions, mortgage banks, mortgage loan originators, pawnbrokers, check printers, and registered non-bank ATMs.

2. **Division of Financial Institutions**: The Division of Financial Institutions regulates, and supervises non-banking financial institutions including credit unions, currency exchanges, title insurance underwriters, and consumer credit services, as well as a variety of other financial institutions.

3. **Division of Professional Regulation**: The Division of Professional Regulation licenses and regulates over 1 million professionals and firms in Illinois including a variety of healthcare-related professions such as doctors, nurses, and veterinarians, as well as a variety of occupational professions such as CPAs, barbers, engineers, and detectives.

4. **Division of Real Estate**: The Division of Real Estate licenses and regulates professionals involved in the buying and selling of property, including real estate brokers, appraisers, auctioneers, community association managers, and home inspectors (IDFPR).

The IDFPR administers three different primary funds. They are as follows:

1. The Real Estate License Administration Fund, which is the fund in which licensee fees are sent.

2. The Real Estate Recovery Fund, which primarily focuses on consumers who are victims of licensees' actions that were unethical, immoral, and/or harmful that caused actual financial harm.

3. The Real Estate Research and Education Fund (REEF), which "may be used for research and for education at state institutions of higher education or other organizations for research and for education to further the advancement of education in the real estate industry" (The Act, 225 ILCS 454/25-25). This also includes scholarships.

There are three main sections of IDFPR Procedures. These include: 1) Complaints 2) Investigation of Complaints and Compliance with Investigation 3) Prosecutions, which includes a) informal conference and b) formal conference.

The Division of Real Estate within IDFPR communicates the following via its webpage as its primary mission:

> The Mission of the Division of Real Estate is to serve, safeguard, and promote the public welfare by ensuring that qualifications and standards for licensed real estate related professions are properly evaluated, uniformly applied, and systematically enforced. We strive to provide efficient service through effective communication and transparency in operations, while maintaining a commitment to excellence with both consumers and the industry. The Division of Real Estate regulates the following six professions and entities: appraisal management companies, auction community, association management, home inspection, real estate appraisal, real estate brokerage.

Who conducts licensee exams? Who issues licenses? Who renews licenses? Who does all of that administrative work in order to make sure licensees are prepared to legally practice real estate? As you've already guessed, it's the IDFPR.

REAL ESTATE ADMINISTRATION AND DISCIPLINARY BOARD

The IDFPR can and does enforce disciplinary sanctions by way of the Real Estate Administration and Disciplinary Board (READ). This board is the regulatory agency that oversees the application of licensing law in the state of Illinois. Its purpose is to protect the public by ensuring that real estate professionals, including brokers, managing brokers, and real estate firms, comply with the state's real estate laws and regulations.

The primary responsibility of the board is to conduct disciplinary proceedings and recommend sanctions on real estate professionals found to have violated state laws or regulations.

> "The Board recommends discipline for violations of the Real Estate Licensing Act of 2000; advises the Director on professional conduct, education requirements and industry trends." (Illinois.gov)

This board plays a significant role in ensuring that the real estate industry in Illinois operates fairly and ethically and that consumers are protected from fraud and other abuses. Disciplinary sanctions mean any action (being imposed upon a licensee) in response to licensee misconduct. The law defines sanctions as penalties, punishments, and other kinds of enforcement that are implemented to incentivize individuals and companies to adhere to the law, rules, and regulations.

With minimal exception, individuals and entities can only legally practice real estate in Illinois if they have a license from the IDFPR. The exceptions to this rule are discussed later in the chapter. Without a license, the practice of real estate in the state is illegal. Here is what The Act says about this in 225 ILCS 454:

> Unlicensed practice; civil penalty. (a) Any person who practices, offers to practice, attempts to practice, or holds oneself out to practice as a managing broker, broker, or residential leasing agent without being licensed under this Act shall, in addition to any other penalty provided by law, pay a civil penalty to the Department in an amount not to exceed $25,000 for each offense as determined by the Department. The civil penalty shall be assessed by the Department after a hearing is held in accordance with the provisions set forth in this Act regarding the provision of a hearing for the discipline of a license. (b) The Department has the authority and power to investigate any and all unlicensed activity. (c) The civil penalty shall be paid within 60 days after the effective date of the order imposing the civil penalty. The order shall constitute a judgment and may be filed and execution had thereon in the same manner from any court of record.

What is the composition of the Real Estate Administrative And Disciplinary Board? The Illinois Appointments government website explains it like this:

The Board shall be composed of fifteen persons appointed by the Governor. Members shall be appointed to the Board subject to the following conditions:

1. All members shall have been residents and citizens of this State for at least six years prior to the date of appointment.

2. Twelve members shall have been actively engaged as managing brokers or brokers or both for at least the 10 years prior to the appointment, two of whom must possess an active pre-license instructor license.

3. Three members of the Board shall be public members who represent consumer interests. None of these members shall be

    a. a person who is licensed under this Act or a similar Act of another jurisdiction,

    b. the spouse or family member of a licensee,

    c. a person who has an ownership interest in a real estate brokerage business, or

    d. a person the Department determines to have any other connection with a real estate brokerage business or a licensee. (Illinois.gov https://www2.illinois.gov/sites/bac/SitePages/AppointmentsDetail.aspx?BCID=971)

Concerning the Real Estate Administrative And Disciplinary Board, 225 ILCS 454/25-10 of The Act states:

"The members' terms shall be for 4 years and until a successor is appointed. No member shall be reappointed to the board for a term that would cause the member's cumulative service to the board to exceed 10 years. Appointments to fill vacancies shall be for the unexpired portion of the term. Those members of the board that satisfy the requirements of paragraph (2) shall be chosen in a manner such that no area of the state shall be unreasonably represented. In making the appointments, the governor shall give due consideration to the recommendations by members and organizations of the profession. The governor may terminate the appointment of any member for cause that in the opinion of the governor reasonably justifies the termination. Cause for termination shall include without limitation misconduct, incapacity, neglect of duty, or missing 4 board meetings during any one fiscal year. Each member of the board may receive a per diem stipend in an amount to be determined by the secretary. While engaged in the performance of duties, each member shall be reimbursed for necessary expenses. Such compensation and expenses shall be paid out of the real estate license administration fund. The secretary shall consider the recommendations of the board on questions involving standards of professional conduct, discipline, education, and policies and procedures under this act. With regard to this subject matter, the secretary may establish temporary or permanent committees of the board and may consider the recommendations of the board on matters that include, but are not limited to, criteria for the licensing and renewal of education providers, pre-license and continuing education instructors, pre-license and continuing education curricula, standards of educational criteria, and qualifications for licensure and renewal of professions, courses, and instructors. The department, after notifying and considering the recommendations of the board, if any, may issue rules, consistent with the provisions of this act, for the administration and enforcement thereof and may prescribe forms that shall be used in connection therewith. Eight board members shall constitute a quorum. A quorum is required for all board decisions. A vacancy in the membership of the board shall not impair the right of a quorum to exercise all of the rights and perform all of the duties of the board. The board shall elect annually, at its first meeting of the fiscal year, a vice chairperson who shall preside, with voting privileges, at meetings when the chairperson is not present. Members of the board shall be immune from suit in an action based upon any disciplinary proceedings or other acts performed in good faith as members of the board." (225 ILCS 454/25-10)

Is there a statute of limitations? Yes. As outlined in 225 ILCS 454/20-115, the IDFPR is permitted to take action against violators within five years following the recorded date of the alleged violation.

> "Time limit on action. No action may be taken by the Department against any person for violation of the terms of this Act or its rules unless the action is commenced within five years after the occurrence of the alleged violation. This limitation shall not apply where it is alleged that an initial application for licensure under this Act contains false or misleading information." (225 ILCS 454/20-115).-

The IDFPR operates with transparency. In fact, there is a monthly report of all people who have been subject to disciplinary actions. It covers a wide variety of professions. Take a moment to view the most recent month now. When you arrive on the site, you will see a list of years. Click on the current year. On the next page, click the most recent month. A new page will open. It is a PDF that has a list of regulated professions. Under each profession will be a list of individuals who were disciplined in that month. It shows their names, registered cities, and violations. Although some violations may include the amount of the monetary fine imposed, the Department does not always publicly release that information.

https://idfpr.illinois.gov/news/disciplines/discreports.html

The Real Estate Recovery Fund

As you learned earlier, the Real Estate Recovery Fund primarily focuses on consumers who are victims of licensees' actions that were unethical, immoral, and/or harmful that caused actual financial harm.

225 ILCS 454/20-90 of The Act shares information about the procedure of the Real Estate Recovery Fund:

> "(a) No action for a judgment that subsequently results in a post-judgment order for collection from the Real Estate Recovery Fund shall be started later than two years after the date on which the aggrieved person knew, or through the use of reasonable diligence should have known, of the acts or omissions giving rise to a right of recovery from the Real Estate Recovery Fund.
>
> (b) When any aggrieved person commences action for a judgment that may result in collection from the Real Estate Recovery Fund, the aggrieved person must name as parties defendant to that action any and all licensees, their employees, or independent contractors who allegedly committed or are responsible for acts or omissions giving rise to a right of recovery from the Real Estate Recovery Fund. Failure to name as parties defendant such licensees, their employees, or independent contractors shall preclude recovery from the

Real Estate Recovery Fund of any portion of any judgment received in such an action. These parties' defendants shall also include any corporations, limited liability companies, partnerships, registered limited liability partnership, or other business associations licensed under this Act that may be responsible for acts giving rise to a right of recovery from the Real Estate Recovery Fund.

(c) (Blank).

(d) When any aggrieved person commences action for a judgment that may result in collection from the Real Estate Recovery Fund, and the aggrieved person is unable to obtain legal and proper service upon the parties defendant licensed under this Act under the provisions of Illinois law concerning service of process in civil actions, the aggrieved person may petition the court where the action to obtain judgment was begun for an order to allow service of legal process on the Secretary. Service of process on the Secretary shall be taken and held in that court to be as valid and binding as if due service had been made upon the parties defendant licensed under this Act. In case any process mentioned in this Section is served upon the Secretary, the Secretary shall forward a copy of the process by certified mail to the licensee's last address on record with the Department. Any judgment obtained after service of process on the Secretary under this Act shall apply to and be enforceable against the Real Estate Recovery Fund only. The Department may intervene in and defend any such action.

(e) (Blank).

(f) The aggrieved person shall give written notice to the Department within 30 days of the entry of any judgment that may result in collection from the Real Estate Recovery Fund. The aggrieved person shall provide the Department with 20 days prior written notice of all supplementary proceedings so as to allow the Department to intervene and participate in all efforts to collect on the judgment in the same manner as any party.

(g) When any aggrieved person recovers a valid judgment in any court of competent jurisdiction in an action in which the court has found the aggrieved person to be injured or otherwise damaged by any licensee or an unlicensed employee of any licensee as a result of fraud, misrepresentation, discrimination, or deceit or intentional violation of this Act by the licensee or the unlicensed employee of the licensee, the aggrieved person may, upon the termination of all proceedings, including review and appeals in connection with the judgment, file a verified claim in the court in which the judgment was entered and, upon 30 days' written notice to the Department, and to the person against whom the judgment was obtained, may apply to the court for a post-judgment order directing payment from the Real Estate Recovery Fund of the amount unpaid upon the judgment, not including interest on the judgment, and subject to the limitations stated in Section

20-85 of this Act. The aggrieved person must set out in that verified claim and subsequently prove at an evidentiary hearing to be held by the court upon the application that the claim meets all requirements of Section 20-85 and this Section to be eligible for payment from the Real Estate Recovery Fund. The aggrieved party shall be required to show that the aggrieved person:

1. Is not a spouse of the debtor or debtors or the personal representative of such spouse.

2. Has complied with all the requirements of this Section.

3. Has obtained a judgment stating the amount thereof and the amount owing thereon, not including interest thereon, at the date of the application.

4. Has shown evidence of the amount of attorney's fees sought to be recovered and the reasonableness of those fees up to the maximum allowed pursuant to Section 20-85 of this Act. An affidavit from the aggrieved party's attorney shall be sufficient evidence of the attorney's fees incurred.

(h) If, after conducting the evidentiary hearing required under this Section, the court finds the aggrieved party has satisfied the requirements of Section 20-85 and this Section, the court shall, in a post-judgment order directed to the Department, order payment from the Real Estate Recovery Fund in the amount of the unpaid balance of the aggrieved party's judgment subject to and in accordance with the limitations contained in Section 20-85 of this Act.

(i) If the Department pays from the Real Estate Recovery Fund any amount in settlement of a claim or toward satisfaction of a judgment against any licensee or an unlicensed employee of a licensee, the licensee's license shall be automatically revoked upon the issuance of a post-judgment order authorizing payment from the Real Estate Recovery Fund. No petition for restoration of a license shall be heard until repayment has been made in full, plus interest at the rate prescribed in Section 12-109 of the Code of Civil Procedure of the amount paid from the Real Estate Recovery Fund on their account, notwithstanding any provision to the contrary in Section 2105-15 of the Department of Professional Regulation Law of the Civil Administrative Code of Illinois. A discharge in bankruptcy shall not relieve a person from the penalties and disabilities provided in this subsection (i).

(j) If, at any time, the money deposited in the Real Estate Recovery Fund is insufficient to satisfy any duly authorized claim or portion thereof, the Department shall, when sufficient money has been deposited in the Real Estate Recovery Fund, satisfy such unpaid claims or portions thereof, in the order that such claims or portions thereof were originally filed, plus accumulated interest at the rate prescribed in Section 12-109 of the Code of Civil

Procedure, provided that amount does not exceed the limits set forth in rules adopted by the Department."

As a consumer, the maximum coverage you can receive from the Recovery Fund is $50,000, but this is only possible if you have lost actual money due to the actions of the licensee.

The Act further states:

"A special fund to be known as the Real Estate Recovery Fund is created in the State Treasury. All fines and penalties received by the Department pursuant to Article 20 of this Act shall be deposited into the State Treasury and held in the Real Estate Recovery Fund. The money in the Real Estate Recovery Fund shall be used by the Department exclusively for carrying out the purposes established by this Act. If, at any time, the balance remaining in the Real Estate Recovery Fund is less than $750,000, the State Treasurer shall cause a transfer of moneys to the Real Estate Recovery Fund from the Real Estate License Administration Fund in an amount necessary to establish a balance of $800,000 in the Real Estate Recovery Fund. These funds may be invested and reinvested in the same manner as authorized for pension funds in Article 1 of the Illinois Pension Code. All earnings, interest, and dividends received from investment of funds in the Real Estate Recovery Fund shall be deposited into the Real Estate License Administration Fund and shall be used for the same purposes as other moneys deposited in the Real Estate License Administration Fund." (225 ILCS 454/25-35)

In addition, ten dollars of every licensee's initial application fee is deposited to the Recovery Fund as the candidate's contribution. Further, to ensure the fund remains viable, all fines levied against licensed and unlicensed individuals who have violated The Act are to be directly deposited to the Recovery Fund.

WHAT ACTIONS REQUIRE AN ILLINOIS REAL ESTATE LICENSE? ARE THERE EXEMPTIONS?

Earlier in this book, you read how The Act defines a broker. Let's review it now. Each of the actions listed below that results in compensation requires a real estate license, whether it is that of a broker or a managing broker. (As a reminder, compensation is defined by The Act in Chapter 8.) Pay special attention to each of the *actions* in the list below.

"Broker" means an individual, entity, corporation, foreign or domestic partnership, limited liability company, registered limited liability partnership, or other business entity other than a residential leasing agent who, whether in person or through any media or technology, for another and for compensation, or with the intention or expectation of receiving compensation, either directly or indirectly:

1. Sells, exchanges, purchases, rents, or leases real estate.

2. Offers to sell, exchange, purchase, rent, or lease real estate.

3. Negotiates, offers, attempts, or agrees to negotiate the sale, exchange, purchase, rental, or leasing of real estate.

4. Lists, offers, attempts, or agrees to list real estate for sale, rent, lease, or exchange.

5. Whether for another or themselves, engages in a pattern of business of buying, selling, offering to buy or sell, marketing for sale, exchanging, or otherwise dealing in contracts, including assignable contracts for the purchase or sale of, or options on real estate or improvements thereon. For purposes of this definition, an individual or entity will be found to have engaged in a pattern of business if the individual or entity by itself or with any combination of other individuals or entities, whether as partners or common owners in another entity, has engaged in one or more of these practices on two or more occasions in any twelve-month period.

6. Supervises the collection, offer, attempt, or agreement to collect rent for the use of real estate.

7. Advertises or represents himself or herself as being engaged in the business of buying, selling, exchanging, renting, or leasing real estate.

8. Assists or directs in procuring or referring of leads or prospects, intended to result in the sale, exchange, lease, or rental of real estate.

9. Assists or directs in the negotiation of any transaction intended to result in the sale, exchange, lease, or rental of real estate.

10. Opens real estate to the public for marketing purposes.

11. Sells, rents, leases, or offers for sale or lease real estate at auction. (225 ILCS 454/1-10)

Those actions above can *only* be performed by a real estate licensee in the State of Illinois. If he or she is not an Illinois real estate licensee, each action above that results in compensation is illegal.

However, there are exemptions from the license requirement. The Act illustrates them in detail in section 225 ILCS 454/5-20, which states:

"Exemptions from managing broker, broker, or residential leasing agent license requirement; Department exemption from education provider and related licenses. The requirement for holding a license under this Article 5 shall not apply to:

1. Any person, as defined in Section 1-10, that as owner or lessor performs any of the acts described in the definition of "broker" under Section 1-10 of this Act with reference to property owned or leased by it, or to the regular employees thereof with respect to the property so owned or leased, where such acts are performed in the regular course of or as an incident to the management, sale, or other disposition of such property and the investment therein, if such regular employees do not perform any of the acts described in the definition of "broker" under Section 1-10 of this Act in connection with a vocation of selling or leasing any real estate or the improvements thereon not so owned or leased.

2. An attorney in fact acting under a duly executed and recorded power of attorney to convey real estate from the owner or lessor or the services rendered by an attorney at law in the performance of the attorney's duty as an attorney at law.

3. Any person acting as receiver, trustee in bankruptcy, administrator, executor, or guardian or while acting under a court order or under the authority of a will or testamentary trust.

4. Any person acting as a resident manager for the owner or any employee acting as the resident manager for a broker managing an apartment building, duplex, or apartment complex, when the resident manager resides on the premises, the premises is his or her primary residence, and the resident manager is engaged in the leasing of the property of which he or she is the resident manager.

5. Any officer or employee of a federal agency in the conduct of official duties.

6. Any officer or employee of the State government or any political subdivision thereof performing official duties.

7. Any multiple listing service or other similar information exchange that is engaged in the collection and dissemination of information concerning real estate available for sale, purchase, lease, or exchange for the purpose of providing licensees with a system by which licensees may cooperatively share information, along with which no other licensed activities, as defined in Section 1-10 of this Act, are provided.

8. Railroads and other public utilities regulated by the State of Illinois, or the officers or full-time employees thereof, unless the performance of any licensed activities is in

connection with the sale, purchase, lease, or other disposition of real estate or investment therein that does not require the approval of the appropriate State regulatory authority.

9. Any medium of advertising in the routine course of selling or publishing advertising, along with which no other licensed activities, as defined in Section 1-10 of this Act, are provided.

10. Any resident lessee of a residential dwelling unit who refers for compensation to the owner of the dwelling unit, or to the owner's agent, prospective lessees of dwelling units in the same building or complex as the resident lessee's unit, but only if the resident lessee (i) refers no more than three prospective lessees in any 12-month period, (ii) receives compensation of no more than $5,000 or the equivalent of two months' rent, whichever is less, in any 12-month period, and (iii) limits his or her activities to referring prospective lessees to the owner, or the owner's agent, and does not show a residential dwelling unit to a prospective lessee, discuss terms or conditions of leasing a dwelling unit with a prospective lessee, or otherwise participate in the negotiation of the leasing of a dwelling unit.

11. The purchase, sale, or transfer of a timeshare or similar vacation item or interest, vacation club membership, or other activity formerly regulated under the Real Estate Timeshare Act of 1999 (repealed).

12. (Blank).

13. Any person who is licensed without examination under Section 10-25 (now repealed) of the Auction License Act is exempt from holding a managing broker's or broker's license under this Act for the limited purpose of selling or leasing real estate at auction, so long as:

   a. that person has made an application for said exemption by July 1, 2000

   b. that person verifies to the Department that he or she has sold real estate at auction for a period of five years prior to licensure as an auctioneer

   c. the person has had no lapse in his or her license as an auctioneer; and

   d. the license issued under the Auction License Act has not been disciplined for violation of those provisions of Article 20 of the Auction License Act dealing with or related to the sale or lease of real estate at auction

14. A person who holds a valid license under the Auction License Act and a valid real estate auction certification and conducts auctions for the sale of real estate under Section 5-32 of this Act.

15. A hotel operator who is registered with the Illinois Department of Revenue and pays taxes under the Hotel Operators' Occupation Tax Act and rents a room or rooms in a hotel as defined in the Hotel Operators' Occupation Tax Act for a period of not more than 30 consecutive days and not more than 60 days in a calendar year or a person who participates in an online marketplace enabling persons to rent out all or part of the person's owned residence.

16. Notwithstanding any provisions to the contrary, the Department and its employees shall be exempt from education, course provider, instructor, and course license requirements and fees while acting in an official capacity on behalf of the Department. Courses offered by the Department shall be eligible for continuing education credit (225 ILCS 454/5-20).

While there are sixteen exemptions detailed in The Act, the first four exemptions are typically the content covered in the exam questions.

WHAT ARE THE LICENSE CATEGORIES AND EACH ONE'S REQUIREMENTS?

The Act holds three categories of real estate licenses in Illinois. They are:

1. Broker

2. Managing broker

3. Residential leasing agent

Broker's License Requirements

As you previously read, a broker is someone or an entity who represents sellers and/or buyers of real estate or real property. The sellers and buyers could be individuals, companies, or firms. This action is done for a commission. The broker, generally, represents the owner. In some states, a broker has the option to work independently, however, as this category is the entry-level license for Illinois, a broker must always be sponsored by and work under the supervision of a sponsoring broker.

The Act lays out the exact requirements for licensure as a broker in 225 ILCS 454/5-27. They are:

A. Every applicant for licensure as a broker must meet the following qualifications:

1. Be at least 18 years of age

2. Be of good moral character

3. Successfully complete a four-year course of study in a high school or secondary school approved by the state in which the school is located, or possess a high school equivalency certificate, which shall be verified under oath by the applicant

4. Provide satisfactory evidence of having completed 75 hours of instruction in real estate courses approved by the Department, 15 hours of which must consist of situational and case studies presented in the classroom or by live, interactive webinar or online distance education courses

5. Personally take and pass a written examination authorized by the Department

6. Present a valid application for issuance of a license accompanied by the fees specified by rule

B. The requirements specified in items (3) and (5) of subsection (a) of this Section do not apply to applicants who are currently admitted to practice law by the Supreme Court of Illinois and are currently in active standing.

C. No applicant shall engage in any of the activities covered by this Act until a valid sponsorship has been registered with the Department.

D. All licenses should be readily available to the public at the licensee's place of business.

E. An individual holding an active license as a managing broker may, upon written request to the Department, permanently and irrevocably place his or her managing broker license on inactive status and shall be issued a broker's license in exchange. Any individual obtaining a broker's license under this subsection (e) shall be considered as having obtained a broker's license by education and passing the required test and shall be treated as such in determining compliance with this Act (225 ILCS 454/5-27).

Managing Broker's License Requirements

"'Managing broker' means a licensee who may be authorized to assume responsibilities as a designated managing broker for licensees in one or, in the case of a multi-office company, more than one office, upon appointment by the sponsoring broker and registration with the Department. A managing broker may act as his or her own sponsor" (225 ILCS 454/1-10). The majority of the time, managing brokers have more training and expertise than brokers do. For example, it's common that a managing broker will handle more advanced, technical, and/or complicated parts of a transaction.

The Act lays out the exact requirements for licensure as a managing broker in 225 ILCS 454/5-28. It states:

A. A. Every applicant for licensure as a managing broker must meet the following qualifications:

1. be at least 20 years of age;

2. be of good moral character;

3. have been licensed at least two consecutive years out of the preceding three years as a broker;

4. successfully complete a four-year course of study in high school or secondary school approved by the state in which the school is located, or a high school equivalency certificate, which shall be verified under oath by the applicant;

5. provide satisfactory evidence of having completed at least 165 hours, 120 of which shall be those hours required pre-licensure and post-licensure to obtain a broker's license, and 45 additional hours completed within the year immediately preceding the filing of an application for a managing broker's license, which hours shall focus on brokerage administration and management and residential leasing agent management and include at least 15 hours in the classroom or by live, interactive webinar or online distance education courses;

6. personally take and pass a written examination authorized by the Department; and

7. submit a valid application for issuance of a license accompanied by the fees specified by rule. The requirements specified in item (5) of subsection (a) of this Section do not apply to applicants who are currently admitted to practice law by the Supreme Court of Illinois and are currently in active standing. (225 ILCS 454/5-28)

Residential Leasing Agent's License Requirements

As you know, a residential leasing agent is a licensee who is employed by a sponsoring broker to engage in licensed activities limited to leasing *residential* real estate. Any leasing of *commercial* properties always requires a broker's or managing broker's license. The Act shares the exact requirements for licensure as a managing residential leasing agent in 225 ILCS 454/5-10. It states:

A. A. Every applicant for licensure as a residential leasing agent must meet the following qualifications:

1. be at least 18 years of age;

2. be of good moral character;

3. successfully complete a four-year course of study in a high school or secondary school or an equivalent course of study approved by the state in which the school is located, or possess a high school equivalency certificate, which shall be verified under oath by the applicant;

4. personally take and pass a written examination authorized by the Department sufficient to demonstrate the applicant's knowledge of the provisions of this Act relating to residential leasing agents and the applicant's competence to engage in the activities of a licensed residential leasing agent;

5. provide satisfactory evidence of having completed 15 hours of instruction in an approved course of study relating to the leasing of residential real property. The Board may recommend to the Department the number of hours each topic of study shall require. The course of study shall, among other topics, cover the provisions of this Act applicable to residential leasing agents; fair housing and human rights issues relating to residential leasing; advertising and marketing issues; leases, applications, and credit and criminal background reports; owner-tenant relationships and owner-tenant laws; the handling of funds; and environmental issues relating to residential real property;

6. complete any other requirements as set forth by rule; and

7. present a valid application for issuance of an initial license accompanied by fees specified by rule.

B. No applicant shall engage in any of the activities covered by this Act without a valid license and until a valid sponsorship has been registered with the Department.

C. Successfully completed course work, completed pursuant to the requirements of this Section, may be applied to the course work requirements to obtain a managing broker's or broker's license as provided by rule. The Board may recommend to the Department and the Department may adopt requirements for approved courses, course content, and the approval of courses, instructors, and education providers, as well as education provider and instructor fees. The Department may establish continuing education requirements for residential licensed leasing agents, by rule, consistent with the language and intent of this Act, with the advice of the Board.

D. The continuing education requirement for residential leasing agents shall consist of a single core curriculum to be prescribed by the Department as recommended by the Board. Leasing agents shall be required to complete no less than eight hours of continuing education in the core curriculum for each two-year renewal period. The curriculum shall, at a minimum, consist of a single course or courses on the subjects of fair housing and human rights issues related to residential leasing, advertising and marketing issues, leases, applications, credit reports, and criminal history, the handling of funds, owner-tenant relationships and owner-tenant laws, and environmental issues relating to residential real estate (225 ILCS 454/5-10).

Like the other licenses, a "licensed residential leasing agent must be sponsored and employed by a sponsoring broker." (225 ILCS 454/5-5b) This is under the supervision of a designated managing broker.

One aspect that sets this license apart from the other two licenses is found in this excerpt from The Act:

> "Notwithstanding any other provisions of this Act to the contrary, a person may engage in residential leasing activities for which a license is required under this Act, for a period of 120 consecutive days without being licensed, so long as the person is acting under the supervision of a sponsoring broker, the sponsoring broker has notified the Department that the person is pursuing licensure under this Section, and the person has enrolled in the residential leasing agent pre-license education course no later than 60 days after beginning to engage in residential leasing activities. During the 120-day period all requirements of Sections 5-10 and 5-65 of this Act with respect to education, successful completion of an examination, and the payment of all required fees must be satisfied. The Department may adopt rules to ensure that the provisions of this subsection are not used in a manner that enables an unlicensed person to repeatedly or continually engage in activities for which a license is required under this Act ."(225 ILCS 454/5-5d)

ARE CORPORATIONS, PARTNERSHIPS, AND LLCS REQUIRED TO HAVE A LICENSE?

Corporations, partnerships and LLCs involved in the real estate industry are required to have a real estate license in order to operate legally.

In 225 ILCS 454/5-15, The Act states:

> Necessity of managing broker, broker, or residential leasing agent license; ownership restrictions.

> A. It is unlawful for any person, as defined in Section 1-10, to act as a managing broker, broker, or residential leasing agent or to advertise or assume to act as such managing broker, broker or residential leasing agent without a license issued in accordance with this Act and a valid sponsorship registered with the Department, either directly or through its authorized designee.

B. No corporation shall be granted a license or engage in the business or capacity, either directly or indirectly, of a broker, unless every officer of the corporation who actively participates in the real estate activities of the corporation holds a license as a managing broker or broker and unless every employee who acts as a managing broker, broker, or residential leasing agent for the corporation holds a license as a managing broker, broker, or residential leasing agent. All nonparticipating owners or officers shall submit affidavits of nonparticipation as required by the Department. No corporation shall be granted a license if any nonparticipating owner or officer has previously been publicly disciplined by the Department resulting in that licensee being currently barred from real estate practice because of a suspension or revocation.

C. No partnership shall be granted a license or engage in the business or serve in the capacity, either directly or indirectly, of a broker, unless every partner in the partnership who actively participates in the real estate activities of the partnership holds a license as a managing broker or broker and unless every employee who acts as a managing broker, broker, or residential leasing agent for the partnership holds a license as a managing broker, broker, or residential leasing agent. All nonparticipating partners shall submit affidavits of nonparticipation as required by the Department. In the case of a registered limited liability partnership (LLP), every partner in the LLP that actively participates in the real estate activities of the limited liability partnership must hold a license as a managing broker or broker and every employee who acts as a managing broker, broker, or residential leasing agent must hold a license as a managing broker, broker, or residential leasing agent. All nonparticipating limited liability partners shall submit affidavits of nonparticipation as required by the Department. No partnership shall be granted a license if any nonparticipating partner has previously been publicly disciplined by the Department resulting in that licensee being currently barred from real estate practice because of a suspension or revocation.

D. No limited liability company shall be granted a license or engage in the business or serve in the capacity, either directly or indirectly, of a broker unless every member or manager in the limited liability company that actively participates in the real estate activities of the limited liability company holds a license as a managing broker or broker and unless every other member and employee who acts as a managing broker, broker, or residential leasing agent for the limited liability company holds a license as a managing broker, broker, or residential leasing agent. All nonparticipating members or managers shall submit affidavits of nonparticipation as required by the Department. No limited liability company shall be granted a license if any nonparticipating member or manager has previously been publicly disciplined by the

Department resulting in that licensee being currently barred from real estate practice because of a suspension or revocation.

E. (Blank).

F. No person, partnership, or business entity shall be granted a license if any owner, officer, director, partner, limited liability partner, member, or manager has been denied a real estate license by the Department in the previous five years or is otherwise currently barred from real estate practice because of a suspension or revocation.

THE ILLINOIS REAL ESTATE LICENSE EXAM AND WHAT YOU CAN EXPECT

The state-authorized testing body works to make the license exam convenient for all candidates. You now have the option to take the exam remotely (from a location of your choice), or at a defined facility. Currently, remote testing is available 24/7. On-site testing is limited to Monday through Friday, usually during the morning hours.

The exam is administered via a computer and is comprised of two segments:

1. A 100-question national exam covering content areas applicable throughout much of the country. You will be given 150 minutes to complete this segment. The minimum score to pass is 70%.

2. A 40-question exam that is state-specific. You will be given 90 minutes to complete this segment. The minimum score to pass is 75%.

The two exam segments may not be taken separately for the first sitting. Both must be completed in the first sitting. You must be prepared to answer 105 questions on the national exam and up to 50 questions on the state-specific exam. These additional questions that will be discarded before scoring. This is done to test the application of newly written questions before they're officially added to the active test bank.

Before taking the license exam, a candidate must:

- Have completed the 75-hour broker pre-license course

- Register and pay in advance

On the day of the exam (on-site), candidates must bring two forms of identification and each form must have the same name. One must be an ID issued by the government and the second ID must have your signature. Examples include a driver's license, passport, a US social security card, debit card with signature on back, credit card with signature on back, and/or a green card. Additionally, each candidate needs to bring a non-programmable, non-scientific calculator. (Some sites may provide calculators.) Beyond a calculator and IDs, candidates may only take his or her wallet, purse, and keys into the testing room. No smartphones, cell phones, or watches are permitted inside the testing room.

When a candidate finishes the exam, he/she immediately receives written notification regarding whether he or she passed or failed. A passed exam report does not provide the actual score the candidate achieved. It merely states passed or failed. Only notifications showing a failed exam display the candidate's score. The failed notification will list the eleven areas the national exam covered and how the candidate fared in each area. This allows the candidate to determine which content he or she needs to review in order to pass the exam in the future. A candidate can retake the exam again up to three times maximum. The exam cannot be taken twice on the same day. When a candidate fails the fourth time, he/she is required to do the pre-license course again prior to re-registering for the exam in the future.

With a pass notification, the candidates also will be able to read about the next step, which is to activate his or her real estate license via IDFPR's online portal. Candidates who passed both segments only have twelve months to activate their licenses. After twelve months, if a candidate has not activated the license, he/she must retake the entire exam. In order to activate the license, the candidate must have a sponsoring broker willing to sponsor him/her.

After passing the exam:

- The candidate logs in and creates his or her online portal

- The named designated managing broker will receive an email asking for verification that the candidate will be joining the office

- Once confirmed by the designated managing broker, the state will produce the license and notify the licensee via email that the license is now ready to be downloaded

- The licensee should then download the license and provide a copy to the designated managing broker

  - The license printout will display his or her name, the name of the designated sponsoring broker, and which type of license is held.

  - The license is public record. Any person can search online and find out whether or not someone actually has a real estate license.

- The new licensee is required to carry a digital or physical copy of the license on his or her person

- The licensee may have multiple copies of the license. For example, some licensees have a copy at home, at the office, and in the glovebox of their vehicles.

LICENSE EXPIRATION AND LICENSE RENEWAL

Real estate licenses in Illinois are required to be renewed every two years. Licenses can be renewed within 90 days of the expiration date of the broker's license. Continuing education requirements must be met as well as the fee must be paid. Education requirements are released by the IDFPR. Once a broker completes the necessary education requirements, he/she is to submit his or her license renewal application, along with Illinois' licensing fee of $150 to the license renewal portal on the IDFPR website. (The managing broker renewal fee is $200.) The license renewal process can take up to two to five hours to show on the website depending on the volume the website is receiving. For licensees who renew after the deadline, the late fee is $50.

First renewal of a broker's license: The first renewal is different. The broker is required to complete forty-five hours of post-license education (online or in person), as established by the IDFPR. The forty-five-hour course is composed of three separate fifteen-hour courses. Class one is transactional issues. Class two is risk management and discipline. Class three is applied broker principles. All three courses must be completed in order for the licensee's first renewal to take place and be effective.

Real estate broker and real estate leasing agent renewals happen in even-numbered years. For managing brokers, the renewals occur in odd-numbered years.

The current renewal fees for an unexpired license for each category are:

- Broker: $150

- Managing broker: $200

- Residential leasing agent: $50

In order for a business entity or branch office renewal, it's important to know that licenses expire on October 31st (Halloween) in every even-numbered year. That's easy to remember because, like Halloween, it's scary if your license expires. *Note: Renewal fees and test fees are always subject to change.*

When is there no renewal fee due?

In 225 ILCS 454/5-50, The Act states the following: Expiration and renewal of managing broker, broker, or residential leasing agent license; sponsoring broker; register of licensees.

(a) The expiration date and renewal period for each license issued under this Act shall be set by rule. Except as otherwise provided in this Section, the holder of a license may renew the license within 90 days preceding the expiration date thereof by completing the continuing education required by this Act and paying the fees specified by the rule.

(b) An individual whose first license is that of a broker received on or after the effective date of this amendatory Act of the 101st General Assembly, must provide evidence of having completed 45 hours of post-license education presented in a classroom or a live, interactive webinar, or online distance education course, and which shall require passage of a final examination.

The Board may recommend, and the Department shall approve, 45 hours of post-license education, consisting of three 15-hour post-license courses, one each that covers applied brokerage principles, risk management/discipline, and transactional issues. Each of the courses shall require its own 50-question final examination, which shall be administered by the education provider that delivers the course.

Individuals whose first license is that of a broker received on or after the effective date of this amendatory Act of the 101st General Assembly, must complete all three 15-hour courses and successfully pass a course final examination for each course prior to the date of the next broker renewal deadline, except for those individuals who receive their first license within the 180 days preceding the next broker renewal deadline, who must complete all three 15-hour courses and successfully pass a course final examination for each course prior to the second broker renewal deadline that follows the receipt of their license.

(c) Any managing broker, broker, or residential leasing agent whose license under this Act has expired shall be eligible to renew the license during the 2-year period following the expiration date, provided the managing broker, broker, or residential leasing agent pays the fees as prescribed by rule and completes continuing education and other requirements provided for by the Act or by rule. A managing broker, broker, or residential leasing agent whose license has been expired for more than two years but less than five years may have it restored by (i) applying to the Department, (ii) paying the required fee, (iii) completing the continuing education requirements for the most recent pre-renewal period that ended prior to the date of the application for reinstatement, and (iv) filing acceptable proof of fitness to have his or her license restored, as set by rule. A managing broker, broker, or residential leasing agent whose license has been expired for more than five years shall be required to meet the requirements for a new license.

(d) Notwithstanding any other provisions of this Act to the contrary, any managing broker, broker, or residential leasing agent whose license expired while he or she was (i) on active duty with the Armed Forces of the United States or called into service or training by the state militia, (ii) engaged in training or education under the supervision of the United States preliminary to induction into military service, or (iii) serving as the Coordinator of Real Estate in the State of Illinois or as an employee of the Department may have his or her license renewed, reinstated or restored without paying any lapsed renewal fees if within two years after the termination of the service, training or education by furnishing the Department with satisfactory evidence of service, training, or education and it has been terminated under honorable conditions.

(e) Each licensee shall carry on his or her person his or her license or an electronic version thereof.

(f) The Department shall provide to the sponsoring broker a notice of renewal for all sponsored licensees by mailing the notice to the sponsoring broker's address of record, or, at the Department's discretion, emailing the notice to the sponsoring broker's email address of record.

(g) Upon request from the sponsoring broker, the Department shall make available to the sponsoring broker, by electronic means at the discretion of the Department, a listing of licensees under this Act who, according to the records of the Department, are sponsored by that broker. Every licensee associated with or employed by a broker whose license is revoked, suspended, or expired shall be considered inactive until such time as the sponsoring broker's license is reinstated or renewed, or the licensee changes employment as set forth in subsection (c) of Section 5-40 of this Act. (225 ILCS 454/5-50)

LICENSE BY RECIPROCITY AND NON-ILLINOIS RESIDENT

In 225 ILCS 454/5-60 of The Act, it states:

Section 5-60. Managing broker licensed in another state; broker licensed in another state; reciprocal agreements; agent for service of process.

A. A managing broker's license may be issued by the Department to a managing broker or its equivalent licensed under the laws of another state of the United States, under the following conditions:

1. the managing broker holds a managing broker's license in a state that has entered into a reciprocal agreement with the Department;

2. the standards for that state for licensing as a managing broker are substantially equal to or greater than the minimum standards in the State of Illinois;

3. the managing broker has been actively practicing as a managing broker in the managing broker's state of licensure for a period of not less than two years, immediately prior to the date of application;

4. the managing broker furnishes the Department with a statement under seal of the proper licensing authority of the state in which the managing broker is licensed showing that the managing broker has an active managing broker's license, that the managing broker is in good standing, and that no complaints are pending against the managing broker in that state;

5. the managing broker passes a test on Illinois-specific real estate brokerage laws; and

6. the managing broker was licensed by an examination in the state that has entered into a reciprocal agreement with the Department.

B. A broker's license may be issued by the Department to a broker or its equivalent licensed under the laws of another state of the United States, under the following conditions:

1. the broker holds a broker's license in a state that has entered into a reciprocal agreement with the Department;

2. the standards for that state for licensing as a broker are substantially equivalent to or greater than the minimum standards in the State of Illinois;

3. (blank);

4. the broker furnishes the Department with a statement under seal of the proper licensing authority of the state in which the broker is licensed showing that the broker has an active broker's license, that the broker is in good standing, and that no complaints are pending against the broker in that state;

5. the broker passes a test on Illinois-specific real estate brokerage laws; and

6. the broker was licensed by an examination in a state that has entered into a reciprocal agreement with the Department.

C. (Blank).

D. D. As a condition precedent to the issuance of a license to a managing broker or broker pursuant to this Section, the managing broker or broker shall agree in writing to abide by all the provisions of this Act with respect to his or her real estate activities within the State of Illinois and submit to the jurisdiction of the Department as provided in this Act. The agreement shall be filed with the Department and shall remain in force for so long as the managing broker or broker is licensed by this State and thereafter with respect to acts or omissions committed while licensed as a managing broker or broker in this State.

E. Prior to the issuance of any license to any managing broker or broker pursuant to this Section, verification of active licensure issued for the conduct of such business in any other state must be filed with the Department by the managing broker or broker, and the same fees must be paid as provided in this Act for the obtaining of a managing broker's or broker's license in this State.

F. Licenses previously granted under reciprocal agreements with other states shall remain in force so long as the Department has a reciprocal agreement with the state that includes the requirements of this Section, unless that license is suspended, revoked, or terminated by the Department for any reason provided for suspension, revocation, or termination of a resident licensee's license. Licenses granted under reciprocal agreements may be renewed in the same manner as a resident's license.

G. Prior to the issuance of a license to a nonresident managing broker or broker, the managing broker or broker shall file with the Department, in a manner prescribed by the Department, a designation in writing that appoints the Secretary to act as his or her agent upon whom all judicial and other process or legal notices directed to the managing broker or broker may be served. Service upon the agent so designated shall be equivalent to personal service upon the licensee. Copies of the appointment, certified by the Secretary, shall be deemed sufficient evidence thereof and shall be admitted in evidence with the same force and effect as the original thereof might be admitted. In the written designation, the managing broker or broker shall agree that any lawful process against the licensee that is served upon the agent shall be of the same legal force and validity as if served upon the licensee and that the authority shall continue in force so long as any liability remains outstanding in this State. Upon the receipt of any process or notice, the Secretary shall forthwith deliver a copy of the same by regular mail or email to the last known business address or email address of the licensee.

H. Any person holding a valid license under this Section shall be eligible to obtain a managing broker's license or a broker's license without examination should that person change their state of domicile to Illinois and that person otherwise meets the qualifications for licensure under this (Act 225 ILCS 454/5-60).

States that share license reciprocity with Illinois are:

- Colorado: Broker license

- Connecticut: Salesperson and broker license

- Florida: Associate and broker license

- Georgia: Salesperson, associate broker, and broker license

- Indiana: Illinois and Indiana only share broker reciprocity (not managing broker)

- Nebraska: Salesperson and broker

- South Dakota: Broker associate and responsible broker

- Wisconsin: Salesperson and broker

While Illinois grants license reciprocity to real estate licensees from Iowa, Iowa does not extend reciprocity to Illinois licensees.

To ensure that you have the most accurate and up-to-date information about reciprocity between states and other relevant details contained within this book, it is recommended that you refer to the IDFPR website for new updates and changes. Keep in mind that reciprocity agreements can change over time, so it is always a best practice to check with the relevant state licensing boards to obtain the most current information available.

What Does a License Cost?

Section 1450.130 of the Rules And Regulations, labeled Fees, conveys:

a. Residential Leasing Agent License and Residential Leasing Agent Student

   1. The application fee for an initial residential leasing agent license is $75.

   2. The renewal fee for an unexpired residential leasing agent license is $50 per year.

   3. The late fee for a residential leasing agent license expired for no more than two years is $50.

   4. The application fee for a residential leasing agent permit is$25.

   5. The restoration fee for a residential leasing agent license expired for more than two years but less than five years is the sum of all lapsed renewal and late fees.

6. A person receiving an initial license during the first renewal period shall not be required to pay the initial renewal fee and will be issued a license expiring on the second renewal deadline.

b. Broker License

1. The application fee for an initial broker license is $150.

2. The renewal fee for an unexpired broker license is $200 per renewal.

3. The late fee for a broker license expired for no more than two years is $75.

4. The restoration fee for a broker license expired for more than two years but less than five years is the sum of all lapsed renewal and late fees.

5. The fee to transfer from a managing broker license to a broker license is $150.

6. A person receiving an initial license within the first renewal period shall not be required to pay the initial renewal fee and will be issued a license expiring on the second renewal deadline.

c. Managing Broker License

1. The application fee for an initial managing broker license is $175.

2. The renewal fee for an unexpired managing broker license is $250 per renewal.

3. The late fee for a managing broker license expired for no more than two years is $75.

4. The restoration fee for a managing broker license expired for more than two years but less than five years is the sum of all lapsed renewal and late fees.

5. A person receiving an initial license during the first renewal period shall not be required to pay the initial renewal fee and will be issued a license expiring on the second renewal deadline.

d. Real Estate Auction Certification

1. The application fee for an initial real estate auction certification is $125.

2. The renewal fee for an unexpired real estate auction certification is $300 per renewal.

3. The late fee for a real estate auction certification expired for no more than 2 years is $75.

4. A person receiving an initial certificate during the first renewal period shall not be required to pay the initial renewal fee and will be issued a certificate expiring on the second renewal deadline.

e. Corporation, Limited Liability Company, Partnership, Limited Partnership, or Limited Liability Partnership License

1. The application fee for an initial corporation, limited liability company, partnership, limited partnership, or limited liability partnership license is $250.

2. The renewal fee for an unexpired corporation, limited liability company, partnership, limited partnership, or limited liability partnership license is $300 per renewal.

3. The late fee for a corporation, limited liability company, partnership, limited partnership, or limited liability partnership license expired for no more than two years is $75.

4. An entity receiving its initial license during the first renewal period shall not be required to pay the initial renewal fee and will be issued a license expiring on the second renewal deadline.

f. Education Provider, Pre-license Instructor and Course License Fees

1. The application fee for an initial education provider license is $1,050.

2. The renewal fee for an unexpired education provider license is $1,100 per renewal.

3. The late fee for an education provider license expired for no more than 2 years is $75.

4. The application fee for an initial pre-license instructor license is $150.

5. The renewal fee for an unexpired pre-license instructor license is $300 per renewal.

6. The late fee for a pre-license instructor license expired for no more than 2 years is $75.

7. The application fee for an initial pre-license course license is $150.

8. The application fee for a revised format pre-license course license is $150.

9. The renewal fee for an unexpired pre-license course license is $150 per renewal.

10. The late fee for a pre-license course license expired for no more than 2 years is $75.

11. The application fee for an initial post-license course license is $150.

12. The application fee for a revised format post-license course license is $150.

13. The renewal fee for an unexpired post-license course license is $150 per renewal.

14. The late fee for a post-license course license expired for no more than 2 years is $75.

15. An education provider, pre-license instructor, pre-license course, or post-license course receiving an initial license during the renewal period shall not be required to pay the initial renewal fee and will be issued a license expiring on the second renewal deadline.

g. Continuing Education, Instructor, and Course License Fees

1. The application fee for an initial CE instructor license is $100.

2. The renewal fee for an unexpired CE instructor license is $200 per renewal.

3. The late fee for a CE instructor license expired for no more than 2 years is $75.

4. The application fee for an initial CE course license is $150.

5. The application fee for a revised format CE course license is $150.

6. The renewal fee for an unexpired CE course license is $150 per renewal.

7. The late fee for a CE course license expired for no more than 2 years is $75.

8. A CE instructor or CE course receiving an initial license during the renewal period shall not be required to pay the initial renewal fee and will be issued a license expiring on the second renewal deadline.

h. General

1. All fees paid pursuant to the Act and this Section shall be made payable to the Department of Financial and Professional Regulation and are non-refundable.

2. The fee for a certification of a licensee's record for any purpose is $35.

3. Applicants for an examination as a residential leasing agent, broker, managing broker, instructor, or real estate auction certification holder shall be required to pay the cost of taking the examination. If a designated testing service is utilized for the examination, the fee shall be paid directly to the designated testing service. Failure to appear for the examination on the scheduled date, at the time and place specified, after the applicant's application for examination has been received and acknowledged, shall result in the forfeiture of the examination fee.

4. The fee for requesting credit for CE obtained while out-of-state (see Section 5-75 of the Act) is $50.

5. The fee for processing a sponsorship transfer is $35.

6. The fee for a copy of a transcript of the proceedings under Section 20-62 of the Act is the cost of a copy of the transcript. A copy of the balance of the record will be provided at the Division's cost of producing the record.

7. The fee for certifying the record referred to in Section 20-73 of the Act is $1 per page.

8. The Division may charge an administrative fee, not to exceed $500, as a part of a compliance agreement issued with an administrative warning letter pursuant to Section 20-20 of the Act.

9. Each university, college, community college, or school supported by public funds in the State of Illinois shall be exempt from the education provider and course licensure fees, provided that the institution meets the following criteria and certifies to the Division that:

   a. The facility is domiciled and supported by public funds in the State of Illinois;

   b. The instructors are approved and licensed by the Department;

   c. The courses are approved and licensed by the Department; and

   d. The program, pre-license, and/or CE is not a for-profit division of the university, college, community college, or school. (Section 1450.130 of the Rules And Regulations)

What happens if a fee is not paid due to a declined transaction or bounced check? The Act in 225 ILCS 454/20-25 answers with the following:

"Returned checks and dishonored credit card charges; fees. Any person who (1) delivers a check or other payment to the Department that is returned to the Department unpaid by the financial institution upon which it is drawn shall pay to the Department; or (2) presents a credit or debit card for payment that is invalid or expired or against which charges by the Department are declined or dishonored, in addition to the amount already owed to the Department, a fee of $50. The Department shall notify the person that payment of fees and fines shall be paid to the Department by certified check or money order within 30 calendar days of the notification. If, after the expiration of 30 days from the date of the notification, the person has failed to submit the necessary remittance, the Department shall automatically revoke the license or deny the application, without hearing. If, after revocation or denial, the person seeks a license, he or she shall apply to the Department for restoration or issuance of the license and pay all fees and fines due to the Department. The Department may establish a fee for the processing of an application for restoration of a license to pay all expenses of processing this application. The Secretary may waive the fees due under this Section in individual cases where the Secretary finds that the fees would be unreasonable or unnecessarily burdensome." (225 ILCS 454/20-25)

CONTINUING EDUCATION

The real estate industry employs Continuing Education (CE) courses. These courses are required in order to facilitate a high quality of professionalism in the industry. In fact, they not only protect the consumers, but they also protect the industry and the licensees. Breaking license law can result in disciplinary action. CE is required to maintain a license in Illinois. The Act requires all licensees to complete continuing education with each renewal. Next, you'll read about the CE requirements for each of the three types of agents found in Illinois.

Residential leasing agents: For license renewal, each residential leasing agent is required to successfully complete the eight-hour Residential Leasing Agent Core class. In this course, the agent will learn about fair housing practices, disparate treatment, leasing agreements and disclosures, updates on criminal background checks, credit reports, license law, and other relevant need-to-know updates. Built into this course is a one-hour training on sexual harassment prevention.

Newly licensed brokers and managing brokers: For CE information concerning, see the chart below. On a regular basis, the IDFPR creates and publishes a summary of the continuing education requirements. The table below is adapted from their publication. In it, we remove the references to the exact years that the IDFPR publication includes.

CONTINUING EDUCATION (CE) FACT SHEET
REAL ESTATE BROKER & MANAGING BROKER RENEWAL

Broker	Managing Broker
Renewal dates: By April 30 on *even-numbered* years	Renewal dates: By April 30 on *odd-numbered* years
Prior to renewing a license, the licensee shall complete the required coursework as described below.	

First Renewal	All Subsequent Renewals
45-hour Post-license course	**24 Hours of Continuing Education**
Note: This includes the required 1-hour Sexual Harassment Prevention Training.	12 hours of broker management (Live)
All Subsequent Renewals	4 hours consisting of core subject matter (Live/LMS1)
12 Hours of Continuing Education	8 hours of elective subject matter (Live/LMS1/Home Study2)
4 hours consisting of core subject matter (Live/LMS1)	1 hour recognizing sexual harassment (Live/LMS1)
8 hours of elective subject matter (Live/LMS1/Home Study2)	*Sexual Harassment program can be* *used as an elective program.*
1 hour recognizing sexual harassment (Live/LMS1)	
Sexual Harassment program can be *used as an elective program.*	

1.LMS (Learning Management System): This is a computer-based presentation that provides module learning and has short quizzes that test the student's comprehension of the material presented.

2.Home study programs require a final exam consisting of twenty-five questions per every two hours of education.

Certification of Compliance with Continuing Education Requirements

1. Each renewal applicant must certify on the renewal application that they have satisfied the CE requirements.

2. Attorneys admitted to practice law pursuant to Illinois Supreme Court rule are exempt from CE and should certify on the renewal application that they have satisfied the CE requirements.

3. The Department may require additional evidence demonstrating compliance with the CE requirements. It is the responsibility of each renewal applicant to retain and produce evidence of such compliance upon request. (IDFPR)

Resources

CE must be obtained through an IDFPR-approved Real Estate Education Provider.

- A list of approved Education Providers offering CE courses may be found at: https://idfpr. illinois.gov/dre/education/rececourselist.html

- A list of approved Education Providers offering Post License Education courses may be found at: https://idfpr.illinois.gov/dre/education/reprelist.html

- Your original date of licensure and current license status may be found using "License Lookup" at: https://online-dfpr.micropact.com/lookup/licenselookup.aspx

- Your list of completed CE courses may be found using the "CE Lookup" at: https://online-dfpr.micropact.com/celookup/

- Sexual Harassment Prevention Training Course FAQs https://idfpr.illinois.gov/content/dam/soi/en/web/idfpr/faq/realestate/dre-updated-shpt-faq-2022.pdf (IDFPR)

IDFPR must approve all real estate education providers. Only state-approved providers and educational institutions may provide CE courses and instruction.

What makes up the mandatory core of the subject matter? It may include, but isn't limited by, the following:

- Advertising

- Agency

- Brokerage agreements and disclosures

- Escrow

- Fair housing

- License law

Elective course options have a wide variety. They may include any of the following topics, along with additional topics not mentioned here: diversity, affordable housing, ethics, current issues, marketing, advertising, taxes, property management, appraisal, commercial real estate, and so on.

THE NECESSITY OF LICENSURE

In 225 ILCS 454/5-15, The Act outlines ownership restrictions for managing brokers, brokers, and residential leasing agent licenses. It reads as follows:

"Section 5-15. Necessity of managing broker, broker, or residential leasing agent license; ownership restrictions.

(a) It is unlawful for any person, as defined in Section 1-10, to act as a managing broker, broker, or residential leasing agent or to advertise or assume to act as such managing broker, broker, or residential leasing agent without a license issued in accordance with this Act and a valid sponsorship registered with the Department, either directly or through its authorized designee.

(b) No corporation shall be granted a license or engage in the business or capacity, either directly or indirectly, of a broker, unless every officer of the corporation who actively participates in the real estate activities of the corporation holds a license as a managing broker or broker and unless every employee who acts as a managing broker, broker, or residential leasing agent for the corporation holds a license as a managing broker, broker, or residential leasing agent. All nonparticipating owners or officers shall submit affidavits of nonparticipation as required by the Department. No corporation shall be granted a license if any nonparticipating owner or officer has previously been publicly disciplined by the Department resulting in that licensee being currently barred from real estate practice because of a suspension or revocation.

(c) No partnership shall be granted a license or engage in the business or serve in the capacity, either directly or indirectly, of a broker, unless every partner in the partnership who actively participates in the real estate activities of the partnership holds a license as a managing broker or broker and unless every employee who acts as a managing broker, broker, or residential leasing agent for the partnership holds a license as a managing broker, broker, or residential leasing agent. All nonparticipating partners shall submit affidavits of nonparticipation as required by the Department. In the case of a registered limited liability partnership (LLP), every partner in the LLP that actively participates in the real estate activities of the limited liability partnership must hold a license as a managing broker or broker and every employee who acts as a managing broker, broker, or residential leasing agent must hold a license as a managing broker, broker, or residential leasing agent. All nonparticipating limited liability partners shall submit affidavits of nonparticipation as required by the Department. No partnership shall be granted a license if any nonparticipating partner has previously been publicly disciplined by the Department resulting in that licensee being currently barred from real estate practice because of a suspension or revocation.

(d) No limited liability company shall be granted a license or engage in the business or serve in the capacity, either directly or indirectly, of a broker unless every member or manager in the limited liability company that actively participates in the real estate activities of the limited liability company holds a license as a managing broker or broker and unless every other member and employee who acts as a managing broker, broker, or residential leasing agent for the limited liability company holds a license as a managing broker, broker, or residential leasing agent. All nonparticipating members or managers shall submit affidavits of nonparticipation as required by the Department. No limited liability company shall be granted a license if any nonparticipating member or manager has previously been publicly disciplined by the Department resulting in that licensee being currently barred from real estate practice because of a suspension or revocation.

(e) (Blank).

(f) No person, partnership, or business entity shall be granted a license if any owner, officer, director, partner, limited liability partner, member, or manager has been denied a real estate license by the Department in the previous 5 years or is otherwise currently barred from real estate practice because of a suspension or revocation." (225 ILCS 454/5-15)

Let's look at a sample scenario that could easily happen in any city. Cranston's neighbor Eric moves to Japan and wants Cranston to take care of the house while he is gone. This includes cleaning, lawn care, finding suitable tenants, and collecting and depositing the rent. Eric will give Cranston his antique furniture as payment when he returns. Does Cranston need a real estate license?

A. Yes, this is a licensed activity. Cranston will need a broker's license and must work under a sponsoring broker.

B. Yes, this is a licensed activity, but he can apply for an exemption as long as he manages less than five units.

C. No, this is not a licensed activity. He is only doing a favor for his neighbor, and he is not receiving cash.

D. No, this is not a licensed activity. Managing single-family dwellings does not require a license.

You selected the correct answer if you chose answer A.

Let's say that Cranston does not possess a real estate license. If the tenant Cranston has placed in the property files a complaint against Cranston, what would be the potential penalties that Cranston might face? The chart below illustrates this.

	Section 5-15	Section 20-20	Remainder of Act
First offense	Class A Misdemeanor		Class C Misdemeanor
Subsequent offense	Class Four Felony		Class A Misdemeanor
Each offense		Maximum fine per offense is $25,000 and includes disciplinary action	

Note: Both the Class A misdemeanor and Class C misdemeanor can include a maximum monetary fine per offense of $25,000. Each one potentially can include disciplinary action. (Sections 5-15 and 20-20).

From the chart above, we can see that if Cranston is found guilty of acting in the capacity of a licensee, he can be subjected to the penalties detailed under Section 5-15 and Section 20-20.

OFFICES AND THE ACT

The Act speaks about offices, including branches and virtual offices in 225 ILCS 454/5-45. It reads as follows:

a. If a sponsoring broker maintains more than one office within the State, the sponsoring broker shall notify the Department in a manner prescribed by the Department for each office other than the sponsoring broker's principal place of business. The brokerage license shall be displayed conspicuously in each office. The name of each branch office shall be the same as that of the sponsoring broker's principal office or shall clearly delineate the office's relationship with the principal office.

b. The sponsoring broker shall name a designated managing broker for each office and the sponsoring broker shall be responsible for supervising all designated managing brokers. The sponsoring broker shall notify the Department in a manner prescribed by the Department of the name of all designated managing brokers of the sponsoring broker and the office or offices they manage. Any changes in designated managing brokers shall be reported to the Department in a manner prescribed by the Department within 15 days of the change. Failure to do so shall subject the sponsoring broker to discipline under Section 20-20 of this Act.

c. The sponsoring broker shall, within 24 hours, notify the Department in a manner prescribed by the Department of any opening, closing, or change in location of any office.

d. Except as provided in this Section, each sponsoring broker shall maintain an office or place of business within this State for the transaction of real estate business, and shall conspicuously display an identification sign on the outside of his or her physical office of adequate size and visibility. Any record required by this Act to be created or maintained shall be, in the case of a physical record, securely stored and accessible for inspection by the Department at the sponsoring broker's principal office and, in the case of an electronic record, securely stored in the format in which it was originally generated, sent, or received and accessible for inspection by the Department by secure electronic access to the record. Any record relating to a transaction of a special account shall be maintained for a minimum of five years, and any electronic record shall be backed up at least monthly. The office or place of business shall not be located in any retail or financial business establishment unless it is clearly separated from the other business and is situated within a distinct area within the establishment.

e. A broker who is licensed in this State by examination or pursuant to the provisions of Section 5-60 of this Act shall not be required to maintain a definite office or place of business in this State provided all of the following conditions are met:

   1. the broker maintains an active broker's license in the broker's state of domicile;

   2. the broker maintains an office in the broker's state of domicile; and

   3. the broker has filed with the Department written statements appointing the Secretary to act as the broker's agent upon whom all judicial and other process or

legal notices directed to the licensee may be served and agreeing to abide by all of the provisions of this Act with respect to his or her real estate activities within the State of Illinois and submitting to the jurisdiction of the Department.

The statements under subdivision (3) of this Section shall be in form and substance the same as those statements required under Section 5-60 of this Act and shall operate to the same extent.

f.   The Department may adopt rules to permit and regulate the operation of virtual offices that do not have a fixed location. (225 ILCS 454/5-45)

In 225 ILCS 454/5-29, The Act talks about what happens when there is no branch office designated managing broker.

"Section 5-29. Temporary practice as a designated managing broker. Upon the loss of a designated managing broker who is not replaced by the sponsoring broker or in the event of the death or adjudicated disability of the sole proprietor of an office, a written request for authorization allowing the continued operation of the office may be submitted to the Department within 15 days of the loss. The Department may issue a written authorization allowing the continued operation, provided that a licensed managing broker or, in the case of the death or adjudicated disability of a sole proprietor, the representative of the estate, assumes responsibility, in writing, for the operation of the office and agrees to personally supervise the operation of the office. No such written authorization shall be valid for more than 60 days unless extended by the Department for good cause shown and upon written request by the broker or representative." (225 ILCS 454/5-29)

RECORDKEEPING REQUIREMENTS

Section 1450.755 in the Rules And Regulations is titled Recordkeeping. Here is what it conveys:

a.   A sponsoring broker shall keep, or cause to be kept, escrow records, transaction records, employment agreements, and records reflecting the payment of compensation, as set forth in this Section.

1.   Escrow Records for Each Interest Bearing and Non-interest Bearing Escrow Account or Account Where Escrow Funds Have Been Deposited. These records shall include:

A.   Journals required by Section 1450.750(i)(1);

B.   Monthly bank statements;

    C. Ledgers required by Section 1450.750(i)(2);

    D. Monthly reconciliations required by Section 1450.750(i)(3); and

    E. Master Log of Escrow Accounts required by Section 1450.750(i)(5).

2. The escrow records required by subsection (a)(1) shall be maintained for five years. The sponsoring broker shall ensure that the escrow records for the immediate prior two-year period are maintained in the sponsoring broker's office and shall be produced within 24 hours after a request by the Division as set forth in Section 1450.750(i)(8). The balance of the records can be available at another location and is subject to request by the Division as set forth in Section 20-20(a)(27) of The Act. Any escrow records more than two years old and stored at a location other than the sponsoring broker's office, whether in hard copy or electronically, shall be available for inspection during normal business hours as soon as available, but no later than 30 days after the Division's request.

3. Records relating to transactions shall be retained by the sponsoring broker in hard copy or electronically.

    A. These records might include copies of:

        i) Residential Property Transactions: Signed contracts, including offers and counteroffers, written release of escrow funds, Dual Agency Authorization, notices of designated agency or no agency, written direction for deposit into interest-bearing special account, power of attorney, disclosures (e.g., lead paint, radon, seller disclosure), closing statements and other transaction records required to be retained by the Act.

        ii) Property Management/Leasing: Any rental finding agreement, property management agreements, leases, periodic accounting or statement to the owner regarding the receipts and disbursements, and any other documents set forth in subsection (a)(3)(A)(i) that are relevant to the transaction.

        iii) Commercial Representation: Tenant or owner representation agreement, letters of intent, leases, any written modifications to an executed lease, and any other documents set forth in subsection (a)(3)(A)(i) t are relevant to the transaction.

    B. The documents set forth in subsection (a)(3) are not all-inclusive and are examples of relevant documents to be retained. Any similar documents pertinent to a particular transaction shall also be retained. Any information contained on the outside of a transaction file shall be considered part of that file.

C. Transaction records shall be maintained for five years. The sponsoring broker shall ensure that any transaction records involving any active or pending transaction or representation, or any transaction in which escrow funds or moneys belonging to others were received and have not yet been disbursed for the immediate prior two years shall be maintained in the office. All transaction records maintained at the office shall be made available for inspection and audit during normal business hours by the Division staff no later than 24 hours after a request for escrow records and related documents. Any transaction records stored at a location other than the office in hard copy or electronically shall be made available for inspection during normal business hours as soon as available within 30 days after the request.

D. Sponsoring brokers may allow their sponsored licensees to maintain duplicate transaction records. However, only the file maintained by the sponsoring broker shall be considered as an official file of the office.

4. Employment agreements, required by Section 10-20 of the Act shall be maintained for five years after the sponsored licensee is no longer associated with the sponsoring broker. The sponsoring broker shall maintain a written employment agreement for every licensee who is employed by or associated with the sponsoring broker. A copy of the employment agreement for each sponsored licensee at a branch office shall be maintained at the respective branch office.

5. Records reflecting the payment of compensation for the performance of licensed activities shall be maintained for five years.

b. All records may be kept in hard copy or electronically. If the records are kept electronically, the sponsoring broker shall ensure that a backup is made at reasonable intervals, but at least once a month, so as to protect the data but no less frequently than monthly. Backups can be kept either at the sponsoring broker's office or offsite. The escrow journal shall be reduced to hard copy at least monthly and kept at the sponsoring broker's office for 60 days.

c. Any disclosure required by the Act or this Part can be made in a paper or, if agreed to by both parties, an electronic format and may use electronic signatures. Copies of all disclosures, whether in hard copy or electronically, must be retained by the sponsoring broker.

d. If escrow records are lost, stolen, or destroyed due to fire, flood, or any other circumstances, the sponsoring broker must:

1. report the loss to the Division's enforcement division within 30 days by signature restricted delivery; and

2. immediately obtain copies of monthly bank statements, deposit and disbursement receipts, and any other available records to reconstruct the loss of escrow records. (http://www.ilga.gov/commission/jcar/admincode/068/068014500G07550R.html)

More on this is covered in 225 ILCS 454/10-27:

> Disclosure of licensee status. Each licensee shall disclose, in writing, his or her status as a licensee to all parties in a transaction when the licensee is selling, leasing, or purchasing any interest, direct or indirect, in the real estate that is the subject of the transaction.

There must be a written employee agreement between every sponsoring broker and the licensees and/or independent contractors that he/she hires. This includes licensed personal assistants, non-practicing licensees, and other sponsoring brokers. Regardless of the position held or title given, there must be an employment agreement between him/her and the sponsoring broker.

AGENCY RELATIONSHIPS: SPONSORING BROKER AND LICENSEE

Here is information from The Act found in 225 ILCS 454/15-35.

Section 15-35. Agency relationship disclosure.

a. A licensee acting as a designated agent shall advise a consumer in writing, no later than beginning to work as a designated agent on behalf of the consumer, of the following:

1. That a designated agency relationship exists, unless there is written agreement between the sponsoring broker and the consumer providing for a different agency relationship; and

2. The name or names of his or her designated agent or agents on the written disclosure, which can be included in a brokerage agreement or be a separate document, a copy of which is retained by the real estate brokerage firm for the licensee.

b. The licensee representing the consumer shall discuss with the consumer the sponsoring broker's compensation and policy with regard to cooperating with brokers who represent other parties in a transaction.

c. A licensee shall disclose in writing to a customer that the licensee is not acting as the agent of the customer at a time intended to prevent disclosure of confidential information from a customer to a licensee, but in no event later than the preparation of an offer to purchase or lease real property.

What is a licensee obligated to disclose to all parties? In no particular order, information required to be disclosed includes:

1. Agency relationship

2. Dual agency

3. Designated agency

4. No agency

5. Material facts

6. Known latent defects (physical in nature)

7. Contemporaneous offers

8. Source/s of compensation

Under The Act, duties of designated agency include, but are not limited to, the following:

- Follow the terms of the agency agreement

- Advocate for your clients' best interests

- Look for a transaction that meets the agreement's terms (or if that is not possible given the circumstances, then search for a transaction that is reasonable and acceptable to the buyer/seller)

- Present all offers to client

- Disclose material facts about the transaction

- Practice reasonable care when performing services

- Know what is confidential and keep it confidential

- Always stay in compliance with The Act and other applicable laws

As you learned in an earlier chapter, dual agency is currently allowed by Illinois law in real estate transactions. However, there must be "informed written consent" between all parties.

ADVERTISING: INDIVIDUAL, TEAMS, AND ONLINE

All advertising must adhere to the law. Each licensee needs to carefully follow the advertising regulations as defined by The Act. The Act covers general advertising requirements in 225 ILCS 454/10-30 and states:

Section 10-30. Advertising.

a. No advertising, whether in print, via the Internet, or through social media, digital forums, or any other media, shall be fraudulent, deceptive, inherently misleading, or proven to be misleading in practice. Advertising shall be considered misleading or untruthful if, when taken as a whole, there is a distinct and reasonable possibility that it will be misunderstood or will deceive the ordinary consumer. Advertising shall contain all information necessary to communicate the information contained therein to the public in an accurate, direct, and readily comprehensible manner. Team names may not contain inherently misleading terms, such as "company," "realty," "real estate," "agency," "associates," "brokers," "properties," or "property."

b. No blind advertisements may be used by any licensee, in any media, except as provided for in this Section.

c. A licensee shall disclose, in writing, to all parties in a transaction his or her status as a licensee and any and all interest the licensee has or may have in the real estate constituting the subject matter thereof, directly or indirectly, according to the following guidelines:

   1. On broker yard signs or in broker advertisements, no disclosure of ownership is necessary. However, the ownership shall be indicated on any property data form accessible to the consumer and disclosed to persons responding to any advertisement or any sign. The term "broker owned" or "agent owned" is sufficient disclosure.

   2. A sponsored or inactive licensee selling or leasing property, owned solely by the sponsored or inactive licensee, without utilizing brokerage services of their sponsoring broker or any other licensee, may advertise "By Owner." For purposes of this Section, property is "solely owned" by a sponsored or inactive licensee if he or she (i) has a 100% ownership interest alone, (ii) has ownership as a joint tenant or tenant by the entirety, or (iii) holds a 100% beneficial interest in a land trust. Sponsored or inactive licensees selling or leasing "By Owner" shall comply with the following if advertising by owner:

A. (A) On "By Owner" yard signs, the sponsored or inactive licensee shall indicate "broker owned" or "agent owned." "By Owner" advertisements used in any medium of advertising shall include the term "broker owned" or "agent owned."

B. (B) If a sponsored or inactive licensee runs advertisements, for the purpose of purchasing or leasing real estate, he or she shall disclose in the advertisements his or her status as a licensee.

C. (C) A sponsored or inactive licensee shall not use the sponsoring broker's name or the sponsoring broker's company name in connection with the sale, lease, or advertisement of the property nor utilize the sponsoring broker's or company's name in connection with the sale, lease, or advertising of the property in a manner likely to create confusion among the public as to whether or not the services of a real estate company are being utilized or whether or not a real estate company has an ownership interest in the property.

D. (d) A sponsored licensee may not advertise under his or her own name. Advertising in any media shall be under the direct supervision of the sponsoring or designated managing broker and in the sponsoring broker's business name, which in the case of a franchise shall include the franchise affiliation as well as the name of the individual firm. This provision does not apply under the following circumstances:

   1. When a licensee enters into a brokerage agreement relating to his or her own real estate, or real estate in which he or she has an ownership interest, with another licensed broker; or

   2. When a licensee is selling or leasing his or her own real estate or buying or leasing real estate for himself or herself, after providing the appropriate written disclosure of his or her ownership interest as required in paragraph (2) of subsection (c) of this Section.

d. No licensee shall list his or her name or otherwise advertise in his or her own name to the general public through any medium of advertising as being in the real estate business without listing his or her sponsoring broker's business name.

e. The sponsoring broker's business name and the name of the licensee must appear in all advertisements, including business cards. In advertising that includes the sponsoring broker's name and a team name or individual broker's name, the sponsoring broker's business name shall be at least equal in size or larger than the team name or that of the individual.

f. Those individuals licensed as a managing broker and designated with the Department as a designated managing broker by their sponsoring broker shall identify themselves to the public in advertising, except on "For Sale" or similar signs, as a designated managing broker. No other individuals holding a managing broker's license may hold themselves out to the public or other licensees as a designated managing broker, but they may hold themselves out to holding a managing broker license. (225 ILCS 454/10-30)

When licensees are creating or preparing advertisements, the ads must include all of the necessary and accurate information. All ads must communicate with their audience (the public) in a clear, direct, and easy-to-understand fashion. At a minimum, all ads will include:

- Name of licensee

- Name of company including franchise affiliation (as it is registered with IDFPR)

- Location of company (city and state)

- Location of advertised property (whether noted by the city or area)

If a licensee is performing the functions and duties of a designated managing broker, he/she must advertise themselves as the designated managing broker. Each sponsoring broker is required to include his or her business name, along with the franchise affiliation in every single advertisement they run.

If the licensee, who is the property owner acting as the principal and selling the property on their own, decides to market the property as a For Sale By Owner, they must indicate the phrase "agent owned" on all marketing materials, including the For Sale sign.

Teams

The Act defines the word team as the following:

> "Team means any two or more licensees who work together to provide real estate brokerage services, represent themselves to the public as being part of a team or group, are identified by a team name that is different than their sponsoring broker's name, and together are supervised by the same managing broker and sponsored by the same sponsoring broker. "Team" does not mean a separately organized, incorporated, or legal entity." (225 ILCS 454/1-10).=

The Act further communicates the following:

- Team names may not contain inherently misleading terms, such as "company," "realty," "real estate," "agency," "associates," "brokers," "properties," or "property."

- The sponsoring broker's business name and the name of the licensee must appear in all advertisements, including business cards. In advertising that includes the sponsoring broker's name and a team name or individual broker's name, the sponsoring broker's business name shall be at least equal in size or larger than the team name or that of the individual.

- In advertising that includes the sponsoring broker's name and a team name or individual broker's name, the sponsoring broker's business name shall be at least equal in size or larger than the team name or that of the individual (225 ILCS 454/10-30).

INTERNET AND RELATED ADVERTISING

What does online advertising include? It includes but is not limited to:

- Your business website/s

- Social media platforms (including YouTube)

- Email

Internet advertising regulations from 225 ILCS 454/10-35 of The Act state:

a. Licensees intending to sell or share consumer information gathered from or through the Internet or other electronic communication media, including, but not limited to, social media and digital forums, shall disclose that intention to consumers in a timely and readily apparent manner.

b. A licensee using the Internet or other similar electronic advertising media must not:

    1. use a URL or domain name that is deceptive or misleading;

    2. deceptively or without authorization frame another sponsoring broker's or Multiple Listing Service website; or

    3. engage in phishing or the deceptive use of metatags, keywords or other devices and methods to direct, drive or divert Internet traffic or otherwise mislead consumers.

Section 1450.720 of the Rules And Regulations, called "Digital or Electronic Advertising and Communication Advertising", explains definitions. They are as follows:

a. For purposes of this Section:

1. "Advertising" or "Marketing Real Property" means use of a website, digital platform, or any form of social media to disseminate:

   A. Information regarding properties listed with a sponsoring broker;

   B. The identity of that sponsoring broker or the individual licensee for each property; and

   C. Information related to those properties.

2. "Advertising" or "Marketing of Licensed Activities" means a website, digital platform, or any form of social media that includes an offer or solicitation to provide licensed activities in connection with marketing or identifying real property for sale or lease.

3. "Scraping or Data Mining" means copying or extracting existing listing information or keywords from a website, digital platform, or any form of social media of another licensee and using or altering that material and posting or displaying it for the benefit of the general public on another digital platform or form of social media or in front of a firewall on another website, without written or electronic permission and disclosure from the original listing licensee.

b. Sponsoring Broker's Advertising or Marketing Real Property

1. A sponsoring broker having permission to advertise or market real property must include the following information on the website, digital platform, or any type of social media where the sponsoring broker's advertisement or marketing appears:

   A. The sponsoring broker's name;

   B. The city or geographic area and state or country where the property being advertised or marketed is located;

   C. The city and state where the sponsoring broker's physical principal office or other offices registered with the Division are located or a direct link that connects to the sponsoring broker's virtual office, website, or digital platform; and

   D. If the sponsoring broker does not hold a real estate license for the jurisdiction where the property is located, the regulatory jurisdictions where the sponsoring broker does hold a real estate license.

2. When a sponsoring broker is advertising a property that is subject to an exclusive

listing agreement with another sponsoring broker, the sponsoring broker seeking to advertise the property shall obtain permission from, and identify in the advertisement, the sponsoring broker with the exclusive listing.

c. Sponsoring Broker's Advertising or Marketing of Real Estate Services

A sponsoring broker advertising or marketing licensed activities or soliciting business in connection with licensed activities must include the following information:

1. The sponsoring broker's name; and

2. The city and state where the sponsoring broker's physical principal office or other offices registered with the Division are located or a direct link that connects to the sponsoring broker's virtual office, website, or digital platform.

d) Licensee's Advertising or Marketing Real Property

Any licensee with permission to advertise or market real property must include the following information on the electronic location where the licensee's advertisement or marketing appears:

1. The licensee's name as licensed with the Division or, if applicable, the name registered with the Division (see Section 1450.150(b)). If the licensee is part of a team, the team name may be substituted for the individual licensee's name;

2. The city or geographic area and state or country where the property being advertised or marketed is located;

3. The sponsoring broker's name;

4. The city and state where the sponsoring broker's physical office registered with the Division is located or, in the case of a virtual office, a direct link that connects to the sponsoring broker's virtual office website or digital platform; and

5. If the licensee does not hold a real estate license for the jurisdiction where the property is located, the regulatory jurisdictions where the licensee does hold a real estate license.

d. Licensee's Advertising or Marketing of Real Estate Services

A licensee advertising, marketing, or soliciting business in connection with licensed activities must include the following information:

1. The licensee's name as licensed with the Division or, if applicable, the name registered with the Division (see Section 1450.150(b)). If the licensee is part of a team, the team name may be substituted for the individual licensee's name;

2. The sponsoring broker's name; and

3. The city and state where the sponsoring broker's physical office registered with the Division is located or, in the case of a virtual office, a direct link that connects to the sponsoring broker's virtual office website or digital platform.

e. Sponsoring Broker - Electronic or Digital Communication

A sponsoring broker engaged in licensed activities using any electronic or digital means of communicating must include the following information in the initial communication with a member of the public or another licensee:

1. The sponsoring broker's name; and

2. The city and state where the sponsoring broker's principal physical office or other offices registered with the Division are located or a direct link that connects to the sponsoring broker's virtual office website or digital platform.

f. Licensee - Electronic or Digital Communication

A licensee engaged in licensed activities using any electronic or digital means of communication must include the following information in the initial communication with a member of the public or another licensee:

1. The licensee's name as licensed with the Division or, if applicable, the name registered with the Division (see Section 1450.150(b)). If the licensee is part of a team, the team name may be used in addition to the individual licensee's name;

2. The sponsoring broker's name; and

3. The city and state where the sponsoring broker's physical office registered with the Division is located or, in the case of a virtual office, a direct link that connects to the sponsoring broker's virtual office website or digital platform.

g. A sponsoring broker or other licensee may link to listing information from another electronic or digital location without approval unless the owner of that electronic or digital location specifically requires consent. Any link must not mislead or deceive the public as to the ownership of any listing information.

h. All licensees, including sponsoring brokers, shall periodically review advertising and marketing information on their websites or digital platforms and update the information as necessary to assure that the information is current and not misleading.

i. All licensees, including sponsoring brokers, using websites or digital platforms for advertising must provide a direct link:

1. To all required disclosures relating to the sponsoring broker's name and other relevant business information; and

2. All terms and conditions of any offers or inducements made pursuant to Section 10-15(c) and (d) of the Act.) A domain name, URL, username, or social media handle does not constitute advertising. (Section 1450.720)

A related topic is blind ads. These types of ads do not identify or contain:

- The name of the sponsoring broker

- The name of the brokerage firm

Blind ads are illegal in Illinois. They are firmly prohibited in any type of real estate activity. Furthermore, blind ads do not disclose any information as to whether the advertiser is a licensee or not. When it comes to containing an address, a PO Box, or contact number, these illegal ads may or may not include that information. A blind ad can be digital or physical.

Like print or offline advertisements, all online advertisements must include:

- Name of licensee

- Name of company including franchise affiliation (as it is registered with IDFPR)

- Location of company (city and state)

- Location of advertised property (whether noted by the city or area)

Online advertising cannot include or use:

- Any URL or domain names that are misleading, deceitful, deceptive or fraudulent.

- A URL that "frames" the website of another real estate brokerage.

- Any tools, software or techniques to trick or mislead people in such a way that has them click to the website.

- Multiple Listing Service/s without written permission.

What about links to listing information from other websites? This means any website that is not your company site. These types of links are permitted. However, you must verify whether the site requires you to obtain permission from them or not prior to placing the links on your company site.

ADVERTISING LANGUAGE

Discriminatory language is wording and communication that discriminates, belittles, and/or excludes others. Property ads (whether promoting a sale or rental) are not permitted to include discriminatory language. This type of language has the power to cause pain, upset, and/or misunderstandings both in personal and professional relationships. This kind of language should be avoided. Furthermore, any language that indicates a limitation or a preference must be avoided. The language used needs to be nondiscriminatory. In other words, inclusive language is to be used consistently both in written advertisements and verbally in business settings. Remember, you consistently are representing yourself and your firm, regardless of where you are and who you speak with. Marketing must never target or call out any one demographic to the exclusion of other demographics. For example, if an ad targets someone solely based on national origin, the ad will be viewed as discriminatory. The best practice is to be inclusive in your advertising. Another good practice is to run advertisement campaigns in a variety of media that is widely and generally circulated. Many agents use the phrase "equal housing opportunity" in their advertisements. Likewise, some elect to use the phrase "We do business in accordance with the Federal Fair Housing Law," which is found in materials from HUD. You always want to use positive and inclusive language in all of your business dealings and advertisements.

To recap, The Act states that each sponsored licensee:

- Must never advertise in only his or her name

- Must never advertise the listing of another sponsoring broker without permission

- Must always include the firm's name in the advertisement

- Must always keep all advertisements clear and updated

- Follow all advertising regulations as defined by The Act

ETHICS IN ADVERTISING

Ethics in advertising stems from:

- License law

- IDFPR

- State law

- Illinois Consumer Fraud and Deceptive Business Practices Act

- Federal law

- TILA

- Better Business Bureau Guidelines

Is it ethical in advertising for licensees to offer free prizes or gifts? The Illinois Consumer Fraud and Deceptive Business Practices Act, in addition to licensing law, states:

> "It is an unlawful practice for any person to promote or advertise any interest in property by means of offering free prizes, gifts, or gratuities to any consumer, unless all material terms and conditions relating to the offer are clearly and conspicuously disclosed at the outset of the offer so as to leave no reasonable probability that the offering might be misunderstood." (815 ILCS 505/2P)

The Illinois Consumer Fraud and Deceptive Business Practices Act also states:

> "It is an unlawful practice for any person to promote or advertise any business, product or interest in property by means of distributing documents designed to simulate checks or other negotiable instruments unless such instrument has printed upon both its front and back, the following statement: "This is not a Check." However, it is not an unlawful practice under this Section for a person to distribute for commercial purposes a sample or specimen of a check or other instrument which is used to solicit orders for the sale of that instrument and which is clearly marked as a non-negotiable sample or specimen." (815 ILCS 505/2X)

DISCIPLINARY ACTIONS: NATURE OF AND GROUNDS FOR DISCIPLINE

As you have read in earlier sections, when a licensee is out of compliance with the rules outlined in The Act and/or is accused of such actions, he/she may be subject to disciplinary action. Although you've already read about this topic in some regards, here is the primary content from The Act found in 225 ILCS 454/20-20, entitled "Nature of and grounds for discipline." It reads as follows:

a. The Department may refuse to issue or renew a license, may place on probation, suspend, or revoke any license, reprimand, or take any other disciplinary or non-disciplinary action as the Department may deem proper and impose a fine not to exceed

$25,000 upon any licensee or applicant under this Act or any person who holds himself or herself out as an applicant or licensee or against a licensee in handling his or her own property, whether held by deed, option, or otherwise, for any one or any combination of the following causes:

1. Fraud or misrepresentation in applying for, or procuring, a license under this Act or in connection with applying for renewal of a license under this Act.

2. The licensee's conviction of or plea of guilty or plea of nolo contendere to: *(Note: solo contendere is Latin and basically translates to "No contest" or "I do not wish to contend.")*

    A. a felony or misdemeanor in this State or any other jurisdiction; or

    B. the entry of an administrative sanction by a government agency in this State or any other jurisdiction. Action taken under this paragraph (2) for a misdemeanor or an administrative sanction is limited to a misdemeanor or administrative sanction that has as an essential element dishonesty or fraud or involves larceny, embezzlement, or obtaining money, property, or credit by false pretenses or by means of a confidence game.

3. Inability to practice the profession with reasonable judgment, skill, or safety as a result of a physical illness, including, but not limited to, deterioration through the aging process or loss of motor skill, or a mental illness or disability.

4. Practice under this Act as a licensee in a retail sales establishment from an office, desk, or space that is not separated from the main retail business and located within a separate and distinct area within the establishment.

5. Having been disciplined by another state, the District of Columbia, a territory, a foreign nation, or a governmental agency authorized to impose discipline if at least one of the grounds for that discipline is the same as or the equivalent of one of the grounds for which a licensee may be disciplined under this Act. A certified copy of the record of the action by the other state or jurisdiction shall be prima facie evidence thereof.

6. Engaging in the practice of real estate brokerage without a license or after the licensee's license or temporary permit was expired or while the license was inactive, revoked, or suspended.

7. Cheating on or attempting to subvert the Real Estate License Exam or a continuing education course or examination.

8. Aiding or abetting an applicant to subvert or cheat on the Real Estate License Exam or continuing education exam administered pursuant to this Act.

9. Advertising that is inaccurate, misleading, or contrary to the provisions of the Act.

10. Making any substantial misrepresentation or untruthful advertising.

11. Making any false promises of a character likely to influence, persuade, or induce.

12. Pursuing a continued and flagrant course of misrepresentation or the making of false promises through licensees, employees, agents, advertising, or otherwise.

13. Any misleading or untruthful advertising, or using any trade name or insignia of membership in any real estate organization of which the licensee is not a member.

14. Acting for more than one party in a transaction without providing written notice to all parties for whom the licensee acts.

15. Representing or attempting to represent, or performing licensed activities for, a broker other than the sponsoring broker.

16. Failure to account for or to remit any moneys or documents coming into his or her possession that belong to others.

17. Failure to maintain and deposit in a special account, separate and apart from personal and other business accounts, all escrow moneys belonging to others entrusted to a licensee while acting as a broker, escrow agent, or temporary custodian of the funds of others or failure to maintain all escrow moneys on deposit in the account until the transactions are consummated or terminated, except to the extent that the moneys, or any part thereof, shall be:

    a. disbursed prior to the consummation or termination (i) in accordance with the written direction of the principals to the transaction or their duly authorized agents, (ii) in accordance with directions providing for the release, payment, or distribution of escrow moneys contained in any written contract signed by the principals to the transaction or their duly authorized agents, or (iii) pursuant to an order of a court of competent jurisdiction; or

    b. deemed abandoned and transferred to the Office of the State Treasurer to be handled as unclaimed property pursuant to the Revised Uniform Unclaimed Property Act. Escrow moneys may be deemed abandoned under this subparagraph (B) only: (i) in the absence of disbursement under subparagraph (A); (ii) in the absence of notice of the filing of any claim in a court of competent jurisdiction; and (iii) if six months have elapsed after the receipt of a written demand for the escrow moneys from one of the principals to the transaction or the principal's duly authorized agent.

The account shall be non-interest bearing, unless the character of the deposit is such that payment of interest thereon is otherwise required by law or unless the principals to the transaction specifically require, in writing, that the deposit be placed in an interest-bearing account.

18. Failure to make available to the Department all escrow records and related documents maintained in connection with the practice of real estate within 24 hours of a request for those documents by Department personnel.

19. Failing to furnish copies upon request of documents relating to a real estate transaction to a party who has executed that document.

20. Failure of a sponsoring broker or licensee to timely provide sponsorship or termination of sponsorship information to the Department.

21. Engaging in dishonorable, unethical, or unprofessional conduct of a character likely to deceive, defraud, or harm the public, including, but not limited to, conduct set forth in rules adopted by the Department.

22. Commingling the money or property of others with his or her own money or property.

23. Employing any person on a purely temporary or single deal basis as a means of evading the law regarding payment of commission to nonlicensees on some contemplated transactions.

24. Permitting the use of his or her license as a broker to enable a residential leasing agent or unlicensed person to operate a real estate business without actual participation therein and control thereof by the broker.

25. Any other conduct, whether of the same or a different character from that specified in this Section, that constitutes dishonest dealing.

26. Displaying a "for rent" or "for sale" sign on any property without the written consent of an owner or his or her duly authorized agent or advertising by any means that any property is for sale or for rent without the written consent of the owner or his or her authorized agent.

27. Failing to provide information requested by the Department, or otherwise respond to that request, within 30 days of the request.

28. Advertising by means of a blind advertisement, except as otherwise permitted in Section 10-30 of this Act.

29. A licensee under this Act or an unlicensed individual offering guaranteed sales plans, as defined in Section 10-50, except to the extent set forth in Section 10-50. *(This list will be continued below once we define what a guaranteed sales plan is.)*

What is a guaranteed sales plan? In the state of Illinois, there is a provision where a broker can offer a seller a guaranteed sales plan. A guaranteed sales plan is a marketing tool where the licensee makes a commitment to the seller that if they cannot find a buyer for the property in a specified period of time, the licensee will purchase the property him/herself.

The Act conveys the following on this topic in 225 ILCS 454/10-50 as follows:

A. Guaranteed sales plans.

    a. As used in this Section, a "guaranteed sales plan" means a real estate purchase or sales plan whereby a licensee enters into one or more conditional or unconditional written contracts with a seller, one of which is a brokerage agreement, and wherein the person agrees to purchase the seller's property within a specified period of time, at a specific price, in the event the property is not sold in accordance with the terms of a brokerage agreement to be entered into between the sponsoring broker and the seller.

    b. A person who offers a guaranteed sales plan to consumers is engaged in licensed activity under this Act and is required to have a license.

    c. A licensee offering a guaranteed sales plan shall provide the details, including the purchase price, and conditions of the plan, in writing to the party to whom the plan is offered prior to entering into the brokerage agreement.

    d. A licensee offering a guaranteed sales plan shall provide to the party to whom the plan is offered evidence of sufficient financial resources to satisfy the commitment to purchase undertaken by the broker in the plan.

    e. A licensee offering a guaranteed sales plan shall undertake to market the property of the seller subject to the plan in the same manner in which the broker would market any other property, unless the agreement with the seller provides otherwise.

f. The licensee may not purchase the seller's property until the period for offering the property for sale has ended according to its terms or is otherwise terminated.

g. Any licensee who fails to perform on a guaranteed sales plan in strict accordance with its terms shall be subject to all the penalties provided in this Act for violations thereof and, in addition, shall be subject to a civil fine payable to the party injured by the default in an amount of up to $25,000.

Now, let's continue with the list that covers the nature of and grounds for discipline according to The Act.

30. Influencing or attempting to influence, by any words or acts, a prospective seller, purchaser, occupant, landlord, or tenant of real estate, in connection with viewing, buying, or leasing real estate, so as to promote or tend to promote the continuance or maintenance of racially and religiously segregated housing or so as to retard, obstruct, or discourage racially integrated housing on or in any street, block, neighborhood, or community.

31. Engaging in any act that constitutes a violation of any provision of Article 3 of the Illinois Human Rights Act, whether or not a complaint has been filed with or adjudicated by the Human Rights Commission.

32. Inducing any party to a contract of sale or lease or brokerage agreement to break the contract of sale or lease or brokerage agreement for the purpose of substituting, in lieu thereof, a new contract for sale or lease or brokerage agreement with a third party.

33. Negotiating a sale, exchange, or lease of real estate directly with any person if the licensee knows that the person has an exclusive brokerage agreement with another broker, unless specifically authorized by that broker.

34. When a licensee is also an attorney, acting as the attorney for either the buyer or the seller in the same transaction in which the licensee is acting or has acted as a managing broker or broker.

35. Advertising or offering merchandise or services as free if any conditions or obligations necessary for receiving the merchandise or services are not disclosed in the same advertisement or offer. These conditions or obligations include without limitation the requirement that the recipient attend a promotional activity or visit a real estate site. As used in this subdivision (35), "free" includes terms such as "award," "prize," "no charge," "free of charge," "without charge," and similar words or phrases that reasonably lead a person to believe that he or she may receive or

has been selected to receive something of value, without any conditions or obligations on the part of the recipient.

36. (Blank)

37. Violating the terms of a disciplinary order issued by the Department.

38. Paying or failing to disclose compensation in violation of Article 10 of this Act.

39. Requiring a party to a transaction who is not a client of the licensee to allow the licensee to retain a portion of the escrow moneys for payment of the licensee's commission or expenses as a condition for release of the escrow moneys to that party.

40. Disregarding or violating any provision of this Act or the published rules adopted by the Department to enforce this Act or aiding or abetting any individual, foreign or domestic partnership, registered limited liability partnership, limited liability company, corporation, or other business entity in disregarding any provision of this Act or the published rules adopted by the Department to enforce this Act.

41. Failing to provide the minimum services required by Section 15-75 of this Act when acting under an exclusive brokerage agreement.

42. Habitual or excessive use of or addiction to alcohol, narcotics, stimulants, or any other chemical agent or drug that results in a managing broker, broker, or residential leasing agent's inability to practice with reasonable skill or safety.

43. Enabling, aiding, or abetting an auctioneer, as defined in the Auction License Act, to conduct a real estate auction in a manner that is in violation of this Act.

44. Permitting any residential leasing agent or temporary residential leasing agent permit holder to engage in activities that require a broker's or managing broker's license.

45. Failing to notify the Department of any criminal conviction that occurs during the licensee's term of licensure within 30 days after the conviction.

46. A designated managing broker's failure to provide an appropriate written company policy or failure to perform any of the duties set forth in Section 10-55.

    a. The Department may refuse to issue or renew or may suspend the license of any person who fails to file a return, pay the tax, penalty or interest shown in a filed return, or pay any final assessment of tax, penalty, or interest, as required by any tax Act administered by the

Department of Revenue, until such time as the requirements of that tax Act are satisfied in accordance with subsection (g) of Section 2105-15 of the Department of Professional Regulation Law of the Civil Administrative Code of Illinois.

b. (Blank).

c. In cases where the Department of Healthcare and Family Services (formerly Department of Public Aid) has previously determined that a licensee or a potential licensee is more than 30 days delinquent in the payment of child support and has subsequently certified the delinquency to the Department may refuse to issue or renew or may revoke or suspend that person's license or may take other disciplinary action against that person based solely upon the certification of delinquency made by the Department of Healthcare and Family Services in accordance with item (5) of subsection (a) of Section 2105-15 of the Department of Professional Regulation Law of the Civil Administrative Code of Illinois.

d. In enforcing this Section, the Department or Board upon a showing of a possible violation may compel an individual licensed to practice under this Act, or who has applied for licensure under this Act, to submit to a mental or physical examination, or both, as required by and at the expense of the Department. The Department or Board may order the examining physician to present testimony concerning the mental or physical examination of the licensee or applicant. No information shall be excluded by reason of any common law or statutory privilege relating to communications between the licensee or applicant and the examining physician. The examining physicians shall be specifically designated by the Board or Department. The individual to be examined may have, at his or her own expense, another physician of his or her choice present during all aspects of this examination. Failure of an individual to submit to a mental or physical examination, when directed, shall be grounds for suspension of his or her license until the individual submits to the examination if the Department finds, after notice and hearing, that the refusal to submit to the examination was without reasonable cause.

If the Department or Board finds an individual unable to practice because of the reasons set forth in this Section, the Department or Board may require that individual to submit to care, counseling, or treatment by physicians approved or designated by the Department or Board, as a condition, term, or restriction for continued, reinstated, or renewed licensure to practice; or, in lieu of care, counseling, or treatment, the Department may file, or the Board may recommend to the Department to file, a complaint to immediately suspend, revoke, or otherwise discipline the license of the individual. An individual whose license was granted, continued, reinstated, renewed, disciplined or supervised subject to such terms, conditions, or restrictions, and who fails to comply with such terms, conditions, or restrictions, shall be referred to the Secretary for a determination as to whether the individual shall have his or her license suspended immediately, pending a hearing by the Department.

In instances in which the Secretary immediately suspends a person's license under this Section, a hearing on that person's license must be convened by the Department within 30 days after the suspension and completed without appreciable delay. The Department and Board shall have the authority to review the subject individual's record of treatment and counseling regarding the impairment to the extent permitted by applicable federal statutes and regulations safeguarding the confidentiality of medical records.

An individual licensed under this Act and affected under this Section shall be afforded an opportunity to demonstrate to the Department or Board that he or she can resume practice in compliance with acceptable and prevailing standards under the provisions of his or her license. (225 ILCS 454/20-20)

Related to the topic of disciplinary action are the terms citation and injunction. A citation is essentially a warning with consequences. In Section 20-20.1 of The Act, it defines and explains citations as:

a. The Department may adopt rules to permit the issuance of citations to any licensee for failure to comply with the continuing education requirements set forth in this Act or as adopted by rule. The citation shall be issued to the licensee, and a copy shall be sent to his or her designated managing broker and sponsoring broker. The citation shall contain the licensee's name and address, the licensee's license number, the number of required hours of continuing education that have not been successfully completed by the licensee within the renewal period, and the penalty imposed, which shall not exceed $2,000. The issuance of any such citation shall not excuse the licensee from completing all continuing education required for that renewal period.

b. Service of a citation shall be made in person, electronically, or by mail to the licensee at the licensee's address of record or email address of record, and must clearly state that if the cited licensee wishes to dispute the citation, he or she may make a written request, within 30 days after the citation is served, for a hearing before the Department. If the cited licensee does not request a hearing within 30 days after the citation is served, then the citation shall become a final, non-disciplinary order, and any fine imposed is due and payable within 60 days after that final order. If the cited licensee requests a hearing within 30 days after the citation is served, the Department shall afford the cited licensee a hearing conducted in the same manner as a hearing provided for in this Act for any violation of this Act and shall determine whether the cited licensee committed the violation as charged and whether the fine as levied is warranted. If the violation is found, any fine shall constitute non-public discipline and be due and payable within 30 days after the order of the Secretary, which shall constitute a final order of the Department. No change in license status may be made by the Department until such time as a final order of the Department has been issued.

c. Payment of a fine that has been assessed pursuant to this Section shall not constitute disciplinary action reportable on the Department's website or elsewhere unless a licensee has previously received two or more citations and paid two or more fines.

d. Nothing in this Section shall prohibit or limit the Department from taking further action pursuant to this Act and rules for additional, repeated, or continuing violations. (225 ILCS 454/20-20.1)

An injunction is a court order. Under the current licensing law, if a licensee is in violation of any aspect of The Act, the state of Illinois has the right to pursue and acquire an injunction. The injunction can legally force the licensee to perform or stop performing a certain action. Concerning injunctions, along with cease-and-desist orders, The Act states:

a. If any person violates any provision of this Act, the Secretary may, in the name of the People of the State of Illinois, through the Attorney General, or the State's Attorney of any county in which the action is brought, petition for an order enjoining the violation or for an order enforcing compliance with this Act. Upon the filing of a verified petition in court, the court may issue a temporary restraining order, without notice or bond, and may preliminarily and permanently enjoin such violation, and if it is established that such person has violated or is violating the injunction, the Court may punish the offender for contempt of court. Proceedings under this Section shall be in addition to, and not in lieu of, all other remedies and penalties provided by this Act.

b. If any person shall practice as a certified professional midwife or hold himself or herself out as a licensed certified professional midwife without being licensed under the provisions of this Act, then any licensed certified professional midwife, any interested party, or any person injured thereby may, in addition to the Secretary, petition for relief as provided in subsection (a).

c. If, in the opinion of the Department, any person violates any provision of this Act, the Department may issue a rule to show cause why an order to cease and desist should not be entered against him or her. The rule shall clearly set forth the grounds relied upon by the Department and shall provide a period of 7 days from the date of the rule to file an answer to the satisfaction of the Department. Failure to answer to the satisfaction of the Department shall cause an order to cease and desist to be issued forthwith. (225 ILCS 64/135)

According to 225 ILCS 454/20-115 in The Act, the IDFPR is permitted to issue citations or injunctions against violators within five years following the recorded date of the alleged violation. Five years is the statute of limitations. Also keep in mind that an alleged violation is only alleged. It is not proven or dismissed until the outcome is final.

Section 225 ILCS 454/20-5 is called the "index of decisions."

> The Department shall maintain an index of formal decisions regarding the issuance, refusal to issue, renewal, refusal to renew, revocation, and suspension of licenses and probationary or other disciplinary action taken under this Act. The index shall be available to the public during regular business hours.

The index of these decisions is available to the public. This allows the state to maintain the goal of complete and total transparency in the real estate industry.

WHAT CAN CAUSE A LICENSE TO BE WITHHELD OR SUSPENDED?

The four causes below can be the basis for a license being withheld, suspended, or even revoked. A withheld license is usually withheld temporarily. A suspended license is also temporary. Revocation means the license is canceled permanently. Let's look at the four causes in detail now.

1. **Tax issues:** "The Department may refuse to issue or renew or may suspend the license of any person who fails to file a return, pay the tax, penalty or interest shown in a filed return, or pay any final assessment of tax, penalty, or interest, as required by any tax Act administered by the Department of Revenue, until such time as the requirements

of that tax Act are satisfied in accordance with subsection (g) of Section 2105-15 of the Department of Professional Regulation Law of the Civil Administrative Code of Illinois." (225 ILCS 454/20-20)

2. **Not paying child support**: "In cases where the Department of Healthcare and Family Services (formerly Department of Public Aid) has previously determined that a licensee or a potential licensee is more than 30 days delinquent in the payment of child support and has subsequently certified the delinquency to the Department may refuse to issue or renew or may revoke or suspend that person's license or may take other disciplinary action against that person based solely upon the certification of delinquency made by the Department of Healthcare and Family Services in accordance with item (5) of subsection (a) of Section 2105-15 of the Department of Professional Regulation Law of the Civil Administrative Code of Illinois." (225 ILCS 454/20-20)

3. **Non-payment of a student loan:** The loan must originate from either ISAC (Illinois Student Assistance Commission) or an Illinois state government agency. You can learn more here: https://www.isac.org If this occurs, the individual will not receive his or her real estate license. When a current/existing licensee fails to pay, he/she has the option for a hearing. Depending on the outcome of the hearing and whether or not a payment plan is created, the licensee may possibly lose his or her license.

4. **Discrimination:** 225 ILCS 454/20-50 shares about "Illegal discrimination" and says:

   When there has been an adjudication in a civil or criminal proceeding that a licensee has illegally discriminated while engaged in any activity for which a license is required under this Act, the Department, upon the recommendation of the Board as to the extent of the suspension or revocation, shall suspend or revoke the license of that licensee in a timely manner, unless the adjudication is in the appeal process. When there has been an order in an administrative proceeding finding that a licensee has illegally discriminated while engaged in any activity for which a license is required under this Act, the Department, upon recommendation of the Board as to the nature and extent of the discipline, shall take one or more of the disciplinary actions provided for in Section 20-20 of this Act in a timely manner, unless the administrative order is in the appeal process.

There may be other reasons for discipline that can arise apart from the causes listed above. Each licensee must be aware of that there are other provisions the state may call upon as a means of disciplinary action.

Scenario: What happens if the sponsoring broker hires a designated managing broker who turns out to do something illegal? Perhaps during the interview process and onboarding, he was great. All the qualities the firm was looking for were present. Then, just at the four-month point of him being engaged as the designated managing broker, he violates the law. Does the sponsoring broker lose their license? Is there a consequence for the firm? If the firm had no knowledge of his illegal actions, the firm likely will not lose its sponsoring broker license. If the firm did have knowledge of his actions, there will be consequences for the firm as the sponsoring broker.

Inside the IDFPR's PDF document entitled "FAQs for Consumers," it outlines several relevant questions and answers that are important for consumers and real estate professionals to know. Here is an excerpt from one of the twenty-nine questions and answers on the PDF.

What disciplinary actions can the Department take? The Department may take any of the following disciplinary actions. This list is not exclusive.

- **Reprimand:** A reprimand is an official public record of discipline but does not restrict the licensee's ability to practice. If monitoring is required, the licensee may have to fulfill additional requirements or conditions.

- **Probation:** Licensees placed on probation are permitted to practice subject to certain terms and conditions, which vary depending on case circumstances. During the probation term, a licensee may be monitored by the Department's Probation Compliance Unit. The probation term may be for a definite period (i.e., automatically expires at the end of a stated term) or indefinite (i.e., a licensee must file a Petition for Restoration after a stated term has passed and prove that probation should be terminated). A licensee's failure to comply with probation terms and conditions may result in further disciplinary action.

- **Suspension:** Suspended licensees are prohibited from practicing during the suspension term and may be subject to certain terms and conditions. The suspension term may be for a definite period (i.e., automatically expires at the end of a stated term) or indefinite (i.e., a licensee must file a Petition for Restoration after a stated term has passed and prove that suspension should be terminated). The term of suspension may be followed by probation.

- **Summary or Temporary Suspension:** When a licensee's continuation in practice poses an imminent danger to the public, the Department may take immediate action by summarily or temporarily suspending a license. The license remains suspended pending a hearing on the case within a required statutory time frame. Summarily or temporarily suspended licensees are prohibited from practice immediately upon being served by the Department.

- **Revocation:** Licensees are prohibited from practice while revoked. If no term is stated, a licensee must wait a minimum of three (3) years to be eligible to file a Petition for Restoration. In limited instances, a license may be permanently revoked and is ineligible for restoration.

- **Refuse to Renew:** Licensees who are refused renewal are ineligible to renew their license and are prohibited from practice after the expiration of the date of their license. A licensee who has been refused renewal may file a Petition for Restoration.

- **Relinquished, Surrendered, or Permanent Inactive:** These terms may or may not be considered discipline; however, a licensee in one of these statuses is not currently authorized to practice in Illinois. License lookup will indicate whether or not the status is disciplinary.

- **Fines:** Fines are disciplinary actions and may be issued in conjunction with one of the above disciplines.

- **Order to Cease & Desist:** An order to cease and desist is issued to an unlicensed individual or entity that is practicing without a license. An order to cease and desist may require the individual or entity to pay a monetary civil penalty. In some cases, the unlicensed activity may be referred to law enforcement for further action. (IDFPR)

The complete PDF is found here: https://idfpr.illinois.gov/content/dam/soi/en/web/idfpr/faq/dpr/faqs-for-consumers.pdf

The Department may issue a disciplinary order. This is a directive by the disciplinary board to a licensee or unlicensed individual that has violated license law to refrain from undertaking that specific action again.

Related to the information above is an IDFPR PDF titled "FAQs for Administrative Hearings." Here are a few excerpts from this important document.

1. I received a formal complaint, what do I do? The formal complaint will provide information about when you must appear before the Department and when you must file an answer. Failing to timely respond may result in a default judgment against you, so you are strongly encouraged to cooperate with the Department. You have the right to be represented by an attorney and are strongly advised to seek representation.

2. What is an informal conference? The purpose of an informal conference is for the parties to informally negotiate and discuss a case to determine if a resolution can be made prior to a formal administrative hearing. You have the right to be represented by an attorney at an informal conference and are strongly advised to seek representation.

3. What is a preliminary hearing? The purpose of a preliminary hearing is to set a date on which all parties expect to be prepared for rulings by the Administrative Law Judge on any preliminary motions. This may be eliminated by agreement of the parties or the Administrative Law Judge.

4. What is an administrative hearing? An administrative hearing is a formal hearing before an Administrative Law Judge during which each party makes opening and closing statements, the Department presents a case in chief, and the Respondent presents their defense. The Administrative Law Judge may rule on the case immediately following the hearing or at a later date. (IDFPR)

If there is a circumstance or scenario in which disciplinary action is not warranted, another option is that the IDFPR may choose to take non-disciplinary action/s. The "FAQs for Administrative Hearings" PDF continues:

The Department may take any of the following non-disciplinary actions. This list is not exclusive.

- **Administrative Warning Letter/Letter of Concern:** An administrative warning letter (AWL) or letter of concern (LOC) may be issued to an individual or entity to bring attention to a specific issue, which may or may not be a violation of law.

- **Agreement for Care, Counseling & Treatment:** An Agreement for Care, Counseling, & Treatment (CCT) is a confidential agreement between a licensee and the Department wherein the licensee seeks recommended treatment. A licensee may continue to practice so long as he/she abides by the terms of the agreement. The agreement remains confidential unless a licensee violates its terms.

- **Non-Disciplinary Order:** A non-disciplinary order is not available to the public but imposes certain terms and conditions on the licensee. Failure to comply with the terms of the non-disciplinary order may result in public discipline.

- **Non-Disciplinary Fee or Administrative Fee:** This fee is a non-disciplinary, non-public action and may be issued in conjunction with a non-disciplinary order. (IDFPR)

You can read the full PDF at this link: https://idfpr.illinois.gov/content/dam/soi/en/web/idfpr/faq/dpr/faqs-for-administrative-hearings.pdf

Concerning disciplinary action, a simple sequence of events looks like this:

1. Case initiation. Someone initiates a case, files a complaint, etc.

2. Investigation

3. Prosecution

4. Disciplinary conference

5. Outcome

Section 225 ILCS 454/20-75 of The Act states:

a. All final administrative decisions of the Department are subject to judicial review under the Administrative Review Law and its rules. The term "administrative decision" is defined in Section 3-101 of the Code of Civil Procedure.

b. Proceedings for judicial review shall be commenced in the circuit court of the court in which the party applying for review resides, but if the party is not a resident of Illinois, the venue shall be in Sangamon County or Cook County.

The IDFPR has an emphasis on good and moral character. This foundation inside of each real estate professional sets up the industry, brokerage, and community for success, honesty, and transparency. The Act does not simply use the phrase "good character." It actually goes in depth. Take a look.

The Act, in 225 ILCS 454/5-25 is titled "Good moral character." It reads as follows:

a. When an applicant has had his or her license revoked on a prior occasion or when an applicant is found to have committed any of the practices enumerated in Section 20-20 of this Act or when an applicant has been convicted of or enters a plea of guilty or nolo contendere to forgery, embezzlement, obtaining money under false pretenses, larceny, extortion, conspiracy to defraud, or any other similar offense or offenses or has been convicted of a felony involving moral turpitude in any court of competent jurisdiction in this or any other state, district, or territory of the United States or of a foreign country, the Board may consider the prior revocation, conduct, or conviction in its determination of the applicant's moral character and whether to grant the applicant a license.

b. In its consideration of the prior revocation, conduct, or conviction, the Board shall take into account the nature of the conduct, any aggravating or extenuating circumstances, the time elapsed since the revocation, conduct, or conviction, the rehabilitation or restitution performed by the applicant, mitigating factors, and any other factors that the Board deems relevant, including, but not limited to:

1. the lack of direct relation of the offense for which the applicant was previously convicted to the duties, functions, and responsibilities of the position for which a license is sought;

2. unless otherwise specified, whether five years since a felony conviction or three years since release from confinement for the conviction, whichever is later, have passed without a subsequent conviction;

3. if the applicant was previously licensed or employed in this State or other states or jurisdictions, the lack of prior misconduct arising from or related to the licensed position or position of employment;

4. the age of the person at the time of the criminal offense;

5. if, due to the applicant's criminal conviction history, the applicant would be explicitly prohibited by federal rules or regulations from working in the position for which a license is sought;

6. successful completion of sentence and, for applicants serving a term of parole or probation, a progress report provided by the applicant's probation or parole officer that documents the applicant's compliance with conditions of supervision;

7. evidence of the applicant's present fitness and professional character;

8. evidence of rehabilitation or rehabilitative effort during or after incarceration, or during or after a term of supervision, including, but not limited to, a certificate of good conduct under Section 5-5.5-25 of the Unified Code of Corrections or a certificate of relief from disabilities under Section 5-5.5-10 of the Unified Code of Corrections; and

9. any other mitigating factors that contribute to the person's potential and current ability to perform the job duties.

c. The Department shall not require applicants to report the following information and shall not consider the following criminal history records in connection with an application for licensure or registration:

1. juvenile adjudications of delinquent minors as defined in Section 5-105 of the Juvenile Court Act of 1987 subject to the restrictions set forth in Section 5-130 of that Act;

2. law enforcement records, court records, and conviction records of an individual who was 17 years old at the time of the offense and before January 1, 2014, unless the nature of the offense required the individual to be tried as an adult;

3. records of arrests not followed by a charge or conviction;

4. records of arrests where the charges were dismissed unless related to the practice of the profession; however, applicants shall not be asked to report any arrests, and

an arrest not followed by a conviction shall not be the basis of a denial and may be used only to assess an applicant's rehabilitation;

5. convictions overturned by a higher court; or

6. convictions or arrests that have been sealed or expunged.

d. If an applicant makes a false statement of material fact on his or her application, the false statement may in itself be sufficient grounds to revoke or refuse to issue a license.

e. A licensee shall report to the Department, in a manner adopted by rule, any plea of guilty, or nolo contendere to forgery, embezzlement, obtaining money under false pretenses, larceny, extortion, conspiracy to defraud, or any similar offense or offenses or any conviction of a felony involving moral turpitude that occurs during the licensee's term of licensure.

What Would You Do?

Pretend you are in the situation that each question below presents. What would you do?

> **You're a licensed broker who wants to leave your brokerage or switch brokerages. How do you accomplish that?**

Changing brokerages is a fairly common practice that takes place every week in the real estate industry. At times, it's not that there's anything bad or wrong with a brokerage, it's that another brokerage is believed to be a better fit for the licensee. Sadly, at times, the circumstances are challenging or difficult and that prompts a licensee to leave. To be clear, this action terminates an employment agreement.

The first step to switch brokerages is to go to the IDFPR website and open up your personal portal. There you will enter the name of the new sponsoring broker and all supporting information. In addition, you will submit the $25 transfer fee required by the state of Illinois. For image and reputation purposes, it is appropriate to advise the designated managing broker of the office you are leaving that you have made the decision to join another office. This is a wise choice as this industry is one of networking and you never want to leave an office on bad terms. When you submit the change on your portal, the prior designated managing broker will be notified by the state of your action and the new managing broker will be asked to confirm that you will now be a sponsored licensee under his or her management.

You're a licensed broker and need to update your information with the IDFPR. How do you do that?

On the IDFPR website, under "Resources and publications," a broker can easily click one of these options: "Change Your Address" or "Change Your Name." The broker simply follows the steps and updates the information. Making sure the IDFPR has current information is the responsibility of each and every broker. These updates need to be done within *24 hours of a broker having a new address, new office location, new cell or land-line number, and/or new email address. *Since communications with the Department are now strictly online, the response time that has been established by the state is 24 hours from the point a change has been made.

Here is a link to the IDFPR's PDF entitled "Online Services Portal: Dashboard." It can walk a broker through navigating the website and making necessary changes. https://www.idfpr.com/Forms/Online/Online%20Services%20Portal%20Dashboard.pdf

What happens if your sponsoring broker's license is rendered inactive or revoked?

A ripple effect occurs. All brokers under the sponsoring broker are considered inactive. As such, they cannot legally engage in the business of real estate. Their licenses revert to active status when the sponsoring broker's license is reactivated, whether through reinstatement or renewal.

As you can see, when there is a question, it is always best to go to the source, which in this industry, is the Real Estate License Act of 2000. It's imperative that all real estate professionals, licensed or not, understand their rights, responsibilities, and how the law works in regard to real estate transactions in Illinois.

You have now finished an extensive final chapter. Congratulations! It's now time for your last chapter quiz.

CHAPTER 30 QUIZ

1. How often does Illinois law require the state legislature required to reinitiate The Act?

    a. Every 5 years
    b. Every 7 years
    c. Every 10 years
    d. Every 15 years

2. Which of the following professionals does the Division of Real Estate license and regulate in Illinois?

    a. Real estate brokers
    b. Appraisers
    c. Auctioneers
    d. Community association managers
    e. All of the above

3. The IDFPR administers four different primary monetary funds. Which of these funds focuses on consumers who have been victims of unlawful or unethical actions by licensees?

    a. The Real Estate Research and Education Fund
    b. The Real Estate License Administration Fund
    c. The Real Estate Consumer Protection Fund
    d. The Real Estate Recovery Fund

4. Robert is a licensee. Two years ago today, someone reported an alleged violation against him. How much longer does the IDFPR have the right to take action against Robert if they choose to do so before the statute of limitations kicks in?

    a. 1 more year
    b. 2 more years
    c. 3 more years
    d. 5 more years

5. Sarah passed the state-approved written exam on her career path of becoming a licensee. She is beyond excited! She currently does not have a managing broker. Can she submit her license application prior to securing a managing broker?

    a. Yes, but she cannot practice until she has a managing broker.
    b. Yes, and then she can practice real estate but must secure a managing broker within 60 days.
    c. No, she must secure a managing broker before she submits her license application.
    d. No, Sarah must complete three years of legal training to ensure that she and the managing broker are protected from liability.

6. Janissa has been a licensee working at the Home Now Brokerage for three years. She found out today that her sponsoring broker had her license revoked. What does this mean for Janissa?

    a. She still holds an active license and can practice real estate.
    b. She still holds an active license and can practice real estate with a few limitations outlined by The Act.
    c. Her license is considered inactive, and she cannot practice real estate.
    d. It depends on the reason why her managing broker's license was revoked.

7. Real estate licenses in Illinois are required to be renewed how often?

    a. Every year
    b. Every two years
    c. Every three years
    d. Every four years

8. Jan is a broker who has been licensed in Connecticut for two years. This past week, she moved to Illinois. Does she have to do any coursework or log classroom time in order to practice real estate in Illinois?

    a. No.
    b. Yes.
    c. No, she is only required to take the state-specific part of the licensing exam.
    d. Yes, she is required to take the state-specific part of the licensing exam along with the 12 hours of continuing education.

9. Concerning continuing education requirements, which of the following is incorrect?

    a. Managing brokers must successfully complete 24 hours.
    b. Brokers must successfully complete 18 hours.
    c. Residential leasing agents must successfully complete 8 hours.
    d. All licensees must take the sexual harassment course.

10. Licensee Jacob is cleaning up his office and organizing his files. His office is a mess. He finds a few stacks of old transaction records. How long must he keep those on file according to The Act?

    a. Two years
    b. Three years
    c. Five years
    d. Seven years

11. Ron is a new licensee. He has a background in digital marketing. He created a logo for himself and wants to use his name with the logo to advertise online. Is Ron permitted to use this unique logo?

    a. Yes, Ron can advertise in his name.
    b. No, a broker cannot advertise in his or her name.
    c. It depends on the brokerage.
    d. Yes, as long as the sponsoring broker's name is equal to or larger than Ron's name.

12. The IDFPR has a database of formal decisions online called the index of decisions. Which of the following statements below is false concerning this database?

    a. It includes information on refusal to renew, revocation, and suspension of licenses.
    b. It includes the names of the offenders.
    c. It's available to the public.
    d. It includes the addresses of the offenders.
    e. Only A and B

13. Michael found out that his license is being withheld by the Department. He is very upset. Which of the following might be the cause of the delay in issuance?

    a. He failed to pay the previous two months of rent on his apartment.
    b. He has not filed state income tax returns for the previous two years.
    c. He is delinquent on his child support payments.
    d. Only B and C
    e. A, B, and C

14. Janet is a sponsoring broker. One of her newest brokers, Jimmy, has been a superstar since he started working at her brokerage six months ago. Jimmy is high energy, a real people person, and even great with the details. However, today, Janet was informed that Jimmy misused the earnest money that he had been entrusted with on a new real estate transaction. This has never happened before in her brokerage. Is it possible that Jimmy's actions will affect her and her license? If so, how?

    a. No, his actions will not affect her license.

    b. His actions could cause her license to be suspended.

    c. If she knew of his actions and failed to correct them, she could face consequences as she is responsible for his actions.

    d. If she did not know of his actions, she wouldn't face consequences.

15. What disciplinary actions can the Department take when someone has violated an aspect of licensing law?

    a. Reprimand, probation, suspension, revocation, refuse to renew, fines, order to cease and desist, and more options.

    b. Reprimand, probation, revocation, and order to cease and desist.

    c. Probation, suspension, revocation, fines, and order to cease and desist.

    d. Reprimand, probation, suspension, revocation, refuse to renew, fines, and order to cease and desist.

16. If an action by a licensee does not warrant disciplinary action, the Department may take non-disciplinary action. Which answer best captures possible outcomes for non-disciplinary action?

    a. Administrative warning letter, agreement for care, counseling and treatment, non-disciplinary order, non-disciplinary fee, or administrative fee.

    b. Verbal reprimand, administrative warning letter, letter of concern, agreement for care, counseling and treatment, non-disciplinary order, non-disciplinary fee, or administrative fee.

    c. Administrative warning letter, letter of concern, agreement for care, counseling and medication, non-disciplinary order, non-disciplinary fee, or administrative fee.

    d. Administrative warning letter, letter of concern, agreement for care, counseling and treatment, non-disciplinary order, non-disciplinary fee, or administrative fee.

17. All fines and penalties that are submitted go to the State Treasury. Which fund are they deposited into?

    a. Real Estate Recovery Fund
    b. Consumer Protection Fund
    c. Disciplinary Action Fund
    d. None of the above

18. The License Act was originally created in 1922. Section 1-5 establishes the intent for The Act. Which of the following is not one of the intents?

    a. To protect the public
    b. To regulate the actions of the licensee and the sponsoring broker
    c. To protect the licensee from unnecessary interference in doing their job from the designated managing broker
    d. To provide a means for evaluating the licensee's competency

19. In order to meet the industry's needs for qualified real estate brokers, which of the following would be a correct statement? The state . . .

    a. Provides for a preliminary period of 150 days, allowing the candidate to practice real estate and learn the strategic issues before taking the state exam.
    b. Does not provide for an apprentice period. The candidate must complete and take the state exam before being able to practice the profession.
    c. Provides a specialized license labeled Broker Mentor that can be used to guide potential candidates into the industry before they pass the state exam.
    d. Ignores the situation entirely, letting the industry create methods to allow candidates to learn the specifics of the industry in a hands-on approach.

20. The law provides for the ability of a property owner to sell their property without the necessity of a license. Sam wants to begin purchasing homes that are in need of renovation so he can fix and flip them. As Sam is acquiring the properties directly from their owners, what is the position of the state regarding this practice?

    a. The law permits purchasing of real estate by an individual but limits the number of transactions to two within a 12-month period without the necessity of having a license.

    b. There are no limitations established by law as to the number of units an individual acting on his or her own behalf is allowed to purchase within a 12-month period.

    c. Illinois law does not address an individual's rights in regard to purchasing real estate but does address the person's right to sell real estate. Sam must be aware that each seller he comes in contact with will be limited to the sale of only one property within a 12-month period.

    d. As long as Sam registers himself with the Secretary of State's office as a qualified real estate investor, there are no provisions of law that limit Sam's ability to purchase or sell real estate within any period of time.

CONCLUSION

THANK YOU FOR READING.

At Inland Real Estate School, we take pride in actively supporting our students.

If you have any questions concerning the material you have read or about your future in real estate, reach out to us.

For media inquiries, speaking engagements, and/or book-related purchases and questions, contact us via email or a social media channel listed below.

SCHOOL INFORMATION:

- Email: school@inlandreschool.com

- Phone: 877-990-8409

- Website: www.InlandRESchool.com

SOCIAL MEDIA CHANNELS:

- Facebook: www.facebook.com/inlandreschool

- David McGowan's LinkedIn: www.linkedin.com/in/educatordavidmcgowan

- Stephanie Krol's LinkedIn: www.linkedin.com/in/stephaniekrol

ADDITIONAL RESOURCES:

- IDFPR: www.idfpr.com

- Exam Smart: www.ExamSmart.com (Study aide)

- CompuCram: www.CompuCram.com (Study aide)

- Real Estate License Act of 2000: The IDFPR has a link with a section called Laws and Rules. This section has links to both the Real Estate License Act and the Real Estate License Rules: https://idfpr.illinois.gov/profs/REALEST.asp

PSI LINKS:

- PSI Homepage: www.PSIOnline.com

- PSI Registration: https://schedule.psiexams.com/

- PSI Exam Schedule Link: www.psiexams.com/ilre

QUIZ ANSWERS

Below, you will find the answers to each quiz.
The correct answers are in bold.

CHAPTER 1 QUIZ ANSWERS

1. There are a number of different loan programs available to the purchaser of a residential home. Which type of mortgage loan program can the purchaser of a townhouse acquire that periodically adjusts the interest rates based on an index that reflects the cost to the lender for lending the money?
    a. **Adjustable rate**
    b. Fixed rate
    c. 30-year fixed
    d. Graduated payment loan

2. Sam and Martha are interested in purchasing an investment building. They have a friend Mark Dillon, who recently acquired his real estate license. If Mark agrees to work with Sam and Martha, the role Mark is going to play is:
    a. The agent of the loan officer, who will provide necessary funds to purchase the property
    b. The attorney, who will provide Sam and Martha with the necessary legal advice regarding the purchase of the property
    c. **The real estate agent charged with the responsibility of representing the best interest of Sam and Martha**
    d. Simply a friend providing advice on what they need to do

3. A real estate agent is someone who has acquired a broker's license and is generally charged with the responsibility to represent the best interest of which party:
    a. Seller of real estate
    b. Buyer of real estate
    c. Landlord
    d. **Whoever has hired (engaged) the broker**

4. Karen, having recently graduated from college, is interested in purchasing a condo rather than moving back in with her parents. In order for her to secure a loan, the lender wishes to verify the current value of the property. Which of the following terms is a professional judgment of the property's value on a specific date?
    a. Home inspection report
    b. **Appraisal**
    c. Estimate
    d. Home value report

5. A real estate licensee is someone who represents sellers and/or buyers of real estate or real property. The sellers and buyers could be:
    a. Individuals
    b. Companies
    c. Firms
    d. **All of the above**

6. Andrew wants to start his own business. As he has an interest in real estate, he thought it might be best to start a real estate brokerage office. If Andrew has the funding necessary to start the business, what other credentials will be required in order to make the business operational? Who has the credentials and can legally exercise the option of starting their own brokerage and employing other real estate agents?

    a.   Any real estate agent who has successfully passed the state broker exam

    b.   Only a broker

    c.   **Only a designated managing broker**

    d.   An attorney working under court-ordered supervision

7. What term is frequently used to represent the action within the real estate industry that reflects the representation of buyers, sellers, landlords, and/or tenants in the pursuit of real estate possibilities?

    a.   **Brokerage**

    b.   Buyer's agency

    c.   Property management agreement

    d.   Licensee

8. Quinton is looking to buy a new home for his family. In order to better understand the markets and available housing, which professional would most likely be the choice to give Quinton some insight and direction into the marketplace?

    a.   Seller's agent

    b.   **Buyer's agent**

    c.   Leasing agent

    d.   Property manager

9. Closing costs are the expenses that are in addition to and on top of the price of the property. They are payable by:

    a.   **The buyer only**

    b.   Both the buyer and seller are responsible for paying their respective closing costs

    c.   Seller only

    d.   Either party depending upon the written agreement by and between the seller's and buyer's attorney

10. The sales contract is the binding agreement between buyer and seller that will ultimately fulfill the desire to deliver the deed. The contract lays out terms and conditions that buyer and seller agree to regarding the transaction. Provisions within this contract that establishes certain obligations of either party are generally considered to be:

    a.   Closing costs

    b.   **Contingencies**

    c.   Preapproval letter

    d.   Power of attorney

11. Which of the following individuals has been granted written authority to execute legal documentation on behalf of the owner who wants to sell/lease the home or property?

    a.   Listing agent

    b.   Seller's agent

    c.   **Attorney-in-fact**

    d.   Buyer's agent

12. When a buyer makes an application for a mortgage, the lender will confirm the buyer's credentials, which might include verifying employment and the financial capability to repay the debt. An essential element of judging the buyer's financial capability is looking at their history of satisfying the debt to other creditors. Which of the four documents used in processing the mortgage loan would give the lender an understanding of the buyer's responsibility for repayment of debt?

    a.   **Credit report**

    b.   Preapproval letter

    c.   Pre-authorization letter

    d.   Satisfaction of mortgage

13. There are different professional associations that licensees may elect to participate in. When a licensee secures their license, which of the following professional associations does the licensee automatically belong to?
    a. The local board of REALTORS®
    b. National Association of REALTORS®
    c. Association of Real Estate Professionals
    d. **There is no professional association the licensee automatically belongs to after securing their real estate license.**

14. Special-purpose properties are generally highly specialized with regard to their use, resulting in a limited supply. Many times, this requires a specialized means of appraisal in order to establish a market value. Which of the following is NOT included in the category of special purpose real property?
    a. Places of worship
    b. Colleges
    c. **Construction sites**
    d. Cemeteries

15. There are five categories of real property. Which of the following would not fall in the realm of real property?
    a. Special purpose
    b. Apartment buildings consisting of five or more units
    c. Rental properties
    d. **Motor homes**

16. Licensees are required to complete continuing education to further enhance their knowledge of real estate law so they can better protect the interest of their clients. The requirements for continuing education must be met before the licensee can renew their licenses. Said requirements are established by:
    a. The designated managing broker
    b. The Federal Government
    c. **The state licensing agency**
    d. The local board in REALTORS® in conjunction with the National Association of REALTORS®

17. Development activities include all of these, except which one?
    a. Renovation
    b. Re-lease of existing buildings
    c. **Home inspections**
    d. Raw land purchases

18. Real estate skill set training and practical education can be provided through:
    a. State-approved educational venues
    b. **The sponsoring broker to ensure the licensee can successfully protect the interests of the consumer**
    c. Professional vocational schools licensed under the state's department of education
    d. Such education is not required so long as the licensee uses simple common sense on how to protect the financial interests of their client

19. Who or what sets the minimum standards and requirements for those who seek to obtain a real estate license?
    a. Sponsoring broker
    b. Board of REALTORS®
    c. Federal Government
    d. **State regulatory agency responsible for the oversight of professional industries**

20. In order for the buyer to fully understand the physical condition of the property, there will generally be a home inspection by a licensed home inspector. Who has the responsibility of paying for the services of this home inspector?
    a. **Buyer**
    b. Seller
    c. Brokerage
    d. Agent or broker

CHAPTER 2 QUIZ ANSWERS

1. Which social science focuses on the production, consumption, and transfer of wealth, and the distribution and consumption of goods and services?
   a. Sociology
   b. **Economics**
   c. Business
   d. Micro-business

2. Real estate economics applies to which of the following?
   a. Residential
   b. Commercial
   c. Industrial
   d. **All of the above**
   e. None of the above

3. Real estate business is an industry consisting of multiple facets. Which of the following would not constitute a facet of the real estate industry as it exists within the market?
   a. Buyer representation
   b. Seller representation
   c. **Lender representation**
   d. Landlord representation

4. The real estate market is able to exist and yet there is a question as to whether or not it can exist and thrive within its own individual bubble. Which of the statements below would best reflect the real estate industry's existence within its own unique bubble?
   a. **The real estate industry is impacted by a number of variables as well as forces that help to define its parameters. Therefore, the real estate industry is of a nature that it cannot exist within its own unique bubble but is directly impacted by influences from other realms including buyer sentiments and industry standards.**
   b. Due to restraints established by society, the real estate industry is limited to the simple act of representing the best interest of a seller in a real estate transaction.
   c. Unlike other industries, the demand for real estate does not have an impact on the availability and pricing of such.
   d. The government does not have any influence over the real estate industry, and as such, is not a factor in defining the parameters and conditions under which business activities can be performed.

5. Which term reflects the amount or quantity of a commodity, product, or service available and the desire of buyers for it?
   a. Supply
   b. Demand
   c. **Supply and demand**
   d. None of the above

6. Supply and demand focus on which of the following?
   a. Price determination
   b. The interaction between homebuyers and sellers
   c. **Both of the above**
   d. None of the above

7. In a competitive market, the house prices can fluctuate until they settle at a point where the quantity demanded (at the current asking price) will equal the quantity that is supplied (also at the current asking price). What does this generate?
   a. Greater supply and demand
   b. Less supply and demand
   c. Interest rate increases
   d. **An economic equilibrium**

8. A city in California has a vibrant job market and is attracting new people who want to settle down there. However, the supply of houses is low. Since the demand is high, how does that affect prices?
   a. House prices usually stay the same.
   b. House prices usually decrease.
   c. **House prices usually increase.**
   d. None of the above

9. Construction companies and project managers are finding it difficult to find and hire the specialists and skilled laborers that they need in order to complete housing projects. What has been created?
   a. **A reduction in the available supply of new housing designed to meet the demands of the consumers.**
   b. A general increase in the demand for real estate because of the creative nature that unskilled specialists can bring to the marketplace.
   c. An environment that discourages potential specialists from entering the construction industry due to government interference in construction standards
   d. The lack of skilled craftspeople in constructing homes does not have any influence on the availability or supply of new housing.

10. When construction costs increase, what almost always happens?
    a. The market stays the same
    b. **The market slows down**
    c. The market speeds up
    d. None of the above

11. The Federal Reserve regulates and supervises the practices of which financial institutions?
    a. Lending institutions
    b. Banking institutions
    c. **Both of the above**
    d. None of the above

12. What is the ultimate goal of the Federal Reserve?
    a. **Banking system stability**
    b. Government accountability
    c. Credit bureau accountability
    d. To control government cash flow

13. For new home construction or expansions, what is the necessary legal approval required in order to complete those projects?
    a. A listing contract executed by a real estate licensee approved by the local municipality to represent the developer in pursuit of a potential buyer.
    b. **Building permit**
    c. An executed sales contract establishing that there is an interested buyer to assume the ownership of the property upon completion of the project.
    d. None of the above

14. Demographics can best be defined as a reflection of which of the following?
    a. The natural need of society to establish a place to live. The extent of the population defines the need for real estate and also governs the nature of the demographics.
    b. Reflects the general concept that the desire to purchase real estate has nothing to do with financial capability but simply the need to provide a financial platform to grow personal wealth.
    c. **The study of the human population including various levels of education, national origin, various age ranges, spending habits, and the potential study of society and subsets.**
    d. A reflection of the direction the money market is taking and how we define the availability of funds in the pursuit of real estate investments.
    e. Population growth generally has the same growth rate in all major US cities.
    f. This is a true statement as society has evolved into a consistency regarding the general growth of the population.
    g. This is true, as the government has established the maximum population density that can be defined and achieved in a given marketplace.
    h. This is false because the general population within the US has not changed for over 100 years.
    i. **This is false as there are a number of factors that impact population growth, such as employment opportunities and housing availability.**

15. Which of the following can influence people to move to a new city?
    a. Good economy in the city
    b. Healthy job market in the city
    c. Low interest rates
    d. **All of the above**

16. A bad economy usually means less movement of:
    a. Money
    b. People
    c. Assets
    d. **All of the above**
    e. None of the above

17. In general terms, when interest rates are low, the demand for real estate will:
    a. **Increase as housing becomes more affordable**
    b. Decrease as the economy is shaky and as such consumers tend to be cautious in purchasing real estate, which many consider to be an unstable investment opportunity.
    c. Hold steady as people oftentimes consider the future as being defined by what happens in the economic climate. If interest rates go down, that is a potential sign of a pending recession or depression.
    d. Hold steady because lenders are now more cautious about loaning money and create more restrictions that limit a buyer's ability to qualify for the debt.

18. When a purchaser is interested in acquiring a new home, and they find themselves in a position where they have to borrow the money from a lender, the lender is concerned with the buyer's ability to meet the monthly debt. Which of the following factors does a lender specifically look at to judge a buyer's eligibility?
    a. The number of foreclosures that had been reported in a specific neighborhood.
    b. The number of siblings that a buyer has that may be used as cosigners or backup resources.
    c. **The buyer's gross income and the commitments the buyer has incurred regarding repayment of other debt.**
    d. The financial strength of the municipality where the property in question is located and as to whether or not the governmental services provided are adequate to meet the needs of any purchaser of the property.

19. Demand for housing has been impacted by a number of different facets. Which of the following would not be considered a factor that could influence the demand for real estate?
    a. Interest rates
    b. Demographics
    c. Population
    d. **Accessibility to the stock market**

CHAPTER 3 QUIZ ANSWERS

1. When someone wants to become a real estate agent, he/she is usually drawn to this career because of a desire for:
    a. Being his or her own boss
    b. Income possibilities
    c. Flexible schedule
    d. **All of the above**

2. A career in real estate includes:
    a. Working with a wide variety of people
    b. Variety
    c. Needing outstanding people skills
    d. **All of the above**

3. Real estate brokers interact with:
    a. Only buyers and sellers
    b. Sponsoring brokers
    c. Property inspectors
    d. **All of the above**

4. AREAA focuses on which of the following?
    a. African Americans
    b. **Asian Americans**
    c. LGBT Americans
    d. Hispanic

5. What is the biggest trade organization in the US?
    a. **NAR**
    b. NAREB
    c. NAHREP
    d. AREAA

6. NAREB, NAHREP, AREAA, and NAGLREP have which characteristics in common?
    a. **Seeking to end discrimination**
    b. Focuses exclusively on commercial real estate
    c. All of the above
    d. None of the above

7. NAREB focuses on which of the following?
    a. **African Americans**
    b. Asian Americans
    c. LGBT Americans
    d. Hispanic
    e. None of the above

8. Does NAR target a specific demographic?
    a. Yes, African Americans
    b. Yes, Asian Americans
    c. Yes, the LGBT community
    d. Yes, Hispanic
    e. **No**

9. NAGLREP focuses on which of the following?
    a. African Americans
    b. Asian Americans
    c. **LGBT Americans**
    d. Hispanic

10. Which of the following is not a commercial real estate organization?
    a. Institute of Real Estate Management (IREM)
    b. National Multifamily Housing Council (NMHC)
    c. The Appraisal Institute
    d. **National Association of Multilingual Attorneys (NAMA)**

CHAPTER 4 QUIZ ANSWERS

1. The definition of land includes:
    a. Houses
    b. Garages
    c. Swimming pools
    d. All of the above
    e. **None of the above**

2. The definition of land also includes:
    a. Soil
    b. Plants
    c. Minerals in the subsurface
    d. **All of the above**

3. Real estate and land are the same thing.
    a. True
    b. **False**

4. Real estate includes:
   a. Only land
   b. **Human-made structures and land**
   c. Only human-made structures
   d. Soil and water

5. An improvement is each of the following except:
   a. A development on the land
   b. **A series of potted plants on the front porch**
   c. Something permanently attached to the land
   d. An addition to the land

6. Fences, houses, other buildings, landscaping, and driveways are classified as which of the following?
   a. **Real property**
   b. Personal property
   c. Appurtenances
   d. Emblements
   e. Chattel

7. An appurtenance is generally immovable.
   a. **True**
   b. False

8. Which answer below most accurately describes personal property?
   a. Something attached or affixed to the land
   b. Movable
   c. Tangible
   d. **Movable and tangible**

9. Another word for personal property is which word below?
   a. **Chattel**
   b. Emblement
   c. Appurtenance
   d. Capitale

10. A Ming vase, having been given to the property owner as a wedding gift, is commonly referred to as which of the following?
    a. Emblement
    b. **Personal property**
    c. Real property
    d. Fee simple defeasible estate

11. Which of the following is an item that is attached to a building that is used in the operation of a business?
    a. **Trade fixture**
    b. Chattel
    c. Emblement
    d. Appurtenance

12. The acronym M.A.R.I.A. is a simple way to recall a framework for figuring out whether something is a fixture or not. What does the acronym M.A.R.I.A. stand for?
    a. Method, add-on, real, intention, agreement
    b. Method, appurtenance, relationship, instance, agreement
    c. **Method, adaptability, relationship, intention, agreement**
    d. Movable, add-on, relationship, intention, agreement

13. Two categories emerge when it comes to crops, plants, and trees. It centers around one question. What is that question?
    a. Who purchased the crops, plants, and/or trees?
    b. **Is annual cultivation required?**
    c. Is the land government owned?
    d. Is the land special purpose?

14. Which answer below is not correct when considering how the Illinois General Assembly defines the term manufactured home?
    a. Factory-assembled
    b. Permanent chassis
    c. **Clear intention**
    d. Movable

15. Mobile homes and manufactured homes found in mobile home parks must be assessed and taxed as chattel.
    a. **True**
    b. False

16. Which statement is false concerning the Real Estate License Act of 2000?
    a. It was amended in 2020.
    b. It's commonly called The Act.
    c. **It does not apply to all real estate professionals.**
    d. It is overseen by the IDFPR.

17. Which type of law has been established by court decisions as a result of lawsuits?
    a. Common law
    b. Local ordinances
    c. License law
    d. **Case law**

18. What is the primary purpose of RELA and laws in general?
    a. **To protect the public**
    b. To generate funding
    c. To oversee real estate taxes
    d. To extend its own reach

19. Which answer is best? Licensing protects consumers from _____.
    a. Real estate professionals lying or cheating
    b. Real estate professionals being incompetent
    c. **All of the above**
    d. None of the above

20. Which word fills in the blank accurately? "Mobile homes and manufactured homes outside of mobile home parks must be assessed and taxed as _____."
    a. Land
    b. Personal property
    c. **Real property**
    d. Real estate

CHAPTER 5 QUIZ ANSWERS

1. Homeownership can possibly provide:
    a. Peace of mind
    b. Stability
    c. New options
    d. **All of the above**
    e. None of the above

2. In the real estate tax cycle, what does the County Clerk do?
    a. Establishes home values
    b. Approves exemptions
    c. Prints and mails tax bills
    d. All of the above
    e. **None of the above**

3. To the IRS, the terms "real estate tax" and "property tax" are the exact same thing.
    a. **True**
    b. False

4. In Illinois, taxes are paid in arrears.
   a. **True**
   b. False

5. Which phrase helps describe a tax credit?
   a. Incurred expenses in a calendar year
   b. Decreasing the taxable income
   c. **Dollar-for-dollar reduction**
   d. It is not recognized in Illinois.

6. If a loss or damage occurs in a 1902 Victorian home that was unforeseen or unintended, what is the specific tax benefit called?
   a. Claim loss
   b. **Accidental loss**
   c. Appurtenances
   d. Home insurance loss

7. Sarah just sold her home. Her profits from the sale of a house were $75,000. Which word defines what this money is called?
   a. **Capital Gains**
   b. Mortgage loan interest deduction
   c. Points and closing costs
   d. Deferment

8. Can people who rent a home or apartment benefit from home office expenses if they own or run a business from their residence or if they are self-employed?
   a. **Yes**
   b. No

9. Any mortgage financed by the FHA requires the borrower to have which of the following?
   a. High credit score
   b. Life insurance policy naming the FHA as the beneficiary
   c. **Mortgage insurance**
   d. All of the above

10. An active duty military member and her family are moving across the country. According to the Tax Cuts and Jobs Act of 2017, can she deduct moving costs on her taxes?
    a. **Yes**
    b. No

11. Which of the following is a simple definition for points?
    a. Standard deduction
    b. Itemized deductions
    c. **Prepaid interest**
    d. None of the above

12. Which of the following describes a 1031 exchange?
    a. Capital gains taxation
    b. Federal solar tax credit
    c. Sales tax issued at closing
    d. **Strategy for tax deferment**

13. Can property that increased in value greatly since its purchase be exchanged for other property?
    a. **Yes**
    b. No

14. One of the main appeals of condo ownership is property ownership without having the responsibility of which of the following?
    a. **Lawn maintenance and repairs**
    b. Real estate taxes
    c. Property taxes
    d. None of the above

15. Which of the following is an example of a converted-use property?
    a. A small factory is now a retail center
    b. An old barn is now a single-family home
    c. A cafe is transformed into a barber shop
    d. **All of the above**

16. In a co-op, unit residents pay their portion of the maintenance and care expenses of the building.
    a. **True**
    b. False
    c. It depends on the co-op
    d. Co-ops are prohibited from charging maintenance fees by law

17. Who oversees the National Flood Insurance Program?
    a. The state government in which the homeowner resides
    b. **Federal Emergency Management Agency**
    c. The Environmental Protection Agency
    d. National Domestic Preparedness Office

18. Which type of housing has numerous purchasers who own a specific amount of time within a given time frame?
    a. Condos
    b. Co-ops
    c. MUDs
    d. **Timeshares**

19. Which type of housing is a designed grouping that contains housing, recreation areas and/or buildings, business/retail centers, along with industrial zones that exist within one subdivision?
    a. A MUD
    b. Converted-use
    c. Manufactured housing
    d. **A PUD**

20. Which of the following are prefabricated homes?
    a. Modular homes
    b. Manufactured housing
    c. Mobile homes
    d. **All of the above**

CHAPTER 6 QUIZ ANSWERS

1. What is the term that describes a relationship in which a broker or licensee, whether directly or indirectly, represents a consumer by his/her consent in a real property transaction?
    a. **Agency**
    b. Brokerage
    c. Dual agency
    d. Broker agreement

2. What term's definition includes finder fees, discounts, and retainer fee?
    a. Referral
    b. **Compensation**
    c. Broker agreement
    d. None of the above

3. Which word below means a person who is not being represented by the licensee?
    a. Consumer
    b. **Customer**
    c. Candidate
    d. None of the above

4. The "minimum services provision" was enacted to:
    a. Ensure the consumer is protected
    b. Make sure licensees accept delivery of all offers from buyers
    c. Compel licensees to care for the absolute best interests of the client
    d. **All of the above**
    e. None of the above

5. "COLD AC" helps you remember your fiduciary duties as a licensee. What does that acronym stand for?
    a. Comprehensive, Obedience, Licensed, Disclosure, Accountability, Confidentiality
    b. Care, Observance, Loyalty, Disclosure, Accountability, Confidentiality
    c. Careful, Obedience, Law-abiding, Disclosure, Accounting, Confidence
    d. **Care, Obedience, Loyalty, Disclosure, Accountability, Confidentiality**

6. What occurs when you have a single real estate licensee that is representing both the buyer and seller simultaneously?
    a. **Being a dual agent**
    b. Being a fiduciary
    c. Being a sponsoring broker
    d. None of the above

7. Known material facts are to be disclosed to only the principal, not all parties.
    a. True
    b. **False**

8. Licensees are required by law to disclose information about physical defects and material facts.
    a. Depends on the circumstances
    b. **True**
    c. False

9. The Residential Real Property Disclosure Report is to be used with which of the following?
    a. Only a single residence
    b. **A 1-4 unit residential property**
    c. A five or more unit residential property
    d. Apartment complexes
    e. None of the above

10. Which type of defects are defined as those defects in the property that the seller is aware of, but that are not visible to the buyer?
    a. **Latent defects**
    b. Patent defects
    c. Dormant defects
    d. Inspection defects

11. Accountability is not a fiduciary duty. It's the job of real estate bookkeepers or in-house support teams.
    a. True
    b. **False**

12. Mixing client money with your own funds is which of the following?
    a. Acceptable
    b. Conversion
    c. Fraud
    d. **Commingling**

13. As a licensee, you are able to share confidential information without the express written authorization given by the client if it's an advantageous decision given the circumstances.
    a. True
    b. **False**

14. You hear another licensee talking to a potential client. He says, "This is the most extraordinary property for this price you'll find within 50 miles of here. The neighborhood is amazing. The social life is phenomenal." What has he most likely just done?
    a. He is lying
    b. He is misrepresenting the listing
    c. **He is puffing**
    d. None of the above

15. What does the Dru Sjodin National Sex Offender Public Website (NSOPW) provide to the public?
    a. A list of sex offenses that have happened in the areas they search
    b. **Where registered sex offenders live**
    c. Where registered sex offenders currently work
    d. All of the above

16. Does Illinois require listing agents to disclose if a registered sex offender lives near a listing?
    a. **No**
    b. Yes

17. Which is an example of a stigmatized property?
    a. A house where a murder took place
    b. A property where lynching happened
    c. A home where someone committed suicide
    d. **All of the above**
    e. None of the above

18. According to The Act, which term means "a sponsored licensee named by a sponsoring broker as the legal agent of a client"?
    a. **Designated agent**
    b. Dual agent
    c. Sponsoring broker
    d. Dual agency

19. Is it possible and legal for two licensees from the exact same real estate company to have the ability to represent opposite parties in the sale of a property?
    a. No
    b. **Yes**

20. You are representing the best interests of the person you are working with as your client unless you have which of the following written declarations?
    a. Nondisclosure agreement
    b. Designated broker
    c. Dual agency
    d. **Notice of no agency**

CHAPTER 7 QUIZ ANSWERS

1. The Act states that "a relationship in which a broker or licensee, whether directly or through an affiliated licensee, represents a consumer by the consumer's consent." What is this known as?
    a. **Agency**
    b. No agency
    c. Power of attorney
    d. Substantive contact
    e. None of the above

2. Which agency relationship is always a fiduciary relationship by nature?
    a. Single agency
    b. Dual agency
    c. Buyer agency
    d. **All of the above**

3. In which way or ways can agency be created?
    a. Expressed
    b. Implied
    c. Written
    d. Verbal
    e. **All of the above**

4. Illinois agents actively work on what is known as a presumption of agency, also known as implied agency.
    a. **True**
    b. False

5. Which word or words accurately fill in the blank? The licensing act is "You are considered to be the agent of the party you are working with, unless some other _____ exists."
   a. Verbal agreement
   b. **Written declaration**
   c. Substantive contact
   d. No agency

6. When you start a conversation with a consumer, especially a potential buyer, and begin inquiring as to what they are looking for and how you can be of assistance, which of the following best describes that scenario?
   a. Single agency
   b. No agency
   c. **Substantive contact**
   d. None of the above

7. A no agency relationship means that there is neither a written agreement nor a fiduciary relationship in existence.
   a. **True**
   b. False

8. In Illinois, agency may be terminated under which of the following circumstances?
   a. Death of the principal
   b. Incapacity of the principal
   c. Breach of contract
   d. **All of the above**

9. All agents authorized by a principal do have the same privileges and levels of authority.
   a. True
   b. **False**

10. According to The Act, which term below is defined as a "sponsored licensee named by a sponsoring broker as the legal agent of a client"?
    a. **Designated agent**
    b. Special agent
    c. General agent
    d. Universal agent

11. What is present when one agent, broker, or firm represents the interests of either one seller or one buyer?
    a. Property management agency
    b. Dual agency
    c. **Single agency**
    d. Buyer agency

12. With a first-year license, Sarah just asked a consumer to sign a dual agency representation. To her surprise, the consumer declined to do so. What can Sarah do?
    a. Create a single agency
    b. Withdraw with liability
    c. **Withdraw with no liability**
    d. Nothing

13. This is an agreement where a buyer and seller in the same transaction are represented by two different agents who work at the same brokerage.
    a. Buyer agency
    b. Property management agency
    c. **Designated agency**
    d. No agency

14. In Illinois, which is accurate concerning agency disclosure?
    a. It is exceptionally important.
    b. It defines the working relationships between the agent and the client.
    c. It is required according to The Act.
    d. **All of the above**

15. What's the purpose of the agency disclosure requirement?
    a. Assurance that all the other sponsored licensees that work in the same company do not obtain information that is confidential or private in nature
    b. To fulfill the law
    c. To stay in alignment with The Act
    d. **All of the above**

16. Are property managers required to have a real estate license in Illinois?
    a. No
    b. **Yes**
    c. Only if by direct request from the owner
    d. It depends on the county where the property is located

17. As the property manager, which action can he/she most likely not perform?
    a. Oversee the property
    b. **Sell the property**
    c. Market the property
    d. Lease the property
    e. None of the above

18. Buyer agency can be which of the following?
    a. Implied
    b. Express
    c. **A and B**
    d. Buyer agency is expressly prohibited by The Act.

19. Special agents are authorized to represent the principal in multiple business transactions.
    a. True
    b. **False**

20. Which of the following licensee designations would not be responsible for the fiduciary duties defined under agency law?
    a. A general agent acting as a designated agent
    b. **Secret agent**
    c. Special agent acting as a designated agent
    d. Designated agent

CHAPTER 8 QUIZ ANSWERS

1. How does a brokerage firm function?
    a. A middleman
    b. A connecting point
    c. A broker
    d. **All of the above**
    e. None of the above

2. A brokerage may only be legally structured as a partnership or an LLC.
    a. True
    b. **False**

3. Two main categories of brokerages are independent and franchises.
    a. **True**
    b. False

4. In order for a broker to qualify to become a managing broker, he/she must be a broker for a minimum of how many years?
    a. One
    b. **Two**
    c. Three
    d. Four
    e. Experience as a broker is not required.

5. How many levels of real estate licenses does Illinois currently have?
    a. Three
    b. **Four**
    c. Five
    d. Six

6. Which word means the services that real estate professionals are deemed competent to perform and which actions they are permitted to take, all while staying in alignment and agreement with the terms of their professional license?
    a. Company handbook
    b. Fiduciary
    c. Legal requirements
    d. **Scope of practice**

7. In Illinois, each and every licensee is directly engaged by which of the following?
    a. **Sponsoring broker**
    b. Brokerage owner
    c. Property owner
    d. Company president

8. Which of the following actions may be performed by a residential leasing agent?
    a. Assist property owner in navigating the difficult and ever-changing nature of the property market
    b. Oversee all paperwork, including the signing of leases
    c. Serve as a landlord to the tenants
    d. **All of the above**

9. According to The Act, whose responsibilities "include directly handling all earnest money, escrows, advertisement approvals, and contract negotiations for all transactions where the designated agent for the transaction has not completed his or her 45 hours of post-license education" by the license renewal date?
    a. Designated agent
    b. Sponsoring broker
    c. **Designated managing broker**
    d. Leasing agent

10. According to The Act, which term "means an individual, entity, corporation, foreign or domestic partnership, limited liability company, registered limited liability partnership, or other business entity other than a residential leasing agent who, whether in person or through any media or technology, for another and for compensation, or with the intention or expectation of receiving compensation, either directly or indirectly"?
    a. Broker
    b. Sponsoring broker
    c. Designated managing broker
    d. **All of the above**
    e. None of the above

11. Any leasing of commercial properties always requires a managing broker's or broker's license.
    a. **True**
    b. False

12. Licensed residential leasing agents may be employed or independent contractors depending on the policy of the sponsoring broker.
    a. **True**
    b. False

13. The phrases company culture, corporate culture, and organizational culture are mostly used interchangeably in everyday language.
    a. **True**
    b. False

14. Almost all brokerages have the same company culture.
    a. True
    b. **False**

15. In The Act, "every brokerage company or entity, other than a sole proprietorship with no other sponsored licensees, shall adopt a company or office policy dealing with" which topics?
   a. The agency policy of the entity
   b. Confidentiality of client information
   c. Required disclosures and use of forms
   d. **All of the above**
   e. None of the above

16. You're chatting with Mike in the break room one day in the brokerage. The conversation quickly turns to clients. He says, "The Johnson family on 15th Avenue are loaded! I had no idea. Their net worth is 1.4 million." What just happened?
   a. **Mike broke his fiduciary duties by disclosing confidential information that could harm his client's negotiating position.**
   b. Harmless water cooler talk
   c. Office gossip
   d. A and B

17. Disclosing confidential information directly violates which of the following?
   a. The licensee's duty of care and loyalty
   b. The licensee's fiduciary duties
   c. The brokerage's handbook
   d. **All of the above**

18. What is a simple and common starting point when creating a goal?
   a. **Start with the vision**
   b. Consider how much time it will take
   c. Consider how much money it will take
   d. None of the above

19. When setting goals, what is important to consider?
   a. How you are wired
   b. Whether you perform best alone or on a team
   c. Your strengths as an extrovert or an introvert
   d. **All of the above**
   e. None of the above

20. KPIs are also known in the context of business planning and goals as which of the following?
   a. Keeping People Involved
   b. Key Profit Indicators
   c. **Key Performance Indicators**
   d. Key Profit Initiative

CHAPTER 9 QUIZ ANSWERS

1. The Act states that "No sponsored licensee shall pay compensation directly to a licensee sponsored by another sponsoring broker for the performance of licensed activities."
   a. **True**
   b. False

2. All compensation earned in a real estate transaction, whether a sale, lease, or property management, shall be paid directly to the sponsoring broker.
   a. **True**
   b. False
   c. More information is needed

3. Which of the following is true about this statement? "One sponsoring broker may pay compensation directly to another sponsoring broker for the performance of licensed activities."
   a. It is from The Act.
   b. It is a legal relationship.
   c. Brokers must be aware of this fact.
   d. **All of the above.**

   e.   None of the above.

4. The Act states: "Notwithstanding any other provision of this Act, a leasing agent may pay compensation to a person currently licensed under the Auction License Act who is in compliance with and providing services under Section 5-32 of this Act."
   a.   True
   b.   **False**
   c.   More information is needed

5. The Act states: "A licensee does not need to disclose to a client the sponsoring broker's compensation policy with regard to utilization of cooperating brokers."
   a.   True
   b.   **False**
   c.   More information is needed

6. The Act states: "A licensee must disclose to a client all sources of compensation related to the transaction received by the licensee from a third party."
   a.   **True**
   b.   False
   c.   More information is needed

7. The Act states: "Compensation may be paid to any unlicensed person in exchange for the person performing licensed activities in violation of this Act."
   a.   Yes
   b.   **No**

8. The Act states: "Every sponsoring broker must have an employment or independent contractor agreement with each licensee the broker sponsors."
   a.   No.
   b.   Yes, and it can be verbal.
   c.   **Yes, and it must be written.**

9. Team members are always compensated the same way, regardless of his or her brokerage.
   a.   True
   b.   **False**
   c.   More information is needed

10. Is it legal for team members in Illinois to compensate each other?
   a.   Yes
   b.   **No**

11. Compensation is always outlined in a written employment agreement. This is determined by each brokerage.
   a.   **True. The sponsoring broker determines the compensation plan.**
   b.   False. It's determined by the law.

12. Concerning compensation, it's common for a master franchisor to charge a certain percentage fee off the top to the licensees who work there.
   a.   **True**
   b.   False

13. A written employment agreement must be between the sponsoring broker and who else that works under her/him?
   a.   Licensees
   b.   Licensed personal assistants
   c.   Non-practicing licensees
   d.   **All of the above**
   e.   None of the above

14. An employment agreement is a written agreement that is between a sponsoring broker and who else?
   a.   Other brokers
   b.   The brokerage owner
   c.   **Sponsored licensee**
   d.   None of the above

15. Daniel is a designated agent who is designated as his seller's sole agent. He has the exclusive right to market the property of the seller. Which type of listing agreement can define Daniel as the designated agent?
    a. Net listing agreement
    b. Exclusive agency listing agreement
    c. Exclusive right to sell listing agreement
    d. **All of the above**

16. In which ways can team members be compensated?
    a. Performance-based
    b. Percentage-based
    c. Flat rate
    d. A combination of A, B, and/or C
    e. **All of the above**

17. Concerning recordkeeping, how many years does a sponsoring broker need to keep escrow records, transaction records, employment agreements, and records showing compensation payments on file?
    a. 3 years
    b. **5 years**
    c. 7 years
    d. 10 years

18. In the state of Illinois, who can legally collect a commission in a real estate transaction?
    a. **Sponsoring broker**
    b. Licensee
    c. Designated broker
    d. Only C and D

19. Janet is a new licensee who is a Type A personality. She starts at a popular brokerage on Monday. Her plan is to keep 100% of the commissions from her sales. Which compensation model will she opt for?
    a. Flat rate
    b. Production-based splits
    c. Salary
    d. **None of the above**

20. Because there are limited cooperative relationships in this sector, there is a higher probability that the buyer is going to have to compensate their own broker. Which realm is this?
    a. Residential
    b. **Commercial**
    c. Property management
    d. None of the above

CHAPTER 10 QUIZ ANSWERS

1. Antitrust laws focus on which of the following?
    a. Stimulating healthy business competition
    b. Prohibiting business practices that restrain trade
    c. Protect consumers
    d. **All of the above**
    e. None of the above

2. According to the FTC, what is the foundation of a vibrant economy?
    a. **Free and open markets**
    b. Healthy competition
    c. A growing economy
    d. None of the above

3. Which piece of legislation outlaws trusts such as monopolies and cartels and was the first of its kind?
    a. The Federal Trade Commission Act
    b. **The Sherman Antitrust Act**
    c. The Clayton Antitrust Act
    d. None of the above

4. Which act outlaws mergers that are anticompetitive, along with discriminatory pricing and cutthroat pricing?
    a. The Federal Trade Commission Act
    b. The Sherman Antitrust Act
    c. **The Clayton Antitrust Act**
    d. None of the above

5. Tying or tie-in agreements exist when:
    a. Price-fixing takes place.
    b. A group boycott is happening.
    c. **The consumer is required to undertake an additional activity in order to obtain the benefit of another.**
    d. Two businesses divide a city by territory.

6. When competitors agree to restrict competition, the result is often an attempt to do which of the following?
    a. **Raise prices**
    b. Lower prices
    c. Create fewer options for buyers
    d. Boycott

7. Which antitrust violation disrupts the normal laws and rhythms of supply and demand?
    a. **Price-fixing**
    b. Boycotting
    c. Affiliated business
    d. Market division

8. A broker must never agree with other brokers on commission rates.
    a. **True**
    b. False
    c. More information is needed

9. What is a secret or illegal cooperation or conspiracy, especially in order to cheat or deceive others called?
    a. Boycotting
    b. **Collusion**
    c. Affiliated business
    d. Phishing

10. What is it called when two or more licensees or businesses choose to conspire against another, or they agree to withhold their business/patronage in order to reduce competition?
    a. **Boycotting**
    b. Collusion
    c. Affiliated business
    d. Phishing

11. You're watching a movie. A character says: "You can only purchase the property on 5th Street if you purchase the office building on 12th Avenue as well." Which word captures what just happened?
    a. Collusion
    b. Disparagement
    c. **Tie-in agreement**
    d. Extortion

12. Two brokerages decide to split the town. Brokerage A takes the east side and Brokerage B takes the west side. What is this antitrust violation known as?
    a. Boycotting
    b. Collusion
    c. Affiliated business
    d. **Market division**

13. If a licensee violates TCPA, whether it is intentional or not, he/she can be held liable for the violation.
    a. **True**
    b. False

14. The Do Not Call Law covers specific guidelines in terms of when it's allowed and not allowed for licensees to contact consumers.
    a. **True**
    b. False

15. When a consumer (lead) is on the Do Not Call Registry and he/she makes inquiries and/or submits applications (in writing or online), a licensee is allowed to contact the consumer for up to _____ months after the inquiry or initial contact was made.
    a. Two
    b. **Three**
    c. Four
    d. Five

16. The Junk Fax Prevention Act of 2005 permits the sending of unsolicited fax advertisements to persons and businesses with which the sender has _____?
    a. **An established business relationship**
    b. A signed contract/agreement
    c. No relationship
    d. None of the above

17. The CAN-SPAM Act of 2003 applies to which of the following?
    a. The CRM of the licensee
    b. Sending one email to all contacts
    c. Sending an email to one recipient
    d. **All of the above**
    e. None of the above

18. What is the creation of email messages that use a forged or fake sender address known as?
    a. **Email spoofing**
    b. Fishing
    c. Clickbait
    d. None of the above

19. As a first-year licensee, you receive an email. At first, you think it's from your new client. Now, you're not sure. You don't remember if she has used this email before or not. What should you do?
    a. Email back and ask her if it's her new email
    b. Ignore it
    c. **Call her to confirm**
    d. None of the above

20. You're at a dinner with several licensees from other brokerages. A licensee you've never met says: "Brokerage A is the worst place to work! That's why I quit! They treat their clients like parts on a factory line. Their brokerage handbook is a joke." You notice other licensees are listening to him now. Which term below best describes what is happening?
    a. **Disparagement**
    b. Character assassination
    c. Gossip
    d. Venting

CHAPTER 11 QUIZ ANSWERS

1. For a property owner, the bundle of rights and the title are the same thing.
    a. True
    b. **False**

2. Shannon and Mike just purchased their new home. After 10 years of living in an apartment, they are very excited. They both want to remodel. Specifically, they want to extend the backyard, build a room over the garage, and put up a metal fence around the property. Since they own the home, can they make those changes as they wish?
   a. Yes
   b. No
   c. **Possibly. However, it depends on local zoning limitations.**

3. Ownership is composed of a variety of rights, usually referred to as the _____.
   a. Brokerage agreement
   b. Deed
   c. **Bundle of rights**
   d. Title rights

4. When it comes to advertising, can a sponsored licensee legally advertise under his or her own name?
   a. Yes
   b. **No**
   c. More information is needed.

5. If a licensee has ownership interest in a property for sale, he/she must _____.
   a. **Inform the potential buyers**
   b. Sign a non-disclosure agreement
   c. Work through another licensee
   d. None of the above

6. What are the four government powers?
   a. Police protection, eminent dominance, transportation, and escheatment
   b. Police protection, eminent dominance, taxation, and escrow
   c. Police power, equity, taxation, and escrow
   d. **Police power, eminent domain, taxation, and escheatment**

7. The Escheats Act says the following. What goes in the blank? "The county treasurer shall keep just and true accounts of all moneys paid into the treasury, and if any person appears within _____ years after the death of the intestate and claims any money paid into the treasury as his or hers, on legal representation such person may file a petition in the circuit court of such county, stating the nature of the claim and praying such money may be paid to the claimant."
   a. 5
   b. **10**
   c. 12
   d. 15

8. Sam recently passed away. He has no heirs and there is no will. His prize possession was his golden retriever named Dixie. In this circumstance, who takes responsibility for the ownership of Dixie?
   a. City
   b. County
   c. **State**
   d. Municipality

9. What is the procedure or process of a government taking ownership of unclaimed property, abandoned property, and estate assets?
   a. Unclaimed property initiative
   b. Government intervention
   c. Appropriation
   d. **Escheatment**

10. What can possibly happen if someone fails to pay his or her taxes?
    a. Penalties
    b. Fees
    c. Garnished wages
    d. **Any of the above**
    e. None of the above

11. In Illinois, real property escheats to the _____.
    a. State
    b. City
    c. **County**
    d. None of the above

12. What can the IRS use in an effort to collect unpaid taxes?
    a. **Automated Collection System**
    b. Automated Carryover System
    c. Back Taxes System
    d. Individual Tax Collection System

13. What is included in the mandatory financial charge that is imposed on taxpayers, whether they are individuals or businesses?
    a. Property taxes
    b. Income taxes
    c. **Both A and B**
    d. None of the above

14. Illinois created the Equity in Eminent Domain Act so that the government must show evidence and reasoning that an area is actually blighted before it can move forward with _____, thereby conveying ownership to a private developer.
    a. Taxation
    b. **Condemnation**
    c. Escheatment
    d. None of the above

15. Local governments can condemn both businesses and residences for private reasons or economic and financial reasons.
    a. True
    b. False
    c. **Depends on the state**

16. Which procedure in Illinois allows an authority to acquire possession of a landowner's property before having to pay just compensation?
    a. Taxation
    b. Condemnation
    c. Escheatment
    d. **A quick-take**
    e. None of the above

17. Sam and Martha have just returned from the closing on their new home. One of the many documents that they were given was the deed. What is the purpose of the seller giving the deed to Sam and Martha?
    a. **Provide legal vesting of the property in the buyer's name**
    b. To provide the buyer with suitable clothing attire for both of them to wear when they celebrate having taken ownership
    c. To create a scenario whereby the King of England has provided Sam with knighthood
    d. To provide Sam's and Martha's children with the legal right of ownership during the lifetime of Sam and Martha

18. Which entity or entities have the power to initiate eminent domain in Illinois?
    a. Illinois Department of Transportation
    b. Illinois counties
    c. Tax Assessor's office
    d. **A and B**
    e. A, B, and C

19. Concerning the topic of condemnation, "just compensation" is required by the _____.
    a. County law
    b. **State law**
    c. Municipal law
    d. None of the above because just compensation is prohibited.

20. What is "the inherent power of a government to exercise reasonable control over persons and property within its jurisdiction in the interest of the general security, health, safety, morals, and welfare except where legally prohibited" known as?
    a. Police state
    b. Condemnation
    c. Curfew law
    d. **Police power**

CHAPTER 12 QUIZ ANSWERS

1. The terms "estate" and "estate in land" are interchangeable.
    a. True
    b. **False**

2. Michael has an interest in real property that he will possess in the future. Which term describes what he has?
    a. **Estate in land**
    b. Estate
    c. Leasehold estate

3. When ownership has been granted by a deed, the recipient is said to have _____ that is inheritable.
    a. **An estate in land**
    b. A leasehold estate
    c. Reversionary rights
    d. None of the above is correct.

4. What are the three types of freehold estates?
    a. Fee simple estates, leasehold estates, and current estates
    b. **Fee simple absolute, fee simple defeasible, and life estates**
    c. Leasehold estates, fee simple defeasible estates, and concurrent estates
    d. Leasehold estates, fee absolute estates, and equitable estates

5. A new licensee is still confused about the four general types of estates. What can you tell him to focus on that can help him remember what makes them different?
    a. Focus on who the owner is
    b. Focus on the deed
    c. **Focus on the duration**
    d. None of the above

6. Which type of estate has an indefinite and indeterminate duration of time? Essentially, this means that it can exist forever, or for a lifetime.
    a. **Freehold estates**
    b. Leasehold estates
    c. Concurrent estates
    d. Equitable estates
    e. All of the above

7. What makes fee simple absolute different from fee simple defeasible?
    a. Fee simple absolute defines a definitive period of time for ownership while fee simple defeasible grants unlimited ownership duration.
    b. **Fee simple absolute provides the least number of restrictions regarding the property ownership while fee simple defeasible defines a specific condition that you must comply with or ignore.**
    c. Fee simple remainder, fee simple defeasible, and life estates all refer to the same legal concept.
    d. None of the above

8. In a leasehold estate, can tenantship be granted indefinitely by the grantor?
    a. Yes
    b. **No. It's only granted for a defined period of time.**
    c. No. It's only for the lifetime of the tenant.
    d. None of the above

9. Janet is the tenant of a leasehold estate. Does this mean she is also the owner?
    a. Yes
    b. **No**
    c. Not enough information is given.

10. Which of the following can be rolling tenancy?
    a. Week to week
    b. Month to month
    c. Year to year
    d. **All of the above**

11. James and Rolland are not related. However, they both own the same property and are both occupants. Which type of estate do they have?
    a. Freehold estate
    b. Leasehold estate
    c. **Concurrent estate**
    d. Equitable estate

12. Which of the following freehold estates feature an indefinite and indeterminate duration of time?
    a. Life estates and fee simple defeasible
    b. Simple derivative
    c. **Fee simple and fee simple defeasible**
    d. All of the above

13. In the context of real estate, which of the following best describes a fee?
    a. **One's legal right to the ownership of land**
    b. One's legal right to sell his or her land
    c. One's legal right to possess the land
    d. None of the above

14. Loretta is a chronic worrier. She has experienced bankruptcy twice as well as a divorce. She is risk-averse. Which type of estate would give her the greatest level of protection and arguably the most peace of mind?
    a. **Fee simple absolute**
    b. Fee simple defeasible
    c. Life estate
    d. Legal life estate

15. Jim is a no-nonsense type of guy who does not like being tied down to a lot of restrictions. If Jim is selling his personal residence, which of the following estates would establish a level of ownership with the least number of restrictions?
    a. **Fee simple absolute**
    b. Fee simple defeasible
    c. Life estate
    d. Legal life estate

16. Tasha wants to sell her land. She has a sprawling, beautiful estate that includes numerous peach trees. As peach orchards have been in her family for generations, she places a restriction that the peach orchards must be maintained. What is this type of arrangement called?
    a. Owner's prerogative
    b. **Special limitation**
    c. Fee simple determinable
    d. Condition subsequent

17. The ownership of a life estate includes which of the following?
    a. **A limited period**
    b. An indefinite period
    c. An agreed-upon duration of time that varies case by case
    d. Any of the above

18. Brian is a life tenant. His nephew had a horrible financial setback and Brian is considering gifting the estate to his nephew so he will at least have a foundation for his life. Does Brian have the right to transfer the estate?
    a. **Yes, but with limited rights**
    b. Yes, with full fee simple absolute rights
    c. No
    d. More information is needed

19. A legal life estate is conventionally and always created by a will or testament.
    a. True
    b. **False**

20. What are the four types of waste?
    a. Volitionary, negligence, ameliorative, and equitable
    b. **Voluntary, permissive, ameliorative, and equitable**
    c. Voluntary, permissive, ameliorative, and erosive
    d. None of the above

CHAPTER 13 QUIZ ANSWERS

1. Which of the following cannot be separated from real estate?
   a. Earth science
   b. Nature
   c. Hurricanes
   d. Nor'easters
   e. **All of the above**

2. A new licensee, Frank, is showing an oceanfront property. The lady who is interested begins asking him about her water rights if she chooses to purchase the property. Which specific topic below will Frank talk about with her?
   a. Riparian rights
   b. Sovereignty of land
   c. **Littoral rights**
   d. None of the above

3. Riparian rights in Illinois are simple and easy to understand because of the state's statutory provisions.
   a. True
   b. **False**

4. Jocelyn just purchased a property that has a stream and a lake. What is she not allowed to do?
   a. Divert or change the stream's course
   b. Put waste in the lake
   c. Build a small dam
   d. **All of the above**
   e. Only A and B

5. Shannon and Mike are newlyweds and recently purchased a beautiful sprawling property that has everything they were searching for. The property is adjacent to a creek. Do they have riparian rights?
   a. **Yes**
   b. No
   c. More information is needed.

6. Are human-made and artificial waterways or bodies of water included with riparian rights?
   a. **Yes**
   b. No
   c. More information is needed.

7. If people are limited to the use kayaks, canoes, and rowboats in a body of water, where do the property owner's riparian rights end?
   a. At the water's edge
   b. **The middle of the body of water**
   c. At the high tide mark
   d. None of the above

8. Frank and Martha have lived on their property for 20 years. They were shocked last month when they discovered that beavers were building a dam on what they call "their creek." They noticed that it was diverting the course of the water. They know that if they do not break the dam or do something to run off the beavers, they will lose land. Since they want to sell in five years, they do not want their property value to decrease. What can they do?
    a. They can remove the beavers, or hire someone to do so.
    b. They can destroy the dam, or hire someone to do so.
    c. Legally, they cannot do anything.
    d. **They can ask for local government assistance to relocate the beavers, and the dam, although it will cost time and money.**

9. Can beachfront property landowners gain and legally own "new" land due to the geological phenomenon of accretion?
    a. **Yes**
    b. No

10. Erosion is only defined as the loss of land caused by natural agents.
    a. True
    b. **False**

11. Large batches of sediment and rocks are flowing from John's shoreline down two miles to his neighbor Sarah's shoreline. What is this called?
    a. **Erosion**
    b. Accretion
    c. Avulsion
    d. Encumbrance

12. Which of the following is the *broadest* term that affects the transferability of a property?
    a. Easement
    b. **Encumbrance**
    c. Encroachment
    d. Liens
    e. Deed restrictions

13. Every encumbrance is a lien.
    a. True
    b. **False**
    c. Not enough information is given.
    d. All of the above

14. Bob is a veteran who has lived at his coastal residence with his wife since 1988. His wife has always wanted an upstairs balcony. For their anniversary this year, Bob decided that he and his sons are going to build it for her. Garry is Bob's neighbor. While Garry and his family are on a two-week vacation, Bob and his sons get to work building the balcony. The balcony blocks Garry's bedroom window view of the beach. When Garry returns, he is livid. Whether intentionally planning to build it when Garry was gone or not, which term describes what Bob has created?
    a. Negative easement
    b. Encumbrance
    c. **Encroachment**
    d. Easement appurtenant

15. What do you call the right to use another person's property for a particular purpose?
    a. Servient tenement
    b. Private easement
    c. **Easement in gross**
    d. None of the above

16. The Thacker family is upset because they do not understand an easement that is on their property. After purchasing, they discovered that the easement has no exact dimensions or location. Which term best describes the type of easement they have?
    a. Negative easement
    b. Public easement
    c. Private easement
    d. **Floating easement**

17. The burdened land is the land that is subject to the easement. It does not receive the benefit. Which term best describes this?
    a. Dominant tenement
    b. **Servient tenement**
    c. Negative easement
    d. None of the above

18. Phil and Lois are a young couple who just signed up for a two-year lease in a homeowners association. Between working full-time jobs and having three kids, they are always busy. During some of their sessions with the leasing agent, they were tired. Sometimes, they simply nodded their heads in agreement, not fully understanding what was being said. Upon moving in, they reviewed their paperwork. One folder was dedicated fully to HOA rules and regulations. Lois had wanted to plant marigolds in the front yard, but according to the rules, she cannot. Phil wanted to put a small shed in the backyard, and likewise, that would be against the rules. They're both frustrated. Which of the following is in place that creates this type of scenario?
    a. Deed restrictions
    b. Title restrictions
    c. **HOA restrictions**
    d. Condemnation

19. In which way can an easement appurtenant not legally be terminated?
    a. Demolition
    b. Abandonment
    c. Condemnation
    d. **Sale of the property**

20. Monica is now in her late 70s. Her husband, who passed away three years ago, was a lifelong fisherman. She and her husband owned their property together for more than 35 years. The acreage is sprawling and has five lakes. They granted fishing licenses to countless individuals through the years. Many of them her husband knew, but she had only met a handful of them. Nowadays, she no longer feels comfortable with strangers on her property. What can she do?
    a. Nothing. She has to wait for each license to expire.
    b. She has to talk to an accountant about the topic of estoppel.
    c. She needs to create a negative easement.
    d. **She can revoke their licenses when she sees fit.**

CHAPTER 14 QUIZ ANSWERS

1. What is the most common goal of a lien?
    a. To gain possession of a property
    b. **To receive money that is due**
    c. To gain collateral
    d. None of the above

2. What do lenders use to protect themselves financially in case the borrower defaults on the loan?
    a. Collateral
    b. Security
    c. **All of the above**
    d. None of the above

3. David had a difficult year financially. His business almost went under. This past week, he learned that the contractor who was installing a new asphalt roof had placed a lien on the property. What type of lien is this?
    a. **Specific**
    b. General
    c. Consensual
    d. Judgment lien

4. Consensual liens are created by a legal contract between the lienee and the lienholder.
    a. **True**
    b. False

5. Jane was a subcontractor on a new home. She did an outstanding job. Two months have passed, and she has not received payment. The homeowner has not answered multiple phone calls and emails. What type of lien does Jane have the right to issue?
    a. Self-employment lien
    b. Unpaid compensation lien
    c. Contractor's lien
    d. **Mechanic's lien**

6. Special assessments are liens designed to gather the public's assistance in paying for a community improvement project. Which of the following statements would apply to a special assessment tax lien?
    a. An infrastructure lien is covered exclusively by local commercial property owners.
    b. Special assessments are used exclusively for the installation of new roadways.
    c. **The most logical means of assessing the public's participation is through using the front foot method.**
    d. Special assessments are always voluntary liens wherein the local municipality hopes for the community's monetary participation.

7. Which lien is a lien against documents and monies/funds in order to secure payment of fees owed for legal services?
    a. **Attorney's lien**
    b. Litigious lien
    c. Legal lien
    d. None of the above

8. The tax assessor sets tax rates and levies, and also decides the dollar amount of the tax bills of property owners who live in his or her county.
    a. True
    b. **False**

9. Bob and Jane are homeowners in Kendall County, Illinois. They just received the paperwork, which states their home's assessed value. They believe it is very high. What can they do?
    a. Nothing
    b. File a lawsuit
    c. **File an appeal**
    d. Sue the seller for providing incorrect information

10. The Senior Citizens Assessment Freeze Homestead Exemption freezes the tax rate as well as the taxable assessment on the homeowner's property.
    a. True
    b. **False**

11. A special assessment is which of the following?
    a. An improvement tax
    b. A way to fund local, specific infrastructure projects
    c. **All of the above**
    d. None of the above

12. All property taxes are real estate taxes.
    a. **True**
    b. False

13. Which of the following describes a judgment lien?
    a. Abstract of judgment
    b. It gives constructive notice
    c. Court ruling
    d. **All of the above**
    e. None of the above

14. Is it possible for a judgment to become a lien?
    a. **Yes**
    b. No

15. A lawsuit has been filed against Kelly. She knows that it may be a year or more before the court case is settled. What is that period of time between filing and securing a judgment called?
    a. Attachment
    b. Bond
    c. Interim
    d. **None of the above**

16. A plaintiff is worried that a defendant will take actions that either damage the defendant's real estate or sell targeted assets for cash and hide the cash in an effort to avoid payment to the plaintiff. Which type of lien can the plaintiff issue?
    a. Landlord's lien
    b. Bail bond lien
    c. **Attachment lien**
    d. Mechanic's lien

17. John died a few months ago. He had a lien on his property. His neighbor Ronald wants to buy John's property. What happens to the lien if Ronald purchases the property?
    a. The entire lien is forgiven.
    b. **The entire lien becomes Ronald's responsibility.**
    c. Fifty percent of the lien goes to Ronald and the remaining fifty percent is forgiven.
    d. None of the above

18. Sam has engaged a general contractor to lay new hardwood floors in his house. Sam is not satisfied with the quality of workmanship and has refused to pay the contractor. In order to protect himself, the contractor has the right to file what type of lien?
    a. A property tax lien to complement the tax lien provided by the government and ensure payment is made.
    b. A customized lien commonly known as a "weed lien."
    c. **A mechanic's lien that provides the contractor with a higher priority subject only to a tax lien.**
    d. A sinister lien designed to allow the contractor to enter the home and recapture all of the improvements that have been placed in the property.

19. Judgment liens exist as a result of a court order. Such liens give the claimant the right to seize any and all assets of the defendant in order to satisfy the debt. Judgment liens are commonly referred to as:
    a. A voluntary specific lien that protects the claimant.
    b. **An involuntary general lien to provide the claimant with the ability to seize all assets to cover the debt.**
    c. An involuntary lien specifically that has no relevance or presence when looking at the priority of liens.
    d. A statutory lien that limits the claimant's rights.

20. John and Martha recently purchased their new home in Romeoville. Their current tax bill amounts to $13,258. They're interested in knowing the market value that was used by the county assessor. They've learned that the equalization factor is 1.76 with an assessed value amounting to 35% of the market value. The current tax rate used by the county is $7.50 per $250 of value. What would the current market value be per county records?
    a. **$717,424**
    b. $710,416
    c. $737,025
    d. $1,717,275

CHAPTER 15 QUIZ ANSWERS

1. When working with a buyer, what does a licensee need to know?
    a. The buyer's needs
    b. The buyer's wants
    c. The buyer's financial ability
    d. **All of the above**

2. Licensees are allowed to change or alter forms and agreements for clients as needed.
    a. True
    b. **False**

3. What is another way to say separate and exclusive ownership?
   a. **Severalty**
   b. Co-ownership
   c. Joint tenancy
   d. Tenancy in common

4. Sarah, a sponsoring broker, is explaining co-ownership to Mike, who is a new licensee. Which of the following terms also means co-ownership?
   a. Concurrent estate
   b. Co-owner/s
   c. Cotenancy
   d. **All of the above**
   e. Only A and B

5. Bob and Jane are getting a divorce. During their marriage, Jane consistently earned more than double what Bob made. They were married in Illinois and have always lived in Illinois. What will happen when their assets are divided up?
   a. Jane will receive more because she earned more money.
   b. Marital property, along with debts will be divided up by 50/50.
   c. **The court will focus on "equitable division."**
   d. None of the above.

6. Jane is talking to her sister on the phone about her divorce from Bob. Her sister says she thinks that Bob had one or more affairs. Jane feels the same way. She does not have proof but thinks it will be possible to find some evidence of the adultery. If Bob did cheat on Jane, will the court take this into consideration?
   a. Yes
   b. **No**

7. What is the best word below to describe when each owner legally owns distinct and separate shares of the exact same property?
   a. Timeshare
   b. Co-ownership
   c. **Tenancy in common**
   d. Undivided fractional interest
   e. None of the above

8. George owns ¼ of a large property on the outskirts of Chicago as a joint tenant. Yesterday, he tragically died in a car wreck. His wife and children are mourning, but know they have to talk about what happens next. Concerning this large property George owns, will it automatically go to his wife and children?
   a. Yes, survivorship is commonplace for tenants in common.
   b. It is possible, but a legal battle will have to take place.
   c. **No, it's impossible. Right of survivorship prevails.**
   d. More information is needed.

9. Emmett owns a large property via joint tenancy. There are six other joint tenants. Today, he heard that one joint tenant, John, has received a judgment. Can this potentially affect Emmett negatively?
   a. Yes
   b. **No**

10. Along with nine other tenants in common, Breonna owns 30% interest in a property. Does that mean she owns 30% of the physical property?
    a. Yes
    b. **No**
    c. Need more information

11. In 1980, a specific piece of property was purchased by four joint tenants. Through the years, two of them died. Now, there are only two joint tenants left, Paul and Peter. Sadly, it looks like Peter is on his deathbed. When he passes, what happens to the land?
    a. Paul has to purchase Peter's portion and interest.
    b. Paul automatically receives Peter's portion and interest.
    c. Paul will own 100% of the property.
    d. A and B
    e. **B and C**
    f. None of the above

12. Which "four unities" create joint tenancies?
    a. Partial interest, investment, time, and tax deed
    b. Possession, interest, time, and taxation
    c. Percentage, interest, time, and title
    d. **None of the above**

13. Which type of business organization allows its owners to know that creditors cannot come after their personal assets and property on behalf of their business entity?
    a. Sole proprietorship
    b. Partnership
    c. Limited partnership
    d. **Corporation**
    e. Limited liability company (LLC)
    f. Cooperative

14. Which of the following describes a judgment lien?
    a. Abstract of judgment
    b. It gives constructive notice
    c. Court ruling
    d. **All of the above**
    e. None of the above

15. Is it possible for a judgment to transform into a lien?
    a. **Yes**
    b. No

16. What are the most common business types used for purchasing commercial real estate?
    a. **Corporations, partnerships, and LLCs**
    b. Corporations and partnerships
    c. Corporations, cooperatives, and LLCs
    d. Corporations, sole proprietorships, and LLCs

17. A plaintiff is worried that a defendant will take actions that either harm the defendant's real estate or sell assets for cash and hide the cash in an effort to not pay the plaintiff. Which lien can the plaintiff issue?
    a. Landlord's lien
    b. Bail bond lien
    c. **Attachment lien**
    d. Mechanic's lien

18. Each timeshare owner is entitled to a specific time period when they can enjoy the benefits of the timeshare. Which answer shows the most common annual time frames?
    a. Five days
    b. One month
    c. **One or two weeks**
    d. None of the above

19. Which type of concept below is modeled after and inspired by mutual funds?
    a. Partnership
    b. Limited partnership
    c. **A real estate investment trust (REIT)**
    d. Corporation
    e. Cooperative

20. Which of the following is true about condominiums?
    a. It is viewed as a separate parcel of real estate.
    b. Each condo owner holds a fee simple title to his or her unit.
    c. Each condo owner has a deed to his or her property.
    d. **All of the above**
    e. None of the above

CHAPTER 16 QUIZ ANSWERS

1. In which listing agreement is the seller only obligated to pay a commission to the licensee who successfully secures a buyer?
   a. **Open listing agreement**
   b. Net listing agreement
   c. Exclusive agency listing agreement
   d. Exclusive right to sell listing agreement

2. In which agreement does the seller set a minimum monetary amount that he/she is willing to accept that allows the broker's commission to be anything in excess of the seller's minimum monetary needs?
   a. Open listing agreement
   b. **Net listing agreement**
   c. Exclusive agency listing agreement
   d. Exclusive right to sell listing agreement

3. Which marketing tool allows licensees to work in cooperation with other brokers in order to provide greater exposure of properties to potential buyers?
   a. His or her CRM (customer relationships management system)
   b. Estate for years
   c. **Multiple listing service**
   d. None of the above

4. Designated agents in Illinois have flexibility and options when it comes to how they want to create and present a comparative market analysis to clients.
   a. True
   b. **False**

5. What is a licensee required to disclose?
   a. Agency relationship
   b. His or her interest
   c. Condition of the property
   d. Material facts
   e. Only A and B
   f. **A, B, C, and D**

6. Agent Jane tried to sell the Rutherford estate for six months. She showed the property to over forty interested parties, but nobody purchased it. It is now sixty days later, and Jane is no longer representing the Rutherfords. However, she just learned that one of the interested parties who Jane physically presented the property to has decided to purchase it. What does Jane need to check in order to confirm that she has a right to compensation?
   a. **The broker protection clause contained within the listing agreement**
   b. Nothing because she has no right to compensation
   c. Her brokerage handbook
   d. None of the above

7. Which type of agreement is where the broker only gets paid if she or he discovers the property that the buyer chooses to purchase? (If the buyer locates the property that he/she wants to buy, he/she owes no compensation to the broker.)
   a. Exclusive buyer agency agreement
   b. Open buyer agency agreement
   c. **Exclusive agency buyer agency agreement**
   d. None of the above

8. What is a negotiation?
   a. A discussion aimed at reaching an agreement
   b. A strategic conversation
   c. A lifelong study
   d. **All of the above**

9. Which term below best describes what exists when a single licensee actively represents the interest of either two separate purchasers or two separate tenants simultaneously pursuing the same property?
    a. Simultaneous offers
    b. Conflict of interest
    c. Liability
    d. **Contemporaneous offers**

10. At times, a licensee and client will prepare to have something to give away in advance during a negotiation. What they give away will not hurt their ultimate goal or negotiating position. This type of negotiation technique is intentionally designed to be distracting. What is it called?
    a. Squirrel
    b. **Red herring**
    c. Advance diversion
    d. Strategic accommodation

11. In Illinois, agency may not be terminated when which of the following circumstances occurs?
    a. Mental incapacity of the principal
    b. Mutual agreement among all involved parties
    c. **Lack of interest or initiative of either party**
    d. The agreement expires

12. The Act reads, "No licensee shall obtain any written brokerage agreement that does not either provide for automatic expiration within a definite period of time or provide the client with a right to terminate the agreement annually by giving no more than 45 days' prior written notice. Any written brokerage agreement not containing such a provision shall be void." Is this true or false?
    a. True
    b. **False**

13. Sponsored licensee Mike has one listing right now. Yesterday, Mike's wife received an offer for her dream job. It's in another city that is two hundred and fifty miles away. She will make triple what she makes now. As a couple, they want her to say yes. This means they need to move soon. Is there a potential outcome that would allow the listing agreement to be terminated amicably?
    a. No. Mike is bound to the terms of his contract.
    b. Mike can explain what's going on and see if the seller is willing to terminate the agreement.
    c. **No, the listing would simply be assigned to another agent.**
    d. None of the above

14. Which of the following can or may need to be used during a negotiation?
    a. Improv
    b. Silence
    c. Empathy
    d. **All of the above**

15. When money is part of a real estate conversation, people can quickly become which of the following?
    a. Interested
    b. Irrational
    c. Defensive
    d. Emotionally triggered
    e. **Any of the above**

16. Which of the following is not required by The Act on written buyer brokerage agreements, whether exclusive or nonexclusive?
    a. Agreed basis or amount of compensation and time of payment
    b. Name of the sponsoring broker and the buyers
    c. **Cell number or business phone numbers of the sponsoring broker and the buyers**
    d. Signatures of the sponsoring broker and the buyers or an authorized signator on behalf of the buyers

17. No licensee shall use real estate contract forms to change previously agreed commission payment terms.
    a. **True**
    b. False

18. If a lack of disclosure is present, what might consequently happen?
    a. Litigation
    b. Disciplinary action for the licensee
    c. A potential deal can collapse
    d. The reputation of the client and/or licensee can be damaged
    e. **All of the above**
    f. Only A and B

19. Is social media messaging a secure practice for when a licensee is communicating with a client?
    a. Yes
    b. **No**
    c. Depends on the brokerage handbook and policies

20. To expand your knowledge of MLS, it's important to know that Illinois law requires a licensee to exercise fiduciary duties when authorized to represent the interest of the client. If the client happens to be a seller, under the concept of care, the broker needs to use every marketing tool legally available to position the property for exposure to potential buyers.
    a. **True**
    b. False

CHAPTER 17 QUIZ ANSWERS

1. Which of the following is not provided as a component when using the rectangular survey?
   a. **The name of the property owner**
   b. The property's exact location
   c. The size of the parcel
   d. The relationship to a defined principal meridian

2. Which measurement system focuses on the boundaries of the property and the area inside of the boundaries?
   a. Lot and block system
   b. **Metes and bounds**
   c. Rectangular survey
   d. None of the above

3. Sarah is a real estate investor. She is considering purchasing a large apartment building that includes its own private gym and park. It is located in a highly populated metropolitan area. Which of the following measuring systems is most likely to be used considering those details?
   a. Rectangular survey
   b. Metes and bounds
   c. **Lot and block system**
   d. None of the above

4. A lot and block survey is sometimes also called which of the following?
   a. Recorded plat survey
   b. Recorded map survey system
   c. Meets map
   d. **A and B**
   e. None of the above

5. A rectangular survey is also known as which of the following?
   a. Public Land Survey System (PLSS)
   b. Government survey system
   c. Geodetic survey system
   d. **All of the above**
   e. None of the above

6. Jill is a surveyor. Every day, she works with longitude and latitude lines. In legal descriptions, they are also known as which of the following, respectively?
   a. **Principal meridian and baseline**
   b. Prime meridian and baseline
   c. POB (point of beginning) and POE (point of ending)
   d. B and C

7. Juan is a surveyor. Currently, he is surveying a new university running track. He starts at the point of beginning (POB), then delineates the sides and angles (boundaries) of the property. Juan continues to the point of ending (POE). Which measurement system is he implementing?
   a. Geodetic survey system
   b. Lot and block system
   c. **Metes and bounds**
   d. Rectangular survey

8. A township is divided into 36 smaller parcels, commonly known as sections. A section of land is one square mile in size, which consists of 660 acres.
   a. True
   b. **False**

9. A principal meridian only runs north to south.
   a. **True**
   b. False

10. Mike is explaining townships to his young daughter. It does not surprise him, as she has always loved geography and math. She asks him what a principal meridian does concerning townships. How would he answer?
    a. **It divides a township between east and west.**
    b. It divides a township between east and west.
    c. It divides a township down the middle.
    d. None of the above.

11. How many principal meridians does Illinois have within its boundaries?
    a. One
    b. **Two**
    c. Three
    d. Four

12. How many principal meridians are within the US?
    a. 12 principal meridians
    b. 24 principal meridians
    c. **37 principal meridians**
    d. 48 principal meridians

13. What is a bearing?
    a. A baseline
    b. The way range lines are divided
    c. **A compass direction**
    d. None of the above

14. What is the distance between range lines that are east or west of the principal meridian?
    a. 4 miles
    b. **6 miles**
    c. 8 miles
    d. 10 miles

15. Township lines create rows. What do you call the lines that create the columns?
    a. **Range lines**
    b. Quarter sections
    c. Township tiers
    d. Bearing lines

16. Morris was a high school assistant principal who recently became a licensee. He is still getting acquainted with the wide

variety of terms and phrases in the world of real estate. In the past, when someone said the word benchmark, he commonly thought of the strengths and weaknesses of students, along with state exams. However, in the world of surveyors and legal descriptions, what are benchmarks?

- a. Temporary reference points used to define the location of a given parcel of land
- b. **Permanent reference points used to define the location of a given parcel of land**
- c. The inaugural bench installed in the local park
- d. Details about the minimum requirements to be a surveyor

17. Why is it rare for a township to be a perfect 36 square miles? Which of the following is the best answer? This is due to . . .
- a. Rivers and other waterways
- b. The Earth's curvature
- c. Most townships are naturally larger than 36 square miles
- d. **A and B**

18. John Adams is considering buying a parcel of land with plans to construct his new home there. The legal description states that the parcel is the north half of the southeast quarter of the southwest quarter of the northeast quarter of section 21. If he purchases the property at $98,000 per acre and the commission payable is 6%, what is the commission due to John's broker?
- a. $31,250
- b. **$29,400**
- c. $28,700
- d. $32,100

19. What makes it possible for surveyors to adjust the width of a township because of the curvature of the Earth when doing a land description?
- a. Township lines
- b. **Correction lines**
- c. Fractional sections
- d. Datum

20. In a legal description, what is the reference point for elevation measurement?
- a. Benchmarks
- b. Correction lines
- c. Township lines
- d. **Datum**

CHAPTER 18 QUIZ ANSWERS

1. A real estate contract is which of the following?
- a. Agreement between two or more parties
- b. Enforceable by law if signed by all parties
- c. Able to be edited by licensees
- d. **Only A and B**
- e. Only A and C

2. Which are governed by US contract law?
- a. Express contracts
- b. Implied contracts
- c. **Express or implied contracts**
- d. None of the above

3. Is an offer a legally binding contract?
- a. Yes
- b. **No**

4. Which statement is false concerning mutual consent?
- a. The seller has the right to accept or reject the offer.
- b. No buyer should be coerced into signing.
- c. Each party enters the agreement of their own free will.
- d. **None of the above.**

5. Can valuable goods be used as consideration in a real estate offer in Illinois?
   a. **Yes**
   b. No

6. Which type of contract encapsulates all terms and conditions, either verbally (orally) or written?
   a. **Express contracts**
   b. Implied contracts
   c. Express or implied contracts
   d. None of the above

7. Michael is a seller. He promises to sell his property for $300,000. Janissa is the buyer. She promises to pay $300,000 for the property. They have entered into a written agreement. What type of contract is this?
   a. **A bilateral contract**
   b. A unilateral contract
   c. Exclusive right to sell
   d. None of the above

8. Which of the following is viewed as a unilateral contract in Illinois?
   a. Exclusive right to sell listing agreement
   b. **Open listing agreement**
   c. Exclusive buyer agency agreement
   d. Exclusive property management agreement

9. The Walden Family worked with Deborah as their broker. They wanted to sell their estate outside of Chicago so they could live full time in Colorado. The estate sold and closed within four weeks. Fortunately, the whole process went as smoothly as possible. The sellers were pleased and so was Deborah. Which type of contract best describes this transaction at this point in time?
   a. Unilateral contract
   b. Executory contract
   c. Implied contract
   d. **Executed contract**

10. Which type of contract is neither enforceable in nor outside of a court of law?
    a. Exclusive agency contract
    b. Valid contract
    c. Voidable contract
    d. **Unenforceable contract**

11. Licensee Brian just discovered that his seller failed to disclose a handful of material facts. The buyer will find out within the hour. Because of this, it's likely that their contract will go from valid to which of the following?
    a. Void
    b. Valid
    c. **Voidable**
    d. Unenforceable

12. In Illinois, if a real estate sales contract is not in writing, it is not enforceable.
    a. **True**
    b. False

13. At what point is a broker discharged from his or her contract?
    a. When the broker breaches the contract
    b. When the contract is successfully fulfilled
    c. If the seller's lender files a foreclosure action
    d. **All of the above**

14. Which legal term is used when a contract moves from being legally binding to having zero legal implications?
    a. Novation
    b. Assignment
    c. **Rescission**
    d. None of the above

15. Broker Williams had an exclusive right to sell listing on seller Caitlin's home. However, her lender filed foreclosure action against her. What is the provision of law that caused the listing contract to be terminated?
    a. Novation
    b. **Operation of law**
    c. Rescission
    d. None of the above

16. Earnest money deposits are not legally required in Illinois.
    a. **True**
    b. False

17. Fill in the blank with the correct answers below. In Illinois, the statute of limitations on oral contracts is _____ years, and for written contracts, it is _____ years.
    a. One and three
    b. Two and four
    c. **Five and ten**
    d. Five and seven

18. Sarah and her husband have equitable title in their dream house. Once the property transaction is executed and completed, what happens?
    a. They continue to have equitable title.
    b. They have legal title.
    c. They legally own the land.
    d. **Both B and C**
    e. Both A and B

19. James wants to buy property. Due to a divorce a few years ago, lending institutions see him as high risk. He showed evidence of his career, but nothing he seemed to do helped. A few banks did offer a loan, but the APR was exceptionally high. James told the property owner about his situation. Rebecca, the property owner, has known James for years and says that she can help with financing. What is this arrangement known as?
    a. Owner/lender option
    b. An illegal form of lending
    c. Property contract
    d. **Land contract**

20. What is a contingency?
    a. A clause in a contract
    b. A specific condition that needs to be met in order to complete the transaction
    c. A clause that protects the buyer and/or seller
    d. **All of the above**
    e. None of the above

CHAPTER 19 QUIZ ANSWERS

1. Which is true concerning a deed?
    a. It is a signed legal document that conveys ownership.
    b. A deed conveys interest, right, and title of real property.
    c. A deed is used for personal property.
    d. It gives the grantee specific rights to a real property asset.
    e. All of the above
    f. **Only A, B, and D**
    g. Only A, C, and D

2. Which of the following are required for a deed to be valid?
    a. The deed must be in writing with the grantor or grantors' signature/s.
    b. The names of the grantee/s and grantor/s are required to be on the deed.
    c. A legal description that is complete and accurate of the property that will be conveyed via the real estate transaction.
    d. **All of the above**
    e. None of the above

3. A grantor has the right to set aside a selection of parts of the property and/or of the estate that he/she is conveying. What are these called?
    a. Exceptions
    b. Reservations
    c. Hold-backs
    d. **A and B**
    e. A and C

4. Acceptance of a deed is required to be done manually in person in the state of Illinois.
    a. True
    b. **False**
    c. Depends on the type of property

5. How is personal property transferred?
    a. Deed
    b. **Bill of sale**
    c. Probate
    d. None of the above

6. Through an inheritance, George receives his deceased grandmother's property. It includes 30 acres, a large house, and a barn. He decided to sell the property and quickly received a highly qualified buyer. George is planning the transfer of title to real property to the buyer within the week. This is George's personal decision that he is making independently of anyone else. What is this exact term called in the world of real estate?
    a. Consideration
    b. **Voluntary alienation**
    c. Involuntary alienation
    d. None of the above

7. What is another way to say words of conveyance?
    a. **Granting clause**
    b. Consideration
    c. Conveyance agreement
    d. None of the above

8. Twenty-two years ago, James moved into an abandoned property that he discovered in an unincorporated area of Kankakee County Illinois. The small property with a tiny house was tucked away at the end of a dead-end dirt road. Now, James is being challenged in court for the ownership. Is James the owner or not, and why?
    a. James is not the owner because of Illinois state law.
    b. **At this point, James has a legal right to the ownership because of adverse possession.**
    c. James is a squatter who will most likely be evicted.
    d. The next of kin to the previous property owner will be contacted and will receive the property. James will have to move out.

9. Ricky has been living off the grid for over two decades. He has lived on a small hidden plot of land in Rocky Mountain National Park. After that many years, does he legally own the small plot of land?
    a. Yes, after twenty years, he is the owner.
    b. Yes, because of adverse possession.
    c. **No. He can never own the land because it's government land.**
    d. Yes, because of A and B.
    e. More information is required to answer the question.

10. Is a real estate transfer declaration required for a valid deed?
    a. **Yes**
    b. No

11. Which of the following is not a requirement for a valid deed?
    a. A blank space of at least 3 ½ inches by 3 ½ inches. The recorder of the deed will use this space to enter the pertinent information when the deed is recorded.
    b. **The grantee's notarized signature.**
    c. The individual who prepares the deed, his or her name and address must be on the deed itself.
    d. An accurate legal description

12. Cynthia wants to record her deed. She is worried that she is getting incomplete information. Which of the following is false concerning recording her deed?
    a. Recording the deed proves that the grantee (buyer) is the legal owner of a property.
    b. It secures her property rights against any legal issues that might come up in the future.
    c. She can buy a title insurance policy prior to recording the deed.
    d. **Recording of the deed hides her identity from public view.**

13. A best practice is for a deed to be acknowledged. Acknowledgment is also known as notarization and is an Illinois law requirement.
    a. **True**
    b. False

14. Which word does this definition match? The courts assume that a party who is interested in a property has knowledge that they, in fact, may not have. This legal presumption is that the party should have known about a legal action that took place because the action was recorded in public records.
    a. Giving notice
    b. Direct knowledge
    c. Actual notice
    d. **Constructive notice**

15. Jake has just relinquished any and all claims and rights (whether real or not) to a former property of his. Most likely, which type of deed was used to convey this ownership?
    a. **Quitclaim deed**
    b. Deed in trust
    c. Special warranty deed
    d. Bargain and sale deed
    e. None of the above

16. Which deed is issued by the court system when there is a successful bidder on a mortgage foreclosure or when we have a successful claim by an individual under the banner of adverse possession?
    a. Mortgage deed
    b. Master deed
    c. Bargain and sale deed
    d. **Sheriff's deed**

17. The Jackson family lives a short drive from Grant Park in Chicago. They're in the process of selling their home. Who will pay the county transfer tax?
    a. The buyer
    b. **The Jackson family (the seller)**
    c. Both buyer and seller
    d. More information is needed.

18. Concerning transfer taxes in Illinois, the state rate is 50¢ per every $1000 dollars. The county rate is 25¢ per every $500, or part thereof. Is that accurate?
    a. Yes
    b. No. The state rate is $1 for every $500.
    c. **No. The state rate is 50¢ for every $500.**
    d. No. The country rate is 50¢ per every $500.

19. What is done when a person dies with a legal will?
    a. Probate court is involved.
    b. Evidence is shown that proves the will is valid legally.
    c. Actions follow the will's instructions.
    d. Heirs have to pay any applicable taxes and fees.
    e. Only A and C
    f. **A, B, C, and D**

20. Shannon's great-aunt died recently. Her aunt left her both personal property and $15,000 cash. Which of the following did Shannon receive?
    a. Bequest
    b. Legacy
    c. Devise
    d. **A and B**
    e. A and C

CHAPTER 20 QUIZ ANSWERS

1. Which document is a signed legal document that conveys interest, right, and title of real property?
    a. Title
    b. **Deed**
    c. Abstract of title
    d. Chain of title

2. Which document can include a complete list of potential liens, encumbrances, lawsuits, claims, or anything of that nature which may have an impact on ownership?
    a. Title
    b. Deed
    c. Abstract of title
    d. **Chain of title**

3. Through what means is ownership transferred from one person or entity to another person or entity?
    a. Title
    b. **Deed**
    c. Abstract of title
    d. Chain of title

4. Are all real estate transactions in the US public record?
    a. **Yes**
    b. No
    c. Depends on the state
    d. Depends on the county where the property is located

5. Jaqueline is interested in purchasing a property. She wants to see the history of the property as related to the sequence of ownership transfers that have taken place over the years. You're her broker. When she asks for this, what is she asking to receive?
    a. Title history
    b. Title report
    c. Abstract of title
    d. Chain of title
    e. **C or D**

6. What is the condensed and summarized history and record of the title?
    a. Title history
    b. Title report
    c. **Abstract of title**
    d. Chain of title

7. The Baker family moved to Illinois and acquired a property on October 15th, 1922. For the creation of an abstract of title, initially how far back in the time would the title examiner search to show the quality of ownership to be conveyed today?
    a. October 15th, 1922
    b. October 15th, 1941
    c. 75 years from the current date of conveyance
    d. **40 years from the current date of conveyance**

8. Cynthia wants to record her deed to ensure she is giving notice to the world of her interest. She is worried that she has incomplete information. Which of the following is false concerning recording her deed?
    a. Recording the deed proves that Cynthia is the legal owner of a property.
    b. It secures her property rights against any legal issues that might come up in the future.
    c. **If the seller refuses to purchase title insurance, Cynthia will be barred from recording her deed because title insurance is the only legal way of establishing ownership.**
    d. Recording makes it accessible to everybody.

9. Frank is an abstractor. Yesterday, he started a new project for the Baker family concerning a piece of property they want to purchase. What might Frank discover during the course of his work concerning the title?
    a. Encumbrances
    b. Zoning violations
    c. Liens
    d. **All of the above**
    e. Only A and B

10. Martha grants to her son Kevin a five-acre parcel of land in Grundy County. Kevin lives in LaSalle County and does not visit the land very often. When researching the entire history of ownership, which document would an interested investor look at to determine the ownership lineage?
    a. The abstract of title reflecting the ownership records of the last 40 years
    b. The chain of title tracing the ownership back to the late 1800s
    c. The plat of survey maintained by the county recorder's office
    d. **A or B**

11. Tom is talking with the next-door neighbor and has learned that the property that both homes have been built on was formerly used as a cemetery. Lately, there has been a lot of discussion regarding the rights to the property by the descendants of individuals previously buried here. Tom is curious to know if there are any restrictions that may exist on the property, that could eventually challenge his rights of ownership. Which of the following could Tom use to learn about prior ownership interests?
    a. **Abstract of title**
    b. Archives of the local church
    c. The local alderman
    d. There are no historical records that can provide Tom with this insight

12. Which word below best fills in the blank of the following sentence? In real estate, a title is a _____.
    a. Form of physical evidence
    b. **Concept**
    c. Legal right
    d. None of the above

13. A deed can be in the name of a single entity (severalty), or in the names of two or more entities (concurrent).
    a. **True**
    b. False

14. Licensee Ted received a title search this morning. As he is reviewing the information, he discovers that, unfortunately, the title has a gap of six years in which there are no recorded public records. Nothing accounts for the ownership during that six-year time frame. What is this gap known as?
    a. **A cloud**
    b. A certainty
    c. An inconsistency
    d. An encumbrance

15. What can be completed in order to confirm the list of all owners from the first recording of the property, as well as determine if the property has any liens, claims, or clouds?
    a. **Title search**
    b. Claims search
    c. Abstract of title
    d. A and C

16. Emma is a client of Licensee Jane. Jane tells Emma that the next step in their process of working together is to do a title search. Emma, a natural overachiever, says that she will do it herself. However, Jane tells her that it would not be in her best interest to do this important project by herself. Who can Jane recommend for running a title search?
    a. A title company
    b. Emma's lender
    c. An attorney
    d. **Any of the above**
    e. None of the above

17. Which of the following is an item that an abstractor could find when doing an abstract of title?
    a. Leasehold interest
    b. Potential claims of adverse possession
    c. **Life estate interest**
    d. Outstanding easement in gross

18. Which statement below is true?
    a. **Neither the abstract of title nor the chain of title ensures the title's validity.**
    b. Only the abstract of title ensures the title's validity.
    c. Only the chain of title ensures the title's validity.
    d. Both the abstract of title and chain of title ensure the title's validity.

19. Which of the following is a professional opinion on the quality of title that is prepared by a title examiner?
    a. Attorney's opinion
    b. **Certificate of title**
    c. Title insurance
    d. A and B

20. Which form of title is the result when a title insurance company finds little to no risk with the title and is willing to insure the title against future claims?
    a. Marketable title
    b. Safe harbor title
    c. Certificate of title
    d. **Insurable title**

CHAPTER 21 QUIZ ANSWERS

1. In which theory is the title held in the name of the lender up until the point at which the last payment is paid?
    a. **Title theory**
    b. Lien theory
    c. Intermediate theory
    d. None of the above

2. In this theory, the title is retained by the borrower. There is an agreement in which the lender can regain the title if and when the borrower defaults. A formal foreclosure process is required in order to obtain the legal title. Which theory is being described?
    a. Title theory
    b. Deed in lieu of foreclosure
    c. **Intermediate theory**
    d. None of the above

3. Jane borrows $100,000 from Michael and signs a document promising to repay the money within five years. What type of agreement is this known as?
    a. Negotiable instrument
    b. Hypothecation
    c. Usury
    d. **Promissory note**

4. Ray is down on his luck. He took multiple financial hits over the last year and the setbacks have pushed him into a financial corner. Currently, he knows he cannot pay his mortgage next month. Embarrassed, he finds himself at a business that does personal loans. After a 30-minute conversation, Ray is looking down at the numbers in front of him. It would be a relief to have the money, but the rates seem astronomical to him. He cannot ever remember seeing an APR so high. Additionally, on page 2, he sees other upfront fees he has to pay. Most likely, what is the best way to describe what he is experiencing?
   a. Logical business principles
   b. Hypothecation
   c. **Predatory lending**
   d. Lis pendens

5. Jean took out a loan for her home. She pledged the real property in order to secure the debt for the loan. If she defaults on her payments, she knows the lender has a legal right to seize her property. Which provision of the mortgage contract gives the lender the right to claim the property when the borrower is in default?
   a. **Hypothecation**
   b. Security and debt
   c. Mortgage
   d. Usury

6. Tom and Jerri are planning to purchase their first house. They're nervous and excited. However, they're also somewhat disoriented by all the new terms and phrases that come along with buying a house. How would you explain what loan origination is and/or what it includes?
   a. Filling out the application.
   b. Submitting the application.
   c. Funds being disbursed.
   d. **All of the above.**
   e. None of the above.

7. Concerning discount points, to whom is the fee paid? Which is the best answer?
   a. **The lender**
   b. The broker
   c. The trustee
   d. The title company

8. Which answer best fills in the blank? A _____ is used when Party A takes out a loan from Party B in order to buy a property and the property is conveyed into a trust.
   a. Land contract
   b. Mortgage document
   c. Lis pendens
   d. **Deed in trust**

9. David is severely behind on his mortgage payments. He is reading his contract now. Which clause gives the lender power to initiate a foreclosure?
   a. **Acceleration clause**
   b. Alienation clause
   c. Prepayment penalty clause
   d. Release clause
   e. Subordination clause

10. Fred is at a licensee training with you. The trainer keeps using the term "due-on-sale clause." Fred cannot figure out what that is. He leans over to you and asks you. You tell him that it's another phrase for which of the following?
    a. Prepayment penalty clause
    b. Acceleration clause
    c. Subordination clause
    d. **Alienation clause**
    e. Release clause
    f. None of the above

11. Jack initiated his mortgage loan six years ago. He has fallen on hard times and is no longer able to make his monthly mortgage payment. Which foreclosure philosophy would allow the lender to sell the property without first securing court authorization?
    a. Judicial foreclosure
    b. **Nonjudicial foreclosure**
    c. Strict foreclosure
    d. None of the above

12. What do we call a legally binding contract between the seller of real estate and the buyer when the seller is providing the financing?
    a. Hypothecation
    b. Lis pendens
    c. **Land contract**
    d. Deed of trust
    e. Property contract

13. In which ways might it be possible for a homeowner who is in default to avoid foreclosure?
    a. A short sale
    b. A deed in lieu of foreclosure
    c. Chapter 13 bankruptcy
    d. **Any of the above**
    e. None of the above

14. A borrower in default, Nancy received notice of foreclosure today. She was served. She now has seven months to pay off the full amount of the loan that is due. What is this known as?
    a. **Equitable right of redemption**
    b. Statutory right of reinstatement
    c. Right of redemption
    d. Statutory right of redemption

15. Which type of bankruptcy can possibly allow a borrower in default to pay what is owned by allowing him/her to pay the ongoing current payments, along with delinquent payments?
    a. Chapter 7
    b. **Chapter 13**
    c. Neither. It's not possible.

16. Which market works with entities like private lenders, lending institutions, and investors that buy and sell existing mortgage promissory notes (previously issued mortgages) and/or securities that are mortgage-backed?
    a. Primary mortgage market
    b. **Secondary mortgage market**
    c. Tertiary mortgage market
    d. None of the above

17. Will is applying for a home loan. His application is being reviewed by a mortgage underwriter this week. What will the underwriter be doing? He/she will . . .
    a. Look up Will's credit score
    b. Research to see whether or not Will has any current or previous foreclosures, judgments, and bankruptcies
    c. Decide whether or not to approve or deny the application
    d. All of the above
    e. **Only B and C**

18. What provision within the mortgage contract provides lenders with a method to recoup some of the lost interest revenue that would have been generated over the full and expected lifetime of the loan, when the loan is paid off early?
    a. Release clause
    b. Premature loan termination
    c. **Prepayment penalty clause**
    d. A and C
    e. None of the above

19. Which type of foreclosure, often referred to as a friendly foreclosure, is a managed agreement between the parties, rather than a requirement of a lawsuit?
    a. **A deed in lieu of foreclosure**
    b. Judicial foreclosure
    c. Nonjudicial foreclosure
    d. Strict foreclosure
    e. None of the above

20. Donald is buying a three-unit building to use as an income property. He does not intend to live on the premises. However, he tells the lender that he will. Donald is most likely engaging in which of the following?
    a. An act of blockbusting
    b. **An act of mortgage fraud**
    c. An antitrust violation
    d. An unethical yet not illegal practice

CHAPTER 22 QUIZ ANSWERS

1. Which best describes what an appraisal is in terms of value?
    a. A proven fact
    b. A guess
    c. **An opinion**
    d. None of the above

2. Only certain states require appraisers to be licensed.
    a. True
    b. **False**

3. How many different types of appraisers does Illinois have?
    a. Two
    b. **Three**
    c. Four
    d. Five

4. Which of the following is false?
    a. A CMA is not an appraisal.
    b. A BPO reflects a real estate licensee's opinion of value.
    c. **A licensee can use the term appraisal written or verbally.**
    d. Neither a CMA nor a BPO is a formal appraisal.

5. Dustin, a new licensee, has been asked to render an opinion of value on a potential listing. To ensure that Dustin's opinion matches that of an appraiser, which three components will both Dustin and the appraiser use in rendering their opinions?
    a. **Recently sold properties, current listings, expired listings**
    b. Recently sold properties, current listings, the neighborhood demographics
    c. Recently sold properties, expired listings, property history
    d. Expired listings, property history, current listings

6. Maxine is studying to become a licensed real estate agent. She read the chapter you just completed. You're studying with her. She asks you which of the following is true. How do you respond?
    a. Some states require no specific format requirements for CMAs and BPOs.
    b. Like legal documents, both of these should be in writing.
    c. **All of the above**
    d. None of the above

7. Appraisals, CMAs and BPOs focus on value. What are the four essential elements or ingredients that show us whether or not a real property has value?
    a. Transferability, demand, use, and scarcity
    b. Transferability, desirability, use, and scarcity
    c. Transferability, desirability, utility, and scarcity
    d. **Transferability, utility, demand, and scarcity**

8. Which of the following sources of information is used in developing an opinion of value used by both an appraiser and a real estate licensee?
   a. Market price
   b. **Market value**
   c. Reasonable price
   d. None of the above

9. Market value is influenced by subjective factors.
   a. **True**
   b. False

10. Steve and Nancy have been house hunting and have narrowed their choices to two. One costs $30,000 more than the other. The large loan it would require makes them a bit uncomfortable. The less expensive house provides greater flexibility as they believe they can do a number of projects to make the home their dream home. What is at work during their conversation and decision-making?
    a. Principle of contribution
    b. Principle of highest and best use
    c. Principle of change
    d. **Principle of anticipation**

11. Which principle applies when a property's maximum value is realized because it fits in harmoniously with its structural and natural surroundings?
    a. Principle of highest and best use
    b. Principle of contribution
    c. Principle of substitution
    d. **Principle of conformity**

12. Which one word correctly completes both of the following blanks? Less _____ means higher value. More _____ means lower value.
    a. Demand
    b. **Supply**
    c. Competition
    d. Change
    e. None of the above

13. Which principle is the main point of the following story? This past summer, Jonathan and Robin decided to invest money into their backyard area. They added a beautiful brick patio with a firepit and a medium-sized pool surrounded by updated landscaping. The total cost will be $45,000. However, they spoke with three advisors and each one shared data showing that it would increase the value of the property from $420,000 to at least $500,000. The reason for this investment is that next summer, the couple is moving to Nashville because Robin's mom lives there. Their oldest son is graduating a month prior, so they will be empty nesters. They think it will be the best time to put the house on the market and move.
    a. **Principle of contribution**
    b. Principle of change
    c. Principle of progression and regression
    d. Principle of anticipation

14. This appraisal method generates an opinion of property value by comparing and contrasting it with similar properties that have been sold and closed recently. It relies on recent sales data and stats from similar properties that have sold. The procedure makes proper adjustments for time, along with differences in size, square footage, acres, and other different conditions. Which approach to value is this describing?
    a. Cost approach
    b. Income capitalization approach
    c. **Sales comparison approach**
    d. Gross rent multiplier

15. Lucas is a property owner who is working with an appraiser. The appraiser tells him about replacement costs and reproduction costs. To calculate those, which method below is most likely to be used by the appraiser?
    a. Unit-in-place method
    b. Quantity survey method
    c. Index method
    d. **Square footage method**

16. Joyce wants to sell her house. She has never sold a house before but is confident she will receive a good price. With her Type A personality, she has always had regular repairs and maintenance performed. Everyone in her neighborhood knows that she also keeps the inside of the house sparkling clean. The house has a large wraparound porch, a large backyard, five bedrooms, one bathroom, and beautiful landscaping. Erica, a local real estate agent, has been invited by Joyce to look at the house in person for the first time. The neighborhood has been in high demand by parents with growing families. Erica's one concern, which will cause the house to have less value, is caused by which of the following?
    a.   Physical deterioration
    b.   **Functional obsolescence**
    c.   External obsolescence
    d.   Economic obsolescence

17. Karen is an investor. She has an eye on a residential property that has four units. Which ratio would be used for an appraisal?
    a.   Gross income multiplier
    b.   Net income multiplier
    c.   **Gross rent multiplier**
    d.   None of the above

18. Which of the following is required to be included in an appraisal report?
    a.   Intended use and purpose of the appraisal report
    b.   The assignment's purpose and type of value
    c.   Effective date when the opinion was rendered
    d.   **All of the above**

19. What is the name of the most commonly used appraisal form for government institutions like Fannie Mae?
    a.   Uniform USPAD appraisal report
    b.   USPAE appraisal report
    c.   Conventional appraisal report
    d.   **Uniform residential appraisal report**

20. A gross rent multiplier measures the investment property's value by dividing the property's selling price by its annual gross rental income.
    a.   **True**
    b.   False

CHAPTER 23 QUIZ ANSWERS

1.   In terms of renting, a lease can be called which of the following?
    a.   Leasing agreement
    b.   Tenant agreement
    c.   Rental agreement
    d.   **All of the above**
    e.   Only A, B, and C

2.   What does the owner (lessor) retain when he/she rents a property to a tenant?
    a.   **Reversionary right**
    b.   Quiet enjoyment
    c.   Disposition
    d.   None of the above

3.   Louisa is a new tenant who is leasing a beautiful residential property. What do her monthly rental payments and the contract grant her?
    a.   Right to use the property
    b.   Possessory rights
    c.   Quiet enjoyment
    d.   Leased fee estate plus reversionary right
    e.   All of the above
    f.   **A, B, and C**

4. James leased a residential single-family home to two brothers who intended to live there. He did not have the best feeling about them, but the property had been sitting vacant for months with no inquiries. Despite his intuition telling him otherwise, he decided to accept the two brothers as tenants. Their tenancy just hit month three and James discovers that they have been manufacturing an illegal drug on site. He calls his lawyer and agent. Most likely, what would they tell him?
   a. The lease must run its course.
   b. The lease can be immediately terminated based on the illegal activity.
   c. James can file for immediate eviction based on the illegal activity.
   d. **B and C**
   e. None of the above.

5. Janet recently moved from Argentina to Illinois. Her friend, Agnus, has a guest house in Illinois and told her she can live there if she agrees to do specific chores, cooking, and maintenance. Janet agreed. Although this is not the norm, it's not uncommon. Agnus will not receive cash rent as payment for Janet to stay there. However, Janet's labor is her rental payment. What is the most accurate term to describe what is happening here?
   a. Illegal activity
   b. **Rental compensation**
   c. Allowance
   d. A Fair Housing violation

6. Leasehold estate is a tenant's exclusive right to occupy and possess the real estate for the time period outlined in the lease. It is not ownership. A leasehold is usually considered personal property. What are the different types of leasehold estates?
   a. Estate for years, estate from period to period, freehold estate
   b. Estate for years, estate from period to period, life estate, and estate at sufferance
   c. **Estate for years, estate from period to period, estate at will, and estate at sufferance**
   d. None of the above

7. Which type of leasehold estate is a type of tenancy created when a tenant and landlord create an agreement that has no end date?
   a. Estate at sufferance
   b. Continuous estate
   c. Estate from period to period
   d. Periodic tenancy
   e. **C and D**
   f. A, C, and D

8. Suzie has passed the date of her lease terms. As a nursing student, she is constantly busy. When she's not working or studying, she is sleeping. The leasing agreement said that her last day was June 30th and now it's September 1st. She has kept paying rent, and the landlord has consistently accepted the payment. What is this called?
   a. Undefined tenancy
   b. Estate at will
   c. Extended tenancy
   d. **Holdover tenancy**

9. Which of the following is false concerning estate at will?
   a. It's also called tenancy at will.
   b. **It has a specific end date or period of time.**
   c. In order to end the estate at will, it's possible that the landlord will need to evict the tenant.
   d. Either party can terminate with proper notice given. If one of the parties dies, the agreement is terminated.
   e. Estate at will can be created by operation of law or by an express agreement between the parties.

10. When creating a long-term lease, to provide the landlord with a reasonable return on their investment, this type of lease is an agreement for a tenant/renter to pay specified rent increases. These increases are based on a predetermined index (CPI) at set dates in the future. What type of lease is this?
    a. Gross lease
    b. Net lease
    c. Percentage lease
    d. **Variable lease**

11. Peter is a disabled veteran. He is downsizing and has decided to move into an apartment building. It's hard to try and maintain his current house and the move will put him a few blocks away from his grandkids. He has been in a wheelchair for over 15 years. He really likes a specific apartment building. The apartment is on the ground floor and the assigned parking space is close. He would like to make a few modifications given his disability. More than likely, who will have to pay for those modifications?
    a. **Peter**
    b. Landlord
    c. Both pay 50% of the cost
    d. His grandchildren

12. This legal term is the process by which Tenant A transfers his or her leasehold interests, rights, and benefits to Tenant B. For example, Frank (Tenant A) has six months remaining on his current lease. He is moving out on June 15th. Heather (Tenant B) is assuming the responsibility of the remaining six months of Frank's lease and is moving in on July 1st. Frank's landlord will legally transfer Frank's interest, rights, and benefits over to Heather. What is this known as?
    a. Lease takeover
    b. Lease transfer
    c. Transference
    d. Assignment
    e. A and B
    f. **A, B, and D**

13. Ted and Terry are a married couple. Terry works at the hospital and received notice last month that they are transferring her to a different hospital in a different town. They have no choice but to move. One benefit is that Ted, an architectural engineer, will also be closer to work. As they are looking for a new apartment in the new city, they are not finding any that they like. They finally found one apartment they like, but both Ted and Terry have concerns about the structural integrity of the property. Which official document can they request to see that can ease their mind, so they have reassurance if they choose to rent there?
    a. Inspection certificate
    b. Certificate of occupancy
    c. Safety certificate
    d. **A, B, and C**

14. Which of the following is not an on-site improvement?
    a. **Curb along the parkway**
    b. Landscaping
    c. Pool
    d. Drainage improvement

15. A tenant is expected to make improvements.
    a. True
    b. **False**

16. Dr. Brenner is a popular therapist in Chicago. He has just learned that the owner of the office building where he rents his office is facing foreclosure. He knows nothing about real estate or how this works, so he is talking to a friend who is a licensee. After his friend explains it, Dr. Brenner feels relieved. Why is it that he will be able to retain his office space despite the owner facing foreclosure? What is inside the lease contract that offers and outlines this protective measure?
    a. Severability clause
    b. **Nondisturbance clause**
    c. Use of premises clause
    d. Continuity clause

17. What is the best answer to the following question? Do leases have to be recorded?
    a. Yes
    b. No
    c. **If a lease is long term like three-plus years, certain states require the lease to be recorded**

18. When a tenant and landlord are in an eviction situation, which notice is the landlord required by law to give the tenant that states a lawsuit is commencing?
    a. Notice to Terminate
    b. Order for Possession
    c. **Forcible Entry and Detainer**
    d. Eviction Notice

19. Eddie is a busy intern at a tech startup. He leaves his apartment at 6 a.m. every day and does not get home until eleven p.m. or later. He realized he forgot to pay his rent. It was due three days ago. How many more days does Eddie have, according to 770 ILCS 95/7.10 of The Act before late payment fees begin?
    a. None
    b. **Two**
    c. Four
    d. Seven

20. Residential leasing agents can earn a commission on a real estate sale.
    a. True
    b. **False**

CHAPTER 24 QUIZ ANSWERS

1. Are property managers required to have a real estate license?
    a. Yes, for every state
    b. Depends on the state
    c. In Illinois, yes
    d. **Only B and C**

2. In which of the following scenarios might E&O coverage protect agents and brokers?
    a. Closing transaction delays as a result of the broker's mismanagement
    b. Discrimination, libel, or slander
    c. Failure of the licensee to advise on a reasonable price
    d. Failure of the licensee to inspect property
    e. Mishandling earnest money, security deposits, or other monies
    f. **All of the above**
    g. A, C, D, and E
    h. A, B, and D

3. Does the law regulate the time duration of a commercial property management representation agreement?
    a. Yes
    b. **No**

4. Suzie is a property manager. Her assistant left her a message saying that the owner wants a printout of a financial document that gives a snapshot in time. It's a financial document that shows bank account balances, security deposits held, money owed to others, and more. Which report is being requested?
    a. Accounts payable report
    b. **Balance sheet**
    c. Cash flow statement
    d. Income and expense statement
    e. None of the above

5. Which financial document shows a month-to-date and year-to-date featuring a detailed breakdown of income, along with itemized expenses with a comparison to the numbers that were budgeted?
    a. Accounts payable report
    b. Balance sheet
    c. Cash flow statement
    d. **Income and expense statement**
    e. Tenant receivables and prepaid report

6. Terry is a new property manager. She is learning about setting rental rates. Which of the following are true considering what she is learning about?
    a. They mostly revolve around supply and demand.
    b. It's important to learn what similar properties in the city/region are charging.
    c. The owner must receive a reasonable ROI.
    d. **All of the above.**
    e. Only A and C.

7. Eddie paid a security deposit of $1400 to lease his apartment 11 months ago. Since he was just promoted at work, he will be staying there at least one more year if not longer. The apartment complex where he rents a unit has over 50 units. Is Eddie's landlord required to pay Eddie interest on his security deposit?
    a. Yes
    b. No
    c. **Yes, or the landlord has to apply the interest as a credit to Eddie's rent every 12 months.**

8. Earnest money constitutes escrow money in which of the following forms?
    a. Personal checks
    b. Cashier's checks
    c. Money orders
    d. Cash
    e. Any form of legal tender
    f. **All of the above**
    g. Only A, B, C, and E

9. What are the categories of property maintenance?
    a. **Routine, preventive, corrective, and emergency**
    b. Mandatory, proactive, reparative
    c. Everyday, electrical, structural, and emergency
    d. None of the above

10. Dimitri commercially manages a small shopping center outside of Chicago. A small consulting firm wants to rent a space. They are requesting a few things to be added, including partitions, another restroom, and lowered ceilings. What is the best way to describe these additions?
    a. Updates
    b. **Tenant improvements**
    c. Tenant renovations
    d. Specialized updates

11. Mikey is a community association manager. He wants to move from Boise to Naperville. He is looking online for job openings that he qualifies for. In which of the following communities can Mikey work?
    a. HOAs
    b. Apartment complexes
    c. Resort communities
    d. Condominium associations
    e. Commercial tenant associations
    f. All of the above
    g. **All of the above except for B**
    h. All of the above except for A and C

12. Tina is crafting her first property management business plan. Which of the following is not going to be part of her research?
    a. Neighborhood market analysis
    b. Regional market analysis report
    c. **Race research**
    d. Comprehensive property assessment

13. Which of the following is the least likely to be on a list of building-related illnesses?
    a. Asthma
    b. Hypersensitivity pneumonitis
    c. **Stomach flu**
    d. Inhalation fever
    e. Rhinosinusitis

14. To be protected by ADA, a person must have a disability. How does ADA define this?
    a. A person with a physical or mental impairment that substantially limits one or more major life activities.
    b. A person who has a history or record of such an impairment.
    c. A person who is perceived by others as having such an impairment.
    d. **All of the above**

15. Phil and Robin have been living in their apartment building in Illinois for over a year. Over the weekend, they were visiting Robin's mom in another state. That Saturday, they received a call saying that their building had caught on fire. Their unit was destroyed. Everything inside was consumed by the fire. They were devastated. They decided to leave early. On the way back, they discovered that they did not really know if their belongings were covered and would be replaced or not. Phil thought this insurance was included when they signed the lease. Robin thought it was an additional insurance. Neither remembered if it was a monthly expense they have. Which of the following is correct?
   a. This insurance is commonly included in leases, and their belongings will be replaced.
   b. **Nothing will be replaced unless they have HO4 insurance.**
   c. The property owner is personally liable to replace their belongings.
   d. None of the above

16. Which type of insurance covers civil insurrections?
   a. **Fire and hazard**
   b. Business interruption insurance
   c. Contents insurance
   d. Casualty

17. Bill is a property manager. He has just learned that an employee has been embezzling funds. Bill is worried about how this will affect the property's future. Which type of insurance or coverage will assist in this type of unfortunate event?
   a. Business interruption insurance
   b. Contents insurance
   c. Casualty
   d. **Surety bonds**

18. What is depreciated cash value also known as?
   a. **Actual cash value**
   b. Replacement cost value
   c. A and B
   d. None of the above

19. Jenna is a property manager. She hired a DJ for an evening event for the benefit of the tenants. At the conclusion of the event, the DJ stores his equipment temporarily in a utility closet in the complex. The property manager locks it, and they go to the office. When they finish talking in the office, they both go back to get his equipment. Unfortunately, they found the lock broken on the ground and all of the DJ's equipment is gone. Since the property owner is most likely to be liable or responsible for the DJ's equipment that was stored on-site, what type of insurance will cover the DJ's stolen equipment?
   a. **Contents insurance**
   b. Business interruption insurance
   c. Surety bonds
   d. Casualty

20. According to the CDC, what are the top three most common disabilities?
   a. Mobility, vision, and independent living
   b. Hearing, vision, and self-care
   c. Cognitive, vision, and independent living
   d. **Mobility, cognitive, and independent living**

CHAPTER 25 QUIZ ANSWERS

1. Which of the following does the IEPA not do?
   a. **Provide grants for safe housing**
   b. Work to protect the health of Illinois residents
   c. Safeguard environmental quality
   d. Fight against pollution

2. Trevon discovered that a crawl space in his house has asbestos. He is telling his family about it. Which of the following is something he would not say because it is not accurate?
   a. Asbestos was commonly used in buildings years ago.
   b. Exposure is highly toxic.
   c. **If asbestos mineral fibers can get trapped in an individual, they can be safely removed by a doctor.**
   d. Mineral fibers enter the body by way of ingestion or inhalation.

3. The licensing requirement for asbestos workers comes from the state in which they reside.
    a. Yes
    b. **No**

4. Which of the following is false concerning the topic of radon in the state of Illinois?
    a. A seller of residential property must provide a radon disclosure to the buyer.
    b. **Radon is a Class-B human carcinogen.**
    c. Radon is the leading cause of lung cancer in non-smokers.
    d. Radon is a radioactive, colorless, odorless, and tasteless gas.

5. Which of the following is true concerning formaldehyde?
    a. It is a colorless gas with a strong odor.
    b. It was used mostly in the past for building materials and countless household products.
    c. It can be found in plywood, particle board, glues, fiberglass, adhesives, permanent-press fabrics, and similar products.
    d. It occurs naturally in the environment.
    e. **All of the above**
    f. Only A, B, and C

6. Most likely, where would radon be found in a residential property?
    a. Crawl spaces
    b. Bedrooms
    c. Kitchens
    d. Basements
    e. B and C
    f. **A and D**

7. As of the publishing of this book, what was listed as the number one environmental hazard that causes illness in babies and children?
    a. Radon
    b. Formaldehyde
    c. Mold
    d. **Lead poisoning**
    e. Asbestos

8. Reginald and Amy purchased their first home nine months ago. Amy just found out she is pregnant! After learning about the exciting news, they started talking about how to ensure that the home is 100% safe for the baby. What recommendations would you make if you were their close friend who happens to be a licensee?
    a. Review your lead paint disclosure
    b. Review the residential real property disclosure
    c. Buy a carbon monoxide detector
    d. **All of the above**

9. Can asbestos removal in Illinois legally be accomplished without a license?
    a. Yes
    b. **No**

10. Where can lead be found?
    a. In water
    b. In the air
    c. In the soil
    d. **All of the above**

11. Carbon monoxide poisoning has similar symptoms to which of the following?
    a. Stomach virus symptoms
    b. **Flu**
    c. Sinus infection
    d. None of the above

12. On a federal level, as of January 1, 2007, each and every homeowner, building owner, and landlord is required by law to install carbon monoxide detectors within 15 feet of any room that is used for sleeping.
    a. True
    b. **False**

13. Although mold can be found almost anywhere, which of the following locations would be the *most* likely place for mold to be present?
    a. Bedroom
    b. Patio room
    c. **Kitchen**
    d. Attic

14. Which of the following is not a health concern of electromagnetic radiation exposure?
    a. DNA damage
    b. Dementia
    c. **Respiratory problems**
    d. Cancer

15. Which of the following sentences describes groundwater accurately?
    a. It is the water under the Earth's surface.
    b. It is the water we can see.
    c. It is water that is naturally safe for drinking.
    d. It is the water that is stored in aquifers.
    e. All of the above
    f. **Only A and D**
    g. Only A, B, and C

16. Is every underground storage tank in the US required to comply with federal EPA regulations?
    a. Yes
    b. **No**

17. What is the primary concern of an underground storage tank?
    a. Explosion
    b. **A leak**
    c. That it does not have an owner or responsible party associated with it, and thus is an orphan site.
    d. None of the above

18. What are the main types of wastes as related to landfills?
    a. Chemical, biological, residential, and commercial
    b. **Domestic, municipal, and industrial**
    c. Domestic and commercial
    d. Biological, residential, and commercial

19. Janissa purchased property last spring. After a few complaints from neighbors, she had someone do an environmental test. She was shocked and angry to discover that her newest property is contaminated. Is Janissa liable for this?
    a. Yes
    b. No
    c. **Not if she is eligible and qualifies with the EPA as an innocent landowner.**
    d. Yes, she could be subject to a monetary penalty equal to five times the purchase price.

20. Which of the following can produce carbon monoxide?
    a. Furnace
    b. Clothes dryers
    c. Fireplaces
    d. Generators
    e. **All of the above**

CHAPTER 26 QUIZ ANSWERS

1. On which levels do housing laws protect people from discrimination?
    a. Federal
    b. State
    c. Local
    d. **All of the above**
    e. Only state and local

2. Which act added sex/gender to the list of protected classes?
    a. The Civil Rights Act of 1968
    b. **The Housing and Community Development Act of 1974**
    c. The Fair Housing Amendments Act of 1988
    d. None of the above

3. The Fair Housing Act protects individuals from discrimination in which of the following scenarios?
    a. Renting a condo
    b. Buying a home
    c. Getting a mortgage
    d. Seeking housing assistance
    e. **All of the above**
    f. Only A, B, and C

4. James moved from Wyoming to Illinois. He is 31 years old. When he was 25, he was convicted of criminal conduct and thus has a criminal record. He wants to rent a room in a small town. Michael owns a large house and has a room for rent within his primary dwelling. Can he deny James the room because of his criminal record?
    a. **Yes, he is within his rights to do so.**
    b. No, he may not.

5. Concerning emotional support animals (ESAs), which of the following is true?
    a. **ESAs do not qualify as service animals under the Americans with Disabilities Act (ADA), but they may be permitted as reasonable accommodations for persons with disabilities under the Fair Housing Act.**
    b. ESAs do qualify as service animals under the Americans with Disabilities Act (ADA)
    c. An ESA can only be a dog.
    d. None of the above

6. Dean is a residential leasing agent for a small apartment complex. Sarah came into the office this morning. She is blind and has a service animal. Dean is concerned it will be a hassle to accept Sarah as a resident because the service animal is a large dog. While pets are allowed, no large dogs are allowed. Does Dean have to accept Sarah if she qualifies financially for the apartment?
    a. **Yes**
    b. No

7. Jean owns a small construction company. She is in the process of drawing up blueprints for a small apartment building with eight units. The location is a small town in Illinois. The land sits on a hill. Is Jane required by law to make the leasing office for the new building accessible to those with disabilities, in wheelchairs for example?
    a. No
    b. **Yes**

8. Which advertisement would be appropriate under the Federal Fair Housing rules for advertising units in a small apartment building?
    a. Catholic applicants only
    b. English speaking only
    c. **Near parks**
    d. No wheelchairs

9. Licensee Robert tells the Jones family that it's in their best interest to move. They are a Caucasian devout Latter-day Saints family. He tells them that the neighborhood is changing because of a lower cost of living as compared to other neighborhoods. Robert also shares that the people buying properties in their neighborhood represent a mix of other religions and races, and that they are forcing the housing values to decline. What is this Fair Housing violation called?
    a. **Blockbusting**
    b. Redlining
    c. Steering
    d. Rerouting

10. In the 1970s, the Singh family moved from Bangalore India to the outskirts of Chicago. Both Mr. and Mrs. Singh had medical degrees and had been accepted by a well-known medical school in Chicago to further their education. While the Singhs were financially qualified and spoke fluent English, it took them over a year to get their purchase financed. Despite easily qualifying financially, for one reason or another, no lending institution would do business with them. It is conceivable that lenders were reluctant to finance them because of their background. Which discriminatory action was most likely taking place?
    a. Blockbusting
    b. **Redlining**
    c. Steering
    d. Panic peddling

11. The Huang family moved from China to Springfield, Illinois, last month. Since then, they have been staying at an Airbnb while scouting out a house to purchase. Mrs. Huang has done endless hours of research in advance. She happily brought a list of neighborhoods when she and her husband met with their first licensee. The licensee looked at the list. Out of the ten neighborhoods, he crossed off seven and said, "One of these three neighborhoods will be best for you." Later, as they toured the three neighborhoods, Mr. and Mrs. Huang noticed that the signs for the commercial businesses were predominantly in Chinese. Which type of discriminatory practice is occurring?
    a. Blockbusting
    b. Redlining
    c. **Steering**
    d. Panic peddling

12. A licensee named Todd has just discriminated against a lesbian couple who are clients. They were speaking with him on the sales floor inside the brokerage office. Two other licensees overheard what he said and were shocked, hurt, and disappointed. Each of them immediately went to the sponsoring broker's office to talk with her about the incident. Which of the following categorizes what Todd did?
    a. Civil rights violation
    b. Office policy that covers Fair Housing laws
    c. **A and B**
    d. None of the above

13. Juan, a Spanish speaker, has a complaint about his current rental situation. He knows what is happening is not fair. Nobody in the office speaks Spanish. Juan's English is limited, although he has been building his speaking and listening skills. He has heard of the Office of Fair Housing and Equal Opportunity. However, he knows he cannot clearly articulate what is happening with someone on the phone as it would be too hard to explain the situation in English. What is most likely his best option?
    a. Ignore the situation
    b. **File a complaint online**
    c. Talk to the property owner again
    d. Call the regional management office

14. Jane lives in a small complex and the property manager personally oversees the office, maintenance, and repairs. Her dishwasher recently broke. She submitted a repair request to the property manager. However, the property manager failed to respond for over three weeks. She reached out to him again, and he once again failed to respond. Jane's next recourse is to file a complaint against the property manager and the complex with the municipal building department. It has now been over six weeks. What can Jane do?
    a. Seek legal advice
    b. Follow up on her first complaint
    c. Jane can file a subsequent complaint
    d. **Any of the above**

15. If you are a licensee who is part of an industry-based organization or association that has a strict code of ethics, what can happen if you break the code?
    a. Nothing.
    b. They can penalize you.
    c. They can revoke your membership.
    d. **B and C**

16. To whom does the Illinois Human Rights Act apply?
    a. Property owners
    b. Property managers
    c. Licensees
    d. **All of the above**
    e. Only B and C

17. Age is a protected class in the Illinois Human Rights Act. At what age is an individual protected?
    a. **40 and up**
    b. 50 and up
    c. 60 and up
    d. 70 and up

18. Which of the following is sexual harassment?
    a. Forwarding emails with sexual content
    b. Requesting sexual favors
    c. Inappropriate touching
    d. **All of the above**

19. The Thorton family has been living in an apartment building for three weeks. Mr. Thornton is a very talkative person. He has been meeting residents in his building and other buildings. He started to notice that all of the residents in his building, Building C, were Christians. He noticed several church and God stickers on vehicles before they arrived, but had assumed that was common for the complex. This week, he started talking with people who live in Building A. The majority of them are Muslim. Which violation does it look like the property manager is guilty of?
    a. Blockbusting
    b. Redlining
    c. **Steering**
    d. Panic peddling

20. Do emotional support animals qualify as service animals under the Americans with Disabilities Act?
    a. Yes
    b. **No**

CHAPTER 27 QUIZ ANSWERS

1. Which of the following is required by RESPA?
    a. An attorney to prepare the loan estimate of closing costs.
    b. **Brokers and lenders to disclose any affiliated business relationships to all parties.**
    c. Brokers and lenders prepare the Closing Disclosure at least three business days prior to closing.
    d. Buyers use settlement service providers recommended by brokers and lenders.

2. Which of the following is not done by the lender/mortgage company representative at a closing?
    a. Examines all loan documents for accuracy and completeness
    b. Verifies mortgagor's employment status prior to closing day
    c. **Delivers evidence that the title is insured**
    d. Provides a check for the loan amount

3. In Illinois, is an acknowledgment required for a valid deed?
    a. **Yes**
    b. No

4. Which of the following is false concerning a title? A title . . .
    a. Is the actual lawful ownership of real property.
    b. Refers to holding the bundle of rights conveyed.
    c. **Is a physical document.**
    d. Is a theory of ownership.

5. Who usually performs a title search?
    a. The buyer
    b. The seller
    c. The licensee
    d. An abstractor
    e. A title company
    f. **D or E**
    g. C or F

6. Jane recently married. She is selling her house in Chicago and moving to Hawaii with her husband. She has no need for her furniture. It is included in the home sale. Which document below will be used to transfer the title of personal property from Jane to the buyer?
    a. **Bill of sale**
    b. Closing Disclosure
    c. Sales contract
    d. Title

7. Which of the following does not show evidence as to the quality of the title being conveyed?
    a. Certificate of Title
    b. Attorney's opinion of title
    c. Title insurance
    d. **Quit claim deed**

8. Which of the following is false concerning a loan estimate?
    a. A loan estimate is sometimes called an "LE."
    b. A loan estimate was previously called a good faith estimate.
    c. **A loan estimate is just as precise as the Closing Disclosure statement.**
    d. A loan estimate groups and categorizes total estimated costs.

9. Which of the following is not typically a shared expense between the buyer and the seller?
    a. HOA fees
    b. **Property survey**
    c. Property taxes
    d. Title insurance fees

10. Mary is a title company representative. She is responsible for preparing a particular closing document that shows every title-related event in the public record for a particular piece of property. What is Mary working on?
    a. **The abstract of title**
    b. Property survey
    c. Property deed
    d. Sales contract

11. If the buyer does not insist upon a professional property inspection, or inspections for termites, who would most likely request these?
    a. Buyer's attorney
    b. Closing agent
    c. Lender's representative
    d. Title company representative
    e. **None of the above**

12. At the closing, the seller is generally responsible for which of the following?
    a. Creating the abstract of opinion
    b. Issuing a letter of opinion
    c. **Paying prorated expenses for the day of closing**
    d. Preparing the settlement statement

13. Which type of evidence of title gives the purchaser or the lender recourse if title defects are later discovered?
    a. Abstract of title
    b. Attorney's opinion
    c. Certificate of title
    d. **Title insurance**

14. Closing day arrives and licensee Viola takes her buyer client on a final walk-through of the property. Viola notices a large section of flooring appears warped. It was not warped on the previous inspection. What should Viola do?
    a. **Bring this to her client's attention**
    b. Contact the listing agent and ask for monetary credit
    c. Not say anything to her client
    d. Suggest to her client that she cancel the transaction
    e. A and C

15. Broker Maria insists that her buyer clients review a home inspection report on a house. This is an example of which of the following?
    a. Engaging in the unauthorized practice of law
    b. **Ensuring the full disclosure of pertinent material facts**
    c. Misleading buyers into making false conclusions
    d. Providing a service outside her field of competence

16. Which statements are true concerning discharge of mortgage?
    a. It is also known as a release of lien.
    b. When the mortgage is paid off, the lender issues a discharge of the mortgage debt.
    c. **A and B**
    d. None of the above

17. Which statements are true concerning marketable title?
    a. They are only used in residential.
    b. It is sometimes called a merchantable title.
    c. It is one in which a reasonable and prudent person would accept as being good, clean, and valid.
    d. **B and C**

18. Which statement below is false concerning the topics of amortization and negative amortization?
    a. Amortization is the process of making regular payments to pay off a loan.
    b. Negative amortization means that your monthly payments are not sufficient to cover the interest, and this causes the total amount you owe to continue to increase.
    c. **Lenders do not work with borrowers who are experiencing negative amortization and it's best for borrowers to seek legal and financial counsel.**
    d. When the borrower is delinquent in making their mortgage payments, the lender may provide the borrower with the option to make a minimum payment, but if chosen, the deferred interest will be added to the outstanding debt and the borrower's overall debt obligation will increase.

19. Which law requires lenders to provide timely information about loan terms and costs?
    a. **The Truth in Lending Act**
    b. The Home Ownership and Equity Protection Act
    c. The Illinois High Risk Home Loan Act
    d. A and C
    e. B and C

20. Licensee Sarah was hopeful to sign up a new seller. The property was immaculate. She expected to get top dollar. However, she just found out there is a construction lien on the property. This makes real property unmarketable. Under which of the following categories does this construction lien fall?
    a. **Cloud**
    b. Right to rescind
    c. Curveball
    d. Hardstop

CHAPTER 28 QUIZ ANSWERS

1. Billy is a senior in high school who is considering becoming a real estate licensee. He has been learning more about the topic and what the life of a licensee is like. Recently, he wrote down several questions to ask his mentor. He is curious about how the government and states control land. What is their main method of overseeing the vast amount of land in the US? Which of the following is the topic or topics he should learn about?
   a. Local ordinances
   b. Land regulation
   c. Zoning
   d. **All of the above**
   e. Only B and C

2. How much land does the Federal Government own?
   a. **About 640 million acres**
   b. About 240 million acres
   c. About 840 million acres
   d. A little over 1000 million acres

3. A small rural town in Illinois has the authority to make and pass its own laws for its municipality as long as those laws are not in conflict with any state and federal laws. What is this called?
   a. **Home rule unit**
   b. Township
   c. Local authority
   d. Municipality limited sovereignty

4. Buying land, building new structures, renovating existing structures, and converting property from one type of use to another are referred to as which of the following?
   a. Property development
   b. Real estate development
   c. Land development
   d. **All of the above**
   e. Only A and B
   f. Only A and C

5. What are the five essential elements in a municipality's comprehensive plan?
   a. Land use, housing needs, community facilities, energy conservation, stewardship
   b. Land use, property use, people movement, community facilities, energy conservation
   c. **Land use, housing needs, people movement, community facilities, energy conservation**
   d. Land use, people movement, raising property taxes, community facilities, energy conservation

6. What are the two primary ways in which zoning is achieved and overseen?
   a. Municipal rulings and voting
   b. **Ordinances and maps**
   c. Jurisdiction meetings and local hearings
   d. Building permits and density control

7. Which of the following is not a type of zoning?
   a. Aesthetic
   b. **Nonprofit**
   c. Combination
   d. Home-based business

8. Local laws, construction standards, how to repair or erect buildings and material requirements are the four key elements of which of the following?
   a. Property development
   b. Land use
   c. Building permits
   d. **Building codes**

9. Betty is a real estate developer. In a meeting with her team, the focus is a new 12-story building. It will be the largest building in a small municipality. As they talk about details, someone asks how many evacuation points will be required. This question falls best inside which of the following categories?
   a. Building permit
   b. Inspection requirements
   c. **Building code**
   d. Safety ordinances

10. Who generally arranges and pays for a municipal presale inspection once a building is completed?
    a. The buyer
    b. **The seller**
    c. Both buyer and seller (50/50)
    d. Insurance company

11. Land development regulations are enacted by each state and local governing body, not by the Federal Government.
    a. **True**
    b. False

12. Which is the usual order of the land development process?
    a. Land-use development, land development plan, subdividing, plats
    b. Land-use development, subdividing, plats
    c. Land development plan, plats, subdividing
    d. **Land development plan, subdividing, plats**

13. Which of the following is not typically included in a plat map?
    a. **Land ownership**
    b. Blocks and streets
    c. Size of the parcel
    d. Configuration of the parcel

14. Licensee Gerardo moved to a new neighborhood. He is an avid jogger. He decides he wants to get to know the area more by jogging. One evening while out on a run, he sees a fence and what he suspects is a human-made stream between a school and a horse farm. For what purpose do the stream and fence exist?
    a. Separation zone
    b. Natural barrier
    c. **Buffer zone**
    d. Property line

15. Jill believes the municipality she lives in has one area suffering from overcrowding and nonstop building. At a town hearing, she is planning to bring this topic up with everyone. Under which category does her topic best fit?
    a. **Density zoning**
    b. Real estate development
    c. Setback
    d. Variance

16. Margaret and Ted always wanted to build a retirement house by a stream. As they were scoping out some land, they found a beautiful vacant spot near a stream. After two weeks, they finally tracked down the property owner and asked if she was willing to sell. They told her their plans. However, the property owner said, "Your house plans sound wonderful. However, no houses can be built by the river. In this area, the closest a house can be is 400 feet." What is the topic of this conversation?
    a. Riparian rights
    b. Density zoning
    c. Variance
    d. **Setback**
    e. A and C
    f. C and D

17. David wants to build a wooden fence on the north side of his property line. This is not allowed by local zoning. However, how might he possibly be able to build his fence with the permission of the municipality?
    a. Zoning permit
    b. **Variance**
    c. Setback
    d. Improvement
    e. Conditional use permit

18. This permit is a government-issued permit by a municipality that allows an individual or company to use a building or property for his or her or its specific purpose. This permit must be obtained before development starts. Requirements must be met in order to obtain it. Which type of permit is this?
    a. Building permit
    b. Developer permit
    c. **Zoning permit**
    d. Special use permit
    e. ADD 20

19. Which of the following is not traditionally considered federally-owned land?
    a. Nellis Air Force Base
    b. Yosemite National Park
    c. **Saint Tobias Catholic Church**
    d. Ronald Reagan UCLA Medical Center

20. Which of the following is false concerning a zoning map?
    a. It is a highly detailed map.
    b. It follows the local laws and divides municipalities into zones.
    c. It shows the different zones and labels them.
    d. **It defines the property owners of record with the county.**

CHAPTER 29 QUIZ ANSWERS

1. Which is correct concerning the length of a mile?
    a. **5,280 linear feet and 1,760 yards**
    b. 4,280 linear feet and 1426 yards
    c. 3,280 linear feet and 1093 yards
    d. None of the above

2. James is with a potential buyer. They looked at a large house for sale. Now, they are driving around the property. James boasts about the property spanning three square miles. The potential buyer says, "I really don't use those measurements much anymore. How many acres is it?" What is the correct response?
    a. 740 acres
    b. 1280 acres
    c. 1740 acres
    d. **1920 acres**

3. Which formula below is incorrect?
    a. **Part = whole ÷ rate**
    b. Whole = part ÷ rate
    c. Part = whole x rate
    d. Rate = part ÷ whole

4. A broker agrees to a sliding scale commission. She will receive 7% on the first $175,000 and 4% on the next $200,000 and 2% on the balance. What is the sales price of the property if she is paid $28,350 in commission?
    a. $510,000
    b. $620,000
    c. **$780,000**
    d. $850,000

5. A two-story modern house in Chicago is 2,500 square feet. The width of the house is 45 feet. What is the house's rounded depth?
   a. 2025
   b. 112,500
   c. **56**
   d. None of the above

6. Janetta is scouting out a retirement home while her husband is traveling. Today's home is a sprawling property with a high white fence enclosing the entirety of the property. She asks the licensee, "What is the linear length of the entire fence?" The licensee knows the fence is a perfect rectangle. Two sides are 300 feet and the other two are 250 feet. Which formula below would help him answer correctly?
   a. 300 x 250
   b. 300 x 2 + 250 x 2
   c. 300 + 300 + 250 + 250
   d. None of the above
   e. **B and C**

7. Betty sells her property for $550,000 and pays 4% commission on the sale price. If the commission is split equally between the listing office and the selling office, how much commission will the listing office retain?
   a. **$11,000**
   b. $18,000
   c. $22,000
   d. $26,000

8. The Smith estate outside of Chicago sold for $450,000. The listing office received $24,750 in commission. What was the brokerage's percentage of commission on this real estate transaction?
   a. **5.5%**
   b. 4.5%
   c. 6.5%
   d. 5%

9. Mike and Jane are upset. They discovered that their property value has decreased. In their small town, the real estate prices have decreased by 11% over the past twelve months. They purchased the house last year for $320,000. Given the decrease in property value, what is their home currently worth?
   a. $264,800
   b. $274,800
   c. $279,800
   d. **$284,800**

10. Although Sarah is a well-known doctor in her community, she and her husband John have a financial obstacle. Last year, John had a horrible medical issue that drained their savings and retirement funds. They want to sell their home and downsize, but they're upset because even with doing that, the current interest rate will make it difficult for them to thrive financially. They want to finance $225,000. The current interest rate is 4.5%. However, they need an interest rate of 3.25%. How much cash will be required to buy down the interest rate in order to allow them to purchase the new home?
    a. **$22,500**
    b. $25,000
    c. $15,000
    d. $5,000

11. Dakota and Betty are exploring selling their current home. They are both retiring over the next six months. Their goal is to purchase a newly constructed condo. It's in a popular neighborhood and they can even walk to several stores and parks. They will need $140,000 of equity from their current home in order to be able to finance the new condo purchase. Their broker has estimated their closing costs will likely amount to $32,000 plus a 6% commission. If their existing mortgage debt is $328,000, what would be the minimum sales price they can accept in order to meet all of these expenses?
    a. $530,000
    b. $482,000
    c. $360,000
    d. **$531,915**

12. Daniela and Eric are searching intensely for a four-unit apartment building. Their goal is to purchase it, live in one unit, and rent out the other three units. They feel that this will help them retire soon in the future as well as have an income-producing asset. Working with their broker, they learned that the asking price is $475,000. However, they're considering offering $440,000. If the couple and the seller ultimately agree on a sales price of $455,000 and the couple wants to put down $75,000, what rounded percentage of the purchase price does the down payment reflect?

    a. 14%
    b. 15%
    c. **16%**
    d. 17%

13. John, a recent divorcée, is now responsible for the home he had previously shared with his wife. He is exploring the option of selling the house. The current tax bill has recently been received and John is looking at how the county calculated the property taxes, trying to figure out approximately what the house might be worth. The tax bill indicates that the paid property taxes were $16,767. It also indicates that the county is applying an equalization factor of 1.83 against the assessed value, which happens to be 42% of the current market value. Assuming there is a $5,000 owner occupant homestead, and the tax rate is $5.34 per $350 of value. Based on these facts, what would you estimate as the market value?

    a. **$1,436,327**
    b. $1,336,275
    c. $1,536,254
    d. $1,245,327

14. Whitney just purchased a four-year fire insurance policy on her current residence. The start date was May 1, 2020. The four-year premium was $2,555 paid on May 1, 2020. Whitney is now selling her home with an anticipated closing date of June 15, 2021. If the buyer intends to assume the responsibility for the current fire insurance policy, what would be the amount of the proration? How would proration be entered into the closing statement? (When solving the problem, use a statutory year.)

    a. $1,903.56
    b. **$1,854.15**
    c. $1,776.76
    d. $1,734.95

15. Broker Viola has been working with potential buyers Alexandra and Phillip Johnson, a couple with children, for five weeks. While she has tirelessly shown the Johnsons multiple properties that were impressive, each one was rejected. Viola presented a new house today. It exceeds the list that the Johnsons had given her weeks earlier. Viola thinks it will be perfect for their growing and blended family. The Johnsons are going to tender an offer of $515,000. The commission payable by the seller is 5.5%. A cooperating broker's share of the commission is set at 55%. Viola will receive 50% of the commission earned by her office. Given those circumstances, how much commission will Viola be paid by her sponsoring broker?

    a. $9,347.38
    b. $8,265.46
    c. **$7,789.38**
    d. $7,354.46

16. Janet wants to sell her house. She has found a new home and due to personal circumstances, she needs to move in ASAP. In order to purchase the new home, Janet has to be able to net a minimum of $335,000 from her existing home. Her outstanding mortgage is $298,000. The anticipated closing costs are $31,000, plus the 5.5% broker's commission. What would be the minimum sales price that Janet could accept in order to be able to purchase the new house?

    a. $698,345
    b. $705,946
    c. $711,644
    d. **$702,646**

17. Buyer Rebecca is working with broker Cindy. Cindy is excited because she has found what Rebecca considers to be the perfect house. Rebecca is confident the seller will accept $375,000. However, Rebecca has a concern. She is worried about how much cash she will need in order to complete the purchase. She wants to keep her down payment low. Her hope is that the lender will accept a 10% down payment. Rebecca has estimated her closing costs at $12,200. She is working under an exclusive buyer agency agreement requiring that she pay broker Cindy 3% of the purchase price. How much cash is Rebecca going to require in order to complete this purchase?

    a. $62,950
    b. **$60,950**
    c. $65,950
    d. $49,700

18. Scotty and Christine are buying a beautiful two-story house in Rockford, Illinois. They agreed on a sales price of $820,000. At the closing, in order to allow Scotty and Christine to record the deed in their name, the sellers need to pay both the state and county transfer taxes. Using the Illinois schedule for both the state and the county taxes, what will the transfer tax consist of in order to allow the purchaser to record the deed?
    a. **$1,230**
    b. $820
    c. $410
    d. $1,620

19. Mickey and Rosanna want to acquire a conventional loan to purchase their first townhouse. They are tendering an offer of $310,000. The lender they are working with wants to charge them 4.25% interest for a 30 year fixed-rate loan. If the amortization factor is 4.53 and the annual taxes are $11,878 with the hazard insurance annual premium of $850, what will their PITI consist of?
    a. $1,404.13
    b. $1,964.97
    c. **$2,464.97**
    d. $2,664.97

20. Which formula below is incorrect?
    a. **% profit = $ profit ÷ $ original purchase price x 1000**
    b. Net operating income = All revenue generated by the property - operating expenses.
    c. Rate = part ÷ whole
    d. Annual interest = $ mortgage x % rate

CHAPTER 30 QUIZ ANSWERS

1. How often does Illinois law require the state legislature to reinitiate The Act?
    a. Every 5 years
    b. Every 7 years
    c. **Every 10 years**
    d. Every 15 years

2. Which of the following professionals does the Division of Real Estate license and regulate in Illinois?
    a. Real estate brokers
    b. Appraisers
    c. Auctioneers
    d. Community association managers
    e. **All of the above**

3. The IDFPR administers four different primary monetary funds. Which of these funds focuses on consumers who have been victims of unlawful or unethical actions by licensees?
    a. The Real Estate Research and Education Fund
    b. The Real Estate License Administration Fund
    c. The Real Estate Consumer Protection Fund
    d. **The Real Estate Recovery Fund**

4. Robert is a licensee. Two years ago today, someone reported an alleged violation against him. How much longer does the IDFPR have the right to take action against Robert if they choose to do so before the statute of limitations kicks in?
    a. 1 more year
    b. 2 more years
    c. **3 more years**
    d. 5 more years

5. Sarah passed the state-approved written exam on her career path of becoming a licensee. She is beyond excited! She currently does not have a managing broker. Can she submit her license application prior to securing a managing broker?
    a. Yes, but she cannot practice until she has a managing broker.
    b. Yes, and then she can practice real estate but must secure a managing broker within 60 days.
    c. **No, she must secure a managing broker before she submits her license application.**
    d. No, Sarah must complete three years of legal training to ensure that she and the managing broker are protected from liability.

6. Janissa has been a licensee working at the Home Now Brokerage for three years. She found out today that her sponsoring broker had her license revoked. What does this mean for Janissa?
    a. She still holds an active license and can practice real estate.
    b. She still holds an active license and can practice real estate with a few limitations outlined by The Act.
    c. **Her license is considered inactive, and she cannot practice real estate.**
    d. It depends on the reason why her managing broker's license was revoked.

7. Real estate licenses in Illinois are required to be renewed how often?
    a. Every year
    b. **Every two years**
    c. Every three years
    d. Every four years

8. Jan is a broker who has been licensed in Connecticut for two years. This past week, she moved to Illinois. Does she have to do any coursework or log classroom time in order to practice real estate in Illinois?
    a. No.
    b. Yes.
    c. **No, she is only required to take the state-specific part of the licensing exam.**
    d. Yes, she is required to take the state-specific part of the licensing exam along with the 12 hours of continuing education.

9. Concerning continuing education requirements, which of the following is incorrect?
    a. Managing brokers must successfully complete 24 hours.
    b. **Brokers must successfully complete 18 hours.**
    c. Residential leasing agents must successfully complete 8 hours.
    d. All licensees must take the sexual harassment course.

10. Licensee Jacob is cleaning up his office and organizing his files. His office is a mess. He finds a few stacks of old transaction records. How long must he keep those on file according to The Act?
    a. Two years
    b. Three years
    c. **Five years**
    d. Seven years

11. Ron is a new licensee. He has a background in digital marketing. He created a logo for himself and wants to use his name with the logo to advertise online. Is Ron permitted to use this unique logo?
    a. Yes, Ron can advertise in his name.
    b. No, a broker cannot advertise in his or her name.
    c. It depends on the brokerage.
    d. **Yes, as long as the sponsoring broker's name is equal to or larger than Ron's name.**

12. The IDFPR has a database of formal decisions online called the index of decisions. Which of the following statements below is false concerning this database?
    a. It includes information on refusal to renew, revocation, and suspension of licenses.
    b. It includes the names of the offenders.
    c. It's available to the public.
    d. **It includes the addresses of the offenders.**
    e. Only A and B

13. Michael found out that his license is being withheld by the Department. He is very upset. Which of the following might be the cause of the delay in issuance?
    a. He failed to pay the previous two months of rent on his apartment.
    b. He has not filed state income tax returns for the previous two years.
    c. He is delinquent on his child support payments.
    d. **Only B and C**
    e. A, B, and C

14. Janet is a sponsoring broker. One of her newest brokers, Jimmy, has been a superstar since he started working at her brokerage six months ago. Jimmy is high energy, a real people person, and even great with the details. However, today, Janet was informed that Jimmy misused the earnest money that he had been entrusted with on a new real estate transaction. This has never happened before in her brokerage. Is it possible that Jimmy's actions will affect her and her license? If so, how?

    a. No, his actions will not affect her license.

    b. His actions could cause her license to be suspended.

    c. **If she knew of his actions and failed to correct them, she could face consequences as she is responsible for his actions.**

    d. If she did not know of his actions, she wouldn't face consequences.

15. What disciplinary actions can the Department take when someone has violated an aspect of licensing law?

    a. **Reprimand, probation, suspension, revocation, refuse to renew, fines, order to cease and desist, and more options.**

    b. Reprimand, probation, revocation, and order to cease and desist.

    c. Probation, suspension, revocation, fines, and order to cease and desist.

    d. Reprimand, probation, suspension, revocation, refuse to renew, fines, and order to cease and desist.

16. If an action by a licensee does not warrant disciplinary action, the Department may take non-disciplinary action. Which answer best captures possible outcomes for non-disciplinary action?

    a. Administrative warning letter, agreement for care, counseling and treatment, non-disciplinary order, non-disciplinary fee, or administrative fee.

    b. Verbal reprimand, administrative warning letter, letter of concern, agreement for care, counseling and treatment, non-disciplinary order, non-disciplinary fee, or administrative fee.

    c. Administrative warning letter, letter of concern, agreement for care, counseling and medication, non-disciplinary order, non-disciplinary fee, or administrative fee.

    d. **Administrative warning letter, letter of concern, agreement for care, counseling and treatment, non-disciplinary order, non-disciplinary fee, or administrative fee.**

17. All fines and penalties that are submitted go to the State Treasury. Which fund are they deposited into?

    a. **Real Estate Recovery Fund**

    b. Consumer Protection Fund

    c. Disciplinary Action Fund

    d. None of the above

18. The License Act was originally created in 1922. Section 1-5 establishes the intent for The Act. Which of the following is not one of the intents?

    a. To protect the public

    b. To regulate the actions of the licensee and the sponsoring broker

    c. **To protect the licensee from unnecessary interference in doing their job from the designated managing broker**

    d. To provide a means for evaluating the licensee's competency

19. In order to meet the industry's needs for qualified real estate brokers, which of the following would be a correct statement? The state . . .

    a. Provides for a preliminary period of 150 days, allowing the candidate to practice real estate and learn the strategic issues before taking the state exam.

    b. **Does not provide for an apprentice period. The candidate must complete and take the state exam before being able to practice the profession.**

    c. Provides a specialized license labeled Broker Mentor that can be used to guide potential candidates into the industry before they pass the state exam.

    d. Ignores the situation entirely, letting the industry create methods to allow candidates to learn the specifics of the industry in a hands-on approach.

20. The law provides for the ability of a property owner to sell their property without the necessity of a license. Sam wants to begin purchasing homes that are in need of renovation so he can fix and flip them. As Sam is acquiring the properties directly from their owners, what is the position of the state regarding this practice?

    a. **The law permits purchasing of real estate by an individual but limits the number of transactions to two within a 12-month period without the necessity of having a license.**

    b. There are no limitations established by law as to the number of units an individual acting on his or her own behalf is allowed to purchase within a 12-month period.

    c. Illinois law does not address an individual's rights in regard to purchasing real estate but does address the person's right to sell real estate. Sam must be aware that each seller he comes in contact with will be limited to the sale of only one property within a 12-month period.

    d. As long as Sam registers himself with the Secretary of State's office as a qualified real estate investor, there are no provisions of law that limit Sam's ability to purchase or sell real estate within any period of time.

ABOUT THE AUTHORS

DAVID A. MCGOWAN, a name synonymous with real estate education, is a true luminary in the field. His story is one of unwavering dedication and a lifelong commitment to shaping the future of real estate professionals.

Founder, President, and CEO:

At the helm of Professional Studies Institute, Inc., DBA Inland Real Estate School, David wears many hats, each representing his passion for educational excellence.

Managing Broker Extraordinaire:

Since 1982 and forward, David was the guiding force behind Inland Commercial Brokerage and several other successful real estate companies, seamlessly blending his roles together as an educator and a leader in real estate. David started the school on behalf of Inland in 2006 and then was given the opportunity to purchase the school in 2010. Even though he acquired the school he remained with Inland in a managing broker capacity taking responsibility for overseeing senior executive management. He currently still serves in the capacity of President of the school as well as the designated managing broker for one division of Inland.

A Legacy of Experience:

With over four decades as a real estate practitioner and an educator, David has accumulated a wealth of knowledge that few can rival. His journey is marked by countless accomplishments and milestones from being in real estate sales, brokerage management, brokerage ownership to a real estate educator and mentor.

A Teacher to Thousands:

Through the years, David has had the privilege of instructing over 30,000 students, each of whom has benefited from his profound insights and guidance. His impact on their careers is immeasurable.

Elevating the Standard:

David's leadership has seen Inland Real Estate School consistently achieve pass rates for Illinois real estate exams that exceed the state average, a testament to his dedication to student success.

A Trailblazer and Advocate:

David's influence extends well beyond the classroom. He has served as the past president of the Northern Illinois Commercial Association of REALTORS® and former regional director of the Real Estate Educators Association. His tenure as the Director of Education for the Chicago Association of REALTORS® has further cemented his status as a pioneer.

A Collaborative Force:

As a member and former director of the Association of Illinois Real Estate Educators, David continues to champion the importance of educational standards in the industry.

Join David on a profound educational journey, and discover the wisdom, dedication, and expertise that have made him an icon in the world of real estate education.

DR. STEPHANIE KROL is a Real Estate Visionary, Educator and Multifaceted Entrepreneur

Dr. Stephanie, is the vice president, co-owner, and COO of Inland Real Estate School, is a living testament to the adage that diversity is the spice of life. Her two decades of educational expertise weaves through the realms of real estate, every facet of traditional on ground, online, for-profit higher education management, school turn around, accreditation, new school creation, curriculum, corporate training and development publishing, health, and wellness, crafting a tapestry of excellence and boundless passion.

A Proven Excellence in Real Estate:

With over 25 years invested in real estate, Dr. Stephanie has established herself as a reputable investor and broker, garnering accolades for her professionalism and commitment to her clients.

An Evolved Entrepreneur:

Dr. Stephanie's entrepreneurial spirit knows no bounds. Her multidimensional approach spans luxury residential, estates, equine facilities, and commercial spaces, forging an expansive network of business owners, property owners, and civic leaders in Chicago, western suburban Illinois, and western Michigan.

A Multi-Award-Winning Educator:

In the sphere of higher education management, Dr. Stephanie shines as a multi-award-winning educator, an esteemed speaker, and a distinguished dean, leaving an indelible mark on the educational landscape.

A Literary Maven:

Dr. Stephanie's creative spirit extends to the world of publishing. She's a full-time certified publishing consultant, and publishing services owner, offering her expertise to authors seeking to bring their work to life. As an author herself, she penned the enlightening and multi-award-winning book, 'What the Pet Food Industry Is NOT Telling You.'

Pioneering in Publishing Services:

Dr. Stephanie's imprint ownership and boutique specialize in self-publishing services, which signify her dedication to helping aspiring authors realize their dreams and help them bridge the path to attaining their goals.

A Wellness Advocate:

With a heart dedicated to health and well-being, she wears the hats of a functional medicine practitioner and a certified health and well-being coach for both humans and their furry friends. As a certified raw dog nutrition specialist and pet health advocate, she champions the health and happiness of pets.

A Global Network in Publishing:

In the publishing realm, Dr. Stephanie is broadening her horizons, connecting with professionals nationally and internationally, fostering collaboration and creativity on a global scale.

Living Her Values:

Today, Dr. Stephanie counts herself fortunate to live her values, follow her passions, and build meaningful relationships along the way. Her journey is a testament to the power of pursuing purpose and doing things her way.

Join Dr. Stephanie on an inspiring journey through real estate, education, publishing, and wellness, and discover the energy and dedication that make her a true trailblazer.

www.ingramcontent.com/pod-product-compliance
Lightning Source LLC
Chambersburg PA
CBHW080413030426
42335CB00020B/2434